Lecture Notes in Computer Science   14347

Founding Editors

Gerhard Goos
Juris Hartmanis

The series Lecture Notes in Computer Science (LNCS), including its subseries Lecture Notes in Artificial Intelligence (LNAI) and Lecture Notes in Bioinformatics (LNBI), has established itself as a medium for the publication of new developments in computer science and information technology research, teaching, and education.

LNCS enjoys close cooperation with the computer science R & D community, the series counts many renowned academics among its volume editors and paper authors, and collaborates with prestigious societies. Its mission is to serve this international community by providing an invaluable service, mainly focused on the publication of conference and workshop proceedings and postproceedings. LNCS commenced publication in 1973.

Gene Tsudik · Mauro Conti · Kaitai Liang ·
Georgios Smaragdakis

Editors

Computer Security –
ESORICS 2023

28th European Symposium
on Research in Computer Security
The Hague, The Netherlands, September 25–29, 2023
Proceedings, Part IV

Springer

Editors
Gene Tsudik
University of California
Irvine, CA, USA

Mauro Conti 🆔
University of Padua
Padua, Italy

Kaitai Liang 🆔
Delft University of Technology
Delft, The Netherlands

Georgios Smaragdakis
Delft University of Technology
Delft, The Netherlands

ISSN 0302-9743 ISSN 1611-3349 (electronic)
Lecture Notes in Computer Science
ISBN 978-3-031-51481-4 ISBN 978-3-031-51482-1 (eBook)
https://doi.org/10.1007/978-3-031-51482-1

This Springer imprint is published by the registered company Springer Nature Switzerland AG
The registered company address is: Gewerbestrasse 11, 6330 Cham, Switzerland

Paper in this product is recyclable.

Preface

We are honoured and pleased to have served as PC Co-Chairs of ESORICS 2023. As one of the longest-running reputable conferences focused on security research, ESORICS 2023 attracted numerous high-quality submissions from all over the world, with authors affiliated with diverse academic, non-profit, governmental, and industrial entities.

After two rounds of submissions, each followed by an extensive reviewing period, we wound up with an excellent program, covering a broad range of timely and interesting topics. A total of 478 submissions were received: 150 in the first round and 328 in the second. 3–4 reviewers per submission in a single blind review driven by selfless and dedicated PC members (and external reviewers) who collectively did an amazing job providing thorough and insightful reviews. Some PC members even "went the extra mile" by reviewing more than their share. The end-result was 93 accepted submissions: 28 and 65, in the first and second rounds, respectively.

The 18-session ESORICS 2023 technical program included: (1) 93 talks corresponding to accepted papers, (2) a poster session, and (3) 3 impressive keynote talks by internationally prominent and active researchers: Virgil Gligor, Carmela Troncoso, and Mathias Payer. The program testifies to the level of excellence and stature of ESORICS.

We offer our deepest gratitude to:

- **Authors** of all submissions, whether accepted or not. We thank them for supporting ESORICS and for their trust in us and the PC to fairly evaluate their research results.
- **General Chairs:** Kaitai Liang and Georgios Smaragdakis, who dealt with (and addressed) numerous logistical and organisational issues. We very much appreciate it!
- **Submission Chairs:** Gabriele Costa and Letterio Galletta, for their super-human efforts and invaluable support during the submission and reviewing processes. We could not have done it without them!
- **Publication Chairs:** Florian Hahn and Giovanni Apruzzese, for handling the proceedings. We are especially grateful to them for handling numerous requests from the authors.
- **Web Chair:** Yury Zhauniarovich for creating and maintaining the conference website.
- **Poster Chair:** Bala Chandrasekaran, for taking care of the poster track.
- **All PC members** and their delegated reviewers, who were the main engine of success of ESORICS 2023 and whose hard work yielded an excellent program.

  - Special thanks to the recipients of the *Outstanding Reviewer Award*: Ferdinand Brasser and Brendan Saltaformaggio, for their exceptional reviewing quality.

In closing, though clearly biased, we believe that ESOIRCS 2023 was an overall success and we hope that all attendees enjoyed the conference.

September 2023

Mauro Conti
Gene Tsudik

Organization

General Chairs

Kaitai Liang   Delft University of Technology, The Netherlands
Georgios Smaragdakis   Delft University of Technology, The Netherlands

Program Committee Chairs

Mauro Conti   University of Padua, Italy & Delft University of
                              Technology, The Netherlands
Gene Tsudik   University of California, Irvine, USA

Submission Chairs

Gabriele Costa   IMT School for Advanced Studies Lucca, Italy
Letterio Galletta   IMT School for Advanced Studies Lucca, Italy

Workshops Chairs

Jérémie Decouchant   Delft University of Technology, The Netherlands
Stjepan Picek   Radboud University & Delft University of
                              Technology, The Netherlands

Posters Chair

Bala Chandrasekaran   Vrije Universiteit Amsterdam, The Netherlands

Publication Chairs

Florian Hahn   University of Twente, The Netherlands
Giovanni Apruzzese   University of Liechtenstein, Liechtenstein

Publicity Chair

Savvas Zannettou   Delft University of Technology, The Netherlands

Sponsorship Chair

Giovane Moura   SIDN/Delft University of Technology,
                                    The Netherlands

Web Chair

Yury Zhauniarovich   Delft University of Technology, The Netherlands

Programme Committee

Gergely Acs	Budapest University of Technology and Economics, Hungary
Massimiliano Albanese	George Mason University, USA
Cristina Alcaraz (only Round 2)	University of Malaga, Spain
Alejandro Cabrera Aldaya	Tampere University of Technology, Finland
Mark Allman	International Computer Science Institute, USA
Elli Androulaki	IBM Zurich, Switzerland
Giovanni Apruzzese	University of Liechtenstein, Liechtenstein
Mikael Asplund	Linköping University, Sweden
Ahmad Atamli	Nvidia, UK
Vijay Atluri	Rutgers University, USA
Kiran Balagani	New York Institute of Technology, USA
Giampaolo Bella (only Round 2)	University of Catania, Italy
Antonio Bianchi	Purdue University, USA
Giuseppe Bianchi	Università di Roma Tor Vergata, Italy
Jorge Blasco	Royal Holloway, University of London, UK
Ferdinand Brasser	SANCTUARY Systems GmbH, Germany
Alessandro Brighente	University of Padua, Italy
Ileana Buhan	Radboud University, The Netherlands
Alvaro Cardenas	University of California Santa Cruz, USA
Xavier Carpent	University of Nottingham, UK
Anrin Chakraborti	Stony Brook University, USA
Sze Yiu Chau	Chinese University of Hong Kong, China
Liqun Chen	University of Surrey, UK

Contents – Part IV

Machine Learning

Software and Systems Security

Machine Learning

Reinforcement Learning Approach to Generate Zero-Dynamics Attacks on Control Systems Without State Space Models

Bipin Paudel$^{(\boxtimes)}$ [ID] and George Amariucai [ID]

Kansas State University, Manhattan, KS 66506, USA
{bipinp,amariucai}@ksu.edu

Abstract. Stealthy attacks on control systems are bound to go unnoticed, which makes them a severe threat to critical infrastructure such as power systems, smart grids, and vehicular networks. This paper investigates a subset of stealthy attacks known as zero-dynamics-based stealthy attacks. While previous works on zero-dynamics attacks have highlighted the necessity of highly accurate knowledge of the system's state space for generating attack signals, our study requires none. We propose a deep reinforcement learning based attacker to generate attack signals without prior knowledge of the system's state space. We develop several attackers and detectors iteratively until the attacker and detectors no longer improve. In addition, we also show that the reinforcement learning based attacker successfully executes an attack in the same manner as the theoretical attacker described in previous literature.

Keywords: Stealthy attacks · Zero-dynamics attack · Deep Reinforcement Learning · Quadratic Tank Model

1 Introduction

Control Systems regulate the behavior of most of the cyber-physical systems, ranging from smart homes to critical infrastructures. Since control systems typically consist of several interconnected components, they exhibit multiple open surfaces for attacks. Multiple such attacks have been recorded to date, including one that targeted one of Iran's nuclear sites, where the attacker gained access to the industrial control systems and damaged around 1000 centrifuges by increasing their speed beyond normal [16], or the 2015 attack on the power grid in Ukraine [4], which left approximately 225,000 people without electricity, causing damage to almost half of the system's substations, which took more than two months to fix. Protecting critical infrastructures against such attacks is therefore crucial to the security of any household, company, or state.

Stealthy attacks are a type of false data injection attacks (FDIAs) on control systems, characterized by the fact that they typically go undetected. While there are many works focused on stealthy attacks, this paper focuses on a specific kind of stealthy attack, also known as a **zero-dynamics** attack. In a zero-dynamics

G. Tsudik et al. (Eds.): ESORICS 2023, LNCS 14347, pp. 3–22, 2024.
https://doi.org/10.1007/978-3-031-51482-1_1

attack, the attack signals are injected into the control signals, eventually disrupting the states of the system in such a way that the immediate effect of the state disruption is not seen in the system's measurements. Zero-dynamics-based attacks in control systems are described in [23], and [12] demonstrates the application of such an attack in power grids.

Several conditions must be fulfilled for a successful zero-dynamics-based attack to occur, as explained in [23]. One of them is that the attacker has access to the state space equations of the system to generate stealthy attack signals [23] – note that [11] demonstrates that the attack can be successful at a reasonable rate even with imperfect system knowledge, so an approximate model should suffice. Furthermore, the systems have to be of non-minimum phase, and only a subset of the states should be measured directly. The latter two conditions are primarily fulfilled in large power systems and smart grids where the supervisory control and data acquisition (SCADA) system does most of the control work based on the subset of the measured states. Nevertheless, due to the high complexity of such systems, it is usually not feasible to derive even approximately accurate state space models of the entire system. In such a case, the standard method for generating the zero-dynamics attack becomes infeasible. To address this problem, we explore the use of a reinforcement learning technique to perform an attack similar to a zero-dynamics one, in situations in which the state space model of the system is unavailable.

The recent advancements in artificial intelligence, particularly deep learning models, have led to a rise in using these models for stealthy attacks in cyber-physical systems. This paper examines the use of a reinforcement learning (RL) framework for training an agent to generate attack signals on a cyber-physical system (CPS) based on the system's current state. Given that such systems operate in a state/action space where the attack signals, state, and measurement values are continuous, we chose the deep reinforcement learning-based framework, which is known to be effective in approximating continuous functions.

To the best of our knowledge, this is the first attempt to investigate a zero-dynamics-based stealthy attack on a cyber-physical system using a deep reinforcement learning framework. We test our approach on the Quadratic Tank Process (QTP) described in [14]. The QTP is a classic example of a multivariable control system consisting of four interconnected water tanks arranged in a specific configuration as shown in Fig. 1. Each of the bottom two tanks has its own water level sensor. The water levels in the four tanks can be controlled by two pumps that regulate (through two pre-set splitting valves) the flow of water into the tanks. The goal of the control system is to maintain the water levels in the tanks at desired setpoints despite disturbances or changes in the system. For the attack to be successful, the agent (or attacker) must be capable of causing at least one of the system state components to diverge while keeping the output measurement constant (the system state is a 4-dimensional vector representing the water levels in the four tanks).

To accomplish our attack-generation goal, we initially constructed an attacker that can successfully move the system's states away from the desired value without being detected by a simple chi-square test statistics based detector. Subsequently, we developed a more robust LSTM-based detector to detect such attacks. We then created new attackers to beat the new detectors, and *added* new detectors to catch the new attacker, and the process continued iteratively until both the attacker and the *composite* detector converged, and no further improvements were observed. At this point, we claimed that the attacker and detector at the convergence stage represented the most effective attackers and detectors for this particular setup.

The main contributions of this paper are as follows:

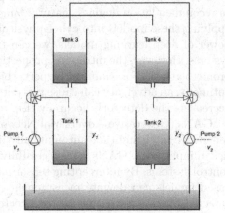

- We developed a framework for training RL-based attackers that learn to approximate theoretical zero dynamics-based attacks. The framework involves training cumulative LSTM-based detectors until they converge to the point where they show no further improvement.
- We empirically showed that our optimal RL-based attacker approximates zero dynamics attackers rather well, in the sense that it diverges the system's states in the same manner (i.e., in the same

Fig. 1. QTP consisting of four connected tanks [12]

direction of the state space) as the theoretical attacks of [12,23].

2   Related Works

The majority of research on the security of cyber-physical systems focuses on false data injection attacks, also known as FDIAs. For example, works such as [3, 6,7] delve into the overall process of creating FDIAs, their impact, and potential mitigation strategies. The effects of FDIAs on electricity market operations are studied in [7], while stealthy attacks on robotic vehicles by disrupting their state estimation techniques are demonstrated in [6].

While much of the existing research on FDIAs has focused on attacks that aim to modify measurements, a zero dynamics attack [23] involves injecting attack signals into the control signals. The authors of [12] demonstrate how zero-dynamics-based stealthy attacks can drive the states of cyber-physical systems based on the quadruple tank process (QTP) beyond the desired value. The same QTP is also used in [22–24].

The authors of [22] provide a comprehensive analysis of several attacks, such as denial-of-service(DoS), replay, false data injection, and zero dynamic attacks, classifying such attacks into three dimensions, and providing insights into how attackers can exploit various vulnerabilities of complex systems. Similarly, [26] studies the trade-off between the increase in the quadratic cost and the stealthiness of the attack based on a linear quadratic Gaussian (LQG) controller. The vulnerability of industrial control systems, such as power systems, to stealthy attacks is well-established. However, protecting power systems can be incredibly challenging due to the outdated and difficult-to-replace equipment. Due to this reason, the need arises for a proper framework to enable risk analysis on each measurement and to identify the buses in a power system that are most vulnerable to attack [24].

Due to the tremendous success of deep learning models in various fields, such as recommendation engines, natural language processing, and computer vision, applying these models into cyber-physical systems is inevitable. By utilizing the power of deep learning models, we can train them to attack and protect these systems. However, the intriguing properties of neural network models make them prone to attack. For example, by perturbing an input to a deep learning detector optimally, an adversary can cause this detector to misclassify an input, eventually decreasing the detector's accuracy [19].

GANs (Generative Adversarial Networks) are a semi-supervised approach to generative modeling that automatically discover and learn patterns or regularities in input data. GANs can successfully conduct stealthy attacks on industrial control systems. By intercepting sensor measurements and control signals, GAN-based models can deviate measurements by a certain threshold without being detected by an existing black box detector [9]. In addition, GANs can be leveraged to attack power systems such that an attack's effects increase while the number of nodes to attack reduces [18]. GAN-based models can also be used for system protection by developing anomaly detectors in industrial control systems [1,15,25].

Deep reinforcement learning models have made their way into the optimal control setting and can often successfully replace the conventional controller. A data-driven, model-free, and closed-loop control agent based on a deep reinforcement learning (DRL) model that controls the voltage in the 200-bus test system was demonstrated in [8]. In addition, [17] also demonstrates the use of reinforcement learning in cyber-physical systems along with several case studies.

Similarly, reinforcement learning techniques can be used to perform FDIAs, as shown in [5], where the authors introduce a novel FDIA to distort the normal operations of a power system regulated by automatic voltage controls (AVCs). The attack is based on a Partially Observable MDP reinforcement learning-based framework where an agent learns to apply actions to collapse the voltage in the system with knowledge of the entire power system.

3   Preliminaries

3.1   Quadruple Tank Process

We consider a discrete time state space representation of the quadratic tank process. In a general form, such a state space representation is defined by the following equations:

$$x_{k+1} = Ax_k + Bu_k + v_k \quad \text{and} \quad y_k = Cx_k + w_k, \tag{1}$$

where x_k, y_k, and u_k are the states, observations, and control signal at time k, respectively.

In control systems, a controller is used to minimize the difference between the actual and desired states of the system. This paper proposes using a linear quadratic Gaussian (LQG) controller comprising a Kalman filter and a linear quadratic regulator (LQR). The LQR helps to drive the system's states to their desired values, while the Kalman filter is used for state estimation since the controller does not have direct access to state values.

The conventional LQR primarily aims to drive the system states to 0. However, to drive the states toward the desired values, we can change the traditional LQR by utilizing the backward recursion technique and solving the matrix Ricatti difference equation to obtain optimal control signal as demonstrated in [11].

3.2 State Space-Based Theoretical Attack

Zero-dynamics-based stealthy attacks based on the state space model are described in [23]. In this version of a zero-dynamics-based attack, the attacker injects the attack signal a_k at time k into the control signal u_k, and the state value at time $k + 1$ becomes

$$x_{k+1} = Ax_k + B(u_k + a_k) + v_k, \tag{2}$$

where $a_k = Fz_k$ is chosen in such a way that the output measurement y_k does not change during the time of an attack.

F is chosen such that $(A + BF)V^* \subseteq V^*$, where V^* is the maximal output-nulling invariant subspace of the system. The algorithm for calculating V^* is described in [2], and one way to obtain F is provided in Appendix A. Finally, z_k is defined by a recursive equation, $z_k = (A + BF)z_{k-1}$. The initial value of z, denoted as z_0, is the Perron eigenvector of $(A + BF)$. As the attack progresses, the contribution of an attack to the diverging states is of the form $(A + BF)^k z_0$. For the attack to work at all, the system should be a non-minimum phase one. If this is the case, then at least one of the system's zeros must be outside the unit circle, leading to one of the eigenvalues of $(A + BF)$ outside the unit circle.

As illustrated above, creating attack signals necessitates an attacker's complete knowledge of the A, B, and C matrices. While it is easier to determine the state space equations for a less intricate system, such as a QTP model, accurately establishing the state space equation for larger and more complicated systems, such as power systems and smart grids, is quite challenging. As a result, a different attack method must be explored when executing zero-dynamics based attacks in these intricate systems.

3.3 Reinforcement Learning (RL)

There are two high-level entities in RL problems: the agent and the environment. The agent observes the current state of the environment, takes action, gets some reward, and gets to a new state. The agent's primary goal is to get the maximum possible reward based on its interaction with the environment.

Markov Decision Process (MDP): The RL problem can be formalized as MDP containing the following elements:

- S, a set of states
- A, a set of actions
- $r : S \times A$, a reward function
- $S \times A \times S' \in [0, 1]$, transition probabilities between the states

The Markov condition states that the future state only depends on the current state and current actions [20].

The main elements of the RL agent are the policy and value functions. A policy is a mapping from a state s to an action a, denoted as $\pi(a|s)$, where π is the policy function. Similarly, a value function $V_\pi(S)$ can be defined for a given state s as follows:

$$V^\pi(s) = \sum_a \pi(s|a) \sum_{s'} \sum_r p(s', r|s, a)(r + \gamma.v_\pi(s')). \tag{3}$$

The following equation is a Bellman equation that returns the expected return for the agent starting from state s and following a policy π. The reward value, denoted by r, is obtained by taking action a while in state s and transitioning to state s'. $\gamma \in [0, 1]$ is a discount factor that diminishes the value of future rewards. RL algorithms use various methods to learn the optimal policy, such as Q-learning, policy gradient methods [21], and actor-critic methods [20].

3.4   Deep Reinforcement Learning

Deep reinforcement learning integrates reinforcement learning with deep Learning. Here, deep learning models are used as function approximations for RL functions, such as value functions and policy functions. In addition, deep learning models can also be used to learn the model dynamics. We will now explore the main functions of deep reinforcement learning.

For a real-world scenario that consists of large-dimensional and continuous state/action pairs, we opt for the value function approximation based on the deep learning model. The value function, in this case, is represented as $V(s; w)$ and is a function approximation given by a neural network model and parameterized by the weight vector w.

Deep RL Based Soft Actor-Critic: Generally, RL problems are concerned with maximizing long-term rewards. In addition, soft actor-critic (SAC) also seeks to maximize the entropy of the policy. SAC is an off-policy actor-critic deep reinforcement learning algorithm based on the maximum entropy RL framework.

Entropy refers to the degree of randomness or uncertainty. In SAC, entropy measures the diversity of policy actions for a given state. High entropy corresponds to the situation in which a policy function's output consists of a range of actions for a particular state. By encouraging high entropy, SAC encourages the policy to explore more diverse actions and avoid getting stuck in suboptimal policies. In other words, maximum entropy helps SAC address the brittleness issue by promoting policy exploration rather than giving a higher probability to any one action.

SAC uses a parametric probability distribution $\pi_\theta(a|s) = Pr(a|s; \theta)$. Consequently, an actor produces a probability distribution over the actions the agent can take in a given state, rather than a deterministic action. The objective function with the expected entropy of the policy over $p_\pi(s_t)$ is represented as

$$J(\pi) = \sum_{t=0}^{T} \mathbb{E}_{(s_t, a_t) \sim p_\pi}[r(s_t, a_t) + \alpha \mathbb{H}(\pi(.|s_t))], \tag{4}$$

where α is the temperature parameter that determines the relative importance of the entropy term against the reward, thus determining the optimal policy's stochasticity. Several advantages of the given objective function are described in [10]. First, this policy is incentivized to explore more; second, this policy can capture multiple modes of near-optimal behavior.

In SAC, neural network-based function approximators are used for both the Q-function and the policy. Furthermore, both these networks are optimized with stochastic gradient descent alternately. The three networks associated with SAC are a *state value function* $V_\psi(s_t)$ parameterized by ψ, a *soft Q-function* $Q_\theta(s_t, a_t)$ parameterized by θ and a *policy function* $\pi_\phi(a_t|s_t)$.

The soft value function is trained to minimize the squared residual error

$$J_v(\psi) = \mathbb{E}_{s,t \sim \mathbb{D}}[\frac{1}{2}(V_\psi(s_t) - E_{a_t \sim \pi_\phi}[Q_\theta(s_t, a_t)$$
$$- \log \pi_\phi(a_t|s_t)])^2], \tag{5}$$

where $\mathbb{D}$ is the distribution from the experience replay.

The soft Q-function is trained to minimize the soft Bellman residual

$$J_Q(\theta) = \mathbb{E}_{(s_t, a_t) \sim \mathbb{D}}[\frac{1}{2}(Q_\theta(s_t, a_t) - \hat{Q}(s_t, a_t))^2], \tag{6}$$

with $\hat{Q}(s_t, a_t) = r(s_t, a_t) + \gamma \mathbb{E}_{s_{t+1} \sim p}[V_{\bar{\psi}(s_{t+1})}]$.

Finally, the policy parameters can be learned by directly minimizing the expected KL-divergence as given in [10], which finally yields the objective function as:

$$J_\pi(\phi) = \mathbb{E}_{s_t \sim \mathbb{D}, \epsilon_t \sim \mathbb{N}}[log\pi_\phi(f_\phi(\epsilon_t; s_t)|s_t) - Q_\theta(s_t, f_\phi(\epsilon_t; s_t))]. \tag{7}$$

The complete algorithm is described in [10], and it alternates between gathering data by interacting with the environment while applying the current policy and updating the function approximators using stochastic gradients from samples taken from a replay buffer.

4   Attacking the Quadruple Tank Process (QTP)

Cyber-physical systems exhibit intricate structures, incorporating components from various companies or vendors across different countries. When one of these components turns malicious, it gains unhindered access to measurements, control signals, and system configurations linked to the entire system. We assume that these compromised components can replicate the target system, a digital twin of the QTP system, which is the subject of the attack [12], but not to the state-space representation of this system. This emulates a real-world attack on a more complex system, where the state-space representation is unavailable. Using the digital twin, the attacker develops a deep reinforcement learning model to orchestrate a zero-dynamics attack.

During the attack process, the attacker only possesses the measurements of the QTP being attacked. Along with these measurements, the attacker estimates state values from the digital twin as explained in Sect. 4.2. Subsequently, an attack signal is generated by the attacker and injected into the control signals. This manipulation causes the measurements to deviate, all while avoiding detection by the detector system. The attack cannot be initiated at the start of the system (i.e., $t = 0s$) due to the transient phase of the system [12]. Therefore, the attack is initiated after the system has reached its steady state.

Subsequently, we develop an LSTM-based detector that analyzes the directly observed measurements to detect any presence of an attack in the system. We then create new attackers to beat the new detectors, and the process continues iteratively until no further improvements are observed.

The following steps explain how we build attackers and detectors iteratively:

1. Start with a chi-square detector (DET_0);
2. Train an attacker ATT_i to beat detectors $DET_{i-1}...DET_0$;
3. Build DET_i to detect ATT_i;
4. Go back to 2.

4.1   Description of the QTP Model

In Sect. 3.1, we described the system model of the quadruple tank. As illustrated in Fig. 1, the system can be modeled by the following differential equations:

$$\frac{dx_1}{dt} = -\frac{a_1}{S_1}\sqrt{2gx_1} + \frac{a_3}{S_1}\sqrt{2gx_3} + \frac{\gamma_1 k_1}{S_1}v_1,$$

$$\frac{dx_2}{dt} = -\frac{a_1}{S_2}\sqrt{2gx_2} + \frac{a_4}{S_2}\sqrt{2gx_4} + \frac{\gamma_2 k_2}{S_2}v_2,$$

$$\frac{dx_3}{dt} = -\frac{a_3}{S_3}\sqrt{2gx_3} + \frac{1-\gamma_2 k_2}{S_3}v_2,$$

$$\frac{dx_4}{dt} = -\frac{a_4}{S_4}\sqrt{2gx_4} + \frac{1-\gamma_1 k_1}{S_4}v_1,$$

where S_i is the cross-section of tank i, x_i is the water level of tank i, v_i is the voltage applied to pump i, causing a flow $k_i v_i$, a_i is the cross-section of the outlet hole and $\gamma_1, \gamma_2 \in (0,1)$ are the flow ratios set by the fixed-position valves.

Based on this model, our next goal is to instantiate the parameters and linearize the model to obtain the state matrices.

$$A = \begin{bmatrix} 0.975 & 0 & 0.042 & 0 \\ 0 & 0.977 & 0 & 0.044 \\ 0 & 0 & 0.958 & 0 \\ 0 & 0 & 0 & 0.956 \end{bmatrix}, B = \begin{bmatrix} 0.0515 & 0 \\ 0 & 0.0447 \\ 0 & 0.0737 \\ 0.085 & 0 \end{bmatrix} \text{ and } C = \begin{bmatrix} 0.2 & 0 & 0 & 0 \\ 0 & 0.2 & 0 & 0 \end{bmatrix}.$$

The maximum value of the height of the tank is 20 cm. The initial height of the tank is given by $x_0 = \hat{x_0} = [0\ 0\ 0\ 0]^T$ and the desired values of the states at steady state are given as $x_d = [10\ 10\ 10\ 10]^T$.

The control system is exposed to various external disturbances in a real-world scenario. This experiment simulates these real-world disturbances through process and measurement noise, modeled as white Gaussian noises with a variance of 10^{-3}.

The system is controlled by an LQG controller, and a Kalman Filter state estimation technique is used to estimate the system states, as described in Sect. 3.1.

4.2 Deep Reinforcement Learning Based Attacker

In our experiment, the control signals correspond to the system's voltage, so the attack signals must be continuous. Therefore, we train the attacker to generate continuous attack signals. In this study, we employ the soft actor-critic (SAC) algorithm as the basis for our attacker, as explained in Sect. 3.4.

The input to the RL-based attacker comprises current observations of the system. In our experiment, the observations (states) for the RL agent are based on a sliding window of size 10 of past observations. We train the attacker to produce attack signals based on a combination of states (x) and measurements (y). However, in a real-world situation, an attacker does not have access to the system's states (x) but only to the measurements (y), and control signals (u). To address this limitation, the attacker runs a parallel copy of the system to estimate the state values (x) while using measurements (y) from the actual system where the attack is being performed. Figure 2 illustrates the attack process. Despite using the state values (x) from another clone system, the process and measurement noises of the two systems are different, as the noises are sampled randomly from a Gaussian distribution. This variation in noise makes it more challenging for an attacker to generate the desired attack signals without detection. Nonetheless, we have observed that the attacker generalizes well in this scenario and can successfully attack the system with a high probability.

The attacker's RL based framework involves multiple Neural Network models to approximate the function of the actor and critic, in addition to another value network. The overall architecture of these networks for all the attackers is shown in Appendix B Table 4.

Reward Shaping. The rewards received by an attacker in a cyber-physical system are proportional to their performance. The states in the system correspond to the height of individual tanks, and if an unobserved state falls outside the range of 0 to 20 cm, the system is considered to have diverged beyond the model's bounds, indicating a successful attack. The agent is rewarded based on the degree of divergence in unobserved states and penalized based on the degree of divergence in observed states. There are three different kinds of rewards the attacker receives at each timestep.

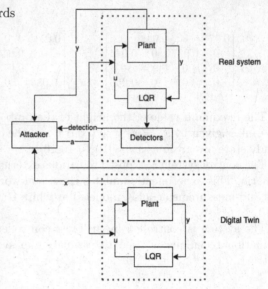

Fig. 2. Architecture of the process during an attack

1. *Success*: A scenario where the attacker successfully attacks the system
   - $reward = -15 + 10 \cdot (2 + d_2)^3$.
2. *Failure*: A scenario where the detector detects an attack before an attack is successful.
   - $reward = -(25 + 10 \cdot (2 + d_1)^3)$ if DET_0 detects an attack
   - $reward \mathrel{-}= (20 + (5 \cdot (i-1)) + (2 + d_1)^3)$ for all n LSTM-based detectors DET_i, $i \in (1, n)$ if DET_i detected an attack.
3. - An attacker receives a small reward at each timestep based on how close it is to a goal. $reward = -15 - a \cdot (1 + d_1)^2 + b \cdot (1 + d_2)^2$.

where d_1 represents the Euclidean distance between the desired and current values of $[x_1, x_2]$, while d_2 represents the Euclidean distance between the desired and current values of $[x_3, x_4]$. Here, x_1 and x_2 are directly measured states, while x_3 and x_4 are non-measured states. Similarly, the values of a and b are different for different attackers, ATT_i, $\forall i \in (1, n)$ as shown in Appendix B Table 5. The reward function incorporates numerical values derived from experimental evaluations, lacking a formal scientific derivation method.

Furthermore, it is worth noting that reward functions in deep reinforcement learning are often non-linear, which enables more intricate connections between the agent's actions and the rewards it obtains. The rationale behind this is that deep reinforcement learning agents operate in high-dimensional spaces where a linear reward function may not be capable of comprehending the complexity of the task or environment.

4.3   Chi-Square Based Anomaly Detector (χ^2)

Our initial detector is a windowed χ^2 test statistics-based detector that detects changes in the variance of the observations. Here, we calculate the sample variance from the $y\_residuals$, which is the difference between the actual and estimated measurements. Our detector is identical to the one employed in [11].

4.4   LSTM Based Detector

Once we successfully create an attacker that can beat the Chi-square-based anomaly detector, we train an LSTM-based detector to identify if the system was being attacked [13]. The time series measurements that correspond to the directly observed states are inputted into the LSTM detector to analyze whether the system was under attack. The architecture of the LSTM-based detector, along with its dataset, is explained below.

Architecture of LSTM. Each measurement at time t is represented by $y^{(t)} = \{y_1^{(t)}, y_2^{(t)}\}$, with $y_1^{(t)}$ and $y_2^{(t)}$ representing the measurements for states x_1 and x_2 respectively. We configured the LSTM detector to have an input size of 50 time series measurements, such that at each timestep t, the input to the LSTM network was a sequence of the most recent 50 measurements, i.e., $Y = \{y^{(t)}, y^{(t-1)}, y^{(t-2)}, ..., y^{(t-49)}\}$. On the other hand, the output consists of a single node representing whether or not the input system is under attack.

The main advantage of the LSTM-based detector over a simple Chi-square-based anomaly detector is that it can learn the trajectory of the directly measured states $y^{(t)} = \{y_1^{(t)}, y_2^{(t)}\}$ of the QTP to identify any anomalies in the system. All the detectors in this paper share the same architecture. The architecture of these LSTM detectors is shown in Appendix B Table 6.

Dataset Collection. The dataset contains two distinct categories of measurements; those taken during an attack and those taken during a non-attack scenario. To obtain measurements for the non-attack scenario, we conducted multiple simulations of the system without any attack and recorded the corresponding measurements. For the attack measurements, we ran the simulation until the system reached a steady state and then launched an attack at timestep 100. We generated measurements for the attack scenario until the system diverged completely or the attack was detected. Additionally, we ensured that our dataset included measurements corresponding to the transient state of the system. While generating these measurements, we added random process and measurement noise to these simulations to make the simulation more realistic and to replicate real-world phenomena.

4.5   Two Proportion Z-Test

We utilize a statistical hypothesis test called the two-proportion z-test to assess the performance of two consecutive attackers or detectors to determine if two proportions are identical where these proportions represent the binomial distribution. To conduct the test, we determine the rate of successful attacks (p) across n trials for the attacker and the rate of successful detection for the detector before any successful attacks across n trials. We then take two independent samples from these proportions and compute the z-statistic, assuming the samples were randomly selected.

$H_0 : p_1 = p_2$, $H_a : p_1 \neq p_2$ and z value is calculated using

$$z = \frac{\hat{p}_1 - \hat{p}_2}{\sqrt{\hat{p}(1 - \hat{p})(\frac{1}{n_1} + \frac{1}{n_2})}}, \text{where } \hat{p} = \frac{n_1\hat{p}_1 + n_2\hat{p}_2}{n_1 + n_2}$$

and $\hat{p}_1$ and $\hat{p}_2$ are the rates of success of the two proportions used during this test, and n_1 and n_2 are the number of trials performed. After calculating the test statistic z, we calculate the corresponding critical region to compare the test statistic. If the absolute value of z-statistic is greater than or equal to the critical value, we can reject the null hypothesis or conclude that the two distributions are not the same.

5 Results

As explained in Sect. 4, we iteratively develop attackers that can overcome all previous detectors and detectors that can recognize the new attacker until further developing new attackers would not improve attack success rates, and developing new detectors would not reduce the probability of an RL-based attacker's success.

5.1 RL Based Attackers

The success rate of attackers is presented in Table 1. From this, we can infer that the attacker can still carry out successful attacks even when the states (x_s) are estimated using the parallel-running digital twin system. Furthermore, we observe that the likelihood of a successful attack decreases as the number of detectors increases, making it more challenging for an attacker to succeed. However, we cannot assert that the system is secure from zero-dynamics attacks unless the successful attack rate is 0%.

Likewise, Table 1 also illustrates the duration it takes for the system to deviate after an attack has been initiated. It is worth noting that our experiment's sampling time is set to one second, meaning that each timestep corresponds to a one-second interval. An increment in the number of detectors results in more time for an attacker to devise an optimal attack signal to accomplish a successful attack on the system. This trend can be seen in the mentioned results table.

The success probabilities of our last two attackers were 1.9% and 0.9%, respectively, which are lower than those of the earlier attackers. Despite this, all the attackers could attack the QTP system successfully. Figure 4 in Appendix C depicts the reward diagram for the five attackers during the training process. Specifically, Figs. 4d and 4e illustrate that the agents were unable to reach the global optima and obtain less reward as compared to the previous attackers.

Table 1. Performance of different attackers. Each attacker's (ATT_i) attack rate indicates their capability to beat collective previous detectors d_{i-1} to d_0.

Attacker	Successful Attack Rate	Timesteps for successful attack
ATT_1	70%	27
ATT_2	59%	42
ATT_3	50%	63
ATT_4	1.9%	49
ATT_5	0.9%	71

5.2   LSTM Based Detectors

Table 2 presents the results of our experiment on the performance of LSTM-based detectors. Each detector in the table is associated with a specific threshold value. If the detector's output is below the threshold, it indicates the presence of an attack; otherwise, it is considered normal. The threshold value was selected to minimize the false positive or false alarm rates. Using this concept, we chose the threshold value that ensures the false positive rate remains below 0.0001.

In addition, selecting the threshold value involves balancing the false positive rate and the true positive rate (TPR). Although the TPR in Table 2 does not seem to be perfect, it should be noted that the system does not fail immediately, and it requires multiple time steps of attack signals to cause system divergence. Additionally, all four detectors in our experiment can detect an attack generated by their corresponding attacker before the attack succeeds at a reasonable rate, as evidenced by the results in Fig. 3 where an arrow pointing from DET_i to ATT_i indicates the successful attack rate of ATT_i against DET_i which is pretty low. Meanwhile, the arrow pointing from ATT_i to DET_i indicates the success rate of an attacker's attack towards its corresponding detector and the detectors preceding it. Consequently, these results illustrate the feasibility of constructing functional LSTM-based detectors tailored to RL-based attackers.

Table 2. Results of LSTM detectors

Name	DET_1	DET_2	DET_3	DET_4
Threshold	0.001	0.001	0.002	0.001
Test set TP	20810	68223	88345	67175
Test set FP	7	4	2	0
Test set FN	8037	21850	1733	13795
Test set TN	89930	89635	89632	90038
Test set FPR	0.00007	0.00004	0.00002	0.0
Test set TPR	0.72	0.76	0.98	0.83

5.3 · Test of Convergence

Figure 3 shows the success rate of attackers against the corresponding detectors as explained in Sect. 4. We conducted a hypothesis test to evaluate the performance of the two consecutive attackers and detectors, as explained in Sect. 4.5. The test was conducted at a 95% confidence level, and we compared the absolute value of the test statistic (Z) with the critical region value of $z_{\alpha/2} = 1.96$. If the absolute value of Z is less than 1.96, we accepted the null hypothesis that the two proportions are equal, which implies that the two subsequent attackers or detectors follow identical binomial distributions.

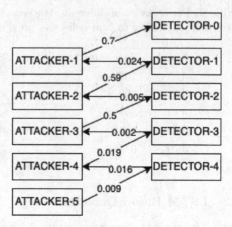

Fig. 3. Convergence of attackers and detectors along with their success rate.

Table 3 displays the results of our hypothesis testing. The results show that the Z-value of 1.4 indicates no significant difference in the success rate of ATT_4 against DET_4 and the success rate of ATT_5 against DET_4 and the previous detectors. On the other hand, the Z-value of 0.51 indicates that the DET_3 (along with the earlier detectors) and DET_4 detection rates against ATT_4 are similar. Through this empirical evidence, we concluded that neither the attacker nor the detector would improve further. Therefore, based on our experiment, we affirmed that the best attacker and the best detector in this scenario are the ATT_5 and the DET_4, respectively.

Table 3. Test significance between consecutive attackers and detectors

Items	Success rate	Z-value	Null Hypothesis
DET_1 against ATT_1 & ATT_2	0.024 & 0.59	−27.4388	Reject
DET_2 against ATT_2 & ATT_3	0.005 & 0.5	−25.477	Reject
DET_3 against ATT_3 & ATT_4	0.002 & 0.019	−4.31	Reject
DET_4 against ATT_4 & ATT_5	0.016 & 0.009	1.4	Accept
ATT_1 against DET_0 & DET_1	0.7 & 0.024	31.45	Reject
ATT_2 against DET_1 & DET_2	0.59 & 0.005	28.6	Reject
ATT_3 against DET_2 & DET_3	0.5 & 0.002	25.68	Reject
ATT_4 against DET_3 & DET_4	0.019 & 0.016	0.51	Accept

5.4   RL vs. Theoretical Attack

In Fig. 5 of Appendix C it is observed that the states (x_3, x_4) that diverge follow the direction of the highest eigenvector associated with the largest eigenvalue of $(A+BF)$, which is the underlying principle of the theoretical attack explained in Sect. 3.2. The cosine similarity between the attack contributions to the diverging states and the highest eigenvector associated with the largest eigenvalue of $(A+BF)$ is shown in the figure. The results demonstrate that for all five attackers, the cosine similarity approaches 1 at the point of system divergence. This outcome indicates that the RL-based attacker emulates the theoretical zero-dynamics attack.

6   Conclusion

We introduced a novel concept of zero-dynamics attack on the QTP process using deep reinforcement learning, which differs from previous works focused on theoretical zero-dynamics based attacks. The theoretical attacks required an attacker to have perfect knowledge of the system state space to generate attack signals. In contrast, our work showed that an RL-based attacker does not require such knowledge and is robust to different system noises. Furthermore, our study highlights the superiority of LSTM-based detectors over chi-square statistics based detectors. We conclude that not all detectors are equally effective in detecting system anomalies. We also used a cosine similarity technique to show that the RL-based attacker imitates a theoretical attacker.

Acknowledgement. This publication was made possible by NPRP grant #12C-33905-SP-165 from the Qatar National Research Fund (a member of Qatar Foundation). The findings achieved herein are solely the responsibility of the authors. We appreciate the anonymous reviewers' valuable suggestions and comments.

A   Proof for Attack Generation

Since matrix D is 0, we replace the solution in [2] as shown below. We need a value of F_2 that satisfies

$$[V \; B] \begin{bmatrix} F_1 \\ F_2 \end{bmatrix} V = AV. \tag{8a}$$

From this, we can easily obtain

$$[V \; B]^+ [V \; B] \begin{bmatrix} F_1 \\ F_2 \end{bmatrix} VV^+ = [V \; B]^+ AVV^+, \tag{8b}$$

where, $[V \; B]^+$ and V^+ represent the Moore-Penrose pseudo-inverses of matrices $[V \; B]$ and V, respectively.

If we choose $\begin{bmatrix} F_1 \\ F_2 \end{bmatrix}$ to be the right-hand side of (8b), that is,

$$\begin{bmatrix} F_1 \\ F_2 \end{bmatrix} = [V\ B]^+ AVV^+, \tag{9}$$

then using one of the properties of the pseudo-inverse, that states that for a general matrix M we have $M^+MM^+ = M^+$, we see that this choice of $\begin{bmatrix} F_1 \\ F_2 \end{bmatrix}$ satisfies (8b). Now substituting the same in the left-hand side of (8a), and using the property that for a general matrix M we have that $MM^+M = M$, we get

$$[VB] \begin{bmatrix} F_1 \\ F_2 \end{bmatrix} V = [V\ B] [V\ B]^+ AV, \tag{10}$$

the right-hand side of which is equal to AV (meaning that our choice of $\begin{bmatrix} F_1 \\ F_2 \end{bmatrix}$ satisfies (8a)) whenever $[VB]$ has linearly independent rows. What remains is to set $F = -F_2$.

B   Architectures and Hyperparameters

Table 4 shows the architecture of neural network models associated with the attackers. The table displays the number of nodes in each subsequent layers of the model, activation function in hidden and output layers, and learning rate and optimizer used to update the model's parameters. Similarly, the Table 5 consists of hyperparameter settings for the neural network models. The target network is updated using a soft update method whose coefficient is 0.005 for each attacker. Similarly, the output of these attackers is scaled using the Tanh activation function. Hence, to get the desired attack signals, we scaled the output by some constant, depicted in the same table. In addition to this, the value of the parameters a and b from the reward function in Sect. 4.2 for each attacker are provided in the table. In addition, Table 6 consists of architectures and hyperparameters of LSTM detectors. All the detectors have the same architecture but differ in learning rate parameter, which is given in the table.

Table 4. Architecture of the neural network models associated with the attackers. Attackers (ATT_1, ATT_2) and (ATT_3, ATT_4 and ATT_5) share the same architecture

	ATTACKERS (1 and 2)			ATTACKERS(3, 4 and 5)		
	Actor	Critic	Value	Actor	Critic	Value
Nodes in each layers	60, 256, 256, 2	60, 256, 256, 1	62, 256, 256, 1	60, 256, 256, 2	60, 256, 256, 1	62, 256, 256, 1
Output layer activation	Tanh	Tanh	Tanh	Tanh	Tanh	Tanh
Hidden layer activation	RELU	RELU	RELU	RELU	RELU	RELU
Learning rate	0.00008	0.0008	0.0008	0.00008	0.0008	0.0008
Optimizer	ADAM	ADAM	ADAM	ADAM	ADAM	ADAM

Table 5. Hyper Parameter Setting for the attackers based on SAC algorithm

Name	ATT_1	ATT_2	ATT_3	ATT_4	ATT_5
Replay buffer size	1,000,000	1,000,000	1,000,000	1,000,000	1,000,000
Discount factor	0.99	0.99	0.99	0.99	0.99
Mini-batch size	256	256	512	512	512
Training episodes(N)	50000	50000	50000	50000	250000
Soft update coefficient	0.005	0.005	0.005	0.005	0.005
Actions scaled by	10	4	3	3	3
reward scale factor	2	2	2	2	2
a in reward function	2	2	10	10	10
b in reward function	2	2	7	7	7

Table 6. Architecture of the LSTM-based detectors

Feature	Value
Number of inputs	2
Number of features in hidden states	512
Number of recurrent layers	1
Feed-forward layers	2 layers with size 256 and 128 respectively
Hidden layer activation	RELU
Output layer activation	Sigmoid
Optimizer	Adam
Batch size	1024
$DETECTOR_1$ Learning rate	0.004
$DETECTOR_2$ Learning rate	0.004
$DETECTOR_3$ Learning rate	0.003
$DETECTOR_4$ Learning rate	0.001

C   Attacker Rewards and Performance

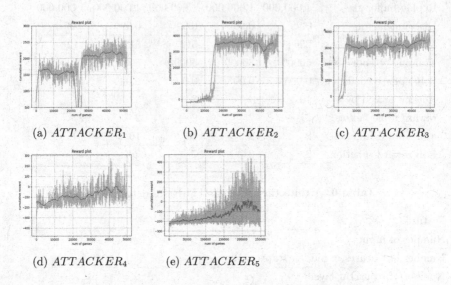

(a) $ATTACKER_1$ (b) $ATTACKER_2$ (c) $ATTACKER_3$

(d) $ATTACKER_4$ (e) $ATTACKER_5$

Fig. 4. Reward plots of five consecutive attackers

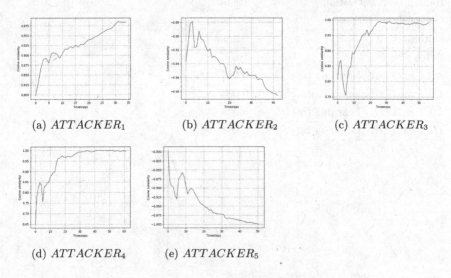

(a) $ATTACKER_1$ (b) $ATTACKER_2$ (c) $ATTACKER_3$

(d) $ATTACKER_4$ (e) $ATTACKER_5$

Fig. 5. Cosine similarity as described in Sect. 3.2.

References

1. Alabugin, S.K., Sokolov, A.N.: Applying of generative adversarial networks for anomaly detection in industrial control systems. In: 2020 Global Smart Industry Conference (GloSIC), pp. 199–203. IEEE (2020)
2. Anderson, B.D.: Output-nulling invariant and controllability subspaces. IFAC Proc. Vol. **8**(1), 337–345 (1975)
3. Aoufi, S., Derhab, A., Guerroumi, M.: Survey of false data injection in smart power grid: attacks, countermeasures and challenges. J. Inf. Secur. Appl. **54**, 102518 (2020)
4. Defense Use Case: Analysis of the cyber attack on the Ukrainian power grid. Electr. Inf. Shar. Anal. Center (E-ISAC) **388**, 1–29 (2016)
5. Chen, Y., Huang, S., Liu, F., Wang, Z., Sun, X.: Evaluation of reinforcement learning-based false data injection attack to automatic voltage control. IEEE Trans. Smart Grid **10**(2), 2158–2169 (2018)
6. Dash, P., Karimibiuki, M., Pattabiraman, K.: Out of control: stealthy attacks against robotic vehicles protected by control-based techniques. In: Proceedings of the 35th Annual Computer Security Applications Conference, pp. 660–672 (2019)
7. Deng, R., Xiao, G., Lu, R., Liang, H., Vasilakos, A.V.: False data injection on state estimation in power systems attacks, impacts, and defense: a survey. IEEE Trans. Industr. Inf. **13**(2), 411–423 (2016)
8. Duan, J., et al.: Deep-reinforcement-learning-based autonomous voltage control for power grid operations. IEEE Trans. Power Syst. **35**(1), 814–817 (2019)
9. Feng, C., Li, T., Zhu, Z., Chana, D.: A deep learning-based framework for conducting stealthy attacks in industrial control systems. arXiv preprint arXiv:1709.06397 (2017)
10. Haarnoja, T., Zhou, A., Abbeel, P., Levine, S.: Soft actor-critic: off-policy maximum entropy deep reinforcement learning with a stochastic actor. In: International Conference on Machine Learning, pp. 1861–1870. PMLR (2018)
11. Harshbarger, S.: The impact of zero-dynamics stealthy attacks on control systems: stealthy attack success probability and attack prevention (2022). https://krex.k-state.edu/dspace/handle/2097/42853
12. Harshbarger, S., Hosseinzadehtaher, M., Natarajan, B., Vasserman, E., Shadmand, M., Amariucai, G.: (A little) ignorance is bliss: The effect of imperfect model information on stealthy attacks in power grids. In: 2020 IEEE Kansas Power and Energy Conference (KPEC), pp. 1–6. IEEE (2020)
13. Hochreiter, S., Schmidhuber, J.: Long short-term memory. Neural Comput. **9**(8), 1735–1780 (1997)
14. Johansson, K.H.: The quadruple-tank process: a multivariable laboratory process with an adjustable zero. IEEE Trans. Control Syst. Technol. **8**(3), 456–465 (2000)
15. Kim, S., Park, K.J.: A survey on machine-learning based security design for cyber-physical systems. Appl. Sci. **11**(12), 5458 (2021)
16. Langner, R.: Stuxnet: dissecting a cyberwarfare weapon. IEEE Secur. Privacy **9**(3), 49–51 (2011)
17. Li, C., Qiu, M.: Reinforcement Learning for Cyber-Physical Systems: With Cybersecurity Case Studies. Chapman and Hall/CRC, London (2019)
18. Liu, Z., Wang, Q., Ye, Y., Tang, Y.: A GAN-based data injection attack method on data-driven strategies in power systems. IEEE Trans. Smart Grid **13**(4), 3203–3213 (2022)

19. Sayghe, A., Zhao, J., Konstantinou, C.: Evasion attacks with adversarial deep learning against power system state estimation. In: 2020 IEEE Power & Energy Society General Meeting (PESGM), pp. 1–5. IEEE (2020)

20. Sutton, R.S., Barto, A.G.: Reinforcement Learning: An Introduction. MIT Press, Cambridge (2018)

21. Sutton, R.S., McAllester, D., Singh, S., Mansour, Y.: Policy gradient methods for reinforcement learning with function approximation. In: Advances in Neural Information Processing Systems 12 (1999)

22. Teixeira, A., Pérez, D., Sandberg, H., Johansson, K.H.: Attack models and scenarios for networked control systems. In: Proceedings of the 1st International Conference on High Confidence Networked Systems, pp. 55–64 (2012)

23. Teixeira, A., Shames, I., Sandberg, H., Johansson, K.H.: Revealing stealthy attacks in control systems. In: 2012 50th Annual Allerton Conference on Communication, Control, and Computing (Allerton), pp. 1806–1813. IEEE (2012)

24. Teixeira, A., Sou, K.C., Sandberg, H., Johansson, K.H.: Secure control systems: a quantitative risk management approach. IEEE Control Syst. Mag. **35**(1), 24–45 (2015)

25. Zenati, H., Foo, C.S., Lecouat, B., Manek, G., Chandrasekhar, V.R.: Efficient GAN-based anomaly detection. arXiv preprint arXiv:1802.06222 (2018)

26. Zhang, R., Venkitasubramaniam, P.: Stealthy control signal attacks in linear quadratic Gaussian control systems: detectability reward tradeoff. IEEE Trans. Inf. Forensics Secur. **12**(7), 1555–1570 (2017)

Secure Split Learning Against Property Inference, Data Reconstruction, and Feature Space Hijacking Attacks

Yunlong Mao[1], Zexi Xin[1], Zhenyu Li[2], Jue Hong[3], Qingyou Yang[3], and Sheng Zhong[1(✉)]

[1] State Key Laboratory for Novel Software Technology, Nanjing University, Nanjing, China
zhongsheng@nju.edu.cn
[2] University of California San Diego, San Diego, USA
[3] ByteDance Ltd., Beijing, China

Abstract. Split learning of deep neural networks (SplitNN) has provided a promising solution to learning jointly for the mutual interest of a guest and a host, which may come from different backgrounds, holding features partitioned vertically. However, SplitNN creates a new attack surface for the adversarial participant. By investigating the adversarial effects of highly threatening attacks, including property inference, data reconstruction, and feature hijacking attacks, we identify the underlying vulnerability of SplitNN. To protect SplitNN, we design a privacy-preserving tunnel for information exchange. The intuition is to perturb the propagation of knowledge in each direction with a controllable unified solution. To this end, we propose a new activation function named R^3eLU, transferring private smashed data and partial loss into randomized responses. We give the first attempt to secure split learning against three threatening attacks and present a fine-grained privacy budget allocation scheme. The analysis proves that our privacy-preserving SplitNN solution provides a tight privacy budget, while the experimental results show that our solution performs better than existing solutions in most cases and achieves a good tradeoff between defense and model usability.

Keywords: Privacy preservation · Inference attack · Reconstruction attack · Feature space hijacking attack · Split learning

1 Introduction

Private data, such as biological information and shopping history, is potentially valuable for commercial usage. Commercial agencies can learn users' preferences and make proper recommendations using their private data. Meanwhile, users could enjoy personalized services by sharing their privacy with service providers. However, both agencies and users are worried about their private data being abused. Besides, since commercial agencies nowadays are dedicated to providing high-quality services in vertical industries, like social networks or online

G. Tsudik et al. (Eds.): ESORICS 2023, LNCS 14347, pp. 23–43, 2024.
https://doi.org/10.1007/978-3-031-51482-1_2

shopping, their user profiles are business-relevant and highly homogeneous. But it commonly requires diversified features for building deep learning models. For these reasons, using multifarious private data for building a satisfying model is essential but challenging.

Fortunately, the collaborative learning paradigm [26] has emerged as a promising solution. Collaborative learning enables participants from different interests to learn a shared model jointly. A well-known collaborative learning paradigm is federated learning [26], focusing on the coordination of distributed participants. Meanwhile, another paradigm split neural network (SplitNN for short) [2,11] is designed explicitly for vertically partitioned features. Participants from different backgrounds could contribute with distinct feature representations. By combining different features, SplitNN is supposed to be more expressive in the real world. Notably, SplitNN has already been used for building industry-level frameworks, such as FATE [39] and Syft [31].

However, collaborative learning paradigms are faced with severe security issues. Roughly speaking, there are three kinds of threats, inference attack [29,35], reconstruction attack [17,34], and poisoning attack [18,37]. An inference attack discloses attributes or membership information of specific data samples of the participants, while a reconstruction attack seeks to generate data samples similar to participants' private data. In [5], the reconstruction attack and the inference attack are studied simultaneously, enabling the host to recover the client's data and allowing an honest-but-curious host to infer the labels with desirable accuracy. Unlike these two kinds of threats, a poisoning attack aims to put harmful data into collaborative learning for malicious purposes rather than stealing private information. Moreover, a feature space hijacking attack considers a malicious participant, enlarging the attack effect of inference and reconstruction. Some excellent defensive solutions have been proposed for federated learning since it is a more general paradigm. According to the techniques used, these solutions can be roughly classified into differential privacy solutions [22,36] and secure multiparty computation solutions [30,42].

Unfortunately, security issues in SplitNN are barely discussed. The workflow of SplitNN has a unique asymmetric design. Therefore, most solutions for secure federated learning are not suitable for SplitNN. Secure multiparty computing solutions like homomorphic encryption can achieve ideal data confidentiality [33,41], but the overhead introduced is still far away from practical uses. It has been proved in [12] that the defense performance of applying differential privacy in a general way to split learning is far away from the expectation when dealing with a feature space hijacking attack (FSHA) [32]. To defend against FSHA, two novel methods are designed in [6] for a split learning client to detect if it is being targeted by a hijacking attack or not. One approach is an active method relying on observations about the learning object, and the other one is a passive method at a higher computing cost. Thus, for the first attempt at privacy-preserving SplitNN for both the server and the client, we offer a unified solution for addressing different threats, including inference, reconstruction, and hijacking attacks. We focus on the abovementioned threats since they share a similar adversarial goal of privacy disclosure, while poisoning attacks need to be studied separately [7,24].

We also note that there is an inherent contradiction [5] between privacy preservation and model usability, especially when private information of two sides should be considered in SplitNN. Through the investigation of the attack effect, we find that the attacker has sufficiently high success rates when disclosing the privacy of either party. To defeat the attacks [17,32,35] and give privacy guarantees on both sides in SplitNN, we make the following contributions:

- We investigate the privacy leakage issue in SplitNN by adapting inference and reconstruction attacks from federated learning. For the first attempt at securing SplitNN against multiple attacks, we propose a unified solution based on a newly designed activation function.
- We offer strong privacy guarantees for both sides of SplitNN. Moreover, a fine-grained privacy budget allocation scheme is given to achieve more efficient perturbations and improve privacy budget utilization.
- We implement and evaluate our solution using real-world datasets for different split learning tasks. The experimental result shows that our solution outperforms existing solutions when concurrently considering privacy preservation and model usability.

2   Problem Statement

2.1   Deep Learning

Given a training dataset X and DNN model parameters θ, a training task is to find approximately optimal θ by minimizing a pre-defined loss function $\mathcal{L}$, regarding input X. We assume that the optimizer used is a mini-batch stochastic gradient descent (SGD) algorithm, which updates θ with a batch input of X iteratively. Assuming the batch size is M, then the total loss of θ for a batch input $x = \{x_i | x_i \in X, i \in [1, M]\}$ should be $\sum_{x \in x} \mathcal{L}(\theta, x)$ in the t-th training iteration. The gradients of θ for model updating should be estimated by $\frac{1}{M} \sum_{x \in x} \nabla_\theta \mathcal{L}(\theta, x)$ approximately. Hence, parameters θ can be updated as $\theta^{t+1} = \theta^t - \frac{1}{M} \sum_{x \in x} \nabla_\theta \mathcal{L}(\theta, x)$. This mini-batch SGD-based optimizing procedure should be repeated until the model usability meets the requirement or the maximal count of iterations reaches.

2.2   Split Learning

SplitNN is an emerging collaborative learning paradigm partitioning the original neural network into different parts. There are commonly two types of participants in SplitNN, the host and the guest. For each training iteration, the forwarding input of the guest should be evaluated locally and passed to the host. Then the backpropagation should be initialized by the host and propagated to the guest. According to related studies [14], there exist several configurations of SplitNN. This paper will focus on the SplitNN design suitable for building models jointly with vertically partitioned features [2]. Assume that host and guest are two companies aiming to predict customer behaviors collaboratively. After an embedding procedure, the host who holds label data merges embedded vectors using a predefined strategy, say averaging. Then the host will finish the rest of the forward propagation and initiate backward propagation. In Table 1, we give a benchmark of SplitNN using different merging strategies for building recommendation models with two public datasets, MovieLens [15] and BookCrossing [43]. For misaligned features where the server and the client may hold different shapes of features for the same data entry, we use zero padding to complement the missing features by zeros to retain the same shape of feature vectors. We give the top-10 hit ratio for the test in Table 1, which are the average of 30 runs in the same setting. During the experiment, we divide the original feature vector of 160 dimensions into two parts. One is 96 dimensional while the other is 64 dimensional. We notice that merging strategies have no significant influence on performance. Thus, averaging will be used as the default setting.

Table 1. Top-10 hit ratio (%) of SplitNN using different merging strategies. Batch size 32, learning rate 0.01. Model architectures are shown in the appendix.

		concat	element-wise					no split
			max	sum	avg.	mul.	min	
MovieLens	padding	56.62	56.26	56.35	56.89	55.23	**57.19**	57.21
	non-padding	55.38	54.75	54.95	**55.72**	54.52	55.08	
Book Crossing	padding	**61.70**	60.84	60.21	61.16	58.99	60.98	61.92
	non-padding	58.80	59.34	**59.44**	59.10	58.85	59.02	

2.3 Threat Model

Unlike updating local models separately in federated learning, participants of SplitNN are required to update local models cooperatively. Interactions between two parties pose new threats to each other [8, 21]. Hence, we will investigate privacy leakage threats from two perspectives. The host and the guest are honest but curious about the private data of each other. They are allowed to do any additional computations when they are following the split learning protocol. Assuming both parties are rational and privacy-aware, they will not exchange information except for the interactive interface. Please note that label leakage attacks and defense in SplitNN have attracted much attention recently. However, these topics are out of our discussion and need to be studied separately. Therefore, both parties may carry out certain attacks to infer or reconstruct each other's private data even simultaneously. The following part introduces the attacks which are considered potential threats against one party or both parties.

Property Inference Attack. Since the host has access to the output of the guest while the guest receives gradients containing private information of the host, an adversary can mount the property inference attack [9, 23] from both parties. Access to the output of the local model on the other side can be seen as a black-box query. In this setting, the adversary can infer properties of private

data by observing query input and the corresponding output. By constructing elaborating shadow models, the adversary can steal substantial information
from the target. In this way, the adversary acquires the capability of inferring
some properties (such as gender and age) of the data samples used for training.
Denoted by F, T, $\mathcal{L}_F$ and l_i the inference model, target model, the loss function
used for F and the label of each data, the adversarial goal is

$$\mathcal{A}_{PIA} = \arg\min_F \sum_{x_i \in X} \mathcal{L}_F(F(T(x_i)), l_i), l_i \in \{0, 1\}. \tag{1}$$

Data Reconstruction Attack. A generative adversarial network (GAN) is
an instance of generative models designed to estimate target data distribution
[13]. Taking advantage of GANs, a data reconstruction attack is proposed in
[17]. The adversary of a reconstruction attack aims to reconstruct the private
training data of other participants in collaborative learning. The host or the guest
or both can be adversarial. To mount the attack, the adversary augments the
training data per iteration by inserting fake samples Z generated by a generator
G. The global model will serve as a discriminator D. The adversary will affect
global model updating by deceiving the target using fake training samples. For
correcting the adversary, the target participant is supposed to put more private
information into the learning. In this game-style training, the adversary may
obtain substantial knowledge to reconstruct data samples as similar to target
data as possible. Thus, the adversarial goal can be given as

$$\mathcal{A}_{DRA} = \min_G \max_D \frac{1}{|X|} \sum_{x \in X} log D(x) + \frac{1}{|X|} \sum_{z \in Z} log(1 - D(G(z))). \tag{2}$$

Feature Space Hijacking Attack. Unlike attacks mentioned above, the feature space hijacking attack [32] considers a malicious adversary capable of manipulating the learning process. With the help of hijacking, the adversary can
improve the performance of inference and reconstruction attacks. In this setting, the adversary can only be the host because label information is needed to
mislead the victim. To mount the attack, the adversary uses a pilot model $\hat{f}$, an
approximation of its inverse function $\hat{f}^{-1}$ with a shadow dataset and a discriminator D to distinguish the output from guest model f and the pilot model $\hat{f}$
during the training process. Then, the malicious host can send a suitable gradient
to hijack the training of an honest guest by setting the goal as

$$\mathcal{A}_{FSHA} = log(1 - D(f(X_{PRIV}))).$$

3   Privacy-Preserving Split Learning

Our solution will be designed to preserve the privacy of the host and the guest
concurrently. Ideally, the guest wants to collaborate with the host under the
condition that the host should disclose no private data and vice versa. However,

unlike conventional model publishing scenarios, the host and guest in SplitNN are required to exchange intermediate results continually. These continuous queries significantly increase the risk of privacy leakage for both sides. Moreover, the attack surface of SplitNN is inside the neural network, which is different from situations studied in end-to-end models [25,40]. Our work offers the first privacy-preserving SplitNN solution for defending against multiple attacks from two directions. The fundamental idea is to construct a bidirectional privacy-aware interface between the host and the guest. Noting that components of a neural network are loosely coupled, any output port may be a candidate for the interface. However, recent studies have proved that activation functions are more adaptive for perturbed operands [10]. Moreover, activation functions have various forms, which are flexible for configuration. As a result, we design a new variant of ReLU as an interface for SplitNN.

3.1 R^3eLU: Randomized-Response ReLU

Inspired by randomized response mechanisms [38], we design a new activation function R^3eLU (randomized-response ReLU) for SplitNN. Specifically, R^3eLU consists of a randomized-response procedure [38] and a Laplace mechanism [4]. This combination is not arbitrary but a complementary result. The original randomized response is good at statistical analysis of item sets. But the activation result of an input sample is commonly a continuous variable. The Laplace mechanism is a classic approach for differential privacy, handling continuous variables. But the perturbation is hard to be controlled, especially when the sensitivity degree of a query function is relatively large. It also means that it is highly risky to adopt the Laplace mechanism to an activation function directly. In SplitNN, we consider the model held by each party as a query function. Remember that both parties need to protect their privacy, so the sensitivity is bounded by the output of the cut layer in the process of forward propagation for the guest and by the gradient in the process of backward propagation for the host.

Recall that the original ReLU is $f(v) = \max(0, v)$, $v \in \mathcal{R}$. A randomized-response variant should yield a proper substitute for replacing real activations with a probability of p. We consider the activations of the cut layer as item sets and apply randomized-response on them. If we yield 0 as the substitute for $v > 0$, then we can inactivate a part of ReLU results, serving as artificial perturbations. But nothing has been changed for $v \leq 0$. Thus, it is not privacy-preserving since $f(v) = 0$ also reveals private information, indicating $v \leq 0$. To enforce a strict privacy policy, we integrate a Laplace mechanism into the ReLU variant by adding noise $z \xleftarrow{r} Laplace(0, \sigma)$. In this way, we can give the definition of R^3eLU as

$$R^3\text{eLU}(v) = \begin{cases} \max(0, v + z), & \text{with probability } p, \\ 0, & \text{with probability } (1 - p). \end{cases} \tag{3}$$

3.2   Forward Propagation with R³eLU

In forward propagation, the guest needs to transfer local forwarding results to the host. At this point, an adversarial host can mount property inference or reconstruction attacks. To stem the leakage, we recommend replacing the original activating function with R³eLU while leaving the rest unchanged. Algorithm 1 gives R³eLU-forward procedure by integrating essential operations. Denoted by v^g (the superscript may be omitted for concision) input of the original ReLU of the guest and N the cardinality of v. The first operation is to select the top K largest elements of v and zero the rest. Then the top-K elements are clipped by a hyper-parameter C. The abovementioned pre-processing is defined as a procedure $ClipK$, taking as input v, constants K and C, outputting $\hat{v}$. We pre-process the inputs of R³eLU to bound the sensitivity. The method $ClipK$ preserves the maximum K absolute values and clips each vector in the l_1 norm for a clipping threshold C. For randomized responding activation states, we calculate the probability

$$p_i = \frac{1}{2} + \frac{\hat{v}_i}{\|\hat{v}\|_\infty} \cdot \left(\frac{e^{\frac{\epsilon_p}{K}}}{1 + e^{\frac{\epsilon_p}{K}}} - \frac{1}{2} \right), \tag{4}$$

where ϵ_p indicates the privacy budget of randomized responding. The state of $\hat{v}_i$ will be deactivated with probability $1 - p_i$ as per R³eLU definition. Finally, a Laplace mechanism with privacy budget ϵ_l is integrated into the R³eLU-forward completing the procedure. Now, the guest will transmit $\tilde{a}^g = \text{R}^3\text{eLU-forward}(v^g, C, K, N, \epsilon_p, \epsilon_l)$ instead of $a^g = \text{ReLU}(v^g)$ to the host.

Algorithm 1: R³eLU-forward procedure.

Input: original input v^g, cardinality N, constants C and K, privacy parameters ϵ_p and ϵ_l, probability p.

Output: activation $\tilde{a}^g$.

1 $\hat{v}^g \leftarrow ClipK(v^g, C, K, N)$ // pre-process
2 **for** $i \leftarrow 1$ **to** N **do**
3 | $r \xleftarrow{r} \mathcal{N}(0,1)$
4 | **if** $r < p_i$ **then**
5 | | $\tilde{a}_i^g \leftarrow \max(\hat{v}_i^g + \text{Lap}(0, \frac{2KC}{\epsilon_l}), 0)$ // activate
6 | **else**
7 | | $\tilde{a}_i^g \leftarrow 0$ // deactivate
8 | **end**
9 **end**
10 **return** $\tilde{a}^g \leftarrow \{\tilde{a}^1, \tilde{a}^2, \ldots, \tilde{a}^N\}$

3.3 Private Backward Propagation

Privacy leakage also exists from the host's perspective. When the host finishes the rest of forwarding propagation after aggregating activations $\tilde{a}^g$ and a^h, the loss produced for backward propagation contains data privacy of the host and guest. According to recent studies of backward propagation [27,34], intermediate results of model updating can cause severe data privacy leakage. Since the loss must be propagated to the guest, it is crucial to prevent the host from being attacked by an adversarial guest. However, the partial loss propagated ranges widely. Integrating a DP mechanism directly into the original ReLU is unrealistic. Due to the randomized-response design, we can construct a privacy-preserving tunnel for backward propagation atop the derivative of R^3eLU.

Recall that the derivative value of ReLU for any input is either one or zero. A randomized-response variant will perturb the binary output randomly. Besides, randomly flipping still discloses real partial losses when value ones are not flipped. Therefore, a Laplace mechanism is used in the backward procedure. Now, we give a randomized-response derivative of R^3eLU

$$\nabla R^3\text{eLU}(\boldsymbol{\delta}^g, \tilde{\boldsymbol{a}}^g, \boldsymbol{v}^g) = \begin{cases} \boldsymbol{\delta}^g + \boldsymbol{z}, & \text{with probability } p, \\ 0, & \text{with probability } (1-p), \end{cases} \tag{5}$$

where $\boldsymbol{\delta}^g$ is the partial loss for the guest model, $\boldsymbol{z}$ is artificial noise. Similar to R^3eLU-forward, R^3eLU-backward also needs some essential operations. Thus, the same $ClipK$ process for top-K selecting and scalar clipping can be adopted for R^3eLU-backward. However, different from R^3eLU, absolute values are used because the partial loss instructs the gradient descent direction. In this case, we have $\hat{\boldsymbol{\delta}}^g = ClipK(\boldsymbol{\delta}^g, C, K, N)$. Moreover, a $Sign$ process is used to obtain signs.

For randomized responding, the probability of retaining an actual loss is

$$p_i = \frac{1}{2} + \frac{|\hat{\delta}_i|}{\|\hat{\delta}_i\|_\infty} \cdot \left(\frac{e^{\frac{\epsilon_p}{K}}}{1 + e^{\frac{\epsilon_p}{K}}} - \frac{1}{2} \right), \tag{6}$$

where ϵ_p is the privacy budget for the randomized response. We now give the backward procedure R^3eLU-backward in Algorithm 2. Please note that although some existing solutions choose to disturb the gradients of two parties, we choose to perturb the partial loss regarding the guest's backpropagation while keeping the partial loss of the host model unchanged. In this way, a slighter influence is caused for the host compared with disturbing all gradients directly.

Algorithm 2: R^{3}elu-backward procedure.

Input: partial loss $\boldsymbol{\delta}^g$, cardinality N, constants C and K, privacy parameters ϵ_p and ϵ_l, probability $\boldsymbol{p}$.

Output: partial loss $\tilde{\boldsymbol{\delta}}^g$.

1   $|\hat{\boldsymbol{\delta}}| \leftarrow ClipK(|\boldsymbol{\delta}|, C, K, N)$ // pre-process

2   **for** $j \leftarrow 1$ **to** N **do**

3      $r \xleftarrow{r} \mathcal{N}(0,1)$

4   **if** $r < p_i$ **then**

5         $\hat{\delta}_i \leftarrow Sign(\delta_i) \cdot |\hat{\delta}_i|$

6   **else**

7         $\hat{\delta}_i \leftarrow 0$ // randomized response

8   **end**

9      $\tilde{\delta}_i^g \leftarrow \hat{\delta}_i^g + \text{Lap}(0, \frac{2KC}{\epsilon_l})$

10 **end**

11 **return** $\tilde{\boldsymbol{\delta}}^g = \{\tilde{\delta}^1, \tilde{\delta}^2, ..., \tilde{\delta}^N\}$

3.4 Dynamic Privacy Budget Allocation

To further reduce privacy loss and improve the utilization of the privacy budget, we recommend allocating the privacy budget for parameters dynamically instead of allocating uniformly. Based on [28], the importance of a parameter during training can be quantified by the error introduced when it is removed from the model. In particular, the importance I_j of $\theta_j \in \boldsymbol{\theta}$ is the squared difference of prediction errors caused by removing θ_j, i.e.,

$$I_j = (\mathcal{L}(\boldsymbol{x}, \boldsymbol{\theta}) - \mathcal{L}(\boldsymbol{x}, \boldsymbol{\theta} \setminus \{\theta_j\}))^2. \tag{7}$$

For efficiency concern, an approximating method is given in [28], estimating the importance I_j by its first-order Taylor expansion as

$$\hat{I}_j = (\nabla_{\theta_j} \mathcal{L}(\boldsymbol{\theta}, x) \cdot \theta_j)^2. \tag{8}$$

Given the importance of each parameter in the cut layer, the importance of a feature can be derived further. Specifically, the importance of a feature U_j, $j \in [1, N_u]$, where N_u is the total number of neurons in the cut layer, can be calculated as joint importance of relevant parameters by summing them up. Thus, $U_j = \sum_{\theta_k \in \boldsymbol{\theta}_{U_j}} \hat{I}_k$, where $\boldsymbol{\theta}_{U_j}$ is the set of all parameters directly connected to the j-th neuron.

Please note that the original importance estimation is designed for a well-trained model and cannot be directly applied to intermediate models during training. To tackle the problem, we give a dynamic estimation method by deriving the original method into a cumulative form. The importance of a feature will be accumulated as the training epoch increases. Specifically, the importance of the j-th neuron in the q-th training epoch is

$$U_j^q = \frac{\sum_{\theta_k \in \tilde{\theta}_j} \hat{I}_k + U_j^{q-1} \times (q \times \lfloor T/n_t \rfloor + (t \bmod n_t) - 1)}{q \times \lfloor T/n_t \rfloor + (t \bmod n_t)}, \tag{9}$$

where n_t indicates the iteration number within a training epoch, T is the maximum training iteration number, and t is the current training iteration. Assuming that $T \mod n_t = 0$, then $q \in [1, T/n_t]$.

Based on the importance estimated, now we can dynamically allocate the privacy budget for different features. The intuition is to give larger budgets to more important features. Before the q-th training epoch begins, we can estimate a feature importance vector $\boldsymbol{U} = \{U_1^q, U_2^q, \ldots, U_{N_u}^q\}$. Accordingly, the privacy budget allocated to each feature will be $\epsilon_j = \epsilon \times U_j^q$, if ϵ is one unit budget. Then the total privacy budget for all features is $\epsilon_F = \sum_{j=\in[1,N_u]} \epsilon_j$. Now, we can set the probability of randomized response for R^{3}eLU-forward and R^{3}eLU-backward using the dynamic budget allocation,

$$p_i = \frac{1}{2} + \frac{U_i^q}{\|\boldsymbol{U}\|_\infty} \cdot \left(\frac{e^{\frac{\epsilon_p}{K}}}{1 + e^{\frac{\epsilon_p}{K}}} - \frac{1}{2} \right). \tag{10}$$

On the other hand, we can also allocate different privacy budgets for different iterations for better budget utilization. Given the total budget ϵ_T for all iterations, we assign the privacy budget $\epsilon_i = \frac{\epsilon_T}{2^i}$ to the i-th iteration as suggested by [3]. Since $\sum_{i=1}^{\infty} \frac{\epsilon_T}{2^i} = \epsilon_T$, according to the sequential composition theory of differential privacy, we can ensure that the whole training process achieves ϵ_T-differential privacy.

We note that the additional computing cost will be caused by the dynamic privacy budget allocation, which is dominated by the computation of the importance of each neuron at the cut layer. As the gradient of the cut layer can be preserved during the process of each backward propagation, the cost generated by the product of the gradients and neurons for each round is $O(N_u)$ where N_u is the number of neurons of the cut layer.

4   Privacy Analysis

We give privacy analysis results regarding the host and the guest, respectively[1].

Corollary 1. *Given privacy budgets ϵ_p and ϵ_l for randomized response and Laplace mechanism respectively, the output of R^3eLU-forward procedure is $(\epsilon_p + \epsilon_l)$-DP.*

Corollary 2. *Split learning for the guest with R^3eLU-forward achieves (ϵ_g, δ_g)-DP, where $\epsilon_g = \gamma\epsilon\sqrt{2T\ln(\frac{1}{\delta_g})} + \gamma\epsilon T(e^{\gamma\epsilon} - 1)$.*

Since we construct R^{3}eLU-forward and R^{3}eLU-backward using the same method, these two procedures have the same analysis result if we constrain that they use the same input. In this way, we can conclude that the output of R^{3}eLU-backward procedure is $(\epsilon_p + \epsilon_l)$-DP, where ϵ_p and ϵ_l are budgets for randomized response and Laplace mechanism, respectively.

---

[1] More details can be found in another version, http://arxiv.org/abs/2304.09515.

Corollary 3. *Split learning for the host with R^3eLU-backward achieves (ϵ_h, δ_h)-DP, where $\epsilon_h = \gamma\epsilon\sqrt{2T\ln(\frac{1}{\delta_h})} + \gamma\epsilon T(e^{\gamma\epsilon} - 1)$.*

We remark that the dynamic privacy budget allocation improves budget utilization without any additional privacy loss. In other words, an important feature gets a higher probability of retaining the activation state than an insignificant feature, which leads to a larger privacy budget. But the total privacy budget of all features remains unchanged.

Corollary 4. *When the guest runs R^3eLU-forward procedure with the dynamic privacy budget allocation, the output is still ϵ-DP, $\epsilon = \epsilon_p + \epsilon_l$.*

Since activation values are clipped with constant C, $\max_{i \in h}\{p_i\}$ will not be affected. Thus, the activation state with the dynamic privacy budget allocation is still ϵ_p-DP. Given the activation state s and sensitivity Δ, then

$$\frac{\Pr[\tilde{a}^g|\hat{v}, s]}{\Pr[\tilde{a}^g|\hat{v}', s]} \leq e^{\sum_{i=1}^{N}(\frac{C\sum_{j=1}^{N}U_j}{\epsilon_l\Delta U_i})} \leq e^{\sum_{i=1}^{N}(\frac{\epsilon_l U_i}{\sum_{j=1}^{N}U_j})} = e^{\epsilon_l} \tag{11}$$

For any arbitrary v and v', the difference of R^3eLU-forward outputs can be bounded by

$$\frac{\Pr[\tilde{a}^g|v]}{\Pr[\tilde{a}^g|v']} = \frac{\Pr[\tilde{a}^g|\hat{v}, s] \cdot \Pr[s|s_a]}{\Pr[\tilde{a}^g|\hat{v}', s] \cdot \Pr[s|s_{a'}]} \leq e^{\epsilon_l} \cdot e^{\epsilon_p} = e^{\epsilon_l + \epsilon_p} \tag{12}$$

5   Evaluation

We evaluate our privacy-preserving SplitNN solution from two aspects, model usability, and privacy loss. To be comprehensive, we will compare our solution with the baseline (without any protection) and the most relevant defensive solutions, i.e., a primitive Laplace mechanism [4] and DPSGD [1], the most well-known privacy-preserving deep learning solution, in the same setting. We will use the same fixed total privacy budget and the same split way (shown in the appendix) for all solutions. For the primitive Laplace mechanism, we simply add Laplacian noise to activations and partial losses to protect the privacy of the guest and host, respectively. For DPSGD, we add artificial noises to gradients of models on either side. For our solution, we set $\epsilon_p = \epsilon_l = \frac{\epsilon}{2}$ and K as half number of features. We set C as 10. We use the dynamic privacy budget allocation for features in our solution and set the initial importance as zero for all features.

All defensive solutions will be evaluated using three real-world datasets, MovieLens [15] and BookCrossing [43] for the recommendation, and MNIST [20] and CIFAR100 [19] for image classification. The *MovieLens* 1-M dataset contains 1 million ratings of 4,000 movies collected from 6,000 users and users' demographic information such as gender and age. The *BookCrossing* dataset includes 278,858 users' demographic information and 1,149,780 ratings of 271,379 books. The *MNIST* database has 70,000 handwriting image examples of digital numbers from 0 to 9. The *CIFAR100* database has 60,000 image examples for 100 classes. Each image example has one superclass as its rough label and one class as its accurate label. We will use batch size 32, a learning rate of 0.01, and an Adam optimizer as default. Since different datasets and defensive solutions may require various epochs for split learning, we will compare the metrics when the learning converges or the privacy budget is drained. All experimental results are averaged across multiple runs.

Before the evaluation, we verify the feasibility of our dynamic importance estimation method. During the verification, we observe the importance estimation of the neurons in the cut layer. The importance estimation of each neuron is calculated as Eq. (9). By accumulating all intermediate results of the importance estimated for neurons, we find that the final importance is almost the same as obtained by the original estimation method on a well-trained model's final state. The importance estimation results of neurons are shown in Fig. 1, proving the correctness of our dynamic importance estimation method and the existence of unbalanced feature importance. As can be seen, the similarity between the accumulated (dynamic) estimation and the original (stable) estimation indicates that our accumulated approach to estimating the importance of a neuron works as well as the original approach.

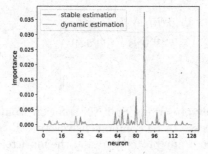

Fig. 1. Estimation results of neuron importance.

Table 2. Model usability results while preserving the privacy of the guest.

ϵ	MovieLens			BookCrossing			MNIST			CIFAR100		
	Laplace	DPSGD	**Ours**	Laplace	DPSGD	**Ours**	Laplace	DPSGD	**Ours**	Laplace	DPSGD	**Ours**
0.1	30.84%	32.29%	**34.03%**	57.02%	55.89%	**58.18%**	17.43%	30.21%	**32.41%**	20.25%	34.21%	**37.87%**
0.5	41.25%	43.69%	**43.87%**	57.67%	56.14%	**58.54%**	27.33%	58.43%	**60.38%**	39.74%	51.36%	**58.22%**
1.0	48.16%	49.09%	**50.56%**	58.02%	56.56%	**58.42%**	31.05%	75.58%	**76.60%**	46.19%	60.48%	**65.32%**
2.0	49.32%	50.38%	**50.49%**	58.74%	56.91%	**59.24%**	38.92%	92.90%	**93.53%**	56.30%	69.72%	**73.35%**
4.0	49.26%	**50.86%**	50.73%	59.01%	57.16%	**59.26%**	95.37%	**95.87%**	94.12%	57.04%	70.86%	**74.41%**

5.1 Model Usability

Since artificial perturbation may affect the learning procedure, we evaluate how SplitNN is affected by privacy-preserving solutions. Two asymmetric parties of

SplitNN may have different influences on learning. Thus, we will evaluate model usability concerning privacy from the perspective of the guest or the host, respectively. We use an averaged test accuracy across all test samples for the evaluation of model usability. Precisely, the test accuracy of a recommendation model is calculated using a top-10 hit ratio, while the test accuracy of an image classifier is its prediction accuracy. In Table 2 and Table 3, we show the model usability results regarding various privacy budget values of the two parties. We note that model accuracy baselines of Movielens, BookCrossing, MNIST and CIFAR100 for SplitNN are 56.62%, 61.70%, 98.00% and 76.20%, respectively.

For the MovieLens model, our solution achieves the best model usability in most cases, especially with a smaller privacy budget. DPSGD has a better result when $\epsilon = 4$ for the guest. But a significant privacy leakage will be caused in this case. For the BookCrossing model, the model usability of our solution is relatively high in cases of protecting the guest and the host. Similarly, DPSGD achieves a better result when $\epsilon = 4$ by sacrificing the host's privacy. Results show some differences for the MNIST model. DPSGD has better results when protecting the host's privacy. The reason is that split learning for an image classification model segments image samples roughly, making our dynamic budget allocation approach malfunction. Meanwhile, DPSGD is not designed to protect partial loss in SplitNN, leading to an optimistic estimation of the threat against the host. On the contrary, our solution has a competitive performance in image classification. For the CIFAR100 model, our method outperforms other protection mechanisms. As the host has the major part of the model, the accuracy drops 5.5% for host protection while only 1.79% for guest protection. These results show that our method with dynamic privacy budget allocation can allocate appropriate privacy budget on different neurons and achieve high accuracy even on complex datasets and models while the primitive Laplace mechanism suffers a 24-percentage points drop in accuracy for CIFAR100 evaluation due to its indiscrimination on all neurons, as shown in Table 3.

Table 3. Model usability results while preserving the privacy of the host.

ϵ	MovieLens			BookCrossing			MNIST			CIFAR100		
	Laplace	DPSGD	Ours	Laplace	DPSGD	Ours	Laplace	DPSGD	Ours	Laplace	DPSGD	Ours
0.1	31.47%	30.68%	**33.98%**	57.37%	57.46%	**58.26%**	27.64%	**33.45%**	32.36%	17.04%	34.22%	**38.96%**
0.5	41.75%	42.31%	**42.67%**	58.62%	58.24%	**58.59%**	55.38%	65.28%	**67.83%**	25.82%	43.96%	**53.72%**
1.0	47.43%	48.29%	**50.39%**	59.49%	58.44%	**59.77%**	71.95%	**89.74%**	88.14%	37.69%	55.28%	**61.48%**
2.0	49.86%	50.43%	**51.47%**	59.34%	59.97%	**60.27%**	89.15%	**92.66%**	92.52%	51.87%	65.67%	**69.60%**
4.0	49.57%	50.09%	**51.62%**	59.55%	**60.75%**	60.66%	94.61%	**95.37%**	95.01%	51.87%	66.89%	**70.70%**

5.2 Privacy Preservation

We evaluate the performance of privacy preservation by comparing attack results against SplitNN with and without the defense. We will mount property inference and data reconstruction attacks against the guest and the host, respectively. The prediction accuracy of the adversary's inference model will be used to measure the performance of the property inference attack. As for the data reconstruction attack, the adversary tries to generate data samples as similar as possible to the target's private data. In this case, a mean squared error (MSE) between a generated sample and a target data sample is commonly used for the adversarial effect measurement.

Table 4. Results of defending the guest against property inference attack.

ϵ	MovieLens			BookCrossing			MNIST			CIFAR100		
	Laplace	DPSGD	**Ours**	Laplace	DPSGD	**Ours**	Laplace	DPSGD	**Ours**	Laplace	DPSGD	**Ours**
0.1	66.99%	77.71%	**60.99%**	**54.76%**	73.29%	55.78%	**43.27%**	53.95%	44.33%	**50.76%**	79.14%	53.97%
0.5	66.16%	74.23%	**64.16%**	**54.97%**	74.52%	56.33%	46.92%	54.23%	**45.59%**	51.47%	79.26%	55.13%
1.0	**67.19%**	78.65%	68.18%	**55.03%**	74.96%	58.65%	47.58%	54.26%	**47.51%**	50.40%	79.37%	55.72%
2.0	68.65%	73.06%	**68.56%**	**54.85%**	74.26%	58.14%	**48.06%**	54.65%	52.87%	60.76%	79.37%	**58.81%**
4.0	**69.14%**	76.18%	71.91%	**54.92%**	74.33%	60.76%	**48.47%**	54.57%	55.73%	60.81%	79.35%	**58.03%**

Table 5. Results of defending the host against property inference attack.

ϵ	MovieLens			BookCrossing			MNIST			CIFAR100		
	Laplace	DPSGD	**Ours**	Laplace	DPSGD	**Ours**	Laplace	DPSGD	**Ours**	Laplace	DPSGD	**Ours**
0.1	53.46%	78.59%	**51.86%**	**54.55%**	74.35%	59.42%	60.34%	80.29%	**48.74%**	50.42%	51.46%	**41.89%**
0.5	53.46%	75.64%	**51.89%**	**54.62%**	74.36%	59.42%	59.82%	81.92%	**49.71%**	50.38%	52.23%	**44.26%**
1.0	53.46%	73.54%	**52.75%**	**54.95%**	74.39%	59.52%	59.74%	82.80%	**50.48%**	49.95%	51.95%	**44.78%**
2.0	**53.47%**	75.05%	59.77%	**54.40%**	74.39%	58.13%	60.38%	88.88%	**50.57%**	50.77%	51.67%	**50.16%**
4.0	**53.48%**	79.28%	56.52%	**54.95%**	74.39%	62.04%	60.62%	89.73%	**50.47%**	51.52%	51.76%	**51.27%**

Defense Against Property Inference Attack. A property inference attack is to infer an existing property (or attribute) of data samples. For example, an adversarial host in our experiments infers the age attribute of the guest's data for a recommendation model. However, the host has no idea of the age distribution since training data is vertically partitioned. We carry out the same property infence attack as [23]. We give evaluation results of the defensive effect of the guest and the host in Table 4 and Table 5, respectively. We use the prediction accuracy of the adversary's inference model as a criterion for evaluation. The higher the prediction accuracy, the more probable success the property inference attack may achieve. In other words, the worse the defensive effect is. As for an image classification model, an unknown patch of image samples will be inferred. The attack accuracy against baselines of MovieLens, BookCrossing, MNIST and CIFAR100 models can achieve above 80%, 79%, 94% and 87% by an adversarial host, 80%, 78%, 57% and 53% by an adversarial guest, respectively. However, our solution can effectively mitigate the adversarial effect during training and decrease the attack accuracy significantly. It should be noted that the primitive Laplace mechanism frustrates the inference attack because the artificial noise added by the Laplace mechanism is indiscriminate, leading to conspicuous damage to the model's usability. Even so, our solution has significant advantages on MovieLens and MNIST datasets. In contrast, the primitive Laplace mechanism cannot protect image classification models, while DPSGD cannot defeat the attack. On the BookCrossing dataset, the primitive Laplace mechanism seems to have a better performance. We infer that the simplicity of the BookCrossing dataset and its corresponding model may lead to this situation. As the noise generated by the primitive Laplace mechanism is haphazard, the model may fail to learn this certain property that the property inference attack aims for. As a result, the property inference attack performs worse on the primitive Laplace mechanism while it maintains a good level of accuracy due to its simplicity. For the CIFAR100 model, While protecting the guest, it seems that at a low privacy budget, the primitive Laplace is better. However, we remind that the model usability is extremely low when applying the primitive Laplace mechanism. Under other situations, our method can effectively decrease the effect of a property inference attack, especially at a low privacy budget.

Table 6. Results of defending the guest against data reconstruction attack.

ϵ	MovieLens			BookCrossing			MNIST			CIFAR100		
	Laplace	DPSGD	**Ours**	Laplace	DPSGD	**Ours**	Laplace	DPSGD	**Ours**	Laplace	DPSGD	**Ours**
0.1	0.2459	0.2455	**0.3223**	0.3216	0.2907	**0.3329**	1.8849	1.8885	**2.0181**	12.5145	2.8622	3.6983
0.5	0.2453	0.2451	**0.3222**	0.3202	0.2902	**0.3329**	1.8024	1.8137	**1.9875**	12.5262	2.8537	3.6891
1.0	0.2453	0.2451	**0.3222**	0.3202	0.2902	**0.3221**	1.7857	1.7509	**1.9533**	3.6419	2.8351	**3.6624**
2.0	0.2452	0.2451	**0.3222**	0.3202	0.2902	**0.3221**	1.7336	1.7469	**1.9391**	2.9453	2.7998	**3.6383**
4.0	0.2452	0.2451	**0.3222**	0.3202	0.2902	**0.3221**	1.7014	1.7440	**1.9206**	2.9502	2.7743	**3.6365**

Table 7. Results of defending the host against data reconstruction attack.

ϵ	MovieLens			BookCrossing			MNIST			CIFAR100		
	Laplace	DPSGD	**Ours**	Laplace	DPSGD	**Ours**	Laplace	DPSGD	**Ours**	Laplace	DPSGD	**Ours**
0.1	0.4032	0.2417	**0.5486**	0.4237	0.2758	**0.5066**	1.2887	1.0875	**1.8257**	13.2849	6.0999	6.5283
0.5	0.4024	0.2419	**0.5357**	0.4222	0.2756	**0.5149**	1.2778	1.0685	**1.7758**	12.8057	5.9302	6.3719
1.0	0.4008	0.2422	**0.5285**	0.4217	0.2743	**0.5235**	1.2602	1.0422	**1.7528**	12.7936	5.9283	6.3531
2.0	0.3982	0.2421	**0.5083**	0.4214	0.2697	**0.5150**	1.2613	1.0333	**1.7334**	6.0397	5.9256	**6.3453**
4.0	0.3960	0.2422	**0.4819**	0.4194	0.2683	**0.5046**	1.2549	0.9996	**1.7262**	6.0143	5.9247	**6.3396**

Defense Against Data Reconstruction Attack. We take advantage of GANs and use the same reconstruction attack as [17]. We show the defense results against an adversarial host and an adversarial guest in Table 6 and Table 7, respectively. We note that the MSE is measured after the attack model has been trained sufficiently in all cases. The MSEs measured for the attack against baselines of MovieLens, BookCrossing, MNIST and CIFAR100 models are 0.2412, 0.2629, 0.9612 and 2.6335 by an adversarial host, 0.2369, 0.2402, 1.6998 and 5.7534 by an adversarial guest, respectively. Please note that these attack results against the baselines are frustrating because the reconstruction attack is hard to succeed in the semi-honest setting. Meanwhile, data samples in the two recommendation datasets are similar and embedded with the same feature vectors. This leads to similar reconstruction results and similar MSEs because the reconstruction of structured data in MovieLens and BookCrossing largely depends on the embedding module. But we can still conclude from the results that our solution has a dominant performance in the defense against reconstruction attacks on either side. For the CIFAR100 model, when at a low privacy budget, the primitive Laplace mechanism sacrifices the prediction accuracy to reach a high difference. However, our method can maintain a satisfying prediction accuracy while protecting against the reconstruction attack.

Defense Against Feature Space Hijacking Attack (FSHA). Please note that property inference and data reconstruction attacks implemented in FSHA [32] hijack the learning objective, offering the adversary an advantage over the previous attacks we have evaluated. In this setting, the malicious attacker trains a generator using SplitNN as a discriminator during the learning process. And a gradient-scaling trick is used to train the generator in FSHA. The sample generating process is essential to FSHA, meaning inference attacks depend on the reconstruction in FSHA. Thus, we will focus on the evaluation of defense against reconstruction attacks. If the generating part fails, the inference attack will be impossible. Since FSHA is comprehensively evaluated using the MNIST dataset, we give defense results of the MNIST model here. In Fig. 2 and Fig. 3, we give the reconstruction results of FHSA mounted by an adversarial host and an adversarial guest against the target samples used in [32], respectively. The second row of the two figures shows the results of FSHA against baselines. The following rows show that our solution can effectively preserve private data for both the guest and the host, even if the privacy budget is relaxed to 4. The results of our solution against FSHA using other datasets and the results of different budget values are in the appendix.

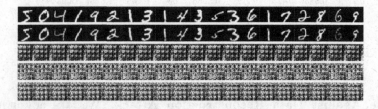

Fig. 2. Reconstruction results of FSHA against the guest's data in the first row. The following rows are attack results against the original SplitNN and our solution ($\epsilon = 0.1, 1.0, 4.0$), respectively.

Fig. 3. Reconstruction results of FSHA against the host's data in the first row. The following rows are attack results against the original SplitNN and our solution ($\epsilon = 0.1, 1.0, 4.0$), respectively.

6   Conclusion

We investigate privacy leakage issues in SplitNN for two parties. By mounting property inference, data reconstruction, and hijacking attacks, we confirm that both the host and the guest in SplitNN are under severe threats of privacy leakage. To mitigate the leakage, we design a new activation function R^3eLU and its derivative in a randomized-response manner. By integrating R^3eLU into SplitNN as an interacting tunnel, we implement R^3eLU-forward and R^3eLU-backward procedures. Through the privacy analysis, we confirm that SplitNN using R^3eLU-forward and R^3eLU-backward provides differential privacy for both two parties. Moreover, we propose a fine-grained privacy budget allocation scheme for assigning privacy budgets dynamically according to the parameters' importance. We finally conclude that our SplitNN solution outperforms the existing privacy-preserving solutions in model usability and privacy preservation through a comprehensive evaluation of different learning tasks. We also note that our solution concentrates on the leakage of private property and data samples. Other privacy issues, like label leakage in SplitNN, should be discussed separately. It is now unclear whether randomized-response solutions can deal with label leakage, which will be our work in the next.

Acknowledgement. The authors would like to thank our shepherd Prof. Stjepan Picek and the anonymous reviewers for the time and effort they have kindly put into this paper. Our work has been improved by following the suggestions they have made. This work was supported in part by the Leading-edge Technology Program of Jiangsu-NSF under Grant BK20222001 and the National Natural Science Foundation of China under Grants NSFC-62272222, NSFC-61902176, NSFC-62272215.

A   Appendix

A.1   Model Architecture

The neural networks we used for MovieLens, BookCrossing, MNIST and CIFAR100 datasets after a split are shown in Table 8. These networks are widely used in related studies. We apply ResNet18 [16] for CIFAR100. We split them according to the interpretation of SplitNN in previous studies [2,32].

Table 8. Model architectures used for evaluation.

MovieLens Model			BookCrossing Model		
Guest Layers	Dim.	Param.	Guest Layers	Dim.	Param. #
Linear(160,128)+ReLU	128	20608	Linear(160,128)+ReLU	128	20608
Host Layers	Dim.	Param.	Host Layers	Dim.	Param.
Linear(160,128)+ReLU	128	20608	Linear(160,128)+ReLU	128	20608
Merge Guest Output			Merge Guest Output		
Linear(128,128)+ReLU	128	16512	Linear(128,256)+ReLU	256	33024
Linear(128,64)+ReLU	64	8256	Linear(256,128)+ReLU	128	32894
Linear(64,3952)+Softmax	3952	256880	Linear(128,17384)+Softmax	17384	2242536

MNIST Model		
Guest Layers	Dim.	Param.
Linear(28*14,128)+BatchNormalization+ReLU	128	50304
Linear(128,64)	64	8256
Host Layers	Dim.	Param.
Linear(28*14,128)+BatchNormalization+ReLU	128	50304
Linear(128,64)+BatchNormalization+ReLU	64	8256
Merge Guest Output		
Linear(64,64)+BatchNormalization+ReLU	64	4160
Linear(64,10)+Softmax	10	650

Cifar100 Model		
Guest Layers	Dim.	Param.
conv1_x = Conv2D(3, 64, kernel=3, padding=1)	[1, 64, 32, 32]	1728
+ BatchNormalization+ReLU	[1, 64, 32, 32]	128
conv2_x = BasicBlock(64, 64, stride=1)	[1, 64, 32, 32]	73984
+ BasicBlock(64, 64, stride=1)	[1, 64, 32, 32]	73984
Host Layers	Dim.	Param.
conv1_x = Conv2D(3, 64, kernel=3, padding=1)	[1, 64, 32, 32]	1728
+ BatchNormalization+ReLU	[1, 64, 32, 32]	128
conv2_x = BasicBlock(64, 64, stride=1)	[1, 64, 32, 32]	73984
+ BasicBlock(64, 64, stride=1)	[1, 64, 32, 32]	73984
Merge Guest Output		
conv3_x = BasicBlock(64, 128, stride=2)	[1, 128, 16, 16]	230,144
+ BasicBlock(128, 128, stride=2)	[1, 128, 16, 16]	295,424
conv4_x = BasicBlock(128, 256, stride=2)	[1, 256, 8, 8]	919,040
+ BasicBlock(256, 256, stride=2)	[1, 256, 8, 8]	1,180,672
conv5_x = BasicBlock(256, 512, stride=2)	[1, 512, 4, 4]	3,673,088
+ BasicBlock(512, 512, stride=2)	[1, 512, 4, 4]	4,720,640
AdaptiveAvgPool2d(1, 1)+Linear(512, 1000)	[1, 100]	51300

A.2   Supplement Results of Evaluation

To further investigate how our solution affects the learning process of SplitNN, we report learning results of a MovieLens recommendation model protecting the privacy of the guest and the host in Fig. 4 and 5, respectively. In each plot, we show trends of training accuracy and testing accuracy as the training epoch increases. When $\epsilon = 0.1$ for the guest or the host, model usability will be influenced seriously. Things get better when the privacy budget increases to 1 for either the guest or the host. We can conclude from the figures that our solution achieves satisfying model usability even with a small privacy budget for either side of SplitNN.

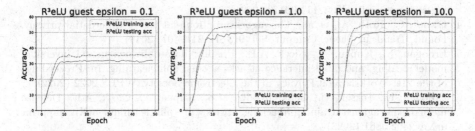

Fig. 4. SplitNN learning curve with the guest's privacy protected by our solution.

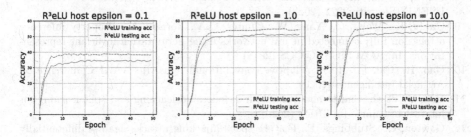

Fig. 5. SplitNN learning curve with the host's privacy protected by our solution.

In Table 9, we give a benchmark of SplitNN using different cut layers with two public datasets, MovieLens [15] and BookCrossing [43]. We also give the top-10 hit ratio for the test in Table 9. We use min as our merging strategy. We combine one linear layer with one ReLU as one cut layer. We notice that there is little difference between different cut layers. However, considering the computational cost at the guest part, it is a good tradeoff between computational cost and model usability to select the first layer as the cut layer.

Table 9. Top-10 hit ratio (%) of SplitNN using different cutlayers.

		layer1	layer2	layer3	layer4	no split
MovieLens	padding	**57.19**	56.97	56.72	57.07	57.21
	non-padding	55.08	55.76	**56.94**	56.75	
Book Crossing	padding	60.98	60.98	61.24	**61.12**	61.92
	non-padding	59.02	58.93	**60.16**	59.83	

References

1. Abadi, M., et al.: Deep learning with differential privacy. In: ACM SIGSAC CCS (2016)
2. Ceballos, I., et al.: Splitnn-driven vertical partitioning. preprint arXiv:2008.04137 (2020)
3. Du, J., Li, S., Chen, X., Chen, S., Hong, M.: Dynamic differential-privacy preserving sgd. preprint arXiv:2111.00173 (2021)
4. Dwork, C., Roth, A., et al.: The algorithmic foundations of differential privacy. Found. Trends® Theor. Comput. Sci. 9(3–4), 211–407 (2014)
5. Erdogan, E., Kupcu, A., Cicek, A.E.: Unsplit: data-oblivious model inversion, model stealing, and label inference attacks against split learning. In: Proceedings of the 21st Workshop on Privacy in the Electronic Society, WPES 2022 (2022)
6. Erdogan, E., Teksen, U., Celiktenyildiz, M.S., Kupcu, A., Cicek, A.E.: Defense mechanisms against training-hijacking attacks in split learning. arXiv preprint arXiv:2302.0861 (2023)
7. Fang, M., Gong, N.Z., Liu, J.: Influence function based data poisoning attacks to top-n recommender systems. In: WWW 2020 (2020)
8. Fu, C., et al.: Label inference attacks against vertical federated learning. In: USENIX Security 2022 (2022)
9. Ganju, K., Wang, Q., Yang, W., Gunter, C.A., Borisov, N.: Property inference attacks on fully connected neural networks using permutation invariant representations. In: ACM SIGSAC CCS (2018)
10. Gao, H., Cai, L., Ji, S.: Adaptive convolutional relus. In: AAAI Conference on Artificial Intelligence (2020)
11. Gao, Y., et al.: End-to-end evaluation of federated learning and split learning for internet of things. In: SRDS (2020)
12. Gawron, G., Stubbings, P.: Feature space hijacking attacks against differentially private split learning. arXiv preprint arXiv:2201.04018 (2022)
13. Goodfellow, I., et al.: Generative adversarial nets. In: NIPS (2014)
14. Gupta, O., Raskar, R.: Distributed learning of deep neural network over multiple agents. J. Netw. Comput. Appl. 116, 1–8 (2018)
15. Harper, A.F.M., Konstan, J.A.: The movielens datasets: history and context. ACM Trans. Interact. Intell. Syst. (2015)
16. He, K., Zhang, X., Ren, S., Sun, J.: Deep residual learning for image recognition. CoRR (2015)
17. Hitaj, B., Ateniese, G., Perez-Cruz, F.: Deep models under the gan: information leakage from collaborative deep learning. In: ACM SIGSAC CCS (2017)
18. Huang, H., Mu, J., Gong, N.Z., Li, Q., Liu, B., Xu, M.: Data poisoning attacks to deep learning based recommender systems. In: NDSS (2021)
19. Krizhevsky, A., Hinton, G., et al.: Learning multiple layers of features from tiny images (2009)
20. LeCun, Y., Bottou, L., Bengio, Y., Haffner, P.: Gradient-based learning applied to document recognition. Proc. IEEE 86(11), 2278–2324 (1998)
21. Li, J., Rakin, A.S., Chen, X., He, Z., Fan, D., Chakrabarti, C.: Ressfl: a resistance transfer framework for defending model inversion attack in split federated learning. In: CVPR (2022)
22. Liu, R., Cao, Y., Chen, H., Guo, R., Yoshikawa, M.: Flame: differentially private federated learning in the shuffle model. In: Proceedings of the AAAI Conference on Artificial Intelligence (2021)

23. Luo, X., Wu, Y., Xiao, X., Ooi, B.C.: Feature inference attack on model predictions in vertical federated learning. In: ICDE (2021)

24. Mao, Y., Yuan, X., Zhao, X., Zhong, S.: Romoa: robust model aggregation for the resistance of federated learning to model poisoning attacks. In: ESORICS (2021)

25. Mao, Y., Zhu, B., Hong, W., Zhu, Z., Zhang, Y., Zhong, S.: Private deep neural network models publishing for machine learning as a service. In: IWQoS (2020)

26. McMahan, B., Moore, E., Ramage, D., Hampson, S., Arcas, B.A.: Communication-efficient learning of deep networks from decentralized data. In: Artificial Intelligence and Statistics (2017)

27. Melis, L., Song, C., De Cristofaro, E., Shmatikov, V.: Exploiting unintended feature leakage in collaborative learning. In: IEEE S&P (2019)

28. Molchanov, P., Mallya, A., Tyree, S., Frosio, I., Kautz, J.: Importance estimation for neural network pruning. In: CVPR (2019)

29. Nasr, M., Shokri, R., Houmansadr, A.: Comprehensive privacy analysis of deep learning: passive and active white-box inference attacks against centralized and federated learning. In: IEEE S&P (2019)

30. Nguyen, T.D., et al.: Flguard: secure and private federated learning. arXiv preprint arXiv:2101.02281 (2021)

31. OpenMined: Syft (2021). https://github.com/OpenMined/PySyft

32. Pasquini, D., Ateniese, G., Bernaschi, M.: Unleashing the tiger: inference attacks on split learning. In: ACM SIGSAC CCS (2021)

33. Pereteanu, G.L., Alansary, A., Passerat-Palmbach, J.: Split he: fast secure inference combining split learning and homomorphic encryption. arXiv preprint arXiv:2202.13351 (2022)

34. Salem, A., Bhattacharya, A., Backes, M., Fritz, M., Zhang, Y.: Updates-leak: data set inference and reconstruction attacks in online learning. In: USENIX Security Symposium (2020)

35. Salem, A., Zhang, Y., Humbert, M., Fritz, M., Backes, M.: ML-leaks: model and data independent membership inference attacks and defenses on machine learning models. In: NDSS (2019)

36. Sun, L., Qian, J., Chen, X.: LDP-FL: practical private aggregation in federated learning with local differential privacy. In: IJCAI (2021)

37. Tolpegin, V., Truex, S., Gursoy, M.E., Liu, L.: Data poisoning attacks against federated learning systems. In: ESORICS (2020)

38. Warner, S.L.: Randomized response: a survey technique for eliminating evasive answer bias. J. Am. Stat. Assoc. **60**(309), 63–69 (1965)

39. Webank: Fate (2021). https://github.com/FederatedAI/FATE

40. Yu, L., Liu, L., Pu, C., Gursoy, M.E., Truex, S.: Differentially private model publishing for deep learning. In: IEEE S&P (2019)

41. Zhang, C., Li, S., Xia, J., Wang, W., Yan, F., Liu, Y.: {BatchCrypt}: efficient homomorphic encryption for {Cross-Silo} federated learning. In: 2020 USENIX Annual Technical Conference (USENIX ATC 2020) (2020)

42. Zheng, Y., Lai, S., Liu, Y., Yuan, X., Yi, X., Wang, C.: Aggregation service for federated learning: an efficient, secure, and more resilient realization. IEEE Trans. Dependable Secure Comput. **20**(2), 988–1001 (2022)

43. Ziegler, C.N., McNee, S.M., Konstan, J.A., Lausen, G.: Improving recommendation lists through topic diversification. In: WWW (2005)

The Power of MEME: Adversarial Malware Creation with Model-Based Reinforcement Learning

Maria Rigaki[✉][iD] and Sebastian Garcia[iD]

Faculty of Electrical Engineering, Czech Technical University in Prague, Prague, Czech Republic
maria.rigaki@fel.cvut.cz, sebastian.garcia@agents.fel.cvut.cz

Abstract. Due to the proliferation of malware, defenders are increasingly turning to automation and machine learning as part of the malware detection toolchain. However, machine learning models are susceptible to adversarial attacks, requiring the testing of model and product robustness. Meanwhile, attackers also seek to automate malware generation and evasion of antivirus systems, and defenders try to gain insight into their methods. This work proposes a new algorithm that combines Malware Evasion and Model Extraction (MEME) attacks. MEME uses model-based reinforcement learning to adversarially modify Windows executable binary samples while simultaneously training a surrogate model with a high agreement with the target model to evade. To evaluate this method, we compare it with two state-of-the-art attacks in adversarial malware creation, using three well-known published models and one antivirus product as targets. Results show that MEME outperforms the state-of-the-art methods in terms of evasion capabilities in almost all cases, producing evasive malware with an evasion rate in the range of 32–73%. It also produces surrogate models with a prediction label agreement with the respective target models between 97–99%. The surrogate could be used to fine-tune and improve the evasion rate in the future.

Keywords: adversarial malware · reinforcement learning · model extraction · model stealing

1 Introduction

As machine learning models are more commonly used in malware detection, there is a growing need for detection tools to combat evasive malware. Understanding attackers' motives is vital in defending against malware, often created for profit. Malware-as-a-Service operations are used to automate the obfuscation and evasiveness of existing malware, and it is safe to assume that attackers will continue to improve their automation and try to create adversarial malware as efficiently as possible [47]. In this work, we are interested in the problem of automating the

G. Tsudik et al. (Eds.): ESORICS 2023, LNCS 14347, pp. 44–64, 2024.
https://doi.org/10.1007/978-3-031-51482-1_3

generation of evasive Windows malware executables primarily against machine learning static detection models.

Creating adversarial malicious binaries that preserve their functionality has been the subject of several works until now. Most works use a set of pre-defined actions that alter the Windows binary file by, e.g., adding benign sections and strings, modifying section names, and other "non-destructive" alterations. The selection of the most appropriate set of actions is learned through reinforcement learning or similar approaches. To our knowledge, all prior work relies on the assumption that the target model (or system) is available to perform unlimited checks or queries to verify whether a malicious binary has evaded the target. However, from the attacker's perspective, fewer queries mean less time to produce malware. They can also lead to lower detection probabilities because they can be stealthier. More adversarial samples can also draw attention from malware analysts about the adversarial modifications performed, leading to better defenses [23]. Therefore, assuming an attacker can do unlimited queries to a target model to modify their malware may not be realistic in evasive malware creation.

We propose an algorithm that combines malware evasion with model extraction (MEME) based on model-based reinforcement learning. The goal of MEME is to learn a reinforcement learning policy that selects the appropriate modifications to a malicious Windows binary file in order for it to evade a target detection model while using a limited amount of interactions with the target. The core idea is to use observations and labels collected during the interaction with the reinforcement learning environment and use them with an auxiliary dataset to train a surrogate model of the target. Then, the policy is trained to learn to evade the surrogate and evaluated on the original target.

We test MEME using three malware detection models that are released and publicly available and on an antivirus installed by default in all Windows operating systems. MEME is compared with two baseline methods (a random policy and a PPO-based policy [36]) and well as with two state-of-the-art methods (MAB [39] and GAMMA [9]). Using only 2,048 queries to the target during the training phase, MEME learns a policy that evades the targets with an evasion rate of 32–73%. MEME outperforms all baselines and state-of-the-art methods in all but one target. The algorithm also learns a surrogate model for each target with 97–99% label agreement with a much lower query budget than previously reported.

The main contributions of this work are:

- A novel combination of two attacks, malware evasion and model extraction in one algorithm (MEME).
- An efficient generation of adversarial malware using model-based reinforcement learning while maintaining better evasion rates than state-of-the-art methods in most targets.
- An efficient surrogate creation method that uses the adversarial samples produced during the training and evaluation of the reinforcement learning agent. The surrogates achieve high label agreement with the targets using minimal interaction with the target models.

2   Threat Model

The threat model for this work assumes an attacker that only has **black-box** access to a target (classifier or AV) during the inference phase and can submit binary files for static scanning. The target provides binary labels (0 if benign, 1 if malicious). The attacker has no or limited information about the target architecture and training process, and they aim to evade it by modifying the malware in a **functionality-preserving** manner, i.e., modifications produce valid executables and do not alter the "maliciousness" of the original file. In the case of classifiers, the attacker may have some knowledge of the extracted features, but this is not the case for antivirus systems. For the model extraction part of the attack, the adversary requires an auxiliary dataset. Given the existence of open source datasets such as [3,15], we consider this a reasonable assumption. Prior work has shown that model extraction is more successful if the auxiliary dataset comes from a similar distribution as the training data distribution of the target [33]. The training data distribution is unknown when the target is an AV or an unknown system, which may lower the attack's efficiency. However, it does not render it useless. Finally, the attacker aims to minimize the interaction with the target by submitting as few queries as possible.

3   Background and Related Work

This section provides background information and summarizes the related work in machine learning malware evasion and model extraction. It also presents some relevant background information on reinforcement learning and the environments used for training agents for malware evasion.

3.1   Reinforcement Learning

Reinforcement Learning (RL) is a sub-field of machine learning where the optimization of a reward function is done by *agents* that interact with an *environment*. The agent performs actions in the environment and receives back *observations* (view of the new state) and a *reward*. The goal of RL is to train a *policy*, which instructs the agent to take certain *actions* to maximize the rewards received over time [41].

More formally, the agent and the environment interact over a sequence of time steps t. At each step, the agent receives a state from the environment s_t and performs an action a_t from a predefined set of actions $\mathcal{A}$. The environment produces the new state s_{t+1} and the reward that the agent receives due to its action. Through this interaction with the environment, the agent tries to learn a policy $\pi(a|s)$ that maps the probability of selecting an action a given a state s, so that the expected reward is maximized. One of the essential aspects of RL is the *Markov property*, which assumes that future states of the process only depend on the current state.

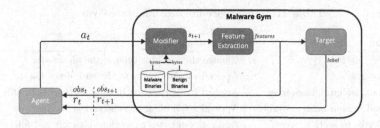

Fig. 1. Malware-Gym Architecture

Some of the most successful RL algorithms are *model-free* approaches, i.e., they do not try to build a model of the environment. A downside of model-free algorithms is that they tend to require a lot of data and work under the assumption that the interactions with the environment are not costly. In contrast, *model-based* reinforcement learning algorithms learn a model of the environment and use it to improve policy learning. A fairly standard approach for model-based RL is to alternate between policy optimization and model learning. During the model learning phase, data is gathered from interacting with the environment, and a supervised learning technique is employed to learn the model of the environment. Subsequently, in the policy optimization phase, the trained model explores methods for enhancing the policy [21].

In terms of security applications, reinforcement learning has been proposed for use in several applications such as honeypots [11,17], IoT and cyber-physical systems [27,43], network security [46], malware detection [13,44], and malware evasion [2,14,22,24,30,31,39]. Most malware evasion papers use Malware-gym or extensions of it to test their proposed algorithms. Therefore we present the basic concepts of the environment in more detail below.

Malware-Gym. The Malware-Gym environment is a reinforcement learning environment based on OpenAI Gym [5], and it was first introduced in [2]. Figure 1 shows the internal architecture of the environment.

The environment encapsulates a target model, which is considered a black box. The target takes as input extracted features from a binary file and outputs a label or a prediction score. The binary file bytes are the state s_t, and the extracted features are the observation o_t, which the agent receives from the environment at time t. The observation is also fed into the target model that outputs a score or a label. The score is transformed into a reward r_t that is returned to the agent that has to decide which action to take, a_t. The action is fed back into the environment, which modifies the binary through the transition function (modifier) to produce the next binary state s_{t+1}, observation o_{t+1}, and reward r_{t+1}. The list of available actions in the latest version of the Malware-Gym can be found in Table 1. The actions listed aim to preserve functionality, and ideally, the modified binary should still be valid. Some of the actions require a benign dataset in order to use strings and sections from benign files.

Table 1. Action space in latest Malware-Gym

Action	Description
modify_machine_type	Change the machine type in the file header
pad_overlay	Append random bytes at the end of the file
append_benign_data_overlay	Append benign section data to the end of the file
append_benign_binary_overlay	Append a full binary to the end of the file
add_bytes_to_section_cave	Add random bytes to sections that are not full
add_section_strings	Add a new section with benign strings
add_section_benign_data	Add a new benign section
add_strings_to_overlay	Append benign strings to the end of the file
add_imports	Add a new library to the import address table
rename_section	Rename a section
remove_debug	Remove debug information from Data Directories
modify_optional_header	Modify operating system info in the PE header
modify_timestamp	Modify the timestamp
break_optional_header_checksum	Change the checksum in the PE header
upx_unpack	Unpack the file using UPX
upx_pack	Pack the file using UPX

The reward is calculated based on the output of the classifier/target. If the score is below a predetermined decision threshold, the binary is considered benign, i.e., it evaded the target, and the returned reward equals 10. If the score exceeds the threshold, the binary is considered malicious, and the reward is calculated as the difference between the previous and current scores. The process continues until the binary is evasive or a predetermined number of maximum iterations is reached. The agent receives the current observation (features) and the reward and decides on the following action unless the malware is evasive, where it moves to the next binary. The agent's goal is to learn a policy π that generalizes well and can be applied to future malicious binaries.

3.2 Malware Evasion

The main goal of malware evasion is to make the malware undetectable by security systems so that it can perform its malicious activities unnoticed. Malware creators continuously develop new techniques to evade detection, which makes it difficult for security experts to keep up with the evolving threat landscape. The concept has evolved to include the evasion of machine learning classifiers and the use of machine learning techniques to evade antivirus (AV) systems. For this work, we are mainly interested in machine learning approaches that attackers may use to generate evasive **fully functional** Windows PE malware so that malware classifiers and AVs can not detect them.

There have been several works on this topic, and detailed taxonomies and definitions can be found in the following surveys [10,25]. Anderson et al. [2] created the Malware-Gym and were the first work that generated adversarial malware that aimed to be functionality-preserving. They used the Actor-Critic model with Experience Replay (ACER) algorithm and tested against the original Ember model. Other works extended the Malware-Gym and tested different algorithms such as Double Deep Q-Network(DQN) [14], Distributional Double DQN [22], and REINFORCE [31].

Apart from testing different algorithms, several authors proposed changes to the reward function [12,22]. MAB-malware [39] is an RL framework based on multi-armed bandits (MAB). MAB and AIMED [22] are the only works that assume that the target model provides only a hard label instead of a prediction score. The different works propose different numbers of permitted modifications, varying from as low as 5 to as high as 80. However, none of the prior work constrains the number of queries to the target or discusses whether unlimited query access is a realistic scenario.

Other black-box attacks for the evasion of malware classifiers proposed different approaches such as genetic algorithms [9], explainability [34], or using simpler but effective techniques such as packing [6].

3.3 Model Extraction

Model extraction or model stealing is a family of attacks that aim to retrieve a model's parameters, such as neural network weights or a functional approximation, using a limited query budget. These attacks are usually tested against Machine Learning as a Service (MLaaS) applications. Most model extraction attacks use learning-based approaches, which query the target model with multiple data samples X and retrieve labels or prediction scores y to create a thief dataset. Using the thief dataset, they train a surrogate model that behaves similarly to the target model in the given task. Model extraction attacks may have different goals [19]. In a *fidelity* attack, the adversary aims to create a surrogate model that learns the decision boundary of the target as faithfully as possible, including the errors that the target makes. These surrogate models can be used later in other tasks, such as generating adversarial samples. In a *task accuracy* attack, the adversary aims to construct a surrogate model that performs equally or better than the target model in a specific task, such as image or malware classification. The attacker's ultimate goal affects the selection of the thief dataset, the metrics for a successful attack, and the attack strategy itself.

Learning-based model extraction attacks use different strategies to select the samples they use for querying the target, such as active learning [7,29], reinforcement learning [28], generative models [35], adversarial samples [45], or just using random data [8]. In the security domain, model extraction has been proposed as the first step of an attack that aims to generate evasive malware [16,33,34]. Both [34] and [33] generate evasive malware in a two-step approach: creating a surrogate and then evading the target. Hu et al. [16] use a Generative Adversarial Network (GAN) and a surrogate detector to bypass a malware detector that works with API calls. Neither [16] and [34] are concerned with the number of queries they are making to the target, while in [33] the authors measured only the query efficiency of the model extraction and not that of the subsequent task of the malware evasion.

Algorithm 1. Malware Evasion and Model Extraction (MEME)

1: **Initialize:** policy π_θ and a surrogate model $\hat{f}_\phi$.
2: **Initialize:** empty dataset $\mathcal{D}_{sur}$ and the auxiliary dataset $\mathcal{D}_{aux}$.
3: **Train:** policy π_θ on the real model f using PPO for n steps and store episode data in $\mathcal{D}_{sur}$.
4: **for** i in 1..k **do**
5:     **Train:** surrogate model $\hat{f}_\phi$ using $\mathcal{D}_{sur}$ and $\mathcal{D}_{aux}$.
6:     **Update:** policy π_θ using PPO with the surrogate for m steps.
7:     **Evaluate:** policy π_θ in real system f for n steps. Add episode data to $\mathcal{D}_{sur}$.
8: **end for**
9: **Output:** policy π_θ and surrogate model $\hat{f}_\phi$.

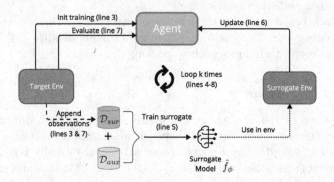

Fig. 2. High-level description of the MEME algorithm. First, there is an initial training that produces a first $\mathcal{D}_{sur}$, which is combined with $\mathcal{D}_{aux}$ to train a surrogate, which is used to improve the agent. The loop is repeated k times.

4   Methodology

The MEME algorithm combines model extraction and reinforcement learning (RL) techniques to improve the generation of evasive malware binaries. The algorithm takes advantage of the fact that the attacker fully controls the binary modifier part of the environment but does not control the target model, which is a black box. However, an attacker can use data collected during the training of the RL agent to create and train a surrogate model of the target. The algorithm is implemented as several training/testing rounds until a final reinforcement learning policy is learned that can produce adversarial binaries for a given target. Figure 2 presents a high-level description of the algorithm, and the detailed listing is presented in Algorithm 1.

Following Algorithm 1, MEME initializes a Proximal Policy Optimization (PPO) RL algorithm [36] (lines 1 and 2) to perform a first train of the PPO policy using the target model and a limited amount of steps (using Malware-Gym). The goal of this step is to store a small number of observations and labels in $\mathcal{D}_{sur}$ (line 3). Then, $\mathcal{D}_{sur}$ is combined with an auxiliary set of labeled data ($\mathcal{D}_{aux}$) that the attacker should possess, and this combined dataset is used to train a surrogate model for the model extraction attack (line 5). The improved surrogate replaces the target model in a new Malware-Gym environment that trains a better policy (agent) for evasion (line 6). Last, the improved policy is evaluated against the original target model (line 7) to obtain the final evasion metrics. In this last step, we take advantage of the queries done to the target to append their output to the D_{sur} dataset.

This loop is repeated for k rounds. During the last round, the evaluation is performed using the malware binary *test set* to produce the final evasion metrics (instead of the malware binary *evaluation set* used in the inner loop). The total number of queries to the target during training is $k * n$, where k is the total number of rounds.

For learning the policy, we use the PPO algorithm, a model-free on-policy gradient method that clips the objective function, limiting the updates done to the policy to avoid too large positive changes or a minimum of negative changes to stabilize it. We used the Stable Baselines3 [32] implementation of PPO that uses an Actor-Critic (A2C) architecture.

To train the surrogate model, using the data collected during the learning or evaluation of the agent in D_{sur} is not enough. The number of samples is not enough since we aim to minimize the queries to the target. In addition, all observations come from the extracted features of the malicious binary dataset or their adversarial modifications. Using only malicious samples is not adequate to train a surrogate model that is a binary classifier. Therefore, using an auxiliary dataset that contains benign samples is necessary. Regarding the model extraction, our attack is closest to the one proposed in [45] since it uses adversarial samples to generate a synthetic dataset for training the surrogate.

Adaptations to the Gym Environment. MEME was implemented around the Malware-Gym environment (Sect. 3.1) in its latest version[1]. Several modifications were applied to the environment to fit the assumptions and constraints for this work:

- The "modify_machine_type" action was removed because our tests showed that it produces invalid binaries for Windows 10 systems.
- All targets were set to return hard labels (0 or 1), not scores.
- Regarding the benign sections, the Malware-Gym implementation used only data from ".text" sections. In our implementation, we use data from other sections if the ".text" section is unavailable.
- The latest environment supports the Ember and Sorel-LGB classifiers as targets. We added new environments to support the Sorel-FFNN, surrogate, and AV targets. The AV requires a web service in a virtual machine that invokes the AV static scanning capabilities.
- For all target environments, we added support for saving the observations (features) and scores during training and evaluation runs so that they can be used for the training of the surrogate.

---

[1] https://github.com/bfilar/malware_rl.

Our version of the environment and the experiments performed as part of this work can be found in (https://github.com/stratosphereips/meme_malware_rl/releases/tag/v1.0). Please note that we are releasing the source code of our implementation for reproducibility and improvement; however, we do not release the trained models or agents to avoid potential misuse.

4.1 Evasion Evaluation Metrics

To evaluate the performance of the evasion models reasonably and realistically, we limited how many queries they do to the target model and how long they run. The idea behind limiting running time is that the ratio at which malware authors create new malware is high, and a method that takes too long to create evasive malware is impractical. Industry measurements such as the ones provided by AV-ATLAS [18] report that 180 new malware are generated per minute. Virus Total [42] provides an even higher measurement of 560 distinct new files uploaded per minute as of the 21st of May, 2023. These global measurements vary but show how quickly new malware variants appear, possibly due to the proliferation of Malware-as-a-Service frameworks. A recent and more conservative measurement from Blackberry mentions that they observe 1.5 new malware samples per minute [40]. Given the above measurements, we decided to constrain the running time of each experiment to four hours in total. Given that the test set consists of 300 malware binaries, this corresponds to 1.25 processed binaries per minute, which is lower than the most conservative reported metric we could find.

The primary metric used to evaluate the malware evasion task was the *evasion rate* $\mathbf{E}$, which is the fraction of malware that becomes evasive within the time window of *four hours* over the total number of malware that were initially detected by each target: $\mathbf{E} = \frac{n_{ev}}{n_{det}}$.

We also report the *average number of binary modifications* required for a malware binary to evade the target. For the Random, PPO, and MEME methods, this is equivalent to the mean episode length over all the detected malware binaries in the test set. The episode length for a non-evasive binary is equal to the maximum number of attempts, and for an evasive one is the number of changes required to become evasive. For the MAB framework, for the evasive binaries, we considered only the minimal binaries with the least amount of actions. The average number of binary modifications was impossible to measure for the GAMMA attack since the SecML framework (through which GAMMA was implemented) does not provide a straightforward way to measure this metric.

4.2 Surrogate Evaluation Metrics

The surrogate models trained in MEME were evaluated using two different metrics: *label agreement* and explainability-based *feature agreement* [38]. The label agreement of two models f and $\hat{f}$, respectively, is defined as the average number of similar predictions over a test set X_{test}, and it is a standard metric for model extraction fidelity attacks [19]:

$$LabelAgreement(f, \hat{f}) = \frac{1}{|X_{test}|} \sum_{x \in X_{test}} \mathbb{1}(f(x) = \hat{f}(x))$$

The feature agreement metric computes the fraction of common features between the sets of top-k features of two explanations. Given two explanations E_t (target) and E_s (surrogate), the feature agreement metric can be formally defined as:

$$FeatureAgreement(E_t, E_s, k) = \frac{|top\_features(E_t, k) \cap top\_features(E_s, k)|}{k}$$

where $top\_features(E, k)$ returns the set of top-k features of the explanation E based on the magnitude of the feature importance values. The maximum value of the feature agreement is 1. For this work, we measured the feature agreement for $k = 10$ and $k = 20$, and the explainability method used was SHAP (SHapley Additive exPlanations) [26]. SHAP employs game theory principles to explain machine learning model outputs by linking effective credit allocation with localized explanations via Shapley values that originated from game theory. SHAP is model-agnostic and has been used effectively in the past for adversarial malware creation [34]. For the LightGBM targets we used TreeSHAP which is designed for tree models, while for Sorel-FFNN we used the KernelSHAP variant.

5   Experimental Setup

To evaluate MEME, several experiments were conducted in different configurations. Four different malware detection solutions were selected as targets to evade. MEME was compared to four other evasion techniques on these four targets.

5.1   Targets

The selection of targets was made to include three highly cited malware detection models together with a real implementation of a popular free Antivirus solution.

1. **Ember.** A LightGBM [20] model that was released as part of the Ember dataset [3] which was used for training that same model. The decision threshold was set to 0.8336, which corresponds to a 1% false positive rate (FPR) on the Ember 2018 test set.
2. **Sorel-LGB.** A LightGBM model that was distributed as part of the Sorel-20M [15] dataset, which was used for training that same model. The decision threshold was set to 0.5, which corresponds to a 0.2% false positive rate (FPR) on the Sorel-20M test set.
3. **Sorel-FFNN.** A feed-forward neural network (FFNN) that was also released as part of the Sorel-20M dataset and was trained using the same data. The decision threshold was set to 0.5, which corresponds to 0.6% false positive rate (FPR) on the Sorel-20M test set.

4. **Microsoft Defender.** An antivirus product that comes pre-installed with the Windows operating system. According to [37], it is the most used free antivirus product for personal computers. All tests were performed using a virtual machine (VM) running an updated version of the product. The VM had no internet connectivity during the binary file scanning.

5.2 Datasets

Our experiments required the use of the following datasets:

1. **Ember 2018.** A dataset that consists of features extracted from one million Windows Portable Executable (PE) files [3]. The dataset is split into training, testing, and "unlabeled sets". The training set consists of 300,000 clean samples, 300,000 malicious samples, and 200,000 "unlabeled" samples. The so-called unlabeled part of the dataset was truly unlabeled in the first version. However, in the 2018 release, the authors provided an *avclass* label for all malicious samples, including those in the unlabeled set. Each sample has 2,381 static features related to byte and entropy histograms, PE header information, strings, imports, data directories, etc.
2. **Sorel-20M.** The Sorel dataset [15] was released in 2020 and contains the extracted features of 20 million binary files (malicious and benign). The feature set used was the same as the one from the Ember dataset.
3. **Malware Binary Files.** In addition to the Ember features used for training the surrogate, we also obtained **1,000 malicious binary** files whose hashes were part of Ember 2018 and we use them for generating the evasive malware with all the methods.
4. **Benign Binary Files.** All methods require a benign set of data from where they extract benign strings, sections, and other elements that are used for the binary modifications. The same set of 100 benign binaries were used in all experiments. The files were obtained from a Windows 10 virtual machine after installing known benign software.

MEME required two versions of the D_{aux} dataset to train the surrogate models. For the Ember and AV surrogates, D_{aux} contains the *unlabeled* part of the Ember dataset. For the Sorel surrogates, D_{aux} contains 200,000 samples from the Sorel-20M validation set. These datasets were chosen to create the surrogate because they were **not** used to train the corresponding targets. During the evaluation, a subset of the Sorel-20M test set was used to evaluate the performance of the Sorel surrogate models. The Ember test set was used to evaluate the Ember and AV models.

The 1,000 malware binaries were split into training and test sets with a 70–30% ratio using five different seeds. The test sets were used to test all the methods, while the 700 binaries in the training set were used to train each of the RL policies for PPO and MEME (these were the binaries to which modifier actions were applied).

5.3 Adversarial Malware Generation Comparison

Concerning the generation of adversarial malware, MEME is compared with four algorithms. Two baseline reinforcement learning algorithms that use the Malware-Gym environment: a random agent and an agent that learns a policy using the *vanilla* Proximal Policy Optimization (PPO) algorithm [36], and two state-of-the-art (SOTA) algorithms: MAB [39] and GAMMA [9]. The two SOTA algorithms were selected based on the fact that they are relatively recently released and the fact that they seem to perform well in the malware evasion task. In addition, their source code is available. The detailed setup used for each of the algorithms, as well as any modifications, are presented below:

1. **Random Agent.** The random agent is the simplest baseline used in our experiments. It uses the Malware-Gym environment and randomly samples the next modification action from the available action space. The agent is evaluated in the test environments using the 300 test malware samples.
2. **PPO.** This is an agent that uses the PPO [36] algorithm as implemented in the Stable-Baselines3 software package. The agent was trained for 2,048 steps on the malware training set and evaluated on the malware test set. To select the hyper-parameters related to PPO training, we used the Tree-structured Parzen Estimator (TPE) method [4] as implemented in the software package Optuna [1]. The TPE algorithm was executed with the Ember dataset, but the settings performed well in the other targets. The tuned hyper-parameters were γ, the learning rate, the maximum gradient norm, the activation function, and the neural network size for the actor and critic models. The search space of each parameter and the final values are presented in the Appendix.
3. **MAB.** RL algorithm that treats the evasive malware generation as a multi-armed bandit problem[2]. It operates in two stages: evasion and minimization. It samples the action space, which includes generic actions (similar to Malware-Gym) and any successful evasive actions along with the specific modifiers, e.g., appending a specific benign section. MAB directly manipulates each binary without generating a learned policy. Therefore, all experiments were conducted directly on the malicious binary test set.
4. **GAMMA.** An algorithm that injects benign binary sections into malicious PE files while preserving their functionality. It modifies features like section count, byte histograms, and strings, leaving features related to, e.g., certificates and debugging data unaffected. By employing genetic algorithms, GAMMA searches for optimal benign sections to reduce the target model's confidence by minimizing the content and location of injected sections. The attack is implemented in the SecML library[3]. Though effective, it has a significantly longer runtime than other tested methods. The attack uses a restricted set of 30 available benign sections and a population size of 20. The λ parameter, impacting the injected data size, was set to 10^{-6}. GAMMA directly operates on each binary and does not generate a learned policy. Hence, all experiments were conducted on the malicious binary test set.

---

[2] https://github.com/weisong-ucr/MAB-malware.
[3] https://github.com/pralab/secml_malware.

5.4   General Experiment Settings

All the algorithms were tested under a common set of constraints. The maximum allowed modifications to a binary file were set to 15 for the RL-based algorithms. Similarly, for GAMMA, the number of iterations was set to 15; for MAB, the number of "pulls" was also 15. The second constraint was to set the maximum running time for all experiments to 4 h. For MAB and GAMMA, this setting means that the algorithms must handle as many malicious binaries as possible in that time. At the same time, for PPO and MEME, this time included both the policy training time and the evaluation time.

For PPO and MEME, we set the query budget to 2,048. This budget does not include the final evaluation queries on the test set. MAB and GAMMA were not constrained in the total number of queries because the respective frameworks do not support the constraint. Finally, all experiments were run with five different seeds. The random seeds controlled the split of the 1,000 malicious binaries into train and test, and therefore, all methods were tested in the same files.

For MEME, the initial training steps n in Algorithm 1 were set to 1,024, and the total number of loops k was two. The surrogate training steps m were set to 2,048 (step 6 of Algorithm 1). MEME utilizes PPO for training and updating the policy (π_θ). The PPO settings remained the same as in the baseline experiments, enabling a comparison of the impact of using a surrogate model for additional PPO training. In total, there were a total of 2,048 queries to the target and 4,096 training steps using the surrogate environment. The surrogate was always a LightGBM model. Surrogate training involved two datasets: $\mathcal{D}_{aux}$ from an external dataset (e.g., Ember 2018 or Sorel-20M) and $\mathcal{D}_{sur}$ generated during lines 3 and 7 of Algorithm 1. These datasets were mixed with a ratio α, a hyperparameter for LGB surrogate tuning. Other hyperparameters, such as the number of boosting trees, learning rate, tree depth, minimum child samples, and feature fraction, were tuned separately for each target using TPE and Optuna. Appendix A provides the detailed search space and selected values. Surrogate models were evaluated using the respective target test sets, and a decision threshold matching target FPR levels was calculated. For the AV target without a representative dataset, the surrogate's decision threshold was set to 0.5.

6   Results

6.1   Malware Evasion

To evaluate MEME, we tested its evasion capabilities compared to four other algorithms. Figure 3 shows the evasion rates of all algorithms against four different targets. Generally, we can see that some targets are more challenging than others. For example, the Sorel-FFNN target seems the hardest to evade, while Ember seems the easiest. MEME outperforms the PPO algorithm in all four targets, with a difference in mean evasion rate between 5–10% depending on the target. This result indicates that creating a surrogate model and running additional training steps is beneficial and produces a better policy. MEME also

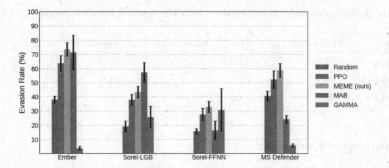

Fig. 3. Mean evasion rates and standard deviations of all methods tested on all targets.

Table 2. Average number of binary modifications to evade the target. The numbers for MAB correspond to the minimal samples created. Random, PPO, and MEME numbers correspond to the mean episode length of the final evaluation on the test set.

Algorithm	Target			
	Ember	Sorel-LGB	Sorel-FFNN	MS Defender
Random	11.53	13.13	13.63	11.84
PPO	8.68	10.91	12.41	9.80
MAB	**5.02**	**6.58**	12.99	11.58
MEME	7.54	10.40	**11.87**	**9.48**

outperforms MAB in three out of four targets and GAMMA in all four, showing stable overall performance. GAMMA is the only method affected by the time constraint and, in most experiments, manages to process less than 100 binaries. However, it performs almost as well as MEME on the Sorel-FFNN. This shows that the RL methods, including MAB, did not learn the simple strategy of *section injection* GAMMA uses, which is part of their action set.

The AV evasion rate was over 50% for both PPO and MEME, with MEME achieving an average evasion rate of 59%. This demonstrates that even though AV is more complex than a single classifier, it can still be bypassed.

In terms of required modifications for a malicious binary to appear benign (Table 2), MEME has the lowest average changes against Sorel-FFNN and Microsoft Defender. MAB performs better with lower average changes against Ember and Sorel-LGB, as it aims to minimize the required actions. However, if MAB struggles with evasion, the average modifications increase. Unfortunately, getting the number of modifications for each binary from the GAMMA attack was not possible since the framework that implements the attack does not provide this metric.

Table 3. Surrogate agreement metrics with the test set for each target model.

Target	Label agr. (%)	Top-10 feature agr. (%)	Top-20 feature agr. (%)
Ember	97.3	90.0	66.3
Sorel-LGB	98.9	72.0	81.0
Sorel-FFNN	98.4	40.0	30.0

6.2 Surrogate Evaluation

Table 3 shows the agreement scores of the surrogate models with their respective targets. The label agreement scores were higher than 97% for all targets. In the feature agreement metrics, 9 out of 10 top features, according to SHAP feature importances, were the same for the Ember target and the respective surrogates. The percentage is slightly lower for Sorel-LGB, with 7.2 out of the top 10 feature agreement and 16.2 out of the top 20. However, the feature agreement metrics get significantly lower regarding the Sorel-FFNN target, even though the label agreement is higher than 98%. This target is also the harder one to evade for the RL-based methods. This level of label agreement was reached with only 2,048 queries, significantly lower than reported in prior work (25k) [33].

7 Discussion

7.1 Performance Considerations

The results showed that it is possible to learn a reinforcement learning policy that evades machine learning classifiers and AVs with limited queries and that the number of modifications required is lower for "easier" targets. However, it must be noted that different frameworks use different implementations of the modifications and slightly different action sets, which may play some role in the results. It may explain why the random agent outscored the SOTA frameworks in two targets. However, the fact that the random agent managed to achieve an evasion rate of 40% on the AV target shows that sometimes deployed products have simple rules and heuristics that can be bypassed by making random changes to a malicious binary.

The created surrogates showed a very high-label agreement with very few queries, but they required an auxiliary dataset. However, obtaining an auxiliary dataset of malicious and benign features is more straightforward than obtaining actual files, especially benign ones. An interesting result is that even with an auxiliary dataset such as Ember, which is almost five years old, it was possible to evade the AV with a high evasion rate.

7.2 The Advantage of Learning a Policy

MEME and PPO use 2,048 queries for training the policy and require additional queries during evaluation. MAB and GAMMA directly act on the binaries without separate training and testing phases. While this may seem advantageous, a trained policy can be applied to any binary, and its generalization abilities are shown using a previously unseen test set. Moreover, the attacker controls the environment and can apply multiple actions using the learned policy, bypassing the target entirely or using the surrogate. Then, they can test the final modified binary on the target, achieving the highest query efficiency of one query per binary.

7.3   Future Work

To extend this work, we can explore improvements and optimizations. One possibility is using an ensemble of surrogates, similar to [21], consisting of diverse model types and architectures. This can enhance the evasion rate and feature explainability but adds complexity and training time.

Another avenue is investigating recurrent PPO or similar algorithms, leveraging recurrent neural networks to learn policies that generate action sequences from states. Any query-efficient method, even non-RL-based, that takes malicious binaries or their extracted features as input and produces modification actions can be explored.

Expanding the targets to include more AVs would help test different malware detection approaches. Additionally, while surrogate models improved MEME's performance, they can provide more target information. Future work involves utilizing surrogates to reduce the RL algorithm's action space based on feature importance or gradient information from neural network surrogates.

8   Conclusions

By employing model-based reinforcement learning, MEME generates adversarial malware samples that successfully evade black-box targets by mimicking the targets with high agreement. Our experiments show that MEME surpasses existing methods in evasion rate, suggesting its potential for various applications, such as testing model robustness and enhancing cybersecurity defenses. Future work may involve exploring ensemble surrogates and other optimizations to enhance MEME's performance further.

Acknowledgments. The authors acknowledge support from the Strategic Support for the Development of Security Research in the Czech Republic 2019–2025 (IMPAKT 1) program, by the Ministry of the Interior of the Czech Republic under No. VJ02010020 – AI-Dojo: Multi-agent testbed for the research and testing of AI-driven cyber security technologies. The authors acknowledge the support of NVIDIA Corporation with the donation of a Titan V GPU used for this research.

Appendix

A. Hyper-parameter Tuning

The search space for the PPO hyper-parameters:

- gamma: 0.01 - 0.75
- max_grad_norm: 0.3 - 5.0
- learning_rate: 0.001 - 0.1
- activation function: ReLU or Tanh
- neural network size: small or medium

Selected parameters: gamma=0.854, learning_rate=0.00138, max_grad_norm= 0.4284, activation function=Tanh, small network size (2 layers with 64 units each).

The search space for the LGB surrogate training hyper-parameters:

- alpha: 1 - 1,000
- num_boosting_rounds: 100-2,000
- learning_rate: 0.001 - 0.1
- num_leaves: 128 - 2,048
- max_depth: 5 - 16
- min_child_samples: 5 - 100
- feature_fraction: 0.4 - 1.0

Selected parameters for the LGB surrogate can be found in Table 4.

Table 4. Hyper-parameter settings for the training of each LGB surrogate

Parameter	Ember	Sorel-LGB	SorelFFNN	MS Defender
alpha	1.26	6.67	1.26	1.26
num_boosting_rounds	200	648	580	500
learning_rate	0.05	0.023	0.067	0.067
num_leaves	1,250	1,175	1,000	1,000
max_depth	15	12	16	16
min_child_samples	1.0	0.45	1.0	1.0

References

1. Akiba, T., Sano, S., Yanase, T., Ohta, T., Koyama, M.: Optuna: a next-generation hyperparameter optimization framework. In: Proceedings of the 25th ACM SIGKDD International Conference on Knowledge Discovery & Data Mining. pp. 2623–2631. KDD 2019, Association for Computing Machinery, New York, NY, USA (2019). https://doi.org/10.1145/3292500.3330701

2. Anderson, H.S., Kharkar, A., Filar, B., Evans, D., Roth, P.: Learning to evade static PE machine learning malware models via reinforcement learning (2018). https://doi.org/10.48550/arXiv.1801.08917, arXiv:1801.08917

3. Anderson, H.S., Roth, P.: EMBER: an open dataset for training static PE malware machine learning models (2018). https://doi.org/10.48550/arXiv.1804.04637, arXiv:1804.04637

4. Bergstra, J., Bardenet, R., Bengio, Y., Kégl, B.: Algorithms for hyper-parameter optimization. In: Advances in Neural Information Processing Systems, vol. 24. Curran Associates, Inc. (2011)

5. Brockman, G., et al.: OpenAI gym (2016). https://doi.org/10.48550/arXiv.1606.01540, arXiv:1606.01540

6. Ceschin, F., Botacin, M., Gomes, H.M., Oliveira, L.S., Grégio, A.: Shallow security: on the creation of adversarial variants to evade machine learning-based malware detectors. In: Proceedings of the 3rd Reversing and Offensive-oriented Trends Symposium, pp. 1–9. ROOTS 2019, Association for Computing Machinery, New York, NY, USA (2020). https://doi.org/10.1145/3375894.3375898

7. Chandrasekaran, V., Chaudhuri, K., Giacomelli, I., Jha, S., Yan, S.: Exploring connections between active learning and model extraction. In: Proceedings of the 29th USENIX Conference on Security Symposium, pp. 1309–1326. SEC 2020, USENIX Association, USA (2020)

8. Correia-Silva, J.R., Berriel, R.F., Badue, C., de Souza, A.F., Oliveira-Santos, T.: Copycat CNN: stealing knowledge by persuading confession with random non-labeled data. In: 2018 International Joint Conference on Neural Networks (IJCNN), pp. 1–8 (2018). iSSN: 2161–4407

9. Demetrio, L., Biggio, B., Lagorio, G., Roli, F., Armando, A.: Functionality-preserving black-box optimization of adversarial windows malware. IEEE Trans. Inf. Forensics Secur. 16, 3469–3478 (2021). https://doi.org/10.1109/TIFS.2021.3082330

10. Demetrio, L., Coull, S.E., Biggio, B., Lagorio, G., Armando, A., Roli, F.: Adversarial exemples: a survey and experimental evaluation of practical attacks on machine learning for windows malware detection. ACM Trans. Priv. Secur. 24(4), 1–31 (2021)

11. Dowling, S., Schukat, M., Barrett, E.: Using reinforcement learning to conceal honeypot functionality. In: Brefeld, U., Curry, E., Daly, E., MacNamee, B., Marascu, A., Pinelli, F., Berlingerio, M., Hurley, N. (eds.) Machine Learning and Knowledge Discovery in Databases, pp. 341–355. Lecture Notes in Computer Science, Springer International Publishing, Cham (2019). https://doi.org/10.1007/978-3-030-10997-4_21

12. Fang, Y., Zeng, Y., Li, B., Liu, L., Zhang, L.: DeepDetectNet vs RLAttackNet: an adversarial method to improve deep learning-based static malware detection model. PLoS ONE 15(4), e0231626 (2020). https://doi.org/10.1371/journal.pone.0231626

13. Fang, Z., Wang, J., Geng, J., Kan, X.: Feature selection for malware detection based on reinforcement learning. IEEE Access 7, 176177–176187 (2019). https://doi.org/10.1109/ACCESS.2019.2957429

14. Fang, Z., Wang, J., Li, B., Wu, S., Zhou, Y., Huang, H.: Evading anti-malware engines with deep reinforcement learning. IEEE Access 7, 48867–48879 (2019). https://doi.org/10.1109/ACCESS.2019.2908033

15. Harang, R., Rudd, E.M.: SOREL-20M: a large scale benchmark dataset for malicious PE detection. arXiv:2012.07634 (2020)

16. Hu, W., Tan, Y.: Generating adversarial malware examples for black-box attacks based on GAN. In: Tan, Y., Shi, Y. (eds.) Data Mining and Big Data, pp. 409–423. Communications in Computer and Information Science, Springer Nature, Singapore (2022). https://doi.org/10.1007/978-981-19-8991-9_29

17. Huang, L., Zhu, Q.: Adaptive honeypot engagement through reinforcement learning of semi-markov decision processes. In: Decision and Game Theory for Security, pp. 196–216. Lecture Notes in Computer Science, Springer International Publishing, Cham (2019). https://doi.org/10.1007/978-3-030-32430-8_13

18. Institute, A.T.: AV-ATLAS - Malware & PUA (2023). https://portal.av-atlas.org/malware

19. Jagielski, M., Carlini, N., Berthelot, D., Kurakin, A., Papernot, N.: High Accuracy and High Fidelity Extraction of Neural Networks. In: SEC 2020: Proceedings of the 29th USENIX Conference on Security Symposium, pp. 1345–1362 (2020)

20. Ke, G., et al.: LightGBM: a highly efficient gradient boosting decision tree. In: Advances in Neural Information Processing Systems, vol. 30. Curran Associates, Inc. (2017)

21. Kurutach, T., Clavera, I., Duan, Y., Tamar, A., Abbeel, P.: Model-ensemble trust-region policy optimization. In: International Conference on Learning Representations (2018)

22. Labaca-Castro, R., Franz, S., Rodosek, G.D.: AIMED-RL: exploring adversarial malware examples with reinforcement learning. In: Dong, Y., Kourtellis, N., Hammer, B., Lozano, J.A. (eds.) Machine Learning and Knowledge Discovery in Databases. Applied Data Science Track, pp. 37–52. Lecture Notes in Computer Science, Springer International Publishing, Cham (2021). https://doi.org/10.1007/978-3-030-86514-6_3

23. Li, D., Li, Q., Ye, Y.F., Xu, S.: Arms race in adversarial malware detection: a survey. ACM Comput. Surv. **55**(1), 15:1-15:35 (2021)

24. Li, X., Li, Q.: An IRL-based malware adversarial generation method to evade anti-malware engines. Comput. Secur. **104**, 102118 (2021). https://doi.org/10.1016/j.cose.2020.102118

25. Ling, X., et al.: Adversarial attacks against Windows PE malware detection: a survey of the state-of-the-art. Comput. Secur. **128**, 103134 (2023). https://doi.org/10.1016/j.cose.2023.103134

26. Lundberg, S.M., Lee, S.I.: A unified approach to interpreting model predictions. In: Advances in Neural Information Processing Systems, vol. 30. Curran Associates, Inc. (2017)

27. Nguyen, T.T., Reddi, V.J.: Deep reinforcement learning for cyber security. IEEE Trans. Neural Networks Learn. Syst. **34**, 3779–3795 (2021). https://doi.org/10.1109/TNNLS.2021.3121870

28. Orekondy, T., Schiele, B., Fritz, M.: Knockoff Nets: stealing functionality of black-box models. In: 2019 IEEE/CVF Conference on Computer Vision and Pattern Recognition (CVPR), pp. 4954–4963 (2019)

29. Pal, S., Gupta, Y., Shukla, A., Kanade, A., Shevade, S., Ganapathy, V.: ActiveThief: model extraction using active learning and unannotated public data. Proc. AAAI Conf. Artif. Intell. **34**(01), 865–872 (2020). https://doi.org/10.1609/aaai.v34i01.5432

30. Phan, T.D., Duc Luong, T., Hoang Quoc An, N., Nguyen Huu, Q., Nghi, H.K., Pham, V.H.: Leveraging reinforcement learning and generative adversarial networks to craft mutants of windows malware against black-box malware detectors.

In: Proceedings of the 11th International Symposium on Information and Communication Technology. pp. 31–38. SoICT 2022, Association for Computing Machinery, New York, NY, USA (2022)

31. Quertier, T., Marais, B., Morucci, S., Fournel, B.: MERLIN - malware evasion with reinforcement LearnINg. arXiv:2203.12980 (2022)

32. Raffin, A., Hill, A., Gleave, A., Kanervisto, A., Ernestus, M., Dormann, N.: Stable-Baselines3: reliable reinforcement learning implementations. J. Mach. Learn. Res. **22**(268), 1–8 (2021)

33. Rigaki, M., Garcia, S.: Stealing and evading malware classifiers and antivirus at low false positive conditions. Comput. Secur. **129**, 103192 (2023). https://doi.org/10.1016/j.cose.2023.103192

34. Rosenberg, I., Meir, S., Berrebi, J., Gordon, I., Sicard, G., Omid David, E.: Generating end-to-end adversarial examples for malware classifiers using explainability. In: 2020 International Joint Conference on Neural Networks (IJCNN), pp. 1–10 (2020). https://doi.org/10.1109/IJCNN48605.2020.9207168, iSSN: 2161-4407

35. Sanyal, S., Addepalli, S., Babu, R.V.: Towards data-free model stealing in a hard label setting. In: 2022 IEEE/CVF Conference on Computer Vision and Pattern Recognition (CVPR), pp. 15284–15293 (2022)

36. Schulman, J., Wolski, F., Dhariwal, P., Radford, A., Klimov, O.: Proximal policy optimization algorithms. arXiv preprint arXiv:1707.06347 (2017)

37. Security.org, T.: 2023 Antivirus market annual report (2023). https://www.security.org/antivirus/antivirus-consumer-report-annual/

38. Severi, G., Meyer, J., Coull, S., Oprea, A.: Explanation-guided backdoor poisoning attacks against malware classifiers. In: 30th USENIX Security Symposium (USENIX Security 21), pp. 1487–1504. USENIX Association (2021)

39. Song, W., Li, X., Afroz, S., Garg, D., Kuznetsov, D., Yin, H.: MAB-malware: a reinforcement learning framework for blackbox generation of adversarial malware. In: Proceedings of the 2022 ACM on Asia Conference on Computer and Communications Security, pp. 990–1003. ASIA CCS 2022, Association for Computing Machinery, New York, NY, USA (2022). https://doi.org/10.1145/3488932.3497768

40. Sussman, B.: New malware is born every minute (2023). https://blogs.blackberry.com/en/2023/05/new-malware-born-every-minute

41. Sutton, R.S., Barto, A.G.: Reinforcement Learning, second edition: An Introduction. MIT Press (2018)

42. Total, V.: VirusTotal - Stats. https://www.virustotal.com/gui/stats

43. Uprety, A., Rawat, D.B.: Reinforcement learning for IoT security: a comprehensive survey. IEEE Internet Things J. **8**(11), 8693–8706 (2021). https://doi.org/10.1109/JIOT.2020.3040957

44. Wu, C., Shi, J., Yang, Y., Li, W.: Enhancing machine learning based malware detection model by reinforcement learning. In: Proceedings of the 8th International Conference on Communication and Network Security, pp. 74–78. ICCNS 2018, Association for Computing Machinery, New York, NY, USA (Nov 2018). https://doi.org/10.1145/3290480.3290494

45. Yu, H., Yang, K., Zhang, T., Tsai, Y.Y., Ho, T.Y., Jin, Y.: CloudLeak: large-scale deep learning models stealing through adversarial examples. In: Proceedings 2020 Network and Distributed System Security Symposium. Internet Society, San Diego, CA (2020)

46. Zolotukhin, M., Kumar, S., Hämäläinen, T.: Reinforcement learning for attack mitigation in SDN-enabled networks. In: 2020 6th IEEE Conference on Network Softwarization (NetSoft), pp. 282–286 (2020). https://doi.org/10.1109/NetSoft48620.2020.9165383
47. Šembera, V., Paquet-Clouston, M., Garcia, S., Erquiaga, M.J.: Cybercrime specialization: an exposé of a malicious android obfuscation-as-a-service. In: 2021 IEEE European Symposium on Security and Privacy Workshops (EuroS&PW, pp. 213–236 (2021). https://doi.org/10.1109/EuroSPW54576.2021.00029

FLGuard: Byzantine-Robust Federated Learning via Ensemble of Contrastive Models

Younghan Lee[1,2], Yungi Cho[1,2], Woorim Han[1,2], Ho Bae[3(✉)],
and Yunheung Paek[1,2(✉)]

[1] ECE, Seoul National University, Seoul, Republic of Korea
{201younghanlee,q1w1ert1,rimwoo98,ypaek}@snu.ac.kr
[2] ISRC, Seoul National University, Seoul, Republic of Korea
[3] Department of Cyber Security, Ewha Woman's University, Seoul, Republic of Korea
hobae@ewha.ac.kr

Abstract. Federated Learning (FL) thrives in training a global model with numerous clients by only sharing the parameters of their local models trained with their private training datasets. Therefore, without revealing the private dataset, the clients can obtain a deep learning (DL) model with high performance. However, recent research proposed poisoning attacks that cause a catastrophic loss in the accuracy of the global model when adversaries, posed as benign clients, are present in a group of clients. Therefore, recent studies suggested byzantine-robust FL methods that allow the server to train an accurate global model even with the adversaries present in the system. However, many existing methods require the knowledge of the number of malicious clients or the auxiliary (clean) dataset or the effectiveness reportedly decreased hugely when the private dataset was non-independently and identically distributed (non-IID). In this work, we propose FLGuard, a novel byzantine-robust FL method that detects malicious clients and discards malicious local updates by utilizing the contrastive learning technique, which showed a tremendous improvement as a self-supervised learning method. With contrastive models, we design FLGuard as an ensemble scheme to maximize the defensive capability. We evaluate FLGuard extensively under various poisoning attacks and compare the accuracy of the global model with existing byzantine-robust FL methods. FLGuard outperforms the state-of-the-art defense methods in most cases and shows drastic improvement, especially in non-IID settings. https://github.com/201younghanlee/FLGuard.

Keywords: Byzantine-Robust · Federated Learning · Poisoning Attacks · Contrastive Learning

1 Introduction

Federated learning (FL) [14,16,20] is an emerging distributed learning scheme in which the clients work collaboratively to train a high-performance model on the

G. Tsudik et al. (Eds.): ESORICS 2023, LNCS 14347, pp. 65–84, 2024.
https://doi.org/10.1007/978-3-031-51482-1_4

server (global model). Instead of sharing the client's private dataset, only the parameters of a model trained locally (local model) are uploaded to the server. In the era of big data, where the private dataset is considered highly valuable, protecting the privacy of the dataset is regulated by General Data Protection Regulation (GDPR) [1]. Therefore, many companies' service, including Apple's Siri [24], Google's Gboard [2] employed FL schemes to provide their services in a privacy-preserving fashion. The clients are required to download the initial global model from the server. Using the private dataset, the local model update (gradient) is learned and then sent to the server for aggregation. For example, FedAvg [21], one of the most commonly deployed FL schemes devised by Google, applies AGR that uses a weighted average of all local model updates from clients to form the global model update. Since the global model is trained using updates from all clients, the premise for FL to operate as designed is that all clients are legitimate and reliable.

However, according to [5], such a premise may no longer hold true due to a major threat to FL, called *Byzantine failure*, that some clients can become adversaries whose aim is to thwart FL and degrade the quality of the global model by generating malicious local model updates. Such attacks, known as *poisoning attacks*, can be categorized mainly into two types: model poisoning attack (MPA) and data poisoning attack (DPA). The prerequisite of MPA is that the entire device of adversaries is compromised. The adversaries directly apply the perturbation vector (p) to the local model updates (g) so that the generated malicious model update (g_m) is given as follows: $g_m = g + \gamma p$, where γ is the scale parameter. For example, LIE [4] demonstrated that a very small γ is sufficient to degrade the accuracy of a global model. More recently, MPAs exploited a new attack surface where the algorithm of AGR is known to adversaries [11,26]. Therefore, researchers converted the challenge of finding an appropriate γ to an optimization problem. DPA assumes that adversaries only have access to private datasets. The adversaries poison the private dataset to hinder the training of the global model. The label-flip attack [11,27] is a typical DPA that intentionally changes the label of data to minimize the loss in the wrong direction.

To defend against both MPA and DPA, researchers proposed byzantine-robust FL schemes that filter out disguising malicious clients. Most of the proposed methods are *statistic-based* using statistical information regarding the local updates to discard malicious clients. For example, Trimmed-Mean (TM) [31] introduced *dimension-wise* filtering that treats each element in local model updates from all clients individually. Furthermore, Multi-Krum (MK) [5] and DnC [26] introduced *vector-wise* filtering in which AGR decides to remove a certain number of clients. SignGuard (SG) [30] uses the gradient statistics as features to filter out the malicious clients through clustering method. FLtrust (FLT) [7], the *validation-based* approach that utilizes the auxiliary dataset as a root-of-trust to validate the uploaded local model updates. However, existing defenses failed to achieve a high global model accuracy when the private dataset of clients was non-IID. Moreover, for the best results, current byzantine-robust FL schemes require prior knowledge regarding FL, such as the number of malicious clients or an auxiliary (clean) dataset for validation.

Due to the high cost of collecting human-annotated datasets, self-supervised learning [8,22], such as contrastive learning (CL) [9,13,15], has erupted as a leading technique in the image classification domain. The main idea of CL is to contrast data against each other by pushing the data for the same representation close to each other and pulling apart that of different representations. Our insight is that the characteristic of CL, which congregates the data of a similar representation in the embedding space, is suitable for detecting the outlier among the local updates. Hence, we adopt CL in FL security domain to establish a novel byzantine-robust FL by detecting and filtering malicious clients. In this paper, we propose FLGuard, a novel byzantine-robust FL scheme with contrastive models. Unlike the conventional CL, we additionally implement the dimension reduction technique to reduce the size of local updates in a tabular data shape. Also, we craft positive pairs by applying Gaussian noise to the local model updates. The rationale behind our approach is that a slight addition of perturbation does not change the true properties of original data in embedding space but rather induces the strong core properties shared between data to stand out and consequently to be extracted with ease. Only after projecting the data to the representations could we reveal the innate features of benign and malicious updates by contrasting data against each other. Finally, we employ clustering methods only to use local updates from clients classified as benign in global model training.

We extensively evaluate FLGuard under various experimental settings. Empirically we demonstrate that FLGuard shows an impressive defensive performance even under non-IID settings without prior knowledge and thrives to achieve three defensive objectives: Fidelity, Robustness, and Efficiency. The high accuracy of the global model is maintained even without the presence of adversaries (fidelity). Especially, FLGuard achieved SOTA defense performance (robustness) under various types of poisoning attacks (DPA and MPA) and dataset distribution. Also, FLGuard does not incur a significant increase in communication cost on the server (efficiency). Moreover, we performed ablation studies to confirm that FLGuard retained its SOTA performance regardless of the number of malicious clients and non-IID degree of the dataset. The following summarizes our contributions:

- We propose FLGuard, a novel byzantine-robust federated learning via an ensemble of contrastive models that operate without prior knowledge regarding the FL scheme (i.e., number of malicious clients, auxiliary dataset).
- We conduct an extensive evaluation of FLGuard on various threat models, datasets, and poisoning attacks. The results show that FLGuard achieves state-of-the-art performance even in non-IID settings.

2 Background

2.1 Federated Learning

In federated learning (FL), the server trains a *global model* (w) without disclosing the private dataset. We consider a widely used FL scenario with a server and N clients with disjoint datasets [14,16,20]. We denote D_n as nth client's private dataset. In FL, the global model is obtained by solving the following optimization problem: $\min_w F(w, D)$ where $D = \cup_{n=1}^{N} D_n$ and F is a loss function. Each client computes the local update (stochastic gradient), $g_n = \frac{\partial F(b,w)}{\partial w}$ over a mini-batch b randomly sampled from D_n and uploads it to the server synchronously. Finally, the server computes the global update (G_{agr}) using the local updates via an aggregation rule. Moreover, each client's private dataset (D_n) can be independently and identically distributed (IID) or non-independently and identically distributed (non-IID) among clients. Many federated learning aggregation rules struggle to achieve a high-performance global model under non-IID (real-world scenario) setting. We evaluate FLGuard under both *IID* and *non-IID* dataset settings among participating clients.

2.2 Poisoning Attack

According to [27], two main factors that divide different types of poisoning attacks are adversaries' objectives and capabilities. The former refers to the intent of adversaries and a result that they can achieve. The latter depends on how much adversaries can thwart the federated learning given a certain level of access to the schemes. **Adversaries' objectives** can be categorized into two: discriminate or indiscriminate. Targeted attacks aim to induce the misclassification of specific sets of samples (discriminate), and untargeted attacks aim to misclassify any data samples (indiscriminate). **Adversaries' capabilities** represent either the adversaries have full access to the malicious client's *model* or have access only to the *data* of malicious clients. Model poisoning attacks (MPAs) have full access to the device of malicious clients and directly poison the local updates (model). Data poisoning attacks (DPAs) have only access to the local private dataset of malicious clients and poison the data samples (data). To prevent recent threats to FL, we focus and evaluate FLGuard on *untargeted MPAs* and extend our attack scope to *DPA*.

2.3 Byzantine-Robust Aggregation Rules

Following [30], we categorize the byzantine-robust aggregation rules into three different groups, which are discussed below. **Statistic-based** defense strategies utilize statistical metrics to determine malicious clients. Trimmed-Mean (TM) [31] is a dimension-wise aggregation rule that uses the mean of the remaining local updates after removing m largest and smallest values. Multi-Krum (MK) [5] adds the local update to the set until there are c number of local updates such that $N - c > 2M + 2$, where M is the upper bound of the number of malicious clients. Bulyan (Bul) [12] executes dimension-wise aggregation using TMean on the selected updates. Divide and Conquer (DnC) [26] removes $e \cdot M$ local updates with the highest outlier score which is calculated using the singular value decomposition. SignGuard (SG) [30] uses a sign-based clustering method that incorporates gradient statistics as features. **Validation-based** and current **learning-based** assume that the auxiliary dataset is available to the defender. FLTrust (FLT) [7] utilizes the auxiliary dataset as a root-of-trust and computes

Table 1. Types of threat models based on adversaries' capability and knowledge

Type	Adversaries' Capability	Adversaries' Knowledge	
		Local Updates of Benign Clients	Server's AGR Algorithm
Type-1 (T1)	Model Poisoning	✓	✓
Type-2 (T2)	Model Poisoning	✗	✓
Type-3 (T3)	Model Poisoning	✓	✗
Type-4 (T4)	Model Poisoning	✗	✗
Type-5 (T5)	Data Poisoning	✗	✗

the trust score (TS) to reduce the impact of poisoning attacks from malicious clients. Spectral anomaly detection [19] utilizes variational autoencoder (VAE) with clean auxiliary dataset to filter out the malicious local updates by measuring the reconstruction errors. FLGuard belongs to *vector-wise filtering, learning-based* byzantine-robust FL. Unlike previous byzantine-robust aggregation rules, FLGuard works *without any prior information* (i.e., number of malicious clients or auxiliary dataset).

2.4 Contrastive Learning and Clustering

Recently, contrastive learning has shown promising results in self-supervised representation learning [10,13]. The fundamental concept is to learning representations through maximizing agreement between augmented views of the same original image (positive pairs) and minimizing between that of the different images (negative pairs). SimCLR [9] consists of a base encoder $f(\cdot)$ that extracts the representations h from the original image x (i.e., $f(x) = h$) and a projection head $g(\cdot)$ that maps the representations h to the latent vector z (i.e., $g(h) = z$). For the contrastive loss function [28], normalized temperature-scaled cross-entropy loss ($NT\text{-}Xent$) is used with x_i, x_j as positive pairs generated by randomly applying one of the augmentation operators. After training, only the base encoder $f(\cdot)$ is used for downstream tasks and a projection head $g(\cdot)$ is discarded. Agglomerative Hierarchical Clustering (AHC) [23] operates by grouping the data based on their similarities and the clusters with the shortest distance are grouped together repeatedly in a bottom-up manner until only a single cluster is formed. Then, the hierarchy tree (dendrogram) is dissected according to the desired number of clusters. FLGuard employs *contrastive models* based on SimCLR with self-supervised learning and uses *clustering mechanism* to detect and discard malicious local updates.

3 Threat Model and Problem Setup

Adversaries' Objective. Adversaries aim to poison the global model by devising malicious local updates and cause a considerable reduction in the accuracy.

As discussed in the previous section, we focus on untargeted (indiscriminate) poisoning attacks. **Adversaries' capability** The adversaries are assumed to occupy M malicious clients among a total of N clients and can access the global model at each FL round. The number of malicious clients is assumed to be less than benign clients (i.e., $\frac{M}{N} < 0.5$) [7,11,26,27,30,32]. Adversaries with model poisoning capability are assumed to have full access to compromised clients, and they can directly manipulate the local updates. On the other hand, adversaries with data poisoning capability can only manipulate the local dataset. As shown in Table 1, threat models from Type-1 to Type-4 fall under model poisoning and Type-5 under data poisoning. **Adversaries' knowledge** Following [26], we consider two aspects of adversaries' knowledge: local updates from benign clients and aggregation rule (AGR) algorithm from the server. There are a total of five different types of threat models, as shown in Table 1. Type-1 represents the *strongest adversaries* with knowledge of both local updates of benign clients and AGR algorithm. While such type of threat model lacks practicality, previous works [4,11] implemented such threat model to demonstrate the severe impact of poisoning attacks on FL. **Defender's objective** The fundamental objective is to design FL scheme that attains byzantine robustness under MPA without compromising FL's fidelity and efficiency. Fidelity: Byzantine-robust FL scheme should not sacrifice the accuracy of the global model in return for the robustness when malicious clients are not involved (Table 2). Robustness: The defender's FL scheme should persist the accuracy of the global model even under the influence of poisoning attacks (Table 2, Table 3 and Table 4). Efficiency: Byzantine-robust FL scheme should not cause a significant overhead that will delay the training of the global model (Fig. 4). **Defender's Capability** We assume the defense mechanism is operated from the server side and the server (defender) has an access to the global model and the local updates of all clients at each FL round. Unlike previous studies [7,26], we further assume that the server does not have any prior knowledge regarding the malicious clients (i.e., the number of malicious clients) or access to the auxiliary dataset. The server is unaware of whether the local updates it receives are from malicious or benign clients.

4   Our FLGuard

4.1   Overview

Figure 1 illustrates the overview of byzantine-robust FL where a single malicious client is present. FL operates essentially in three steps, both from the server and client sides. Explanations with asterisks denote the part in which FLGuard is different from plain FL without a defense mechanism against adversaries.

Step 1: *Server Side*: The server initializes the global model (w) at random in the first round of FLGuard (Line 1 in Algorithm 1). The global model is off-loaded to all clients in FL for synchronization. *Client Side*: The clients download the global model (w) from the server (Line 1 in Algorithm 2). **Step 2:** *Server Side*: Unlike other FL schemes in which the server awaits the clients to

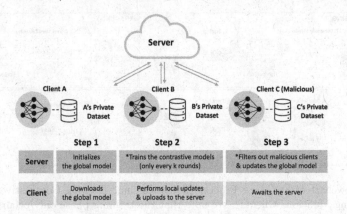

Fig. 1. Overview of byzantine-robust FL. Steps described in asterisk (*) denote the design novelty of our FLGuard

---

Algorithm 1. FLGuard

Intput: Total number of clients N, number of FL rounds R, number of local iterations I, loss function F, private dataset D, batch size b, global learning rate η, local learning rate α, FLGuard parameter k

Output: Global model w_R

1: $w_0 \leftarrow$ initialize at random
2: **for** each FL round $r = 1, 2, ..., R$ **do**
3:    **for** each client $n = 1, 2, ..., N$ **in parallel do**
4:      $g_n \leftarrow$ **LocalUpdate**$(w_{r-1}, I, D_n, b_n, F, \alpha)$
5:    **end for**
6:    $G \leftarrow$ set of current local updates $g_1, g_2, ..., g_N$
7:    $G_{train} \leftarrow$ set of local updates for last k FL rounds
8:    **if** $r \bmod k = 0$ **then**
9:      $ContrastiveModels, Scaler \leftarrow$ **Training**(G_{train})
10:   **end if**
11:   $G_{lv}, G_{rd} \leftarrow$ **Preprocessing**$(G, Scaler)$
12:   $C_{good} \leftarrow$ **Filtering**$(G_{lv}, G_{rd}, ContrastiveModels)$
13:   $G_{filtered} \leftarrow G[C_{good}]$
14:   $G_{agr} \leftarrow \frac{1}{|C_{good}|} \cdot \sum G_{filtered}$
15:   $w_r = w_{r-1} - \eta \cdot G_{agr}$
16: **end for**

---

upload the local updates, FLGuard capitalizes on such an idle state to train the contrastive models. FLGuard only trains the new model every k rounds of FL as the same contrastive models can be used for multiple FL rounds (Line 7–10 in Algorithm 1). Further details on the training phase are explained in Sect. 4.3. *Client Side*: The clients perform local updates (g_n) on the global model with mini-batch sampled from their private dataset (D_n). All clients perform in parallel and send calculated local updates to the server (Line 2–6 in Algorithm 2 in Appendix A.1). **Step 3:** *Server Side*: In the final step, the server filters

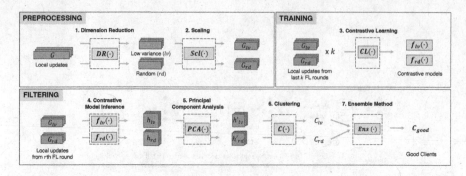

Fig. 2. Flowchart of FLGuard Process (Preprocessing, Training Contrastive Models, and Filtering Malicious Clients). We note that the training phase only occurs every k FL rounds to generate new contrastive models

out malicious local updates and removes them from updating the global model (Algorithm 3 in Appendix A.1). The details of each function in the filtering phase of FLGuard are explained in Sect. 4.4. Finally, the server aggregates the filtered local updates by averaging to form the global update (G_{agr}) (Line 12–15 in Algorithm 1). *Client Side*: The clients await until the next round of FL while the server updates the global model.

Figure 2 summarizes the process of FLGuard, which consists of three parts: preprocessing, training, and filtering. In the preprocessing phase, we prepare local updates by applying popular data preprocessing techniques. In the training phase, we utilize contrastive learning to generate contrastive models that extract local updates' representation. In the filtering phase, through the clustering and ensemble method, FLGuard only collects benign clients (C_{good}).

4.2   Preprocessing Local Updates

Dimension Reduction and Scaling. Previous study reported that the robustness of FL is compromised with high dimension (i.e., *the curse of dimensionality* [26]) and utilized a random filter. However, we additionally implement a low variance filter in FLGuard that removes features with low variance to avoid dismissing the elements that represent the unique aspect of local updates depending on the origin (malicious or benign clients). Given a set of local updates of clients (G), we compute variance (i.e., $\sigma^2 = \sum(x_i - \mu)^2 / N$ where N = number of clients) of each element among local updates and remove the element with low variance to fit the dimension of 3,072. Scaling the data is necessary to prevent the data with a large magnitude from dominating the data with a small magnitude. As the values of local updates are unbounded in magnitude, an appropriate scaling technique must be applied. We observed that the local updates are either positive or negative. Therefore, we implement a max-absolute (MaxAbs) scaler to maintain the sign of local updates. MaxAbs ($x_{scaled} = \frac{x}{max(|x|)}$) scales the data to a range from -1 to 1. As shown in Fig. 2, G_{lv} and G_{rd} are the final results of preprocessing phase.

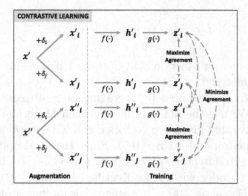

Fig. 3. Illustration of Contrastive Learning including Augmentation. $f(\cdot)$ and $g(\cdot)$ represent the contrastive models (encoders) and the projection heads

4.3   Training Contrastive Models

Contrastive Learning. Collecting a vast labeled dataset for training is expensive as human supervision is required. Especially in the FL scenario, dealing with high-dimensional local updates as the training dataset makes collecting the annotated dataset seems unfeasible. Therefore, we utilize self-supervised learning, which automatically labels the dataset by learning the difference in representations of inputs. In the training phase, we adopt contrastive learning, which enforces the data of similar representations closer and different representations further away by maximizing the agreement of positive pairs and minimizing the agreement of negative pairs. Our implementation of contrastive learning is based on SimCLR [9] with modifications to suit the security domain. The main difference is that the local updates are tabular data. Augmentation strategy, applied to the original data to form positive and negative pairs, is vital for learning good representations of the data. Inspired by [3,29], we choose to add Gaussian noise ($X \sim \mathcal{N}(\mu, \sigma^2)$) by using a masking ratio as means of augmenting the original tabular data (local updates). We generate two augmented data (views) per each original data by randomly adding Gaussian noise with $\sigma^2 = 0.01$ and maksing ratio of 0.1. The augmented views obtained from the same original data are treated as positive pairs (i.e., $x_i' \leftrightarrow x_j'$ and $x_i'' \leftrightarrow x_j''$ in Fig. 3). The negative pairs are simply formed by pairing each data with all other data in the batch except for itself. The orange dotted line in Fig. 3 represents the negative pairs. For example, with 32 as the batch size (B), we create a total of 32 positive pairs and 1,984 negative pairs (i.e., $2(B\text{-}1)$ negative pairs per one sample).

Training the contrastive models $f(\cdot)$ and the projection heads $g(\cdot)$ require the pairs of augmented views and the loss function ($NT\text{-}Xent$) applied to the space mapped by the projection heads can be written as below Eq. (1).

$$l(z_{i,j}) = -\log \frac{\exp(sim(z_{i,j})/\tau)}{\sum_{k=1}^{2B} \mathbb{1}_{[k \neq i]} \exp(sim(z_{i,k})/\tau)} \tag{1}$$

$$L = \frac{1}{2B} \sum_{i,j=1}^{B} [l(z_{i,j}) + l(z_{j,i})] \tag{2}$$

where $\mathbb{1}_{[k \neq i]}$ is an indicator function that outputs 1 if and only if $k \neq i$ and τ is a temperature parameter.

The final loss (L) is computed by averaging over all pairs in the batch as shown in Eq. (2). We use the dot product between l2 normalized two vectors (i.e., cosine similarity) that given two vectors a and b, $sim(a, b) = a^T b / \|a\|_2 \cdot \|b\|_2$ as the similarity function and set $\tau = 0.01$. Since the local updates are tabular data, we design the architecture of contrastive models $f(\cdot)$ by following [29] with a single layer encoder with leaky-Rectified Linear Unit (leaky-ReLU) as activation function ($\mathbb{1}_{[x<0]} \alpha x + \mathbb{1}_{[x>=0]} x$ where $\mathbb{1}$ is an indicator function, and α is a small constant). The projection head $g(\cdot)$ is a 2-layer multi-layer perceptron (MLP) which is discarded once the contrastive models are trained due to the information lost from the contrastive loss. Note that the last layers of both the encoder and projection head are linear, with a dimension of 3,072. Finally, as shown in Fig. 2, we create two contrastive models $f_{lv}(\cdot)$ and $f_{rd}(\cdot)$ depending on the results of filters used in preprocessing.

Contrastive Model Training Interval. As the values of local updates vary throughout FL rounds, employing the same contrastive models trained with earlier rounds to filter out malicious local updates from the later rounds would not guarantee the best performance. Therefore, we update our contrastive models in FLGuard every k FL rounds where k is a parameter to adjust the interval of updating contrastive models. From a certain round in FL, we use local updates from the last k FL rounds (e.g., from 1 to 5) to train the contrastive models which are used for the next k rounds (e.g., from 6 to 10) to filter the malicious clients. For example, for 1,500 total FL rounds, updating new contrastive models occurs 300 times when k is set to 5 (i.e., every 5 FL rounds).

4.4   Filtering Malicious Clients

In the filtering phase of FLGuard, we utilize both contrastive models only to collect local updates from good clients (i.e., C_{good}). More specifically, we apply principal component analysis (PCA) and clustering algorithms on the representations of local updates to filter out malicious clients. **Contrastive Model Inference** As shown in Fig. 2, in each FL round, we project the local updates G_{lv} and G_{rd} to representation h_{lv} and h_{rd} with the contrastive models $f(\cdot)$. We only use the encoder trained in the training phase for the inference and discard the projection head. **Principal Component Analysis (PCA)** For dimension reduction process, we empirically set on the number of components equal to two and we obtained dimension-reduced h'_{rd} and h'_{lv} as the results. **Clustering** We form two clusters with the latent space representations and assume that the larger is from benign clients. The results of clustering are groups of benign clients (C_{lv} and C_{rd}) depending on different representations (h'_{lv} and h'_{rd}). In this paper, we design

FLGuard using agglomerative hierarchical clustering (AHC) with single linkage metric to measure the distance between the clusters. **Ensemble Method** To maximize the robustness of FLGuard, we implement the ensemble method with two different clusters which are formed by two different contrastive models. We only select clients that are classified as benign by both contrastive models (i.e., $C_{good} = C_{rd} \cap C_{lv}$). Finally, the local updates uploaded by clients in C_{good} are used to train the global model.

5   Evaluation

5.1   Experimental Setup

Datasets. To distribute the training data among participating clients [7], we divide the clients into n groups (i.e., the number of classes in a dataset). Then, a sample from the dataset with label K is assigned to group K with probability q and to any other group with $\frac{1-q}{n-1}$. Finally, samples in the same group are uniformly distributed to each client. We note that the probability (q) is the parameter that determines the distribution of the private dataset among clients. For example, if $q = \frac{1}{n}$, the private training dataset are independent and identically distributed (IID), otherwise non-IID. The greater the value of q, the higher degree of non-IID. ① MNIST [18] contains gray-scale digit images of 10 classes. MNIST-0.1 ($q = 0.1$) indicates IID and MNIST-0.5 ($q = 0.5$) simulates non-IID. ② CIFAR-10 [17] is a 10-class RGB image classification dataset and the training data are IID among participating clients. ③ FEMNIST [6] is a 62-class character recognition classification dataset consisting of 3,400 clients and each client has a different number of images (non-IID). For FL training, we randomly select 60 clients in each round to participate [26]. We set the percentage of malicious clients in each round to be 20% of total clients [7,26,30]. The details of FL parameter setting for each dataset can be found in Appendix A.1.

5.2   Evaluated Poisoning Attacks

A general approach to model poisoning attacks (MPAs) is as the following. Firstly, adversaries compute an average of available benign local updates (g_b). The availability depends on the type of threat model as explained in Sect. 3. After selecting an appropriate perturbation vector (p), the scale (γ) is multiplied before being added to g_b. Finally, the malicious clients upload $g_m = g_b + \gamma p$ to the server. In this paper, following [26], we implement two types of perturbation vectors (p): ① Inverse unit vector ($\boldsymbol{uv} = -\frac{g_b}{\|g_b\|_2}$) ② Inverse sign ($sgn = -\text{sgn}(f_{avg}(g))$). We evaluate FLGuard against various MPAs including optimization approaches [11,26] and adaptive attacks [26] where AGR is known to the adversaries (i.e., threat model T1 and T2). In particular, we design an adaptive attack on FLGuard to evaluate the robustness under a severe attack in which the adversaries can obtain the contrastive models trained. In terms of perturbation vector, we set $p = sgn$ for optimization approaches and adaptive attacks. Moreover, when AGR is unknown to the adversaries (i.e., threat model T3 and T4), we evaluate FLGuard against Little Is Enough (LIE) [4], Min-Max and Min-Sum [26], and Sign-Flip Attack (SF) [25]. Also, Label-Flip attack [7,11,27] is one of the data poisoning attacks. The malicious local updates are generated using the local private dataset with flipped labels from malicious clients. The details of each evaluated attacks can be found in Appendix A.2.

5.3   Experimental Result

Fidelity. In order for byzantine-robust FL to be suitable in a real-world scenario, the fidelity of FL scheme must not be violated when no adversaries are present. The abbreviation for AGR can be found in Sect. 2.3. We evaluated the fidelity of FLGuard (FLG) by comparing the global model accuracy with other AGRs and consider FedAvg as the baseline. FedAvg achieved 97.24%, 73.54%, 97.16%, and 84.11% for MNIST-0.1, CIFAR-10, MNIST-0.5, and FEMNIST respectively. As shown in *No Attack* column in Table 2, the accuracy trained by FLGuard is higher than other AGRs and as high as FedAvg. For all four datasets, the accuracy of the global model trained by FLGuard only drops by less than 1% compared to that of FedAvg. Especially in MNIST-0.1, FLGuard did not induce any drop in accuracy and in FEMNIST, FLGuard managed to achieved even higher accuracy than FedAvg as all malicious clients were filtered out (84.11% for FedAvg and 84.74% for FLGuard). In CIFAR-10, the accuracy drops was only 0.81% for FLGuard while DnC, FLTrust, and SignGuard drop by 1.10%, 2.80%, and 2.90%. FLGuard outperforms others because the filtering performance is better compared to DnC and SignGuard and FLTrust operates in dimension-wise manner that considers all local updates to train the global model. Therefore, we conclude that the fidelity of FLGuard is achieved for all four datasets.

Robustness. FLGuard has been extensively tested under many threat models with various poisoning attacks including MPAs (Table 2 and Table 3) and DPA (Table 4). The robustness of FLGuard is analyzed based on three criteria: types of threat model, dataset distribution, and types of attacks. **Robust under different types of threat models**. Among 24 cases in Type-1 (i.e., the strongest threat model) FLGuard achieved the best performance in 18 cases (75%). In Type-2, where adversaries are unaware of local updates of benign clients, FLGuard outperformed in 87.5% (21/24) of total cases. We concluded that FLGuard is robust to MPAs even under strongest adversaries and outperforms other defenses by up to 79.5% (vs. FLT in FEMNIST). In Type-3 (i.e., unknown AGR algorithm), FLGuard outperformed other defenses in 71% (17/24) of total cases and in Type-4 (i.e., weakest adversaries) FLGuard achieved the best accuracy in 67% of cases (21/28). In particular, FLGuard improved the global model accuracy up to 78.45% in Type-4 (vs. FLT in FEMNIST). Finally, we expand the evaluation to DPA (Type-5) by executing label-flip attacks (SLF and DLF). Table 4 shows FLGuard achieves state-of-the-art performance in 5 out of 8 cases. **Robust under both IID and non-IID**. For IID dataset (MNIST-0.1 and CIFAR-10), FLGuard achieved the best accuracy in 76% of all cases (41/54). Additionally, in non-IID settings where many byzantine-robust FL are known to fail in achieving a high

Table 2. Comparison of accuracy from byzantine-robust AGRs against no attack (Fidelity) and MPAs (Robustness) under threat model Type-1 & Type-2

Dataset (Distr.)	AGR	No Attack	Type-1						Type-2					
			STAT-OPT		DYN-OPT		Adaptive		STAT-OPT		DYN-OPT		Adaptive	
			Krum	TM	Krum	TM	DnC	FLG	Krum	TM	Krum	TM	DnC	FLG
MNIST -0.1 (IID)	TM	96.98	89.83	96.16	87.60	90.30	86.85	96.33	86.67	95.56	87.30	87.28	96.90	95.31
	MK	96.37	84.33	95.86	84.11	96.45	83.87	94.68	83.95	94.58	83.83	96.45	96.61	96.60
	Bul	95.92	88.29	93.65	88.94	95.19	87.36	96.10	86.67	93.34	90.71	95.21	94.56	93.04
	DnC	97.06	93.43	96.77	96.83	**96.88**	96.83	95.54	91.72	96.53	96.69	96.75	97.00	94.74
	FLT	95.96	94.72	95.50	95.27	93.69	95.54	93.32	92.94	95.25	94.93	93.73	94.06	93.41
	SG	97.20	95.90	**96.85**	92.63	96.81	93.32	96.47	91.56	**96.92**	89.33	**96.96**	97.22	95.39
	FLG	**97.24**	96.83	96.79	96.85	96.83	**96.90**	**96.85**	**96.85**	96.85	**96.88**	96.83	**97.26**	**97.06**
CIFAR -10 (IID)	TM	71.92	58.16	46.53	63.82	52.11	69.32	71.83	58.73	44.48	58.89	53.33	59.88	71.39
	MK	71.41	31.82	45.11	41.94	71.49	51.58	69.56	41.66	41.92	49.49	71.06	68.06	69.58
	Bul	56.62	31.84	40.38	35.86	49.39	41.96	67.51	33.12	38.35	36.47	48.15	50.89	64.89
	DnC	72.44	72.73	71.55	64.94	72.65	47.28	70.88	72.22	72.85	70.76	71.96	72.08	70.84
	FLT	70.74	71.00	56.98	65.02	70.80	67.45	71.47	70.27	53.04	71.29	70.54	71.06	68.99
	SG	70.64	66.72	72.52	68.63	69.66	70.21	69.70	60.88	72.71	68.71	72.38	70.86	70.68
	FLG	**72.73**	73.44	72.71	73.86	73.60	72.48	72.02	73.19	72.99	73.15	73.44	73.30	72.36
MNIST -0.5 (Non -IID)	TM	95.96	87.44	95.19	87.95	90.00	88.23	96.33	83.10	93.45	84.19	87.18	96.12	95.31
	MK	96.19	56.43	94.93	52.72	96.33	62.74	94.68	59.01	93.26	58.22	96.33	96.08	94.60
	Bul	94.38	86.89	94.93	88.43	93.75	88.13	96.10	85.17	94.62	88.11	93.65	94.46	93.04
	DnC	96.57	85.35	**96.92**	91.40	96.81	93.38	95.54	85.47	96.75	87.36	96.85	96.63	94.74
	FLT	95.47	88.74	93.65	93.87	89.02	93.95	93.32	88.15	94.03	93.45	88.35	93.99	93.41
	SG	**96.94**	89.14	95.84	92.65	96.94	91.74	**96.47**	93.93	96.94	92.78	96.73	**97.02**	95.39
	FLG	96.79	**96.81**	96.49	**96.83**	96.96	**96.71**	96.06	**96.67**	96.96	**96.67**	96.96	97.00	**96.71**
FE -MNIST (Non -IID)	TM	80.62	56.78	76.10	62.52	63.69	49.44	80.06	73.98	76.73	74.28	75.68	78.84	81.11
	MK	83.69	5.05	78.60	5.02	83.71	4.87	81.00	5.67	78.13	4.85	83.74	8.81	81.34
	Bul	69.89	53.41	72.77	53.13	66.74	53.47	75.95	48.89	74.98	53.53	67.20	56.50	79.63
	DnC	83.87	6.97	82.76	4.85	84.03	4.87	80.71	5.26	81.06	4.98	83.63	26.79	80.65
	FLT	81.83	4.60	83.30	35.79	4.58	52.83	80.07	4.68	83.61	36.88	4.46	5.09	79.98
	SG	83.56	80.37	**84.19**	10.12	83.58	8.87	**82.15**	8.75	83.96	8.77	83.40	77.64	81.73
	FLG	**84.74**	84.14	83.80	**84.30**	**84.19**	**83.22**	81.86	**83.12**	84.02	82.11	83.94	81.51	83.44

accuracy global model, FLGuard also achieved the best accuracy in 76% of all case (41/54). In particular, we note that FLGuard achieved impressive results in FEMNIST. For example, against Min-Max (sgn), FLGuard achieved 82.63% compared to 5.25%, 6.17%, and 8.13% in previous defenses (DnC, FLTrust, and SignGuard). Furthermore, FLGuard demonstrated a notable absence of catastrophic failure in comparison to other defense mechanisms. For instance, when examining FEMNIST dataset, FLGuard exhibited mean and standard deviation values of 83.58 and 0.89, respectively, whereas Signguard yielded values of 62.68 and 32.54. **Robust against various types of poisoning attacks**. As explained above, we evaluated AGRs against both MPAs and DPAs. While FLGuard exhibited its robustness across all types of poisoning attacks, the defense against optimization and adaptive attacks (best in 39/48 cases) and Min-Sum (14/16) attacks was particularly outstanding. However, FLGuard achieved relatively lower accuracy against LIE attack (8/16).

Table 3. Comparison of global model accuracy from byzantine-robust AGRs against and MPAs (Robustness) under threat model Type-3 & Type-4

Dataset (Distr.)	AGR	Type-3						Type-4						SF
		LIE		Min-Max		Min-Sum		LIE		Min-Max		Min-Sum		
		uv	sgn	uv	sgn	uv	sgn	uv	sgn	uv	sgn	uv	sgn	
MNIST -0.1 (IID)	TM	96.90	**97.00**	91.80	87.13	94.62	89.51	96.49	96.51	88.25	86.40	90.50	90.10	88.72
	MK	**97.02**	96.45	87.78	84.13	90.26	85.21	96.31	96.45	86.79	83.77	89.53	85.02	87.87
	Bul	96.90	96.12	89.63	91.72	92.23	83.64	95.45	96.06	86.99	91.42	92.21	85.98	92.23
	DnC	96.85	96.94	**96.88**	96.79	94.99	86.53	96.88	96.77	96.81	96.67	93.10	86.83	96.85
	FLT	95.35	95.70	93.97	95.35	95.43	95.50	95.74	95.86	93.41	95.23	93.41	95.11	89.65
	SG	96.98	96.81	96.12	91.68	**96.69**	95.52	**97.38**	**96.94**	95.58	90.28	96.33	93.43	96.61
	FLG	96.90	96.83	96.85	**96.83**	96.53	**96.88**	96.83	96.83	**96.83**	**96.88**	**96.67**	**96.85**	**96.90**
CIFAR 10 (IID)	TM	72.65	71.61	57.65	60.65	69.36	69.07	73.42	**75.28**	64.85	59.33	68.34	64.67	57.73
	MK	71.31	71.55	65.32	44.18	65.69	56.39	70.64	70.35	59.21	43.32	64.02	46.61	62.62
	Bul	73.42	53.86	38.80	37.58	45.21	41.07	64.96	54.44	39.31	38.70	40.28	42.67	48.54
	DnC	72.24	71.23	71.61	71.29	70.94	55.05	72.24	73.09	71.83	71.57	71.49	60.13	**73.54**
	FLT	72.24	68.22	71.29	70.54	72.24	57.57	71.00	66.11	70.27	71.45	70.45	57.35	69.83
	SG	72.50	70.68	60.11	69.99	70.05	69.87	72.81	71.96	58.85	68.43	69.95	68.51	53.06
	FLG	**73.60**	**73.13**	**72.95**	**73.50**	**72.38**	**72.50**	**74.25**	72.85	**72.87**	**72.97**	**72.06**	**72.87**	72.06
MNIST -0.5 (Non -IID)	TM	97.04	96.88	92.55	87.36	95.37	88.86	96.23	96.29	91.80	83.52	95.21	86.97	86.93
	MK	97.08	96.33	89.35	54.20	95.45	65.44	95.88	96.33	88.31	56.55	93.81	64.27	93.63
	Bul	96.73	95.03	86.49	89.87	84.64	80.64	95.01	95.01	86.32	88.84	94.80	80.88	89.91
	DnC	97.10	96.88	96.53	96.73	95.35	80.22	96.59	96.77	**95.03**	**96.79**	93.51	79.00	96.63
	FLT	94.50	94.18	88.68	93.28	91.70	76.22	94.30	94.30	90.16	92.98	90.10	82.47	91.34
	SG	**97.18**	96.92	95.03	93.69	**96.33**	92.98	96.85	96.69	92.31	92.13	95.25	89.79	96.29
	FLG	96.90	96.96	96.59	96.96	96.27	96.33	97.10	96.96	94.40	96.63	95.39	96.47	96.90
FE MNIST (Non -IID)	TM	83.12	83.95	72.09	57.64	81.26	64.11	82.21	83.17	73.62	71.05	80.49	72.24	79.73
	MK	83.86	72.30	80.18	4.85	82.90	9.33	83.68	**83.80**	78.13	4.87	82.79	11.25	78.23
	Bul	82.60	71.41	58.29	61.21	72.34	34.50	80.86	72.28	57.43	60.39	73.09	45.37	68.70
	DnC	83.93	83.59	83.34	44.11	83.36	5.69	83.84	83.63	80.93	5.25	83.51	5.42	81.44
	FLT	**84.92**	81.97	4.64	59.68	76.16	58.83	83.66	4.85	6.64	6.17	5.63	6.40	14.27
	SG	83.90	83.56	80.09	8.73	83.58	76.80	83.79	83.74	80.10	8.13	83.27	10.80	78.43
	FLG	84.32	**84.04**	**84.07**	**84.39**	**84.19**	82.62	**83.90**	82.41	**83.47**	82.63	**84.08**	**83.53**	**83.79**

Efficiency. We discuss efficiency by comparing the number of rounds and the total time required to train the global model [7]. The defender aims to implement byzantine-robust AGR without incurring extra overhead. As shown in Fig. 4, FLGuard does not pose extra communication costs (extra FL rounds) for the clients since the accuracy of the global model under attacks saturates as fast as FedAvg without poisoning attacks. We also measured the time taken to train the contrastive models and filter out the malicious clients with a Linux machine running on a Xeon Gold 6226R with 16 cores, 256 GB of RAM, and NVIDIA RTX A6000 GPU. For FEMNIST, given $k = 5$, the training time was 22.1 s, and the filtering time was 78 ms. As FLGuard capitalizes the idle time on the server (waiting for the clients to upload the local update) to train the contrastive models, the extra overhead is minimal given a suitable computational power.

Table 4. Comparison of global model accuracy from byzantine-robust AGRs against DPAs under threat model Type-5

AGR	Type-5							
	SLF	DLF	SLF	DLF	SLF	DLF	SLF	DLF
	MNIST-0.1		CIFAR-10		MNIST-0.5		FEMNIST	
TM	95.50	96.02	62.72	47.93	94.81	95.78	80.39	75.21
MK	96.45	96.45	71.21	70.58	96.25	96.31	83.47	84.37
Bul	95.78	95.68	46.49	53.31	94.30	94.56	68.39	72.17
DnC	96.67	**96.83**	71.23	72.18	96.67	96.33	84.15	83.52
FLT	95.80	95.64	68.97	70.19	94.89	95.29	79.34	81.84
SG	96.81	96.81	**71.67**	72.48	**96.77**	**96.90**	85.08	84.55
FLG	**96.83**	**96.83**	68.06	**72.63**	96.16	95.72	**85.18**	**84.67**

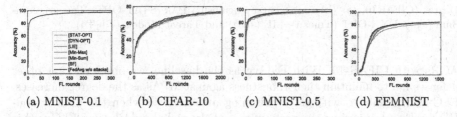

(a) MNIST-0.1   (b) CIFAR-10   (c) MNIST-0.5   (d) FEMNIST

Fig. 4. Global Model Accuracy vs. FL rounds for FLGuard with various MPAs and FedAvg without attacks

5.4 Ablation Study

Impact of Number of Malicious Clients. Sub-figures of (a) to (d) (i.e., first row) in Fig. 5 depict the impact of different fractions of malicious clients present in FL that varies from 0% to 40% which is an extreme adversarial setting [7,26,30]. The performance of the global model trained with other defense mechanisms deteriorates as the proportion of malicious clients increases. This effect is particularly pronounced when the percentage of malicious clients is high (40%), where the decline in accuracy is significant for T1 and T2 attacks. In contrast, FLGuard maintains its robustness even as the proportion of malicious clients increases across all types of attacks. Notably, when facing the Min-Sum attack, only FLGuard managed to keep the accuracy close to that of FedAvg without attacks, while other FL methods saw a sharp decline to less than 10%.

Impact of Non-IID Degree. Training the global model with non-IID setting in FL is a challenge that has been studied vigorously recently and as the degree of non-IID increases, it becomes more difficult to train a global model with high accuracy. Sub-figures of (e) to (h) (i.e., second row) in Fig. 5 illustrate the impact of non-IID degree on FLGuard compared with other byzantine-robust

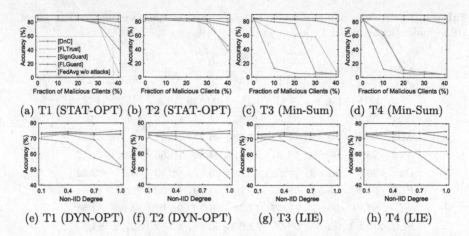

Fig. 5. Impact of Fraction of Malicious Clients (FEMNIST, (a)–(d)) and Non-IID Degree (CIFAR10, (e)–(h)) on Accuracy against MPAs (STAT-OPT (Tmean), Min-Sum (*sgn*), DYN-OPT (Tmean), LIE (*sgn*)) and Threat Models (T1–T4)

AGRs with CIFAR-10. With FedAvg as the baseline, we observed that other defenses fail to maintain their robustness against MPAs as the degree increases. FLGuard is able to withstand poisoning attacks even when the data is non-IID to a great extent as the performance of the global model using FLGuard is consistent and similar to that of FedAvg.

6   Conclusion and Future Work

FLGuard is a novel byzantine-robust FL technique that employs contrastive learning to formulate the challenge of detecting and removing malicious clients as a self-supervised learning problem. Thus, unlike other byzantine-robust FL schemes, FLGuard operates without prior knowledge about FL schemes or auxiliary datasets. The contrastive models are trained. Specifically, it adopts an ensemble of contrastive models trained with different dimension reduction methods and a clustering method to collect local model updates from only benign clients. We conducted an extensive evaluation with various experimental settings, including IID and non-IID datasets and various poisoning attacks (i.e., MPAs and DPAs) under five different threat models. The results demonstrate that FLGuard outperforms existing defense mechanisms by achieving three defender's objectives: fidelity, robustness, and efficiency. In particular, FLGuard has improved the accuracy of the global model with non-IID datasets by a huge margin. Moreover, our ablation study reveals that the performance of FLGuard is maintained even when a large fraction of clients are compromised and the degree of non-IID is high. We further note that FLGuard can be further improved by increasing the number of negative pairs used in contrastive learning. Also, we observed cases where dimension-wise filtering performed better than vector-wise defenses. Hence, we can devise a hybrid approach to combine the two for a stronger byzantine-robust FL scheme which we leave as future work.

Acknowledgements. This work was supported by Institute of Information & communications Technology Planning & Evaluation (IITP) grant funded by the Korea government (MSIT) (No. 2021-0-02068, Artificial Intelligence Innovation Hub, No. RS-2022-00155966, Artificial Intelligence Convergence Innovation Human Resources Development, No. 2022-0-00516, Derivation of a Differential Privacy Concept Applicable to National Statistics Data While Guaranteeing the Utility of Statistical Analysis (Ewha Woman's University and Seoul National University) and the artificial intelligence semiconductor support program to nurture the best talents (IITP-2023-RS-2023-00256081), Also, it was supported by the BK21 FOUR program of the Education and Research Program for Future ICT Pioneers, Seoul National University in 2023 and Inter-University Semiconductor Research Center (ISRC).

A   Appendix

A.1   FLGuard Algorithms and Parameter Settings for Experiments

Algorithm 2 illustrates the algorithm for updating the local model and returning the local updates for the server to gather. Algorithm 3 depicts the filtering process of FLGuard through the usage of contrastive models and clustering. We set the parameter $e = 1.5$ for DnC and collect the root dataset as the same distribution as the overall training dataset for FLTrust. For FLGuard, we set learning rate $= 0.001$, epoch $= 5$, batch size $= 32$ and $k = 5$ for all experiments.

Algorithm 2. LocalUpdate(w, I, D, b, F, α)

1: $w_0 \leftarrow w$
2: **for** each local iteration $i = 1, 2, ..., I$ **do**
3:     each mini-batch b sampled from D
4:     $w_i \leftarrow w_{i-1} - \alpha \cdot \frac{\partial F(b, w_{i-1})}{\partial w_{i-1}}$
5: **end for**
6: **return** $w_I - w$

Algorithm 3. Filtering($G_{lv}, G_{rd}, ContrastiveModels$)

1: $h_{lv}, h_{rd} \leftarrow$ **ContrastiveModels**(G_{lv}, G_{rd})
2: $h'_{lv}, h'_{rd} \leftarrow$ **PCA**(h_{lv}, h_{rd}, var)
3: $C_{lv}, C_{rd} \leftarrow$ **Clustering**(h'_{lv}, h'_{rd})
4: $C_{good} \leftarrow C_{lv} \cap C_{rd}$ {Ensemble Method}
5: **return** C_{good}

Table 5. FL parameter settings for various datasets. η for CIFAR10 is with weight decay of 5E-4 and momentum of 0.9

	Details	MNIST	CIFAR-10	FEMNIST
R	# FL Rounds	300	2,000	1,500
N	# Total Clients	100	50	3,400
M	# Malicious Clients	20	10	680
P	# Participating Clients	N		60
b	Batch Size	250	32	250
η	Global Learning Rate	0.001	0.01	0.001
Opt	Optimizer	Adam	SGD	Adam
$Arch$	Global Model Architecture	FCN	ResNet-14	ConvNet

A.2   Details of Evaluated Attacks

Optimization Approaches [27] consist of two types: static and dynamic. Such approaches assume that the aggregation rule for FL is known to the adversaries. **Static optimization (STAT-OPT)** [11] searches for a sub-optimal γ in generating malicious local updates g_m. The objective is to bypass the aggregation rule (i.e., classified as benign) and enable the malicious local updates (g_m) to participate in training the global model. **Dynamic approach (DYN-OPT)** [26] operates under the same constraints but differs in that DYN-OPT dynamically finds the largest γ for the specific AGR. Therefore, DYN-OPT is a stronger attack that circumvents the byzantine-robust AGR better. **Adaptive Attacks** [26] against DnC and FLGuard are reported separately. The adaptive attack against DnC operates similarly to DYN-OPT in that the largest γ for a specific known AGR is obtained. However, FLGuard updates the contrastive models every k FL rounds which makes designing the adaptive attack more challenging. In other words, the mechanism of AGR used to design the adaptive attacks is replaced with new contrastive models that project the local update to a different representation map. Therefore, in designing the adaptive attack against FLGuard, we assume that the adversaries can obtain the contrastive models every k FL rounds and use DYN-OPT to find the largest γ. **Little Is Enough (LIE)** [4] crafted malicious updates that are within the population variance but yet cause byzantine failure in FL based on an observation that the practical variance of local model updates is high. LIE successfully degrades the accuracy of the global model with a very small γ to bypass the previous defense mechanisms. **Min-Max** [26] aims to place malicious model update (g_m) close to the benign ones (g_b) by finding a suitable γ. Hence, the maximum distance of g_m to any other g is bounded by the maximum distance between two g_b. **Min-Sum** [26] operates similar to Min-Max but with different upper bound constraint in finding γ. Min-Sum bounds the sum of squared distances between g_m and all other g_b by the sum of squared distances of any two g_b. **Sign-Flip Attack (SF)** reveres the local updates in the opposite direction without adjusting the size. This is a special case of the reversed gradient attack [25]. **Label-Flip attack** is one of the data poisoning attacks. The malicious local updates are generated using data with flipped labels. Static Label-Flip (SLF) [7,11] flips the original label of data c to $n-1-c$, where n is the total number of labels. Dynamic Label-Flip (DLF) [27] trains a surrogate model with the available benign data and flips the original label to the least probable label output from the surrogate model.

References

1. 2018 reform of EU data protection rules. https://ec.europa.eu/commission/sites/beta-political/files/data-protection-factsheet-changes_en.pdf
2. Federated learning: Collaborative machine learning without centralized training data (2017). https://ai.googleblog.com/2017/04/federated-learning-collaborative.html
3. Bahri, D., Jiang, H., Tay, Y., Metzler, D.: Scarf: self-supervised contrastive learning using random feature corruption. arXiv preprint arXiv:2106.15147 (2021)
4. Baruch, G., Baruch, M., Goldberg, Y.: A little is enough: circumventing defenses for distributed learning. In: Advances in Neural Information Processing Systems, vol. 32 (2019)
5. Blanchard, P., El Mhamdi, E.M., Guerraoui, R., Stainer, J.: Machine learning with adversaries: byzantine tolerant gradient descent. In: Advances in Neural Information Processing Systems, vol. 30 (2017)
6. Caldas, S., et al.: Leaf: a benchmark for federated settings. arXiv preprint arXiv:1812.01097 (2018)
7. Cao, X., Fang, M., Liu, J., Gong, N.Z.: Fltrust: byzantine-robust federated learning via trust bootstrapping. arXiv preprint arXiv:2012.13995 (2020)
8. Caron, M., Misra, I., Mairal, J., Goyal, P., Bojanowski, P., Joulin, A.: Unsupervised learning of visual features by contrasting cluster assignments. Adv. Neural. Inf. Process. Syst. **33**, 9912–9924 (2020)
9. Chen, T., Kornblith, S., Norouzi, M., Hinton, G.: A simple framework for contrastive learning of visual representations. In: International Conference on Machine Learning, pp. 1597–1607. PMLR (2020)
10. Chen, T., Kornblith, S., Swersky, K., Norouzi, M., Hinton, G.E.: Big self-supervised models are strong semi-supervised learners. Adv. Neural. Inf. Process. Syst. **33**, 22243–22255 (2020)
11. Fang, M., Cao, X., Jia, J., Gong, N.: Local model poisoning attacks to {Byzantine-Robust} federated learning. In: 29th USENIX Security Symposium (USENIX Security 2020), pp. 1605–1622 (2020)
12. Guerraoui, R., Rouault, S., et al.: The hidden vulnerability of distributed learning in byzantium. In: International Conference on Machine Learning, pp. 3521–3530. PMLR (2018)
13. He, K., Fan, H., Wu, Y., Xie, S., Girshick, R.: Momentum contrast for unsupervised visual representation learning. In: Proceedings of the IEEE/CVF Conference on Computer Vision and Pattern Recognition, pp. 9729–9738 (2020)
14. Kairouz, P., et al.: Advances and open problems in federated learning. Found. Trends® Mach. Learn. **14**(1–2), 1–210 (2021)
15. Khosla, P., et al.: Supervised contrastive learning. Adv. Neural. Inf. Process. Syst. **33**, 18661–18673 (2020)

16. Konečnỳ, J., McMahan, H.B., Yu, F.X., Richtárik, P., Suresh, A.T., Bacon, D.: Federated learning: strategies for improving communication efficiency. arXiv preprint arXiv:1610.05492 (2016)

17. Krizhevsky, A., Hinton, G.: Learning multiple layers of features from tiny images (2009)

18. LeCun, Y., Bottou, L., Bengio, Y., Haffner, P.: Gradient-based learning applied to document recognition. Proc. IEEE **86**(11), 2278–2324 (1998)

19. Li, S., Cheng, Y., Wang, W., Liu, Y., Chen, T.: Learning to detect malicious clients for robust federated learning. arXiv preprint arXiv:2002.00211 (2020)

20. McMahan, B., Moore, E., Ramage, D., Hampson, S., Arcas, B.A.: Communication-efficient learning of deep networks from decentralized data. In: Artificial Intelligence and Statistics, pp. 1273–1282. PMLR (2017)

21. McMahan, B., Moore, E., Ramage, D., Hampson, S., Arcas, B.A.Y.: Communication-efficient learning of deep networks from decentralized data. In: Singh, A., Zhu, J. (eds.) Proceedings of the 20th International Conference on Artificial Intelligence and Statistics. Proceedings of Machine Learning Research, vol. 54, pp. 1273–1282. PMLR (2017)

22. Misra, I., Maaten, L.V.D.: Self-supervised learning of pretext-invariant representations. In: Proceedings of the IEEE/CVF Conference on Computer Vision and Pattern Recognition, pp. 6707–6717 (2020)

23. Müllner, D.: Modern hierarchical, agglomerative clustering algorithms. arXiv preprint arXiv:1109.2378 (2011)

24. Paulik, M., et al.: Federated evaluation and tuning for on-device personalization: system design & applications (2021). https://doi.org/10.48550/ARXIV.2102.08503

25. Rajput, S., Wang, H., Charles, Z., Papailiopoulos, D.: Detox: a redundancy-based framework for faster and more robust gradient aggregation. In: Advances in Neural Information Processing Systems, vol. 32 (2019)

26. Shejwalkar, V., Houmansadr, A.: Manipulating the byzantine: optimizing model poisoning attacks and defenses for federated learning. In: NDSS (2021)

27. Shejwalkar, V., Houmansadr, A., Kairouz, P., Ramage, D.: Back to the drawing board: a critical evaluation of poisoning attacks on production federated learning. In: IEEE Symposium on Security and Privacy (2022)

28. Sohn, K.: Improved deep metric learning with multi-class n-pair loss objective. In: Advances in Neural Information Processing Systems, vol. 29 (2016)

29. Ucar, T., Hajiramezanali, E., Edwards, L.: Subtab: subsetting features of tabular data for self-supervised representation learning. In: Ranzato, M., Beygelzimer, A., Dauphin, Y., Liang, P., Vaughan, J.W. (eds.) Advances in Neural Information Processing Systems, vol. 34, pp. 18853–18865. Curran Associates, Inc. (2021)

30. Xu, J., Huang, S.L., Song, L., Lan, T.: Signguard: byzantine-robust federated learning through collaborative malicious gradient filtering. arXiv preprint arXiv:2109.05872 (2021)

31. Yin, D., Chen, Y., Kannan, R., Bartlett, P.: Byzantine-robust distributed learning: towards optimal statistical rates. In: International Conference on Machine Learning, pp. 5650–5659. PMLR (2018)

32. Zhao, B., Sun, P., Wang, T., Jiang, K.: Fedinv: byzantine-robust federated learning by inversing local model updates (2022)

Machine Learning for SAST: A Lightweight and Adaptable Approach

Lorenz Hüther[1]([✉]) [iD], Karsten Sohr[1] [iD], Bernhard J. Berger[2] [iD],
Hendrik Rothe[3], and Stefan Edelkamp[4] [iD]

[1] Computer Science Department, Software Engineering Group, University of Bremen,
Bibliothekstraße 5, 28359 Bremen, Germany
{lorenz1,sohr}@uni-bremen.de
[2] Institute of Embedded Systems, Hamburg University of Technology,
Am Schwarzenberg-Campus 3 (E), 21073 Hamburg, Germany
bernhard.berger@tuhh.de
[3] Team Neusta GmbH, Konsul-Smidt-Straße 24, 28217 Bremen, Germany
h.rothe@neusta.de
[4] Artificial Intelligence Center, Czech Technical University in Prague,
Charles Square 13, 120 00 Prague, Czech Republic
edelkste@fel.cvut.cz

Abstract. In this paper, we summarize a novel method for machine learning-based static application security testing (SAST), which was devised as part of a larger study funded by Germany's Federal Office for Information Security (BSI). SAST describes the practice of applying static analysis techniques to program code on the premise of detecting security-critical software defects early during the development process. In the past, this was done by using rule-based approaches, where the program code is checked against a set of rules that define some pattern, representative of a defect. Recently, an increasing influx of publications can be observed that discuss the application of machine learning methods to this problem. Our method poses a lightweight approach to this concept, comprising two main contributions: Firstly, we present a novel control-flow based embedding method for program code. Embedding the code into a metric space is a necessity in order to apply machine learning techniques to the problem of SAST. Secondly, we describe how this method can be applied to generate expressive, yet simple, models of some unwanted behavior. We have implemented these methods in a prototype for the C and C++ programming languages. Using tenfold cross-validation, we show that our prototype is capable of effectively predicting the location and type of software defects in previously unseen code.

Keywords: SAST · Machine Learning · Static Analysis · Software Defect Prediction

G. Tsudik et al. (Eds.): ESORICS 2023, LNCS 14347, pp. 85–104, 2024.
https://doi.org/10.1007/978-3-031-51482-1_5

1 Introduction

The term Static application security testing (SAST) refers to the use of static analysis techniques for the detection of security-critical software defects. A key property of SAST is that the program being analyzed is not executed to determine potential defects. Instead, SAST tools apply predefined analysis rules that model different security threats. Recently, an increasing trend has been observed, where researchers apply machine learning techniques to the problem of SAST [11,14,18]. Hence, this approach to the problem does not require rules to be conceived explicitly, but instead, statistical methods are used to separate benign from defective code. A lot of the methods described in the literature rely on complex models, which are hard to retrain on new data. To make matters worse, if the authors do not publish the datasets used to train the models or the tools used in the preprocessing of the data, this already daunting task becomes even more challenging for practitioners. This is problematic, since data changes over time and new threats and therefore new data, may call for adjustments w.r.t existing models. To alleviate this problem, we therefore devise a new method that allows us to generate lightweight models, which can be easily adapted if necessary. We have developed a prototype that implements this method, while fully embracing this property by means of a built-in feedback loop that allows practitioners to retrain the models on the fly, using confirmed findings. In summary, our contributions in this paper are the following:

1. We describe a method which relies on the control flow to embed program code into a metric space.
2. We show how we apply this embedding to generate lightweight models using supervised and unsupervised machine learning techniques.
3. We have developed a prototypical implementation of our method that will be released to the public under an open-source license.
4. We evaluated our method on the Juliet test suite using tenfold cross-validation. The evaluation shows that our method can effectively detect different types of software defects that are reflected in the control flow.

The rest of the paper is structured as follows: In Sect. 2, we introduce the techniques and data structures from the domains of static code analysis and machine learning that lay the foundation of our method. Section 3 covers the working principles behind our method, i.e., the embedding of program code into a metric space and the generation of our lightweight models. In Sect. 4 we then present the experimental setup and the results of our evaluation, which will be at the center of the ensuing discussion found in Sect. 5. After our method has been thoroughly expounded, Sect. 6 will briefly cover another method and work out some similarities, but also key differences. Finally, Sects. 7, 8 and 9 cover possible threats to the validity of our results, an outlook in terms of further research and the conclusion of this paper.

2   Background

Surveys on machine learning in the field of SAST show that the vast majority of primary studies appear to employ supervised machine learning algorithms [11,18], an observation that is also backed by our research [14]. With supervised ML-based SAST, a model is learned on select code samples, where it is known whether each particular sample is defective or not. After this training phase, the model is applied to previously unseen code, in hopes that it has learned general patterns from the training data that allow for the detection of software defects. A prime example of such a supervised approach to ML-based SAST, can be considered the VulDeeP-ecker paper devised by Li et al., being one of the most cited publications in this regard. The authors use an LSTM neural network that was trained on various software defects in order to discover vulnerabilities in previously unseen code [17]. Despite being a highly cited paper, the VulDeePecker approach is not without problems, however. Since being learned on all tokens of the training programs, including parentheses, semicola, etc., their model inadvertently picked up on false correlations, as was uncovered by Arp et al. [3].

Another, albeit much less common approach to the problem of ML-based SAST, makes use of unsupervised machine learning methods, where a labeled ground truth is not necessary. Instead, analysis rules are deduced from the same code base that is being analyzed. There are a few examples that use clustering methods to discover software defects in program code. Ahmadi et al., for instance, use a two-step clustering method, where the authors would first cluster the code into semantically similar constructs. Then they search for outliers within the previous clusters by employing a second, more precise clustering technique [1]. Another example in this respect is the approach described by Yamaguchi et al., where the authors employ clustering methods to automatically generate search patterns for the detection of taint-style vulnerabilities [23].

Regardless of the machine learning technique used, these SAST approaches share some fundamental commonalities. That is, a) they require some means of mapping the program code into a metric space and b) due to the limitations of machine learning methods w.r.t. the dimensionality of the input data, these methods must divide the code into smaller segments [10]. This may seem trivial at first considering that, on a syntactic level, the program code forms a consecutive sequence of instructions. Based on this assumption, it would then be possible to partition the code into equally sized vectors, where each instruction would be mapped to some dimension as a numerical value, for instance. In reality, however, such representation would be far from ideal, since it entirely neglects the underlying semantics and truncates the code at arbitrary points. Therefore, a more refined strategy is to perform a control flow analysis on the code. This way the instructions can be embedded in the same consecutive order in which they would be executed during runtime. Moreover, there are a lot of software defects that manifest in the control flow, such as missing return values or null pointer checks. If modeled interprocedural, even more defects may be detected, such as missing calls to sanitization functions.

Our prototype therefore uses the interprocedural control flow graph (ICFG) at it's base, a common data structure in the field of static analysis that models a program's control flow interprocedurally [16]. Moreover, it can usually be generated with acceptable effort, making it ideal for our purposes. For the implementation of our prototype, we chose the SVF library to generate ICFGs with, which is built upon the LLVM compiler infrastructure project and offers a comprehensive collection of algorithms and data structures for static analysis [21]. As a consequence, the library requires program code to be compiled into LLVM's intermediate program representation (LLVM-IR) first. To better understand the kind of information an ICFG holds, consider the example in Listing 1.1.

```
01 void foo(void){              04 int main(int argc, char *argv[]){
02      printf("foo");          05      void (*f)(void) = NULL;
03 }                            06      if (argc > 1) f = &foo;
                                07      if (f) f();
                                08 }
```

Listing 1.1. A small example program in the C programming language.

As can be seen, the listing shows a small program, written in the C programming language, comprising two procedures: main() and foo(). In order to construct an ICFG from the program, we begin by attending to each procedure individually, modeling the local control flow by first inserting two unique nodes that mark the distinct entry and exit points of a procedure. Then, for every statement in a procedure, a node is added and the flow of control is modeled by directed edges. Nodes that correspond to consecutive statements in the program are connected by a single (unconditional) edge, when they are guaranteed to be executed in sequence. For conditional control flow statements it is unknown, which branch will be taken during execution. Therefore, two edges are inserted, connecting the control flow statement to the next statement that would be executed if the associated condition evaluates to true and another edge for the case that the condition evaluates to false. Vice versa, if two execution branches merge again, two edges are inserted that connect the last statements of each branch to the unconditional successor.

This models the local control flow and if it was our goal to construct a CFG, we could stop here. However, many software defects span multiple procedures, hence it is necessary to also model the passing of control between procedures. This is done by drawing directed edges from every call site of a procedure to its unique entry node and in reverse, edges from its exit node back to the call site [16]. This may sound simple at first, but this problem is complicated by the fact that it is not always known, which procedure is actually called during runtime. Notice, how in Listing 1.1, the call to foo() in line 07 is made via a pointer that is declared in line 05, but only initialized in line 06 if a command line argument is supplied. To model the interprocedural control flow, it is therefore necessary to perform a so-called points-to analysis (PTA) that tries to determine sets of potential targets that pointer variables may point to during runtime. Multiple algorithms exist to this end, with varying degrees of precision. However, this problem is undecidable and may therefore only ever be approximated. We use SVF to this end, which offers a large variety of algorithms with different properties. Figure 1 depicts the fully constructed ICFG for the example program provided in Listing 1.1. The local control flow is marked using solid lines, whereas the dashed lines correspond to the interprocedural control flow. Also notice, how we aggregated unconditional sequences of statements in a single node, for brevity's sake.

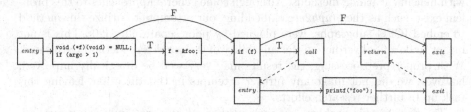

Fig. 1. The ICFG that corresponds to the example given in Listing 1.1

3   Our Approach

As outlined in Sect. 2, we have developed a novel method that allows us to observe a program's control flow in a metric space, whereby enabling us to model SAST problems on an example-based approach. In this section, we describe the methods used to map an ICFG into a metric space. Based on this step, we then show in Sect. 3.2, how this method may be employed to generate models that pertain to different classes of software defects and how they can be used to find similar defect patterns in previously unseen code.

3.1   Embedding Method

The application of machine learning methods to SAST is a difficult problem due to some inherent restrictions of the available machine-learning techniques and the structural properties of program code. Beginning with the side of the machine-learning methods, there are some strict limitations in terms of the dimensionality of the input data. This phenomenon is often referred to as the "curse of dimensionality", a term initially coined by Bellman [5,10]. This yields two implications that are of particular importance for our method: Firstly, distance metrics, such as the Euclidean distance, lose usefulness in high dimensional spaces and the *K-Means* algorithm, which we make use of in Sect. 3.2, relies on this metric [22]. Secondly, with increasing dimensionality of the input space, the number of necessary observations, for a supervised model to generalize well, grows as well [10]. Therefore, keeping the dimensionality of the input data low is crucial when finding a suitable embedding method for program code. Put in other words, using machine learning, we can only observe the program through a very small window at a time.

As elaborated in Sect. 2, we begin our analysis by first generating the program's ICFG, a more meaningful program representation that allows us to use the available dimensions of the input space more effectively. Unfortunately, we inadvertently run into another problem, using this program representation. As ICFGs are complex graph structures, where nodes may be connected by multiple incoming and outgoing edges, they have no canonical representation in the vector space. In other words, there is no direct way of embedding graphs for use with machine learning methods. Although some general approaches to this problem exist, such as the *graph2vec* embedding, our attempts to utilize this method to embed ICFG subgraphs, were plagued by poor separability [20]. This is not meant to be a final verdict on the suitability of the *graph2vec* method to this end. With proper preprocessing, the results may very well be drastically improved, however, we did not make any further attempts in this direction, leaving this task up to further research efforts.

To alleviate this problem, we instead devised our own embedding method, where we restrict ourselves to traversals along the graph edges. Each traversal corresponds to a single execution path in the program. To do so, we formulated our traversals as follows: For every procedure in the ICFG, we retrieve its unique entry node as a starting point and extract every individual path from there on, descending and returning from the functions called along the way, until either the exit node of the same procedure is reached or the current path reaches a length of 75 nodes. We found that limiting the depth of each walk in this way results in acceptable runtimes, while not restricting the path extraction too much. This value has not been determined empirically, however, such that this endeavor would make for a good subject w.r.t. future research. As for the Juliet test suite, the dataset we use to train our prototype, this limit was reached in 1.6% of all cases, while the average path length was close to 48 nodes.

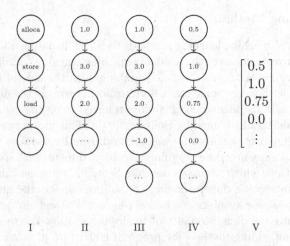

Fig. 2. The steps involved in the embedding of an ICFG.

For each path extracted, we continue by collecting all nodes and map them onto numerical values, e.g., by their instruction. Since, every traversal underlies a strict total order, we can assign a dimension in a vector space to each node in ascending traversal order. We pad the paths to the length of the longest path that was extracted and finally, normalize the values including the padding. The above Fig. 2 summarizes the steps involved in the embedding of the individual ICFG paths visually. From left to right, we can see the unaltered path in **I** before being embedded in **II**, padded in **III** and normalized in **IV**. The final vector representation is marked **V**.

3.2 Model Generation

Using the embedding method outlined in Sect. 3.1, we now explain how we use this method to generate models that can be employed to detect defect patterns in source code. Before we do so, however, we first need a ground truth from which the models can be fitted.

There are two basic types of ground truths available: synthetic and realistic. Whereas the former is manually crafted, the latter comprises code samples that have been extracted from real software projects. Realistic datasets could therefore be considered much more reflective of actual vulnerabilities found in software projects, since they have been generated from such. The synthetic datasets, being hand-crafted, are possibly more akin to textbook examples and might not encapsulate the complexity of real software defects to their full extent. This may sound like realistic datasets should be unconditionally preferred, however, their realism comes at a price. Firstly, since often being generated in an automated fashion, there is a risk that they contain benign code samples that have been wrongfully labeled defective. While this is amendable, there is a much bigger problem, pertaining to the class of benign samples. As these too are generated from actual software projects, they have to be sampled from code that is assumed to be benign. While it is easy to prove that a program is defective—since showing the existence of a single defect within that code suffices—it is much harder to prove that a program is free of any defect. Hence, one can never say with certainty that the benign class of realistic datasets is indeed free of defects. Realistically this is very unlikely. A model that is trained on such datasets might suffer from decreased predictive performance due to this kind of label noise. Finally, realistic datasets may also lack vital context, due to being extracted from large and complex programs. For these reasons, we determined that the lack of realism synthetic datasets may suffer from was less problematic than the disadvantages that come with realistic datasets. Hence, for our prototype we chose the Juliet test suite for the C and C++ programming languages as the ground truth that our models would be trained on. The Juliet test suite is a synthetic dataset, which comprises 64,099 individual test cases, covering over 100 types of defects [6]. Each test case comes as a self-contained program that is buildable using standard tool-chains. Test cases always have a single entry point, their main function, from where other functions are called. These functions may then call further functions. For each test case there is a benign version that showcases the correct behavior, as well as a defective version that contains a defect. Since these test cases are too comprehensive to provide concrete examples in this paper, we would like to refer interested readers to the NIST's website, where the Juliet test suite is hosted, and individual test cases may be viewed[1].

With a ground truth at hand, it is now time to discuss the generation of the models used for the detection of defective code. As elaborated in Sect. 3.1, we can use our embedding method, to map individual execution paths from a program's ICFG into a vector space. When generating our models, we are trying to abstract from the concrete behavior that each of these paths depict and extract their common, abstract behavior. The Juliet test suite consists of different collections of test cases, organized by their type of defect. We can thus assume that paths extracted from the same defect class have some underlying commonalities in terms of abstract behavior. When generating our models we take advantage of this property by attending to each defect class in the Juliet test suite individually, generating one model per class. Hence, for every class, we begin by processing its test cases as outlined in Sect. 3.1: building its ICFG, extracting individual paths and mapping them onto real-valued vectors.

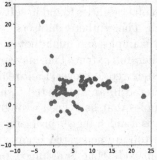 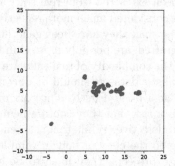

(a) A two-dimensional scatter plot of the benign (green) and vulnerable (red) paths of the Juliet test suite within the same vector space (see Section 3.1).

(b) The same embedded paths from Figure 3a after removing all benign paths. In this example, the models are generated from the vulnerable paths of the Juliet Test Suite only.

Fig. 3. Paths from the Juliet test suite's CWE-690 class of test cases, embedded in a vector space. (Color figure online)

We then continue by randomly sampling 50% of both, benign and defective paths and reserve this set for later use as our test dataset. The remaining paths will be our training dataset, which also comprises benign as well as defective paths. As will be shown, both parts of the split play an equally important part in the generation of the models, hence why we deemed a 50/50 split to be appropriate. However, experimenting with different ratios may be worthwhile

---

[1] https://samate.nist.gov/SARD/test-suites/112.

investigating in future research. When observed in the same space, one can see that the different behaviors of the paths are separable, depicted above in Fig. 3a. Each data point marked in green represents a benign path extracted from the Juliet test suite's CWE-690 class of test cases, while red data points represent the defective paths. It must be noted that in this example, the paths have been subjected to the UMAP dimensionality reduction method to be able to show them in a two-dimensional scatter plot, hence this depiction is likely inaccurate [19]. Since we are only interested in modeling unwanted behavior, we discarded the benign paths for the remainder of this explanation, as can be seen above in Fig. 3b.

Despite being extracted from the same CWE class and only using the defective paths, they are still not entirely homogeneous, forming clusters in the vector space. If we were to continue with the paths as is, we would likely learn a model that is too imprecise, as the program behavior it abstracts from is still too diverse. Hence, we need to further dismantle the concrete behavior into smaller units. This is done by application of the K-Means clustering algorithm to the paths, parametrized with $k = 8$, i.e., we instruct the algorithm to fit the data into eight distinct clusters [4]. In experiments, we evaluated this number to likely strike a good balance in terms of the abstraction level. While increasing the k-parameter further lead to better predictive performance, doing so also entailed diminishing returns, with gains drastically decreasing at a k between 8 and 13. Therefore, choosing a k that is too high would likely lead to an overfitting effect, as we would move closer to the actual behavior depicted by the individual paths. On a final remark, we must also highlight that this value may be different for other datasets.

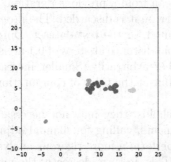

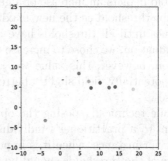

(a) The paths from Figure 3b after being clustered using the K-Means clustering algorithm, parametrized with $k = 8$. Each color represents a different cluster.

(b) Using the geometric mean of each cluster, their centroids are calculated. This constitutes the first part of the models.

Fig. 4. The process of finding the centroids within the paths from the previous example.

Figure 4a above shows the same paths as before, after the *K-Means* algorithm has been applied, where each color represents a different cluster. We then continue by computing the geometric mean of each cluster. The idea is that if paths lie in the same cluster, then they must be semantically very similar. As a result, the geometric mean of such cluster may be viewed as the mean value of the combined behaviors of all paths within that cluster. Figure 4b above displays the geometric means of the clusters from before. They form the first part of our models.

If we were now to observe unseen paths from a program we want to analyze within the same vector space, we could measure the distance of each path to the geometric centers. A path excerpting a close distance to one of these centers has an increased risk of also being defective. However, in order to be able to tell benign paths from defective paths, it is necessary to first define some threshold around the centers, so that paths that fall below this threshold can be reported as potential risks. We can find the optimal threshold if we conceive this problem as an optimization problem, where it is the goal to find a balance between the true positive rate (TPR) and the true negative rate (TNR). To this end, we use a method, devised by Johnson et al., which aims to maximize the geometric mean of the TPR and TNR to determine the optimal threshold [15]. Using the test dataset from the beginning, we employ this method as follows:

Firstly, we measure the distance of each path from the test dataset, benign and defective, to each of the previously generated centers. The smallest distance marks the radius of the smallest threshold and vice versa, the largest distance marks the largest threshold. Then beginning with the smallest threshold we compute the confusion matrix for this threshold and derive its TPR and TNR. Finally, we determine the geometric mean of the TPR and TNR. If the current threshold depicts an increase of a geometric mean from a previous iteration, we store the threshold as the new maximum, otherwise it is discarded. The process continues until all thresholds have been computed for the test dataset. During our evaluation, we chose to increase the threshold distance at steps of 0.1 at each iteration, however, this value was chosen rather arbitrarily. Smaller increases could potentially yield slightly better models, but at the price of computational expenses.

While technically posing the optimal thresholds, they may not necessarily conform to a practitioner's individual requirements, calling for manual adjustments. For instance, when it is imperative to perform a more rigorous analysis, the size of the thresholds should be increased. This, in turn, decreases the number of false negatives, however, at the cost of an increase in false positives. Conversely, when a more swift and less complete analysis is required, decreasing the size of the thresholds will decrease the number of false positives, at an increased rate of false negatives. With the thresholds being determined, our model is complete, and we can apply it to previously unseen code. Figure 5a shows the same paths from before, along with their thresholds, marked in red.

To apply this model, we must first process the software under analysis as outlined in Sect. 3.1, thereby generating a number of ICFG paths. Then, between each path and each geometric center, the Euclidean distance is computed. If for any of the geometric centers the distance is determined to fall below its threshold, the affected path is filed as potentially defective and a report is made. Figure 5b depicts this situation. Here, the red saltires mark previously unseen paths that lie within the thresholds and are consequently considered a potential defect. The green crosses, on the other hand, mark those paths that lie outside the thresholds. Hence, they are considered safe.

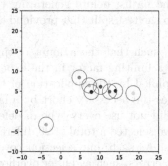 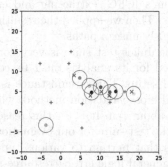

(a) Using the benign and vulnerable paths from the test split, the optimal thresholds can be determined for the centroids from Figure 4b.

(b) Using the centroids and their according thresholds, it is possible to then observe unseen paths in the same vector space. Paths within the thresholds are considered problematic.

Fig. 5. The threshold-based detection of paths that potentially contain software defects. (Color figure online)

As elaborated, we generate a single model for every class of defect defined by the Juliet test suite. Therefore, to cover every class of defect in our analysis as well, we must apply each model to every execution path extracted from the software under analysis. Algorithm 1, in the appendix, depicts this process in the form of pseudocode.

4 Evaluation

In order to evaluate our method, we have determined its predictive performance using the tenfold cross-validation method, as is standard practice. In addition we have also tested our method against real vulnerabilities found in actual open source software and compared the results against those of three other conventional SAST tools, as well as the academic FICS tool, developed by Ahmadi et al. [1].

Since for the tenfold cross-validation, different training and test splits are used for the evaluation, it is paramount to ensure a strict separation of the splits. To do so, we started at the very bottom of the pipeline and created the splits at the source code level. That is, for each type of defect in the Juliet test suite, we began by partitioning the test cases into ten equally sized sets. Then, we generated separate main files for the training and test datasets. The file for the training dataset would call the test cases, contained in nine of the sets, whereas the file for the test dataset would call those of the remaining set. Then we swap sets and repeat the steps until every partition would be used exactly once as the test dataset. Using these splits, we then processed every training dataset as outlined in the previous Sects. 3.1 and 3.2, i.e., building the program's ICFG, extracting and embedding the paths, before generating the models. Then we applied the resulting models to the test split that provided the previously unseen paths.

The Juliet test suite is very comprehensive, such that the amount of time required for its analysis must be considered as a limiting factor in the experimental setup. This circumstance is further amplified by the application of the tenfold cross-validation method, which multiplies the necessary effort by a factor of about ten. It is for this reason that we did not use every type of defect from the test suite for our evaluation. Instead, we selected a total of 20 different classes that pertain to various types of defects. As such, our selection covers more general logic errors, resource-management errors, such as buffer overflows and numeric errors. Since the Juliet test suite is of synthetic nature, it can be assumed that all code labeled benign is indeed benign and vice versa, all code labeled defective is indeed defective. Consequently, we make assumptions about all dimensions of the confusion matrix, from which we derived the *accuracy, precision, recall* and *F1-score*, depicted in Table 1 in the appendix. There it can be seen that the separability varies drastically between different classes of defects. This is to be expected as not all types of defects manifest equally strong in the control flow.

As elaborated, we have also tested our method against a number of real vulnerabilities, found in four different open source software projects. To this end, we relied on a dataset by Fan et al. that was built from CWE reports [9]. Not only, does this dataset contain the according CWE class for each sample, but it also refers to the affected versions via commit hashes for the respective git repositories. To cover a variety of different software domains, we included defects reported for the network service application *miniupnp*, the image conversion libraries *libtiff* and *openjpeg* and finally *zlib*, a compression library. Due to time limitations, we had to restrict ourselves to a total of 44 bug reports, spanning 12 different CWE classes. Unfortunately, the same problems that apply to training datasets, described in Sect. 3.2, equally apply to test datasets. That is, if generated from real software projects it may be only possible ascertain the presence of defects in the defective class of code samples, but not the absence thereof in the benign class. In order to still be able to make some statements on how our method behaves in a realistic scenario, we decided to perform an oracle test, where we would only determine, if a defect can be found using our method. However, we would make no assumptions about false positives or true negatives.

We proceeded by checking out one of the affected versions and running our prototype against the code, before moving on to the next version, until each of the 44 had been processed. To determine how well our method fares against other solutions, we repeated the same test using the previously introduced FICS tool, by Ahmadi et al. [1] and three conventional SAST tools. While our prototype successfully reported two buffer related vulnerabilities, FICS correctly detected three other, equally buffer related defects. Of the conventional tools, none succeeded in reporting any of the 44 defects present in the dataset. The full table containing the results of this evaluation can be found in Table 2 in the appendix.

5   Discussion

As the evaluation has shown, we have developed a novel method for ML-based SAST that is capable of discerning different program behaviors in the vector space. This way, we were able to effectively predict vulnerable code patterns within the Juliet test suite for the C and C++ programming languages. One of the key benefits of this approach is that it does away with complex machine learning methods, which simplifies the training process. For our prototype we have chosen to persist our models as simple lists of ICFG paths, as this granted us the flexibility to add or remove paths at will. Therefore, once a new program's ICFG has been generated and its paths extracted, making modifications to an existing model is as simple as appending new paths to this list. For all 48, 413 individual paths that we have extracted from the Juliet test suite, we found that the entire process of computing the geometric centers as well as the according thresholds takes less than a minute on a modest Intel i7-7700K processor. Our prototype integrates this workflow in a simple and straight-forward fashion by allowing practitioners to mark findings in a user interface for later incorporation in the model.

As for the oracle test, we unfortunately suspect that the test dataset used may have been biased towards cases that are hard to detect statically. One reason for this may be that the analyzed software systems have been subjected to other static analysis tools in the past. GitHub, for instance, offer their SAST solution free of charge for open source and research projects [12]. Hence, this scenario would be conceivable. Another reason why these defects may be especially difficult to detect is that the dataset was generated from CVE-reports. Alexopoulos et al. report that the lifetime of vulnerabilities in FOSS often exceeds several years, suggesting that these kinds of defects may be particularly complex and hard to discover for SAST tools and developers alike [2]. Moreover, since FICS has detected entirely different defects, the oracle test has also highlighted the potential of combining our method with other ML-based SAST methods for improved detection rates. Interested readers may obtain a copy of our prototype via Germany's Federal Office for Information Security [14].

6   Related Research

Now that our method has been thoroughly expounded, we would like to draw the attention to another method introduced by Cui et al., to highlight some of its similarities, but more importantly, its differences. Cui et al. extract important identifiers from known vulnerable code, which they assign a weight based on their importance. The authors then normalize the identifiers using the K-Means clustering algorithm. These terms serve as the slicing criteria for their next step, where the authors continue by extracting the CFG and the abstract syntax tree (AST) for every procedure in the software under analysis, using LLVM. From this, the authors then construct a new data structure, which they refer to as the weighted feature graph (WFG). This graph is an amalgamation of both graphs, where the CFG is preserved in its entirety and for every basic block its corresponding AST is mapped onto a vector using the bag of words method. The authors then use a bipartite graph matching algorithm in order to compare the WFGs that were extracted from the software under analysis against WFGs of known vulnerabilities to detect new vulnerabilities [8].

This approach showcases some parallels to ours in the sense that it uses the K-Means clustering algorithm in the preprocessing of the data. Moreover, the authors use the CFG and LLVM's internal AST representation as the basis for their analysis. However, on closer inspection, these similarities prove to be of superficial nature, with our method differing in the following key areas: Firstly, unlike Cui et al., we perform a PTA on the source code, hence our method is capable of resolving function pointers. Function pointers are used in callback patterns, which are frequently found in C and C++ software. Furthermore, our technique uses an ICFG, i.e., the interprocedural version of the CFG. The ICFG and its properties have been covered in Sect. 3.1. This way, we are not only able to resolve calls that are made by pointer references, but we can also descend into the function that was called when extracting the program data. Furthermore, we embed entire execution paths over the opcodes of the instructions that lie there on. Due to this step, we do not have to resort to bipartite graph matching and instead rely solely on the Euclidean distance to determine the similarity between two execution paths.

7   Limitations and Threats to Validity

The most salient threat lies in the generalizability of our approach, i.e., how well our method is able to discern between benign and vulnerable code across a large variety of actual software projects. Unfortunately, finding such an answer is not simple because the same aforementioned problems with realistic datasets also pertain to test datasets, see Sect. 3.2. Even in the case that our method generalizes poorly from the concrete code samples it has been trained on, we would like to argue that the approach would still be useful if used appropriately. Then, instead of learning models on a broad variety of defects, it would likely be recommendable to use fewer and, more specifically, very similar samples of the type of defect. This way, our approach could have potential uses in the detection of code clones. However, further research is required to establish the usefulness of our approach in this regard.

Another limitation of our method lies in the way in which we extract paths from the programs. Since we use the ICFG to extract all possible paths, between the entry and exit node of each procedure, the scalability of our method largely depends on two factors: The number of procedures within the program and the number of control flow branches within each procedure. As explained, for our prototype we have limited the depth of our paths to a maximum of 75 nodes. Therefore, the worst case scenario would be a procedure that is comprised of at least 75 (consecutive) nested if-statements, creating a binary tree with 2^{75} leaf-nodes. That is the number of unique paths to traverse the graph. Naturally such graph would be far too large to be traversed. Aside from this theoretical example, we have never found this to be an issue when analyzing real software projects using the prototype, however. Still, the extraction phase remains a computationally demanding task. Moreover, we did not investigate the effects the path length may excerpt on the generalizability of our method. Ideally, multiple models would have to be created, using different path lengths, and finally compared against each other on the basis of real-world applications.

Aside from the method itself, another factor that excerpts a strong influence on the generalizability of the models is the datasets they are learned on. As established in Sect. 3.2, we use the synthetic Juliet test suite to train our models. This has its merits, but unfortunately comes with the detriment of potentially not being very realistic. This, in turn, could pose a negative impact on the generalizability of our approach as well. The prototype aims to mitigate this problem to some degree, by the introduction of *a feedback loop*, which allows practitioners to use prior findings to adjust the models. While not having a definitive solution to the problem at hand, we hope that this feedback loop may help in the creation of better datasets in the future.

Lastly, there is a chance that we overfitted our models during training. As stated in Sect. 3.2.

8 Further Research

The research on our method, as well as the development of our prototype has highlighted some areas, where further research is urgently necessary in order for ML-based SAST to succeed in the future. As elaborated, we made attempts to address some of these problems, however, we could not do so in an exhaustive manner. Firstly, and probably most urgent, is the development of better datasets for training and testing purposes. Unfortunately, this task is not as easy as it may seem and may only be approached through larger community efforts. A dataset that could be considered ideal would comprise the properties of being a) *realistic*, in a sense that the contained code samples are reflective of real code that is found in the wild b) *correct*, such that every sample is labeled correctly and c) *complete*, where each code sample is compilable using standard compilers. This requirement may be weakened to stipulate that each sample must at least contain all referenced data structures and type definitions, as well as the immediate procedures called from the sample.

Secondly, for the C and C++ programming languages, only a few open-source tools that offer conventional static analysis algorithms appear to exist. We would like to argue that, from a data-centric perspective, these kinds of algorithms are as important for ML-SAST as they are for conventional SAST. Poor preprocessing of the training data, due to a lack of adequate analysis options, implies a risk of equally poor-performing models. However, more research is necessary to evince the actual effects of this. We would hope that the increasing popularity of ML-based SAST approaches also leads to an accelerated development in terms of analysis tools.

On a more concrete level, we also see some direct connection opportunities for further research in terms of our own method and the prototype. Since our prototype only considers defects that make themselves visible in the program's ICFG, we see potential in the extension of our method by means of other data structures, such as the system dependence graph by Horwitz et al. [13]. This type of graph representation offers the benefit of not only reflecting a program's interprocedural control, but also data-dependence. Moreover, we have so far only applied our method to C and C++ programs. However, we see no reason as to why this method may not be applied to other programming languages, as well. The Juliet test suite is also available for the Java programming language, which would therefore make for a good starting point.

9   Conclusion

In this paper, we have presented two novel methods in the context of ML-based SAST. Firstly, we introduced an embedding method that uses a program's interprocedural control flow graph to represent individual execution paths in the vector space. Secondly, we have shown how this method may be employed to generate models for unwanted program behavior and then use these models to find similar examples of such behavior in previously unseen code. Our evaluation suggests that our method is capable of effectively separating benign and defective program behavior in the vector space. Still, we find a lot of questions exist in the area of ML-SAST that remain to be answered. We hope that our contributions are helpful to researchers and practitioners alike. On a final remark, we would also like to the German Federal Office for Information Security (BSI) for funding this Study. Once reviewed, the prototype will be made available to the public via the BSI's GitHub repository. The full study may be obtained from the BSI's website [7,14].

Appendix

Algorithm 1. The algorithm used to find paths excerpting some defect characteristics in previously unseen code.

```
paths ← extractPaths(icfg)
models ← generateModels()
reports ← []

for all path in paths do
    for all model in models do
        centers ← model.getCenters()
        for all center in centers do
            distance ← euclidean(path, center)
            if distance < center.getThreshold() then
                report ← makeReport(path, model, distance)
                reports.append(report)
            end if
        end for
    end for
end for
```

Table 1. Results of the intrinsic evaluation.

Test Suite	Recall	Precision	F1-Score	Accuracy
CWE-36	0.816	0.766	0.79	0.686
CWE-78	0.26	0.912	0.405	0.272
CWE-121	0.393	0.778	0.522	0.483
CWE-122	0.345	0.789	0.48	0.426
CWE-124	0.374	0.81	0.512	0.431
CWE-126	0.43	0.86	0.573	0.468
CWE-127	0.434	0.797	0.562	0.466
CWE-134	0.468	0.979	0.633	0.483
CWE-190	0.741	0.965	0.838	0.752
CWE-191	0.736	0.965	0.835	0.748
CWE-194	0.332	0.602	0.428	0.402
CWE-195	0.375	0.604	0.463	0.39
CWE-197	0.236	0.654	0.347	0.292
CWE-369	0.781	1.0	0.877	0.783
CWE-400	0.632	0.978	0.768	0.646
CWE-401	0.953	0.994	0.973	0.955
CWE-415	0.831	0.958	0.89	0.881
CWE-590	0.567	0.788	0.659	0.596
CWE-690	0.855	0.905	0.879	0.895
CWE-789	0.66	0.997	0.794	0.661

Table 2. Results of the oracle test for the FICS tool, our method as well as three conventional tools that were aggregated into a single column. True positive findings are marked with a "+"-symbol, negative results with a "−"-symbol. Cases where a tool failed to process the code entirely are marked with a "o"-symbol.

CWE ID	Project	Commit	FICS	Our Method	Conventional Tools
CWE-119	miniupnp	79cca974a4c2ab1199786732a67ff6d898051b78	o	+	−
CWE-388	miniupnp	140ee8d2204b383279f854802b27bdb41c1d5d1a	o	−	−
CWE-125	miniupnp	b238cade9a173c6f751a34acf8ccff838a62aa47	o	−	−
CWE-119	miniupnp	7aeb624b44f86d335841242ff427433190e7168a	o	−	−
CWE-476	miniupnp	cb8a02af7a5677cf608e86d57ab04241cf34e24f	o	−	−
CWE-119	libtiff	ce6841d9e41d621ba23cf18b190ee6a23b2cc833	−	−	−
CWE-787	libtiff	5ad9d8016fbb60109302d558f7edb2cb2a3bb8e3	−	−	−
CWE-125	libtiff	ae9365db1b271b62b35ce018eac8799b1d5e8a53	−	−	−
CWE-119	libtiff	3ca657a8793dd011bf869695d72ad31c779c3cc1	−	+	−
CWE-119	libtiff	b18012dae552f85dcc5c57d3bf4e997a15b1cc1c	−	−	−
CWE-119	libtiff	5c080298d59efa53264d7248bbe3a04660db6ef7	−	−	−
CWE-119	libtiff	9657bbe3cdce4aaa90e07d50c1c70ae52da0ba6a	−	−	−
CWE-125	libtiff	9a72a69e035ee70ff5c41541c8c61cd97990d018	−	−	−
CWE-125	libtiff	1044b43637fa7f70fb19b93593777b78bd20da86	−	−	−
CWE-191	libtiff	5397a417e61258c69209904e652a1f409ec3b9df	−	−	−
CWE-369	libtiff	43bc256d8ae44b92d2734a3c5bc73957a4d7c1ec	−	−	−
CWE-369	libtiff	438274f938e046d33cb0e1230b41da32ffe223e1	−	−	−
CWE-189	libtiff	c7153361a4041260719b340f73f2f76	−	−	−
CWE-190	libtiff	787c0ee906430b772f33ca50b97b8b5ca070faec	−	−	−
CWE-787	libtiff	391e77fcd217e78b2c51342ac3ddb7100ecacdd2	−	−	−
CWE-369	libtiff	3c5eb8b1be544e41d2c336191bc4936300ad7543	−	−	−
CWE-119	libtiff	6a984bf7905c6621281588431f384e79d11a2e33	−	−	−
CWE-125	openjpeg	c16bc057ba3f125051c9966cf1f5b68a05681de4	−	−	−
CWE-119	openjpeg	e078172b1c3f98d2219c37076b238fb759c751ea	−	−	−
CWE-416	openjpeg	940100c28ae28931722290794889cf84a92c5f6f	−	−	−
CWE-787	openjpeg	dcac91b8c72f743bda7dbfa9032356bc8110098a	+	−	−
CWE-119	openjpeg	afb308b9ccbe129608c9205cf3bb39bbefad90b9	+	−	−
CWE-787	openjpeg	e5285319229a5d77bf316bb0d3a6cbd3cb8666d9	−	−	−
CWE-787	openjpeg	2cd30c2b06ce332dede81cccad8b334cde997281	−	−	−
CWE-119	openjpeg	baf0c1ad4572daaa89caa3b12985bdd93530f0dd7	−	−	−
CWE-369	openjpeg	d27ccf01c68a31ad62b33d2dc1ba2bb1eeaafe7b	−	−	−
CWE-119	openjpeg	397f62c0a838e15d667ef50e27d5d011d2c79c04	−	−	−
CWE-119	openjpeg	162f6199c0cd3ec1c6c6dc65e41b2faab92b2d91	−	−	−
CWE-125	openjpeg	15f081c89650dccee4aa4ae66f614c3fdb268767	+	−	−
CWE-400	openjpeg	8ee335227bbcaf1614124046aa25e53d67b11ec3	−	−	−
CWE-190	openjpeg	c58df149900df862806d0e892859b41115875845	−	−	−
CWE-20	openjpeg	c277159986c80142180fbe5efb256bbf3bdf3edc	−	−	−
CWE-369	openjpeg	c5bd64ea146162967c29bd2af0cbb845ba3eaaaf	−	−	−
CWE-190	openjpeg	5d00b719f4b93b1445e6fb4c766b9a9883c57949	−	−	−
CWE-125	openjpeg	ef01f18dfc6780b776d0674ed3e7415c6ef54d24	−	−	−
CWE-189	zlib	d1d577490c15a0c6862473d7576352a9f18ef811	−	−	−
CWE-189	zlib	e54e1299404101a5a9d0cf5e45512b543967f958	−	−	−
CWE-189	zlib	9aaec95e82117c1cb0f9624264c3618fc380cecb	−	−	−
CWE-189	zlib	6a043145ca6e9c55184013841a67b2fef87e44c0	−	−	−

References

1. Ahmadi, M., Farkhani, R.M., Williams, R., Lu, L.: Finding bugs using your own code: detecting functionally-similar yet inconsistent code. In: 30th USENIX Security Symposium (USENIX Security 2021), pp. 2025–2040 (2021)
2. Alexopoulos, N., Brack, M., Wagner, J.P., Grube, T., Mühlhäuser, M.: How long do vulnerabilities live in the code? A large-scale empirical measurement study on FOSS vulnerability lifetimes. In: 31st USENIX Security Symposium (USENIX Security 2022) (2022)
3. Arp, D., et al.: Dos and Don'ts of machine learning in computer security. In: 31st USENIX Security Symposium (USENIX Security 2022), pp. 3971–3988 (2022)
4. Arthur, D., Vassilvitskii, S.: K-means++: the advantages of careful seeding. In: Proceedings of the Eighteenth Annual ACM-SIAM Symposium on Discrete Algorithms, SODA 2007, pp. 1027–1035. Society for Industrial and Applied Mathematics, USA (2007)
5. Bellman, R.: Dynamic Programming. Princeton University Press, Princeton (1984)
6. Black, P.E.: Juliet 1.3 test suite: changes from 1.2. Technical report, NIST TN 1995, National Institute of Standards and Technology, Gaithersburg, MD (2018). https://doi.org/10.6028/NIST.TN.1995
7. BSI: Bundesamt für Sicherheit in der Informationstechnik - GitHub Organization. https://github.com/BSI-Bund
8. Cui, L., Hao, Z., Jiao, Y., Fei, H., Yun, X.: VulDetector: detecting vulnerabilities using weighted feature graph comparison. IEEE Trans. Inf. Forensics Secur. **16**, 2004–2017 (2021). https://doi.org/10.1109/TIFS.2020.3047756
9. Fan, J., Li, Y., Wang, S., Nguyen, T.N.: A C/C++ code vulnerability dataset with code changes and CVE summaries. In: Proceedings of the 17th International Conference on Mining Software Repositories, MSR 2020, pp. 508–512. Association for Computing Machinery, New York (2020). https://doi.org/10.1145/3379597.3387501
10. Géron, A.: Hands-on Machine Learning with Scikit-Learn, Keras, and TensorFlow: Concepts, Tools, and Techniques to Build Intelligent Systems, 2nd edn. O'Reilly Media Inc., Beijing (2019)
11. Giray, G., Bennin, K.E., Köksal, Ö., Babur, Ö., Tekinerdogan, B.: On the use of deep learning in software defect prediction. J. Syst. Softw. **195**, 111537 (2023). https://doi.org/10.1016/j.jss.2022.111537
12. GitHub Inc.: CodeQL. GitHub Inc. (2021)
13. Horwitz, S., Reps, T., Binkley, D.: Interprocedural slicing using dependence graphs. ACM SIGPLAN Not. **23**(7), 35–46 (1988)
14. Hüther, L., et al.: Machine learning in the context of static application security testing - ML-SAST. Technical report, Federal Office for Information Security, Federal Office for Information Security, P.O. Box 20 03 63, 53133 Bonn (2022)
15. Johnson, J.M., Khoshgoftaar, T.M.: Thresholding strategies for deep learning with highly imbalanced big data. In: Wani, M.A., Khoshgoftaar, T.M., Palade, V. (eds.) Deep Learning Applications, Volume 2. AISC, vol. 1232, pp. 199–227. Springer, Singapore (2021). https://doi.org/10.1007/978-981-15-6759-9_9
16. Landi, W., Ryder, B.G.: Pointer-induced aliasing: a problem classification. In: Proceedings of the 18th ACM SIGPLAN-SIGACT Symposium on Principles of Programming Languages, POPL 1991, pp. 93–103. Association for Computing Machinery, New York (1991). https://doi.org/10.1145/99583.99599

17. Li, Z., et al.: VulDeePecker: a deep learning-based system for vulnerability detection. In: Proceedings 2018 Network and Distributed System Security Symposium (2018). https://doi.org/10.14722/ndss.2018.23158
18. Marjanov, T., Pashchenko, I., Massacci, F.: Machine learning for source code vulnerability detection: what works and what isn't there yet. IEEE Secur. Priv. **20**(5), 60–76 (2022). https://doi.org/10.1109/MSEC.2022.3176058
19. McInnes, L., Healy, J., Melville, J.: UMAP: Uniform Manifold Approximation and Projection for Dimension Reduction (2020)
20. Narayanan, A., Chandramohan, M., Venkatesan, R., Chen, L., Liu, Y., Jaiswal, S.: Graph2vec: Learning Distributed Representations of Graphs (2017)
21. Sui, Y., Xue, J.: SVF: interprocedural static value-flow analysis in LLVM. In: Proceedings of the 25th International Conference on Compiler Construction, Barcelona, Spain, pp. 265–266. ACM (2016). https://doi.org/10.1145/2892208.2892235
22. Xia, S., Xiong, Z., Luo, Y., WeiXu, Zhang, G.: Effectiveness of the Euclidean distance in high dimensional spaces. Optik **126**(24), 5614–5619 (2015). https://doi.org/10.1016/j.ijleo.2015.09.093
23. Yamaguchi, F., Maier, A., Gascon, H., Rieck, K.: Automatic inference of search patterns for taint-style vulnerabilities. In: 2015 IEEE Symposium on Security and Privacy, pp. 797–812 (2015). https://doi.org/10.1109/SP.2015.54

Two Models are Better Than One: Federated Learning is Not Private for Google GBoard Next Word Prediction

Mohamed Suliman(✉) and Douglas Leith

Trinity College Dublin, The University of Dublin, College Green,
Dublin 2 D02 PN40, Ireland
{sulimanm,doug.leith}@tcd.ie

Abstract. In this paper we present new attacks against federated learning when used to train natural language text models. We illustrate the effectiveness of the attacks against the next word prediction model used in Google's GBoard app, a widely used mobile keyboard app that has been an early adopter of federated learning for production use. We demonstrate that the words a user types on their mobile handset, e.g. when sending text messages, can be recovered with high accuracy under a wide range of conditions and that counter-measures such a use of mini-batches and adding local noise are ineffective. We also show that the word order (and so the actual sentences typed) can be reconstructed with high fidelity. This raises obvious privacy concerns, particularly since GBoard is in production use.

Keywords: federated learning · privacy

1 Introduction

Federated Learning (FL) is a class of distributed algorithms for the training of machine learning models such as neural networks. A primary aim of FL when it was first introduced was to enhance user privacy, namely by keeping sensitive data stored locally and avoiding uploading it to a central server [17]. The basic idea is that users train a local version of the model with their own data, and share only the resulting model parameters with a central coordinating server. This server then combines the models of all the participants, transmits the aggregate back to them, and this cycle (i.e. a single FL 'round') repeats until the model is judged to have converged.

A notable real-world deployment of FL is within Google's Gboard, a widely used Android keyboard application that comes pre-installed on many mobile handsets and which has >5 Billion downloads [1]. Within GBoard, FL is used to train the Next Word Prediction (NWP) model that provides the suggested next words that appear above the keyboard while typing [11].

M. Suliman—Now at IBM Research Europe - Dublin.

G. Tsudik et al. (Eds.): ESORICS 2023, LNCS 14347, pp. 105–122, 2024.
https://doi.org/10.1007/978-3-031-51482-1_6

In this paper we show that FL is not private for Next Word Prediction. We present an attack that reconstructs the original training data, i.e. the text typed by a user, from the FL parameter updates with a high degree of fidelity. Both the FedSGD and FederatedAveraging variants of FL are susceptible to this attack. In fairness, Google have been aware of the possibility of information leakage from FL updates since the earliest days of FL, e.g. see footnote 1 in [17]. Our results demonstrate that not only does information leakage indeed happen for real-world models deployed in production and in widespread use, but that the amount of information leaked is enough to allow the local training data to be fully reconstructed.

We also show that adding Gaussian noise to the transmitted updates, which has been proposed to ensure local Differential Privacy (DP), provides little defence unless the noise levels used are so large that the utility of the model becomes substantially degraded. That is, DP is not an effective countermeasure to our attack[1]. We also show that use of mini-batches of up to 256 sentences provides little protection. Other defences, such as Secure Aggregation (a form of multi-party computation MPC), Homomorphic Encryption (HE), and Trusted Execution Environments (TEEs), are currently either impractical or require the client to trust that the server is honest[2] in which case use of FL is redundant.

Previous studies of reconstruction attacks against FL have mainly focussed on image reconstruction, rather than text as considered here. Unfortunately, we find that the methods developed for image reconstruction, which are based on used gradient descent to minimise the distance between the observed model data and the model data corresponding to a synthetic input, do not readily transfer over to text data. This is perhaps unsurprising since the inherently discrete nature of text makes the cost surface highly non-smooth and so gradient-based optimisation is difficult to apply successfully. In this paper we therefore propose new reconstruction approaches that are specialised to text data.

It is important to note that the transmission of user data to a remote server is not inherently a breach of privacy. The risk of a privacy breach is related to the nature of the data being sent, as well as whether it's owner can be readily identified. For example, sending device models, version numbers, and locale/region information is not an immediate concern but it seems clear that the sentences entered by users, e.g. when typing messages, writing notes and emails, web browsing and performing searches, may well be private. Indeed, it is not only the sentences typed which can be sensitive but also the set of words used (i.e.

---

[1] DP aims to protect the aggregate training data/model against query-based attacks, whereas our attack targets the individual updates. Nevertheless, we note that DP is sometimes suggested as a potential defence against the type of attack carried out here.

[2] Google's Secure Aggregation approach [5] is a prominent example of an approach requiring trust in the server, or more specifically in the PKI infrastructure which in practice is operated by the same organisation that runs the FL server since it involves authentication/verification of clients. We note also that Secure Aggregation is not currently deployed in the GBoard app despite being proposed 6 years ago.

even without knowing the word ordering) since this can be used for targeting surveillance via keyword blacklists [3].

In addition, most Google telemetry is tagged with an Android ID. Via other data collected by Google Play Services the Android ID is linked to (i) the handset hardware serial number, (ii) the SIM IMEI (which uniquely identifies the SIM slot) and (iii) the user's Google account [14,15]. When creating a Google account users are encouraged to supply a phone number and for many people this will be their own phone number. Use of Google services such as buying a paid app on the Google Play store or using Google Pay further links a person's Google account to their credit card/bank details. A user's Google account, and so the Android ID, can therefore commonly be expected to be linked to the person's real identity.

2 Preliminaries

2.1 Federated Learning Client Update

Algorithm 1 gives the procedure followed by FL participants to generate a model update. The number of local epochs E, mini-batch size B, and local client learning rate η can be changed depending on the FL application. When $E = 1$ and the mini-batch size is equal the size of the training dataset, then it is called FedSGD, and any other configuration corresponds to FedAveraging, where multiple gradient descent steps occur on the client.

Algorithm 1: Federated Learning Client Update

Input: θ_0: The parameters of the global model, training loss function ℓ.
Output: θ_1: The model parameters after training on the client's data.
Procedure *clientUpdate*
   $\theta_1 \leftarrow \theta_0$;
   $\mathcal{B} \leftarrow$ (split dataset into batches of size B);
   for local epoch i from 1 to E **do**;
     for batch $b \in \mathcal{B}$ **do**;
      $\theta_1 \leftarrow \theta_1 - \eta\nabla\ell(\theta_1; b)$;
   return θ_1;

2.2 Threat Model

The threat model is that of a honest-but-curious adversary that has access to (i) the FL model architecture, (ii) the current global FL model parameters θ_0, and (iii) the FL model parameters, θ_1, after updating locally using the training data of an individual user. The FL server has, for example, access to all of these and so this threat model captures the situation where there is an honest-but-curious FL server.

We do not consider membership attacks against the global model, although knowledge of θ_0 allows such attacks, since they have already received much attention in the literature. Instead we focus on local reconstruction attacks i.e. attacks that aim to reconstruct the local training data of a user from knowledge of θ_0 and θ_1. In the GBoard Next Word Prediction task the local training data is the text typed by the user while using apps on their mobile handset e.g. while sending text messages.

2.3   GBoard NWP Model

Figure 1 shows the LSTM recursive neural net (RNN) architecture used by Gboard for NWP. This model was extracted from the app.

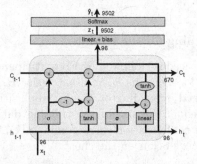

Fig. 1. Schematic of LSTM architecture. LSTM layer takes as input dense vector x_t representing a typed word and outputs a dense vector h_t. This output is then mapped to vector z_t of size 9502 (the size of the dictionary) with the value of each element being the raw logit for the corresponding dictionary word. A softmax layer then normalises the raw z_t values to give a vector $\hat{y}_t$ of probabilities.

The Gboard LSTM RNN is a word level language model, predicting the probability of the next word given what the user has already typed into the keyboard. Input words are first mapped to a dictionary entry, which has a vocabulary of $V = 9502$ words, with a special <UNK> entry used for words that are not in the dictionary, and <S> to indicate the start of a sentence. The index of the dictionary entry is then mapped to a dense vector of size $D = 96$ using a lookup table (the dictionary entry is one-hot encoded and then multiplied by a $\mathbb{R}^{D \times V}$ weighting matrix W^T) and applied as input to an LSTM layer with 670 units i.e. the state C_t is a vector of size 670. The LSTM layer uses a CIFG architecture without peephole connections, illustrated schematically in Fig. 1. The LSTM state C_t is linearly projected down to an output vector h_t of size D, which is mapped to a raw logit vector z_t of size V via a weighting matrix W and bias b. This extra linear projection is not part of the orthodox CIFG cell structure that was introduced in [10], and is included to accommodate the model's tied input and output embedding matrices [22]. A softmax output layer finally maps this to an

$[0, 1]^V$ vector $\hat{y}_t$ of probabilities, the i'th element being the estimated probability that the next word is the i'th dictionary entry.

3   Reconstruction Attack

3.1   Word Recovery

In next word prediction the input to the RNN is echoed in it's output. That is, the output of the RNN aims to match the sequence of words typed by the user, albeit with a shift one word ahead. The sign of the output loss gradient directly reveals information about the words typed by the user, which can then be recovered easily by inspection. This key observation, first made in [26], is the basis of our word recovery attack.

After the user has typed t words, the output of the LSTM model at timestep t is the next word prediction vector $\hat{y}_t$,

$$\hat{y}_{t,i} = \frac{e^{z_i}}{\sum_{j=1}^{V} e^{z_j}}, \quad i = 1, \ldots, V$$

with raw logit vector $z_t = W h_t + b$, where h_t is the output of the LSTM layer. The cross-entropy loss function for text consisting of T words is $J_{1:T}(\theta) = \sum_{t=1}^{T} J_t(\theta)$ where

$$J_t(\theta) = -\log \frac{e^{z_{i^*}(\theta)}}{\sum_{j=1}^{V} e^{z_j(\theta)}},$$

and i_t^* is the dictionary index of the t'th word entered by the user and θ is the vector of neural net parameters (including the elements of W and b). Differentiating with respect to the output bias parameters b we have that,

$$\frac{\partial J_{1:T}}{\partial b_k} = \sum_{t=1}^{T} \sum_{i=1}^{V} \frac{\partial J_t}{\partial z_{t,i}} \frac{\partial z_{t,i}}{\partial b_k}$$

where

$$\frac{\partial J_t}{\partial z_{t,i_t^*}} = \frac{e^{z_{i^*}}}{\sum_{j=1}^{V} e^{z_j}} - 1 < 0,$$

$$\frac{\partial J_t}{\partial z_{t,i}} = \frac{e^{z_i}}{\sum_{j=1}^{V} e^{z_j}} > 0, \quad i \neq i_t^*$$

and

$$\frac{\partial z_{t,i}}{\partial b_k} = \begin{cases} 1 & k = i \\ 0 & \text{otherwise} \end{cases}$$

That is,

$$\frac{\partial J_{1:T}}{\partial b_k} = \sum_{t=1}^{T} \frac{\partial J_t}{\partial z_{t,k}}$$

It follows that for words k which do not appear in the text $\frac{\partial J_{1:T}}{\partial b_k} > 0$. Also, assuming that the neural net has been trained to have reasonable performance then e^{z_k} will tend to be small for words k that do not appear next and large for words which do. Therefore for words i^* that appear in the text we expect that $\frac{\partial J_{1:T}}{\partial b_{i^*}} < 0$.

The above analysis focuses mainly on the bias parameters of the final fully connected layer, however similar methods can be applied to the W parameters. The key aspect here that lends to the ease of this attack is that the outputs echo the inputs, unlike for example, the task of object detection in images. In that case, the output is just the object label.

This observation is intuitive from a loss function minimisation perspective. Typically the estimated probability $\hat{y}_{i^*}$ for an input word will be less than 1. Increasing $\hat{y}_{i^*}$ will therefore decrease the loss function i.e. the gradient is negative. Conversely, the estimated probability $\hat{y}_i$ for a word that does not appear in the input will be small but greater than 0. Decreasing $\hat{y}_i$ will therefore decrease the loss function i.e. the gradient is positive.

Example: To execute this attack in practice, simply subtract the final layer parameters of the current global model θ_0 from those of the resulting model trained on the client's local data, θ_1, as shown in Algorithm 2. The indices of the negative values reveal the typed words. Suppose the client's local data consists of just the one sentence "learning online is not so private". We then train model θ_0 on this sentence for 1 epoch, with a mini-batch size of 1, and SGD learning rate of 0.001 (FedSGD), and report the values at the negative indices in Table 1.

Table 1. Values of the final layer parameter difference at the indices of the typed words. Produced after training the model on the sentence "learning online is not so private", $E = 1, B = 1, \eta = 0.001$. These are the only indices where negative values occur.

word	i	$(\theta_1 - \theta_0)_i$
learning	7437	-0.0009951561
online	4904	-0.0009941629
is	209	-0.000997875
not	1808	-0.0009941144
so	26	-0.0009965639
private	6314	-0.0009951561

Algorithm 2: Word Recovery

Input: θ_0: The global model's final layer parameters, θ_1: The final layer
  parameters of a model update
Output: User typed tokens w
Procedure *recoverWords*
  $d \leftarrow \theta_1 - \theta_0$;
  $w \leftarrow \{i \mid d_i < 0\}$;
  return w;

3.2   Reconstructing Sentences

The attack described previously retrieves the words typed, but gives no indication of the order in which they occurred. To reveal this order, we ask the model[3].

The basic idea is that after running multiple rounds of gradient descent on the local training data, the local model is "tuned" to the local data in the sense that when it is presented with the first words of a sentence from the local training data, the model's next word prediction will tend to match the training data and so we can bootstrap reconstruction of the full training data text.

In more detail, the t'th input word is represented by a vector $x_t \in 0, 1^V$, with all elements zero apart from the element corresponding to the index of the word in the dictionary. The output $y_{t+1} \in [0, 1]^V$ from the model after seeing input words $x_0, \ldots, x_t$ is a probability distribution over the dictionary. We begin by selecting x_0 equal to the start of sentence token <S> and x_1 equal to the first word from our set of reconstructed words, then ask the model to generate $y_2 = Pr(x_2|x_0, x_1; \theta_1)$. We set all elements of y_2 that are not in the set of reconstructed words to zero, since we know that these were not part of the local training data, re-normalise y_2 so that its elements sum to one, and then select the most likely next word as x_2. We now repeat this process for $y_3 = Pr(x_3|x_0, x_1, x_2; \theta_1)$, and so on, until a complete sentence has been generated. We then take the second word from our set of reconstructed words as x_1 and repeat to generate a second sentence, and so on.

This method generates as many sentences as there are extracted words. This results in a lot more sentences than were originally in the client's training dataset. In order to filter out the unnecessary sentences, we rank each generated sentence by its change in perplexity, from the initial global model θ_0 to the new update θ_1.

The Log-Perplexity of a sequence $x_0, ..., x_t$, is defined as

$$PP_\theta(x_0, ..., x_t) = \sum_{i=1}^{t} (-\log Pr(x_i|x_0, ..., x_{i-1}; \theta)),$$

---

[3] It is perhaps worth noting that we studied a variety of reconstruction attacks, e.g., using Monte Carlo Tree Search to perform a smart search over all words sequences, but found the attack method described here to be simple, efficient and highly effective.

and quantifies how 'surprised' the model is by the sequence. Those sentences that report a high perplexity for θ_0 but a comparatively lower one for θ_1 reveal themselves as having been part of the dataset used to train θ_1. Each generated sentence is scored by their percentage change in perplexity:

$$Score(x_0, ..., x_t) = \frac{PP_{\theta_0}(x_0, ..., x_t) - PP_{\theta_1}(x_0, ..., x_t)}{PP_{\theta_0}(x_0, ..., x_t)}.$$

By selecting the top-n ranked sentences, we select those most likely to have been present in the training dataset.

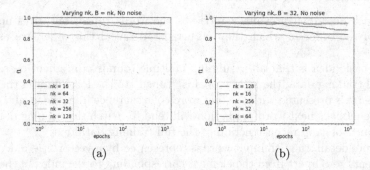

(a)   (b)

Fig. 2. Word recovery performance over time with full batch and mini-batch training. The upper bound on the F1 score for the different datasets is related to how many words in the training set are also in the model dictionary. (a) shows the F1 score over time with $B = n_k$ full batch training. At epoch 1 (FedSGD), the F1 is high and stays constant as you train for longer (FedAveraging). Using a mini-batch $B = 32$ (b) has no effect on the attack (in the case where $n_k = 16, B = 16$).

4   Performance of Attacks Against Vanilla Federated Learning

4.1   Experimental Setup

We make use of the LSTM RNN extracted from Gboard as the basis of our experiments. The value of it's extracted parameters are used as the initial 'global' model θ_0; the starting point of the updates we generate. There are several variables that go into producing an update: the number of sentences in the dataset, n_k, the number of epochs E, the batch size B, and the local learning rate η. Note that when $E = 1$ and $B = n_k$, this corresponds to a FedSGD update, and that any other configuration corresponds to a FedAveraging update. Unless explicitly mentioned otherwise, we keep the client learning rate $\eta = 0.001$ constant for all our experiments. All sample datasets used consist of 4 word long sentences, mirroring the average length of sentences that the Gboard model was trained with [11].

To evaluate the effectiveness of our attack, the sample datasets we use are taken from a corpus of american english text messages [19], which includes short sentences similar to those the Gboard LSTM extracted from the mobile application was trained on. We perform our two attacks on datasets consisting of $n_k = 16, 32, 64, 128,$ and 256 sentences. Converting a sentence into a sequence of training samples and labels $(\mathbf{x}, y)$ is done as follows:

- The start-of-sentence token <S> is prepended to the beginning of the sentence, and each word is then converted to it's corresponding word embedding. This gives a sequence $x_0, x_1, \ldots, x_T$ of tokens where x_0 is the <S> token.
- A sentence of length T becomes T training points

$$((x_0, x_1), y_2), ((x_0, x_1, x_2), y_3), \ldots, ((x_0, x_1, \ldots, x_{T-1}), y_T)$$

where label $y_t \in [0, 1]^V$ is a probability distribution over the dictionary entries, with all elements zero apart from the element corresponding to the dictionary index of x_t

Following [11] we use categorical cross entropy loss over the output and target labels. After creating the training samples and labels from a dataset of n_k sentences, we train model θ_0 on this training data for a specified number of epochs E with a mini-batch size of B, according to Algorithm 1 to produce the local update θ_1. We then subtract the final layer parameters of the two models to recover the words, and iteratively sample θ_1 according to the methodology described in Sect. 3.2 to reconstruct the sentences, and take the top-n_k ranked sentences by their perplexity score.

4.2   Metrics

To evaluate performance, we use the F1 score which balances the precision and recall of word recovery with our attack. We also use a modified version of the Levenshtein ratio i.e. the normalised Levenshtein distance [16] (the minimum number of word level edits needed to make one string match another) to evaluate our sentence reconstruction attack. Ranging from 0 to 100, the larger the Levenshtein ratio, the closer the match between our reconstructed and the ground truth sentence.

4.3   Measurements

Word Recovery Performance. Figure 2 shows the measured performance of our word recovery attack for both the FedSGD and FedAveraging variants of FL for mini-batch/full batch training and as the dataset size and training time are varied. It can be seen that none of these variables have much of an effect on the F1 score achieved by our attack, which remains high across a wide range of conditions. Note that the maximum value of the F1 score is not one for this data but instead a smaller value related to how many of the words in the dataset are also present in the model's vocabulary. Some words, e.g. unique nouns, slang, etc., do not exist in the model's 9502 word dictionary, and our word recovery attack can only extract the <UNK> token in their place, limiting how many words we can actually recover.

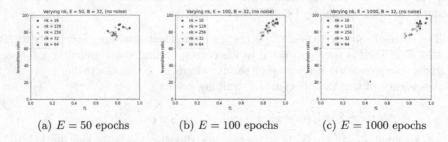

(a) $E = 50$ epochs   (b) $E = 100$ epochs   (c) $E = 1000$ epochs

Fig. 3. Sentence reconstruction performance. Each point corresponds to a different dataset colour coded by it's size. The y-axis gives the average Levenshtein ratio of the reconstructed sentences. The x-axis is the F1 score between the tokens used in the reconstructed sentences and the ground truth. The closer a point is to the top-right corner, the closer the reconstruction is to perfect.

Sentence Reconstruction Peformance. Figure 3 shows the measured performance of our sentence reconstruction attack. Figures 3a, 3b, and 3c show that as you train for more epochs (50, 100, and 1000 respectively) the quality of the reconstructed sentences improves. This is intuitive as the models trained for longer are more overfit to the data, and so the iterative sampling approach is more likely to return the correct next word given a conditioning prefix.

However, longer training times are not necessary to accurately reconstruct sentences. It can be seen from Fig. 4(b) that even in the FedSGD setting, where the number of epochs $E = 1$, we can sometimes still get high quality sentence reconstructions by modifying the model parameters θ_1 to be $\theta_1 + s(\theta_1 - \theta_0)$, with s being a scaling factor. Since $\theta_1 = \theta_0 - \eta \nabla \ell(\theta_0; b)$ with FedSGD,

$$\theta_1 + s(\theta_1 - \theta_0) = \theta_0 - \eta(1 + s)\nabla \ell(\theta_0; b)$$

from which it can be seen that scaling factor s effectively increases the gradient descent step size.

5   Existing Attacks and Their Defences

5.1   Image Data Reconstruction

Information leakage from the gradients of neural networks used for object detection in images appears to have been initially investigated in [28], which proposed the Deep Leakage from Gradients (DLG) algorithm. An image is input to a neural net and the output is a label specifying an object detected in the image. In

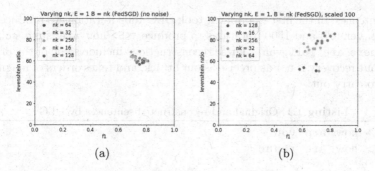

Fig. 4. FedSGD sentence reconstruction performance without (a) and with (b) scaling.

DLG a synthetic input is applied to the neural net and the gradients of the model parameters are calculated. These gradients are then compared to the observed model gradients sent to the FL server and gradient descent is used to update the synthetic input so as to minimise the difference between its model gradients and the observed model gradients.

This work was subsequently extended by [9,12,24–27] to improve the stability and performance of the original DLG algorithm, as well as the fidelity of the images it generates. In [12,25], changes to the optimisation terms allowed for successful data reconstruction at batch sizes of up to 48 and 100 respectively. Analytical techniques of data extraction [4,20] benefit from not being as costly to compute as compared to optimization based methods. Additionally, these analytical attacks extract the exact ground truth data, as compared to DLG and others who often settle to image reconstructions that include artefacts.

5.2 Text Data Reconstruction

Most work on reconstruction attacks has focused on images and there is relatively little work on text reconstruction. A single text reconstruction example is presented in [28], with no performance results. Probably the closest work to the present paper is [8] which applies a variant of DLG to text reconstruction from gradients of transformer-based models (variants of BERT [23]). As already noted, DLG tends to perform poorly with text data and the word recovery rate achieved in [8] is generally no more than 50%.

In our attack context, DLG can recover words but at much smaller scales than we have demonstrated, and takes longer to find these words. There is also no guarantee that DLG can recover words and place them in the correct order. In [28], it is noted that the algorithm requires multiple restarts before successful reconstruction. Additionally, DLG operates by matching the single gradient of a batch of training data, therefore it only works in the FedSGD setting, where $E = 1$. We show the results of DLG in Listing 1.1 on gradients of $B = 1$, and 2 4 word sentences. In the first example, it took DLG 1000 iterations to produce "<S> how are venue", and 1500 iterations to produce "<S> how are sure cow, <S> haha where are Tell van". These reconstructions include some of the original words, but recovery is not as precise as our attack, and takes orders of magnitude longer to carry out.

Listing 1.1. Original and reconstructed sentences by DLG

```
<S> how are you
<S> how are venue

<S> how are you doing
<S> how are sure cow
<S> where are you going
<S> haha where are Tell van
```

Work has also been carried out on membership attacks against text data models such as GPT2 i.e. given a trained model the attack seeks to infer one or more training data points. See for example [6,7]. But, as already noted, such attacks are not the focus of the present paper.

5.3   Proposed Defences

Several defences have been proposed to prevent data leakage in FL.

Abadi et al. [2] proposed Differentially Private Stochastic Gradient Descent (DP-SGD), which clips stochastic gradient decent updates and adds Gaussian noise at each iteration. This aims to defend against membership attacks against neural networks, rather than the reconstruction attacks that we consider here. In [18] it was applied to train a next word prediction RNN motivated by mobile keyboard applications, again with a focus on membership attacks. Recently, the same team at Google proposed DP-FTRL [13] which avoids the sampling step in DP-SGD.

Secure Aggregation is a multi-party protocol proposed in 2016 by [5] as a defence against data leakage from the data uploaded by clients to an FL server. In this setting the central server only has access to the sum of, and not individual updates. However, this approach still requires clients to trust that the PKI infrastructure is honest since dishonest PKI infrastructure allows the server to perform a sybil attack (see Section 6.2 in [5]) to reveal the data sent by an individual client. When both the FL server and the PKI infrastructure are operated by Google then Secure Aggregation requires users to trust Google servers to be honest, and so offers from an attack capability point of view offers no security benefit. Recent work by Pasquini et al. [21] has also shown that by distributing different models to each client a dishonest server can recover individual model updates. As a mitigation they propose adding local noise to client updates to obtain a form of local differential privacy. We note that despite the early deployment of FL in production systems such as GBoard, to the best our knowledge, there does not exist a real-world deployment of secure aggregation. This is also true for homomorphically encrypted FL, and FL using Trusted Execution Environments (TEEs).

6 Performance of Our Attacks Against Federated Learning with Local DP

Typically, when differential privacy is used with FL noise is added by the server to the aggregate update from multiple clients i.e. no noise is added to the update before leaving a device. This corresponds to the situation considered in Sect. 4. In this section we now evaluate how local differential privacy, that is, noise added either during local training (DPSGD) or to the final model parameters θ_1, before its transmission to the coordinating FL server, affect the performance of both our word recovery and sentence reconstruction attacks.

Algorithm 3: Local DPSGD

Procedure *clientUpdateDPSGD*

    $\theta_1 \leftarrow \theta_0$;

    $\mathcal{B} \leftarrow$ (split dataset into batches of size B);

    for local epoch i from 1 to E **do**;

      for batch $b \in \mathcal{B}$ **do**;

        $\theta_1 \leftarrow \theta_1 - \eta\nabla\ell(\theta_1; b) + \eta\mathcal{N}(0, \sigma)$;

    return θ_1;

Algorithm 3 outlines the procedure for DPSGD-like local training, where Gaussian noise of mean 0 and standard deviation σ is added along with each gradient update. Algorithm 4 details the typical FL client update procedure but adds Gaussian noise to the final model θ_1 before it is returned to the server. In our experiments, everything else as described in Sect. 4 is kept the same.

Algorithm 4: Local Single Noise Addition

Procedure *clientUpdateSingleNoise*

    $\theta_1 \leftarrow \theta_0$;

    $\mathcal{B} \leftarrow$ (split dataset into batches of size B);

    for local epoch i from 1 to E **do**;

      for batch $b \in \mathcal{B}$ **do**;

        $\theta_1 \leftarrow \theta_1 - \eta\nabla\ell(\theta_1; b)$;

    return $\theta_1 + \mathcal{N}(0, \sigma)$;

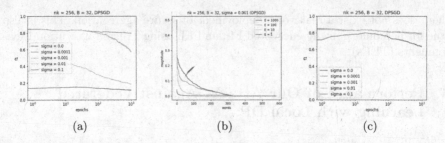

(a)   (b)   (c)

Fig. 5. Word recovery behaviour when Gaussian noise is all to local FL updates: (a) vanilla word recovery performance, (b) disparity of magnitudes between those words that were present in the dataset and those 'noisily' flipped negative, (c) word recovery performance when filtering is used.

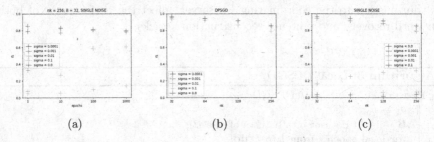

(a)   (b)   (c)

Fig. 6. Word recovery results for two local DP methods. (a) shows how added noise to the final model parameters affects the attack for different training times. With DPSGD-like training, noise levels of up to $\sigma = 0.1$ are manageable with our magnitude threshold trick, resulting in F1 scores close to those had we not added any noise at all. With FedSGD updates then for noise of up to $\sigma = 0.0001$ added to the final parameters, we can still recover words to a high degree of precision and recall.

6.1   Word Recovery Performance

Figure 5a shows the performance of our word recovery attack against DPSGD-like local training for different levels of σ. For noise levels of $\sigma = 0.001$ or greater, it can be seen that the F1 score drops significantly. What is happening is that the added noise introduces more negative values in the difference of the final layer parameters and so results in our attack extracting more words than actually occurred in the dataset, destroying its precision. However, one can eliminate most of these "noisily" added words by simple inspection. Figure 5b graphs the sorted magnitudes of the negative values in the difference between the final layer parameters of θ_1 and θ_0, after DPSGD-like training with $B = 32, n_k = 256$, and $\sigma = 0.001$. We can see that the more epochs the model is trained for, the more words are extracted via our attack. Of the around 600 words extracted after 1000 epochs of training, only about 300 of them were actually present in the dataset. On this graph, those words with higher magnitudes correspond to the ground truth words. It can be seen that we therefore can simply cutoff any words extracted beyond a specified magnitude threshold. This drastically improves the performance of the attack, see Fig. 5c. It can be seen that even for $\sigma = 0.1$, we now get word recovery results close to those obtained when we added no noise at all.

Figure 6a shows the performance of our word recovery attack when noise is added to the local model parameters θ_1 in the FedAveraging setting, with $n_k = 256$, and $B = 32$. When $\sigma \geq 0.01$, it can be seen that the performance drops drastically[4], even when we use the magnitude threshold trick described previously. With FedSGD (Figs. 6b and 6c), we see that with DPSGD-like training, these levels of noise are manageable, but for single noise addition, there are only so many words that are recoverable before being lost in the comparatively large amounts of noise added.

For comparison, in the FL literature on differential privacy, the addition of Gaussian noise with standard deviation no more than around 0.001 (and often much less) is typically considered, and is only added after the update has been transmitted to the coordinating FL server.

6.2   Sentence Reconstruction Performance

Figure 7 shows the measured sentence reconstruction performance with both DPSGD-like training (Figs. 7a and 7b) and when noise is added to the final parameters of the model (Figs. 7c and 7d). By removing the noisily added words and running our sentence reconstruction attack, we get results close to those had we not added any noise for up to $\sigma = 0.1$. For the single noise addition method, as these levels of noise are not calibrated, $\sigma = 0.1$ is enough to destroy the quality of reconstructions, however these levels of noise also destroy any model utility.

7   Additional Material

The code for all of the attacks here, the LSTM model and the datasets used are all publicly available on github here.

8   Summary and Conclusions

In this paper we introduce two local reconstruction attacks against federated learning when used to train natural language text models. We find that previously proposed attacks (DLG and its variants) targeting image data are ineffective for text data and so new methods of attack tailored to text data are

---

[4] Note that in DPSGD the added noise is multiplied by the learning rate η, and so this factor needs to be taken into account when comparing the σ values used in DPSGD above and with single noise addition. This means added noise with standard deviation σ for DPSGD corresponds roughly to a standard deviation of $\eta\sqrt{EB}\sigma$ with single noise addition. For $\eta = 0.001$, $E = 1000$, $B = 32$, $\sigma = 0.1$ the corresponding single noise addition standard deviation is 0.018.

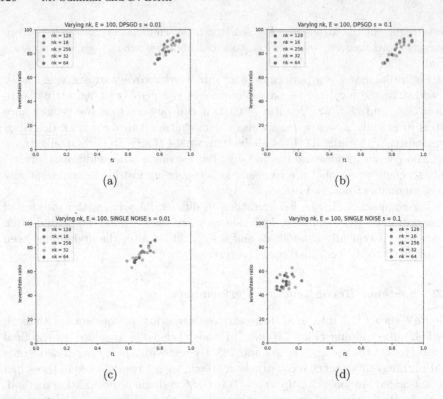

Fig. 7. Sentence reconstruction performance with local DP for FedAveraging. The top two Figures (a and b) show the reconstruction performance for different datasets colour coded by their size for DPSGD-like training, with $E = 100$, $B = 32$. Here we see no real effect in our results compared to the noise-free case. The bottom two figures show the effect of single noise addition on sentence reconstruction for the same setting.

necessary. Our attacks are simple to carry out, efficient, and highly effective. We illustrate their effectiveness against the next word prediction model used in Google's GBoard app, a widely used mobile keyboard app (with >5 Billion downloads) that has been an early adopter of federated learning for production use. We demonstrate that the words a user types on their mobile handset, e.g. when sending text messages, can be recovered with high accuracy under a wide range of conditions and that counter-measures such a use of mini-batches and adding local noise are ineffective. We also show that the word order (and so the actual sentences typed) can be reconstructed with high fidelity. This raises obvious privacy concerns, particularly since GBoard is in production use.

Secure multi-party computation methods such as Secure Aggregation and also methods such as Homomorphic Encryption and Trusted Execution Environments are potential defences that can improve privacy, but these can be difficult to implement in practice. Secure Aggregation requires users to trust that the server is honest, despite the fact that FL aims to avoid the need for such trust.

Homomorphic Encryption implementations that are sufficiently efficient to allow large-scale production use are currently lacking.

On a more positive note, the privacy situation may not be quite as bad as it seems given these reconstruction attacks. Firstly, it is not the raw sentences typed by a user that are reconstructed in our attacks but rather the sentences after they have been mapped to tokens in a text model dictionary. Words which are not in the dictionary are mapped to a special <UNK> token. This means that the reconstructed text is effectively redacted, with words not in the dictionary having been masked out. This suggests that a fruitful direction for future privacy research on FL for natural language models may well lie in taking a closer look at the specification of the dictionary used. Secondly, we also note that changing from a word-based text model to a character-based one would likely make our attacks much harder to perform.

References

1. Gboard – the Google Keyboard (2022). https://play.google.com/store/apps/details?id=com.google.android.inputmethod.latin. Accessed 24 Oct 2022
2. Abadi, M., et al.: Deep learning with differential privacy. In: Proceedings of the 2016 ACM SIGSAC Conference on Computer and Communications Security (2016)
3. Ball, J.: NSA collects millions of text messages daily in 'untargeted' global sweep (2014)
4. Boenisch, F., Dziedzic, A., Schuster, R., Shamsabadi, A.S., Shumailov, I., Papernot, N.: When the curious abandon honesty: Federated learning is not private. arXiv preprint arXiv:2112.02918 (2021)
5. Bonawitz, K., et al.: Practical secure aggregation for federated learning on user-held data. arXiv preprint arXiv:1611.04482 (2016)
6. Carlini, N., Liu, C., Erlingsson, Ú., Kos, J., Song, D.: The secret sharer: evaluating and testing unintended memorization in neural networks. In: Proceedings of the 28th USENIX Conference on Security Symposium, SEC 2019, USA, pp. 267–284. USENIX Association (2019)
7. Carlini, N., et al.: Extracting training data from large language models. In: 30th USENIX Security Symposium (USENIX Security 2021), pp. 2633–2650 (2021)
8. Deng, J., et al.: Tag: gradient attack on transformer-based language models. arXiv preprint arXiv:2103.06819 (2021)
9. Geiping, J., Bauermeister, H., Dröge, H., Moeller, M.: Inverting gradients - how easy is it to break privacy in federated learning? In: Advances in Neural Information Processing Systems (2020)
10. Greff, K., Srivastava, R.K., Koutník, J., Steunebrink, B.R., Schmidhuber, J.: LSTM: a search space odyssey. IEEE Trans. Neural Netw. Learn. Syst. **28**(10), 2222–2232 (2017)
11. Hard, A., et al.: Federated learning for mobile keyboard prediction. arXiv preprint arXiv:1811.03604 (2018)
12. Jin, X., Chen, P.-Y., Hsu, C.-Y., Yu, C.M., Chen, T.: Catastrophic data leakage in vertical federated learning. In: Advances in Neural Information Processing Systems, vol. 34 (2021)
13. Kairouz, P., McMahan, B., Song, S., Thakkar, O., Thakurta, A., Xu, Z.: Practical and private (deep) learning without sampling or shuffling. arXiv preprint arXiv:2103.00039 (2021)

14. Leith, D.J.: Mobile handset privacy: measuring the data iOS and android send to apple and google. In: Proceedings of Securecomm (2021)
15. Leith, D.J., Farrell, S.: Contact tracing app privacy: what data is shared by Europe's GAEN contact tracing apps. In: Proceedings of IEEE INFOCOM (2021)
16. Marzal, A., Vidal, E.: Computation of normalized edit distance and applications. IEEE Trans. Pattern Anal. Mach. Intell. **15**(9), 926–932 (1993)
17. McMahan, B., Moore, E., Ramage, D., Hampson, S., y Arcas, B.A.: Communication-efficient learning of deep networks from decentralized data. In: Artificial Intelligence and Statistics (2017)
18. McMahan, H.B., Ramage, D., Talwar, K., Zhang, L.: Learning differentially private recurrent language models. In: International Conference on Learning Representations (2018)
19. O'Day, D.R., Calix, R.A.: Text message corpus: applying natural language processing to mobile device forensics. In: 2013 IEEE International Conference on Multimedia and Expo Workshops (ICMEW) (2013)
20. Pan, X., Zhang, M., Yan, Y., Zhu, J., Yang, M.: Theory-oriented deep leakage from gradients via linear equation solver. arXiv preprint arXiv:2010.13356 (2020)
21. Pasquini, D., Francati, D., Ateniese, G.: Eluding secure aggregation in federated learning via model inconsistency. arXiv preprint arXiv:2111.07380 (2021)
22. Press, O., Wolf, L.: Using the output embedding to improve language models. In: Proceedings of the 15th Conference of the European Chapter of the Association for Computational Linguistics: Volume 2, Short Papers, Valencia, Spain, pp. 157–163. Association for Computational Linguistics (2017)
23. Vaswani, A., et al.: Attention is all you need. In: Advances in Neural Information Processing Systems (2017)
24. Wang, Y., et al.: Sapag: a self-adaptive privacy attack from gradients. arXiv preprint arXiv:2009.06228 (2020)
25. Yin, H., Mallya, A., Vahdat, A., Alvarez, J.M., Kautz, J., Molchanov, P.: See through gradients: image batch recovery via gradinversion. In: Proceedings of the IEEE/CVF Conference on Computer Vision and Pattern Recognition, pp. 16337–16346 (2021)
26. Zhao, B., Mopuri, K.R., Bilen, H.: idlg: improved deep leakage from gradients. arXiv preprint arXiv:2001.02610 (2020)
27. Zhu, J., Blaschko, M.: R-gap: recursive gradient attack on privacy. arXiv preprint arXiv:2010.07733 (2020)
28. Zhu, L., Liu, Z., Han, S.: Deep leakage from gradients. In: Annual Conference on Neural Information Processing Systems (NeurIPS) (2019)

Privacy-Preserving Split Learning
via Pareto Optimal Search

Xi Yu, Liyao Xiang$^{(\boxtimes)}$ (iD, Shiming Wang, and Chengnian Long

Shanghai Jiao Tong University, Shanghai, China
{yuxi2017,xiangliyao08,my16wsm,longcn}@sjtu.edu.cn

Abstract. With the rapid development of deep learning, it has become a trend for clients to perform split learning with an untrusted cloud server. The models are split into the client-end and server-end with features transmitted in between. However, features are typically vulnerable to attribute inference attacks to the input data. Most existing schemes target protecting data privacy at the inference, but not at the training stage. It remains a significant challenge to remove private information from the features while accomplishing the learning task with high utility.

We found the fundamental issue is that utility and privacy are mostly conflicting tasks, which are hardly handled by the linear scalarization commonly used in previous works. Thus we resort to the multi-objective optimization (MOO) paradigm, seeking a Pareto optimal solution according to the utility and privacy objectives. The privacy objective is formulated by the mutual information between feature and sensitive attributes and is approximated by Gaussian models. In each training iteration, we select a direction that balances the dual goal of moving toward the Pareto Front and toward the users' preference while keeping the privacy loss under the preset threshold. With a theoretical guarantee, the privacy of sensitive attributes is well preserved throughout training and at convergence. Experimental results on image and tabular datasets reveal our method is superior to the state-of-the-art in terms of utility and privacy.

Keywords: Split learning · Privacy · Pareto optimal

1 Introduction

Deep learning shows an impressive performance in various fields such as computer vision and natural language processing, benefiting from the complicated model architectures and massive training data. It is often infeasible for data owners to perform the entire end-to-end training with limited computing resources such as mobile devices. A popular solution is the *split learning*, where the model is partitioned into two parts: the client-end and the server-end. Data owners locally encode their private inputs into features with the client-end encoder model and resort to an untrusted server to further process the features and complete the

G. Tsudik et al. (Eds.): ESORICS 2023, LNCS 14347, pp. 123–142, 2024.
https://doi.org/10.1007/978-3-031-51482-1_7

training or inference tasks. An eavesdropper or the server can infer sensitive attributes of the private inputs from features. The clients would often specify some sensitive attributes, such as gender, age, etc. to remove from the features before sending them to the server. Hence removing sensitive information from the features without affecting the learning tasks is a critical issue.

To resolve the issue, previous approaches have been proposed to either 'hide' the features by crypto techniques such as Homomorphic Encryption(HE) [16] and Secure Multi-Party Computation(SMPC) [24], or by learning-based methods which train the encoder to remove the sensitive attributes from features [6,8,9,13,25]. The former brings significant computation and communication overhead, especially in deep networks. The latter unfortunately does not guarantee privacy throughout the training, as the sensitive information removal requires the learning w.r.t. the privacy loss to converge.

Our scheme follows the line of learning-based approaches but non-trivially preserves privacy over training. It is inspired by the most recent progress in multi-task learning (MTL), a well-established paradigm for learning multiple correlated tasks. A long-neglected fact in the current adversarial learning literature is that preserving the privacy of sensitive attributes and completing the learning task are mostly conflicting objectives, as the learning task may implicitly require the sensitive attributes and thus it is fairly hard to remove such attributes without hurting the task utility. It is notoriously difficult to balance conflicting goals with the conventional linear scalarization method, mostly used in previous works. Hence we formulate our problem as an MOO, set the client's preference vector over privacy versus utility, and search for an Exact Pareto Optimal (EPO) [10] solution w.r.t. the two objectives to find specific tradeoffs given preferences. Pareto optimal solutions mean that, in MOO, no objective value can be further improved without degrading some others.

The privacy objective is formulated by the mutual information loss, similar to [8,13]. We transform the intractable mutual information to the Kullback-Leibler Divergence (KL-divergence) between the feature distributions. To calculate the KL-divergence, we assume each feature is sampled from a Gaussian distribution, and adopt a reparametrization trick [1] to make it differentiable. As sampling and computing in the high-dimensional space are costly, we run Principal Component Analysis (PCA) to extract low-dimensional representations for computing the mutual information loss. The utility objective is essentially the learning task loss.

Although a Pareto optimal solution may present a better tradeoff in utility and privacy, it does not guarantee the training stage privacy. We propose to fill the gap by explicitly controlling the optimization trajectory to keep the privacy loss below the tolerance threshold throughout training. Specifically, instead of directly approaching the Pareto Front as in Fig. 1(a), we let the client first pre-train its encoder to reduce the privacy loss below the preset threshold Th, as in Fig. 1(b). In each of the following training iterations, we search for an appropriate direction to balance the goals of (1) moving toward the Pareto front and (2) towards the preference vector. The utility gradually improves by a controlled ascent in the privacy loss until reaching Th. Once the privacy constraint is activated, we continue looking for a direction without increasing the privacy loss; if such a direction cannot be found, the optimization stops at a point closest to the preference vector and Pareto Front. As shown in Fig. 1(b), the utility loss steadily decreases in traversing the Pareto Front while the trajectory is consistently below the privacy threshold, protecting sensitive attributes throughout the training.

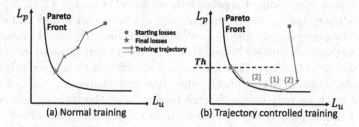

Fig. 1. Trajectory-Controlled EPO compared to normal training. Our method guarantees privacy during training by tracing the Pareto front and curbing the privacy loss (L_p) below Th. L_u refers to the utility loss. The indices (1) and (2) in (b) refer to different optimization steps.

Highlights of our contributions are as follows. First, we innovatively use MOO to handle conflicting tasks in privacy-preserving split learning problem and seek an EPO solution for a better tradeoff between utility and privacy. Second, we propose a trajectory-controlled optimization approach by tracing the utility-privacy Pareto Front with the privacy constraint, thereby protecting sensitive attributes during training with theoretical guarantees. Finally, experiments on image and tabular data verify our approach, showing superiority in utility and privacy against training and inference attacks, compared to the state-of-the-art.

2   Related Works

We focus on prior works defending against attribute inference attacks in the split learning scenario.

2.1   Adversarial Training-Based Defense

One line of works are adversarial training-based defense [9,22,23], which simulates a game between the attacker and defender with conflicting privacy goals. Specifically, the client-end's encoder pits against a simulated attacker by misleading it into making the wrong predictions about the sensitive attributes. The encoder is expected to generate features that preserve the client's attribute privacy as the adversarial training ends. However, Pittaluga et al. [15] point out that adversarial training can hardly reach a theoretical stationary point, so such defense is not robust against adaptive attackers that continue to update its classifier after the defense strategy is fixed. Label Flip Loss [15] proposes to mitigate the problem by reducing the attacker's prediction confidence, despite the prediction being correct or not. However, the empirical improvement is minor overall.

2.2 Information Theoretical Defense

An alternative approach is to limit the sensitive information contained in the client's features, eliminating the privacy threat from the root [8,12,13,25]. Specifically, they try to reduce the mutual information between features and sensitive attributes to preserve user privacy, while maximizing the mutual information between features and utility label. However, the aforementioned works share two common defects. First, they use linear scalarization to balance privacy and utility goals, which performs poorly when handling conflicting goals. Additionally, these methods only ensure feature privacy after the training convergences but leave training privacy an open question. In comparison, our method searches for the Pareto optimal solution instead to achieve a specific tradeoff and protects the client's data privacy during training by trajectory-controlled optimization.

3 Preliminaries

3.1 Split Learning

Split learning [3] enables multiple parties to train a model collaboratively without sharing raw data. As shown in Fig. 2(a), the whole deep learning model is partitioned into an encoder f_θ assigned to the client-end and a subsequent classifier g_Φ deployed on the server-end. During one training epoch, the clients forward their private input X through the encoder and transmit the feature $f_\theta(X)$ to the server. The server continues to forward the feature through its classifier and runs back-propagation to compute gradient updates for g_Φ and then f_θ.

Split learning greatly reduces the client's privacy risk and computation cost. The clients transmit the smashed feature instead, which prevents raw input exposure and saves transmission bandwidth. In addition, the server shares the training burden, which allows clients with limited computing resources such as Internet of Things (IoT) devices to participate in deep learning.

3.2 Multi-task Learning and Multi-objective Optimization

MTL allows several tasks to be learned at the same time in a single model. A popular training approach is to minimize a weighted sum of losses for different tasks, referred to as *linear scalarization*. Despite the concise form, this method often fails to handle conflicting tasks common in real-world applications [10].

To better balance conflicting tasks, Sener et al. [18] propose to solve the MTL problem by MOO. Instead of pursuing optimality for all tasks simultaneously, MOO attains optimal tradeoffs called *Pareto optimal solutions*. Each solution is a non-dominated tradeoff point where no loss can be further reduced without deteriorating other objectives. Together these solutions compose the *Pareto Front* of the learning problem. The state-of-the-art approach of MOO with high preciseness and efficiency is the Exact Pareto Optimal (EPO) search [10]. Given a vector $r = (r_1, \cdots, r_n)$ indicating the client's preference for different objectives, EPO search finds the solution which is in the intersection of the ray $r^{-1} = (1/r_1, \cdots, 1/r_n)$ and the Pareto Front if it exists.

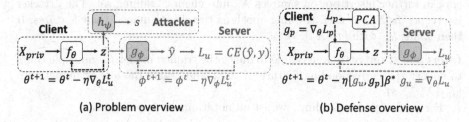

(a) Problem overview   (b) Defense overview

Fig. 2. Problem formulation and defense overview. g_u, g_p denote the gradient of utility loss, and privacy loss, respectively and β^* is the solution to (12). The client, server, and attacker are represented by black, blue, and red respectively. The server can also be an attacker. (Color figure online)

4   Problem Formulation and Threat Model

We focus on the typical split learning scenario where multiple clients train a deep learning model collaboratively. Due to privacy concerns, any raw data or feature transmission that potentially exposes the clients' sensitive information should be avoided during the model *training* and *inference* stages. We formally show the problem setting in Fig. 2(a). The three parties involved are the *client*, *server*, and *attacker*. A deep learning model is split into a client-end encoder f_θ and a server-end classifier g_Φ. The clients encode their private input X_{priv} into feature $z = f_\theta(X_{\text{priv}})$ before sending them to the server for model update (training) or label prediction (inference).

Unfortunately, transmitting features is still prone to privacy leakage. An honest-but-curious inside attacker in the server or a man-in-the-middle attacker receives the feature z and can infer clients' sensitive attributes s. This is known as the *attribute inference attack*. Previous work shows that the attacker is widely successful in inferring sensitive attributes including gender, age, race, etc. [7,17, 20]. The attribute inference attack works because a model trained for a simple task tends to overlearn attributes that are irrelevant to the objective task [19].

Next, we instantiate representative attack methods categorized into training and inference stages, according to whether the attacker utilizes the training trajectory of the model. In both cases, we assume the attacker owns an auxiliary dataset X_{aux} following a similar distribution to the clients' X_{priv} and marked with sensitive attribute labels. The attacker trains a decoder model h_ψ over X_{aux} and known sensitive attribute labels.

Training stage attacks including Decoding Simulator Attack (DSA) [21] and Data Poison Attack (DPA). The DSA attacker intercepts the clients' private feature $f_\theta(X_{\text{priv}})$ at each training epoch. It trains a shadow encoder $\tilde{f}$ with X_{aux} so that the shadow features $\tilde{f}(X_{\text{aux}})$ and real features are hard to distinguish by a discriminator model. That is, the shadow encoder approximates the feature distribution of the real encoder from its training trajectory. Simultaneously, the attacker trains the decoder model h_ψ to infer sensitive attributes with $(\tilde{f}(X_{\text{aux}}), s)$. Besides attaining the encoder's training trajectory, DPA attackers can further insert poison samples X_p into clients' training set. The attacker intercepts $f_\theta(X_p)$ at each training epoch as the clients upload their features. It then trains h_ψ with $(f_\theta(X_p), s)$.

Inference stage attacker is able to query the trained model $f_{\theta*}$ multiple times to collect the corresponding feature of X_{aux} and trains the attack model with $(f_{\theta*}(X_{\text{aux}}), s)$.

For ease of understanding, we list all notations in Appendix A.

5 Methodology

In face of attribute inference attacks, we propose training the encoder with the following goals: 1) *Privacy*: attackers fail to infer the sensitive attribute s from features during training or inference. 2) *Utility*: the features should complete the original learning tasks with high performance.

Intuitively, the feature $z = f_\theta(X_{\text{priv}})$ should contain little information about s while much information about the utility label y. By describing the utility and privacy objectives as mutual information losses $I(\cdot; \cdot)$, we formulate the problem as one to maximize the utility while curbing the privacy leakage. Expressed by the conventional linear scalarization, the objective is

$$\max_\theta \quad I(z; y) - \lambda I(z; s) \tag{1}$$

where λ controls the tradeoff between privacy and utility. We follow previous work [4,13] to transform objective (1) into differentiable utility loss $\mathcal{L}_u$ and privacy loss $\mathcal{L}_p$ in Sect. 5.1. The difficulty lies in balancing the conflicting goals of privacy and utility, which have been neglected in most previous works. We argue that with careful manipulation of the optimization trajectory, the privacy leakage through z could be restrained, throughout the training process and at the convergence. The trick is to formulate the problem as a MOO and perform a controlled EPO search and the detail is provided in Sect. 5.2, i.e., each update step of the client's encoder is selected in a direction where the privacy loss is restricted below a given level while the utility loss steadily decreases. Finally, we present the overall privacy-preserving split learning algorithm with guaranteed privacy in Sect. 5.3. Our defense overview is shown in Fig. 2(b).

5.1 Privacy and Utility Losses

Since it is infeasible to formulate the mutual information of high-dimensional variables in (1), as a proxy, we resort to maximizing the tractable lower bound $\mathcal{L}$ of $I(z; y)$ and minimizing the upper bound $\mathcal{U}$ of $I(z, s)$ as in [13]. The lower and upper bounds are as follows and the detailed derivation can be found in Appendix B.

$$\mathcal{L} = H(y) + \max_{\phi} \mathbb{E}_{z,y} \log q_{\phi}(y|z), \quad \mathcal{U} = \sum_{a} \sum_{b \neq a} p(s_a)p(s_b)D_{KL}[p(z|s_a)||p(z|s_b)].$$
(2)

In $\mathcal{L}$, $H(y)$ denotes the entropy of y, and $q(y|z)$ is a conditional distribution. For $\mathcal{U}$, p denotes the probability distribution of sensitive attributes (with a, b denoting the different actual values of the attribute), and D_{KL} means the KL-divergence. Since $H(y)$ is a constant, we only need to optimize the second term of $\mathcal{L}$, which is equivalent to minimizing the cross-entropy utility loss $L_u = CE(g_{\phi}(f_{\theta}(x)), y)$.

The upper bound $\mathcal{U}$ is still too complicated to compute and requires the approximation of output distributions. Considering the deterministic feature of a given input, we add a zero-mean Gaussian noise to the feature and approximate $p(z|s_k)$ with a Gaussian Mixture Model (GMM): $p(z|s_k) = \frac{1}{N_k} \sum_{i=1}^{N_k} p(z|x_i)$, where k represents the specific sensitive attribute value and N_k denotes the corresponding number of features. The KL-divergence in (2) hence becomes KL-divergence between two GMMs. However, it is still too complicated and thus we further approximate the GMM with Gaussian distribution $\hat{p}$ as in [4] and the upper bound $\mathcal{U}$ becomes a differentiable privacy loss

$$L_p = \frac{1}{N^2} \sum_{a} \sum_{b \neq a} N_a N_b D_{KL}[\hat{p}(z|s_a)||\hat{p}(z|s_b)]$$
(3)

where N is the number of samples. Hence following (1), our objective now becomes minimizing the utility loss L_u and the privacy loss L_p at the same time.

Nevertheless, if the encoded features are high-dimensional for ML models, it will bring heavy computation overhead when calculating GMM losses. In this case, we adopt PCA to reduce the dimension of $f_{\theta}(x)$ to $f'_{\theta}(x)$. Due to the dimension reduction, $f'_{\theta}(x)$ no longer follows GMM but we simply estimate them by Kernel Density Estimation (KDE) with Gaussian kernels [2]. The features z transmitted to the server are still computed using $f_{\theta}(x)$.

5.2 Trajectory-Controlled Pareto Optimal Search

As aforementioned, linear scalarization cannot handle conflicting objectives well. Protecting data privacy and preserving data utility simultaneously is just such a conflicting problem. Additionally, existing MOO-based methods can only ensure feature privacy in the inference stage and training privacy is out of scope. In this section, we will demonstrate in detail how we take advantage of trajectory-controlled Pareto optimal search for guaranteeing privacy throughout training.

We begin by analyzing the relationship between privacy loss and the attack success rate. As mentioned in [25], the theoretical connection between attribute inference accuracy and mutual information is as follows:

$$\Pr[\hat{s} = s] \leq 1 - \frac{H(s)}{\log |\mathcal{S}|} + \frac{I(z;s) + \log 2}{\log |\mathcal{S}|}, \tag{4}$$

where $\mathcal{S}$ means the space of all possible values of s. Hence with a smaller $I(z;s)$, the upper bound of the attack success rate is lower. It means that if L_p is kept at a low level throughout the training process, the privacy of the sensitive attribute is preserved.

To establish control over L_p, we resort to a gradient-based MOO algorithm – Trajectory-Controlled Pareto Optimal (TCPO) search, which traces the Pareto Front by gradually decreasing utility loss with a controlled ascent of the privacy loss. Here we consider a more general case where the number of losses are more than two. Let $l = (l_1, \cdots, l_m) \succeq 0$ represents the non-negative losses of m different utility and privacy tasks. We define a preference order by the preference vector $r \in \mathbb{R}_+^m$ that, for any $i, j \in [m]$, if $r_i \geq r_j$, then $l_i \leq l_j$, suggesting task i is more important than task j. An EPO solution [10] is defined w.r.t. r as:

$$\mathcal{P}_r = \{\theta^* \in \mathcal{P} | r_1 l_1^* = r_2 l_2^* = \cdots = r_m l_m^*\}, \tag{5}$$

where $l_i^* = l_i(\theta^*)$ at convergence, and $\mathcal{P}$ denotes the set of Pareto optimal solutions. The definition suggests that the solution is the intersection between the Pareto Front and the ray $r^{-1} := (1/r_1, 1/r_2, \cdots, 1/r_m)$.

Since our goal is to suppress the privacy leakage, we set the preference vector as follows: $r_i = 1$ if l_i is the utility loss, otherwise $r_i = 0$. By definition, the ideal solution satisfying (5) can never be obtained, and thus the utility loss would always be decreasing by the criteria. Given r, the optimization process includes: initializing the encoder so that the privacy constraint is satisfied, and two iterative steps of approaching the r^{-1} ray and the Pareto Front. Suppose the gradient matrix of the losses is $G = [g_1, g_2, \cdots, g_m]$, and $C = G^T G$. In each step, we select the update direction of θ as $d = G\beta$, where β denotes the linear weights of gradients. In the following, we detail each of the steps.

At the initialization step, we locally pre-train the encoder to minimize the privacy loss under the threshold Th before uploading any feature. As soon as the client begins to upload, the features are vulnerable to attacks. Hence it is important to restrain the privacy leakage from the first round of updates.

In the following optimization step, we apply a non-uniformity loss to approach the r^{-1} ray, which is expressed by the deviation from the r^{-1} ray [11]:

$$\mu_r(l) = \mu(l, r^{-1}) = 1 - \frac{\langle l, r^{-1} \rangle^2}{||l||^2 ||r^{-1}||^2}. \tag{6}$$

It is easy to verify that μ is always positive by Cauchy-Schwarz inequality. Letting $c = \frac{2\langle l, r^{-1} \rangle}{||l||^3 ||r^{-1}||} (c > 0)$, the gradient direction of μ with respect to l is:

$$\frac{\partial \mu_r(l)}{\partial l} = c\left(\frac{\langle l, r^{-1} \rangle}{||l|| ||r^{-1}||} l - \frac{||l||}{||r^{-1}||} r^{-1} \right) \triangleq ca, \tag{7}$$

where c is a constant, and a is the anchor direction. The derivative of μ with respect to θ is

$$\frac{\partial \mu_r(l)}{\partial \theta} = \frac{\partial \mu_r(l)}{\partial l} \frac{\partial l}{\partial \theta} = ca^T G^T. \tag{8}$$

With simple derivation, we have the following claim: the loss vector l and the anchor direction a are always orthogonal, i.e., $a^T l = 0$ and a is scale-invariant to r^{-1}. Also, in minimizing μ, the following lemmas hold:

Lemma 1. *([11]) If the direction d satisfies $a^T G^T d \geq 0$, then there exists a step size $\eta_0 > 0$ such that:*

$$\mu_r(l(\theta - \eta d)) \leq \mu_r(l(\theta)), \quad \forall \eta \in [0, \eta_0]. \tag{9}$$

We can find such a d in the descent direction of μ_r by solving the following quadratic programming problem:

$$\min_{\beta \in [-1,1]^m} ||C\beta - a||_2^2. \tag{10}$$

The range of β is set to reduce the search space. Formally, we have

Lemma 2. *The direction d found by (10) satisfies $a^T G^T d \geq 0$.*

The proof of the lemma can be found in Appendix C. The lemma suggests that solving (10) would always yield a direction which does not increase μ_r in the worst case ($a^T G^T$ is in the same hyperplane with d). Combined with Lemma 1, we could always find a direction to approach the preference ray r^{-1} by solving (10). However, searching for a direction to decrease the non-uniformity loss is not enough. We need to keep the privacy loss under a threshold, meaning that if some privacy loss L_p ever violates the privacy constraint, the loss should be prevented from further increasing. In that case, the gradient of $L_p - g_p$ should be in the same hyperplane of d, i.e., $g_p^T d \geq 0$.

Apart from approaching the preference ray, it is required to find a direction d to decrease losses of all tasks, meaning that d preferably agrees with the descent directions of all losses: $G^T d \succeq 0$. To search such a d is to solve

$$\min_{\beta \in [-1,1]^m} ||C\beta - l||_2^2, \quad \text{s.t.} \quad \frac{C\beta}{||C\beta||} = \frac{l}{||l||}. \tag{11}$$

Formally, we have

Lemma 3. *If the gradient matrix G is full rank, then the direction d solved by (11) satisfies $G^T d \succeq 0$ and $a^T G^T d = 0$.*

The proof is in Appendix D. Hence by solving (11), we find a direction to decrease all losses without increasing the non-uniformity loss. The former is indicated by $G^T d \succeq 0$ and the latter is derived from Lemma 1. In practice, G is a full rank matrix in most cases because few targeted tasks are highly related to each other.

To sum up, we initialize the local encoder so that the privacy leakage falls under a given threshold. Then we iteratively perform two steps of descent. If the current losses are near the Pareto front, we decrease the non-uniformity loss to approach the preference ray. Otherwise, we decrease the task losses to draw close to the Pareto front. Meanwhile, we use an indicator function $\mathbb{1}_{Th}$ to denote the privacy loss surpassing a given threshold Th and $\mathbb{1}_{opt}$ to indicate a Pareto optimal point is reached. Our optimization is to seek the linear weights

$$
\beta^* = \arg \min_{\beta \in [-1,1]^m} ||C\beta - a\mathbb{1}_{opt} - l(1 - \mathbb{1}_{opt})||_2^2,
$$

$$
\text{s.t.} \quad (1 - \mathbb{1}_{opt})(\frac{C\beta}{||C\beta||} - \frac{l}{||l||}) = 0, \tag{12}
$$

$$
g_p^T G\beta \mathbb{1}_{Th} \geq 0.
$$

By solving (12), we obtain the update direction for the local encoder. Different from direct gradient descent, the privacy loss is in controlled ascent from time to time to minimize the non-uniformity loss, but is kept under the threshold by the inequality constraint of (12). Different from the conventional Pareto optimal search which merely ensures the optimality at convergence, our method keeps track of the Pareto front and thus obtains a much lower privacy loss throughout the optimization, as illustrated in Fig. 1.

Theorem 1. *Letting $\theta \in \mathcal{P}$ be a Pareto optimal solution in the optimization, the direction $d = G\beta^*$ found by (12) is not 0 if the privacy constraint is not activated. Meanwhile, the non-uniformity loss μ keeps decreasing.*

The proof of Theorem 1 is found in Appendix E. According to Theorem 1, our optimization would not stop prematurely at a local Pareto optimal solution. Instead, it keeps searching for new Pareto optimal solutions with a smaller non-uniformity loss without violating the privacy constraint. If the training process activates the privacy constraint, denoted by $\mathcal{F} = \{C\beta | g_p^T G\beta \geq 0\}$, and if the orthogonal projection of a on $\mathcal{S} \cap \mathcal{F}$ is not 0, then (12) can still find a direction d to decrease μ, otherwise the optimization terminates.

5.3   Privacy-Preserving Training

Our proposed algorithm is detailed in Algorithm 1. Before uploading any feature to the cloud, the client locally updates its encoder to minimize the privacy loss until meeting the privacy constraint (Line 2–7). The starting point obviously satisfies the privacy requirement. At each iteration of training (Line 9–15), the client samples features and send them to the cloud. The cloud feeds feature z into its model and sends back the error gradient w.r.t. the utility loss to the client. Backpropagating both utility loss and privacy loss through the encoder, the client obtains g_u and g_p. Given the current gradient $G = (g_u, g_p)$, the client searches the descent direction $d = G\beta$ by (12). Finally, the client's encoder gets updated. The key to preserving privacy for the training data lies in Line 15 which searches the descent direction. The direction is chosen to reach the preferred utility and privacy at convergence while keeping the leakage under the tolerance threshold.

Computation Complexity. The most time-consuming part of our algorithm lies in the computation of the privacy loss L_p which is dominated by the feature dimension D and the number of private attributes M, totaling $O(D^3 M^2)$.

Algorithm 1: Privacy-Preserving Learning with Trajectory Control

---

Input: Training dataset $D_{train} = \{x_i, y_i, s_i\}_{i=1}^{N}$, local encoder f_θ, cloud
classifier g_ϕ, noise standard deviation σ, number of training iterations
T, privacy loss threshold Th

Output: encoder f_θ, cloud classifier g_ϕ

1 Initialize θ, ϕ
2 **while** $L_p > Th$ **do**
3   Sample a minibatch b from D_{train}
4   Send each $x \in b$ to the encoder f_θ to get $f_\theta(x)$
5   Compute the privacy loss L_p by (3) given $\mathcal{N}(f_\theta(x), \sigma^2)$
6   Update θ to minimize L_p
7 **end**
8 **for** $t \in [1, T]$ **do**
9   Sample a minibatch b from D_{train}
10   Send each $x \in b$ to encoder f_θ to get $f_\theta(x)$
11   Run PCA for $f_\theta(x)$ to obtain $f_\theta'(x)$ and use KDE for distributions
       estimation
12   Compute privacy loss L_p by (3) using estimated distributions
13   Sample $z \sim \mathcal{N}(f_\theta(x), \sigma^2)$ and send z to cloud classifier g_ϕ
14   Cloud: update ϕ w.r.t. L_u and send back the error gradients
15   Backpropagate L_u and L_p through the encoder to acquire the gradient
       matrix G
16   Calculate linear coeffients β by (12) and update θ using Adam optimizer
17 **end**

---

6   Experiments and Evaluation

Through experiments on a variety of datasets and tasks, we aim to answer the following questions:

Q1: Is our split learning defense effective against attribute inference attacks? How does it protect sensitive attributes at the training and inference stages?

Q2: Does our defense maintain utility for training and inference tasks?

Q3: Does our defense improve the privacy-utility tradeoff compared to existing methods?

6.1   Experimental Setup

Our algorithm is implemented on PyTorch 1.12.0 and all experiments are done on Intel(R) Xeon(R) Gold 6240C with GPU GeForce RTX 3090.

Datasets and Tasks. We choose representative datasets and tasks to evaluate our approach. In the category of image data, we use the widely-adopted CelebA containing over 200K images labeled with 40 binary attributes to perform attribute classification. We also select two tabular datasets, the Health Heritage dataset containing 55K medical records, and the Census Income (Adult) dataset containing 48K personal information records with 14 attributes, for classification tasks. Each dataset is split into three non-overlapping parts: the client's training dataset X_{train}, the client's testing dataset X_{test}, and the attacker's auxiliary dataset X_{aux} on a 4:1:2 ratio.

The privacy and utility attributes of different datasets are listed in Table 1. The 'Age' attribute has nine possible values, the 'Relationship' attribute has six possible values while all others are binary attributes.

Table 1. Privacy and utility attributes for different datasets.

Dataset	CelebA	Health	Adult
Privacy attribute	Male/Attractive/WearingLipstick	Age/Gender	Sex/Relationship
Utility attribute	Smiling	Charlson	Income>50K

Attack Methods. We implement three different attribute inference attack methods on X_{aux}. Two training stage attacks include DSA [21] and DPA as described in Sect. 4. In comparison, DSA is relatively weaker and it merely succeeds on the image data but fails on the tabular data. Hence we only launch DSA to the image data in our experiments. DPA implementation follows the convention by poisoning 5% of the training data. The inference phase attack is implemented as a black-box attack as detailed in Sect. 4, referred to as 'Basic' later.

Table 2. Tradeoff parameters for the baselines.

Dataset	Private Attribute	AdvTrain (ω)	AdvTrain+Label Flip (ω)	Infocensor (λ)
CelebA	Male	$\{1,3,5\}$	$\{0.5,1,3\}$	$\{0.1,0.3,0.4\}$
	Attractive	$\{1,3,5\}$	$\{0.5,1,3\}$	$\{0.1,0.3,0.4\}$
	WearingLipstick	$\{1,3,5\}$	$\{0.5,1,3\}$	$\{0.1,0.3,0.4\}$
Health	Age	$\{0.5,1,3,5\}$	$\{0.1,0.5,1\}$	$\{0.01,0.05,0.1\}$
	Gender	$\{1,3,10,20\}$	$\{3,5,10\}$	$\{0.05,0.1,0.3\}$
Adult	Sex	$\{1,3,10\}$	$\{1,3,5\}$	$\{0.1,0.3,0.5,0.8\}$
	Relationship	$\{1,3,5\}$	$\{1,2,3\}$	$\{0.1,0.3,0.5,0.8\}$

Baselines. We compare our approach with three state-of-the-art privacy-preserving methods against black-box attribute inference attacks: 1) Adversarial training [9] (ADV) pits against a simulated adversary who tries to infer the sensitive attribute information from the intermediate features until the simulated adversary fails to do so. 2) Adversarial training with label flip [15] (ADV2) improves upon the conventional adversarial training by treating the opposite of the label that the current attacker predicts as the true label. The encoder seeks to reduce the attacker's confidence in classifying sensitive attributes and thus weakening its capability. Both 1) and 2) control the utility-privacy tradeoff with a weight hyperparameter ω. 3) Infocensor [25] is an information theoretical approach that minimizes the mutual information between the features and sensitive attributes. It controls the utility-privacy tradeoff with hyperparameter λ. Since all three baselines present different tradeoffs at varied hyperparameters, for a comprehensive view, we test the methods under a wide range of ωs and λs as listed in Table 2.

Evaluation Metrics. The utility metric is the classification accuracy whereas the privacy metric is the attack accuracy of private attributes. For training data privacy, the highest attack accuracy throughout the entire training process is recorded. For testing data privacy, we let the attacker infer the private attribute from the intermediate feature and report the mean attack accuracy on the test set.

Models and Hyperparameters. For tabular datasets, we employ a two-layer Multi-Layer Perceptron (MLP) as the encoder, and a three-layer MLP for the cloud classifier. For the image dataset, we use a convolutional neural network that consists of a three-convolutional-layer encoder and a cloud classifier with one convolutional layer followed by four fully-connected layers. We choose the attack decoder's network structure the same as the cloud classifier for the three kinds of attacks. Additionally for DSA, the shadow encoder shares the same structure with the encoder while the discriminator contains two convolutional layers and two residual blocks following [14]. We train all the models using the Adam optimizer with the learning rate set to 0.001 by default. The framework-specific hyperparameters for the three baselines and our method are tuned individually for optimal performance. For our method, privacy thresholds Th are set to 0.005, 0.003, and 0.001, and σ is set to 10 on CelebA and 1 on tabular datasets.

6.2 Effect of Trajectory-Controlled Pareto Optimal Search

We verify the effectiveness of our design against the conventional linear scalarization objective in training CelebA. The same utility and privacy losses are adopted in both defense objectives. For linear scalarization, the training objective is $\min L_u + \lambda L_p$. Results of the best privacy performance and within $1 - 2\%$ utility decline are reported in Tab. 3. As it shows, our method not only achieves better privacy (lower attack success rate) against basic attacks in the inference stage, but also is superior to linear scalarization against DSA and DPA in the training stage. For a closer inspection, we depict the training loss curves for the two methods in Fig. 3. It is clear that with a similar final utility level, our method maintains a low privacy loss throughout the training. It can also be interestingly observed that, the final privacy level of ours always stays close to Th. It is a verification to the contrapositive of Theorem 1 that, if $d = 0$, the privacy constraint is activated, i.e., at convergence, the privacy level is always around Th.

Table 3. Utility and privacy results (%) on CelebA. 'Linear' refers to the linear scalarization objective being used in privacy-preserving split learning.

CelebA	Male				Attractive				WearingLipstick			
	Utility	Basic	DSA	DPA	Utility	Basic	DSA	DPA	Utility	Basic	DSA	DPA
No defense	92.27	93.41	84.42	90.42	92.27	79.12	74.83	77.17	92.27	89.91	83.65	88.18
Linear	91.57	62.54	59.19	61.39	91.28	62.99	54.42	61.76	91.45	64.02	53.21	62.93
Ours	91.29	61.42	56.44	58.17	91.22	61.53	53.26	58.18	91.41	63.14	52.68	61.09

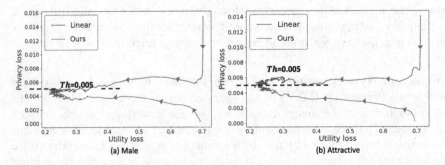

Fig. 3. Training losses trajectory on CelebA. Arrows indicate the iteration sequence. Linear scalarization weight $\lambda = 0.5$. We use uniform filter1d with window size 3 to smooth all the curves.

6.3 Privacy Against Attacks

We show the performance of our method against different training and inference phase attacks. If the privacy is fully preserved, the inference attacker has no choice but to random guess the value of the private attribute, the success rate of which is the proportion of the most common value at best. We refer to such a success rate as 'random' and mark them in italics in Table 4 and 5. Due to the variety of utility-privacy tradeoffs, we report the results of the best privacy performance and within 1–2% utility decline in each method in the two tables.

Table 4 shows the results of CelebA. The line of 'No defense' suggests that all three attacks (basic attack at the inference phase, DSA, and DPA at the training phase) achieve high attack accuracy. Our method significantly lowers the attack accuracy, drawing them close to the accuracy of random guesses, while remaining utility as high as that of no defense. It shows that our method greatly preserves user privacy against all three attacks yet without disrupting the original tasks in both inference and training stages (**Q1**& **Q2**). Note that adversarial training-based methods are not very effective against black-box attacks in the inference stage. Also formulated by information theoretical loss, the privacy objective for Infocensor seems to be well satisfied at the inference stage, but is below par in facing the training stage attacks, showing that Infocensor's strategy hardly meets privacy-preserving training. A similar conclusion holds for tabular data in Table 5 that, our method has superior utility and privacy across all methods, especially with a constantly low attack accuracy during training.

Table 4. Utility and privacy results (%) on CelebA. The best results are marked in bold. 'Basic''ADV''ADV2' refer to the basic black-box attack at the inference stage, adversarial training, and adversarial training with label flip, respectively. The ideal privacy is represented by 'random guesses' in italics.

celebA	Male(58.32)				Attractive(51.25)				WearingLipstick(52.76)			
	Utility	Basic	DSA	DPA	Utility	Basic	DSA	DPA	Utility	Basic	DSA	DPA
No defense	92.27	93.41	84.42	90.42	92.27	79.12	74.83	77.17	92.27	89.91	83.65	88.18
ADV	91.68	89.98	64.39	61.25	91.46	76.91	57.42	61.78	91.69	86.25	58.65	65.42
ADV2	90.89	81.13	59.09	60.12	91.15	71.21	55.62	61.43	91.05	76.88	58.22	64.71
Infocensor	91.37	62.59	58.45	61.79	91.17	62.95	54.27	63.5	91.46	**63.08**	53.09	63.14
Ours	91.29	**61.42**	**58.42**	**58.17**	91.22	**61.53**	**53.26**	**58.18**	91.41	63.14	**52.68**	61.09

Table 5. Utility and privacy results (%) on tabular datasets. The best results are marked in bold. The ideal privacy is represented by 'random guesses' in italics.

Health Heritage	Age(16)			Gender(54.23)		
	Utility	Basic	DPA	Utility	Basic	DPA
No defense	82.9	31.02	30.07	82.9	59.68	58.39
ADV	82.28	30.03	26.13	82.28	58.66	56.23
ADV2	81.47	28.09	25.58	81.36	56.28	55.88
Infocensor	81.27	**22.86**	24.54	81.2	54.86	55.16
Ours	81.36	23.02	**23.16**	81.12	**54.53**	**55.07**
Adult	Sex(66.7)			Relationship(40)		
	Utility	Basic	DPA	Utility	Basic	DPA
No defense	82.68	80.12	77.45	82.68	73.31	67.43
ADV	82.07	78.03	69.39	81.86	71.18	58.26
ADV2	81.72	74.65	68.81	81.75	66.89	57.2
Infocensor	81.94	**66.2**	68.52	81.48	51.98	51.59
Ours	81.95	66.48	**66.39**	81.57	**50.84**	**49.64**

6.4   Privacy-Utility Tradeoffs

For fair and integral comparison, we report results on CelebA under a variety of utility-privacy tradeoffs by tuning the hyperparameters in our method as well as the baselines. As we increase the weight of the privacy task or lower the privacy threshold, data privacy improves but utility declines. The results are visualized in Fig. 4 where the ideal utility-privacy tradeoff is at the right-bottom corner.

As Fig. 4 shows, our method constantly gives a better tradeoff than existing approaches against all attacks (**Q3**), which indicates that our method is able to protect split learning in both training and inference stages. For inference stage attacks, the advantage is the most significant against adversarial training-based methods. For example, in protecting the private attribute 'Male', at a similar utility performance, our method reduces the attack accuracy by over 20%. This is because adversarial training hardly achieves the equilibrium in the attacker-defender game, and thus does not defend adaptive attack strategies. Adversarial training with label flip improves this by obfuscating labels, which drops the attack accuracy by over 5%, but is still far from enough. The performance of Infocensor is marginally inferior to ours in (a)(d) against attacks at the inference phase, but the gap becomes larger in the rest in face of attacks at the training. Particularly for DPA, the stronger training-stage attack, our method has a clear advantage over all baselines, showing the power of rigorous trajectory control over training. Above all, our method delivers a more desirable tradeoff between utility and privacy, staying closer to the right-bottom corner.

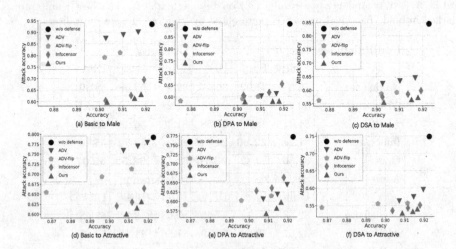

Fig. 4. The privacy-utility tradeoffs on CelebA.

7   Conclusion

We propose a privacy-preserving split learning framework following the paradigm of multi-objective optimization. Different from the conventional linear scalarization in previous works, we seek a Pareto optimal solution to the conflicting goals of utility and privacy while strictly curbing the privacy leakage in training. Our algorithm is essentially a gradient-based, trajectory-controlled Pareto optimal search. Evaluation on different data shows the superior privacy performance of our method against attribute inference attacks both in the training and inference stages, yet without utility decline.

Acknowledgements. This work was supported in part by NSF China (62272306, 62136006, 62032020), and a specialized technology project for the pre-research of generic information system equipment (31511130302).

A   Notations

We list all notations in this paper in Table 6 for better understanding.

B   Proof for Loss Formulation

Proof. **Lower bound of $I(z; y)$.** According to [13], for any conditional distribution $q(y|z)$, it holds that

$$I(z; y) \geq H(y) + \mathbb{E}_{z,y} \log q(y|z). \tag{13}$$

Hence the lower bound of $I(z; y)$ can be defined as

$$\mathcal{L} = H(y) + \max_{\phi} \mathbb{E}_{z,y} \log q_{\phi}(y|z). \tag{14}$$

The model with parameter ϕ is exactly the classifier performing the original task using uploaded feature z. For fixed z, the better the classifier is trained, the better estimation result it will achieve. Since $H(y)$ is a constant, we only need to optimize the second term of $\mathcal{L}$, which can be translated into minimizing the cross entropy loss. Denoting the cross entropy loss as $CE(\cdot)$, the utility loss can be defined as:

$$L_u = CE(g(f(x)), y).$$

Upper Bound of $I(z; s)$. Assuming s is a discrete variable, the mutual information can be written as

$$I(z; s) = \sum_a p(s_a) \int p(z|s_a) \log \frac{p(z|s_a)}{\sum_b p(s_b)p(z|s_b)} dz. \tag{15}$$

Table 6. Notations used in this paper

Notations	Description
m	number of tasks
z	intermediate feature
s	sensitive attribute
f_θ	client side model
g_ϕ	server side model
h_ψ	attacker model
L_u	utility loss
L_p	privacy loss
$\mathcal{P}$	Pareto optimal set
r	preference vector
G	gradient matrix
C	$G^T G$
β	linear combination coefficient of the gradients
d	optimization direction
l	loss vector
μ_r	non-uniformity
a	anchor direction
$Col(\cdot)$	column space
$Null(\cdot)$	null space
$p(\cdot)$	probability distribution

By Jensen's Inequality, $I(z; s)$ is upper bounded by:

$$\mathcal{U} = \sum_a \sum_{b \neq a} p(s_a) p(s_b) KL[p(z|s_a)||p(z|s_b)]. \tag{16}$$

C   Proof of Lemma 2

Proof. We prove by contradiction. The formula in (10) can be written as

$$||C\beta - a||_2^2 = ||G^T d||_2^2 + ||a||_2^2 - 2a^T G^T d. \tag{17}$$

If $a^T G^T d < 0$ at convergence, then $||C\beta - a||_2^2 > ||a||_2^2$, which is greater than the result at $d = 0$. Hence it contradicts with the fact that the current solution is optimal. Thus $a^T G^T d \geq 0$ holds by solving (10).

D   Proof of Lemma 3

Proof. When $\text{rank}(C) = \text{rank}(G) = m$, we can always find β^* such that $C\beta^* = l$. Due to the range constraint of β, we need to scale β^* to the range of $[-1, 1]^m$

without altering the direction of $C\beta^*$. Hence we could get $G^T d = C\beta = kl \succ 0(k > 0)$, and $a^T G^T d = ka^T l = 0$. The last equality holds due to our claim that $a^T l = 0$.

E   Proof of Theorem 1

Proof. If θ is a Pareto optimal solution in optimizing (12), by Pareto Criticality ([5], ch4), G has rank $m - 1$. Hence rank(C) = rank(G) = $m - 1$. Note that $a \neq 0$ at this point, otherwise the optimization terminates for $d = 0$.

Let $\mathcal{S} = \{C\beta | \beta \in [-1,1]^m\}$, $Col(C)$ be the column space of C, and $Null(C)$ be the null space of C. It is clear that $\mathcal{S} \subseteq Col(C)$, and $Col(C)$ and $Null(C)$ are orthogonal complement spaces. By minimizing the objective of (12), $C\beta$ turns out to be the best approximation of a on $\mathcal{S}$. Now we prove by contradiction. Assuming $d = 0$, we have $C\beta = G^T d = 0$. Thus the orthogonal projection of a on $\mathcal{S}$ is 0. Hence the orthogonal projection of a on $Col(C)$ is 0, which means $a \in Null(C)$. Due to the orthogonality of a and l, $l \in Col(C)$, which means $\exists \alpha$ s.t. $C\alpha = G^T G\alpha = l \succeq 0$. So we can find a direction $d = G\alpha$ to decrease all losses, which is contradictory to the condition of Pareto optimality. Therefore, d is not 0.

According to Lemma 1, Lemma 2 and Lemma 3, the direction d found by (12) always satisfies $a^T G^T d \geq 0$, so with proper step size, μ keeps decreasing.

References

1. Doersch, C.: Tutorial on variational autoencoders. arXiv preprint arXiv:1606.05908 (2016)
2. Duong, T., Hazelton, M.L.: Convergence rates for unconstrained bandwidth matrix selectors in multivariate kernel density estimation. J. Multivar. Anal. **93**(2), 417–433 (2005)
3. Gupta, O., Raskar, R.: Distributed learning of deep neural network over multiple agents. J. Netw. Comput. Appl. **116**, 1–8 (2018)
4. Hershey, J.R., Olsen, P.A.: Approximating the Kullback Leibler divergence between gaussian mixture models. In: 2007 IEEE International Conference on Acoustics, Speech and Signal Processing-ICASSP 2007, vol. 4, pp. IV–317. IEEE (2007)
5. Hillermeier, C.: Nonlinear Multiobjective Optimization: A Generalized Homotopy Approach, vol. 135. Springer Science & Business Media, Cham (2001)
6. Jia, J., Gong, N.Z.: {AttriGuard}: a practical defense against attribute inference attacks via adversarial machine learning. In: 27th USENIX Security Symposium (USENIX Security 18), pp. 513–529 (2018)
7. Kosinski, M., Stillwell, D., Graepel, T.: Private traits and attributes are predictable from digital records of human behavior. Proc. Natl. Acad. Sci. **110**(15), 5802–5805 (2013)
8. Li, A., Duan, Y., Yang, H., Chen, Y., Yang, J.: TIPRDC: task-independent privacy-respecting data crowdsourcing framework for deep learning with anonymized intermediate representations. In: Proceedings of the 26th ACM SIGKDD International Conference on Knowledge Discovery & Data Mining, pp. 824–832 (2020)

9. Liu, S., Du, J., Shrivastava, A., Zhong, L.: Privacy adversarial network: representation learning for mobile data privacy. Proc. ACM Interact. Mob. Wear. Ubiquit. Technol. **3**(4), 1–18 (2019)

10. Mahapatra, D., Rajan, V.: Multi-task learning with user preferences: Gradient descent with controlled ascent in pareto optimization. In: International Conference on Machine Learning, pp. 6597–6607. PMLR (2020)

11. Mahapatra, D., Rajan, V.: Exact pareto optimal search for multi-task learning: touring the pareto front. arXiv preprint arXiv:2108.00597 (2021)

12. Moyer, D., Gao, S., Brekelmans, R., Galstyan, A., Ver Steeg, G.: Invariant representations without adversarial training. In: Advances in Neural Information Processing Systems, vol. 31 (2018)

13. Osia, S.A., Taheri, A., Shamsabadi, A.S., Katevas, K., Haddadi, H., Rabiee, H.R.: Deep private-feature extraction. IEEE Trans. Knowl. Data Eng. **32**(1), 54–66 (2018)

14. Pasquini, D., Ateniese, G., Bernaschi, M.: Unleashing the tiger: inference attacks on split learning. In: Proceedings of the 2021 ACM SIGSAC Conference on Computer and Communications Security, pp. 2113–2129 (2021)

15. Pittaluga, F., Koppal, S., Chakrabarti, A.: Learning privacy preserving encodings through adversarial training. In: 2019 IEEE Winter Conference on Applications of Computer Vision (WACV), pp. 791–799. IEEE (2019)

16. Rivest, R.L., Shamir, A., Adleman, L.: A method for obtaining digital signatures and public-key cryptosystems. Commun. ACM **21**(2), 120–126 (1978)

17. Salamatian, S., et al.: Managing your private and public data: Bringing down inference attacks against your privacy. IEEE J. Select. Top. Signal Process. **9**(7), 1240–1255 (2015)

18. Sener, O., Koltun, V.: Multi-task learning as multi-objective optimization. In: Advances in Neural Information Processing Systems, vol. 31 (2018)

19. Song, C., Shmatikov, V.: Overlearning reveals sensitive attributes. In: 8th International Conference on Learning Representations, ICLR 2020 (2020)

20. Weinsberg, U., Bhagat, S., Ioannidis, S., Taft, N.: Blurme: inferring and obfuscating user gender based on ratings. In: Proceedings of the Sixth ACM Conference on Recommender Systems, pp. 195–202 (2012)

21. D Xiaochen, Z.: Feature inference attacks on split learning with an honest-but-curious server, Ph.D. thesis, National University of Singapore (2022)

22. Xie, Q., Dai, Z., Du, Y., Hovy, E., Neubig, G.: Controllable invariance through adversarial feature learning. In: Advances in Neural Information Processing Systems, vol. 30 (2017)

23. Yang, T.Y., Brinton, C., Mittal, P., Chiang, M., Lan, A.: Learning informative and private representations via generative adversarial networks. In: 2018 IEEE International Conference on Big Data (Big Data), pp. 1534–1543. IEEE (2018)

24. Yao, A.C.: Protocols for secure computations. In: 23rd Annual Symposium on Foundations of Computer Science (SFCS 1982), pp. 160–164. IEEE (1982)

25. Zheng, T., Li, B.: Infocensor: an information-theoretic framework against sensitive attribute inference and demographic disparity. In: Proceedings of the 2022 ACM on Asia Conference on Computer and Communications Security, pp. 437–451 (2022)

Security of NVMe Offloaded Data
in Large-Scale Machine Learning

Torsten Krauß[(✉)] [iD], Raphael Götz [iD], and Alexandra Dmitrienko [iD]

University of Würzburg, Sanderring 2, 97070 Würzburg, Germany
{torsten.krauss,raphael.goetz,alexandra.dmitrienko}@uni-wuerzburg.de

Abstract. Large-scale machine learning (LSML) models, such as the
GPT-3.5 that powers the well-known ChatGPT chatbot, have revolutionized our perception of AI by enabling more natural, context-aware,
and interactive experiences. Yet, training such large models nowadays
requires multiple months of computation on expensive hardware, including GPUs, orchestrated by specialized software, so-called LSML frameworks. Due to the model size, neither the on-device memory of GPUs
nor the RAM is capable of holding all parameters simultaneously during training. Therefore, LSML frameworks dynamically offload data to
NVMe storage and reload the information just in time.

In this paper, we investigate the security of NVMe offloaded data
in LSML against poisoning attacks and present *NVMevade*, the first
untargeted poisoning attack on NVMe offloads. NVMevade allows the
attacker to reduce the model performance, as well as slow down or even
stall the training process. For instance, we demonstrate that an attacker
can achieve a stealthy increase of 182% in training time, thus, inflat-
ing costs for model training. To address this vulnerability, we develop
NVMensure, the first defense that guarantees the integrity and freshness
of NVMe offloaded data in LSML. By conducting a large-scale study,
we demonstrate the robustness of NVMensure against poisoning attacks
and explore runtime efficiency and security trade-offs it can provide. We
tested 22 different NVMensure configurations and report an overhead
between 9.8% and 64.2%, depending on the selected security level. We
also note that NVMensure is going to be effective against *targeted* poisoning attacks which do not exist yet but might be developed in the
future.

Keywords: Large-Scale Machine Learning · NVMe Offload ·
Poisoning Attacks

1 Introduction

Machine Learning (ML) enables the extraction of knowledge from datasets,
which can then be utilized for prediction or classification tasks on unseen data.
Usually, increased model sizes and larger datasets result in a greater amount of
encapsulated knowledge in the ML model.

© The Author(s), under exclusive license to Springer Nature Switzerland AG 2024
G. Tsudik et al. (Eds.): ESORICS 2023, LNCS 14347, pp. 143–163, 2024.
https://doi.org/10.1007/978-3-031-51482-1_8

ML involving large Deep Neural Networks (DNNs), commonly known as Deep Learning (DL), produces models with multiple layers and numerous model parameters. With its capability to extract and encapsulate extensive knowledge, DL surpasses alternative methods across diverse domains, including image classification [22], speech recognition [15], text generation [5], language processing [9], as well as fraud and malware detection [11,17]. Scenarios, where the model and dataset exceed easily manageable sizes are referred to as large-scale machine learning (LSML).

Currently, there is a noticeable arms race focused on the size and capacity of large-scale machine learning (LSML) models. This trend can be observed from the development of models such as GPT [40] with 110 million parameters trained in 2018, followed by GPT-2 [41] (1.5 billion, 2019), Megatron-LM [53] (8.3 billion, 2019), Turing-NLG [25] (17.2 billion, 2020), and GPT-3 [5] (175 billion, 2020), which is currently utilized in the free version of ChatGPT [30]. However, the progression continues, with models like Megatron-Turing [54] (530 billion, 2022) and GPT-4 [6,31] (around 1 trillion, 2023) surpassing their predecessors and setting the trend for even larger models. Training such models is not feasible in standard ML environments like PyTorch [34]. Instead, specialized LSML frameworks like DeepSpeed [48] are employed. Additionally, optimized hardware such as NVIDIA DGX clusters [29] is necessary to provide the required computational power. Given the size of the models and the volume of data involved in training, LSML frameworks incorporate parallelism strategies to distribute the training process across multiple hardware instances and accelerators. This parallelism is crucial even in high-performance hardware setups. While performance is prioritized, the security aspects are neglected, which, as we show in this paper, leads to vulnerabilities to poisoning attacks [55].

Poisoning attacks come in two flavors: 1) *untargeted* attacks [19,61,62] strive to negatively impact the prediction performance of the model, while 2) *targeted* attacks [2,8,51] aim to embed trojan behavior into the model. Both attack versions can have visible effects on the final model or remain stealthy. As the size of models increases, it becomes easier to introduce stealthy poisonings since the inner workings of the model are often opaque. However, for those training LSML models, the trained models are valuable intellectual property, and the quality and security of the model predictions are of utmost importance. Improved performance translates to a competitive advantage, while reliable and secure predictions are vital for establishing trust in the technology's future use. Therefore, preventing or at least recognizing poisoning attacks is a necessary and critical step in LSML training, as such attacks can significantly impact both business value and end-user security. Ideally, countermeasures should focus on attack prevention rather than detection since eliminating poisonings may require costly model re-training on extensive hardware infrastructure [43].

Challenges and State-of-the-Art Solutions. The manipulation of the LSML training process by adversarial actors presents a significant challenge, leading to undesired model behavior and financial losses. These attacks encompass various vectors, including poisoned datasets, malicious code changes, and adversarial perturbations on communication channels. Efforts have been made to secure a significant portion of DNN training through technical measures. To ensure benign datasets, human experts or automatic filtering mechanisms [14,35,36] can eliminate potentially malicious data from the training set. Recent research, such as Slalom [57], Graviton [59], HETEE [64], and HIX [20], has proposed protection strategies for secure computation on GPUs and trustworthy code execution on CPUs [23,39]. These advancements help ensure that ML training, fueled by benign data, produces benign models. However, to generate models of maximal size, state-of-the-art LSML frameworks like DeepSpeed [48] employ techniques where idle portions of training data are temporarily offloaded to Nonvolatile Memory Express (NVMe) storage and reloaded onto the CPU or GPU for further training in a just-in-time manner [44,45,49]. While the offloaded data presents an attractive target for attacks on the training process, no previous work has explored the feasibility of such attacks or proposed defenses so far.

Contributions. To emphasize and address the aforementioned issue, this paper provides the following contributions:

- **Attack on NVMe Offloads:** We develop *NVMevade*, the first untargeted poisoning attack on NVMe offloaded data, highlighting the vulnerability of NVMe offload in LSML frameworks to such attacks. We present compelling evidence that our attack can effectively achieve the following outcomes, regardless of the structure of the offloaded data: i) Completely disrupt the training process, necessitating retraining. ii) Reduce prediction performance, resulting in a competitive disadvantage. iii) Slow down the training process without impacting prediction performance, leading to increased computational costs. We successfully implement NVMevade for the DeepSpeed framework, showcasing its ability to quickly terminate the training process, discreetly degrade model performance, and significantly prolong training time by 182%. These outcomes would inevitably lead to considerable financial losses within LSML setups.
- **Security for NVMe Offloads:** We present *NVMensure*, our defense mechanism designed to detect and mitigate poisoning attempts on NVMe offloaded data during training. This method exhibits resilience not only against untargeted poisoning attacks such as NVMevade but also against potential targeted attacks that may emerge in the future. NVMensure ensures the integrity and freshness of the data, providing protection against attacks such as NVMevade. Importantly, it allows the model creator to adjust the trade-off between security and training speed according to their specific requirements.
- **Large-Scale Study:** We have implemented NVMensure for the DeepSpeed framework and conducted a comprehensive evaluation of its runtime and storage efficiency. This involved assessing 22 different versions of the defense, allowing us to identify critical bottlenecks and propose enhancements. To mitigate runtime and memory overhead, we have leveraged space-efficient data structures and employed integrity mechanisms that provide various levels of collision resistance. By combining these methods with multi-core execution to utilize idle CPU resources, we have achieved an acceptable overhead ranging

from 9.8% to 64.2%, depending on the desired security level. Our optimizations effectively reduce the computational impact and storage requirements, while ensuring the defense remains highly effective.

NVMensure is orthogonal to previous works on securing CPU-based [23,39] and GPU-based ML workloads [20,57,59,64], and can be combined with them. Hence, NVMensure is a crucial component for enhancing the overall security of LSML.

2   Background

Below, we introduce the reader to DeepSpeed [48], the de facto framework for large-scale distributed ML training [24] before providing background information about poisoning attacks in ML.

Large-Scale Machine Learning with DeepSpeed. LSML models such as Megatron-Turing [54] would require more than ten terabytes of memory, surpassing the capacity of current GPUs.[1] Thus, LSML frameworks incorporate various forms of parallelism that enable the partitioning of data and computations across multiple hardware devices and accelerators. Thereby, data [44], pipeline [27], and model [53] parallelism strategies facilitate efficient computation during training by leveraging powerful hardware setups like NVIDIA DGX clusters [29]. However, with increasing model size, the limiting factor of training environments is not the computational power, but the GPU memory.

Addressing this problem, DeepSpeed [48], an open-source LSML framework developed by Microsoft in 2020, has become the industry standard for large-scale distributed ML [24]. DeepSpeed's pioneering NVMe offload capability has been key in achieving this milestone, enabling the training of large-scale models. Other frameworks focusing on one specific strategy, like model parallelism in Megatron-LM [53], lack the ability to train independently at such a scale. Hence, the project creators collaborated and integrated multiple methods, including Megatron-LM, into DeepSpeed. Offering ZeRO-Infinity [45], DeepSpeed resolves memory issues by offloading idle training data (model parameters, optimizer states, and gradients) from GPU and CPU to cost-efficient NVMe storage[2]. On-demand, the DeepNVMe [45] library prefetches and broadcasts the offloads to CPUs and GPUs as needed. In this paper, we propose NVMevade, an attack on NVMe offloads, and introduce NVMensure as a defense.

Poisoning Attacks in Machine Learning. Poisoning attacks on ML models [56,60] can be classified into two categories based on the adversary's objectives: Untargeted attacks and targeted (or backdoor) attacks. Untargeted attacks aim to hinder the convergence of the global model. As an example, an untargeted attack can assign false labels to samples in the training dataset. Alternatively, the adversary can also manipulate the code running the training process itself, e.g., by manipulating model parameters or intermediate values like gradients.

---

[1] A NVIDIA A100 GPU [28] provides 80 GB of on-device memory.
[2] NVMe is an interface specification for PCIe attached Flash and SSD storage devices.

The attacker can choose to completely destroy the model or employ a stealthy approach that reduces the model's accuracy or slows down the training process, thereby increasing computational effort. On the other hand, targeted or back-door attacks aim to introduce a backdoor trap into the model. These attacks typically consist of a trigger in the input data and a target prediction chosen by the adversary. The goal is to maintain the model's benign prediction performance while embedding the hidden malicious behavior.

Backdoor attacks often pose a higher risk since the resulting model surprisingly misbehaves, but in LSML high performance is a crucial competitive advantage making untargeted attacks also very attractive for adversaries. Both attacks can be cured by retraining or fine-tuning, but in LSML this involves high costs, making untargeted attacks a substantial danger. This paper conducts untargeted attacks in LSML by manipulating NVMe offloaded model parameters or intermediate values and proposes NVMensure as a defense method against both untargeted and targeted poisoning attacks.

3 NVMevade - Untargeted Poisoning Attack on NVMe

In this section, we introduce NVMevade, the first untargeted poisoning attack that manipulates NVMe offloaded data exposing vulnerabilities of current LSML frameworks. NVMevade offers three distinct operation modes that allow for the complete cessation of the training process or the discreet degradation of model performance and training efficiency through techniques such as bit-flips or replay attacks on NVMe-offloaded data.

3.1 System Model

Figure 1 provides a visualization of an LSML setup, illustrating the four general steps of an LSML training process. It also demonstrates the scope of NVMevade (and NVMensure), as well as their integration with related works, offering comprehensive end-to-end security for LSML training.

Considered System. We consider a general LSML training process as depicted in Fig. 1 and consisting of four steps: 1) The training data is supplied to the computation device, typically a server equipped with CPUs and RAM. 2) During training, certain computations are subsequently offloaded to GPUs for accelerated processing. This involves copying model parameters to the GPUs' on-device memory. 3) When the GPU memory is fully utilized, causing it to become the system bottleneck, the LSML framework addresses this issue by offloading idle portions of the model parameters and training-internal intermediate values to separate files in NVMe storage so that upcoming computations can be conducted on the GPUs. 4) When needed for ongoing model training, the framework loads offloaded data back onto the GPU.

Attackers Goals and Capabilities. The attacker targets model creators that possess enough data to train a LSML model. Thereby, he strives to negatively impact the training process by manipulating the data offloaded to the

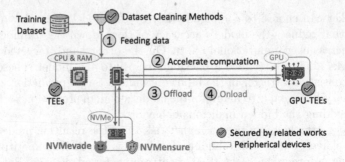

Fig. 1. LSML system overview depicting NVMevade's and NVMensure's scope. Parts of the system can be secured by related works (cf. Sect. 5).

NVMe. Specifically, depending on the concrete goal, one of the following three effects should be triggered by conducting perturbations on the offloaded data: (i) destruction of the model performance or termination of the training process, (ii) stealthy model performance reduction, or (iii) stealthy slowdown of the training speed. These objectives should be accomplished solely through user-level access[3] to the NVMe offloaded data, without requiring access to the CPU, RAM, or other peripheral devices involved in the training process, such as GPUs. The attack needs to be conducted in the timing window between offload and onload of the respective data.

3.2 Design of NVMevade

In Fig. 2, we illustrate the design of NVMevade, which comprises four steps: 1) The attacker conducts a thorough scan of the NVMe storage to identify new offloads. Thereby, LSML frameworks store different parameters in separate files. 2) The adversary loads the newly offloaded data from the NVMe to his own RAM, then 3) poisons the data by using one of the three possible strategies, which we will describe below as *poisoning modes*. 4) Finally, the original data on the NVMe are replaced with the poisoned version.

Poisoning Modes. Depending on the effect that the attacker wants to trigger, NVMevade offers three modes, as can be retraced in Fig. 2:

- *Mode 1: Model Destruction.* This mode applies multiple random bit-flips to the NVMe offloaded data, aiming to transform the model into a naïve classifier or halt the learning process altogether. In mode 1, where all bytes are aggressively poisoned, NVMevade is agnostic to the particular LSML framework implementation and does not consider any knowledge of data types or formats.

---

[3] We posit that the attacker has effectively circumvented OS access controls, thus obtaining necessary user-level permissions to access and manipulate NVMe files.

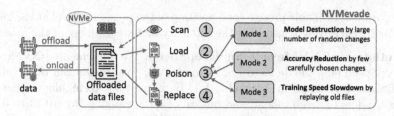

Fig. 2. Overview of NVMevade.

- *Mode 2: Accuracy Reduction.* To reduce the prediction performance without interrupting the training process or producing any noticeable traces for the model creator, mode 2 applies a reduced (in comparison to mode 1) number of bit-flips at the byte level. To achieve a trade-off between reduction performance and stealthiness, the attacker parameterizes the attack by defining parameters (cf. Appendix Table 6) that specify the level of poisoning. Thereby, the type of offloaded parameters is considered, making it the only part of the paper which is not agnostic to DeepSpeed.
- *Mode 3: Training Speed Slowdown.* Conducting a replay attack allows an attacker to slow down the training process while remaining stealthy to the model creator. By capturing offloaded data and replaying them later on, more realistic poisoned data are loaded from the NVMe, exerting a negligible effect on the model performance.[4] The data is replaced at the granularity of files and without consideration of exact file contents, thus remaining agnostic to the implementation of any particular LSML framework.

Among the three modes, mode 1 is very effective but can be detected by monitoring. Further, countermeasures like backups can minimize negative effects. While mode 1 already highlights the vulnerability of NVMe offloads, modes 2 and 3 pose a higher risk in real-world scenarios, due to their stealthiness.

Parameter Configurations. To poison the offloads in mode 1 and 2, we apply bit-flips using a random mask and XOR operation. Six parameters listed in Appendix Table 6 control the extent of poisoning. Namely, for each file, we traverse all bytes considering only a portion of those bytes with respect to P_1. Then, since DeepSpeed is configured with float16 parameters, we check if the actual byte is the upper or lower half of the parameter. For each of the bytes (upper or lower), we decide on the amount of poisoning based on the probability in P_2 and P_3 and start by poisoning the least significant bits (LSBs) of the byte to reduce the influence in the final parameter. For example, in the case of 25% for P_3, the two LSBs of the upper byte are combined with a random mask. When poisoning a byte, we increase a respective counter for upper or lower bytes and stop poisoning upper or lower bytes if a respective threshold ($P4$ and $P5$) is surpassed. Finally, P_6 limits the time window of poisoning data at a stretch.

---

[4] The replay attack naturally also affects the model performance, but the effect was very marginal and not recognizable in our experiments.

These parameters enable precise configuration of the poisoning level at the lowest granularity, effectively controlling the intensity and stealthiness of the attack.

Instantiation of NVMevade for DeepSpeed. We implemented NVMevade for DeepSpeed [48], the de facto LSML framework. We present our observations and challenges in detail in Appendix A.1. Here, we want to highlight, that the timing window between offload and onload of data, ranging from 0.33 to 0.95 s (average of 0.37 s) in our experiments, was sufficient to conduct the attacks and hence did not pose a technical obstacle.

3.3   Evaluation

To efficiently test our approaches, we simulate the NVMe offload of LSML training in a small-scale setup. Specifically, we used a server with 32GB RAM running Ubuntu 20.04 equipped with a single Nvidia Quadro P2200 GPU with 5GB GPU memory and a Western Digital 256 GB NVMe. As LSML framework, Deep-Speed [48] is leveraged to train a T5-small [42] model on translation tasks using the wmt16 (ro-en) dataset [4]. The AdamW optimizer and DeepSpeed's WarmupLR learning rate scheduler were used together with float16 mixed precision training and ZeRO-Infinity [45], which enables the NVMe offload.

Metrics. LSML models are predominantly language models in present times. To evaluate the performance of these models, we assess their prediction accuracy on a test set, indicated by the loss (e.g., cross-entropy) computed through the forward path on the test data. A lower loss value signifies better model performance and quality. The sacreBLEU score [38] is a computationally efficient and highly comparable version of BLEU, widely used for automatic machine translation evaluation. It demonstrates a strong correlation with human evaluations, where a score of 100 represents a perfect prediction and a score of 0 indicates a complete mismatch. Regarding the training speed, one can analyze the training samples per second (SPS), that are processed by the ML system. Further, the seconds per epoch (SPE) indicates the duration for one iteration over the training dataset.

Mode 1: Model Destruction. To conduct mode 1 attacks, we set all parameters to a maximum as listed in Appendix Table 6, resulting in the highest level of poisoning, meaning that all offloaded bytes were randomly changed. Once the attack started, DeepSpeed was faced with overflows resulting in skipping of the optimizer step and a complete stop within a few skips, in our case 15. Therefore, all previously unsaved training steps are lost. If we switch off DeepSpeed's internal overflow skipping procedure, the model becomes naïve within a few optimizer steps. Hence, depending on the internals of the LSML framework, NVMevade's mode 1 destroys the model or, in the case of DeepSpeed, stops the entire training procedure, showing the vulnerability of NVMe offloaded data.

Mode 2: Accuracy Reduction. To achieve a stealthy model performance reduction, extensive fine-tuning of the parameters is required, which we list in Appendix Table 6. The parameters allow only minimal poisoning since even a small number of bit flips can cause massive damage to a model [63]. By executing the attack, we achieved a substantial increase in loss on the test set from 3.3 to 6.8615 and a drastic reduction in the sacreBLEU score [38] from 23.9 to 0.0199, indicating a near-complete mismatch in all predictions. However, by modifying random seed of our test setup, which impacts the ML process and NVMevade, we observed a reduced influence of the attack. This resulted in a loss of 3.9932 and a sacreBLEU score of 5.8927 and shows, that the manual fine-tuning of the parameters is very sensitive as no continuous schema could be identified so far. Simultaneously to the attack, no recognizable warning being a sign for an attack was produced by DeepSpeed[5], thus increasing the stealthiness compared to mode 1, where DeepSpeed stopped the training process. However, since the model performance is reduced, loss and accuracy values calculated during training would be conspicuous. Our findings illustrate the potential to degrade model performance during training without interrupting the process. However, selecting suitable parameters is nontrivial. It necessitated 35 fine-tuning steps to identify optimal parameters for a successful stealthy attack. Merely reducing noise in mode 1 proved insufficient and resulted either in model destruction or had no impact making a more complex strategy necessary. While future research might propose advanced poisoning strategies to prevent expensive parameter fine-tuning, our defense, NVMensure, guards against all such variations. Consequently, further exploration in this area is not pursued.

Mode 3: Training Speed Slowdown. To conduct this attack, NVMevade caches offloaded files and as soon as the scanning procedure of NVMevade reports a subsequent NVMe offload with the same file name, the data are replaced with the historical file, thus resulting in a replay attack. Thereby, we could reduce the samples per second (SPS) from 11.802 to 8.910, leading to a total training time for one epoch being 03:44 min instead of 02:49. As visualized in Table 1, the training efficiency was reduced by 24.5% and the resources for training are leveraged for 32.5% longer. We discovered that our attack faced challenges with the timing constraint, specifically the time between offload and onload. In certain cases, the replay attack was not executed quickly enough. Consequently, we shifted our focus to model parameters based on the offloaded file name, as intermediate training parameters with the same name were often not offloaded twice, leaving no opportunity for a replay attack. Thus, we could worsen those rates by only attacking model parameters to a 69.4% decrease in SPS and 182% increased training time, which could lead to substantial financial losses for model creators. Further, mode 3 addresses the downsides of mode 2, since neither loss nor sacreBLEU score were affected significantly and no visible clues could be detected in DeepSpeed's console output making the attack completely stealthy.

In summary, NVMevade successfully poisons NVMe offloaded data, enabling aggressive or stealthy attacks that reduce training time and model performance. These outcomes lead to financial losses for the model creator, underscoring the importance of prevention in real-world setups.

---

[5] For stealthiness evaluation, we compared the execution log (console output) with and without attack. We only found different timestamps and minimal loss value changes, which is normal in different runs.

Table 1. Effectiveness of NVMevade's mode 3.

	SPS	SPE (in minutes)	Loss	sacreBLEU
Without attack	11.802	02:49	3.3812	23.9366
NVMevade mode 3	8.910	03:44	3.3812	23.9366
	(−24.5%)	(+32.5%)	(±0%)	(±0%)
NVMevade mode 3	3.607	09:14	3.3812	23.9366
(only model parameters)	(−69.4%)	(+182%)	(±0%)	(±0%)

4 NVMevade - Preventing Poisoning Attacks on NVMe

In this section, we present NVMensure, a new defense mechanism designed to counteract poisoning attacks (both targeted and untargeted) on NVMe offloads in LSML. This defense adopts the same system model as described in Sect. 3.1. NVMensure guarantees data integrity by performing checksum calculations during offload and subsequent validation during onload. Additionally, NVMensure ensures freshness by promptly invalidating checksums after validation. To accommodate diverse requirements, NVMensure offers the flexibility to balance security with storage and runtime efficiency. This is achieved through the implementation of various integrity mechanisms for checksum calculation and the utilization of space-efficient data structures.

4.1 Design of NVMensure

As depicted in Fig. 3, NVMensure is comprised of eight distinct steps, which are divided between offload and onload: 1) When DeepSpeed initiates an offload, NVMensure carries out a data integrity mechanism (DIM) to compute a checksum (CS). 2) This checksum is then inserted into a data structure (DS) residing in the RAM. 3) The regular offload to the NVMe continues thereafter. 4) Once DeepSpeed triggers an onload, a second checksum is created from the data

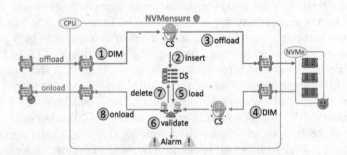

Fig. 3. Overview of NVMensure. A data integrity mechanism (DIM) computes checksums (CSs) which are stored in a data structure (DS) on the RAM during offload and validated during onload.

Table 2. NVMensure's data structures.

	Advantages	Disadvantages
DS_1: List	- No False Positives - **Most secure**	- Linear increase of size - Potential bottleneck when scaling up
DS_2: Bloom Filter [3]	- Constant size - Simple implementation - Most size efficient	- No element deletion resulting in a high false positive rate (FPR)
DS_3: Counting Bloom Filter [16]	- Constant size - Allows deletion of elements - Lower FPR than DS_2 due to deletion of elements	- Less size efficient than DS_2 - Low FPR
DS_4 Cuckoo Filter [12]	- Constant size - **More size efficient than DS_3** - Allows deletion of elements - Lower FPR than DS_2 (deletion)	- Less size efficient than DS_2 - Low FPR

loaded from the NVMe. 5) The checksum associated with the respective offload is retrieved from the data structure. 6) Both checksums are compared, and if they differ, an alarm is raised.[6] This ensures integrity, as only valid checksums are present within the data structure. 7) The checksum corresponding to the offload is immediately removed from the data structure, ensuring freshness, as the utilized checksum becomes invalid on removal. 8) The validated data is utilized for training purposes.

Storage-Efficient Data Structures. In LSML setups, where multiple gigabytes of data are offloaded, the size of the data structure holding the checksums can present challenges and become a bottleneck for the system. To mitigate this issue and to optimize the memory usage of NVMensure, the defender has the option to select from four different data structures, which are listed with advantages and disadvantages in Table 2. Our baseline, offering the highest level of security, is a straightforward list (DS_1). The remaining three alternatives consist of space-efficient probabilistic data structures, which reduce the memory requirements, but sacrifice some security since they introduce a false positive rate (FPR) dependent on the number of elements they store. Thereby, the Cuckoo Filter [12] (DS_4) poses the fastest alternative with minimal security sacrifices.

Runtime-Efficient Integrity Mechanisms. Like any other security mechanism, NVMensure introduces additional overhead. To balance runtime efficiency and security, the defender is provided with a choice of five different integrity mechanisms, each offering varying levels of collision resistance and computational complexity. All of these considered mechanisms require the attacker to adapt their perturbations in a manner that results in a checksum collision with

---

[6] In our experiments the training then stopped. Certainly, real-world scenarios can roll back to a certain checkpoint and continue training automatically.

Table 3. NVMensure's data integrity mechanisms.

	Advantages	Disadvantages
DIM_1 BLAKE2bp [1]	- **SHA-3 security standard** - High-performance (multi-threaded)	- New and unestablished
DIM_2 SHA-256 [13]	- Collision resistant hash function - More established than DIM_1	- Computationally complex - Some vulnerabilities known
DIM_3 MD5 [50]	- Simplicity & wide adaption - Runtime efficiency	- Less secure than DIM_1 & DIM_2 - Collision & preimage attacks
DIM_4 CRC-32 [37]	- Simplicity & cross-domain adaption - Faster than DIM_1 - DIM_3	- Limited error detection - Not designed for intentional attacks
DIM_5 LRC [18]	- Most simple solution - **Fastest solution**	- Designed for consecutive errors - Lowest security level

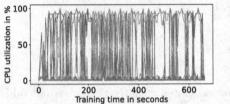 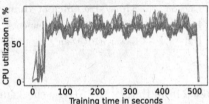

Fig. 4. Comparison of the CPU utilization per core for BLAKE2bp. One color represents one CPU core. On the left, one BLAKE2bp instance runs on a single thread, on the right eight instances are processed by eight threads. The multi-threaded version improves resource utilization by leveraging idle CPU cores.

the benign data, to execute a successful and covert attack. The feasibility of achieving this task depends on the chosen mechanism and the time window the offloads reside on the NVMe, typically spanning only a few seconds. Therefore, to encompass the full spectrum of the trade-off, it is reasonable to also consider algorithms that do not provide formal collision resistance. Such methods can still effectively detect poisoning attacks like NVMensure and offer the potential for significant performance advantages over more intricate approaches. We present a comprehensive overview of integrity mechanisms, along with their respective advantages and disadvantages, in Table 3. Among these mechanisms, BLAKE2bp [1] (DIM_1) stands out as the fastest collision-resistant option. On the other hand, while the Longitudinal Redundancy Check [18] (LRC, DIM_5) is the overall fastest version, it sacrifices a significant degree of security.

4.2   Instantiation of NVMevade for DeepSpeed

We implemented NVMensure inside DeepSpeed's DeepNVMe [45] library, utilizing efficient algorithm implementations for optimal performance. We present details in Appendix A.2. During our experiments, we found that the runtime is mainly affected by single-core CPU utilization. To address this, we implemented LRC as the fastest and BLAKE2bp as the most secure integrity mechanisms, leveraging multiple CPU cores. By splitting the offloaded data into equal segments and calculating checksums concurrently on different cores in different threads, we optimize the utilization of idle CPU resources and greatly enhance the performance of these versions. This positive effect can be observed in Fig. 4.

4.3 Evaluation

To assess the effectiveness of our defense, we utilize the identical experimental setup as in Sect. 3.3. To assess the performance of NVMensure, we conducted extensive benchmarking on all 20 combinations of data structures and integrity mechanisms. Additionally, we evaluated the two additional versions that leverage multi-core execution. During evaluation, we measure the runtime efficiency by analyzing the samples processed per second (SPS) and the duration of one epoch (SPE). The results are presented in Table 4 and discussed below. Additionally, we track the utilization statistics of the GPU, RAM, and CPU to identify any bottlenecks and to illustrate the impact of NVMensure on the system.

Table 4. Comparison of SPS and SPE to the baseline without defense, categorized by data structures and integrity mechanism, including the BLAKE2bp and LRCmulti-core versions (M-C).

Data Structure	Integrity Mechanism	SPS	SPE (in minutes)	SPS decrease in %
Without NVMensure		**11.802**	**02:49.45**	**0%**
List	BLAKE2bp [1]	3.233	10:18.55	72.6%
	SHA-256 [13]	2.457	13:22.58	79.1%
	MD5 [50]	1.160	29:17.00	90.1%
	CRC-32 [37]	3.826	08:42.67	67.5%
	LRC [18]	6.134	05:26.05	48.0%
	(M-C) BLAKE2bp [1]	**4.224**	**07:53.50**	**64.2%**
	(M-C) LRC [18]	**10.642**	**03:07.92**	**9.8%**
Bloom Filter [3]	BLAKE2bp [1]	3.128	10:30.88	73.4%
	SHA-256 [13]	2.491	13:22.85	78.9%
	MD5 [50]	1.124	30:14.00	90.4%
	CRC-32 [37]	3.816	08:44.07	67.6%
	LRC [18]	6.163	05:24.53	47.7%
Counting Bloom Filter [16]	BLAKE2bp [1]	3.257	10:05.78	72.4%
	SHA-256 [13]	2.461	13:21.20	79.1%
	MD5 [50]	1.136	30:14.00	90.3%
	CRC-32 [37]	3.817	08:44.02	67.6%
	LRC [18]	6.175	05:23.90	47.6%
Cuckoo Filter [12]	BLAKE2bp [1]	3.254	10:14.69	72.4%
	SHA-256 [13]	2.460	13:21.72	79.1%
	MD5 [50]	1.115	30:42.00	90.5%
	CRC-32 [37]	3.806	08:45.42	67.7%
	LRC [18]	6.153	05:25.04	47.8%

Storage Efficiency. We did not observe significant differences in RAM utilization, hence the choice of data structure should be based primarily on its security. The reason for this is that in our small-scale setup, a relatively small amount of files is created on the NVMe and reused for subsequent offloads of the same parameter. We, anticipate that the data structure choice will significantly impact RAM memory usage when scaling up, potentially becoming a bottleneck.

Runtime Efficiency. Analyzing the measurements presented in Table 4, we observe that the runtime impact of the data structure used is negligible. For instance, the decrease in SPS for BLAKE2bp across different data structures is consistently around 3.2, with values of 3.233, 3.128, 3.257, and 3.254 for DIM_1, DIM_2, DIM_3, and DIM_4, respectively. This pattern is similarly observed for all other integrity mechanisms. However, within each data structure, significant efficiency differences can be observed among different integrity mechanisms. For instance, in the case of the list data structure, LRC achieved a speed of 6.134 SPS, making it 5.28 times faster than MD5 with 1.160 SPS and 1.98 times faster than BLAKE2bp with 3.233 SPS. LRC emerged as the fastest integrity mechanism, while MD5 exhibited the slowest performance. Notably, MD5 was even slower than SHA-256 due to our utilization of a kernel implementation for SHA-256. These findings highlight that, depending on the desired balance between security and runtime efficiency, BLAKE2bp is the most sensible choice for prioritizing security, whereas LRC is preferable for maximizing performance. Furthermore, by introducing a multi-core execution of the integrity mechanism, we achieved significant runtime improvements for both algorithms. As a result, we observed performance enhancements ranging from 9.8% to 64.2%, depending on the desired level of security.

Security Considerations. To bypass NVMensure, an attacker must generate a collision on the integrity mechanism by providing modified NVMe offloaded data that produces the same checksum as the unmodified data. SHA-256 and BLAKE2bp are both highly collision-resistant cryptographic hash functions, rendering collisions infeasible, especially with regard to the tight time window. Our experiments reveal that data is typically residing on the NVMe between 0.33 and 0.95 s (with an average of 0.37 s). Therefore, BLAKE2bp is the optimal choice regarding security due to its exceptional collision resistance. Concerning LRC and CRC-32, generating collisions is achievable within polynomial time, which makes these integrity mechanisms only effective against unsophisticated attacks. Notably, within our experiments, the LRC version detected all NVMevade attacks, demonstrating its efficacy against unadapted attacks.

Probabilistic data structures involve a trade-off between storage efficiency and security, as indicated by the false positive rate (FPR). In our experiments, with a total of 12,548 NVMe offloads in one epoch, the Counting Bloom and Cuckoo Filters, capable of deleting outdated entries, stored up to 127 entries concurrently, resulting in FPRs of 0.02% and 0.0002%, respectively. However, the Bloom Filter lacks element deletion functionality and saved all 12,548 entries simultaneously, leading to a high FPR of 99.7% despite its 19,172-bit capacity. These FPRs show that using probabilistic data structures in NVMensure is acceptable, as long as they support element deletion, without significantly compromising security.

The data's freshness is guaranteed as each checksum remains valid only for a single validation process and is promptly invalidated by removing it from the data structure. Consequently, attempts to substitute new offloads with previously copied data are rendered ineffective, making replay attacks ineffective.

Scaling to Large-Scale Environments. Our experiments were conducted on a small-scale setup, as described in Sect. 3.3, due to limited access to expensive large-scale hardware. However, we anticipate that larger deployments will be more beneficial for our defense, as its runtime overhead will be reduced in larger systems. In large-scale setups, CPU power is typically not a limiting factor, unlike in our small-scale setup. Consequently, idle CPU resources in larger setups can be utilized to handle the additional computational effort required by our defense. This expectation is supported by observations we made when comparing DeepSpeed [48] with and without activated NVMe offload in our small-scale setup. In large-scale setups, NVMe offload improves computational efficiency and enables the use of larger model architectures. However, in our small-scale system, the runtime efficiency of NVMe-enabled version is reduced by 83.43%, as shown in Table 5, due to increased communication overhead and CPU load. Similarly, our defense introduces additional CPU load, suggesting a similar positive effect when scaling up. Regarding memory consumption, the choice of data structure is not critical in small-scale systems. However, when scaling up, the number of offloads and corresponding checksums within the data structure increases. This can become a bottleneck if using a data structure that grows linearly with the number of offloads, such as a list. Then, the Cuckoo Filter [12] is a suitable alternative as it reduces the memory footprint depending on the configuration. Generally, Cuckoo Filters aim to achieve false positive rates on the order of 1% or less. Moreover, the computational complexity of a list is $O(n)$ while that of a Cuckoo Filter is $O(1)$, demonstrating even better runtime efficiency.

Table 5. Small-scale setup comparison of DeepSpeed with and without offload.

	SPS	SPE (in minutes)
DeepSpeed without NVMe offload	71.239	00:28.07
DeepSpeed with NVMe offload	11.802	02:49.45
Impact	**−83.43%**	**+5926%**

5 Related Work

Below, we examine related works, including targeted poisoning attacks against as well as LSML frameworks and existing security methods for various components of an LSML system (cf. Fig. 1), outlining potential synergies with our research.

Targeted Poisoning Attacks. NVMensure has been specifically designed to ensure robust security against all types of poisoning attacks, including sophisticated targeted poisoning. Although no instances of such attacks on NVMe offloaded data have been demonstrated thus far, the potential for their development in future work exists. Techniques employed in cutting-edge methods like TBT [46], ProFlip [7], and T-BFA [47], which utilize bit-flips via Rowhammer [26], may be considered for adaptation. However, these white-box attacks require full model access and intricate architectural understanding. They are also offline attacks, which poison a DNN post-training by flipping key bits based on factors such as the model's loss. Adapting these methods for NVMe offloaded data is challenging due to the tight timing constraint and limited model access.

In contrast, NVMevade offers three variations of untargeted poisoning attacks during training, requiring control solely over offloaded model portions or training parameters, and demanding minimal ML expertise. Meanwhile, NVMensure effectively detects any modifications made to the NVMe offloaded data, offering protection against potential future targeted poisoning attacks that may emerge

Frameworks Powering LSML. DeepSpeed [48] has emerged as the leading LSML framework, thanks to its unique NVMe offload feature enabling training of giant models. Other existing projects and frameworks for LSML focus on parallelism strategies to distribute data and computation across hardware instances [24] but lack the NVMe offload feature. Many of these projects, such as NVIDIA'sMegatron-LM [53] for model, PipeDream [27] for pipeline, and ZeRO [44] for data parallelism, have been integrated into DeepSpeed.

Dataset Cleaning Methods. Benign models require poison-free datasets, leading to the use of filtering-based approaches for reactive defense against data poisoning attacks.[7] Outlier detection in the input space [35] is one such method, but also classification algorithms can be used to filter malicious samples [36]. For additional information, we direct the reader to [14].

Security of CPU and RAM. Several frameworks [23,32,39,58] secure the CPU-based training process by using a Trusted Execution Environment (TEE) like Intel SGX [10]. Another proposed solution is Perun [33], which relies on TMP [21] to attest the entire OS, ensuring trust also for accelerators. Albeit those approaches introduce overhead, advancements in CPU power and TEE memory capacity in next-generation hardware can address this bottleneck.

Secure Execution on GPUs. Several works have addressed secure ML computation offloading to GPUs. Slalom [57], enables outsourcing of linear model layer computation from a TEE to GPUs. Graviton [59], proposed for single-GPU setups, extends TEE security guarantees to GPUs, although some technical effort is needed to support multiple GPUs. HETEE [64] introduces a container running on separate trusted hardware to control access to untrusted accelerators, while HIX [20] modifies the GPU driver within a TEE to ensure trusted code usage.

Overall, the aforementioned methods are orthogonal to NVMensure and can be combined to create a comprehensive security architecture that protects all components of an LSML system. This technical effort exceeds the scope of this work but is possible for real-world scenarios.

---

[7] Since LSML models are normally trained on publicly available data that can be scrutinized by experts, dataset privacy is not a concern.

6   Conclusion

In this paper, we analyzed the security of large-scale machine learning (LSML) and recent advancements in securing distributed ML training. While security frameworks for CPU and GPU training exist, the NVMe offload mechanism introduced in DeepSpeed, which enables efficient GPU memory utilization and training of billion parameter models, lacked attention in terms of security.

In this work, we are the first to examine the security of NVMe offloads pointing out the vulnerable to untargeted poisoning attacks. To demonstrate this weakness, we propose NVMevade, which uses three distinct methods to exploit NVMe offloads and negatively affect model performance and training speed. To close the vulnerability, we propose NVMensure, the first defense against poisoning attack, targeted or untargeted, on NVMe offloads in LSML. We implement attack and defense for the DeepSpeed library, demonstrate the NVMensure's effectiveness, and explore security-performance trade-offs one can achieve when opting for various integrity protection methods and data structures.

Acknowledgment. We thank the Private AI Collaborate Research Institute which is co-sponsored by Intel Labs (www.private-ai.org) for partially supporting this research.

A   Instantiation for DeepSpeed

Below, we provide implementation details of our approaches for DeepSpeed [48].

A.1   NVMevade

Table 6 depicts the parameters of NVMevade for attack modes 1 and 2. Further, we want to report, that our scanning process confirmed that DeepSpeed offloads three types of data: model parameters, optimizer states, and gradients. Following, we provide additional information for the different attack modes.

Table 6. NVMevade's parameters for bit-flips in attack mode 1 and 2.

NVMevade's Parameters	Mode 1	Mode 2
P_1: Percent of poisoned bytes within each offloaded file	100%	0.0016%
P_2: Percent of poisonings within lower bytes of float16 parameters	100%	100%
P_3: Percent of poisonings within upper bytes of float16 parameters	100%	25%
P_4: Threshold of poisonings for lower bytes in percentage of the file	100%	0.0002%
P_5: Threshold of poisonings for upper bytes in percentage of the file	100%	0.0027%
P_6: Continuous poisoning time window	100%	100%

Mode 1 and 2. During the poisoning process via bit-flips, we simultaneously attacked all offloaded data. The most impactful perturbations were made in intermediate training parameters, namely gradients and optimizer states, leading to immediate gradient overflows. In benign training, DeepSpeed scales gradients using a scaling factor to address gradient underflows. However, in NVMevade's implanted overflow scenario, the current training step is skipped, the scaling factor is halved, and the training is halted. When the scaling factor reaches a configured minimum, the entire DeepSpeed process is interrupted with an exception, typically occurring within a few steps of malicious overflows. When adjusting the parameters for mode 2, the objective is to minimize the occurrence of overflows while ensuring a significant level of detrimental modifications, thereby preventing the training process from abruptly terminating.

Mode 3. Due to DeepSpeed's implementation of a basic sanity check on file sizes, adjusting file size might be necessary if a newly offloaded file with the same name but different size appears during replay attacks. The adjustment can be done via Python's truncate function to reduce size or zero-padding to increase it. Yet, our experiments didn't encounter this scenario.

A.2   NVMensure

NVMensure is implemented in C++ within the DeepNVMe [45] library. The runtime of integrity mechanisms varies depending on the implementation. MD5 and BLAKE2bp employ C++ reference implementations, while SHA-256 utilizes a highly efficient kernel implementation accessed through the kernel's crypto API. We implemented CRC-32 [52] and LRC [18] by ourselves in C++.

References

1. Aumasson, J.-P., Neves, S., Wilcox-O'Hearn, Z., Winnerlein, C.: BLAKE2: simpler, smaller, fast as MD5. In: Jacobson, M., Locasto, M., Mohassel, P., Safavi-Naini, R. (eds.) ACNS 2013. LNCS, vol. 7954, pp. 119–135. Springer, Heidelberg (2013). https://doi.org/10.1007/978-3-642-38980-1_8
2. Bagdasaryan, E., Shmatikov, V.: Blind backdoors in deep learning models. In: USENIX Security (2021)
3. Bloom, B.H.: Space/time trade-offs in hash coding with allowable errors. Commun. ACM **13**(7), 422–426 (1970)
4. Bojar, O., et al.: Findings of the 2016 conference on machine translation. In: Proceedings of the First Conference on Machine Translation (2016)
5. Brown, T., et al.: Language models are few-shot learners. In: NeurIPS (2020)
6. Bubeck, S., et al.: Sparks of Artificial General Intelligence: Early experiments with GPT-4. arXiv preprint arXiv:2303.12712 (2023)
7. Chen, H., Fu, C., Zhao, J., Koushanfar, F.: ProFlip: targeted trojan attack with progressive bit flips. In: IEEE/CVF ICCV (2021)
8. Chen, X., Liu, C., Li, B., Lu, K., Song, D.: Targeted Backdoor Attacks on Deep Learning Systems Using Data Poisoning. arXiv preprint arXiv:1712.05526 (2017)
9. Collobert, R., Weston, J.: A unified architecture for natural language processing: deep neural networks with multitask learning. In: ICML (2008)
10. Costan, V., Devadas, S.: Intel SGX explained. Cryptology ePrint Archive (2016)
11. El Merabet, H., Hajraoui, A.: A survey of malware detection techniques based on machine learning. IJACSA (2019)

12. Fan, B., Andersen, D.G., Kaminsky, M., Mitzenmacher, M.D.: Cuckoo filter: practically better than bloom. In: CoNEXT (2014)
13. Gallagher, P., Director, A.: Secure Hash Standard (SHS). FIPS PUB (1995)
14. Goldblum, M., et al.: Dataset security for machine learning: data poisoning, backdoor attacks, and defenses. IEEE PAMI 45(2), 1563–1580 (2022)
15. Graves, A., Mohamed, A.R., Hinton, G.: Speech recognition with deep recurrent neural networks. In: ICASSP (2013)
16. Guo, D., Liu, Y., Li, X., Yang, P.: False negative problem of counting bloom filter. IEEE Trans. Knowl. Data Eng. 22(5), 651–664 (2010)
17. Hilal, W., Gadsden, S.A., Yawney, J.: Financial fraud: a review of anomaly detection techniques and recent advances. Expert Syst. Appl. 193, 116429 (2022)
18. International Organization for Standardization: Information processing — Use of longitudinal parity to detect errors in information messages. ISO Standard ISO 1155, ISO (2001)
19. Jagielski, M., Oprea, A., Biggio, B., Liu, C., Nita-Rotaru, C., Li, B.: Manipulating machine learning: poisoning attacks and countermeasures for regression learning. In: IEEE S&P (2018)
20. Jang, I., Tang, A., Kim, T., Sethumadhavan, S., Huh, J.: Heterogeneous isolated execution for commodity GPUs. In: ASPLOS (2019)
21. Kinney, S.L.: Trusted Platform Module Basics: Using TPM in Embedded Systems. Elsevier (2006)
22. Krizhevsky, A., Sutskever, I., Hinton, G.E.: ImageNet classification with deep convolutional neural networks. In: NeurIPS (2017)
23. Le Quoc, D., Gregor, F., Singh, J., Fetzer, C.: SGX-PySpark: secure distributed data analytics. In: WWW (2019)
24. Mechanics, M.: What runs ChatGPT? Inside Microsoft's AI supercomputer | Featuring Mark Russinovich (2023). https://youtu.be/Rk3nTUfRZmo
25. Microsoft Research: Turing NLG: A 17 Billion Parameter Language Model by Microsoft (2021). https://www.microsoft.com/en-us/research/blog/turing-nlg-a-17-billion-parameter-language-model-by-microsoft/
26. Mutlu, O., Kim, J.S.: RowHammer: a retrospective. IEEE TCAD 39(8), 1555–1571 (2020)
27. Narayanan, D., et al.: PipeDream: generalized pipeline parallelism for DNN training. In: ACM SOSP (2019)
28. Nvidia: A100 GPU (2023). https://www.nvidia.com/en-us/data-center/a100/
29. Nvidia: DGX Systems (2023). https://www.nvidia.com/de-de/data-center/dgx-systems/
30. OpenAI: Chatgpt (2023). https://openai.com/research/chatgpt
31. OpenAI: GPT-4 Technical Report. arXiv preprint arXiv:2303.08774 (2023)
32. Orenbach, M., Lifshits, P., Minkin, M., Silberstein, M.: Eleos: ExitLess OS services for SGX enclaves. In: EuroSys (2017)
33. Ozga, W., Quoc, D.L., Fetzer, C.: Perun: Secure Multi-Stakeholder Machine Learning Framework with GPU Support. arXiv preprint arXiv:2103.16898 (2021)
34. Paszke, A., et al.: PyTorch: an imperative style, high-performance deep learning library. In: NeurIPS (2019)
35. Paudice, A., Muñoz-González, L., Gyorgy, A., Lupu, E.C.: Detection of Adversarial Training Examples in Poisoning Attacks through Anomaly Detection. arXiv preprint arXiv:1802.03041 (2018)
36. Peri, N., et al.: Deep k-NN defense against clean-label data poisoning attacks. In: Bartoli, A., Fusiello, A. (eds.) ECCV 2020. LNCS, vol. 12535, pp. 55–70. Springer, Cham (2020). https://doi.org/10.1007/978-3-030-66415-2_4

37. Peterson, W.W., Brown, D.T.: Cyclic codes for error detection. In: Proceedings of the IRE (1961)
38. Post, M.: A call for clarity in reporting BLEU scores. In: Proceedings of the Third Conference on Machine Translation: Research Papers (2018)
39. Quoc, D.L., Gregor, F., Arnautov, S., Kunkel, R., Bhatotia, P., Fetzer, C.: SecureTF: a secure TensorFlow framework. In: ACM/IFIP Middleware (2020)
40. Radford, A., Narasimhan, K., Salimans, T., Sutskever, I., et al.: Improving language understanding by generative pre-training. In: OpenAI (2018)
41. Radford, A., Wu, J., Child, R., Luan, D., Amodei, D., Sutskever, I., et al.: Language models are unsupervised multitask learners. OpenAI Blog (2019)
42. Raffel, C., et al.: Exploring the limits of transfer learning with a unified text-to-text transformer. JMLR **21**(1), 5485–5551 (2020)
43. Rajbhandari, S., et al.: DeepSpeed-MoE: Advancing Mixture-of-Experts Inference and Training to Power Next-Generation AI Scale. arXiv preprint arXiv:2201.05596 (2022)
44. Rajbhandari, S., Rasley, J., Ruwase, O., He, Y.: ZeRO: memory optimizations toward training trillion parameter models. In: SC 2020 (2020)
45. Rajbhandari, S., Ruwase, O., Rasley, J., Smith, S., He, Y.: ZeRO-Infinity: Breaking the GPU Memory Wall for Extreme Scale Deep Learning. arXiv preprint arXiv:2104.07857 (2021)
46. Rakin, A.S., He, Z., Fan, D.: TBT: targeted neural network attack with bit trojan. In: IEEE/CVF CVPR (2020)
47. Rakin, A.S., He, Z., Li, J., Yao, F., Chakrabarti, C., Fan, D.: T-BFA: targeted bit-flip adversarial weight attack. IEEE PAMI **44**(11), 7928–7939 (2022)
48. Rasley, J., Rajbhandari, S., Ruwase, O., He, Y.: DeepSpeed: system optimizations enable training deep learning models with over 100 billion parameters. In: SIGKDD (2020)
49. Ren, J., et al.: ZeRO-offload: democratizing billion-scale model training. In: USENIX ATC (2021)
50. Rivest, R.: The MD5 Message-Digest Algorithm. IETF (1992)
51. Saha, A., Subramanya, A., Pirsiavash, H.: Hidden trigger backdoor attacks. In: AAAI (2020)
52. Sarwate, D.V.: Computation of cyclic redundancy checks via table look-up. Commun. ACM **31**(8), 1008–1013 (1988)
53. Shoeybi, M., Patwary, M., Puri, R., LeGresley, P., Casper, J., Catanzaro, B.: Megatron-LM: Training Multi-Billion Parameter Language Models Using Model Parallelism. arXiv preprint arXiv:1909.08053 (2020)
54. Smith, S., et al.: Using DeepSpeed and Megatron to Train Megatron-Turing NLG 530B, A Large-Scale Generative Language Model (2022)
55. Tian, Z., Cui, L., Liang, J., Yu, S.: A comprehensive survey on poisoning attacks and countermeasures in machine learning. ACM Comput. Surv. **55**(8), 1–35 (2022)
56. Tian, Z., Cui, L., Liang, J., Yu, S.: A comprehensive survey on poisoning attacks and countermeasures in machine learning. ACM CSUR (2022)
57. Tramèr, F., Boneh, D.: Slalom: fast, verifiable and private execution of neural networks in trusted hardware. In: ICLR (2018)
58. Tsai, C.C., Porter, D.E., Vij, M.: Graphene-SGX: a practical library OS for unmodified applications on SGX. In: USENIX ATC (2017)
59. Volos, S., Vaswani, K., Bruno, R.: Graviton: trusted execution environments on GPUs. In: USENIX OSDI (2018)
60. Xia, G., Chen, J., Yu, C., Ma, J.: Poisoning attacks in federated learning: a survey. IEEE Access **11**, 10708–10722 (2023)

61. Xiao, H., Biggio, B., Brown, G., Fumera, G., Eckert, C., Roli, F.: Is feature selection secure against training data poisoning? PMLR (2015)
62. Yang, C., Wu, Q., Li, H., Chen, Y.: Generative Poisoning Attack Method Against Neural Networks. arXiv preprint arXiv:1703.01340 (2017)
63. Yao, F., Rakin, A.S., Fan, D.: DeepHammer: depleting the intelligence of deep neural networks through targeted chain of bit flips. In: USENIX Security (2020)
64. Zhu, J., et al.: Enabling rack-scale confidential computing using heterogeneous trusted execution environment. IEEE S&P (2020)

PassGPT: Password Modeling and (Guided) Generation with Large Language Models

Javier Rando[1](✉)(iD), Fernando Perez-Cruz[1,2](iD), and Briland Hitaj[3](iD)

[1] ETH Zürich, Andreasstrasse 5, 8092 Zürich, Switzerland
jrando@ethz.ch
[2] Swiss Data Science Center, Andreasstrasse 5, 8092 Zürich, Switzerland
fernando.perezcruz@sdsc.ethz.ch
[3] SRI International, New York, NY 10165, USA
briland.hitaj@sri.com

Abstract. Large language models (LLMs) successfully model natural language from vast amounts of text without the need for explicit supervision. In this paper, we investigate the efficacy of LLMs in modeling passwords. We present **PassGPT**, an LLM trained on password leaks for password generation. PassGPT outperforms existing methods based on generative adversarial networks (GAN) by guessing twice as many *previously unseen* passwords. Furthermore, we introduce the concept of *guided password generation*, where we leverage PassGPT sampling procedure to generate passwords matching arbitrary constraints, a feat lacking in current GAN-based strategies. Lastly, we conduct an in-depth analysis of the entropy and probability distribution that PassGPT defines over passwords and discuss their use in enhancing existing password strength estimators.

Keywords: Password Guessing · LLMs · Generative AI

1 Introduction

Passwords remain the authentication mechanism of choice despite the ever-increasing number of alternative technologies [36,45], primarily thanks to passwords being easy to deploy and remember. Furthermore, most applications rely on passwords as a fallback mechanism when other methods do not succeed. Considering their prevalence, password leaks [22,48] are one of the main threats institutions (and individuals) face. Not only do password leaks enable adversaries to break into systems, but they also make it possible to research and identify hidden patterns within human-generated passwords that guide the creation and refinement of effective password cracking tools [1,30].

Machine learning (ML) has played (and continues to play) a prominent role in extracting and learning meaningful features from vast password leaks,

Code and models can be accessed at https://github.com/javirandor/passgpt.

© The Author(s), under exclusive license to Springer Nature Switzerland AG 2024
G. Tsudik et al. (Eds.): ESORICS 2023, LNCS 14347, pp. 164–183, 2024.
https://doi.org/10.1007/978-3-031-51482-1_9

resulting in major contributions primarily towards two main areas of research:
(1) password guessing [24,25,31,33,34] and (2) password strength estimation
mechanisms [10,19,20,25,43].

Large Language Models (LLMs) have demonstrated tremendous effectiveness
in natural language processing (NLP) and understanding (NLU). These models
are based on the *Transformer* architecture; well-known examples include the
Generative Pre-trained Transformer (GPT) models [9,28], PaLM [13] or LLaMA
[42]. Given their recent success, we pose the following question: **How effectively
can *LLMs* capture the underlying characteristics and cues hidden in
the complex nature of human-generated passwords?**

To answer this question, we present and thoroughly evaluate an LLM-based
password-guessing model called **PassGPT**. Suitable for both password guessing and password strength estimation, PassGPT is an *offline* password-guessing
model based on the GPT-2 architecture [37]. Offline password guessing considers an adversary possessing a set of password hashes and not restricted by the
number of attempts, techniques, and resources. Tools and techniques that *intel-
ligently* reduce the guessing time in these settings become highly relevant. In this
vein, LLM-based approaches, such as PassGPT, can augment existing tools and
capture characteristics of human-generated passwords, reducing the (manual)
effort of domain experts. When compared with prior work on deep generative
models [24,33], PassGPT guesses 20% more *unseen passwords*, and demonstrates
good generalization capabilities to novel leaks. Moreover, we enhance PassGPT
with vector quantization [54]. The resulting architecture is **PassVQT**, which
can increase the perplexity of generated passwords.

Unlike previous deep generative models that generate passwords as a whole,
PassGPT sequentially samples each character, thus enabling the novel task of
guided password generation. This method ensures a more granular (character-
level) guided search space exploration, where generated passwords are sampled based on arbitrary constraints. Finally, PassGPT, in contrast with GANs,
explicitly represents the probability distribution over passwords. We show that
password probabilities align with state-of-the-art password strength estimators:
PassGPT assigns lower probabilities to more robust passwords. We also look
for passwords that can be easily guessed by generative approaches, even though
they are considered "strong" by strength estimators. We discuss how password
probabilities under PassGPT can be valuable for enhancing existing strength
estimators.

1.1 Contributions and Remarks

Given the nature of LLMs and the probabilistic nature of DL-based password
generation, we position ourselves in **offline password guessing**. Such a setup
is in line with prior work in the domain [17,24,31,34,35]. In these scenarios,
the adversary has one or more password hashes obtained from a target system
and their primary goal is to obtain the plaintext version corresponding to the
respective password/s hash [7]. In general, a powerful adversary can employ
a series of heuristics [2–4,17,29,46] using a combination of tools [1,30]. While

doing so, the adversary seeks to reduce the search space and avoid a worst-case scenario in which they must enumerate all potential guesses, i.e., brute-force.

In this work, we narrow down our experiments and comparisons to *deep generative models* for offline password guessing. We acknowledge the field is broader than that (e.g., Markov models and online guessing), but we restrict ourselves to comparable architectures. We aim to provide additional tools in the password-guessing landscape rather than establishing a default go-to architecture. We summarize our contributions as follows:

- We introduce PassGPT, an autoregressive transformer that obtains state-of-the-art results in password generation and generalization to unseen datasets.
- We show how PassGPT enables a novel approach to password generation under arbitrary constraints: *guided password generation*.
- We examine password probabilities under PassGPT and how they align with strength. We discuss how this metric could be used to improve current strength estimators.
- We present PassVQT, a similar architecture enhanced with vector quantization to increase generation perplexity.

2 Background and Related Work

In this paper, we make heavy use of LLMs and generative AI. In this section, we introduce the concepts relevant to generative models (Sect. 2.1) and *transformer* models (Sect. 2.2). We conclude by discussing progress in password guessing and strength estimation, focusing on works that use deep generative models (Sect. 2.3).

2.1 Deep Generative Models

Deep generative models are a class of deep learning (DL) techniques designed to *autonomously* grasp the characteristics underlying a set of samples from a distribution, i.e., training set, and to generate new samples from that distribution [21,41]. The primary distinction between the two major categories of generative models is how they represent probability distributions. Generative models can be either (1) implicit or (2) explicit. *Implicit* models do not estimate the training data distribution directly; instead, they learn a function that generates samples similar to the ground truth. Generative Adversarial Networks (GANs) [21] are the most notable example. *Explicit* models, on the other hand, explicitly model the underlying distribution of the training data that can be later accessed [40]. Our models fall under this second category.

Generative Adversarial Networks [21]. GANs consist of two main components: (1) a generator $G(\mathbf{z}; \theta_g) : \mathbb{R}^n \to \mathbb{R}^n$, a neural network that takes in random noise from a prior p_z and generates samples resembling the training data and (2) a discriminator $D(\mathbf{x}; \theta_d) : \mathbb{R}^n \to [0,1]$, also a neural network, trained to distinguish between training samples and outputs from the generator.

Both G and D are trained adversarially in a zero-sum game until the generator produces samples that are indistinguishable from real ones (see Eq. 1). GANs can approximate sharp distributions and generate high-quality samples without defining a likelihood function.

$$\min_G \max_D V(D, G) = \mathbb{E}_{\mathbf{x} \sim p_{\text{data}}(x)}[\log D(\mathbf{x})] + \mathbb{E}_{\mathbf{z} \sim p_z(z)}[\log(1 - D(G(\mathbf{z})))] \quad (1)$$

Autoregressive Generative Models (AGMs). These explicit generative models make it possible to sample from the target distribution. They do so by specifying a probability density function over the data and decomposing it into the product of conditionals via the chain rule of probability. These conditionals can be parametrized using neural networks with parameters θ that take as input the preceding entries in the sequence (see Eq. 2). Unlike implicit generative models, this definition makes it possible to train these models using *maximum likelihood estimation*. Our models match this definition.

$$p(\mathbf{x}) \approx p(\mathbf{x}; \theta) = \prod_{i=0}^{n} p(x_i | x_0, \ldots x_{i-1}; \theta) = \prod_{i=0}^{n} p(x_i | x_{<i}; \theta). \quad (2)$$

2.2 Transformers

Choosing the right neural network to model conditional probabilities in deep autoregressive models has received a lot of attention in recent research [8]. Two commonly used architectures are *recurrent neural networks* (RNNs) [39] and *transformers* [44]. Transformers are the most successful because of faster, more stable, and parallelizable training [44].

Transformers rely entirely on the attention mechanism [40] to model dependencies within the input sequence regardless of distance. The original transformer [44] consists of an encoder and a decoder, both comprising multiple layers of self-attention and feed-forward neural networks. The main difference between the encoder and the decoder lies in how they consume the input. The encoder uses all information in the input sequence to generate a latent representation for each token, while the decoder can only use information from previous tokens. Recent work has proposed using only the decoder for autoregressive language modeling, where words are generated conditioned only on previous ones. GPT models [9,37] have revolutionized NLP by relying solely on transformer decoders.

2.3 Related Work

This section focuses primarily on using deep generative models for *password guessing* and *password strength estimation*.

Password Guessing is a widely studied class of attacks [18,26], where the adversary either has a limited number of guesses (*online password guessing*) or is already in possession of a copy of the password hashes and needs to break them (*offline password guessing*). In both these scenarios, the adversary seeks to crack passwords before they run out of budget, i.e., the number of tries in an online service, or computing resources available for offline guessing.

The research community has explored different approaches to guessing passwords efficiently. Tools like Hashcat [1] or John the Ripper [30] employ heuristics, such as mangling-rules, dictionary attacks, association attacks, hybrid attacks, and more [2–5,29]. Further work in the domain has proposed and evaluated the use of Markov models [17,27], probabilistic context-free grammars (PCFG) [46], (deep) neural networks [14,25,32,35], or composition of techniques [53]. Our work focuses on the use of generative deep neural networks.

Deep Generative Models for Password Guessing. To the best of our knowledge, PassGAN [24] is the first work implementing generative models, in particular GANs, for password guessing. PassGAN uses the improved Wasserstein GAN (IWGAN) [23] to learn the underlying distribution of the RockYou password leak [51] and then evaluates the model performance on additional leaks like LinkedIn data [49]. Pasquini et al. [35] suggested an improved version of Pass-GAN by adding random noise to the input representation to improve training stability. Follow-up work has explored different architectures, obtaining similar results. For instance, PassFlow employs normalizing flows instead of GANs [31]. PassGPT is a contribution to this line of work. Unlike existing methods that generate passwords as a whole and do not explicitly model the password distribution, PassGPT leverages autoregressive language models to define an explicit distribution over passwords and enables the sampling of each character independently to match arbitrary constraints.

Password Strength Estimation aims to define a password robustness metric against guessing [11,43]. Similarly to password guessing, this has resulted in a variety of different approaches such as Markov models [12,16], PCFGs [46], or neural networks [25]. Our work uses the *lightweight* estimator zxcvbn [47], as recommended by Carnavalet et al. [11].

3   Experimental Setup

In Sect. 2.3, we introduced the central problem we are exploring: password guessing. This section presents the datasets (Sect. 3.1) and novel architectures (Sect. 3.2) used throughout our experiments.

3.1   Datasets

We chose datasets previously utilized in password guessing work and security research[1] that enable comparison of our techniques. The diverse characteristics of these password sets enhance the robustness of our evaluation and demonstrate generalization capabilities. Table 1 summarizes the key information about

---

[1] This work makes use of publicly available password datasets. We consider this practice to be ethical and consistent with prior security research, e.g., [24,25,35].

each dataset. The largest leaks that we consider for training are RockYou and LinkedIn, as done by previous work [24,31,35].

We split the previous datasets into training and test sets using the same approach as PassGAN [24] and follow-up work [35]. For RockYou, we take the list of all passwords of at most 10 and 16 characters, respectively. In this leak, passwords may appear more than once. We take 80% of this list as training data. From the remaining 20%, we keep as test data all passwords that are not contained in the training split, keeping only passwords with low frequency. The most commonly used password in the test set appears only 7 times in the entire leak. The average frequency of test passwords is 1.03. In comparison, the most frequent password in RockYou –123456– appears 290,731 times, and the average frequency in the entire leak is 2.28. This method allows us to test our model's generation abilities on low-probability passwords that were not seen during training.

Since the LinkedIn leak does not provide information about password frequency, we take 80% as training data and the remaining 20% for evaluation. We ensure that no password appears in both sets. Additionally, we define *cross-evaluation* test sets by removing RockYou training passwords from the LinkedIn evaluation set and vice versa to evaluate generalization to unseen distributions.

Finally, we also consider the MySpace, phpBB, and Hotmail [51] leaks as evaluation sets. We perform the analogous cross-evaluation procedure to remove RockYou and LinkedIn training data from all of them.

Table 1. Main facts about the datasets used in this work.

Name	Unique passwords	Year
LinkedIn [49]	60,505,270	2012
RockYou [50,51]	14,344,391	2009
phpBB [51]	184,318	2009
MySpace [51]	37,144	2006
Hotmail [51]	8,931	Unknown

3.2   Our Models

Transformers are a versatile and broad family of deep-learning models, as discussed above in Sect. 2.2. For password guessing, we are interested in autoregressive generative models (see Sect. 2.1). *PassGPT* and *PassVQT* model the probability of a character in a password, given the previous ones: $p(x_i|x_0,\cdots,x_{i-1};\theta)$. Sampling sequentially from this distribution can generate likely passwords. Our models operate over a vocabulary, Σ, comprising 256 ASCII characters.

Neural networks require a vector representation of tokens as input. We define a *tokenizer* as a function that maps every character σ in the vocabulary to an integer,

$$\text{tokenizer} : \Sigma \mapsto [0, |\Sigma| - 1]. \tag{3}$$

Then, a vector representation is created for each token σ using a one-hot encoding of its image under the tokenizer function. This results in a vector of dimension $|\Sigma|$, with all entries equal to zero and a single entry equal to 1 at position $\text{tokenizer}(\sigma)$.

PassGPT, depicted in Fig. 1, is an implementation of the GPT-2 architecture [38]. GPT models utilize the decoder component of transformers and are trained to predict the next token in a sequence autoregressively. To predict a specific character x_i in a password, the transformer decoder considers only previous characters $x_0, \ldots, x_{i-1}$ as input and outputs a latent vector with dimension d ($d = 768$ in our work). This latent vector is then mapped into a real vector of dimension $|\Sigma|$ through a linear layer and further transformed into a probability distribution over the vocabulary using the *softmax* function. The output distribution over the vocabulary represents $p(x_i|x_{<i}; \theta)$. This distribution is optimized using cross-entropy loss with respect to the one-hot-encoding representation of the true character found at that position.

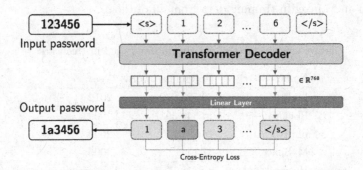

Fig. 1. *PassGPT* autoregressively predicts the input character at position n using all previous tokens. Green indicates correct prediction; red indicates incorrect. (Color figure online)

Once the network is trained, it provides us with a parameterized distribution over our vocabulary conditioned on previous tokens, namely, $p(x_i|x_{<i}; \theta)$. For generation purposes, we can start from the start-of-password token, <s>, and find $p(x_1|x_0 = \text{<s>})$. This assigns a probability to every character in our vocabulary to be the first token in the password. If we sample from this distribution, we can fix the first character and repeat the process to find the second one by computing $p(x_2|x_0, x_1)$. The sampling process for a password finishes when the end-of-password token, </s>, is sampled from the distribution at any given step. Unlike training, this process is sequential.

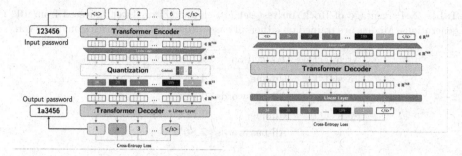

Fig. 2. Overview of PassVQT showing (left) an end-to-end model trained to compress passwords into a quantized latent space, where each code represents a fixed vector of dimension 768 and (**right**) an autoregressive GPT model that parameterizes the conditional distribution of indices. The latter is trained once the first one has converged and is required for generation. Transformer decoders in both models are independent.

PassVQT enhances the transformer architecture with vector-quantization of the latent space. In the computer vision domain, this has been shown to improve sample quality [54]. PassVQT follows the architecture designed by Yu et al. [54]. While modeling the same conditional distribution as PassGPT, we aim to assess whether quantization can provide additional benefits. In this architecture, depicted in Fig. 2, a transformer encoder maps each input token to a latent representation with a dimension of 768. This latent representation is then mapped to 10 dimensions using a linear layer and quantized using k-means and a codebook with N entries. The quantized 10-dimensional vectors are mapped back to 768 dimensions through a linear layer and serve as input to a transformer autoregressive decoder. This decoder is trained to reconstruct the input password character by character, using only the quantized representations for previous tokens.

Once the encoder-decoder network has converged, the model can reconstruct input passwords from a compressed quantized latent representation. If we model the distribution of latent codes, we can sample from it to produce a likely sequence of codes, which the decoder can then transform into likely passwords. For this, we train an autoregressive *codes model* over the quantized representation of the training dataset. During inference, we create new passwords by sampling sequences of codes from the *codes model* and transforming them into passwords using the original decoder. The encoder is no longer needed.

Training Details. We implement both architectures using the HuggingFace library [52] and inherit optimized hyperparameters from GPT-2. We find that performance increases with model size with diminishing returns. For PassGPT and both the PassVQT encoder and decoder, we use transformer models with 12 attention heads, 8 layers, and a latent space of 768 dimensions. Additionally, for PassVQT, a codebook size of 300 provides the best performance compared to smaller and larger alternatives. Both architectures are trained for 1 epoch with

Table 2. Percentage of RockYou test set (10 characters or fewer) guessed from 10^7 generations. Models are trained on either all passwords or unique entries from RockYou.

Architecture	Trained on	% Test set guessed
PassGPT	Unique	**4.25%**
	All passwords	0.53%
PassVQT	Unique	0.14%
	All passwords	**2.86%**

AdamW optimizer and a starting learning rate of 5e−5 with linear decay during training[2].

4   Evaluation

Our foremost contribution focuses on password generation. This section compares PassGPT and PassVQT with state-of-the-art deep generative models and demonstrates their generalization to different datasets without the need for further training. We also examine the probabilities and entropies of passwords under PassGPT to provide insights into its capabilities and modeled distribution. Finally, we analyze the alignment of these probabilities with password-strength estimators and discuss how they can be used to improve strength estimation.

4.1   Password Generation

For a fair comparison with PassGAN [24] and its improved version (PassGAN+) [35], we train PassGPT and PassVQT using 80% of passwords of at most 10 characters in the RockYou leak. The evaluation of the generation process is determined by the percentage of passwords from a disjoint test set that the models can generate. In this case, the test set comprises the unique passwords in the remaining 20% of the RockYou leak that are not in the training set.

We consider two variations of the training set: (1) unique passwords and (2) all occurrences. PassGPT demonstrates superior generalization when trained on unique passwords, as detailed in Table 2. Conversely, PassVQT experiences difficulty generating in-distribution passwords when trained on unique entries but significantly improves upon incorporating their absolute occurrences. We believe incorporating all password occurrences can yield a more robust quantization of latent representations for common patterns.

We sample increasingly large pools of password guesses from PassGPT (trained on unique passwords) and PassVQT (trained on all passwords) and calculate the percentage of the RockYou test split they recover. Results in Table 3 show that PassGPT outperforms all other models. It recovers 41.9% of the test

---

[2] We focus on the concept rather than on subtle performance gains. Further hyperparameter tuning is very costly and provides little value for this work.

set among 10^9 guesses, whereas state-of-the-art GAN models matched 23.33%. PassVQT performance surpasses that of the original PassGAN and stays close to that of the PassGAN improved version.

Table 3. Percentage of the RockYou test split (<10 characters) matched by samples from various models. PassGAN* stands for the improved PassGAN presented in [35]. Results for GANs were taken directly from original papers [24,35] and not reproduced. Last column is the union of 10^N guesses from both models to compare their overlap.

Guesses	PassGAN	PassGAN*	PassVQT	PassGPT	PassGPT ∪ PassVQT
10^4	0.01%	–	0.004%	0.01%	0.01%
10^5	0.05%	–	0.05%	0.05%	0.10%
10^6	0.38%	–	0.45%	**0.50%**	0.93%
10^7	2.04%	–	2.90%	**4.25%**	6.39%
10^8	6.73%	9.51%	10.30%	**19.37%**	22.70%
10^9	15.09%	23.33%	21.46%	**41.86%**	44.66%

Another important factor in password generation evaluation is the ability to generate novel and distinct samples. We compared the percentage of unique passwords generated by our models to those from PassGAN; results are shown in Fig. 3. PassGPT retains the highest percentage of unique passwords (60%), whereas PassVQT drops to 20% of unique passwords among 10^9 guesses. Since PassVQT was trained on all occurrences of passwords, common passwords are more likely to be generated under its distribution, reducing the number of novel passwords. PassGAN stays between them with approximately 40% unique entries.

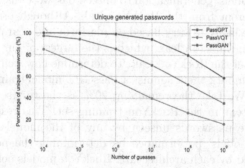

Fig. 3. Log-Linear plot of unique passwords generated by different architectures.

4.2   Generalizing to Longer Passwords and Unseen Distributions

Our models outperform state-of-the-art deep generative models in a common setup. To further evaluate the effectiveness of our models, we extend the modeling to longer passwords, which are more representative of real-world distributions. We train PassGPT and PassVQT on passwords with up to 16 characters (including longer passwords primarily increases entries that are difficult to guess). We again train the models using both unique and all occurrences of the data. PassGPT, as before, performs best when trained on unique samples. Surprisingly, PassVQT now obtains better performance when trained on unique passwords. After training on this new distribution, models retain similar accuracy. From 10^8 guesses, PassGPT and PassVQT recover 15.5% and 8.57% of the test set, respectively, compared to 19.37% and 10.30% in the 10-character setting. From now on, we will focus on 16-character models for a richer analysis.

Table 4. Percentage of passwords from the LinkedIn test split guessed. Columns indicate training distribution. The test set does not contain passwords in the RockYou training set.

Guesses	PassGPT		PassVQT
	RockYou	LinkedIn	RockYou
10^4	0.001%	0.001%	0.001%
10^5	0.012%	0.010%	0.012%
10^6	0.11%	0.10%	0.13%
10^7	1.03%	0.94%	1.10%
10^8	6.03%	6.80%	5.41%

To assess the models' generalization to unseen password distributions, we test them on leaks different from the RockYou leak. Although users tend to reuse passwords, they are likely to vary based on platform and year of creation [6,15]. We first analyze the LinkedIn leak, which is the largest of our samples and was obtained 3 years after the RockYou leak. To determine how well RockYou models generalize, we benchmark them against a PassGPT model trained solely on 80% of LinkedIn data. We take the remaining 20% as the test set after excluding any passwords present in the RockYou training set. This results in a test set of over 11M unique passwords unseen by any of the models during training. We evaluate the models' performance by determining the percentage of test passwords generated by each architecture. RockYou models achieve comparable results to the LinkedIn-trained PassGPT, as shown in Table 4, demonstrating the ability of autoregressive models to parameterize rich distributions that generalize beyond the training leak without the need for retraining.

Finally, we evaluate the RockYou and LinkedIn models to determine which training leak leads to a better generalization. The models are tested on three additional datasets: phpBB, MySpace, and Hotmail (refer to Sect. 3.1), after removing passwords present in either the RockYou or LinkedIn training sets. The results are shown in Table 5. RockYou models exhibit superior performance, with password recovery rates of 9.45%, 11.39%, and 7.22% from 10^8 guesses.

Table 5. Percentage of phpBB, MySpace, and Hotmail leaks generated by PassGPT trained on RockYou, compared with PassGPT trained on LinkedIn. Evaluation is performed on the entire leak after entries contained in the RockYou training set are removed.

Guesses	PassGPT trained on RockYou			PassGPT trained on LinkedIn		
	phpBB	MySpace	Hotmail	phpBB	MySpace	Hotmail
10^4	0.002%	0%	0%	0%	0%	0%
10^5	0.02%	0%	0.02%	0.008%	0%	0%
10^6	0.20%	0.22%	0.18%	0.10%	0.10%	0.05%
10^7	1.80%	2.06%	1.24%	0.77%	0.94%	0.61%
10^8	9.45%	11.39%	7.13%	6.02%	6.57%	4.67%

4.3 Guided Generation

We propose a novel approach to password generation: *guided password generation*. Unlike previous deep generative methods that generate passwords as a whole, PassGPT models each token separately, granting full control over each character. This allows the generation process to meet specific constraints. Some examples of these constraints are: password length, fixed characters (e.g., "a" at first position), and templates (e.g., four lowercase letters and two numbers). This can be achieved by restricting the sampling distribution $p(x_i|x_0, \cdots, x_{i-1})$ to consider only the probability mass assigned to a subset of interest $\Sigma' \subset \Sigma$; for instance, limiting Σ' to lowercase letters for the first four tokens. The resulting password generation is guided by these constraints while still likely under the modeled password distribution. Table 6 shows various templates and their corresponding generations produced by PassGPT.

Table 6. *Guided generation* examples from PassGPT. Templates formatted using l for lowercase, u for uppercase, d for digit, p for punctuation, and * for any character.

llllll	lllldd	ullppdd	uuuu**dd
orange	manb13	Nms__12	PARLA198
iluvma	sall89	Zac&&09	CELAN777
gikiyd	lowm12	Chl@(18	QWER1234

4.4   Probabilities and Entropies Estimates by PassGPT

One of the main advantages of autoregressive models is having access to an explicit representation of the modeled distribution. We exploit this property to provide further intuitions behind the PassGPT generation process.[3] The probability of a password is estimated as the product of the conditional probability for each sampled character, which is more conveniently represented as the log probability (Eq. 4). Furthermore, the entropy measures the uncertainty in the model for each token and is calculated according to Eq. 5.

$$\log_{10} p(\mathbf{x}; \theta) = \sum_{i=1}^{n} \log_{10} p(x_i | x_1, \ldots x_{i-1}; \theta). \tag{4}$$

$$H(X_i) = \sum_{x_i \in \Sigma} p(x_i | x_{<i}; \theta) \cdot \log_2 p(x_i | x_{<i}; \theta). \tag{5}$$

We computed the log probability and entropy for every position in all unique passwords (<16 characters) in the RockYou dataset using PassGPT. Examples of passwords with different probabilities under the model can be found in Appendix A. Figure 4a depicts the entropy distribution for characters found at specific positions in passwords of length 16. The entropy of the first character is slightly above five; it is constant since $p(x_1 | x_0 = \texttt{<s>})$ is equal across passwords. The median entropy decreases as we move towards the last positions because the model reduces uncertainty as more characters are observed. Figure 4b illustrates how the log-probability of passwords decreases with length, with the median log-probability dropping by approximately 1 unit for each additional character. This corresponds to an average probability of 0.1 for each new character.

We can analyze password probabilities under the model compared to brute-force search. Our vocabulary Σ contains 256 characters. Therefore, the log-probability of discovering a password of length 3 through brute force can be approximated as $\log_{10}(1/256^3) \approx -7.5$. This value is close to the median log-probability under PassGPT. However, the utility of generative methods becomes evident when we deal with longer passwords that are computationally infeasible to uncover through exhaustive search. For instance, the log-probability of successfully recovering a 16-character password using brute-force attacks is -38.5. In contrast, the median log-probability under PassGPT hovers around -18. This indicates that finding a 16-character password using PassGPT is approximately 10^{20} times more likely than relying on random guessing.

4.5   Discussion: PassGPT Vs PassVQT

We wrap up this section with a brief discussion about the main differences between PassGPT and PassVQT and when to use each of them. Details can

---

[3] For PassVQT, this is not possible, as the modeled distribution is in the codebook space, and different codes can lead to the same password generation.

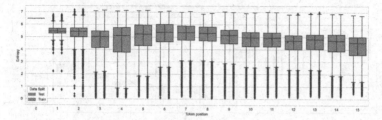

(a) Entropy distribution per token for passwords of length 16 under PassGPT.

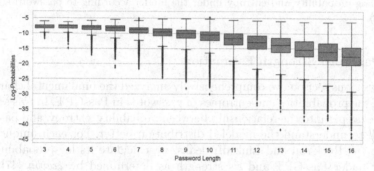

(b) Log-probabilities with respect to length for all passwords in RockYou.

Fig. 4. Entropy and log-probability of passwords in the RockYou leak under PassGPT

be found in Appendix B. These models can surpass state-of-the-art deep generative models and generalize to unseen distributions. Focusing on models trained on 16 characters, we can highlight several differences:

1. PassVQT generates longer passwords than PassGPT.
2. PassGPT guesses weaker passwords, while PassVQT matches stronger passwords.
3. PassGPT generates more unique passwords than PassVQT: 60% vs 20%.
4. PassGPT can generate passwords faster than PassVQT: 12h vs. 24h to generate 10^8 samples on 1 NVIDIA RTX3090.

All things considered, PassGPT seems better at modeling the actual leaked distribution and generating in-distribution samples. On the other hand, PassVQT is "more imaginative" and creates stronger passwords with a similar distribution to that of the leaked file. Nevertheless, the sampling process of both models can be tweaked to pursue specific goals. For instance, if we want to reduce out-of-distribution samples, we can perform top-k sampling for each character, considering only the most likely tokens under the model to avoid long-tail passwords. Similarly, to incentivize the generation of stronger and less likely passwords, we can increase the temperature of the *softmax* function or avoid sampling from the top-k most likely tokens.

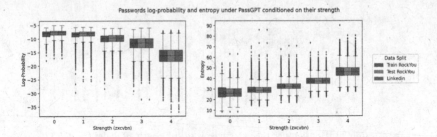

Fig. 5. Log-probability and entropy under the model according to password strength (zxcvbn)

4.6 Password Strength Estimation

In the previous section, we comprehensively analyzed the fundamental characteristics of the probabilities and entropies of passwords in PassGPT. In this section, we delve deeper into the relationship between probability, entropy, and password strength to understand the modeled distribution better. For each unique password in the RockYou and LinkedIn leaks, we calculate its log-probability and entropy under PassGPT and its strength as determined by *zxcvbn* [47]. This method assigns a score ranging from 0 (very weak) to 4 (very strong). The distribution of log-probabilities and entropies for each strength score is illustrated in Fig. 5. The results show that PassGPT assigns lower probability and higher entropy to stronger passwords, demonstrating that weak passwords are more likely in the modeled distribution.

Finally, we manually examine outliers in the distributions to better understand when PassGPT does not align with *zxcvbn*. Our analysis revealed three distinct phenomena where the model assigns low probabilities to passwords considered weak by *zxcvbn*. These examples are hard to model for PassGPT but easy to detect using dictionary attacks.

1. Pattern repetition. These passwords are composed of a sequence that is repeated several times. Examples: ":X:X:X:X:X:X", "qwertqwertqwert".
2. Replacement of characters in common words by similar symbols. A dictionary attack is successful in finding these passwords. Examples: "k1m83rly" (from "kimberly") or "r00sevelt" (from "roosevelt").
3. Reversed words. These can also be easily detected by *zxcvbn* but are unlikely under the model distribution. Example: "llabtooF" (from "Football").

On the other hand, there are very strong passwords, according to *zxcvbn*, that obtain high probabilities under the model. We can also identify predominant phenomena:

1. Passwords containing non-English words. *zxcvbn* tries to decompose them as English words unsuccessfully. For example, the password "teamomiamorcito" is formed by the Spanish words "te amo mi amorcito" ("I love you my love"). However, *zxcvbn* parses it as "team", "omi", "amorcito".

2. Love-related passwords. "iloveyou" is one of the most common passwords in RockYou. When analyzing passwords with strength 4 that obtained high probabilities, we found copious variations of it. Examples: "ilovematt4eva", "ilovetoby4eva", "ilovetyler4ever", "ilovehotmail", "iloveyousomuch". The suffixes "4ever" and "4eva" are very common among these passwords.

It is crucial for strength estimators to minimize the number of false negatives, i.e., classifying passwords that can be guessed by any existing technique as strong. Our analysis revealed instances of very strong passwords with high probabilities under PassGPT, indicating that they are likely to be discovered by such a model. We believe that incorporating the log-likelihood from generative models into existing password strength estimators could provide valuable supplementary information and improve the accuracy of these systems for high-stake scenarios.

5   Conclusions

In this work, we investigated the use of large language models to model password distributions without explicit supervision. We introduced two autoregressive architectures that model the conditional distribution of characters based on previous ones: PassGPT and PassVQT. PassGPT might be preferable because it provides access to an explicit probability distribution, is simpler, and provides faster generation. However, PassVQT might still be helpful for scenarios where we want to express more variability and generate more complicated passwords that are still close to the training distribution.

Advantages of autoregressive models over state-of-the-art GAN generators include *guided password generation* and access to an explicit probability distribution. We have analyzed how the log-probabilities of passwords under PassGPT align with their strength and how this metric could be used to mitigate limitations in strength estimators.

Overall, this work seeds many promising research directions in the field of password modeling using large language models that are to be explored by future research.

A   Passwords at the Quantiles of the Distribution

In Fig. 6, we illustrate passwords located at the quantiles of the probability distribution defined by PassGPT for different lengths.

B   PassGPT vs PassVQT

Table 7 illustrates how many passwords are guessed by each method conditioned on their strength. Figure 7 depicts a histogram of the length of passwords generated by each architecture. PassVQT generates longer and more difficult passwords, but PassGPT fits better the distribution of easy passwords, improving its overall performance.

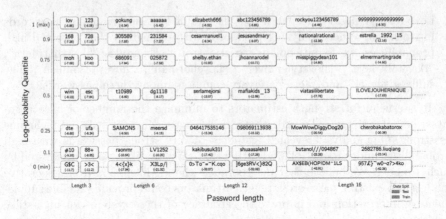

Fig. 6. Passwords in RockYou located at the quantiles of the probability distribution for different password lengths.

Table 7. Detailed statistics on the matched passwords by different models from Rock-You test set (<16 characters) depending on their strength.

Strength	Total	Guessed by			Not guessed
		PassGPT ∩ PassVQT	PassGPT	PassVQT	
0	2,035	41 (2.0%)	481 (23.7%)	28 (1.4%)	1485 (73%)
1	752,137	150,945 (20.1%)	111,704 (14.9%)	66,004 (8.8%)	423,484 (56.3%)
2	926,826	45,337 (4.9%)	50,704 (5.5%)	53,782 (5.8%)	777,003 (83.8%)
3	558,029	4,501 (0.8%)	7,831 (1.4%)	8,832 (1.6%)	536,865 (96.2%)
4	158,635	88 (0.06%)	194 (0.1%)	152 (0.09%)	158,201 (99.7%)
	2,397,662	200,912 (8.38%)	170,914 (7.12%)	128,798 (5.37%)	1,897,038 (79.12%)

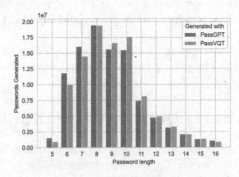

Fig. 7. Histogram of generated password length by each model on a subset of 10^8 samples.

References

1. Hashcat: Advanced password recovery. https://hashcat.net/hashcat/
2. Hashcat: Advanced password recovery - Attacks Wiki. https://hashcat.net/wiki/

3. Hashcat: Advanced password recovery - Mask attack. https://hashcat.net/wiki/doku.php?id=mask_attack

4. Hashcat: Advanced password recovery - Rule-based attack. https://hashcat.net/wiki/doku.php?id=rule_based_attack

5. Hashcat: Advanced password recovery - Slow candidates mode. https://github.com/hashcat/hashcat/blob/master/docs/slow-candidates-mode.md

6. Bailey, D.V., Dürmuth, M., Paar, C.: Statistics on password re-use and adaptive strength for financial accounts. In: Abdalla, M., De Prisco, R. (eds.) SCN 2014. LNCS, vol. 8642, pp. 218–235. Springer, Cham (2014). https://doi.org/10.1007/978-3-319-10879-7_13

7. Blocki, J., Harsha, B., Zhou, S.: On the economics of offline password cracking. In: 2018 IEEE Symposium on Security and Privacy (SP), pp. 853–871. IEEE (2018)

8. Bond-Taylor, S., Leach, A., Long, Y., Willcocks, C.G.: Deep generative modelling: a comparative review of vaes, gans, normalizing flows, energy-based and autoregressive models. IEEE Trans. Pattern Anal. Mach. Intell. **44**, 7327–7347 (2021)

9. Brown, T., et al.: Language models are few-shot learners. Adv. Neural. Inf. Process. Syst. **33**, 1877–1901 (2020)

10. de Carné de Carnavalet, X., Mannan, M.: From very weak to very strong: analyzing password-strength meters. In: Network and Distributed System Security Symposium (NDSS 2014). Internet Society (2014)

11. Carnavalet, X.D.C.D., Mannan, M.: A large-scale evaluation of high-impact password strength meters. ACM Trans. Inf. Syst. Secur. (TISSEC) **18**(1), 1–32 (2015)

12. Castelluccia, C., Dürmuth, M., Perito, D.: Adaptive password-strength meters from markov models. In: NDSS (2012)

13. Chowdhery, A., et al.: Palm: scaling language modeling with pathways. arXiv preprint arXiv:2204.02311 (2022)

14. Ciaramella, A., D'Arco, P., De Santis, A., Galdi, C., Tagliaferri, R.: Neural network techniques for proactive password checking. IEEE Trans. Depend. Secure Comput. **3**(4), 327–339 (2006)

15. Das, A., Bonneau, J., Caesar, M., Borisov, N., Wang, X.: The tangled web of password reuse. In: NDSS, vol. 14, pp. 23–26 (2014)

16. Dell'Amico, M., Michiardi, P., Roudier, Y.: Password strength: an empirical analysis. In: 2010 Proceedings IEEE INFOCOM, pp. 1–9. IEEE (2010)

17. Dürmuth, M., Angelstorf, F., Castelluccia, C., Perito, D., Chaabane, A.: OMEN: faster password guessing using an ordered markov enumerator. In: Piessens, F., Caballero, J., Bielova, N. (eds.) ESSoS 2015. LNCS, vol. 8978, pp. 119–132. Springer, Cham (2015). https://doi.org/10.1007/978-3-319-15618-7_10

18. Feldmeier, D.C., Karn, P.R.: UNIX password security - ten years later. In: Brassard, G. (ed.) CRYPTO 1989. LNCS, vol. 435, pp. 44–63. Springer, New York (1990). https://doi.org/10.1007/0-387-34805-0_6

19. Golla, M., Beuscher, B., Dürmuth, M.: On the security of cracking-resistant password vaults. In: Proceedings of the 2016 ACM SIGSAC Conference on Computer and Communications security, pp. 1230–1241 (2016)

20. Golla, M., Dürmuth, M.: On the accuracy of password strength meters. In: Proceedings of the 2018 ACM SIGSAC Conference on Computer and Communications Security, pp. 1567–1582 (2018)

21. Goodfellow, I., et al.: Generative adversarial nets. In: Advances in Neural Information Processing Systems, vol. 27. Curran Associates, Inc. (2014). https://proceedings.neurips.cc/paper/2014/file/5ca3e9b122f61f8f06494c97b1afccf3-Paper.pdf

22. Greenbag, A.: Hackers are passing around a megaleak of 2.2 billion records (2019). https://www.wired.com/story/collection-leak-usernames-passwords-billions/
23. Gulrajani, I., Ahmed, F., Arjovsky, M., Dumoulin, V., Courville, A.C.: Improved training of wasserstein gans. Adv. Neural Info. Process. Syst. **30** (2017)
24. Hitaj, B., Gasti, P., Ateniese, G., Perez-Cruz, F.: PassGAN: a deep learning approach for password guessing. In: Dèng, R.H., Gauthier-Umaña, V., Ochoa, M., Yung, M. (eds.) ACNS 2019. LNCS, vol. 11464, pp. 217–237. Springer, Cham (2019). https://doi.org/10.1007/978-3-030-21568-2_11
25. Melicher, W., Ur, B., Segreti, S.M., Komanduri, S., Bauer, L., Christin, N., Cranor, L.F.: Fast, lean, and accurate: modeling password guessability using neural networks. In: 25th USENIX Security Symposium (USENIX Security 16), pp. 175–191 (2016)
26. Morris, R., Thompson, K.: Password security: a case history. Commun. ACM **22**(11), 594–597 (1979)
27. Narayanan, A., Shmatikov, V.: Fast dictionary attacks on passwords using time-space tradeoff. In: Proceedings of the 12th ACM Conference on Computer and Communications Security, pp. 364–372 (2005)
28. OpenAI: Chatgpt: Optimizing language models for dialogue (2022). https://openai.com/blog/chatgpt/
29. Openwall: John the ripper markov generator. https://openwall.info/wiki/john/markov
30. Openwall: John the ripper password cracker. https://www.openwall.com/john/
31. Pagnotta, G., Hitaj, D., De Gaspari, F., Mancini, L.V.: PassFlow: Guessing passwords with generative flows. In: 2022 52nd Annual IEEE/IFIP International Conference on Dependable Systems and Networks (DSN). pp. 251–262. IEEE (2022)
32. Pal, B., Daniel, T., Chatterjee, R., Ristenpart, T.: Beyond credential stuffing: password similarity models using neural networks. In: 2019 IEEE Symposium on Security and Privacy (SP), pp. 417–434. IEEE (2019)
33. Pasquini, D., Ateniese, G., Bernaschi, M.: Interpretable probabilistic password strength meters via deep learning. In: Chen, L., Li, N., Liang, K., Schneider, S. (eds.) ESORICS 2020. LNCS, vol. 12308, pp. 502–522. Springer, Cham (2020). https://doi.org/10.1007/978-3-030-58951-6_25
34. Pasquini, D., Cianfriglia, M., Ateniese, G., Bernaschi, M.: Reducing bias in modeling real-world password strength via deep learning and dynamic dictionaries. In: 30th USENIX Security Symposium (USENIX Security 21), pp. 821–838 (2021)
35. Pasquini, D., Gangwal, A., Ateniese, G., Bernaschi, M., Conti, M.: Improving password guessing via representation learning. In: 2021 IEEE Symposium on Security and Privacy (SP), pp. 1382–1399. IEEE (2021)
36. Paterson, K.G., Stebila, D.: One-time-password-authenticated key exchange. In: Steinfeld, R., Hawkes, P. (eds.) ACISP 2010. LNCS, vol. 6168, pp. 264–281. Springer, Heidelberg (2010). https://doi.org/10.1007/978-3-642-14081-5_17
37. Radford, A., Narasimhan, K., Salimans, T., Sutskever, I., et al.: Improving language understanding by generative pre-training (2018)
38. Radford, A., Wu, J., Child, R., Luan, D., Amodei, D., Sutskever, I., et al.: Language models are unsupervised multitask learners. OpenAI blog **1**(8), 9 (2019)
39. Rumelhart, D.E., Hinton, G.E., Williams, R.J.: Learning internal representations by error propagation. California Univ San Diego La Jolla Inst for Cognitive Science, Technical report (1985)
40. Sutskever, I., Vinyals, O., Le, Q.V.: Sequence to sequence learning with neural networks. Adv. Neural Inf. Process. Syst. **27** (2014)

41. Tomczak, J.M.: Deep Generative Modeling. Springer, Heidelberg (2022). https://doi.org/10.1007/978-3-030-93158-2
42. Touvron, H., et al.: Llama: open and efficient foundation language models. arXiv preprint arXiv:2302.13971 (2023)
43. Ur, B., et al.: How does your password measure up? the effect of strength meters on password creation. In: USENIX Security Symposium, pp. 65–80 (2012)
44. Vaswani, A., et al.: Attention is all you need. Adv. Neural Inf. Process. Syst. **30** (2017)
45. Wayman, J.L., Jain, A.K., Maltoni, D., Maio, D.: Biometric Systems: Technology, Design and Performance Evaluation. Springer, Heidelberg (2005). https://doi.org/10.1007/b138151
46. Weir, M., Aggarwal, S., De Medeiros, B., Glodek, B.: Password cracking using probabilistic context-free grammars. In: 2009 30th IEEE Symposium on Security and Privacy, pp. 391–405. IEEE (2009)
47. Wheeler, D.L.: zxcvbn: low-budget password strength estimation. In: USENIX Security Symposium, pp. 157–173 (2016)
48. Whitney, L.: Billions of passwords leaked online from past data breaches (2021). https://www.techrepublic.com/article/billions-of-passwords-leaked-online-from-past-data-breaches/
49. Wikipedia: 2012 linkedin hack (2023). https://en.wikipedia.org/wiki/2012_LinkedIn_hack. Accessed 21 Jan 2023
50. Wikipedia: Rockyou (2023). https://en.wikipedia.org/wiki/RockYou#Data_breach. Accessed 21 Jan 2023
51. WikiSkull: Password datasets (2023). https://wiki.skullsecurity.org/index.php/Passwords. Accessed 21 Jan 2023
52. Wolf, T., et al.: Transformers: state-of-the-art natural language processing. In: Proceedings of the 2020 Conference on Empirical Methods in Natural Language Processing: System Demonstrations, pp. 38–45. Association for Computational Linguistics (2020). https://www.aclweb.org/anthology/2020.emnlp-demos.6
53. Xu, M., Wang, C., Yu, J., Zhang, J., Zhang, K., Han, W.: Chunk-level password guessing: towards modeling refined password composition representations. In: Proceedings of the 2021 ACM SIGSAC Conference on Computer and Communications Security, pp. 5–20 (2021)
54. Yu, J., et al.: Vector-quantized image modeling with improved vqgan. arXiv preprint arXiv:2110.04627 (2021)

Learning Type Inference for Enhanced Dataflow Analysis

Lukas Seidel[1,3] ⓘ, Sedick David Baker Effendi[2,4(✉)] ⓘ, Xavier Pinho[1],
Konrad Rieck[3], Brink van der Merwe[2], and Fabian Yamaguchi[1,2]

[1] QwietAI, San Jose, USA
jlseidel@qwiet.ai
[2] Stellenbosch University, Stellenbosch, South Africa
dbe@sun.ac.za
[3] Technische Universität Berlin, Berlin, Germany
[4] Whirly Labs, Cape Town, South Africa

Abstract. Statically analyzing dynamically-typed code is a challenging endeavor, as even seemingly trivial tasks such as determining the targets of procedure calls are non-trivial without knowing the types of objects at compile time. Addressing this challenge, *gradual typing* is increasingly added to dynamically-typed languages, a prominent example being TypeScript that introduces static typing to JavaScript. Gradual typing improves the developer's ability to verify program behavior, contributing to robust, secure and debuggable programs. In practice, however, users only sparsely annotate types directly. At the same time, conventional type inference faces performance-related challenges as program size grows. Statistical techniques based on machine learning offer faster inference, but although recent approaches demonstrate overall improved accuracy, they still perform significantly worse on user-defined types than on the most common built-in types. Limiting their real-world usefulness even more, they rarely integrate with user-facing applications.

We propose CodeTIDAL5, a Transformer-based model trained to reliably predict type annotations. For effective result retrieval and re-integration, we extract usage slices from a program's code property graph. Comparing our approach against recent neural type inference systems, our model outperforms the current state-of-the-art by 7.85% on the ManyTypes4TypeScript benchmark, achieving 71.27% accuracy overall. Furthermore, we present JoernTI, an integration of our approach into Joern, an open source static analysis tool, and demonstrate that the analysis benefits from the additional type information. As our model allows for fast inference times even on commodity CPUs, making our system available through Joern leads to high accessibility and facilitates security research.

Keywords: Type Inference · Representation Learning · Static Analysis · Static Taint Tracking · Dataflow Analysis

L. Seidel and S.D. Baker Effendi—Contributed equally to this work.

G. Tsudik et al. (Eds.): ESORICS 2023, LNCS 14347, pp. 184–203, 2024.
https://doi.org/10.1007/978-3-031-51482-1_10

1   Introduction

Dynamically typed languages are continually rising in popularity, with JavaScript and Python consistently in the top 5 languages learned by developers [10]. While easier to learn and modify, these loosely typed languages do not benefit from compile-time error detection, optimizations, and IDE support, as statically typed languages do [8,12,26]. Statically typed languages often suffer from much of the same shortcomings when library dependencies are not available and whole-program analysis is not an option [4], with hidden type declarations and class members leading to incomplete intermediate representations. If accessing all the dependencies of a project is not an option, this issue is then compounded by the growing catalog of open-source libraries and developers' inclination to make use of third-party code [44]. Overall, this incomplete view of the typing system of a given code base presents static program analysis with substantial challenges. Traditional Static Application Security Testing (SAST) tools rely on type information to identify the attacker surface and sensitive data, and may fall short when they fail to infer it for given variables. When analyzing the flow of data throughout a program, e.g., in order to find paths leading to XSS or the leak of sensitive information, the tool needs to be able to verify which method is implemented by what class, in order to track that flow recursively. If now the method belongs to an external class, but it is unknown what type from what library or if there are multiple local classes implementing the same interface in different ways, the SAST tool is faced with a problem if the exact type of a variable is missing. Statistical type inference can assist in deriving type suggestions for objects in dynamically typed languages, and a variety of machine learning and rule-based approaches were explored in recent years [13,20,42]. But although these novel approaches were able to offer improvements time after time, implementation of such tools in real-world applications, actually used by developers, is heavily lacking. With only very recent work looking at integrations into development environments [37] and not a single published use case for program security analysis, this drastically increases the barrier to entry.

In this paper, we propose a new, holistic type inference system for dynamic languages: We combine automated extraction of relevant data using an open source multi-language code analysis platform, Joern [30], with a Transformer model for type inference following an encoder-decoder architecture. Our approach is implemented for JavaScript, which can use the inferred type information in subsequent static analysis tasks. Our proposed type inference mechanism outperforms the current state-of-the-art in machine-learning-based type inference by up to 7.85%. Even where it is not significantly better overall, our system still shows favorable performance where inference is most needed, i.e., on custom user-defined types. Moreover, by training the model on annotated TypeScript code and then running inference as part of Joern's analysis on JavaScript, we show that re-integrating inferred types into the static analysis engine can improve dataflow recovery, allowing a developer to analyze their program in a more complete manner.

In conclusion, our work makes the following contributions, advancing the current state of probabilistic type inference of dynamic languages for static analysis:

1. We propose *CodeTIDAL5*: A CodeT5+ model for **T**ype **I**nference for enhanced **D**ataflow **A**nalysis via **L**anguage modeling. Our machine learning model for type inference in JavaScript achieves above-state-of-the-art accuracy with a generative approach and increased context sizes. Its open type vocabulary allows the model to provide useful hints even on types it has not seen during training.

2. We present *JoernTI*, an integrated type inference subsystem for Joern, and demonstrate the benefits in practice. The module queries CodeTIDAL5 to then re-integrate inferred types into the internal code representation for subsequent analysis steps. We show that additional type annotation coverage may lead to better dataflow analysis results.

3. We implement usage slicing in Joern: based on abstract syntax information, our system generates usage vectors that can be used to efficiently locate and re-integrate inferred type information. We publish a dataset containing usage slices of 300 000 open source projects: https://doi.org/10.5281/zenodo.8321614.

2   Background

2.1   Code Property Graphs and Code Analysis

The Code Property Graph (CPG) is a versatile data structure that combines multiple traditional program representations to form a holistic representation of a program's source code. Yamaguchi et al. [45] combine Abstract Syntax Trees (ASTs), Control Flow Graphs (CFGs), and Program Dependence Graphs (PDGs) into a single structure in order to capture relationships between syntax, control flow, and data dependencies in a unified view. CPGs may also incorporate symbol and type information, enabling comprehensive interprocedural and whole-program analysis. Moreover, many dataflow tasks can be solved with graph traversal, e.g., IFDS (interprocedural, finite, distributive, subset) [33,34], hence, CPGs offer a natural foundation for complex program analysis.

Joern [30] is the artifact of Yamaguchi et al.'s CPG associated research and supports the analysis of various programming languages. Joern provides a Scala-based, domain-specific querying language to query against CPGs that allows security analysts to write succinct, high-level queries to traverse the CPG and match graph patterns indicative of potential vulnerabilities or violations of coding best practices. A major advantage is that Joern performs fuzzy parsing, making it robust to missing code and useful for partial program analysis tasks, not requiring a complete compilation environment. By providing a unified representation of the code structure and its semantics, CPGs also enable effective tracing of data- and control-flow through an application, helping to identify potentially problematic semantic patterns that more limited representations might miss. In order to trace the flow of data in an inter-procedural way, techniques such as taint tracking are used to model the impact of input parameters on the returned values of a function [35]. Recursively, knowledge of dataflow for all used functions is required. To this end, at least a partially-qualified method name is necessary to tag the correct function as a sensitive source or sink during taint analysis or in re-using the correct method summaries. Ultimately, knowledge of an object's runtime type will reduce the number of procedures to consider and improve both the precision of subsequent analysis.

2.2 Statistical Type Inference

In contrast to strongly typed languages such as Java or Rust, *gradually typed* languages do not strictly require the programmer to provide annotations for all variables but statically check types at compile-time if provided. While type annotations and static type checking are optional in these gradually typed languages, such as TypeScript, they have a significant impact on the code quality [9, 26]. Therefore, inferring types is an important task in gradually or even dynamically typed languages, where types are not explicitly declared at all and might even change over the lifetime of a variable. Automated type inference can reduce the manual effort required to add annotations to existing TypeScript code or to provide type hints to otherwise completely untyped JavaScript in a static analysis context. This is possible, as JavaScript syntax is completely compatible with TypeScript and even implementations of popular open source libraries are re-used between the two languages, leading to the usage of the same classes or interfaces. The TypeScript compiler, for example, can transpile JavaScript to TypeScript, enabling static type checking and its benefits for JavaScript code bases [2]. It also introduces rudimentary rule-based type inference, which unfortunately does not add a lot of value for complex or user-defined types, leaving many variables labelled as the ambiguous any type [42].

The domain of statistical or *neural type inference* has become well established as of late in an effort to statically recover type information for variables in application code using machine learning [13, 20, 25, 29, 42, 46]. These models range from those that use simple token sequences with text models without constraints, such as DeepTyper [13] and TypeBert [20], or with constraints, such as OptTyper [25] and TypeWriter [29], to Graph Neural Network (GNN) based models that account for syntactic and semantic relations between code entities such as LambdaNet [42] and the R-GNN family [46]. While some work tries to introduce additional information by noting the constraints of the type in the context of the target object's usage [25, 29], we find that insufficient data is being learned on precise contextual hints such as how exactly the target object interacts within the surrounding procedure. Jesse et al. [20] address the type inference problem by using a much larger, BERT-style [7] model and more training data than previous work, but this runs the risk of impractically large inference times and resource demand.

Although mentioned work progressed the academic state-of-the-art in type inference rapidly in recent years, virtually no work directly explores means to integrate their approaches into enhancing downstream tasks such as taint analysis. This heavily restricts usability and limits adaptation, since even if proposed solutions are significantly better than readily available systems such as the TypeScript compiler's inference capabilities, developers do not have access to them outside a very limited set of tools such as FlexTyper [37].

2.3   Large Language Models

In recent years, Large Language Models (LLMs), machine learning models with millions up to hundreds of billions trainable parameters, have introduced substantial improvements in many Natural Language Problem (NLP) tasks [3,7,28,31]. Training is performed on natural language text input in a self-supervised manner, i.e., learning objectives, so-called labels, for a given input are automatically retrieved from the raw input. No manual labelling effort is required for generative pre-training performed in such a way, facilitating training on vast amounts of data.

Another crucial building block in the success of LLMs are *Transformers* [36]. At a Transformer's core, the self-attention mechanism allows the model to weigh the relevance of each element in the input sequence when processing a particular element, capturing the dependencies between elements regardless of their distance from each other. Unlike recurrent neural networks, such as the widely adopted LSTMs [14] that process data sequentially, Transformers can process all data points in the input sequence simultaneously. This allows for high parallelization and makes Transformers particularly well-suited for modern hardware accelerators such as GPUs, leading to significant speed-ups in training time and facilitating scalability. Two flavors of Transformer models are predominant: *GPT* [31] is trained to generate the most probable next word, given a sequence of preceding words. *BERT* [7] is a bidirectional approach, not only considering previous context but also subsequent words. Where GPT is a decoder-only architecture, focusing on generating new text from its learned embeddings, BERT-style models typically only consist of encoders, whose main task is to capture contextual information as a continuous representation. GPT is commonly used for language modeling, e.g., for programming code synthesis [24]. BERT on the other hand excels at understanding context and is used for tasks such as sentiment analysis.

We base our approach on *T5* [32], a unified encoder-decoder architecture introduced by Google. T5 was created to explore the boundaries of transfer learning by converting all problems into text-to-text, allowing it to be flexible to a number of NLP tasks. More specifically, we make use of Salesforce's CodeT5+ [38,39], considering its identifier-aware pre-training showing comprehensive semantic understanding on the CodeXGLUE [22] programming tasks. A variety of pre-trained LLMs are readily available as open source, e.g., at Hugging Face [16].

3   Motivation

Despite the rapid advancements in the precision of current state-of-the-art neural type inference models' ability to infer object types, there are still a number of limitations prohibiting their widespread adoption. TypeBert's [20] main premise is to reduce the so-called inductive bias of inputs to a machine learning model. Instead of computing sophisticated input formats, involving hand-crafted type constraint systems or explicitly encoding relations between syntax and semantic [42], the authors scale up the number of parameters and the amount of raw data and let the model learn representations on their own. Although this approach indeed works well, such token classification approaches still require careful processing of the output, although they already take the most straightforward format as input, i.e., raw code snippets. In order to make use of the results in another environment, variable names, declarations and their positions in code files must be carefully matched against the respective token vectors. No available system has the ability to be queried for the type of a single object in a clearly defined format, limiting integration potentials into other platforms. Therefore, broadly accessible type inference systems that are actually available where developers need them, e.g., the inference passes of the TypeScript compiler, lag behind academic progress by years.

We identify the following main roadblocks as the primary reasons for lack of adoption of current state-of-the-art probabilistic type inference systems:

[R1] **Limited Performance on User-Defined Types.** Although increasing the overall type annotation coverage is definitely a laudable goal, annotations for built-in types are rarely the critical piece of information missing. In the place where type annotations are most crucial, where users are working with user-defined classes, are where available approaches are falling short. At the same time, precisely these types are necessary for improving the precision of downstream static analysis starts.

[R2] **High-Effort Setups.** Many of the recently proposed solutions require complex setups to compile and run their application, and even if in a runnable state, the systems only handle highly specific in- and output formats requiring manual effort to receive applicable results.

[R3] **No Integration with Existing Platforms.** Even the most usable of the available systems require a manual transfer from the type inference application to the user's IDE or a code analysis platform. This heavily restricts usability and adaptation, as the introduced overhead is unacceptable to most every-day users.

While subsets of these roadblocks were partially addressed by prior work, to the best of our knowledge no approach tackled all of them systematically. Consequently, with this work we aim to overcome them in a unified and highly usable system.

4   Design

In the following, we discuss design decisions and core aspects of our usage slicing procedure, the machine learning model we train for type inference and its integration in Joern.

4.1   Code Property Graph Usage Slicing

Where program slicing in general is the act of reducing a program to a subset of its information relevant for the current task, code property graph usage slicing reduces a full CPG of a given code base to a subset of useful nodes. More specifically, the goal of CPG *usage slicing* is to extract meaningful information describing how an instantiated object interacts within a procedure while being robust to missing type and data-flow information. This may be seen as similar to TypeT5's [40] *usage graph*, but we omit "potential usages", remain intraprocedurally bound while still including variable usages captured by closures. We compute CPG usage slices using abstract syntax information (as opposed to full-blown dataflow slicing [15]), including dynamic calls invoked from this object or calls the current object is an argument for. Supplementary call graph and type information is used when available. The method source code and these usage vectors build the foundation of our machine learning model. It is important to note that a slice starts at some kind of definition of a variable and ends before any reassignment, so that we can guarantee a slice is representative of a single type.

Our approach rests on two concepts: variables and types. Variables are defined by a set S, and types by a set T. Consider all types to make up the set T, and specific types form subsets of T, where variables at a specific point in a program may only belong to a single type $t \in T$. Examples of primitive types are integer ($\mathbb{Z}$) and boolean ($\mathbb{B}$), as they represent a single word of data. There may exist a type Foo that defines integer and boolean members, which would imply these primitive types are a subset of Foo. Similarly, a collection of one or more characters (Σ) may fall in the string type set ($\Sigma*$). We use $\varnothing$ to denote the null type, but also include types such as void in Java, undefined in JavaScript, None in Python, etc. which may appear in method signatures or type arguments. To denote the *set of all types*, we use $\mathbb{U}$ (similar to any in JavaScript, Object in Java, etc.)

With these concepts, we can now introduce our definition set D. A definition $d \in D$ can be described as the tuple (s, t) where $s \in S, t \in T$. This is more formally defined in Eq. 1, and is similar to what is used in [25].

$$(s,t) = d \in D \tag{1}$$

We now present Listing 1.1 as our running example and to illustrate the concepts described in this section. Within the scope of the closure at line 4, we see three referenced variables from within the function: req, res, and params. From outside the scope of this closure, we capture documentClient. This slice excludes the implementation of the child closure at line 6, but will trace usages of `documentClient` as it is captured in this procedure.

```javascript
1 const db = require("db.js");
2 const documentClient = db.documentClient;
3
4 const handler = (req, res) => {
5   const params = req.body.params;
6   documentClient.query(params, function(err, data) {
7     if (err) console.log(err);
8     else console.log(data);
9   });
10 };
11
12 export default handler;
```

Listing 1.1. A JavaScript example of a generic HTTP request handler performing a query to a DynamoDB instance. A flow exists from `req`, over `params` into `query()`.

As is, without type information, the associated types of our variables would be the any type ($\Sigma*$). This is commonly how slices appear in practice. With type information, our variables become (`documentClient`, `DocumentClient`), (`req`, `NextApiRequest`), (`res`, `NextApiResponse`), (`params`, `Object`), (`err`, `Error`), and (`data`, `Object`). TypeScript programs enable us to populate these tuples with type information more often.

Finally, the usage slice is a 3-tuple consisting of two definitions and a set of calls. The definitions are (i) the object call, identifier, or literal that defines the data of the target object, named d_{def}, and (ii), the target object of the classification, named d_{tgt}. If d_{def} is a parameter, then $d_{def} = d_{tgt}$. The calls are those which d_{tgt} invokes or is an argument to.

4.2   Machine Learning Model

Architecture. Conceptually, our model is meant to learn from semantic relationships, e.g., variable naming conventions and class names. As we deliberately aim to deduce clues on an object's type from the semantic principles of how developers name variables or a class's methods, we opt for an encoder-decoder Transformer model for contextual text processing and generation.

The proposed machine learning model for type inference, hereinafter referred to as *CodeTIDAL5*, is based on Saleforce's CodeT5+ [38] models. We use the smallest version of the model family with 220M trainable parameters. CodeT5+ is an encoder-decoder model trained on various uni- and bimodal pre-training objectives: To initialize the model, it is first pre-trained with causal language modeling and denoising objectives on large amounts of source code from Github. As a result, the model learns a robust semantic model for programming code and its relation to natural language. Other pre-training objectives include text-to-code causal language modeling, a bimodal task in which both encoder and decoder are activated, generating code snippets from natural language descriptions or vice-versa. The authors argue, that this type of objective is effective in closing the pretrain-finetune gap for downstream tasks such as code summarization [39]. CodeT5+ achieves state-of-the-art results on programming tasks such as natural language code search, in which a model needs to find the most semantically related code from a natural description, and code completion. We model the type inference problem as a sequence-to-sequence task, tagging variable locations of interest in raw code snippets and letting the model generate token-based type predictions per tag.

We make use of Hugging Face's `transformers` library [43] for model implementation and training. The library implements various state-of-the-art optimizations and best practices, e.g., FlashAttention [5] that introduces substantial speedups and memory reductions to Transformers.

Input and Output Representations. During inference, we extract usage information from our usage slices to accurately match objects with their occurrences in raw source code. Given a JavaScript or TypeScript code base, comprehensive usage slices can be extracted with Joern's `joern-slice` capability. We annotate an object's declaration and usage locations in the source code of a given function for which we want to retrieve type suggestions with special token tags, signaling relevance of a certain variable to the model. This annotated code snippet is subsequently prefixed with a task description. We finally transform the input into its numerical representation, using CodeT5's tokenizer.

The model generates its output token-by-token, responding with a list of tag-to-prediction assignments of the form `"<extra_id_0> Array"`. Code snippets without any tags receive `"No types to infer."` as a label during training. An input context length of 512 tokens was used during training and evaluation, and output length is restricted to 128 tokens. As opposed to BERT-style models with a token classification head on top, such as TypeBert [20], this theoretically allows the model to produce type suggestions outside the corpus of types it has seen during training. We investigate the occurrence and usefulness of such hallucinations in Sect. 5.2.

Training. For training and testing purposes, we make use of the ManyTypes-4TypeScript dataset [19]. The test split comprises 662 055 TypeScript functions with a total of 8 696 679 type annotations, featuring 50 000 different types. After pre-processing and tokenization for the sequence-to-sequence task, we have 1 758 378 samples in the training set. We fine-tune CodeTIDAL5 for a total of 200k steps.

4.3 Integration in Joern

At the core of the CPG is a language agnostic AST schema from which subsequent analysis and semantics are built upon. The first component of building a CPG is the *language frontend* that uses a parser and abstracts the source code to the AST. Once the AST is complete, subsequent analysis is performed and the graph is then annotated with additional nodes and edges. These subsequent

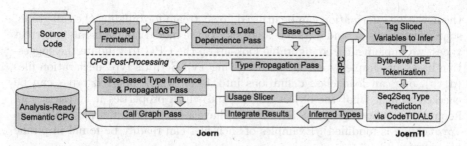

Fig. 1. High-level overview of Joern submodules and integration of our type inference system.

analyses are called "passes" and an example is the CFG pass which accepts the AST and annotates it with CFG edges. Similarly, data-dependence depends on the CFG as input, so once the CFG pass is complete, the control-dependence and reaching-definitions passes are run to construct the intraprocedural CPG.

We implement our analysis in a post-processing pass that accepts the intraprocedural CPG and extracts usage slices, which are then given to Code-TIDAL5 for type inference. The pipeline is illustrated by Fig. 1.

Type Propagation Pass. The type propagation pass is a simple flow-insensitive type recovery algorithm whereby variables, parameters, and fields are associated with types they are assigned to or annotated with. This information is kept in a map which is valid for the scope of the file. For example, if a variable x = 1 is encountered, we associate x with an integer, but if we later see x ="foo" then we append the set of associated types with string. The result would be that x = [integer, string]. However, if at the end of the type propagation, we note that x = [integer] then we can be almost certain it is of that type. While this kind of algorithm is often run as a fixed-point calculation, this is run for a small fixed number of iterations to recover the majority of simple types quickly, while CodeTIDAL5 can recover the rest. This type propagation also gathers type hints for procedure parameters and return values from caller-callee pairs, as well as what occurs within the procedure body itself. This is also why we need to then propagate the inferred types once we receive our results from CodeTIDAL5, in order to make sure interprocedural usages reflect the inferred types.

JoernTI Server. We implement JoernTI, a Python package acting as a queryable server, offering access to slice-based type inference. We implement an enhanced type inference Joern pass which, after the type propagation pass, slices the program and sends a payload of usage slices with their corresponding scope's raw source code, called a "program usage slice", to the JoernTI server. The response produced by CodeTIDAL5 is a collection of variables and their inferred types. The inference results are then integrated into the CPG, where the new type information can be utilized downstream for building the call graph, source-sink tagging, and dataflow analysis. As the model may generate incorrect types, we implement a configurable look-up on the CPG to validate the suggestion based on simple type constraints. Using TypeScript's type declaration files (`d.ts`), one can load class definitions into Joern where inferred types can be checked against what the object invokes and which properties it accesses, e.g., `Request` has a `body` property but does not have a `connect()` method (unless the `.prototype` is modified). Examples of such files can readily be found in public repositories [6].

5   Evaluation

In the following, we compare the performance of CodeTIDAL5 against state-of-the-art probabilistic type inference systems for JavaScript/TypeScript. As a real-world evaluation, we use CodeTIDAL5 in partial-program analysis environments and validate the number of notable types recovered, especially those of which would be useful in taint analysis tasks.

5.1   Type Inference Generalization

We compare our approach against the following systems:

1. **LambdaNet** [42]: A robust baseline for machine-learning-based type inference systems, whose dataset was commonly re-used in subsequent work.
2. **TypeBert** [20]: An early but very successful approach to address the domain, mainly as a Natural Language Modeling problem with Transformers. We use the author's Hugging Face implementation [18].
3. **GCBert-4TS** [19]: A GraphCodeBERT [11] base model fine-tuned on the ManyTypes4TypeScript dataset, currently leading the CodeXGLUE [22,23] benchmark for type inference. We again use the author's Hugging Face implementation [17].

Datasets. We evaluate all approaches on variables with user-provided types from the original LambdaNet (LN) dataset [42], comprised of 60 TypeScript GitHub Repositories, and on the ManyTypes4Typescript (MT4TS) dataset [19]. We use the MT4TS dataset as is.

For LambdaNet, we construct a high-quality dataset split. We extract predictions from the openly accessible experiment data for the paper [41]. In accordance with our goal to use type inference for dataflow analysis, we remove uninteresting objects from the dataset. First, we remove the non-expressive type annotations `Function` and `void` from the sample set. Secondly, we only consider variables with usages besides assignments. We also remove objects being part of class definitions, as we will infer types inside any function which uses or accesses such class members and, again, their occurrence purely as part of a definition is uninteresting from a dataflow point of view. Furthermore, we aim for a more challenging

Table 1. Performance comparison of ML-based Type inference systems for TypeScript on the LambdaNet [42] dataset. Size in number of trainable parameters.

Model	Top-1 Acc %			Size
	User-Defined	Top-100	Overall	
LambdaNet	46.89	64.79	61.18	N/A
TypeBERT	51.50	73.30	68.90	360M
GCBert-4TS	46.89	**80.62**	**73.81**	162M
CodeTIDAL5	**53.20**	79.77	73.61	220M

dataset, better reflecting real-world use cases of type inference where already annotated types are of no interest: While we use user-provided type annotations as a ground truth, we mask these annotations during inference for TypeBert, GCBert-4TS and CodeTIDAL5. For this, we obfuscate all object instantiations where a type's name can be derived from the **new** call, as well as manual type annotations.

Metrics. We report Top-1 accuracy for the following type subsets, in accordance with previous work: The **Top-100** subset includes the 100 most frequent built-in types. Examples are `String` or `Array`. **User-Defined Types** are locally, i.e., within the same scope, defined classes or enums. We derive this category from the original LN experiments, and hence do not report this metric for MT4TS. As LambdaNet excludes external types from their prediction space, types from imported libraries are not considered, limiting the dataset's scope.

For evaluation on the LN dataset, for all approaches we perform greedy matching: Specifically, we infer the type of a variable at multiple locations where it is used in the source, instead of only, e.g., at instantiation, and choose the highest confidence match in order to evaluate a label against the ground truth for a variable. On MT4TS, we only consider exact matches per unique variable usage location. In accordance with previous work, we exclude labels with the ambiguous **any** tag, and consider `UNK` predictions as incorrect.

Results. Performance comparisons of CodeTIDAL5 against state-of-the-art neural inference systems for TypeScript are presented in Tables 1 and 2. On the more diverse and larger ManyTypes4TypeScript dataset, our approach achieves an overall improvement of 7.85% in type prediction accuracy against the current best published model GCBert-4TS. TypeBert's comparatively low accuracy is probably explained by the reduced context size. Where GCBert-4TS and Code-TIDAL5 see a context window of 512 code tokens at a time, TypeBert is trained to only process inputs of 256 tokens. On all benchmarks, CodeTIDAL5 is at least on-par with GCBert-4TS, besting all other evaluated approaches by wide margins. Although overall accuracy on the LN dataset did not show improvements, our approach's performance on user-defined types is significantly better.

Table 2. Performance comparison on the ManyTypes4TypeScript dataset.

Model	Top-1 Acc %	
	Top-100	Overall
TypeBERT	48.92	28.07
GCBert-4TS	87.22	63.42
CodeTIDAL5	**90.03**	**71.27**

5.2 Efficacy of JoernTI

The following section investigates the integration of CodeTIDAL5 into Joern as discussed in Sect. 4.3. We conduct partial program analysis, that is, no library dependencies are retrieved and integrated into the analysis and only application code is passed to Joern. This downstream task illustrates a less resource intensive program analysis task, where CodeTIDAL5 compensates for the missing external type dependencies. All experiments were conducted on an M1 MacBook Pro (2020), 16 GB RAM.

Inference of Missing Types. We infer types on 10 open-source JavaScript repositories from GitHub and manually review the inferred results. The slices given CodeTIDAL5 to infer types for were ones where type information could not be easily resolved via the simple type propagation strategy already in place. We label the suggested types under the following four categories:

1. Correct: The inferred type is an exact match with the actual type.
2. Partial: The inferred type behaves similarly to the actual type or is its interface or supertype, e.g. `__ecma.Request` versus inferring `NextApiRequest`.
3. Useful: The actual type is not a defined type in the current context, but is plausible, e.g. `Object{name: String, pass: String, email: String}` versus inferring `User`.
4. Incorrect: The inferred type is completely incorrect.

To justify the value of the *partial* and *useful* categories, we use examples from the manual review. Consider two popular JavaScript REST frameworks: Express.js and Next.js. When defining routes, both accept handler functions defined with two parameters, where many tutorials and the official documentation often name these two parameters `req` and `res` for the request and response variables respectively. We find that CodeTIDAL5 may confuse the types from HTTP request frameworks such as Express.js `Request` with the Next.js `NextApiRequest`. Semantically speaking, both types perform the same roles, and we did not find CodeTIDAL5 confusing a response type with a request type. In these circumstances, we use the label *partial*, since if the intention is to tag an HTTP response or request, then CodeTIDAL5 provides the correct subtype. For the *useful* category, we describe a case in Project 1 where no classes are defined within the application and the developer simply uses the raw responses from

Table 3. The results of manual reviewing 1093 type inference results from JoernTI. Selected projects can be found in the Appendix (cf. 4).

Category	Manual Labelling Results %			
	Correct	Partial	Useful	Incorrect
Built-in	76.60	0.00	1.25	22.14
User-Defined	63.63	10.43	6.15	19.79
Overall	72.10	3.57	2.93	21.41

the Postgres database responses. As CodeTIDAL5 is based on CodeT5+, which has some understanding of identifiers of commonly defined types, it suggests the non-existent type Customer for an identifier customer. Heuristically, we can consider a type of this name to hold sensitive Personally Identifiable Information (PII) such as a home address or email.

Improvement of Dataflow Analysis. We conduct a case study in order to demonstrate how better type information may lead to enhanced analysis results in Joern. Consider the following scenario: As security researchers, we are looking for potential database injections (CWE-943) in the context of AWS' DynamoDB [1]. This scenario is illustrated by our running example in Listing 1.1. Knowing that the bodies of incoming events are a potentially attacker-controlled source, we develop the following Joern query:

```
1 def src = cpg.identifier
2   .typeFullName(".*(express.|NextApi|__ecma.)Request")
3   .inFieldAccess.code(".*\\.body\\..*")
4 def sink = cpg.identifier
5   .where(_.and(_.typeFullName(".*DocumentClient"),
6          _.argumentIndex(0)) // Receivers are at 0
7   ).inCall.name("query")
8 sink.reachableBy(src)
```

Listing 1.2. Joern query to find a dataflow from an unsanitized request body from multiple frameworks to a DynamoDB query.

The query looks for a dataflow from a special element, in this case parameters tainted by an object of types __ecma.Request, __express.Request, or NextApiRequest, into database query logic. Without proper sanitization, this may lead to a NoSQL injection. First, we create a CPG for the above-mentioned source code without the JoernTI backend. Querying this CPG yields an empty list as the result, as no dataflow can be found without the missing type information. Computing the CPG with JoernTI enabled, CodeTIDAL5 is able to correctly infer type NextApiRequest for the req variable. Running the same query again on the new CPG, the dataflow is correctly identified, and we can continue analyzing the potential vulnerability. As we compute the dataflow based on matches by type knowledge and interprocedural taint tracking, the query generalizes to diverse code no matter the syntactical structure.

Results. We show the results for type inference and manual inspection in Table 3. Each entry is counted *per-definition* and not *per-occurrence* of the target object. We load a TypeScript declaration file for built-in types to filter inferences that violate the type constraints of the slice, and omit any object, UNK or void type inferences as unhelpful. End-to-end, the rate was 8.72 predictions per second. We observe 72.10% correctly inferred types, which matches our MT4TS benchmark. It is noteworthy that certain types, such as JavaScript Event types, were often incorrectly classified due to little context within their usage. For one code base, we were able to retrieve Result types from database queries which may contribute to more accurate sensitive source discovery. The model performed well on inferring user-defined types from libraries such as Express.js, Next.js, MongoDB, Postgres, and the AWS SDK, which is likely due to the popularity of these technologies. The investigated projects showed an average of 61.59% typed nodes, including user annotations and inferences from the simple type propagation pass. After inference with CodeTIDAL5, JoernTI on average contributes 8.58% absolute more types on complex real-world software, inferring types at locations we otherwise would have no information for.

Concluding with our case study, we effectively demonstrate how and where SAST tools such as Joern benefit from additional type information. The types inferred with CodeTIDAL5 directly lead to the discovery of a new dataflow, uncovering a potential NoSQL injection with high generalization potential.

6   Related Work

Neural Type Inference. All three models used in our evaluation (Sect. 5) make use of statistical approaches with deep learning models to infer types from code. In addition to these models for TypeScript, there are models designed to infer types for Python, such as HiTyper [27] and TypeT5 [40]. DeepTyper [13] was a pioneering model in the direction of neural type inference for JavaScript, but was soon surpassed by the likes of LambdaNet [42] and OptTyper [25]. A concern in the direction of work towards statistical methods for type inference is the difficulty in teaching models to understand the logical constraints of code and type systems. While, in practice, it appears that these models work well in hybrid settings where a developer can validate the results [37, 40], some approaches tried incorporating constraints directly. Both LambdaNet and HiTyper incorporate type dependencies in the form of graphs and use type constraints as part of the learning and inference pipeline. More recently, models such as TypeBert, DiverseTyper [21], TypeT5, and GCBert-4TS [19] used LLMs to achieve precise type inference. As these models can take into account context and understand the language of naming strategies in code, with a large enough database to train from, these prove effective at predicting popular library types. These approaches usually make no attempt to constrain the model itself, but instead prune poor predictions after the types are inferred. TypeT5, developed concurrently with our work, additionally uses static analysis to construct dynamic contexts for inference, somewhat similar in intuition to CodeTIDAL5. It is notable, however, that these type dependency graphs in LambdaNet and HiTyper, as well as the usage graphs in TypeT5 do not appear to be language-specific and may generalize among other languages when trained on large enough corpora.

End-to-End Statistical Type Inference for Developers. FlexType [37] is a GraphCodeBERT-based type inference plug-in with the aim to address the issue of being able to utilize this kind of model on a consumer-level laptop. The authors mention that models such as HiTyper and LambdaNet have large hardware requirements comparable to that of workstations or GPU servers. We share a common goal with CodeTIDAL5, i.e., to offer powerful type inference while requiring compute resources akin to a CI/CD runner or laptop. FlexType's downstream goal is to integrate into an IDE to enhance a developer's experience by inferring types during development, while ours is focused on recovering library types of interest which may be associated with sensitive data sources and sinks.

7   Conclusion

We presented CodeTIDAL5, a neural type inference model based on CodeT5 that uses source code context as well as precise slices to query variable types in JavaScript/TypeScript. Additionally, we demonstrated the plug-and-play capability of CodeTIDAL5 using JoernTI, a queryable server for remote type inference, available as an open-source extension to Joern. We demonstrate the value of neural type inference on real-world partial-program analysis by recovering types for popular third-party libraries. Our experiments show that our approach leads state-of-the-art (SOTA) in the LambdaNet dataset for user-defined types by 6.31% and is on-par with SOTA overall but exceeds SOTA by 7.85% on the ManyTypes4TypeScript dataset. The proposed system is able to boost Joern's existing type propagation, resulting in 8.6% more typed nodes on real-world code bases and leading to improved downstream static analysis capabilities.

Future Work. While we demonstrated the capability of our neural type inference approach on JavaScript/TypeScript, the pipeline is language agnostic as it follows on the CPG directly. In future work, we expect it to be possible to reproduce this work on other Joern-supported languages with minimal modifications and to explore approaches for a single, unified model inferring types for multiple programming languages.

Availability. The source code of CodeTIDAL5 and JoernTI, as well as evaluation code and experiment data, is publicly available at:
https://github.com/joernio/joernti-codetidal5.

Acknowledgements. The authors gratefully acknowledge funding from the European Union's Horizon 2020 research and innovation programme under project TESTABLE, grant agreement No. 101019206, from the German Federal Ministry of Education and Research (BMBF) under the grant BIFOLD (BIFOLD23B), the National Research Foundation (NRF), and Stellenbosch University Postgraduate Scholarship Programme (PSP). We would also like to thank Kevin Jesse for help with the MT4TS dataset and models and the anonymous reviewers for the feedback on our work.

Appendix

Table 4. The GitHub subdirectories of each manually reviewed open-source web application or library. Notable technologies include React, Express, Chroma, MongoDB, Meteor, AWS, and Postgres.

#	GitHub Subdirectory
1	/skirupa/Bank-Management-System
2	/najathi/shopping-app-mongodb
3	/Hamidreza-khushab/express-server
4	/meesont/node-house-scoring-system
5	/Dynatrace/AWSDevOpsTutorial
6	/Hthe-scan-project/vulnerable-app-nodejs-express
7	/qrohlf/trianglify
8	/themeteorchef/base
9	/jaredhanson/passport
10	/OWASP/NodeGoat

References

1. Amazon Web Services. AWS DynamoDB: NoSQL Database (2023). https://aws.amazon.com/dynamodb/
2. Bierman, G., Abadi, M., Torgersen, M.: Understanding typescript. In: Jones, R. (ed.) ECOOP 2014 - Object-Oriented Programming. LNCS, vol. 8586, pp. 257–281. Springer, Heidelberg (2014). https://doi.org/10.1007/978-3-662-44202-9_11
3. Brown, T., et al.: Language models are few-shot learners. In: Larochelle, H., Ranzato, M., Hadsell, R., Balcan, M., Lin, H. (eds.) Advances in Neural Information Processing Systems. vol. 33. Curran Associates, Inc. (2020)
4. Dagenais, B., Hendren, L.: Enabling static analysis for partial java programs. In: Proceedings of the 23rd ACM SIGPLAN Conference on Object-Oriented Programming Systems Languages and Applications, pp. 313–328 (2008)
5. Dao, T., Fu, D.Y., Ermon, S., Rudra, A., Ré, C.: FlashAttention: fast and memory-efficient exact attention with IO-awareness. In: Advances in Neural Information Processing Systems (2022)

6. DefinitelyTyped. DefinitelyTyped: repository for high quality TypeScript type definitions. https://github.com/DefinitelyTyped/DefinitelyTyped

7. Devlin, J., Chang, M.W., Lee, K., Toutanova, K.: BERT: pre-training of deep bidirectional transformers for language understanding. In: Proceedings of the 2019 Conference of the North American Chapter of the Association for Computational Linguistics: Human Language Technologies, Volume 1 (Long and Short Papers), pp. 4171–4186. Association for Computational Linguistics, Minneapolis (2019)

8. Gao, Z., Bird, C., Barr, E.T.: To type or not to type: quantifying detectable bugs in javascript. In: 2017 IEEE/ACM 39th International Conference on Software Engineering (ICSE), pp. 758–769. IEEE (2017)

9. Gao, Z., Bird, C., Barr, E.T.: To type or not to type: quantifying detectable bugs in Javascript. In: Proceedings of the 39th International Conference on Software Engineering (ICSE 2017), pp. 758–769. IEEE Press (2017)

10. GitHub. The state of the octoverse: open source software survey (2023). https://octoverse.github.com/

11. Guo, D., et al.: Graphcodebert: pre-training code representations with data flow. arXiv preprint (2020)

12. Hanenberg, S., Kleinschmager, S., Robbes, R., Tanter, É., Stefik, A.: An empirical study on the impact of static typing on software maintainability. Empir. Softw. Eng. 19(5), 1335–1382 (2014)

13. Hellendoorn, V.J., Bird, C., Barr, E.T., Allamanis, M.: Deep learning type inference. In: Proceedings of the 2018 26th ACM Joint Meeting on European Software Engineering Conference and Symposium on the Foundations of Software Engineering, pp. 152–162 (2018)

14. Hochreiter, S., Schmidhuber, J.: Long short-term memory. Neural Comput. 9(8), 1735–1780 (1997)

15. Horwitz, S., Reps, T., Binkley, D.: Interprocedural slicing using dependence graphs. ACM Trans. Progr. Lang. Syst. 12(1) (1990)

16. Huggingface: List of pre-trained models on huggingface (2023). https://huggingface.co/transformers/v3.3.1/pretrained_models.html

17. Jesse, K.: GraphCodeBERT on Huggingface (2023). https://huggingface.co/kevinjesse/graphcodebert-MT4TS

18. Jesse, K.: TypeBert on Huggingface (2023). https://huggingface.co/kevinjesse/typebert

19. Jesse, K., Devanbu, P.T.: ManyTypes4TypeScript: a comprehensive typescript dataset for sequence-based type inference. In: 2022 IEEE/ACM 19th International Conference on Mining Software Repositories (MSR), pp. 294–298 (2022)

20. Jesse, K., Devanbu, P.T., Ahmed, T.: Learning type annotation: Is big data enough? In: Proceedings of the 29th ACM Joint Meeting on European Software Engineering Conference and Symposium on the Foundations of Software Engineering, pp. 1483–1486 (2021)

21. Jesse, K., Devanbu, P.T., Sawant, A.: Learning to predict user-defined types. IEEE Trans. Softw. Eng. 49(4), 1508–1522 (2023)

22. Lu, S., et al.: Codexglue: a machine learning benchmark dataset for code understanding and generation. arXiv preprint arXiv:2102.04664 (2021)

23. Microsoft. Codexglue benchmark for understanding programming code. https://microsoft.github.io/CodeXGLUE/. Accessed 16 May 2023

24. Nijkamp, E., et al.: Codegen: an open large language model for code with multi-turn program synthesis. arXiv preprint (2022)

25. Pandi, I.V., Barr, E.T., Gordon, A.D., Sutton, C.: Opttyper: probabilistic type inference by optimising logical and natural constraints. arXiv preprint arXiv:2004.00348 (2020)
26. Park, J.: Javascript API misuse detection by using typescript. In: Proceedings of the Companion Publication of the 13th International Conference on Modularity, pp. 11–12 (2014)
27. Peng, Y., et al.: Static inference meets deep learning: a hybrid type inference approach for python. In: Proceedings of the 44th International Conference on Software Engineering, pp. 2019–2030 (2022)
28. Peters, M.E., et al.: Deep contextualized word representations. In: Proceedings of the 2018 Conference of the North American Chapter of the Association for Computational Linguistics: Human Language Technologies, Volume 1 (Long Papers). Association for Computational Linguistics, New Orleans (2018)
29. Pradel, M., Gousios, G., Liu, J., Chandra, S.: Typewriter: neural type prediction with search-based validation. In: Proceedings of the 28th ACM Joint Meeting on European Software Engineering Conference and Symposium on the Foundations of Software Engineering, pp. 209–220 (2020)
30. QwietAI. Joern: code analysis tool. https://github.com/joernio/joern
31. Radford, A., Narasimhan, K.: Improving language understanding by generative pre-training (2018)
32. Raffel, C., et al.: Exploring the limits of transfer learning with a unified text-to-text transformer. J. Mach. Learn. Res. **21**(1) (2020)
33. Reps, T.: Program analysis via graph reachability. University of Wisconsin, Tech. rep. (1998)
34. Reps, T., Horwitz, S., Sagiv, M.: Precise interprocedural dataflow analysis via graph reachability. In: Proceedings of the 22nd ACM SIGPLAN-SIGACT Symposium on Principles of Programming Languages, pp. 49–61 (1995)
35. Sagiv, M., Reps, T., Horwitz, S.: Precise interprocedural dataflow analysis with applications to constant propagation. Theoret. Comput. Sci. **167**(1), 131–170 (1996)
36. Vaswani, A., et al.: Attention is all you need. In: Guyon, I., et al. (eds.) Advances in Neural Information Processing Systems, vol. 30. Curran Associates, Inc. (2017)
37. Voruganti, S., Jesse, K., Devanbu, P.: FlexType: a plug-and-play framework for type inference models. In: Proceedings of the 37th IEEE/ACM International Conference on Automated Software Engineering, pp. 1–5 (2022)
38. Wang, Y., Le, H., Gotmare, A.D., Bui, N.D.Q., Li, J., Hoi, S.C.H.: Codet5+: open code large language models for code understanding and generation (2023)
39. Wang, Y., Wang, W., Joty, S., Hoi, S.C.: CodeT5: identifier-aware unified pre-trained encoder-decoder models for code understanding and generation. arXiv preprint arXiv:2109.00859 (2021)
40. Wei, J., Durrett, G., Dillig, I.: Typet5: Seq2seq type inference using static analysis. In: International Conference on Learning Representations (2023)
41. Wei, J., Goyal, M., Durrett, G., Dillig, I.: Lambdanet experiment data. https://github.com/MrVPlusOne/LambdaNet/blob/master/LambdaNet-Experiments.zip. Accessed 16 May 2023
42. Wei, J., Goyal, M., Durrett, G., Dillig, I.: Lambdanet: probabilistic type inference using graph neural networks. arXiv preprint arXiv:2005.02161 (2020)
43. Wolf, T., et al.: Transformers: State-of-the-art natural language processing. In: Proceedings of the 2020 Conference on Empirical Methods in Natural Language Processing: System Demonstrations, pp. 38–45. Association for Computational Linguistics (2020)

44. Xu, B., An, L., Thung, F., Khomh, F., Lo, D.: Why reinventing the wheels? An empirical study on library reuse and re-implementation. Empir. Softw. Eng. **25**, 755–789 (2020)
45. Yamaguchi, F., Golde, N., Arp, D., Rieck, K.: Modeling and discovering vulnerabilities with code property graphs. In: 2014 IEEE Symposium on Security and Privacy, pp. 590–604 (2014)
46. Ye, F., Zhao, J., Sarkar, V.: Advanced graph-based deep learning for probabilistic type inference. arXiv preprint arXiv:2009.05949 (2020)

Efficient Pruning for Machine Learning Under Homomorphic Encryption

Ehud Aharoni[1], Moran Baruch[1], Pradip Bose[2], Alper Buyuktosunoglu[2], Nir Drucker[1(✉)], Subhankar Pal[2], Tomer Pelleg[1], Kanthi Sarpatwar[2], Hayim Shaul[1], Omri Soceanu[1], and Roman Vaculin[2]

[1] IBM Research, Haifa, Israel
nir.drucker@ibm.com
[2] IBM T. J. Watson Research Center, Yorktown Heights, USA
subhankar.pal@ibm.com

Abstract. Privacy-preserving machine learning (PPML) solutions are gaining widespread popularity. Among these, many rely on homomorphic encryption (HE) that offers confidentiality of the model and the data, but at the cost of large latency and memory requirements. Pruning neural network (NN) parameters improves latency and memory in plaintext ML but has little impact if directly applied to HE-based PPML.

We introduce a framework called **HE-PEx** that comprises new pruning methods, on top of a packing technique called tile tensors, for reducing the latency and memory of PPML inference. HE-PEx uses *permutations* to prune additional ciphertexts, and *expansion* to recover inference loss. We demonstrate the effectiveness of our methods for pruning fully-connected and convolutional layers in NNs on PPML tasks, namely, image compression, denoising, and classification, with autoencoders, multilayer perceptrons (MLPs) and convolutional neural networks (CNNs).

We implement and deploy our networks atop a framework called HElayers, which shows a **10–35%** improvement in inference speed and a **17–35%** decrease in memory requirement over the unpruned network, corresponding to **33–65%** fewer ciphertexts, within a **2.5%** degradation in inference accuracy over the unpruned network. Compared to the state-of-the-art pruning technique for PPML, our techniques generate networks with **70%** fewer ciphertexts, on average, for the same degradation limit.

Keywords: Homomorphic encryption · Neural networks · Machine learning · Pruning · Tile tensors · Privacy-preserving computation

1 Introduction

Data privacy and confidentiality are crucial in today's information-driven world. Outsourcing sensitive data to a third-party cloud environment, while complying with regulations such as GDPR [13], is the need of the hour for many companies and organizations, such as banks and medical establishments. One promising

© The Author(s), under exclusive license to Springer Nature Switzerland AG 2024
G. Tsudik et al. (Eds.): ESORICS 2023, LNCS 14347, pp. 204–225, 2024.
https://doi.org/10.1007/978-3-031-51482-1_11

solution is the use of homomorphic encryption (HE), which allows for the evaluation of certain functions on encrypted inputs. Corporations and academic organizations are already investing resources into developing secure and efficient solutions [4,27]. However, the major challenge constraining faster adoption is that HE applications involving a large number of operations are significantly slower and have higher memory requirements than their plaintext counterparts [1].

Non-client–aided, or non-interactive, HE is a popular choice for privacy preserving machine learning (PPML) inference and runs on systems that involve at least one client and one server. Here, the clients desire the privacy of their input data (e.g., images), and the server performs inference over an encrypted machine learning (ML) model, which has been trained with proprietary data. Typical HE schemes perform computation using a single-instruction, multiple data (SIMD) paradigm, for speed and efficiency. For instance, in CKKS [11], $\frac{N}{2}$ input elements are packed into a polynomial of degree N. A recent work, called HElayers [2], proposes efficient packing for multi-dimensional inputs using a technique called *tile tensors*. This method decomposes the input into tiles that are then each packed into a separate ciphertext.

In order to improve inference speed and memory, neural networks (NNs) use a common technique called *pruning*, for convolutional filters, fully connected (FC) weights, or even entire nodes in a trained model [17,22]. The challenge arises when we attempt to re-use plaintext ML pruning strategies for non-client–aided HE under SIMD packing. Naïve application of such a strategy fails due to the fundamental reason that while pruning may introduce zeros, if the zeros lie in a ciphertext with even one other non-zero, then the ciphertext cannot be eliminated. Thus, pruning 85% of the NN weights (85% sparsity), for instance, may lead to the elimination of only 17% of the ciphertexts (17% *tile sparsity*).

Our Solution. We propose a framework called **HE-PEx** for pruning homomorphically encrypted NNs that produces deployment-ready models with superior tile sparsity and small inference losses. Our contributions are as follows:

- We introduce a set of novel methods to perform pruning for NN models under HE with SIMD packing, which combines four main primitives: *prune, permute, pack*, and *expand*. We propose a novel co-permutation algorithm that reorders the structure of the network to improve the tile sparsity, without impacting the network accuracy and with minimum overhead.
- We integrate our techniques into HElayers [2] to develop a holistic framework that takes in an NN model and automatically produces a pruned and packed network that meets various user constraints, such as accuracy, latency, throughput, and memory requirement.
- We adapt a state-of-the-art (SotA) pruning method, Hunter [10], to support NNs under non-interactive HE. This serves as a baseline for our experiments.
- We implement and compare several schemes on four PPML networks with three datasets for different tile shapes, comparing inference accuracy and ciphertext reduction fractions. We additionally report our results on a large NN trained to detect COVID-19 from CT scans under HE.

Our techniques produce networks with tile sparsities of up to **95%** (average **61%**) across the datasets and NNs, within a limit of 2.5% degradation in network accuracy/loss. These improve upon the SotA by an average of **70%**. By leveraging this sparsity, we demonstrate a **10–35%** (**17–35%**) improvement in measured inference speed (resp., memory), compared to the unpruned model, for a privacy-preserving image denoising application run using HElayers. For a higher degradation limit of 5%, these improvements are up to **41%** (**41%**).

2   Related Work

Yang et al. [30] propose a new FPGA design that can efficiently handle sparse ciphertexts. It assumes a network that is pruned based on some standard pruning method and leverages the fact that some ciphertexts happen to encrypt zeros. Chou et al. [12] use pruning to reduce the number of weights, and quantization to convert them to powers-of-two, resulting in sparse polynomial representations. However, their method applies to encoded plaintexts only and is demonstrated for PPML use-cases where the model is unencrypted. Popcorn [29] considers the pruning of convolution layers in the context of Paillier encryption [25] and XONN [26] considers it in the context of garbled circuits (GCs), however their algorithms are different from ours and do not consider packing with tile tensors. NN pruning was also considered by Gong et al. [14] in the context of PPML, where the goal was to maintain the privacy of the data in the training dataset. However, neither the model nor the data is encrypted and their privacy aspect lies with the data used for training, not inference.

A recent work called Hunter [10] applies pruning to NNs in an HE-packing–aware manner. It considers the way the data is encoded and encrypted into the HE ciphertexts, which reduces the number of ciphertexts during computation. The packing-based pruning method of Hunter uses the specific packing choice of the client-aided solution GAZELLE [18], where the client evaluates the activation functions. HE-PEx, instead, targets a non-interactive scenario in which the server computes the activation layers and, therefore, should perform an online sequence of encrypted matrix multiplications. We adapt the Hunter scheme to this scenario, naming it P2T, and compare with our methods. While we focus on non-interactive scenarios, we argue that HE-PEx is equally valuable in a client-aided case. The main differences between HE-PEx and Hunter are:

- HE-PEx targets a non-client-aided solution using HElayers [2], whereas Hunter targets a client-aided solution called GAZELLE [18].
- HE-PEx introduces a novel permutation algorithm to improve tile sparsities.
- HE-PEx uses an expansion technique that improves the inference accuracy of the NN models without affecting their tile sparsities.
- HE-PEx combines the prune, permute and expand strategies into a holistic framework that yields better results than simple packing-aware pruning.

3   Background

This section provides background on HE and a recent method of packing cipher-texts called tile tensors, which we leverage for efficient pruning in PPML inference. We conclude this section with our assumed threat model.

3.1   Homomorphic Encryption

An HE scheme is an encryption scheme that enables computation on encrypted data. Modern HE instantiations such as CKKS [11] rely on the hardness of the Ring-LWE problem and support SIMD operations. They provide the standard public-key encryption methods (Gen, Enc, Dec), where Enc encrypts an s-slot vector M to a ciphertext $[M]$ and Dec decrypts a ciphertext $[M]$ to an s-slot vector. An HE scheme is correct if for every vector M, $M = Dec([M])$ and is approximately correct (as in CKKS) if for some small $\epsilon > 0$ that is determined by the key it follows that $|M(i) - Dec([m])(i)| \leq \epsilon$. In addition, CKKS provides the homomorphic addition ($\oplus$) and multiplication ($\cdot$) functions, where $Dec([M] \oplus [M'])_i \approx M_i + M'_i$, and $Dec([M] \cdot [M'])_i \approx M_i * M'_i$, respectively. It also provides a rotation (Rot) function, where $Dec(Rot([M], n))_i \approx M_{i+n \pmod s}$.

Non-Interactive Homomorphic Encryption. Many frameworks offer PPML inference solutions using HE or a combination of it with multi-party computations (MPC) protocols [5]. Protocols that exclusively use HE, such as [2,21], are called non-interactive or non-client–aided protocols.

In the client-aided approach, the client assists the server, e.g., to compute a non-polynomial function, such as ReLU, that is not supported natively in HE. Here, the server asks the client to decrypt the intermediate ciphertext, perform the ReLU computation, and re-encrypt the data. This approach is implemented, for example, in GAZELLE [18] and nGraph-HE [9]. In client-aided solutions, the server utilizes MPC to hide the intermediate results from the client.

The main drawbacks of client-aided solutions are that the client must stay online during the computation, and that the repeated data transfers between the client and the server may induce variability in inference latency. Moreover, prior works demonstrate that this approach may involve security risks [3] and is susceptible to model-extraction attacks [20]. To this end, our focus is on non-client-aided solutions, where the computation is done entirely under HE. However, we stress that our proposed methods are also applicable to interactive solutions.

3.2   Ciphertext Packing Using Tile Tensors

HE schemes that operate on ciphertexts in a SIMD fashion, such as
CKKS [11], allow encrypting a fixed-
size vector into a single ciphertext,
and the HE operations on the ciphertext are performed slot-wise on the
elements of the plaintext vector. The
use of SIMD also makes it faster to
execute on modern processors that
support efficient vector operations.
To leverage this, we pack several
input elements in each ciphertext.
The choice of packing method can
dramatically affect the latency (computation time), throughput (number

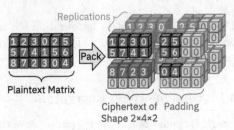

Fig. 1. An example of packing a 3×6 matrix
in a tile tensor format that operates over 8
ciphertexts (16 slots each). The matrix is
zero-padded over dimensions 1 and 2, and
is replicated three times over dimension 3.
See [2] for further information.

of computations performed per unit time), communication costs (e.g., server-
client bandwidth requirement), and memory requirement.

A recent work, HElayers [2], proposes a mechanism called *tile tensor* that
packs tensors (e.g., matrices) into fixed-size chunks, called tiles. The authors
of [2] demonstrate the use of tile tensors to implement various NN layers.
For example, they implement encrypted inference on an HE-friendly variant
of AlexNet [19]. We target HElayers and the tile tensor method of packing due
to its generality and flexibility, which allows running networks of diverse sizes
under HE.

HElayers demonstrates that the same tensor can be packed into tiles of different shapes, as long as they have the same size. For instance, while a matrix may
be naïvely packed into column-vectors or row-vectors, it can also be packed into
2D tiles, as long as the tile size matches the number of slots in the ciphertext. In
addition, tile tensors allow for other manipulations, such as duplicating elements
along one or more dimensions. This is necessary, for instance, when there is a
batch dimension to the input and the weights need to be replicated to construct
3D tiles. Figure 1 shows one way to pack a 3×6 matrix into a 3D tile tensor with
three replications of the original matrix. Further, note that the security level of
the scheme depends on the size of the tile and not on the individual dimensions.

Importance of Considering Various Tile Shapes. The HElayers work
shows that different tile shapes lead to different trade-offs; see a summary of
results in Table II and Table III of [2]. For instance, one tile shape may require
more memory but be optimal in terms of execution time, while another shape
may trade-off execution time for less memory. To this end, the framework proposed in [2] uses an optimizer to navigate the space of valid tile shapes and
discover the one that is optimized for a given objective function.

Overarching Challenge. In the context of NN pruning under HE, packing the
parameters of an NN model into tiles raises an important challenge: *pruning is
effective only if it produces sparsity at the granularity of entire ciphertext tiles,*

and not at that of a single parameter (e.g., neuron, or weight) which is the case for plaintext NNs. This is the exact problem that HE-PEx sets out to address. To this end, we define the term *tile sparsity* as the fraction or percentage of zero tiles (i.e., tiles that contain all zero values) out of all the tiles in the NN model.

3.3   Threat Model

This paper follows the commonly used threat model for using HE (e.g., in [2]), but our methods can almost automatically apply to other threat models. The model involves two parties: a data owner with a pre-trained NN model and private data samples, and a cloud server for running HE inference. The data owner generates an HE key-pair, keeps the secret key, and sends the public key and the (possibly encrypted) NN model to the cloud. Later, the user can securely perform inference by encrypting private samples and uploading them to the cloud, which runs inference and returns the encrypted results for decryption. During the computation, the cloud learns nothing about the underlying encrypted samples of the user or about the encrypted weights of the model owner, although it does learn the structure of the NN, which is provided in the clear by the data-owner.

As the user is also the model-owner, privacy attacks like membership inference over pruned data [31] are not applicable. For other threat models, the mitigation technique in [31] can be applied in our case. We assume secure protocols for inter-party communication, such as TLS 1.3, and consider computationally-bounded and semi-honest adversaries who faithfully execute protocols. We modify the data arrangement before encryption without impacting the semantic security of the underlying HE scheme. We use 128-bit security in our experiments.

4   The HE-PEx Framework

We describe our framework and its confidentiality implications in this section. We provide a description of integrating HE-PEx as part of HElayers [2] in Appendix A.2.

4.1   Prune, Pack, Permute and Expand Methods

We propose several schemes that prune, re-train and pack an NN model before deploying it. We list these in Fig. 2. Each method starts by training a NN; it could train from scratch or start with a pre-trained model. We then prune its neurons, weights, or channels, based on some criterion. We consider a few standard methods that we summarize in Table 1. In the rest of the paper, we name the various pruning techniques using the convention {*scope/criterion/target*}.

Our pruning methods accept a *pruning fraction* as input, which is the fraction of the target (weight/neuron/channel) to prune. We do not consider bias pruning, as biases are generally a small fraction of the parameters in the network. The pruning criteria we consider include *(i)* uniform-random pruning, i.e., randomly pruning neurons/channels or setting weights to zeros, and *(ii)* pruning based on a threshold, i.e., the L1-norm of a weight, weights in a channel, or the input/output weights of a neuron. We describe additional criteria for P2T, P4, and P4E later.

The scope of pruning indicates whether the pruning is done layer-by-layer, or all at once. When using the random criterion, the scope does not have an effect. However, it has a major effect when considering, e.g., L1-based pruning, particularly if there is a large variance in the weights across the different layers. Here, if we prune some fraction of the network, it might be the case that only the initial layer weights get pruned. To summarize, we consider five pruning configurations based on valid combinations of the parameters in Table 1, namely, $Lc/L1/Wei$, $Gl/L1/Wei$, $-/Rnd/Wei$, $Lc/L1/Neu$ (or $Lc/L1/Chan$)[1] and $-/Rnd/Wei$.

All of the strategies, except for P2T, first perform pruning using one of the pruning configurations listed above. P2T uses a tile-based pruning configuration that is distinct from these. Here, we first pick a tile shape and split every matrix into tiles, as illustrated in Fig. 1. For every tile, we compute the minimum/maximum/average metric of its absolute values and prune a fraction of the tiles with the lowest values of this metric. We refer to these options under the (reduction)

P2 :	Train → **P**rune		→ Retrain → **P**ack
P2T :	Train → **P**rune^{tile}		→ Retrain → **P**ack
P3 :	Train → **P**rune → **P**ermute		→ Retrain → **P**ack
P3E :	Train → **P**rune → **P**ermute	→ **E**xpand → Retrain → **P**ack
P4 :	Train → **P**rune → **P**ermute → **P**rune^{pack}		→ Retrain → **P**ack
P4E :	Train → **P**rune → **P**ermute → **P**rune^{pack}	→ **E**xpand → Retrain → **P**ack

Fig. 2. Pruning schemes composed of prune, permute, expand, and pack methods.

Table 1. Scope, criterion and target of pruning in each of the pruning schemes. See explanation in Sect. 4.1.

P2T	Scope	Local (Lc), Global (Gl)
	Criterion	Average/Maximum/Minimum of tile (T-Avg/T-Max/T-Min)
	Target	Weight (-) [tile granularity]
P2, P3, P3E	Scope	Local (Lc), Global (Gl)
	Criterion	L1 (L1), Rand (Rnd)
	Target	Weight (Wei), Neuron (Neu)/Channel (Chan)
P4, P4E	Scope	Local (Lc), Global (Gl) [1st and 2nd prune]
	Criterion	L1 (L1), Rand (Rnd) [1st prune], threshold fraction of zeros in a tile, above which the tile is pruned [2nd prune]
	Target	Weight (Wei), Neuron (Neu)/Channel (Chan) [1st prune]

---

[1] $Gl/L1/Neu$ and $Gl/L1/Chan$ were not evaluated since PyTorch limits the scope of global pruning to unstructured methods only.

criteria in Table 1 and denote this pruning as $\underline{P}rune^{tile}$ in Fig. 2. This forms our adaptation of the Hunter [10] scheme in the context of tile tensors [2].

P2T prunes complete tiles (i.e., packing-aligned pruning) right away and, therefore, there is no need to perform further steps, such as $\underline{P}ermute$, $\underline{P}rune^{pack}$, or $\underline{E}xpand$. However, a major disadvantage of P2T is that because each tile may harbor a wide range of weights, important weights may get pruned out. Intuitively, a non-packing-aligned pruning scheme may be more efficient in terms of removing the "unimportant" weights. However, the pruned values are not necessarily organized in a way that is packing-friendly and would lead to cancellation of tile operations. Therefore, we propose additional steps to mitigate this.

The permute and expand operations are illustrated in Fig. 3. The *permute* operation permutes the rows and columns of the weight matrices after the pruning operation to essentially congregate the zero elements together. The detailed algorithm that we deploy is described in Sect. 4.2. The *expand* operation is a partial reversal of the pruning operation, where we search for tiles that contain both zeros and non-zeros, and we un-prune the zero elements inside them. The motivation behind this action lies in the motivation for pruning, which is to reduce the number of active tiles; if a tile is not reduced, i.e., it has non-zero elements, then we cannot ignore it, and because we do not gain any performance benefits, it is best to fully utilize its elements to improve the model accuracy.

The aforementioned strategies form the foundations of the schemes that are abbreviated as P2, P2T, P3, and P3E in Fig. 2. To complete the set, we construct two more schemes, called P4 and P4E. In P4, instead of expanding the model as in P3E, we perform a second packing-aware pruning step to remove tiles that contain "mostly" zeros. These tiles are selected based on whether they contain more than a threshold fraction of zeros (an additional criterion for this scheme in Table 1). P4E adds an expand operation after the second pruning step in P4.

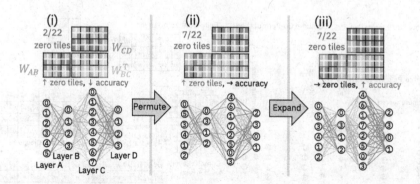

Fig. 3. Illustration of permutation and expansion for the P3E scheme when considering a 4-layer network with 6,4,8,4 neurons in layers A-D, resp. We divide the weight matrices into 2×2 tiles and prune $54/88 = 61\%$ of the weights. The pruned NN *(i)* has a tile sparsity of only $2/22 \approx 10\%$ zero tiles. Permutation *(ii)*, improves it to $7/22 = 35\%$. Expansion *(iii)* (with re-training) restores most of the accuracy loss.

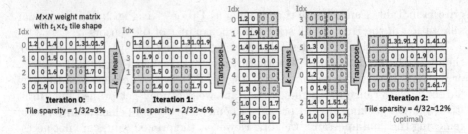

Fig. 4. Permutation of a single 4×8 weight matrix considering tiles of shape 2×2, with zero tiles highlighted. We show the algorithm on the weight matrix instead of the mask matrix, for illustration. Here, two k-means iterations are sufficient to reach the solution with the maximum tile sparsity (optimality tested using exhaustive search).

4.2   Layer Co-Permutation for Improved Pruning

We propose an efficient way of increasing the tile sparsity of an NN model, given a pruned NN and a tile shape. We first discuss the algorithm for a single weight matrix (FC layer) and then extend it to NNs with multiple FC and Conv layers.

Given a pruned matrix, one may ideally desire shuffling the values to arrange the zeros and non-zeros into separate tiles. However, it is not possible to arbitrarily swap two values without changing the function that the matrix encodes. **Our key insight** is that one can, instead, shuffle the rows and columns of the matrix to improve the tile sparsity, *without affecting the functionality.* For an FC layer, it is easy to understand row-column permutations as reordering the order of the neurons of the layers that neighbor the weight matrix, e.g., in Fig. 3 *(i)–(ii)*. One naïve way to obtain a permuted matrix that maximizes the tile sparsity with this method is through exhaustive search. However, this has a complexity of $\mathcal{O}(M!N!)$ for an $M \times N$ matrix, which is prohibitive for large matrices.

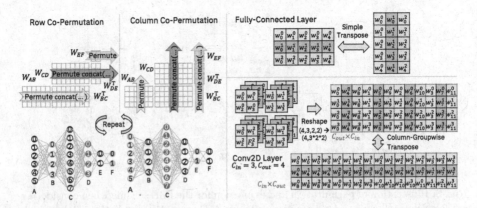

Fig. 5. Left. Illustration of weight co-permutation in a multi-layered FC-only network with weight matrices $W_{AB}, \ldots, W_{EF}$. The row and column permutation phases separately permute three different sets of matrices, where the permute operations correspond to permuting the highlighted neurons. **Right.** Illustration of weight transposition in the context of FC *(top)* and Conv *(bottom)* layers.

To make this problem tractable, we propose to permute the rows and columns based on iterative clustering algorithms. We propose a variant of k-means, which we illustrate in Fig. 4. Specifically, we split the weight array into rows, convert them to binary mask vectors (non-zeros become 1 s) and perform k-means ($k = \lceil \frac{t_1}{M} \rceil$) using a distance function that, for two mask vectors (or, points) a_i and b_i, computes the number of non-zero groups of size $\lceil \frac{t_2}{N} \rceil$ in the vector ($a_i \& b_i$). We term this as *Grouped Hamming* distance; Appendix A.1 shows a comparison with a few other variants. Further, we implement a balancing scheme that reassigns points from centroids with $>t_1$ points to centroids that have the minimum distance to the point. After running k-means, the reordered points are transposed, $\{t_1, M\}$ and $\{t_2, N\}$ are swapped, and the process is repeated till convergence.

Multi-Layer Permutation. The issue with permuting each layer of the network *independently* using the aforementioned technique is that a new "permute" layer must be added after each of the original layers for functional correctness of the network, which can easily remove any benefits from improving the tile sparsity. We obviate the need for these "permute" layers by modifying our technique to permute connected layers in tandem. We refer to this as layer *co-permutation*.

Consider the network in Fig. 5. Here, shuffling the neurons in layer B implies co-permuting the rows of W_{BC}^T and the rows of the preceding weight matrix, W_{AB}, as opposed to permuting each matrix separately. Similarly, permuting the neurons of layer D translates to permuting $concat(W_{CD}, W_{DE}^T)$. In the next iteration, we permute the columns of the re-grouped sets of weights, which corresponds to permuting the neurons in layers A, C, and E. This process is repeated till convergence. As is evident, this technique essentially discovers a re-arranged network such that the packing method can discard the maximum number of ciphertexts (of tiles) that contain only zeros, thus benefitting both memory and latency, and without affecting the model (and, thus, accuracy/loss).

Extension to Conv Layers. In our actual implementation, we transpose each weight matrix before applying row-wise k-means to groups of matrices, rather than switching between row- and column-wise k-means each iteration. While this transpose operations implies a simple transposition for FC layers (Fig. 5 topright), the technique is more involved when applied to 2D convolution (Conv) layers. Precisely, the Conv layer is reshaped to reduce it to a 2D tensor and each group of $C_{out} \times C_{in}$ (or, $C_{in} \times C_{out}$, for alternate iterations) sub-matrix is transposed within the larger tensor. At a higher level, this permutes the channels of the activations consumed and produced by the Conv layer. Note that the reshape and transpose operations are done prior to model deployment (during training) and, thus, do not add any overhead during inference.

Permuting Activations. Along with the permuted model, our algorithm produces two permutation matrices, P_{in} and P_{out}, which are multiplied with the input and output, resp., at the client end, in the clear. The overhead of these two plaintext operations is negligible compared to HE computation. For convolutional neural networks (CNNs), the presence of pooling after the last Conv layer renders the co-permutation of a Conv and FC layer-pair difficult. Therefore, we append a single "permute" (MatMul) layer before the first FC layer, which is not expected to have much overhead as it is extremely sparse (e.g., ~97% zero 16×16 tiles for AlexNet). Alternatively, one can fuse it with the first FC layer.

4.3   Privacy Considerations

The confidentiality of the model or the user data is agnostic to the use of HE-PEx, because the pruning phase happens in plaintext before uploading any data to the server. Once the data is encrypted, its security relies on the semantic security of the underlying HE algorithm, which means that the server can perform any operation on the ciphertexts without revealing the underlying plaintexts. Another advantage of using a non-interactive design is that it relies only on the HE primitive and does not rely on additional cryptographic primitives such as GCs, oblivious transfer (OT), or secret sharing (SS).

By pruning a model, we only reduce the amount of memory, and computation that a server needs to perform; we do not introduce new cryptographic mechanisms. Following [10], and most prior works in HE, we assume that no meaningful leakage happens from using a pruned model, except for the model architecture, which includes the position of zero tiles and is visible with HE. With that being said, we believe that further research in this area will be valuable.

5   Experimental Setup

Network Architectures. We evaluate our methods on the four applications in Fig. 6 and list their parameters in Appendix A.2. Multi-layer Perceptrons (MLPs) and CNNs are commonly used for classification tasks using FC (linear) layers. CNNs are specifically designed to process pixel data and additionally use 2D convolution layers. Autoencoder networks can learn to compress and reconstruct data, through dimensionality reduction. They are also used for image denoising by learning noise from images and then eliminating it for new images. Following [7], we substitute (i) ReLU activations with polynomial activations, and (ii) max-pooling with average-pooling, to make the NNs amenable to HE math.

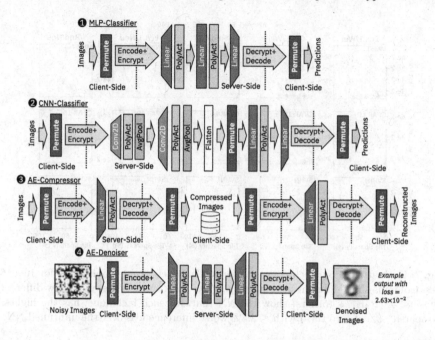

Fig. 6. Privacy-preserving neural network architectures evaluated in this work. To help with an intuitive understanding of the test loss, for the AE-Denoiser, we included an example input and output image that was produced by a model with 70% tile sparsity.

As an additional demonstrator, we showcase our P4E technique on a 21-layer HE-friendly AlexNet, as in [2], trained using trainable activations as in [7].

Datasets. We experiment using the following datasets: MNIST that has 60,000 28×28 images of handwritten digits, CIFAR-10, a collection of 50,000 small color images of everyday objects, and SVHN, an image dataset with >600,000 house number images from Street View [24]. Following [2,6], the AlexNet network is trained on the COVIDx CT-2A dataset [16] containing 194,922 chest CT slices.

Tile Shapes. Without loss of generality, we perform our experiments with tile tensors of dimensions $[t_1, t_2(= t_1), t_3]$, where t_1, t_2 correspond to the width and height of tiles in the weight matrices, and t_3 is the batch size. We fix the ciphertext poly-degree (N) to 32,768, which allows it to hold $\frac{N}{2} = 16,384$ values. We set $t_1 \in \{8, 16, 32, 64\}$ and adapt t_3 so that $(t_1 \cdot t_2 \cdot t_3 = \frac{N}{2})$. The choice of tile shape trades-off latency, throughput, and memory, as described in [2].

Evaluation Metrics. We vary the pruning fraction in 0.5–5% increments and plot the tile sparsity, i.e., % of resulting zero ciphertexts after packing the NN weights, against the cross-entropy test loss (or accuracy) of the NN. We also report the inference latency and memory requirement using HElayers. We define an upper limit for the inference test loss/accuracy degradation over the unpruned NN as 2.5%. However, this is left as a parameter for the model-owner to decide.

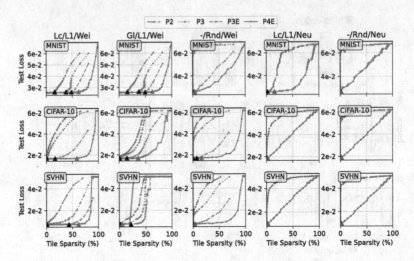

Fig. 7. Evaluation of our techniques on the autoencoder-based denoiser NN for 16×16 tiles. Columns show different pruning *scopes/criteria/targets* while rows show different datasets. ▲ (P4E)/▲ (others) show the NN that, for each technique, has the highest tile sparsity (% of zero tiles) with $\leq 2.5\%$ worse inference loss over the unpruned NN.

Platforms. Appendix A.2 lists the platforms used for our experiments.

6   Evaluation

We present the evaluation of our best pruning methods for each of the networks in Fig. 6 and compare them to our baseline [10]. We then report results from deploying our best method on a PPML inference scenario using HElayers [2].

6.1   Analysis of Our Pruning Schemes

We now compare our P2, P3, P3E, and P4E pruning schemes for each of our {*scope/criterion/target*} configurations (Table 1). Figure 7 compares these for four tile shapes, on the basis of test loss/accuracy and tile sparsity, for the AE-Denoiser NN. We note that an ideal pruning scheme should maximize the tile sparsity of the NN model for minimum degradation in test loss/accuracy.

We present our analysis in the order of the worst to the best pruning scheme. First, we note that P2, which is standard for plaintext NN pruning, fails for network pruning under HE across all networks, datasets, and schemes, thus motivating the need to consider improving the tile sparsity instead of regular sparsity (Sect. 1). In particular, neuron pruning ({*Lc/L1/Neu*} and {*-/Rnd/Neu*}) with P2 quickly break down in terms of loss, without generating more than a few zero tiles. After permutation (P3/P3E/P4E), the network becomes almost fully-dense, i.e., except for the tiles at the right or bottom edge of the weight tensor,

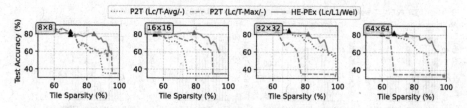

Fig. 8. Inference accuracy vs. tile sparsity (% of zero tiles) comparison using our best pruning technique (P3E for Conv and P4E for FC with Lc/L1/Wei, labeled HE-PEx) against P2T variants for a 21-layer AlexNet NN on the COVIDx CT-2A dataset. The tile shapes are shown in the top-right corner of each subplot. ▲ (HE-PEx)/△ (P2T) shows the network configuration that has the highest tile sparsity (% of zero tiles) within at most 2.5% worse accuracy compared to the original (unpruned) network.

which are taken care of by expansion (P3E/P4E). With P3, our methods improve the number of zero tiles, but not the test loss.

The -/*Rnd/Wei* configuration, which randomly prunes weights in the network, is oblivious to the importance (value) of the weights and, thus, is not as robust as L1-norm–based pruning. Permutation (P3/P3E/P4E) helps, but not by much, as the distribution after permutation is also uniform-random. P4E, with the combination of two pruning rounds with permutation and expansion, performs the best, but as we will see, other schemes outperform random pruning.

The local and global L1-norm based weight pruning schemes, *Lc/L1/Wei* and *Gl/L1/Wei*, demonstrate the best overall trade-off of test loss and tile sparsity, as shown with the colored markers. We also observe that permutation is more effective for the local-scope case than for the global scope. For this NN, local pruning outperforms global pruning, however this is not always the case, as we will see. Overall, P4E is our most effective scheme, as it is able to push the pruning envelope beyond just prune+permute with an additional layer of *careful* pruning. As a trade-off, P4E introduces a new hyperparameter, i.e., the threshold for Prune[pack], which we set to 93.8% based on a set of experiments (Appendix A.1).

Best Overall Scheme. Our best scheme, referred to as HE-PEx henceforth, uses P4E for FC layers, but P3E for Conv layers; this is because Conv layers are more sensitive to the second pruning round (Prune[pack]). Alternatively, hyperparameter search techniques can be used to explore different values of the pruning threshold for Prune[pack] to mitigate this, but this is not explored in our paper.

Local vs. Global Pruning. Prior work [8] shows that global pruning outperforms local pruning by avoiding new hyperparameters associated with per-layer pruning fractions. However, recent works, such as [28], have demonstrated that global pruning may lead to *layer-collapse* that breaks the network, as we can clearly see in the P4E plot for SVHN with *Gl/L1/Wei* configuration in Fig. 7. We observe the efficiency of local vs. global pruning for tile sparsity to be dependent on the architecture and the dataset in our experiments.

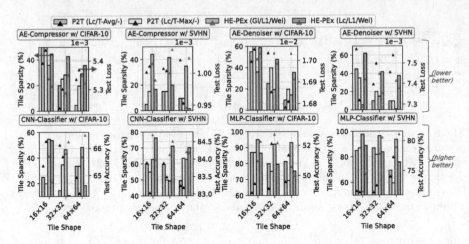

Fig. 9. *Left axis.* Best tile sparsity (% of zero tiles) for within-2.5% degradation in inference accuracy/loss over the unpruned NN. *Right axis.* Absolute inference accuracy/loss vs. tile shape comparison using our best pruning technique (P3E for Conv and P4E for FC, labeled HE-PEx) against P2T variants. Bars show zero tile % and ▲ (HE-PEx)/▲ (P2T) markers show the corresponding inference accuracy/loss. Global-scope P2T variants are not shown as they perform much worse than local-scope variants.

6.2 Comparison with P2T Strategies

We now compare our best pruning method with our adaption of Hunter [10] to a non-interactive solution, which we refer to as P2T. We construct four variants of P2T: *Gl/T-Avg/-*, *Gl/T-Max/-*, *Lc/T-Avg/-* and *Lc/T-Max/-*. All of these use packing-aware pruning as the first step, with the scope and reduction criterion specified by the first two parameters in the scheme name (Sect. 4.1), resp.

We first report the results for the HE-friendly AlexNet network trained on the COVIDx CT-2A dataset, in Fig. 8. Here, the local-scope variants outperform the global-scope schemes, as is true of P4E from Sect. 6.1, and thus we do not plot those. Our best scheme achieves a tile sparsity of **75–84%** with, at worse, a **2.5%** degradation in inference accuracy over the unpruned NN. The efficacy of the P2T schemes, however, degrades as the tile size increases. This is because the variance of magnitudes of weights in each tile grows with the size of the tile, i.e., the larger the tile, the greater the probability that it holds a set of "important" weights along with "unimportant" ones. Pruning all of these weights at once in P2T leads to severe accuracy degradation, since important weights are pruned out. These results showcase the benefits of our prune, permute and expand methods, in lieu of blind packing-aware pruning schemes, such as P2T.

We now report a summary of our results across the four NNs in Sect. 6. Figure 9 shows the best tile sparsity achieved for <2.5% worse test accuracy (or loss) on CIFAR-10 and SVHN. Overall, we observe that HE-PEx improves the tile sparsity of each NN by **48%**, **57%**, and **104%** over P2T across the three tile sizes, resp. In the few cases where there is a smaller improvement, our methods still produce models that are more accurate than those obtained using P2T.

Key Takeaway. Our methods produce NNs with tile sparsities of **95%** for the MLP-Classifier, **61%** for the CNN-Classifier, **41%** for the AE-Compressor, and **47%** for the AE-Denoiser, averaged over the two datasets, for <2.5% degradation in inference accuracy/loss over the unpruned network. These NNs have drastically smaller latency and memory requirements, which we will see in Sect. 6.4.

6.3   Impact of Permutation

To visualize the benefits of permutation, we plot histograms of the percentage of tiles that have a certain percentage of zeros in them. This is shown for AlexNet with *Lc/L1/Wei* pruning of 97.5% of the weights, in Fig. 10.

As shown in green in the figure, after pruning these weights as part of the first prune step, we see a Gaussian distribution centered at 97.5%, with a squashed tail. Here, only 3.9% of the tiles have *all* zeros. After permutation, (orange histogram), we observe a two-fold set of benefits. First, and more obviously, the weight tensors are rearranged so that more zeros are clustered together, thus increasing the tile sparsity

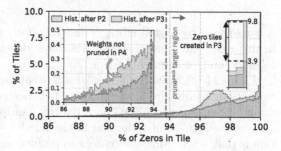

Fig. 10. Histograms of zero values in 32×32 tiles of the layers of AlexNet trained on the COVIDx CT-2A dataset, after performing Lc/L1/Wei pruning.

from 3.9% to 9.8%. Second, trained non-zero weights have migrated from sparse tiles into denser tiles. Particularly, tiles with density less than the Prune^{pack} threshold in P4 have increased (see the 86–94% region in Fig. 10), which leads to better inference accuracy after re-training. As one would expect, these benefits become more prominent with larger t_1, t_2 dimensions of the tile.

6.4   Impact on Latency and Memory

Figure 11 (left) shows the normalized latency and memory reduction, along with the test loss of the network, when running inference HE using HElayers integrated with HE-PEx, for the AE-Denoiser on CIFAR-10. Here, we vary the tile shape as $t_1 = t_2 = \{8, 16, 32, 64\}$ and fix the batch dimension, t_3, to $\{256, 64, 16, 4\}$, resp., (Sect. 5). Our results show memory and latency reductions of **10–35%** and **17–35%**, resp., compared to the unpruned model, within a **2.5%** degradation in test loss, which increase to become up to **41%** if a **5%** degradation is acceptable. The benefits are higher for smaller tile shapes, as the tile sparsity is greater for smaller tiles. However, smaller tile shapes require a large t_3, and therefore a large batch size of the inputs [2]. It is possible to zero-pad along the third dimension if there are insufficient inputs per batch; however,

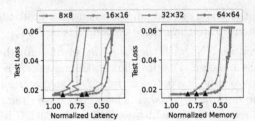

Fig. 11. Trade-offs of latency and memory requirement vs. test loss (*left/center*) and HE operation count before and after pruning (*right*) for the AE-Denoiser NN with the CIFAR-10 dataset for different tile shapes, measured using HElayers with the SEAL HE library. ▲ markers show the NN configurations that have the smallest latency (left) or memory (center) for a loss degradation of at worst 2.5% over the unpruned NN.

it would lead to wasted storage, and therefore, a larger tile shape is preferred in this case. The final choice of tile shape depends on the batch size, latency, memory, and/or throughput (see [2]).

Figure 11 (right) shows a breakdown of the number of HE additions and multiplications before and after pruning. As expected, pruning reduces **29–66%** of the HE additions and **53–67%** of the HE multiplications. Our experiments did not show a significant reduction in the number of HE rotations. One explanation is that when using tile tensors to perform matrix multiplication, even with pruning, we still need to execute the rotate-and-sum algorithm [2]. Another observation is with the right-most point in latency graph for the 8×8 tile shape in Fig. 11; this point corresponds to a 99% tile sparsity and yet has a normalized latency of 0.37. The residual latency exists because although we reduce 67% of the multiplications that are part of the matrix multiplication operations of the NN, the *output* of an FC layer is unlikely to include zero tiles. Therefore, we still have to perform the activations, which involve additional multiplications.

7   Conclusion

This work motivated the challenges associated with employing plaintext pruning techniques for PPML networks and presented a set of methods for efficiently pruning NNs for PPML inference under HE. Our solution, called HE-PEx, combines four critical primitives: *pruning, permutation, expansion,* and *packing.* Specifically, we introduced a novel permutation algorithm that rearranges the NN weights to improve pruning efficiency, without affecting the accuracy. We described how HE-PEx operates in non-interactive HE inference use cases and integrated it with HElayers [2]. The integrated framework takes as input the unpruned NN and produces a deployment-ready pruned NN that meets an objective function composed of accuracy, latency, and memory requirement.

We demonstrated our techniques on a set of four PPML applications with four datasets. We adapted a SotA pruning technique called Hunter [10] for non-interactive HE and compared our best scheme against theirs, in terms of inference accuracy (or loss) vs. tile sparsity in the pruned NN. Across different tile shapes, NNs, and datasets, our framework produced pruned models with **70%** larger tile sparsity on average, over Hunter, within an inference accuracy/loss degradation threshold of **2.5%** over the unpruned NNs. Our implementation on top of HElayers showed up to **35%** reduction in inference latency and memory requirement, over the unpruned NN, for a PPML image denoising application.

A   Appendix

A.1   Additional Evaluation

Selection of P4E prune^{pack} Threshold. We justify our choice of selecting a threshold for the prune^{pack} step (threshold % of zeros in the tile, above which the tile is pruned) of P4E by running a sweep and reporting the results in Fig. 12, for our AE-Compressor with CIFAR-10. The behavior is similar for other networks and datasets. We observe that large values of the threshold do not introduce sufficient new zero tiles to make any meaningful improvement upon P3E. At the other extreme, too small values of this threshold aggressively remove weights, leading to degradation in test loss. We select 93.8% as our choice here, but posit that our results can be further improved by tuning this as a hyperparameter.

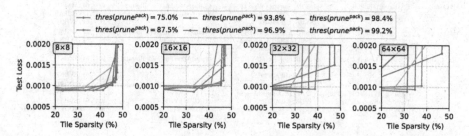

Fig. 12. Test loss vs. tile sparsity (% of zero tiles) for different prune^{pack} thresholds of our P4E scheme, considering four tile shapes using the AE-Compressor with CIFAR-10.

Comparison of Permutation Algorithms. We compare different permutation algorithms for the permute step in HE-PEx.

Figure 13 shows the results of AlexNet with *Lc/L1/Wei* pruning of 97.5% of the weights, which is the same scenario discussed in Sect. 6.3. As expected, "Random Reordering" for the row-column co-permutation provides little-to-no benefit, due to the sheer number of possible permutations of the entire network. Interestingly, *k*-Means alone only improves the benefits to <10%. Moreover, the use of a "Grouped Hamming" variant (Sect. 4.2) does not show significance for the smaller tile shapes. However, as seen in the 64 × 64 case, grouped Hamming distance is critical for grouping zeros together for large tile shapes. Finally, the impact of balancing the clusters in *k*-Means is paramount, as it brings in the critical information of the first dimension of the tile shape into the optimization algorithm. In summary, our permutation algorithm variant improves the tile sparsity by ∼**4–1,000%** for this network.

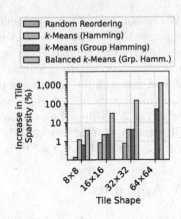

Fig. 13. Increase in tile sparsity (log scale) with different permutation algorithms for AlexNet on the COVIDx CT-2A dataset, after *Lc/L1/Wei* pruning.

Table 2. Network configurations and hyperparameters. [HL = hidden layer]

Network	Activation Function	Configuration	Learning Rate Scheduler	Learning Rate, Batch Size
AE-Compressor	2nd degree tanh [15]	128 HL neurons (MNIST) {256,128,256} HL neurons (SVHN, CIFAR-10)	CosineAnnealingWarmRestarts $T_0 = 5, \eta_{min} = 10^{-4}$	$10^{-3}, 64$ (MNIST) $10^{-3}, 128$ (CIFAR-10) $10^{-4}, 64$ (SVHN)
AE-Denoiser	2nd degree tanh [15]	128 HL neurons (MNIST) {256,128,256} HL neurons (SVHN, CIFAR-10)	CosineAnnealingWarmRestarts $T_0 = 5, \eta_{min} = 10^{-4}$	$10^{-4}, 32$ (MNIST) $10^{-4}, 64$ (SVHN, CIFAR-10)
MLP-Classifier	2nd degree tanh [15]	128 HL neurons (MNIST) {256,128} HL neurons (SVHN, CIFAR-10)	CosineAnnealingWarmRestarts $T_0 = 5, \eta_{min} = 10^{-4}$	$10^{-3}, 64$ (MNIST) $10^{-3}, 128$ (CIFAR-10) $10^{-4}, 64$ (SVHN)
CNN-Classifier	Square (MNIST, SVHN, CIFAR-10) Trained polynomials [7] (COVIDx CT-2A)	32 HL input channels (MNIST) {32,64} HL input channels (SVHN, CIFAR-10) See [7] (COVIDx CT-2A)	CosineAnnealingWarmRestarts $T_0 = 5, \eta_{min} = 10^{-4}$ (MNIST, SVHN, CIFAR-10) ExponentialLR, $\gamma = 0.99$ (COVIDx CT-2A)	$10^{-3}, 64$ (MNIST) $10^{-3}, 128$ (CIFAR-10) $10^{-4}, 64$ (SVHN) $10^{-6}, 128$ (COVIDx CT-2A)

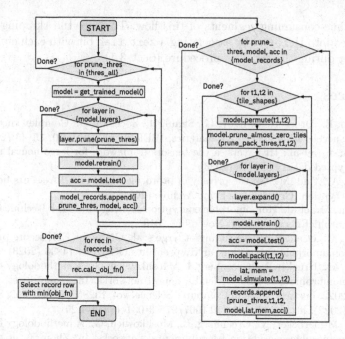

Fig. 14. Flowchart illustrating the P4E strategy with local pruning scope for the prune step and global scope for prune[pack]. This is executed as a pre-deployment step on the entity that has access to the plaintext network parameters.

A.2   Experimental Setup

Our experiments involving the methods in Sect. 4.1 are done on a cluster of systems equipped with Tesla A100 GPUs and Xeon Gold 6258R CPUs. We used PyTorch version 1.11.0 accelerated with CUDA 11.6. For end-to-end evaluation using HElayers [2], we used a 44-core Xeon CPU E5-2699 @2.20 GHz machine with 750 GB memory. We observed that for our pruned networks, not all of the cores were fully utilized and performance saturated around 8 cores. Thus, for a fair comparison, we limited the system to use 8 cores for all of our experiments. We use a modified HElayers [2] with the CKKS SEAL [23] implementation targeting 128-bit security, and the reported results are the average of 10 runs.

Network Configurations and Model Hyperparameters. Table 2 shows details of the activation functions used in each network, the network architecture, and training hyperparameters for each of the networks and datasets in Sect. 5.

Enhancing HElayers. We integrate HE-PEx with HeLayers [2] and show a flowchart for P4E in Fig. 14. This can be extended as needed to our other strategies. We illustrate a grid search approach in the flowchart with {*thres_all*} and {*tile_shapes*} being a pre-selected set of values. The output of the framework is a deployment-ready model that meets an objective function based on accuracy, latency, throughput, and memory. A local search strategy may be considered to navigate the state space with fewer training and permutation rounds, which are the most time-consuming segments of this flow. The zero-tile–skipping logic is programmed into HeLayers by associating a `zero_flag` bit with each ciphertext, which is set during the HE *Enc* procedure (Sect. 3.1).

References

1. Aharoni, E., Drucker, N., Ezov, G., Shaul, H., Soceanu, O.: Complex encoded tile tensors: accelerating encrypted analytics. IEEE Secur. Priv. **20**, 35–43 (2021)
2. Aharoni, E., et al.: HELayers: a tile tensors framework for large neural networks on encrypted data. PoPETs (2023)
3. Akavia, A., Vald, M.: On the privacy of protocols based on CPA-secure homomorphic encryption. Cryptology ePrint Archive (2021)
4. Albrecht, M., et al.: Homomorphic encryption security standard. Technical report, HomomorphicEncryption.org, November 2018
5. Baruch, M., et al.: Sensitive tuning of large scale CNNs for E2E secure prediction using homomorphic encryption. arXiv preprint arXiv:2304.14836 (2023)
6. Baruch, M., Drucker, N., Greenberg, L., Moshkowich, G.: A methodology for training homomorphic encryption friendly neural networks. In: Zhou, J., et al. (eds.) ACNS 2022. Lecture Notes in Computer Science, vol. 13285, pp. 536–553. Springer, Cham (2022). https://doi.org/10.1007/978-3-031-16815-4_29
7. Baruch, M., Drucker, N., Greenberg, L., Moshkowich, G.: A methodology for training homomorphic encryption friendly neural networks. In: Zhou, J., et al. (eds.) ACNS 2022. LNCS, vol. 13285, pp. 536–553. Springer, Cham (2022). https://doi.org/10.1007/978-3-031-16815-4_29
8. Blalock, D., Gonzalez Ortiz, J.J., Frankle, J., Guttag, J.: What is the state of neural network pruning? Proc. Mach. Learn. Syst. **2**, 129–146 (2020)
9. Boemer, F., Costache, A., Cammarota, R., Wierzynski, C.: NGraph-HE2: a high-throughput framework for neural network inference on encrypted data. In: Proceedings of the 7th ACM Workshop on Encrypted Computing & Applied Homomorphic Cryptography, WAHC 2019. Association for Computing Machinery (2019)
10. Cai, Y., Zhang, Q., Ning, R., Xin, C., Wu, H.: Hunter: HE-friendly structured pruning for efficient privacy-preserving deep learning. In: Proceedings of the 2022 ACM on Asia Conference on Computer and Communications Security (CCS) (2022)
11. Cheon, J.H., Kim, A., Kim, M., Song, Y.: Homomorphic encryption for arithmetic of approximate numbers. In: Takagi, T., Peyrin, T. (eds.) ASIACRYPT 2017. LNCS, vol. 10624, pp. 409–437. Springer, Cham (2017). https://doi.org/10.1007/978-3-319-70694-8_15
12. Chou, E., Beal, J., Levy, D., Yeung, S., Haque, A., Fei-Fei, L.: Faster cryptonets: Leveraging sparsity for real-world encrypted inference. arXiv preprint (2018)
13. EU General Data Protection Regulation: Regulation (EU) 2016/679 Directive 95/46/EC (General Data Protection Regulation). Official Journal of the European Union **119** (2016). http://data.europa.eu/eli/reg/2016/679/oj
14. Gong, Y., et al.: A privacy-preserving-oriented DNN pruning and mobile acceleration framework. In: Proceedings of the 2020 on Great Lakes Symposium on VLSI (2020)
15. Gottemukkula, V.: Polynomial activation functions (2019). https://openreview.net/pdf?id=rkxsgkHKvH
16. Gunraj, H., Wang, L., Wong, A.: COVIDNet-CT: a tailored deep convolutional neural network design for detection of COVID-19 cases from chest CT images. Front. Med. **7**, 608525 (2020)

17. Han, S., Mao, H., Dally, W.J.: Deep compression: compressing deep neural networks with pruning, trained quantization and Huffman coding. In: 4th International Conference on Learning Representations, ICLR 2016 (2016)
18. Juvekar, C., Vaikuntanathan, V., Chandrakasan, A.: GAZELLE: a low latency framework for secure neural network inference. In: 27th USENIX Security Symposium, pp. 1651–1669. USENIX Association, Baltimore, August 2018
19. Krizhevsky, A., Sutskever, I., Hinton, G.: ImageNet classification with deep convolutional neural networks. Neural Inf. Process. Syst. **25** (2012)
20. Lehmkuhl, R., Mishra, P., Srinivasan, A., Popa, R.A.: Muse: secure inference resilient to malicious clients. In: USENIX Security 2021. USENIX Association (2021)
21. Lou, Q., Jiang, L.: HEMET: a homomorphic-encryption-friendly privacy-preserving mobile neural network architecture. In: Proceedings of the 38th International Conference on Machine Learning, vol. 139, pp. 7102–7110. PMLR (2021)
22. Luo, J.H., Wu, J., Lin, W.: ThiNet: a filter level pruning method for deep neural network compression. In: Proceedings of the IEEE International Conference on Computer Vision, pp. 5058–5066 (2017)
23. Microsoft: SEAL (release 3.5). https://github.com/Microsoft/SEAL
24. Netzer, Y., Wang, T., Coates, A., Bissacco, A., Wu, B., Ng, A.Y.: Reading digits in natural images with unsupervised feature learning (2011)
25. Paillier, P.: Public-key cryptosystems based on composite degree residuosity classes. In: Stern, J. (ed.) EUROCRYPT 1999. LNCS, vol. 1592, pp. 223–238. Springer, Heidelberg (1999). https://doi.org/10.1007/3-540-48910-X_16
26. Riazi, M.S., Samragh, M., Chen, H., Laine, K., Lauter, K., Koushanfar, F.: XONN: XNOR-based oblivious deep neural network inference. In: 28th USENIX Security Symposium, pp. 1501–1518. USENIX Association, Santa Clara, August 2019
27. The HEBench Organization: HEBench (2022). https://hebench.github.io/
28. Wang, C., Zhang, G., Grosse, R.: Picking winning tickets before training by preserving gradient flow. arXiv preprint arXiv:2002.07376 (2020)
29. Wang, J., Jin, C., Meftah, S., Aung, K.M.M.: Popcorn: Paillier Meets Compression For Efficient Oblivious Neural Network Inference (2021)
30. Yang, Y., Kuppannagari, S.R., Kannan, R., Prasanna, V.K.: FPGA accelerator for homomorphic encrypted sparse convolutional neural network inference. In: 2022 IEEE 30th Annual International Symposium on Field-Programmable Custom Computing Machines (FCCM), pp. 1–9 (2022)
31. Yuan, X., Zhang, L.: Membership inference attacks and defenses in neural network pruning. In: USENIX Security 2022

Software and Systems Security

SoK: A Tale of Reduction, Security, and Correctness - Evaluating Program Debloating Paradigms and Their Compositions

Muaz Ali[1](✉), Muhammad Muzammil[2], Faraz Karim[3], Ayesha Naeem[4], Rukhshan Haroon[5], Muhammad Haris[6], Huzaifah Nadeem[7], Waseem Sabir[6], Fahad Shaon[8], Fareed Zaffar[6], Vinod Yegneswaran[9], Ashish Gehani[9], and Sazzadur Rahaman[1]

[1] University of Arizona, Tucson, USA
muaz@arizona.edu
[2] Stony Brook University, Stony Brook, USA
[3] Georgia Institute of Technology, Atlanta, USA
[4] Boston University, Boston, USA
[5] Tufts University, Medford, USA
[6] LUMS, Lahore, Pakistan
[7] University of Pittsburgh, Pittsburgh, USA
[8] Data Security Technologies, Richardson, USA
[9] SRI International, Menlo Park, USA

Abstract. Automated software debloating of program source or binary code has tremendous potential to improve both application performance and security. Unfortunately, measuring and comparing the effectiveness of various debloating methods is challenging due to the absence of a universal benchmarking platform that can accommodate diverse approaches. In this paper, we first present DEBLOATBENCH_A (<u>Debloating</u> <u>benchmark</u> for <u>applications</u>), an extensible and sustainable benchmarking platform that enables comparison of different research techniques. Then, we perform a holistic comparison of the techniques to assess the current progress.

In the current version, we integrated four software debloating research tools: CHISEL, OCCAM, RAZOR, and PIECE-WISE. Each tool is representative of a different class of debloaters: program source, compiler intermediate representation, executable binary, and external library. Our evaluation revealed interesting insights (i.e., hidden and explicit tradeoffs) about existing techniques, which might inspire future research. For example, all the binaries produced by OCCAM and PIECE-WISE were correct, while CHISEL significantly outperformed others in binary size and Gadget class reductions. In a first-of-its-kind composition, we also combined multiple debloaters to debloat a single binary. Our performance evaluation showed that, in both ASLR-proof and Turing-complete gadget expressively cases, several compositions (e.g., CHISEL-OCCAM, CHISEL-OCCAM-RAZOR) significantly outperformed the best-performing single tool (i.e., CHISEL).

G. Tsudik et al. (Eds.): ESORICS 2023, LNCS 14347, pp. 229–249, 2024.
https://doi.org/10.1007/978-3-031-51482-1_12

Keywords: Program Debloating · Debloating Comparison · Benchmark

1   Introduction

With the growing success of the software industry, and the availability of several competing platforms to support, modern software has become bloated [23]. Since most of the software are monolithic by design, they may contain functionalities that end-users do not need. This extra functionality can not only cause performance issues but also become a security risk [11,38,53]. To avoid these issues, BusyBox [1] offers manually debloated, resource-optimized clones of software with minimal functionality, which are specially suited for embedded systems.

There has been an extensive research to automate this process [4–9,13,16,17, 22,26,29,31,35–37,39–42,44–46,50,52]. Given, a *target program* and *its deployment context*, an automatic program debloating (a.k.a *software specialization*) tool debloats the program itself [5–9,13,16,17,22,26,31,33,35–37,39,40,42,44–46,52] or its execution environment (e.g., Kernel [4,29,41], Firmware [50], etc.) *automatically*. While the main goal of all the automated software debloating tools is to remove as much unnecessary code as possible while attempting to preserve the intended functionality, it still remains challenging to properly evaluate the correctness and compare their performance. The primary reason behind this is – due to the lack of a unified benchmark platform, path to setting up diverse tools for analysis is unclear and seems expensive [39].

Platform for Evaluation. This paper takes the first step towards creating an extensible and sustainable benchmarking framework named DEBLOATBENCH$_A$, for automated software debloating. We designed DEBLOATBENCH$_A$ to evaluate program debloaters targeting software written in C/C++, since most of the efforts in software debloating [5–8,13,22,31,36,37,39,42,44–46,52] are dedicated to C/C++ domain. This design choice also enables the broadest impact, as applications written in C/C++ are more widely used [25], and offer more attack surface than others [10,12,43].

While our DEBLOATBENCH$_A$ framework is more general, the current version integrates a set of software debloating research tools that represent four different classes: CHISEL [22] (source code), OCCAM [31,33] (compiler intermediate representation), RAZOR [37] (executable binary) and PIECE-WISE [39] (external library). Our current target program suite contains 10 coreutils programs from ChiselBench [22], 3 graphical user interface (GUI)-based, and 2 network-facing programs. Note that, DEBLOATBENCH$_A$ is designed to provide an *easy-to-use* command-line interface to run the different debloating tools that are integrated into it. DEBLOATBENCH$_A$ can be downloaded and run with as few as 3 commands. For wide applicability, the ease of adding new tools or enhancing the target application suite is a core requirement. So among other things, DEBLOATBENCH$_A$ is customizable and extensible by design.

Evaluating Program Debloating Methods. To inform and inspire future research, we conducted a thorough study with the set of debloaters integrated with DEBLOATBENCH$_A$. In particular, we examined the correctness, and changes in memory usage, on-disk size, security-relevant gadgets, and running time of the binaries produced by the debloaters. We found the tools based on static analysis (e.g., OCCAM, PIECE-WISE) produced binaries that passed all tests while binaries from debloaters that used dynamic analysis (e.g., CHISEL, RAZOR) failed an increasing number of tests as the aggressiveness of debloating was raised. CHISEL failed to generate binaries for all non-coreutils programs. RAZOR failed on 3 out of 5 non-coreutils binaries too. This indicates a fundamental limitation of test-case-driven debloaters to handle GUI-based or network-facing programs. Our gadget analysis focused on ASLR-proof attack bootstrapping and Turing-complete categories of micro-gadget classes [24]. There was an inverse relationship between the average correctness of a tool's output and its debloating effectiveness (measured by in-memory and on-disk resource usage) and gadget reduction in the binaries derived. A surprising finding was that PIECE-WISE increases binary size while unable to reduce any gadget classes. RAZOR increases binary size in general and could not reduce any gadget classes for non-coreutils programs. Three of the four tools ran quickly enough that they could be integrated into a software staging workflow, while the fourth took several orders of magnitude longer, making it impractical for most use cases. Leveraging this insight, we created the first-of-its-kind compositions of multiple tools to debloat a single binary. Our experimental evaluation on 10 coreutils indicates that compositions can achieve better reductions of gadget classes than the best single tool. It is worth noting that, DEBLOATBENCH$_A$ is an outcome of several years of a group of junior and senior researchers' effort. As part of the development of DEBLOATBENCH$_A$ and evaluation of program debloating tools, we directly fixed and reported several bugs in CHISEL and OCCAM and invented a new technique to measure ROP gadgets for PIECE-WISE.

Our contributions can be summarized as follows:

- We develop a new *easy-to-extend* framework named DEBLOATBENCH$_A$ to evaluate software debloating techniques. We created a set of 82 different variants of 10 unix programs/coreutils, 3 GUI-based, and 2 network-facing applications (total 15) for robust analysis. We integrated four different tools (i.e., CHISEL, OCCAM, RAZOR and PIECE-WISE) covering four different classes of debloaters. We are in the process of open-sourcing DEBLOATBENCH$_A$.
- We perform a holistic comparative analysis of these four debloaters under various metrics. Our evaluation shows that all the binaries produced by OCCAM and PIECE-WISE were correct. In contrast, CHISEL significantly outperformed others in binary size and Gadget class reductions, while failing to produce correct binaries for all non-coreutils programs.
- To leverage the strength of multiple debloaters, we performed a novel composition analysis in which we created several pipelines to use multiple tools to debloat a single binary. Our performance evaluation of tool composition showed that, in both ASLR-proof and Turing-complete gadgets expressively cases, several compositions (e.g., CHISEL-OCCAM, CHISEL-OCCAM-RAZOR) significantly outperformed the best single tool (CHISEL).

2   Debloating Methods

DEBLOATBENCH$_A$ supports application- and library-level software debloating. Since, evaluating kernel-level debloating would require a different set of machinery than application- and library-level debloating, we exclude it from our benchmark. Table 1 summarizes various application- and library-level program debloaters highlighting the tools that are included in our benchmark.

Table 1. Comparison of different classes of program debloaters in terms of their target, analysis method, level of automation, and the availability. Here, "✓" indicates *yes* or *supported*, "✓*" indicates *experimental feature*, "-" indicates *not supported* or *no*. "●" indicates *fully automated* and "◐" indicates *partially automated*.

Debloating Class	Tools	Target		Type			Input			Analysis		Automated?	Opensourced?
		Application	Library	Source	LLVM IR	Binary	Configuration	Testcases	Annotation	Static	Dynamic		
Source	CHISEL [22]	✓	-	✓	-	-	-	✓	-	✓	-	●	✓
	C-Reduce [42]	✓	-	✓	-	-	-	✓	-	✓	-	●	✓
	Perses [46]	✓	-	✓	-	-	-	✓	-	✓	-	●	✓
	DOMGAD [52]	✓	-	✓	-	-	✓	-	-	✓	-	●	✓
	DEBOP [51]	✓	-	✓	-	-	✓	-	-	✓	-	●	✓
LLVM IR	OCCAM [31,33]	✓	✓*	-	✓	✓	✓	-	-	✓	-	●	✓
	Trimmer [6,7,44]	✓	-	-	✓	-	✓	-	-	✓	-	●	-
	LLPE [45]	✓	-	-	✓	-	-	-	✓	✓	-	◐	✓
	LMCAS [8]	✓	-	-	✓	-	✓	-	-	✓	-	●	-
Binary	RAZOR [37]	✓	✓*	-	-	✓	-	✓	-	-	✓	●	✓
	Ancile [13]	✓	✓	-	-	✓	✓	✓	-	-	✓	●	-
Library	PIECE-WISE [39]	-	✓	✓	-	-	-	-	-	✓	-	●	✓
	BlankIt [36]	-	✓	-	✓	-	-	-	-	-	✓	●	-
	Nibbler [5]	-	✓	-	-	✓	-	-	-	✓	-	●	-

2.1   Application-Level Program Debloating

Application-level program debloaters can be categorized as follows: source-level [22], intermediate representation (IR)-level [31,33] and binary-level [37] debloaters.

Source-Level Program Debloating. Most of the source-level program debloating methods (e.g., CHISEL [22], C-REDUCE [42], and PERSES [46]) use variants of the delta-debugging algorithm for debloating. Delta-debugging uses a set of testcases to encompass the usage profile of the program after debloating, which has a potential to over-fit [52]. To address this issue, Xin *et al.* proposed more conservative methods (e.g., DOMGAD [52], DEBOP [51]) to preserve functional generality. *However, as acknowledged by Xin et al.* [52], CHISEL [22] *represents the state-of-the-art, in terms of code reduction performance. There-fore, we included* CHISEL *in our benchmark as the candidate representative for source-level program debloating tools.*

IR-Level Program Debloating. Existing IR-based program debloating tools operate on LLVM bitcode and leverages partial evaluation for code reduction. For example, OCCAM [31,33] combines partial evaluation and type theory to remove unnecessary code. It supports cross-module analysis with multiple passes – first, summarizing cross-module dependencies and then using it for specialization. Similarly, TRIMMER [6,7,44] , LLPE [45], LMCAS [8] also uses partial evaluation as the core technique for specialization. *As* OCCAM *is the only open-sourced tool supporting automated analysis, we included* OCCAM *as the representative for IR-level program specialization tools.*

Binary-Level Program Debloating. Program debloating methods for exe-cutable binaries rely on execution tracing, triggered by carefully chosen testcases (e.g., RAZOR [37]) or fuzzing (e.g., Ancile [13]). For example, RAZOR first runs the binary with the given test cases and uses *Tracer* to collect execution traces. It then decodes the traces to construct the program's CFG, which contains only the executed instructions. In addition to debloating context (i.e., intended func-tionalities), Ancile [13] requires a set of testcases to seed the fuzzer. *Because of being open source, we included* RAZOR *in our benchmark to represent binary-level program debloaters.*

2.2 Library-Level Program Debloating

Library-level program debloating has three flavors – *i*) static [5], *ii*) load-time [39] and *iii*) runtime-debloating [36]. Given a set of applications, static debloating tools (e.g., Nibbler [5]) debloats dynamically linked libraries statically, which replaces the original set of libraries permanently. Load-time debloaters redact (e.g., PIECE-WISE[39]) functions while loading the target library into the mem-ory. Runtime debloaters load (e.g., BlankIt [36]) certain functions only if they are required at runtime. *For our evaluation, we chose* PIECE-WISE, *since its the only tool whose code is opensourced.*

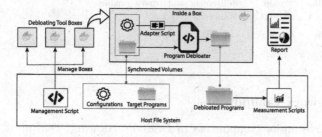

Fig. 1. DEBLOATBENCH$_A$ framework overview.

3   Components of the DEBLOATBENCH_A Framework

In this section, we describe the components of the DEBLOATBENCH_A framework.

Framework Overview. Figure 1 provides an overview of our DEBLOATBENCH_A framework. Our design followed the open-close principle [32] to ensure extensibility without affecting usability and sustainability. We adopted a container-based approach to building DEBLOATBENCH_A framework to provide isolation of environments across different debloaters. We created separate containers for each of them. We use a command-line tool-based management system (known as *orchestrator*) to build and manage the life cycle of these containers. Each input program in DEBLOATBENCH_A has a corresponding configuration file describing various metadata (e.g., testcase location, build script location, etc.) about the program. Different program specialization tools use different formats for input program metadata. Each container has a corresponding adapter script to convert DEBLOATBENCH_A's input program configuration files into its own format.

Table 2. Target application suite and their deployment contexts considered in DEBLOATBENCH_A. All the cells with different flags represents *the set of deployment contexts* named as variants (82 in total). The first 10 applications are coreutils, next 3 applications are GUI-based and the rest of the 2 are network based applications.

	Selected Arguments and Combinations						#Variants (82)
bzip2	-fc	-kc	-ksc	-ksfc	-sc	-sfc	6
chown	-c	-R	-Rc	-Rv	-v		5
mkdir	-m a=r	-m a=rw	-m a=rwx	-mp a=r	-mp a=rw	-mp a=rwx	6
sort	-c	-cf	-cfn	-cfr	-cn	-cr	11
	-f	-fn	-fr	-n	-r		
uniq	-c	-cd	-cdw N	-cu	-cuw N	-cw N	11
	-d	-dw N	-u	-uw N	-w N		
grep	-v	-E	-F	-i	-m		5
gzip	-c	-d	-f	-t			4
tar	-cf	-tvf	-xf				3
date	-d	-u	-r	-Rd	-ud		5
rm	-r	-f	-rf	-i			4
gm	negate	monochrome	flop	flip	contrast		5
vlc	noaudio	loop	fullscreen	starttime	novideo		5
gv	scale	noantialias	fullscreen	color			4
putty	telnet	ssh	m	load			4
nginx	-t	-s	-p	-c			4

3.1   Framework Components

There are three major components in DEBLOATBENCH_A, i.e., input programs, debloating tools, orchestrators, and measurement scripts. Input programs, orchestrators and measurement scripts reside in the host file system. Debloaters and their corresponding adapter scripts reside inside isolated containers.

Debloating Tools. Each of the debloaters in DEBLOATBENCH$_A$ are built within an isolated docker container. Container images freeze the execution environment. While each tool requires an input program and corresponding metadata to perform debloating, they use different means to accept those inputs (Table 1). DEBLOATBENCH$_A$ uses a configuration file to collect inputs corresponding to an input program. We created scripts to parse DEBLOATBENCH$_A$'s configuration file and generate inputs for individual tools. These scripts are called *adapter scripts*. Adapter script of a tool bridges it with DEBLOATBENCH$_A$.

Target Program Suite. In our current version, we selected 10 coreutils/linux utility programs from ChiselBench [22] on which all the selected tools run correctly to produce meaningful results. To evaluate their generalizability, we selected 3 GUI-based and 2 network-facing programs. With the goal of capturing diversity, we chose a diverse of deployment contexts for each of the applications. We term the combination of a target application and a specific deployment context a *variant*. Table 2 summarizes the set of 82 variants that constitute the complete workload.

Testcases. With the target program to debloat, program debloaters also take testcases (i.e., CHISEL, RAZOR, PIECE-WISE) or a configuration file (i.e., OCCAM) as input. Note that, the number of test cases impacts the training time for test case-dependent tools, hence it is important to pick quality test cases to maximize the coverage without impacting the performance. Given the application's running configuration, generating high-quality test-cases is an active area of research. Since this is an orthogonal problem, such automation is beyond the scope. Therefore, we relied on manually created test cases. To produce binaries with CHISEL, RAZOR, and PIECE-WISE, we created a set of 726 test cases. We also created a total of 1007 number of testcases to check the correctness[1]. They are summarized in Table 3 in Appenfix. While preparing these testcases, we aimed to capture diverse behavior in order to maximize the coverage.

Measurement Scripts. We measure the performance of program debloaters with the following five metrics: *i*) correctness of the debloated binaries *ii*) decrease in binary size, *iii*) Security analysis in the lens of gadgets reduction and *iv*) debloating time. Note that, we did not use CVEs for security evaluation, mostly because CVEs are correlated with the functionalities. Elimination of them are more likely to be influenced by the selection of functionalities than a tool.

In-Memory Gadget Counting. PIECE-WISE debloats external libraries in the unit of functions while loading into the memory. We use *gdb* to find missing *functions* in the debloated version loaded in the memory. After collecting that information, we create a new version of the library by replacing the missing function bodies with *NOP*s. Finally, we use this version of the library to collect ROP gadgets using the ROPgadget tool [3].

---

[1] Some of the test cases are taken from Razor Benchmarks [37].

4 Experimental Setup in DEBLOATBENCH$_A$

As discussed in Sect. 2, for performance comparison, we incorporated the following four debloaters into DEBLOATBENCH$_A$, i.e., CHISEL [22], OCCAM [31,33], RAZOR [37] and PIECE-WISE [39], which covers four different paradigms. Next, we discuss our experimental setup to evaluate them. We conducted two set of experiments to measure the performance of i) standalone tools and ii) their composition. Finally, we discuss the metrics that we used to compare performance.

4.1 Standalone Mode

Setting Up CHISEL: From the CHISEL authors we learned that CIL [34] was used to merge the C files for the input programs in the earlier version of CHISEL. To run CHISEL successfully, we reused the merged C files for 10 coreutils programs from CHISELBENCH. For the other 5 large programs, we leveraged its build system integration functionality.

Setting Up OCCAM: A wide range of policies is supported by OCCAM to debloat binaries. Each policy results in a different debloated binary ranging from *aggressive* to *no* specialization. After running a sanity checking experiment to find the best configuration, we selected the *onlyonce* for measuring and comparing OCCAM's performance.

Setting up RAZOR: RAZOR's performance is largely dependent on the choice of heuristic used by the *Pathfinder* module. Since, RAZOR is relatively faster than other tools, for RAZOR we created multiple version of binaries corresponding to each of the heuristics and selected the version with maximum correctness for performance analysis and comparison with other tools.

Setting Up PIECE-WISE: For PIECE-WISE, we used the pre-built compiler and loader provided with the Docker container. We used `musl-libc` v1.1.15 as the library dependency for each of the input programs in our application suite and then debloated `musl-libc` with PIECE-WISE. To create non-PIECE-WISE compiled binaries, we used the same docker container that PIECE-WISE repository provides and downloaded unmodified LLVM and Clang along with `musl-libc`, with the exact same versions that PIECE-WISE used.

4.2 Composition Mode

Since various specialization tools in DEBLOATBENCH$_A$ operate on different forms of application code (i.e., source, IR, binary or library), it is possible to run multiple tools to debloat a single program. For example, CHISEL debloats at the source code level, and the resulting binary can be further debloated using RAZOR, which performs debloating at the binary level. Building upon this idea, we formulate the following 4 unique compositions of tools and use them to debloat the DEBLOATBENCH$_A$'s input program suite: i) CHISEL to OCCAM, ii) CHISEL to OCCAM to RAZOR, iii) CHISEL to RAZOR and iv) OCCAM to RAZOR.

As PIECE-WISE requires both source code and the binary to perform debloating, it can only be composed with CHISEL. We also tried PIECE-WISE to CHISEL pipeline with limited success that we discuss in Sect. 5.3. For a given metric, we compare the performance of compositions with the best-performing individual tools.

5   Evaluation of Debloaters

Research Questions: To understand the utility of software debloating tools, we considered the following issues. **RQ1:** Does a debloating approach adversely impact the correctness of target applications? **RQ2:** How effective is each debloater at reducing the size of individual programs? **RQ3:** What is the effect of debloating on the gadget-related security of target programs? **RQ4:** How usable are each of the debloating approaches in practice? **RQ5:** Does composing debloaters offer any further improvement?

We term the combination of a target application and a specific deployment context a *variant*. Table 2 summarizes the set of 82 variants that constitute the complete workload. Each variant gives rise to a different debloated binary. In the analyses below, a debloater is applied to all variants of a program, with the average result reported. *During our evaluation, we observed that the debloaters significantly failed to produce results for meaningful comparison on non-coreutils programs. Hence, we report their results separately for RQ1 to RQ4 and we only use 10 coreutils programs to answer RQ5.*

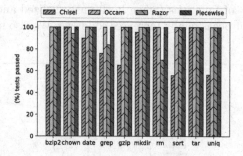

Fig. 2. Each debloater was applied to all variants of a target program. The average fraction of tests passed for each target is reported here.

5.1   Evaluation Results on 10 Coreutil Programs

RQ1: Tool Correctness. We use testcases to measure the correctness of a given debloater, which implies that whether a specific debloated binary is *correct* is an under-estimate. Figure 2 reports the results of our correctness evaluation. The debloating approaches that employ static analysis – i.e., OCCAM and PIECE-WISE – passed 100% of the tests. In contrast, the debloaters that rely on dynamic analysis did not – CHISEL passed 80.4% of the tests, while RAZOR produced correct results for 94.8% of the cases. OCCAM produces the best correctness results because of its static partial evaluation-based approach that conservatively retains all the functionality for a given argument. CHISEL performs worse because of its overly-reliance on the provided testscripts.

We undertook the exercise of augmenting the training cases provided with each debloater for the target applications (Fig. 3). Our experience indicated that a debloated binary created with more training cases retains more behavioral diversity, allowing it to pass more correctness tests. However, the level of improvement varied significantly from one target application to another. To quantify this, we report on the fraction of tests that passed for each of the targets as a function of the number of training cases utilized. The results for RAZOR and CHISEL are shown in Fig. 3. These results are based on one variant of a given target program that represent the main functionality (e.g. chown's -c variant) as opposed to the average of all the variants. The general trend says that more training cases yielded increased debloating correctness.

RQ2: Size Reduction. A primary goal of debloating a target application is to reduce its size by eliminating code that will not be used in a particular deployment. The effect is on the binary size on disk. CHISEL and OCCAM eliminate code at the source and compiler intermediate representation levels, respectively. This usually reduces the size of the resulting binaries. In contrast, RAZOR retains the original binary and extends it with transformed code, while PIECE-WISE adds metadata representing the program's control flow graph to the binary. These effects are easily observed in Fig. 6(b). Since OCCAM's partial evaluation can increase the number of functions (when both unspecialized and specialized versions are retained), it occasionally increases code size. We also measure the effect

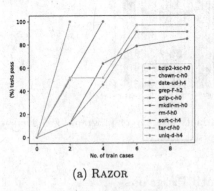

(a) RAZOR

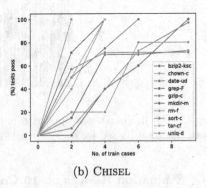

(b) CHISEL

Fig. 3. (a) The correctness of RAZOR's debloating is a function of the training cases used. The variant and heuristic level used is denoted in the legend. h0 indicates no heuristic used. Note that sort, uniq, rm, mkdir, and chown hit 100% correctness on two train cases. (b) The correctness of CHISEL's debloating is a function of the training cases provided to its oracle test script.

on binary size of varying the number of train cases for RAZOR and CHISEL as shown in Fig. 4. We note that increasing the number of train cases can sometimes lead to a relative increase in size reduction for CHISEL (gzip, sort).

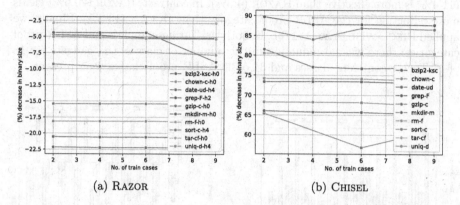

(a) RAZOR   (b) CHISEL

Fig. 4. (a) The reduction in binary size on disk by RAZOR vs. the number of training cases used. (b) The reduction in binary size on disk by CHISEL vs. the number of training cases used. Note that positive values indicate reductions, while negative ones are size increases. For this experiment, the same data is used from Fig. 3.

RQ3: Gadget Expressivity. Raw ROP gadget count and code size is not a reliable metric for estimating the vulnerability of a binary [14,15]. Homescu *et al.* [24] argued that gadgets can be categorized into classes (based·on the type of functionality provided), with just a single member from each class sufficing for the assembly of specific categories of attacks. They constructed classes of "micro-gadgets" (restricted to maximum lengths of 3 bytes) that provide the basis for

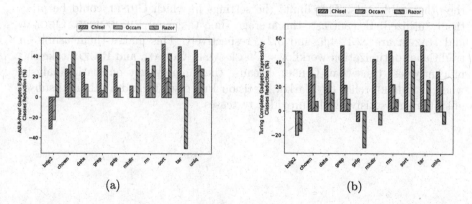

(a)   (b)

Fig. 5. (a) ASLR-proof ROP gadget expressivity and (b) Turing-complete ROP gadget expressivity reduction.

each category. We report on the effect of debloating on the changes in the two categories of ASLR-proof and Turing-complete expressivity. These are reported in Fig. 5. In both categories, CHISEL yields the highest reduction (of 28.2% and 36.6% on average, respectively). For the Turing-complete category, OCCAM (11.4%) is more effective than RAZOR (4.3%). In contrast, RAZOR (20.6%) yields more reduction for the ASLR-proof category than OCCAM (13.3%). Finally, we applied PIECE-WISE to musl libc. In both the Turing-complete and ASLR-proof categories, there was no reduction in the number of classes, i.e., gadgets for 16 of 17 Turing-complete classes and 34 of 35 ASLR-proof classes were present.

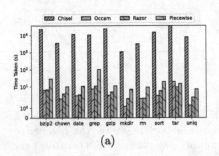
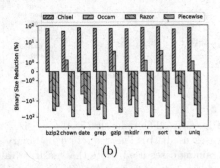

(a)   (b)

Fig. 6. (a) Average time to debloat all variants of a target application with each debloater. Note that the y-axis is logarithmic to accommodate the large differences in time taken. (b) Effect on binary size on disk after applying different debloaters to each target program. Note that positive decreases indicate binary size reduction.

RQ4: Tool Usability. To gain insight into the settings where each debloater could potentially be deployed, the time it takes to run on all the variants in our workload was measured. The results are in Fig. 6 (a). CHISEL takes several orders of magnitude (with an average of around 13,000 s) more time than the other debloaters. This limits the settings in which CHISEL could be practically utilized. In contrast, the average time taken by PIECE-WISE, OCCAM, and RAZOR are 22.1, 4.9, and 5.2 s, respectively. This makes them usable in traditional optimization workflows. PIECE-WISE, OCCAM, and RAZOR take significantly less time than CHISEL because they mainly rely on static analysis, whereas CHISEL relies on Markov Decision Processes to find a minimal subset of statements satisfying the provided testcases.

Summary: Evaluation results on coreutils programs

- **Correctness:** CHISEL: *80.4%*, OCCAM: *100%*, Razor: *94.8%*, PIECE-WISE: *100%*. *Static analysis-based debloaters produce more correct binaries than dynamic analysis-based debloaters.*
- **Size on disk:** CHISEL *and* OCCAM *cause reductions. However, by extending the original binary,* RAZOR *and* PIECE-WISE *increases the size.*
- **Gadget Expressivity:** CHISEL *outperformed others in both categories: ASLR-proof (28.2%), and Turing-complete (36.6%).*
- **Debloat Time:** CHISEL *takes several orders of magnitude (3.75 hours) more than others. The average time taken by* PIECE-WISE, OCCAM, *and* RAZOR *are 22.1, 4.9, and 5.2 seconds, respectively.*

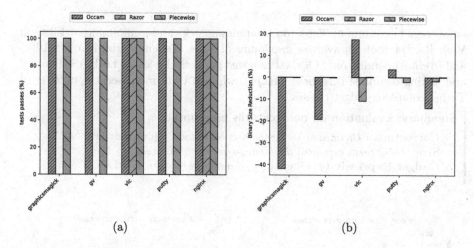

(a)   (b)

Fig. 7. For non-coreutils programs: (a) Average fraction of tests passed. (b) Average binary size reduction.

5.2 Evaluation Results on 5 Non-coreutils Programs.

Here, we present the evaluation results on non-coreutils programs. To evaluate the correctness (**RQ1**) we used 247 test cases for 22 variants of 5 non-coreutils programs. We debloated these applications inside containers. For their correctness testing, we used the host system because of the difficulty of handling GUI applications inside the containers. Our evaluation shows that only OCCAM and PIECE-WISE produced correct binaries that passed all the test cases. RAZOR produced correct binaries for two of them (vlc and nginx), while failing to debloat others. Finally, CHISEL failed on all of the target programs. Surprisingly, all of the debloaters increased binary size to some extent (**RQ2**). Correctness and binary size reduction results are summarized in Fig. 7.

The maximum average debloating time (**RQ3**) for PIECE-WISE was 129.67 s (on Graphicsmagick) and the minimum was 13.66 s (on Gvpdf). OCCAM took

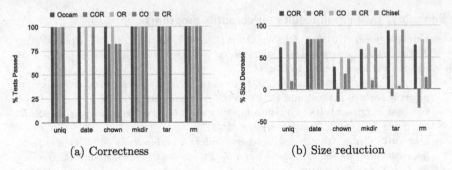

(a) Correctness   (b) Size reduction

Fig. 8. (a) Average fraction of tests passed after applying a debloater composition to a target application. (b) Average binary size reduction using debloater composition.

an average maximum of 95.6 s (on Graphicsmagick) and a minimum of 1.3 s (on Vlc). RAZOR took an average maximum of 120 s. As summarized in Fig. 10(c) and (d) in Appendix, only OCCAM removed gadgets classes for both ASLR-proof and Turing-complete categories **(RQ4)**, while RAZOR increased the number of Turing-complete gadget classes.

Summary: Evaluation on non-coreutils programs

- **Correctness:** *Dictated by static analysis-based tools (*OCCAM *and* PIECE-WISE*).*
- **Size:** *All of them increased the binary size (except* OCCAM *on Vlc).*
- **Gadget Expressivity:** OCCAM *significantly outperformed others.*

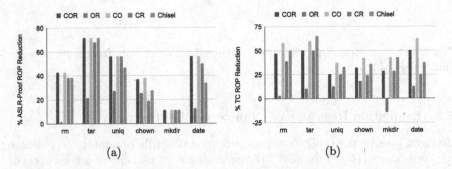

(a)   (b)

Fig. 9. (a) ASLR-proof ROP gadget expressivity reduction using debloater composition. (b) Turing-complete ROP gadget expressivity reduction using debloater composition.

5.3 RQ5: Debloater Composition

For meaningful comparison, we only used coreutils programs to evaluate debloater compositions. In Figs. 8, and 9, the three-stage pipeline is referred to as COR to denote CHISEL to OCCAM to RAZOR. Further, each pair of these three debloaters can be composed without the third one. We evaluated these three combinations as well. In the figures, they are denoted by OR for OCCAM to RAZOR, CO for CHISEL to OCCAM, and CR for CHISEL to RAZOR. After applying two or more debloaters in succession, the resulting binary must function correctly. Figure 8(a) reports the average fraction of tests passed after each combination of debloaters is applied to a target application. The correctness testing of individual debloaters (reported in Sect. 5.1) found that CHISEL was the most likely to produce a binary that failed a check. These variants were eliminated when testing the composition of debloaters. On the other hand, OCCAM is used as a baseline since binaries derived from its output passed all tests.

The maximum average binary size reduction by any single tool is 70.4% (from CHISEL). The combination of CHISEL followed by OCCAM slightly outperforms it with an average reduction of 74.6%. (The combination of all three debloaters only yields an average reduction of 67.5%.) For the Turing-complete gadget expressivity case, the single tool with the maximum average improvement was again CHISEL with 36.6%. However, in this case, the CHISEL-OCCAM-RAZOR composition yielded a slightly better 38.8% while the CHISEL-OCCAM combination provided a substantially better reduction of 50.5%. In the ASLR-proof gadget expressivity case, the single tool with the highest reduction was CHISEL with 28.2% (Fig. 9). Here, CHISEL-OCCAM, CHISEL-RAZOR, and CHISEL-OCCAM-RAZOR combinations all outperformed with reductions of 45.9%, 40.4%, and 45.8%, respectively.

CHISEL to PIECE-WISE **Pipeline** . After debloating with CHISEL, out of 10 target programs, we were successful in compiling five of them with PIECE-WISE compiler. Among these programs, PIECE-WISE was not able to compile all the variants of `grep`, `date`, and `tar`. This is due to the incompatibility between `musl-libc` and `glibc`, where CHISEL uses `glibc` and PIECE-WISE uses `musl-libc` for compilation.

Summary: Composition of Debloaters

– **Correctness:** *Produces correct binaries for non-*CHISEL *pipelines.*
– **Size:** CHISEL-OCCAM *pipeline outperformed the best individual tool (*CHISEL*).*
– **Gadgets:** *In both ASLR-proof and Turing-complete gadget expressively cases, several compositions (e.g.,* CHISEL-OCCAM, CHISEL-OCCAM-RAZOR*) significantly outperformed the best tool (*CHISEL*).*

6 Discussion

We first discuss the impact of design choices on the performance and the usability of program specialization tools in the light of our evaluation. Then, we discuss the limitations of this study.

6.1 Impact of Design Choices

Dependency on Test-Cases in CHISEL: Our evaluation revealed that, in terms of the correctness of the debloated binary, CHISEL is the weakest of all the techniques. This is mostly because of CHISEL's strong reliance on test scripts that it uses to guide the debloating. Also, these scripts can be tricky to get right and CHISEL can misbehave sometimes even when the scripts are seemingly correct. In our experiments, on average, over 96% of the debloating time is spent in running the property test script.

Partial Evaluation in OCCAM: Our experience shows that the partial evaluation [27] significantly reduced the usability of OCCAM. It only allows non-conflicting flags to be present in a debloated binary. We call two flags to be non-conflicing, if both of them can be used simultaneously in the same execution. So for two conflicting flags, one needs to create two variants. However, it is worth noting that configuration-based program debloating enabled by partial evaluation in OCCAM are easy to setup. This is because it does not require careful and tedious use of testcases, where the quality of the tests impacts the overall usability of the debloated binary.

Tracing-Based Reduction in RAZOR: A dominant trend in the analysis of RAZOR debloating was that the number of correctness tests passed would remain low for several heuristics (i.e., *no heuristic*, *zCode*, and *zCall*) and high for others (i.e., *zFunc* and *zLib*). This implies that the benefits of using different heuristics need to be fully assessed to choose the heuristic that produces the correct binary to retain reasonable functionality. Figure 10(a) illustrates the overall relationship between heuristic levels and the percentage of test cases passed in each coreutils program. Moreover, RAZOR's training time is dependent on the number of train cases provided to it. Figure 10(b) in Appendix shows how the number of train cases impacts the time taken to train RAZOR for each of the 10 target programs.

Load-Time Reduction in PIECE-WISE: At compile time PIECE-WISE computes the program dependency graph and appends it in the .dep section in the ELF header, which is used for reduction in load-time. This significantly increases the size. For some applications, the large increase in size can outweigh the benefit.

6.2 Limitations of This Study

In the current version, DEBLOATBENCH$_A$ chose a single tool per category and provides an in-depth analysis. However, tool coverage can easily be extended. The current choice of selecting target applications was hindered by existing debloaters' capabilities, which can be extended too. We created an extensive number of test cases to maximize the coverage for training and testing, however, it is hard to guarantee.

7 Related Work

C/C++ Program Specialization. There are three broad classes of program specialization, i.e., source-level (e.g., CHISEL [22], C-REDUCE [42], and PERSES [46] and DOMGAD [52]), IR-level (e.g., TRIMMER [6,7,44] , LLPE [45], LMCAS [8], OCCAM [31,33]) and binary-level (e.g., RAZOR [37]). Performance comparisons in most of these tools are done with either the state-of-the-art tools in their category or none. Library specialization tools (e.g., PIECE-WISE [39], BlankIt [36], Nibbler [5]) also followed a similar trend. RAZOR [37] and LMCAS [8] are two exceptions. RAZOR compared its performance with CHISEL on runtime, binary correctness as well as code, ROP gadget and CVE reduction. LMCAS [8] compared the runtime with OCCAM, CHISEL and RAZOR, while the performance on other metrics were compared with OCCAM. To the best of our knowledge, DEBLOATBENCH$_A$ is the first benchmark to systematically scrutinize tools across all the categories to underscore the strength and weaknesses of each of the methods. Our evaluation also highlights that a composition of multiple methods has a great potential to achieve better performance than any of the individual tools.

Environment/OS-Level Debloating. MULTIK [29] and SHARD [4] offers application specific kernel-level debloating. CIMPLIFIER [41] uses dynamic analysis to detect logically distinct applications inside a container and automatically breaks it into smaller containers. LIGHTBLUE [50] leverages static analysis to perform application-guided firmware debloating. CDE [20] leverages execution tracing to identify the dependencies of an application for seamless porting. In a concurrent work, recently, Hassan *et al.* developed a framework named DEBLOATBENCH$_C$ to evaluate container debloaters [21].

Program Specialization for Other Languages. Researchers have also explored program debloating for other languages. For example, Piranha [40] targets Objective-C. JSHRINK [16]; JSCLEANER [17], LACUNA [35], Muzeel [30], Stubbifier [48] and [49] target JavaScript; JRed [26], JAX [47], BloatLid [18] Depclean [2] and [9] target Java- and PHP-based applications, respectively. A body of work exists on byte code reduction as well [19, 28].

8 Conclusion

We presented DEBLOATBENCH$_A$, an extensible and sustainable benchmarking framework for rigorous evaluation of program debloaters. We integrated CHISEL, OCCAM, RAZOR and PIECE-WISE into the framework and performed a holistic comparative study. Our analysis shows that conservative static analysis tools produce correct binaries (e.g., OCCAM, PIECE-WISE), while aggressive dynamic analysis tools (e.g., CHISEL) perform better in reducing size and gadget classes. A surprising finding was PIECE-WISE failed to reduce any gadget classes while increasing the binary size. Also, test-cased-driven tools performed worse on non-coreutils programs. Our analysis of multi-tool composition at different stages opens up avenues for future explorations.

Acknowledgements. This material is based upon work supported by the National Science Foundation (NSF) under Grant ACI-1440800 and the Office of Naval Research (ONR) under Contracts N68335-17-C-0558 and N00014-18-1-2660. Any opinions, findings, conclusions, or recommendations expressed in this material are those of the authors and do not necessarily reflect the views of NSF or ONR. We thank Muhammad Hassan,

Abdullah Naveed, Talha Tahir, Muhammad Farrukh, and Ahsan Amin for their help in preparing and testing the large application suite.

Appendix

Table 3. The number of train and correctness testcases we used during our experiment for each of the input programs.

Applications	#Train cases	#Correctness cases
bzip2	45	198
chown	20	35
mkdir	10	69
sort	55	77
uniq	55	55
grep	20	25
gzip	36	132
tar	33	99
date	50	50
rm	16	20
gm	125	75
gv	120	75
vlc	125	75
putty	7	10
nginx	9	12
(Total)	726	1007

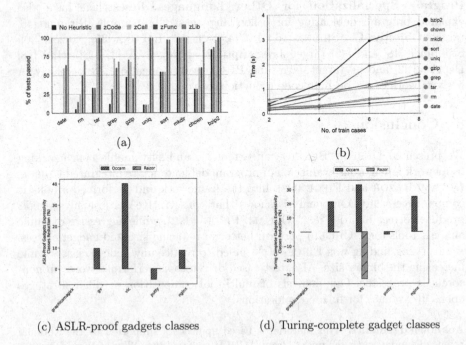

(a)

(b)

(c) ASLR-proof gadgets classes

(d) Turing-complete gadget classes

Fig. 10. For coreutils, (a) average fractions of test passed for different heuristics in RAZOR and (b) relationship between the time taken to train RAZOR and the number of train cases. For non-coreutils, (c) ASLR-proof ROP gadget expressivity and (d) Turing-complete ROP gadget expressivity reduction.

References

1. Busy box. https://busybox.net/
2. Depclean. https://github.com/castor-software/depclean
3. Ropgadget tool. https://github.com/JonathanSalwan/ROPgadget
4. Abubakar, M., Ahmad, A., Fonseca, P., Xu, D.: Shard: fine-grained kernel specialization with context-aware hardening. In: 28th USENIX Security Symposium (2019)
5. Agadakos, I., Jin, D., Williams-King, D., Kemerlis, V.P., Portokalidis, G.: Nibbler: debloating binary shared libraries. In: ACSAC, pp. 70–83 (2019)
6. Ahmad, A., Anwar, M., Sharif, H., Gehani, A., Zaffar, F.: Trimmer: context-specific code reduction. In: 37th IEEE/ACM Conference on Automated Software Engineering (ASE) (2022)
7. Ahmad, A., et al.: Trimmer: an automated system for configuration-based software debloating. IEEE Trans. Softw. Eng. (TSE) 48(9) (2022)
8. Alhanahnah, M., Jain, R., Rastogi, V., Jha, S., Reps, T.: Lightweight, multi-stage, compiler-assisted application specialization. In: 7th European Symposium on Security and Privacy. IEEE (2022)
9. Azad, B.A., Laperdrix, P., Nikiforakis, N.: Less is more: quantifying the security benefits of debloating web applications. In: 28th USENIX Security Symposium (2019)
10. Bessey, A., et al.: A few billion lines of code later: using static analysis to find bugs in the real world. Commun. ACM 53(2), 66–75 (2010)
11. Bhattacharya, S., Rajamani, K., Gopinath, K., Gupta, M.: The interplay of software bloat, hardware energy proportionality and system bottlenecks. In: Hot-Power'11, pp. 1–5 (2011)
12. Bierbaumer, B., Kirsch, J., Kittel, T., Francillon, A., Zarras, A.: Smashing the stack protector for fun and profit. In: Janczewski, L.J., Kutyłowski, M. (eds.) SEC 2018. IAICT, vol. 529, pp. 293–306. Springer, Cham (2018). https://doi.org/10.1007/978-3-319-99828-2_21
13. Biswas, P., Burow, N., Payer, M.: Code specialization through dynamic feature observation. In: Joshi, A., Carminati, B., Verma, R.M. (eds.) CODASPY '21, pp. 257–268 (2021)
14. Brown, M.D., Pande, S.: Is less really more? Towards better metrics for measuring security improvements realized through software debloating. In: 12th USENIX Workshop (CSET 19) (2019)
15. Brown, M.D., Pruett, M., Bigelow, R., Mururu, G., Pande, S.: Not so fast: understanding and mitigating negative impacts of compiler optimizations on code reuse gadget sets. Proc. ACM Program. Lang. 5(OOPSLA) (2021)
16. Bruce, B.R., Zhang, T., Arora, J., Xu, G.H., Kim, M.: JShrink: in-depth investigation into debloating modern Java applications. In: Devanbu, P., Cohen, M.B., Zimmermann, T. (eds.) ESEC/FSE, pp. 135–146. ACM (2020)
17. Chaqfeh, M., Zaki, Y., Hu, J., Subramanian, L.: JScleaner: de-cluttering mobile webpages through Javascript cleanup. In: Huang, Y., King, I., Liu, T., van Steen, M. (eds.) WWW, pp. 763–773. ACM/IW3C2 (2020)
18. Dewan, A., Rao, P., Sodhi, B., Kapur, R.: BloatLibD: detecting bloat libraries in Java applications. In: 16th Conference on the Evaluation of Novel Approaches to Software Engineering (2021)
19. GuardSquare: Proguard. https://github.com/Guardsquare/proguard

20. Guo, P.J., Engler, D.R.: CDE: using system call interposition to automatically create portable software packages. In: Nieh, J., Waldspurger, C.A. (eds.) USENIX ATC (2011)

21. Hassan, M., et al.: Evaluating container debloaters. In: IEEE Secure Development Conference, SecDev 2023, Atlanta, GA, USA, 18–20 October 2023. IEEE (2023)

22. Heo, K., Lee, W., Pashakhanloo, P., Naik, M.: Effective program debloating via reinforcement learning. In: 2018 ACM CCS, pp. 380–394 (2018)

23. Holzmann, G.J.: Code inflation. IEEE Softw. **32**(2), 10–13 (2015)

24. Homescu, A., Stewart, M., Larsen, P., Brunthaler, S., Franz, M.: Microgadgets: size does matter in Turing-Complete Return-Oriented programming. In: USENIX WOOT '12 (2012)

25. Javed, F., Afzal, M.K., Sharif, M., Kim, B.S.: Internet of things (IoT) operating systems support, networking technologies, applications, and challenges: a comparative review. IEEE CS&T **20**(3), 2062–2100 (2018)

26. Jiang, Y., Wu, D., Liu, P.: JRed: program customization and bloatware mitigation based on static analysis. In: IEEE COMPSAC, pp. 12–21 (2016)

27. Jones, N.D.: An introduction to partial evaluation. ACM Comput. Surv. **28**(3), 480–503 (1996)

28. Kalhauge, C.G., Palsberg, J.: Logical bytecode reduction. In: ACM SIGPLAN PLDI, pp. 1003–1016. ACM (2021)

29. Kuo, H., et al.: Multik: a framework for orchestrating multiple specialized kernels. CoRR abs/1903.06889 (2019)

30. Kupoluyi, T., Chaqfeh, M., Varvello, M., Hashmi, W., Subramanian, L., Zaki, Y.: Muzeel: a dynamic Javascript analyzer for dead code elimination in today's web. arXiv preprint arXiv:2106.08948 (2021)

31. Malecha, G., Gehani, A., Shankar, N.: Automated software winnowing. In: 30th ACM Symposium on Applied Computing (SAC) (2015)

32. Martin, R.C.: The open-closed principle. More C++ Gems **19**(96) (1996)

33. Navas, J., Gehani, A.: OCCAMv2: combining static and dynamic analysis for effective and efficient whole program specialization. Commun. ACM **66**(4) (2023)

34. Necula, G.C., McPeak, S., Rahul, S.P., Weimer, W.: CIL: intermediate language and tools for analysis and transformation of C programs. In: Horspool, R.N. (ed.) Conference on Compiler Construction (2002)

35. Obbink, N.G., Malavolta, I., Scoccia, G.L., Lago, P.: An extensible approach for taming the challenges of Javascript dead code elimination. In: Oliveto, R., Penta, M.D., Shepherd, D.C. (eds.) Conference on Software Analysis, Evolution and Reengineering (2018)

36. Porter, C., Mururu, G., Barua, P., Pande, S.: Blankit library debloating: getting what you want instead of cutting what you don't. In: ACM SIGPLAN PLDI, pp. 164–180 (2020)

37. Qian, C., Hu, H., Alharthi, M., Chung, P.H., Kim, T., Lee, W.: Razor: a framework for post-deployment software debloating. In: USENIX Security (2019)

38. Quach, A., Erinfolami, R., Demicco, D., Prakash, A.: A multi-OS cross-layer study of bloating in user programs, kernel and managed execution environments. In: Kim, T., Wang, C., Wu, D. (eds.) Workshop on Forming an Ecosystem Around Software Transformation (2017)

39. Quach, A., Prakash, A., Yan, L.: Debloating software through piece-wise compilation and loading. In: USENIX Security, pp. 869–886 (2018)

40. Ramanathan, M.K., Clapp, L., Barik, R., Sridharan, M.: Piranha: reducing feature flag debt at UBER. In: Rothermel, G., Bae, D. (eds.) ICSE-SEIP, pp. 221–230. ACM (2020)

41. Rastogi, V., Davidson, D., Carli, L.D., Jha, S., McDaniel, P.D.: Cimplifier: automatically debloating containers. In: Bodden, E., Schäfer, W., van Deursen, A., Zisman, A. (eds.) European Software Engineering Conference/Foundations of Software Engineering (2017)
42. Regehr, J., Chen, Y., Cuoq, P., Eide, E., Ellison, C., Yang, X.: Test-case reduction for C compiler bugs. In: ACM PLDI, pp. 335–346 (2012)
43. Shacham, H.: The geometry of innocent flesh on the bone: return-into-libc without function calls (on the x86). In: Ning, P., di Vimercati, S.D.C., Syverson, P.F. (eds.) ACM CCS 2007, pp. 552–561. ACM (2007)
44. Sharif, H., Abubakar, M., Gehani, A., Zaffar, F.: Trimmer: application specialization for code debloating. In: 33rd IEEE/ACM International Conference on Automated Software Engineering (ASE) (2018)
45. Smowton, C.S.: I/O Optimisation and elimination via partial evaluation. Technical report, UC, CL, December 2014
46. Sun, C., Li, Y., Zhang, Q., Gu, T., Su, Z.: Perses: syntax-guided program reduction. In: ICSE 2018, pp. 361–371 (2018)
47. Tip, F., Laffra, C., Sweeney, P.F., Streeter, D.: Practical experience with an application extractor for Java. SIGPLAN Not. **34**(10), 292–305 (1999)
48. Turcotte, A., Arteca, E., Mishra, A., Alimadadi, S., Tip, F.: Stubbifier: debloating dynamic server-side Javascript applications. CoRR abs/2110.14162 (2021)
49. Vázquez, H.C., Bergel, A., Vidal, S.A., Pace, J.A.D., Marcos, C.A.: Slimming Javascript applications: an approach for removing unused functions from Javascript libraries. Inf. Softw. Technol. **107**, 18–29 (2019)
50. Wu, J., et al.: LightBlue: automatic profile-aware debloating of Bluetooth stacks. In: 30th USENIX Security Symposium (2021)
51. Xin, Q., Kim, M., Zhang, Q., Orso, A.: Program debloating via stochastic optimization. In: ICSE-NIER '20, pp. 65–68 (2020)
52. Xin, Q., Kim, M., Zhang, Q., Orso, A.: Subdomain-based generality-aware debloating. In: 35th IEEE/ACM ASE (2020)
53. Xu, G., Mitchell, N., Arnold, M., Rountev, A., Sevitsky, G.: Software bloat analysis: finding, removing, and preventing performance problems in modern large-scale object-oriented applications. In: FSE/SDP, pp. 421–426 (2010)

On the (In)Security
of Manufacturer-Provided Remote
Attestation Frameworks in Android

Ziyi Zhou, Xuangan Xiao, Tianxiao Hou, Yikun Hu[✉], and Dawu Gu[✉]

Shanghai Jiao Tong University, Shanghai, China
{jou.dzyi,xgxiao,tomhou2002,yikunh,dwgu}@sjtu.edu.cn

Abstract. To provide a tamper-proof mechanism for mobile apps to check the integrity of the device and their own code/data, Android phone manufacturers have introduced Manufacturer-provided Android Remote Attestation (MARA) frameworks. The MARA framework helps an app conduct a series of integrity checks, signs the check results, and sends them to remote servers for a remote attestation. Nonetheless, we observe that real-world MARA frameworks often adopt two implementations of integrity check (hardware-based and software-based) for compatibility consideration, and this allows an attacker to easily conduct a downgrade attack to force the app to utilize the software-based integrity check and forge checking results, even if the Android device is able to employ hardware-supported remote attestation securely. We demonstrate our MARA bypass approach against MARA frameworks (i.e., Google SafetyNet and Huawei SafetyDetect) on real Android devices, and design an automated measurement pipeline to analyze 35,245 popular Android apps, successfully attacking all 104 apps that use these MARA services, including well-known apps and games such as TikTok Lite, Huawei Wallet, and Pokémon GO. Our study reveals the significant risks against MARA frameworks in use.

Keywords: Remote Attestation · Android Device Integrity · Android App Integrity

1 Introduction

On the Android platform, ensuring the integrity of the device environment is crucial for app developers. For instance, most payment and banking apps examine whether the runtime environment is tampered (e.g., the device is "rooted"). If so, they refuse to run, in order to reduce the potential risks to users' property and privacy [3,4]. Many game apps also need root detection to prevent game cheating [1,2]. Moreover, some mobile advertisers would like to verify whether ad clicks are coming from real devices to prevent click fraud [5]. In addition to device integrity, many app developers also hope to verify the app integrity to prevent app repackaging which may cause intellectual property infringement or ad insertion [6,8].

G. Tsudik et al. (Eds.): ESORICS 2023, LNCS 14347, pp. 250–270, 2024.
https://doi.org/10.1007/978-3-031-51482-1_13

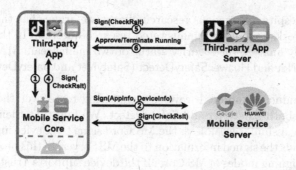

Fig. 1. Workflow of MARA.

It is, however, difficult to implement a secure integrity check by only utilizing the app client. Malicious users could easily modify or disable the integrity check functions to circumvent such defenses. To guarantee a tamper-proof integrity check for Android apps, Android phone manufacturers have implemented integrity check frameworks at the OS level and provided easy-to-use APIs for apps to retrieve integrity check results. We refer to these integrity check frameworks as **Manufacturer-provided Android Remote Attestation** (MARA) frameworks as they have adopted the Remote Attestation (RA) [30] scheme to prevent check results from being tampered or forged. Two commercially available MARA framework implementations, Google SafetyNet [24] and Huawei SafetyDetect [25] are widely used in Android phones sold in the United States and mainland China, respectively. Such MARA frameworks are often parts of the Mobile Service (MS) Cores, that is, the Google Mobile Service Core (GMS Core) [12] and the Huawei Mobile Service Core (HMS Core) [14].

The overview of the MARA's workflow is shown in Fig. 1. When an app calls the MARA API provided by the MS Core, MS Core collects information about the device and the app, signs and then sends these information to the Mobile Service server, and ultimately returns an integrity check result signed by the MS server. If the result indicates, for example, that the device is an emulator instead of a physical device, the app server will return specific commands to the app (e.g., asking the app to terminate execution).

To the best of our knowledge, no previous work has comprehensively and accurately evaluated the security of popular MARA frameworks. Aldoseri *et al.* [33] theoretically analyzed the security of some MARA protocols. They, however, only focused on the high-level design and did not analyze the actually implemented version of the deployed MARA framework. We observe that many of the implementation details **did not** fully follow the protocol specification, as shown in Sect. 3.2, and this would lead to severe security violations even though the original protocol has been verified. Some researches [26,27,29] focused on the internal mechanism of Google SafetyNet, but they did not conduct a security analysis and did not discuss other MARA frameworks. Other researches [28,32] detected the misuse of Google SafetyNet API in Android apps and did not analyze the security of the MARA frameworks themselves.

Our Work. Despite all previous research efforts, we argue that the security of MARA frameworks remains an unanswered research question. In this paper, we comprehensively analyze the security status of two mainstream MARA services – Google SafetyNet and Huawei SafetyDetect (SafetyNet and SafetyDetect in short, respectively).

We first conduct a thorough reverse engineering to recover the underlying mechanisms of both SafetyNet and SafetyDetect. We find that their attestation protocols follow a similar weakness: the MS Core signs the device and app information, and sends the signed information to the MS Server. In this process, MARA allows for two signing modes of MS Core. If the device supports TrustZone, then a hardware-backed KeyStore [23] will be employed during the signing process; otherwise, the signing is entirely executed by the software-level MS Core. We refer to the check result in these two signing modes as *hardware-based check result* and *software-based check result*, respectively. A severe security vulnerability here is that **the hardware-based integrity check cannot be enforced**. That is, most app servers unconditionally accept a software-based check result, even if the device supports hardware-based integrity check. If we deceive the app server that the current device does not support hardware-based attestation, then a software-based check result is accepted, regardless of the actual situation. Since **the software-based signing process can be emulated**, if the MARA protocol is determined, attackers can impersonate MS Core to sign arbitrary messages and cheat the MS Server to return a benign result to both the caller app and the app server. This has finally led to a decrease in the security of the MARA mechanism.

We design an automated measurement pipeline and utilize it to analyze 35,245 top popular apps, confirming that 104 apps, including popular apps and games such as TikTok Lite, Huawei Wallet, Pokémon GO, and NBA LIVE, use the MARA service. Our test shows that there does exist **a generic downgrade attack to bypass MARA**: our software-emulated bypassing approach succeeds against all these apps, which demonstrates the insecurity of the widely used MARA protection.

In a nutshell, this paper makes the following contributions:

- An in-depth reverse engineering to reveal the underlying mechanism of typical MARA frameworks.
- The identification of a common design flaw in these frameworks, which can be exploited to bypass MARA protection.
- A large-scale measurement on real-world apps to evaluate the associated security risks.

Ethical Considerations. We have reported the issue of Google SafetyNet to Google Bug Hunters [36] in May 2022, and Google Security Team has filed the bug based on our report. For the issue of Huawei SafetyDetect, we have reported it to CNCERT/CC[1], and CNCERT/CC has verified our findings and documented related vulnerability under CNVD-2023-57655.

---

[1]   National Computer Network Emergency Response Technical Team/Coordination Center of China, the national CERT of China and responsible for handling severe cyber-security incidents [35].

2 Background

2.1 Remote Attestation

Remote Attestation (RA) [30,31] is a mechanism to verify the integrity and trustworthiness of remote computing devices or systems. A typical remote attestation procedure [30] involves three main parties: the **Attester** is the device or system being attested and generates believable information about itself ("Evidence"); the **Verifier** verifies the Evidence and generates the "Attestation Result"; the **Relying Party** makes the final decision based on the Attestation Result from the Verifier.

On Android, there are several manufacturer-developed implementations for remote attestation. We call them Manufacturer-provided Android Remote Attestation (MARA) frameworks. In these MARA frameworks, mobile devices and their apps typically act as the Attester, the manufacturer's Server usually acts as the Verifier, and the Relying Party is the App Server.

2.2 Mobile Service Core

MARA frameworks are often implemented in the Mobile Service Cores (MS Cores), such as Google Mobile Service Core (GMS Core) [12] and Huawei Mobile Service Core (HMS Core) [14]. These MS Cores are usually integrated into the OS. The phones produced by Google, Huawei and their licensed co-operators [15, 16] are pre-installed with MS Cores since shipped from the factory. For other phones, phone users can also easily install MS Cores by themselves. Since apps like Google Play Store [17], YouTube [18], and Huawei Health [20] can only be used after MS Core is installed, MS Cores have over billions of users [22] and cover almost all countries around the world [21]. This has expanded the impact of security issues within GMS Core and HMS Core.

2.3 Integrity on Android

On Android, integrity protection mainly concerns three aspects:

(1) Device Integrity. Device integrity refers to whether the software and hardware environment of a device has not been unauthorizedly tampered with. Specifically for Android, actions that compromise device integrity include rooting, unlocking the bootloader, changing the SELinux status, using emulators to impersonate a device, and so on. Since running the app on compromised devices can adversely affect the app's service [1–5], ensuring the device integrity is necessary for app developers.

(2) App Integrity. On Android, app integrity mainly refers to whether the app is identical to its official version. The most typical attack behavior that compromises app integrity is app repackaging, which can bring many security risks [6,7]. The repackaged app differs from the original app in aspects such as the APK file digest and app signing certificate fingerprint [48].

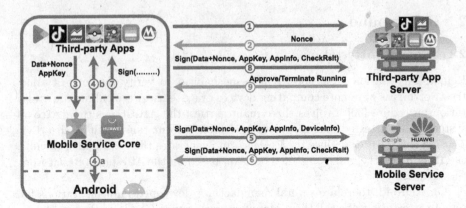

Fig. 2. Key design of the MARA scheme.

(3) Data Integrity. The integrity of certain sensitive data (such as a gamer's score) transmitted from mobile apps to app servers needs to be safeguarded, as attackers may attempt to tamper with these data through network man-in-the-middle (MITM) attacks.

3   MARA Frameworks Demystification

In this section, we introduce the underlying mechanism of two typical MARA frameworks, namely Google SafetyNet and Huawei SafetyDetect. Through reverse engineering, we found that their attestation protocols followed a similar scheme, as described in Sect. 3.1. In Sect. 3.2 and 3.3, we introduce the detailed attestation protocols of SafetyNet and SafetyDetect respectively.

3.1   MARA Scheme

Key Design. Figure 2 presents the high-level design of MARA schemes.

First, the Third-party App on the user's mobile phone obtains a *Nonce* from the App Server (Step ① and ②). Then, the App calls the MARA API, together with *Data+Nonce* and *AppKey* as the parameters (Step ③). Here, *Data* refers to the sensitive data that the App wants to protect from being tampered with, such as the gamer's score. The *Data* will be concatenated with the *Nonce*. *AppKey* is exclusive to a specific app and is pre-assigned to app developers by the manufacturer. It is a fixed string and is usually hard-coded in the App.

Following this, the Mobile Service Core will retrieve the properties of the device (Step ④a) and the App (Step ④b) to get the *DeviceInfo* and the *AppInfo*. Afterwards, the *DeviceInfo* and *AppInfo*, along with the *Data+Nonce* and *AppKey*, will be signed and sent to the Mobile Service Server (Step ⑤). The signing process typically involves a signing key that has been pre-negotiated between the Mobile Service Core and the Mobile Service Server. After verifying the signature, Mobile Service Server will check the integrity of the device based on the *DeviceInfo* and generate *CheckRslt*. Mobile Service Server will then sign the *CheckRslt*, along with the *Data+Nonce*, *AppKey*, and *AppInfo*, using its private key. This signed message will ultimately be obtained by the App Server (Step ⑥, ⑦ and ⑧).

App Server need to verify the Mobile Service Server's signature and check the *Nonce*. Finally, based on the integrity of the device and app, App Server needs to make decisions (Step ⑨). Device integrity can be retrieved directly from the *CheckRslt* and app integrity needs to be judged by comparing *AppInfo* with that of the legitimate app client.

Integrity Protection. Through the above process, MARA Service can provide caller app with integrity protection in three aspects:

(1) Device Integrity Check. Third-party App Server can judge the integrity of the device based on the *CheckRslt* received in Step ⑧. Such a check aims at avoiding the risk of running on a compromised device (e.g., a rooted device or a device whose bootloader is unlocked). The main checking items for device integrity are listed in Appendix A.1.

(2) App Integrity Check. The Third-party App Server receives the *AppInfo* in Step ⑧. Mobile Service Server's signature ensures that *AppInfo* has not been tampered with. Such a check primarily aims at preventing app repackaging [6]. Checking items for app integrity are listed in Appendix A.2.

(3) Data Integrity Protection. In some cases, attackers may tamper with sensitive data sent by the app client through a network man-in-the-middle (MITM) attack. To mitigate this situation, in Step ③, the *Data* is sent to Third-party App Server after being signed. Thus, cheaters can no longer directly tamper with the *Data*.

3.2 Details About SafetyNet

To utilize SafetyNet service, the Third-party App need to integrate the SafetyNet SDK developed by Google. Figure 3 shows the protocol flow of the SafetyNet attestation step-by-step. The whole process can be divided into three phases:

(1) Initialize. This phase corresponds to Step ① to Step ③ in Fig. 2. In this phase, Third-party App passes *Data+Nonce* to GMS Core through SafetyNet SDK.

(2) Obtain Signed Check Result. This phase corresponds to Step ④ to Step ⑥ in Fig. 2. Through this phase, GMS Core will obtain the *CheckRslt* signed by GMS Server.

Specifically, after receiving the App's invocation, GMS Core will download the program file of a customized virtual machine (VM) (Step 5 to 6), and launch the VM) (Step 7). The *VM Program* is an APK-compressed file named "the.apk". It will be saved in GMS Core's private directory. After launched, VM will download customized VM bytecode from GMS Server (Step 8 to 9) and retrieve some device properties through executing these bytecode (Step 10). Finally, VM will get *DeviceInfo₂*.

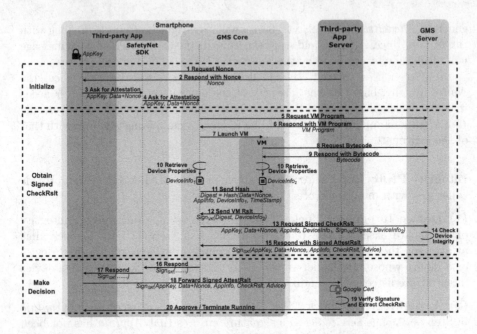

Fig. 3. The protocol flow of SafetyNet attestation.

On the other hand, GMS Core will also retrieve some other device properties and get $DeviceInfo_1$ (Step 10). Afterwards, GMS Core will calculate the SHA-256 value of a protobuf [66] message containing $Data+Nonce$, $AppInfo$, $DeviceInfo_1$ and $TimeStamp$ to get $Digest$ and send $Digest$ to VM (Step 11). The VM will sign $Digest$ and $DeviceInfo_2$ using VK (short for "VM Key"). This VK is embedded in the VM bytecode and the signing algorithm is HS256. We suppose that the reason for carrying out the signing process within VM is because VM offers a higher level of security. Through signing $Digest$, the device properties retrieved by GMS Core and VM, namely $DeviceInfo_1$ and $DeviceInfo_2$, both get authenticated.

The VM-signed message will be forwarded to GMS Server in request for $CheckRslt$ (Step 13). GMS Server will check device integrity based on $DeviceInfo_1$ and $DeviceInfo_2$ (Step 14), and respond with the signed $CheckRslt$ and $Advice$. $Advice$ is a string explaining why the SafetyNet attestation fails, such as "LOCK_BOOTLOADER,RESTORE_TO_FACTORY_ROM" (Step 15).

(3) Make Decision. This phase corresponds to Step ⑦ to Step ⑨ in Fig. 2. In this phase, the signed $CheckRslt$ will be forwarded to Third-party App Server (Step 16 to 18). App Server will verify the signature using Google's public key [38], and make decisions based on $CheckRslt$, $AppInfo$, and $Nonce$ (Step 19 to 20).

3.3 Details About SafetyDetect

Similarly, the Third-party App needs to integrate the SafetyDetect SDK. Figure 4 shows the protocol flow of the SafetyDetect attestation.

(1) Initialize. This phase has no significant difference from the initialization phase of SafetyNet.

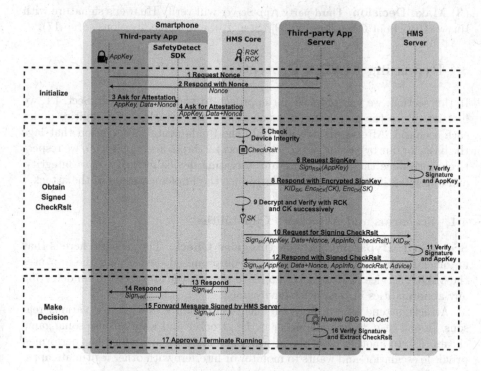

Fig. 4. The protocol flow of SafetyDetect attestation.

(2) Obtain Signed Check Result. Similar to the corresponding phase of SafetyNet, HMS Core will obtain the *CheckRslt* signed by HMS Server through this phase.

Specifically, HMS Core will retrieve device properties, judge whether the device has been compromised, and generate *CheckRslt* (Step 5). Afterwards, by proceeding from Step 6 to Step 9, HMS Core will obtain a *SK* (short for "SignKey") from the HMS Server. This *SK* will later be used to sign *CheckRslt*. In Step 6, HMS Core signs *AppKey* with *RSK* and sends it to HMS Server. Here, *RSK* refers to "RootSignKey", which is a signing key pre-stored in HMS Core and remains fixed. The signing algorithm is HS256. Upon receiving the request from HMS Core, HMS Server verifies the signature and *AppKey* (Step 7) and responds with KID_{SK}, $Enc_{RCK(CK)}$, and $Enc_{CK(SK)}$ (Step 8). Here, KID_{SK} is the Key ID of *SK*; *RCK* refers to "RootCryptoKey" and is a fixed crypto key pre-stored in HMS Core. HMS Core uses *RCK* to decrypt $Enc_{RCK(CK)}$ and uses *CK* to decrypt $Enc_{CK(SK)}$ (Step 9). The algorithm used for encrypting *CK* and *SK* is AES-GCM, so in Step 9, HMS Core will also verify the *Tag*s during decryption.

Finally, HMS Core obtains *SK*, which will be cached and reused within a period. HMS Core use it to sign *CheckRslt* (Step 10). HMS Server will verify the signature and *AppKey* (Step 11), sign *CheckRslt* with *HK* (short for "Huawei Key") and send it back (Step 12).

(3) Make Decision. Third-party App Server will verify Huawei's signature with Huawei CBG Root CA certificate [39] (Step 16), and make decisions (Step 17).

4   Bypassing MARA Protection

In this section, we will propose our approach to bypass MARA. In Sect. 4.1, we first introduce the attack scenarios as well as the attacker's capabilities under each scenario. Afterwards, we illustrate the fundamental observation that lays the basis for our bypassing approach in Sect. 4.2. From Sect. 4.3 to 4.5, we respectively introduce the attack procedure targeting device integrity, data integrity, and app integrity. In Sect. 4.6, we introduce the implementation of the attack.

4.1   Scenarios and Attacker's Capabilities

Scenario 1: Bypassing Device Integrity Check. The scenario here is that an official app has been installed on a compromised device, and the app uses the MARA service. The attacker hopes to prevent the app server from detecting any abnormalities in the device environment.

Attackers tend to run apps on such compromised devices for various reasons. In one case, the phone owner is the attacker and wants to use some game cheats [13]. In another case, the attacker is a malware [37] which has performed privilege escalation and wants to monitor or interfere with other legitimate apps.

Attacker's Capability. In this scenario, we assume that the attacker has **root privilege** on the device. This assumption is reasonable because if the device is compromised, it means that the device has already been rooted, bootloader-unlocked, or flashed with a custom ROM. These circumstances all enable the attacker to easily obtain root privilege.

Scenario 2: Bypassing App Integrity Check. This scenario involves a repackaged app being installed on a non-rooted device and the app has integrated the MARA service. The attacker aims to make the repackaged app appear as the official version.

In reality, there are many cases of app repackaging. For example, some attackers may repackage popular apps to embed advertisements [8] and trick users into clicking on them.

Attacker's Capability. In this scenario, we assume that the attacker **can repackage** the app. Note that we neither require the attacker to have root privileges nor do we require them to possess the developer's *App Signing Key* [48].

Scenario 3: Bypassing Data Integrity Protection. In this scenario, the attacker hopes to tamper with the *Data* exchanged between the app and the app server by performing a network man-in-the-middle attack. MARA service prevents attackers from directly intercepting and tampering with the network data, as the attackers cannot forge the signature of MS Server.

In real-life situations, for important data such as the gamer's score, apps typically use HTTPS for transmission. Therefore, in order to perform network interception, the attacker needs to insert a MITM certificate into the Android System Trust Store [40] and inject code into the victim's app process to bypass Certificate Pinning [41]. Both of these two operations require root privilege.

Attacker's Capability. In this scenario, we assume that the attacker has **root privilege** on the device. Such an assumption is reasonable because if an attacker is able to decrypt and manipulate HTTPS packets, they must have already obtained root privilege.

4.2 Fundamental Observation

There is a fundamental observation that lays the basis for our attacks against these MARA frameworks. The observation is that, **most app servers do not have a mandatory requirement for hardware-based check result**. Through reverse engineering, we found that the *DeviceInfo* sent by MS Core in Step ⑤ of Fig. 2 contains two parts: software-based and hardware-based. The hardware-based part will only be available if the device is equipped with TrustZone; otherwise, only the software-based part will appear.

Taking GMS Core as an example. If the device supports hardware-based attestation, the VM inside GMS Core will retrieve a certificate chain from the device's hardware-backed KeyStore [23] and put it into $DeviceInfo_2$ (see Fig. 3). One certificate in this chain contains device information in its Extension Data, such as the verifiedBootState and the verifiedBootHash. Therefore, through this certificate chain, the GMS Server can obtain the device's bootloader status. For example, if the bootloader is unlocked, the GMS Server may consider that the device has been compromised.

We conducted tests on over 35,000 popular apps and found that, among the apps where we have confirmed the use of MARA service, **none of them has a mandatory requirement for hardware-based check result**. In other words, as long as a benign software-based check result is returned, the app server will not stop the app's running or prompt any security risks. We suppose this is because the apps aim to be compatible with a wider range of devices. This can lead to a downgrade attack: if the attacker can make the app server believe that the device does not support hardware-based attestation and always provide a benign software-based check result to the app, then the attacker can bypass such MARA.

We can implement a "trusted device" to launch the attack: such a "trusted device" is considered to be trusted by MS Server; but in reality, this "trusted device" is compromised, and the attacker can use it to forge MS Core's signature on arbitrary data.

4.3 Bypassing Device Integrity Check

As described in Sect. 4.1, we assume that the attacker has root privilege. Therefore, the attacker can tamper with the data sent and received by the Third-party

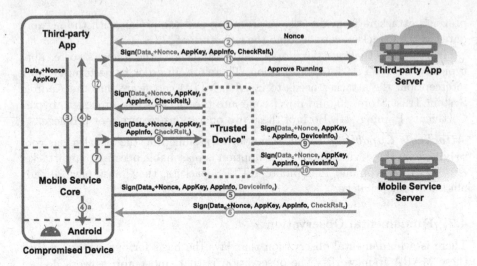

Fig. 5. Bypassing device integrity check and data integrity protection.

App through code injection. The attacker aims to make the compromised device be regarded to be trusted by MS Server. We use $DeviceInfo_c$ and $DeviceInfo_t$ to refer to the compromised device's $DeviceInfo$ and that of the trusted device, respectively. $CheckRslt_c$ and $CheckRslt_t$ have corresponding meanings as well. The process of bypassing device integrity check is illustrated in Fig. 5.

From Step ① to Step ⑥ in Fig. 5, the attestation process is proceeding normally. The "Trusted Device" intercepts the return value (Step ⑧) before App receives it from GMS Core (Step ⑦). The reason for choosing Step ⑧ instead of an earlier step such as Step ③ is that, at Step ⑧, the entire $AppInfo$ can be obtained by the "Trusted Device", which facilitates the construction of the request in Step ⑨. Afterwards, the "Trusted Device" obtains the signed $CheckRslt_t$ from the Mobile Service Server (Step ⑩), and replaces the signed $CheckRslt_c$ with the signed $CheckRslt_t$ (Step ⑪).

4.4   Bypassing App Integrity Check

As described in Sect. 4.1, in this scenario, we assume that the attacker can repackage the app. The repackaged app is installed onto a non-rooted device. We use $AppInfo_o$ and $AppInfo_r$ to refer to the $AppInfo$ of the official app and the repackaged app, respectively. The process of bypassing app integrity check is illustrated in Fig. 7 in Appendix B.

4.5   Bypassing Data Integrity Protection

Due to the shared assumption between scenario 1 and scenario 3 (see Sect. 4.1), we merge the two processes into a single Fig. 5 to save space. We use $Data_c$ and $Data_o$ to refer to the compromised $Data$ and the original $Data$, respectively. As described in Sect. 4.1, the attacker needs root privilege to intercept the HTTPS data packets, which means that the device has been compromised. Therefore, the "Trusted Device" also needs to replace $DeviceInfo_C$ with $DeviceInfo_t$ to bypass device integrity check.

4.6 Attack Implementation

Whether it is in scenario 1, 2, or 3, the implementation of the attack mainly involves two parts: (1) Injecting code into the victim app to intercept the return value from the MS Core; (2) Implementing a "Trusted Device" to sign on arbitrary data.

Code Injection. We integrated the SDKs of SafetyNet and SafetyDetect, and developed two demo apps as the victim apps. In scenario 1 and scenario 3, since the attacker has **root privilege** on the device, we use Frida [42] to perform dynamic instrumentation on the victim apps. In scenario 2, we decompile and recompile the victim apps using ShakaApktool [43], and insert our logic into the original apps through smali [46] code.

Implementation of "Trusted Device". For HMS, we implement such a "Trusted Device" through a protocol-emulating script. The script is implemented in Python and runs on a laptop. For GMS, the $DeviceInfo_2$ is generated by executing the VM's bytecode (Step 10 in Fig. 3) and the bytecode obtained from the GMS Server is different each time (Step 9 in Fig. 3). Thus, in order to implement a "Trusted Device", we need an Android OS environment to support the running of the VM. We implement such an environment based on Magisk [52]. Specifically, We patched an official firmware (ROM[2]) with Magisk, which will create a virtual /system partition under the /data partition. Magisk then redirects GMS Core's calls from the original /system partition to the virtual /system partition and unmounts any root privilege-related file systems to ensure that the retrieved DeviceInfo is benign. We flashed this patched ROM into a OnePlus 5T phone, allowing this virtual environment to be hosted on this phone.

5 Evaluation

5.1 Effectiveness of Our Bypassing Approach

Experimental Setup. To evaluate the effectiveness of our bypassing approach, we tested our bypassing approach on 10 Android smartphones. The 10 devices were running on different operating systems, ranging from Android 5 to Android 11, and covered different brands including Huawei, Xiaomi, OnePlus, Lenovo, and Nokia. These phones are all rooted to facilitate the experiment on bypassing device integrity checks. Details about the smartphones are listed in Table 3 in Appendix C.

---

[2] OnePlus5T Hydrogen_43_OTA_065_all_2012030405_03dba2c095454647.

Experiment Steps. We install GMS Core and HMS Core (if they are not pre-installed) on all these mobile phones and try to bypass the device integrity check and app integrity check based on our approach. Testing for bypassing data integrity protection is not necessary because (1) it has the same assumptions as bypassing device integrity check (see Sect. 4.1); (2) according to Sect. 4.3 and 4.5, as long as the attacker can implement a "trusted device" and bypass device integrity check, he can control the *Data+Nonce* sent by the "trusted device" to the MS Server and thus bypass data integrity protection.

Comparison with Existing Tools in the Wild. As a comparison, we found the two most mentioned MARA bypassing implementations from the XDA forum [49]: Universal SafetyNet Fix [50] and Shamiko [51]. Overall, both Universal SafetyNet Fix and Shamiko take effect by **interfering with the MS Core's retrieval of the device information (during Step ④a in Fig. 2). They target the MS Core.** In contrast, our method takes effect **between Step ⑦ and Step ⑧** in Fig. 2. **Our method targets the victim app.**

Table 1. Success rate of our bypassing approach compared with Universal SafetyNet Fix and Shamiko.

Byapssssing approach	Test item		Device No									
			#1	#2	#3	#4	#5	#6	#7	#8	#9	#10
Universial SafetyNet Fix	Device Int.	GMS	✓	–	✓	✗	✓	–	–	✗	–	–
		HMS	✓	✓	✓	✓	✗	✓	✓	✗	✗	✗
	App Int.						✗					
Shamiko	Device Int.	GMS	✓	–	✓	✗	✓	–	–	✗	–	–
		HMS	✓	✓	✓	✓	✗	✓	✓	✗	✗	✗
	App Int.						✗					
our approach	Device Int.	GMS	✓	–	✓	✓	✓	–	–	✓	–	–
		HMS	✓	✓	✓	✓	✓	✓	✓	✓	✓	✓
	App Int.						✓					

"Int." is short for "Integrity"; ✓: Succeeded in bypassing check; ✗: Failed to bypass check; –: Failed to invoke the attestation API due to MS Core's internal error.

Experiment Results. The experiment results are shown in Table 1.

Bypassing Device Integrity Check. On some phones, compatibility issues between the OS and the GMS Core have resulted in the failure of the SafetyNet service. Although having tried multiple combinations of GMS Core and ROM, we were still unable to make GMS Core execute correctly on these phones. Apart from these 5 issues, our approach succeed in all the other 15 cases.

Regarding the Universal SafetyNet Fix and Shamiko, they succeed in 9 out of 15 cases related to device integrity. Both Universal SafetyNet Fix and Shamiko need to unlock the victim device's bootloader. Therefore, they cannot be applied to devices #4, #9, and #10 as the root privilege on these devices is obtained through vulnerabilities (e.g., CVE-2020-0069 [53] on device #4), instead of through unlocking the bootloader and flashing a custom ROM. On device #5, HMS Server returned the advice of "RESTORE_TO_FACTORY_ROM" in the *CheckRslt*, which might be due to the detection of abnormal SELinux status. On device #8, both GMS and HMS detected abnormalities in the bootloader status and returned advice like "RESTORE_TO_FACTORY_ROM, LOCK_BOOTLOADER".

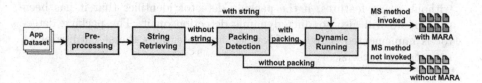

Fig. 6. Overview of our analysis pipeline for identifying affected apps.

Bypassing App Integrity Check. Based on the assumption we presented in Sect. 4.1, in this scenario, the attacker does not have root privilege but can repackage the victim app. Therefore, neither Universal SafetyNet Fix nor Shamiko can be used. Our method only requires the attacker to interfere with the victim app, thus enabling the attacker to bypass the app integrity check through app repackaging.

5.2   Large-Scale Measurement Study

First, we conducted a measurement study on real-world apps to identify apps that use MARA services. Then, we analyzed involved security issues.

Dataset. To better reflect the usage of MARA frameworks worldwide, we crawled all the applications in the top lists of APKPure [54] and Chinese 360 Mobile Market [55]. After removing the losses during download, we collected a total of 35,245 apps, of which 20,253 came from APKPure (including 47 categories) and 14,992 came from the 360 Mobile Market (including 21 categories).

Measurement Approach. We employed a mix of static and dynamic analysis mechanisms to identify the apps that use MARA services. The overall pipeline of our approach is illustrated in Fig. 6. We first use static analysis to filter out potential apps and then conduct dynamic analysis to further confirm the results.

(1) Preprocessing. There are two steps in preprocessing: further filter out corrupted apps and extract APKs from XAPK [58] files for subsequent static analysis.

(2) String Retrieving and Packing Detection.
The result of straightforwardly retrieving the signatures of classes and methods is far from satisfying due to code obfuscation (e.g., ProGuard [56]) and app packing [34].

- Code obfuscation will remove the signatures of classes and methods from the app code, thus we choose to retrieve constant strings. We use Apktool [44] to decompile the app's code and use grep [45] with regular expressions to retrieve strings inside the MARA SDKs. Apps with string features will be dynamically analyzed.
- App packing can hide almost all static code features, including constant strings. To tackle this issue, we implemented a packing detector. For apps without string features, if the packing detector identifies that it has been packed, we will also conduct dynamic detection on it. The packing detector is implemented based on Soot [47] and integrates the signatures of 11 mainstream packers.

(3) Dynamic Running. We use Monkey [57] to generate UI events and drive the tested app to run on a OnePlus 5T device. Meanwhile, we use Frida [42] to hook the MS process. If the app invokes the MARA service during its running process, the corresponding methods in the MS process will be invoked. To prevent the MS process from being killed and causing our hooking to fail, we regularly use an app to call the MS process to keep it active at all times. In addition, we noticed that many apps utilize the SafetyNet service when users log in via a Google account. Therefore, we logged in to our Google account on the device in advance to facilitate triggering the SafetyNet service.

Table 2. Overview of app measurement results

MARA	Total Apps	Static Analysis			Dynamic Analysis	
			String Retrieving	Packing Detection		
SafetyNet	35,245	potential	4,296	11,234	use	73
					don't use	11,161
		unsuspicious	30,949	24,011		
SafetyDetect	35,245	potential	226	7,158	use	31
					don't use	7,127
		unsuspicious	35,019	28,087		

Results and Findings. Our app measurement results are shown in Table 2. In total, among the 35,245 top Android apps, we identified 73 apps that have used the SafetyNet service and 31 apps using the SafetyDetect. These apps include some top most popular applications and games, such as TikTok Lite, Huawei Wallet, China Merchants Bank, Pokémon GO, NBA LIVE, and so on. Detailed information on our measurement result is available at https://github.com/zhouziyi1/MARA.

To detail, when detecting SafetyNet-related apps, our string retrieving process enables us to locate 4,296 candidates. The packing detection process helps us locate 6,938 additional candidates. To this end, we have a total number of 11,234 candidates through the static analysis process. Our dynamic running confirmed that 73 out of these 11,234 apps indeed invoke the SafetyNet service. For SafetyDetect, we ultimately confirmed 31 apps.

Through further manual inspection, we found that most MARA invocations occur when users log in. For example, among the 31 SafetyDetect-related apps, 24 apps call SafetyDetect service when users log in, while the remaining 7 apps call the service as soon as the user launches the app.

Case Studies

(1) Pokémon GO. Pokémon GO [9] is one of the most popular and highest-grossing mobile games worldwide, with over 572 million downloads [11] and $6 billion in player spending [10]. It allows players to catch nearby "Pokémon" based on players' geographical location. If players can use mock locations instead of real ones, they can cheat in the game. One type of mock location tool [59–62] does not require root privilege, but they can be easily blocked by Pokémon GO. Another type of mock location tool [63] requires root privilege and is more difficult to detect. To block such mock location tools, Pokémon GO utilizes the SafetyNet service. Specifically, when a user logs into Pokémon GO with a Google account, Pokémon GO calls the SafetyNet API and checks the integrity of the current device. If the current device has been rooted, Pokémon GO prohibits the user from logging in. We implemented our attack method (as described in Sect. 4.6) on a rooted Mi 8 phone and successfully bypassed Pokémon GO's root detection. This allows us to successfully perform location spoofing using Fake GPS Location Spoofer [63].

(2) Huawei Wallet. Huawei Wallet is a payment app with over 100 million active users [64]. To prevent root malware (such as [37,53,65]) from threatening users' property and privacy, Huawei Wallet checks the device's integrity using the SafetyDetect service right after app's startup. If the device doesn't meet the security requirements, Huawei Wallet displays a prompt to the user. The app will only continue running after the user confirms the risk. We successfully deceived the SafetyDetect service with our bypassing approach (as described in Sect. 4.6) on a OnePlus 9R phone, making it difficult for users to realize the existence of malware. Afterwards, malware with root privilege can access files in the private directory of Huawei Wallet, stealing user account information, program logs, cookies, and other sensitive data.

6   Conclusion

In this paper, we conducted an in-depth security study on Google SafetyNet and Huawei SafetyDetect, two mainstream Manufacturer-provided Android Remote Attestation (MARA) frameworks, and found a new way to bypass their integrity check. *Compared with existing bypassing implementations in the wild, our bypassing approach can succeed on more devices.* To further evaluate the real-world impact of our identified issues, we performed a large-scale measurement over a set of top popular apps, and analyzed related security implications to the apps that integrate MARA service.

Acknowledgments. The authors would like to thank the anonymous reviewers for their valuable feedback to improve the manuscript. This work is partially supported by Shanghai Pujiang Program (No. 22PJ1405700), the National Key Research and Development Program of China (No. 2021YFB3101402) and the Project of Shanghai Science and Technology Innovation Action Program under Grant (No. 22511101300). The authors would like to thank the support from the ZhiXun Crypto Testing Group as well. We also express our sincere appreciation to Professor Douglas Leith from Trinity College Dublin for his patient and detailed responses to our emails. He addressed our confusion regarding his previous research works and generously shared his experimental details with us. Furthermore, we are grateful to Professor Lei Xue from Sun Yat-sen University for his extensive expertise and patient assistance in resolving the technical difficulties we encountered during the experiments. Their contributions have been instrumental in the successful implementation of this study.

Appendix A   Integrity Checking Items

A.1   Device Integrity Checking Items

- SU Files
- SeLinux Status
- Bootloader Status
- Root Frameworks
- Hooking Frameworks
- Emulators

A.2   App Integrity Checking Items

- App Package Name
- App Certificate Fingerprint
- Apk File Digest

Appendix B   Bypassing app integrity check

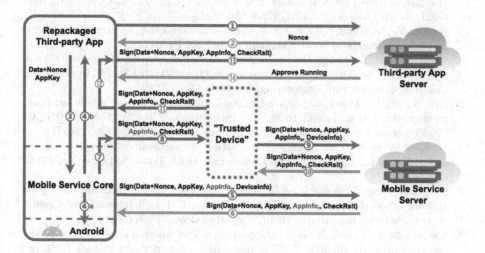

Fig. 7. Bypassing app integrity check.

Appendix C   Device details

Table 3. Details about the Android devices used in Sect. 5.1

No	Model number	Android version	Build number	Bootloader status	GMS version	HMS version
#1	OnePlus 9R	11	Oxygen OS 11.2.4.4.LE28DA	unlocked	21.06.13	6.8.0.332
#2	Xiaomi Mi CC9 Pro	11	MIUI 13.0.4 Stable 13.0.4.0(RFDCNXM)	unlocked	21.21.16	6.8.0.332
#3	Oneplus 5T	10	H2OS 10.0.3	unlocked	22.12.15	6.8.0.332
#4	Nokia X5	9	00CN_2_15A_SP02	locked	22.12.15	6.8.0.332
#5	Xiaomi Mi 8	9	MIUI 10 9.8.22 Beta	unlocked	22.12.15	6.8.0.332
#6	OnePlus 5	9	H2OS 9.0.5	unlocked	22.12.15	6.8.0.332
#7	Motorola P30	8.1.0	ZUI 4.0.374 Stable	unlocked	20.12.16	6.8.0.332
#8	Xiaomi Mi 5	8.0.0	MIUI 10.8.11.22 Beta	unlocked	20.12.16	6.8.0.332
#9	Huawei Mate 9	7	EMUI 5.0	locked	10.2.98	6.10.4.300
#10	Lenovo K5 Note	5.1.1	VIBE UI V3.0	locked	10.0.84	6.8.0.332

References

1. Tian, Y., Chen, E., Ma, X., et al.: Swords and shields: a study of mobile game hacks and existing defenses. In: Proceedings of the 32nd Annual Conference on Computer Security Applications, pp. 386–397 (2016)

2. Karkallis, P., Blasco, J., Suarez-Tangil, G., Pastrana, S.: Detecting video-game injectors exchanged in game cheating communities. In: Bertino, E., Shulman, H., Waidner, M. (eds.) ESORICS 2021. LNCS, vol. 12972, pp. 305–324. Springer, Cham (2021). https://doi.org/10.1007/978-3-030-88418-5_15

3. Nguyen-Vu, L., Chau, N.T., Kang, S., et al.: Android rooting: an arms race between evasion and detection. Secur. Commun. Netw. **2017** (2017)

4. Chen, S., Fan, L., Meng, G., et al.: An empirical assessment of security risks of global android banking apps. In: Proceedings of the ACM/IEEE 42nd International Conference on Software Engineering, pp. 1310–1322 (2020)

5. Sun, S., Yu, L., Zhang, X., et al.: Understanding and detecting mobile ad fraud through the lens of invalid traffic. In: Proceedings of the 2021 ACM SIGSAC Conference on Computer and Communications Security, pp. 287–303 (2021)

6. Li, L., Bissyandé, T.F., Klein, J.: Rebooting research on detecting repackaged android apps: Literature review and benchmark. IEEE Trans. Software Eng. **47**(4), 676–693 (2019)

7. Song, W., Ming, J., Jiang, L., et al.: App's auto-login function security testing via android OS-level virtualization. In: 2021 IEEE/ACM 43rd International Conference on Software Engineering (ICSE), pp. 1683–1694. IEEE (2021)

8. Xue, L., Zhou, H., Luo, X., et al.: Happer: unpacking Android apps via a hardware-assisted approach. In: 2021 IEEE Symposium on Security and Privacy (SP), pp. 1641–1658. IEEE (2021)

9. Pokémon GO. https://play.google.com/store/apps/details?id=com.nianticlabs.Pokemongo&hl=en_US. Accessed 14 May 2023

10. Pokémon Go hits $6 billion in player spending. https://play.google.com/store/apps/details?id=com.nianticlabs.Pokemongo&hl=en_US. Accessed 14 May 2023

11. Pokémon Go Revenue and Usage Statistics (2023). https://www.businessofapps.com/data/pokemon-go-statistics/. Accessed 14 May 2023

12. Android - Google Mobile Services. https://www.android.com/gms/. Accessed 14 May 2023

13. Fake GPS Location Spoofer. https://play.google.com/store/apps/details?id=com.incorporateapps.fakegps.fre. Accessed 14 May 2023

14. HMS Core. https://developer.huawei.com/consumer/en/hms/. Accessed 14 May 2023

15. Mobile Application Distribution Agreement (Android). https://www.sec.gov/Archives/edgar/containers/fix380/1495569/000119312510271362/dex1012.htm. Accessed 14 May 2023

16. HMS Core (APK) Preloading Guide: Ecosystem Cooperation. https://developer.huawei.com/consumer/en/doc/development/hmscore-common-Guides/overview-0000001222509146. Accessed 14 May 2023

17. Google Play Store. https://apkpure.com/google-play-store/com.android.vending. Accessed 14 May 2023

18. YouTube. https://play.google.com/store/apps/details?id=com.google.android.youtube. Accessed 14 May 2023

19. HUAWEI Wallet. https://consumer.huawei.com/en/mobileservices/wallet/. Accessed 14 May 2023

20. HUAWEI Health. https://consumer.huawei.com/en/mobileservices/health/. Accessed 14 May 2023

21. HMS Core 5.0 launched for the global developers. https://www.huaweicentral.com/hms-core-5-0-launched-for-the-global-developers-comes-with-7-new-kits-and-services/. Accessed 14 May 2023

22. Google I/O 2023: What's new in Google Play. https://io.google/2023/program/9019266d-186c-4a61-9cc5-b1c665eb40fb/. Accessed 21 May 2023
23. Verifying hardware-backed key pairs with Key Attestation. https://developer.android.com/training/articles/security-key-attestation. Accessed 14 May 2023
24. Protect against security threats with SafetyNet. https://developer.android.com/training/safetynet. Accessed 14 May 2023
25. Safety Detect. https://developer.huawei.com/consumer/en/hms/huawei-safetydetectkit/. Accessed 14 May 2023
26. Mulliner, C., Kozyrakis, J.: Inside Android's SafetyNet Attestation. Black Hat EU (2017)
27. Thomas, R.: DroidGuard: a deep dive into SafetyNet. Black Hat Asia (2022)
28. Examining the value of SafetyNet Attestation as an Application Integrity Security Control. https://census-labs.com/news/2017/11/17/examining-the-value-of-safetynet-attestation-as-an-application-integrity-security-control/. Accessed 14 May 2023
29. How I discovered an easter egg in Android's security and didn't land a job at Google. https://habr.com/en/articles/446790/. Accessed 14 May 2023
30. RFC 9334: Remote ATtestation procedureS (RATS) Architecture. https://datatracker.ietf.org/doc/rfc9334/. Accessed 14 May 2023
31. Coker, G., Guttman, J., Loscocco, P., et al.: Principles of remote attestation. Int. J. Inf. Secur. **10**, 63–81 (2011)
32. Ibrahim, M., Imran, A., Bianchi, A.: SafetyNOT: on the usage of the SafetyNet attestation API in Android. In: Proceedings of the 19th Annual International Conference on Mobile Systems, Applications, and Services, pp. 150–162 (2021)
33. Aldoseri, A., Chothia, T., Moreira-Sanchez, J., et al.: Symbolic modelling of remote attestation protocols for device and app integrity on android. In: 18th ACM ASIA Conference on Computer and Communications Security. Association for Computing Machinery (ACM) (2023)
34. Duan, Y., Zhang, M., Bhaskar, A.V., et al.: Things you may not know about android (un) packers: a systematic study based on whole-system emulation. In: NDSS (2018)
35. CNCERT/CC: National Computer Network Emergency Response Technical Team/Coordination Center of China. https://www.cert.org.cn/publish/english/index.html. Accessed 14 May 2023
36. Google Bug Hunters. https://bughunters.google.com/. Accessed 14 May 2023
37. A Very Powerful Clipboard: Analysis of a Samsung in-the-wild exploit chain. https://googleprojectzero.blogspot.com/2022/11/a-very-powerful-clipboard-samsung-in-the-wild-exploit-chain.html. Accessed 15 May 2023
38. Upcoming Change: New certificate chain in the API response signature. https://groups.google.com/g/safetynet-api-clients/c/-2ShuYt5kFg. Accessed 17 May 2023
39. SysIntegrity API. https://developer.huawei.com/consumer/en/doc/development/Security-Guides/dysintegritydevelopment-0000001050156331. Accessed 15 May 2023
40. CA-certificates. https://android.googlesource.com/platform/system/ca-certificates/. Accessed 15 May 2023
41. Pin certificates. https://developer.android.com/training/articles/security-config#CertificatePinning. Accessed 15 May 2023
42. Frida. https://frida.re/. Accessed 15 May 2023
43. ShakaApktool. https://github.com/rover12421/ShakaApktool. Accessed 15 May 2023

44. Apktool: A tool for reverse engineering Android APK files. https://ibotpeaches. github.io/Apktool/. Accessed 15 May 2023
45. Grep. https://www.gnu.org/software/grep/manual/grep.html. Accessed 15 May 2023
46. Smali. https://github.com/JesusFreke/smali/wiki. Accessed 15 May 2023
47. Soot. http://soot-oss.github.io/soot/. Accessed 15 May 2023
48. Application Signing. https://source.android.com/docs/security/features/apksign ing. Accessed 15 May 2023
49. XDA Portal & Forums. https://www.xda-developers.com/. Accessed 15 May 2023
50. Universal SafetyNet Fix. https://github.com/kdrag0n/safetynet-fix. Accessed 15 May 2023
51. Shamiko v0.7.2. https://github.com/LSPosed/LSPosed.github.io/releases. Accessed 15 May 2023
52. Magisk. https://github.com/topjohnwu/Magisk/releases. Accessed 27 May 2023
53. CVE-2020-0069. https://nvd.nist.gov/vuln/detail/CVE-2020-0069. Accessed 27 May 2023
54. APKPure: Download APK on Android with Free Online APK Downloader. https://apkpure.com/. Accessed 27 May 2023
55. 360 Mobile Assistant. http://m.app.so.com/. Accessed 27 May 2023
56. ProGuard: Java Obfuscator and Android App Optimizer. https://www. guardsquare.com/proguard. Accessed 27 May 2023
57. UI/Application Exerciser Monkey. https://developer.android.com/studio/test/ other-testing-tools/monkey. Accessed 27 May 2023
58. XAPK file. https://apkpure.com/xapk.html. Accessed 27 May 2023
59. FGL Pro. https://play.google.com/store/apps/details?id=com.ltp.pro.fakelocati on&hl=en_US&gl=US. Accessed 27 May 2023
60. Fake GPS Location-GPS JoyStick. https://play.google.com/store/apps/details? id=com.theappninjas.fakegpsjoystick&hl=en. Accessed 27 May 2023
61. Cha Cha Helper. https://www.xxzhushou.cn/?channelid=352666. Accessed 27 May 2023
62. Moloc. https://www.coolapk.com/apk/top.xuante.moloc. Accessed 27 May 2023
63. Fake GPS Location Spoofer. https://play.google.com/store/apps/details?id=com. incorporateapps.fakegps.fre. Accessed 27 May 2023
64. Huawei has the highest number of active smartphone users globally: how is this possible? https://www.gizchina.com/2022/08/27/huawei-has-the-highest-number-of-smartphone-users-globally-how-is-this-possible/. Accessed 27 May 2023
65. One of China's most popular apps has the ability to spy on its users. https:// edition.cnn.com/2023/04/02/tech/china-pinduoduo-malware-cybersecurity-analy sis-intl-hnk/index.html. Accessed 27 May 2023
66. Protocol Buffers. https://protobuf.dev/. Accessed 30 May 2023

DScope: To Reliably and Securely Acquire Live Data from Kernel-Compromised ARM Devices

Zhe Chen, Haiqing Qiu, and Xuhua Ding[(⊠)]

Singapore Management University, Singapore, Singapore
{zhechen,hqqiu,xhding}@smu.edu.sg

Abstract. Live data acquisition from a mobile device controlled by a corrupted kernel is challenging as the adversary can block data reporting from the inside and also sabotage external I/O interactions. This paper proposes DScope as a reliable live data acquisition system for ARM devices without trusting their kernels. It ensures that a device user can always launch DScope to securely extract the needed virtual memory data when the device is under attack. Besides its reliability, DScope also preserves kernel semantic and support user-customized acquisition routines. We have built a prototype of DScope on a Raspberry Pi 4 development board and have also tested DScope's reliability against various forms of denial of service attacks. Our experiments show that a user can dynamically import data acquisition routines to the device to extract kernel objects and runtime stacks from an attack scene or a kernel crashing site.

1 Introduction

Live data acquisition is integral to incident response, forensics and even crash diagnosis as it provides the raw material for software semantics derivation and attack intelligence extraction. Since data acquisition is often in the presence of an adversary, the procedure is required to be *secure*. Namely, the data is retrieved genuinely from locations demanded by the user. The procedure should not be spoofed or tampered with by the adversary in the device. Equally important to security is the assurance of data retrieval with the same logical-to-physical location mappings as used by the kernel. We term it as *mapping consistency*. For volatile data, the logical location refers to the virtual address in the kernel code referencing the object. An acquisition tool using mappings different from the target may fetch data from wrong physical pages and data analysis cannot be made through the same perspective as the kernel.

The challenges to attain security and mapping consistency in data acquisition mirror those in virtual machine introspection (VMI). In the literature, VMI can be classified into in-VM introspection [22,24] and out-of-VM introspection [8,10, 20]. As noted in [4,15], the former technique uses a consistent mapping, however, without security assurance against a compromised kernel. While the latter can

© The Author(s), under exclusive license to Springer Nature Switzerland AG 2024
G. Tsudik et al. (Eds.): ESORICS 2023, LNCS 14347, pp. 271–289, 2024.
https://doi.org/10.1007/978-3-031-51482-1_14

cope with the kernel adversary, it has no guarantee of mapping consistency. Similarly, a device's runtime data can be acquired in-device by relying on a kernel module or out-of-device by using a special external hardware equipment attached, e.g., a JTAG debugger. The conflicting requirement between security and mapping-consistency in VMI also arises in device data acquisition when the adversary resides in the kernel. The adversary can tamper with the in-device agent to fake the reported data or uses its own address mappings to explore the semantic gap [15], thus undermining the soundness of the collected data. TrustDump [25] overcomes the challenge by freezing the untrusted kernel and walks through its paging hierarchy using an agent protected by ARM TrustZone. While suitable for page-granularity memory dump, it is not efficient and feasible for fine-grained live memory object acquisition, e.g., observing the dynamic of cred objects of all processes during corrupted kernel execution.

A remarkable difference between device and VM data extraction lies in *reliability*. Namely, a data acquisition procedure can always be launched and carried out against denial-of-service attacks. High reliability is a desirable feature for live forensics and incident response. Several schemes [13,30,31] rely on a hardware watchdog or timer to ensure a security-critical task to be reliably launched. Nonetheless, we consider on user demand data acquisition, which makes periodical checking less appealing. More importantly, these schemes do not need to consider runtime denial-of-service attacks since the launched task controls the entire platform. GAROTA [2] assures a reliable launch by protecting the interrupt delivery route in micro-control units which have a simpler architecture than middle or high-end ARM devices such as phones.

In this paper, we propose DSCOPE, a virtualization based system for live data acquisition. DSCOPE uses a daemon running in EL2, with the size orders of magnitude smaller than a full-fledged hypervisor like Xen-on-ARM [14]. The device user can reliably launch a data acquisition session according to her demand in the presence of a kernel adversary. Without terminating the kernel or shutting down the device, the user securely connects the device with her trusted PC via a serial cable and imports her data acquisition agent to the device. The agent's execution uses the kernel's current address mappings to read/write kernel memory and transports the results to the PC. DSCOPE ensures that the agent import and execution are not subject to the kernel's attacks, including denial-of-service attacks. We have implemented a prototype of DSCOPE on a Raspberry Pi development board with an ARM64 processor. We assess its reliability by running several experiments including benign kernel crashes as well as denial-of-service attacks that attempt to sabotage I/O interfaces, block interrupt delivery, and withhold CPU cores. All experiments show that DSCOPE is reliable and practical, with an insignificant performance overhead upon a normal device.

2   Background and Related Work

2.1   Background on ARM Virtualization

ARM virtualization extension supports physical memory virtualization, interrupt virtualization and timer virtualization. ARMv7 and subsequent versions use the Stage-II address translation tables for the hypervisor to define mappings between intermediate physical addresses (IPA) to physical addresses (PA), while the kernel uses the Stage-I address translation tables to map virtual addresses (VA) to IPA. The hypervisor can control the kernel's access to memory by setting stage-II page table. Once memory virtualization is enabled, a memory access requires traversal of both translation tables.

The Generic Interrupt Controller (GIC) [3] is a centralized resource for supporting and managing interrupts in a system that includes at least one processor. As a central controller, GIC can disable, enable or generate processor interrupts from hardware interrupt source. It is compatible with multiprocessor environments and ARM architecture virtualization extensions. Logically, the GIC system includes these two functional components: Distributor and CPU interfaces. The Distributor centralizes all interrupt sources, determines the priority of each interrupt, and for each CPU interface, forwards the interrupt with the highest priority to the associated CPU core. GICv2 and subsequent versions support for ARM interrupt virtualization with which the hypervisor can intercept and dispatch interrupts to the kernel.

2.2   Related Work

Our work is related to software reliability against component failures. The popular approach to reliability is Software Fault Isolation (SFI) [28] with the idea that errors are contained within certain region of the system. For instance, several works [9,11,17] use memory isolation as the building block. It is more challenging to consider failures due to attacks in system software. Nooks [26] uses a copy version of kernel page table for untrusted kernel extension which is only endowed read permission on kernel space so that misbehaving kernel extension cannot directly modify kernel data. ARMLock [34] uses domain access control register (DACR) to create multiple sandboxes for isolating each software or kernel extension. AION [1] provides availability for enclave code execution by introducing a new instruction which ensures an atomic execution for a number of CPU cycles. Cider [31] and Lazarus [13] propose authenticated hardware watchdog to ensure a compromised IoT device to be reset. RT-TEE [30] uses a secure timer to ensure that tasks in the ARM Secure World get the time slices. GAROTA [2] protects the secure interrupt delivery to ensure that the root-of-trust code to be launched when the prescribed interrupt is triggered. In the first three schemes, the activate tasks are not subject to attacks due to the hardware protection, whereas GAROTA validates the code integrity of the root-of-trust. Nonetheless, none of them needs to protect the availability of a task running with the same privilege as the adversary.

TrustZone-based Trustdump [25] reliably dumps volatile data in the Normal World. It routes all interrupts to the Secure World which hosts a memory dumping agent. During memory dumping, the kernel in the Normal World is stopped from execution because the device has only one core. To access the kernel's virtual memory, the dumping agent traverses the paging hierarchy used by the kernel starting from the banked TTBR1 register. Trustdump is more suitable for dumping static memory pages than traversing a kernel object list, due to the overhead of software-implemented paging hierarchy walking. Moreover, it cannot be used for *live* acquisition where the malicious kernel is still running. SMMdump [29] is applied on x86 platforms only and only considers physical memory dumping instead of virtual memory pages.

In a broader sense, this paper is related to virtualization based secure systems where a full-fledged hypervisor (e.g., KVM [7] and Xen [14]) or a micro-hypervisor dedicated for security (e.g., XMHF [27]) is used to enforce system-wide control over the memory and I/O devices. For instance, SecVisor [21], Lares [19] and Hypernel [16] deals with kernel code integrity. Overshadow [5], InkTag [12] and AppShield [6] consider user-space memory page isolation against an untrusted OS. FIMCE [32] provides a secure execution environment with a pool of isolated memory pages and an isolated CPU core, so that it defeats the stifling attack and the virtual processor ID (VPID) attack. Our work will use techniques in FIMCE [32] as one of the building blocks.

3   The Design of DScope

We begin with the problem formulation and then present the architecture of DSCOPE followed by detailed descriptions of its components.

3.1   Problem Description

We consider the scenario that a user kickstarts a live data acquisition from an IoT device whose kernel either malfunctions or is compromised by malware. For instance, the user activates the session when the device becoming irresponsive to user actions or after receiving an alert raised by an intrusion detection system.

Target Device. DSCOPE is designed for mobile and IoT devices using an ARM64 multicore device with virtualization extension (supporting vGIC). The device is equipped with a USB or UART port for external communications. DSCOPE can be exported x86 platforms with modest modification.

Trust Model. We trust the device's hardware and firmware including BIOS, all of which behave as expected. We trust the bootloaders and the associated secure bootup procedure. Namely, the bootloaders ensure the launching time integrity of the hypervisor in the normal world. We also assume that code and data in the Exception Level 2 (EL2) are not susceptible to attacks. We trust the PC used for interrogating the device and receiving the acquired data.

Threat Model. The adversary in our consideration is malicious software that runs arbitrary code with kernel privilege on the target device. Its objective is to obstruct, disrupt and tamper with data acquisition. It may launch denial-of-service attacks such as masking interrupts, replacing the original kernel interrupt handler to exclusively occupy CPU cores, and misconfiguring some I/O interfaces to prevent the device from interacting with external PCs. It may attempt to feed faked data to the acquisition tool. Physical attacks are out of scope.

Goals. We aim to solve to the problem with *security, reliability* and *mapping-consistency*. We also expect the solution scheme to be *performance-friendly*, in the sense that (a) it does not take a significant performance toll to the device's day-to-day operations; and (b) it can be launched promptly and extracts data at a high speed. This requirement is due to that, despite the recent hardware advances, IoT devices are still more resource constraint than desktop computers.

The main challenge is to achieve four aforementioned goals altogether. A secure data acquisition mechanism can be obtained by using a special external hardware attached to the memory bus or by tasking the hypervisor or software in TEE. Nonetheless, the data extractor does not use the kernel's address mappings to reference the memory. One might propose a trusted agent in the device to bridge the semantic gap. As noted by Jain et. al. [15] on in-VM introspection schemes [22,24], the agent is not hardly secure against the kernel adversary, not to mention reliability.

3.2   The Design of DScope

Basic Workflow. We design DSCOPE as a hypervisor-based data acquisition scheme realizing all four goals. The basic workflow is as follows. To start an acquisition session, the user generates a hardware interrupt using a button on the device. The interrupt triggers the hypervisor to launch of a fully isolated environment on a CPU core. This environment, termed as Device Operation Environment (DOE), imports a data acquisition agent from the external PC and executes it with the same virtual-to-physical address mappings as the kernel. At any time, the user can respond to attacks by manually triggering the prescribed hardware interrupt. During data acquisition, the hypervisor and the DOE only occupy one CPU core with other cores controlled by the (malicious) kernel (Fig. 1).

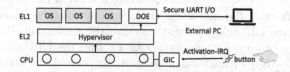

Fig. 1. A system overview of the architecture of DSCOPE.

The Approach. By and large, we attain the security and reliability by leveraging the hypervisor's privilege of configuring the hardware (e.g., GIC) and system settings (e.g., the stage 2 translation tables), whereas the mappings consistency of data acquisition is realized by the system architecture of DOE. Since various virtualization-based techniques for security purposes have been proposed in the literature, our primary challenge is about reliability assurance. Specifically, we face the following challenges: (i) how to ensure that the user can *always* activate the hypervisor to start the acquisition session? (ii) how to ensure that the acquisition agent's execution inside the DOE is *not* sabotaged by DoS attacks from the malicious kernel running in other cores?

The solution to these challenges cannot significantly impact the device's performance in its routine operations. For instance, it is not a satisfactory solution for the hypervisor to persistently hold one CPU core since the device with four cores potentially suffers 25% performance drop. Our basic approach is to leverage several features of ARM vGIC to empower the hypervisor the priority of interrupt filtering. The hypervisor runs as a daemon and stays dormant most of the time. Unlike in x86 platforms, ARM virtualization does not allow selected events to trap the CPU to the hypervisor. Thus, the hypervisor in DSCOPE is "waken" by all interrupts. However, except the activation interrupt, other interrupts are rerouted to the kernel to process to minimize the performance impact.

We cope with the mapping-consistency and reliability of the DOE by improving and combining techniques used in ImEE [33] and FIMCE [32]. The former provides mapping-consistency for an out-of-VM introspection whose system setting does not match DOE. The latter provides a fully-isolated environment using a hypervisor, however, without reliability protection. As show later, we follow the approach in FIMCE to construct the DOE and enhances its reliability by blocking unsolicited interrupts. Within the DOE, we adapt the approach used in ImEE to enclose the kernel's paging hierarchy for the agent to use.

3.3 The Hypervisor

GIC Configuration. During device boot-up, the DSCOPE hypervisor maps the GIC's CPU interfaces for all cores to the corresponding vCPU interfaces and enables interrupt virtualization. As a result, all external hardware interrupts are delivered to EL2 of core 0. An IRQ number chosen by the user is reserved for data acquisition activation. Note that the choice should allow the user to manually trigger the interrupt at any point of time. We call it the *Activation-IRQ*. A potential denial-of-service attack is to generate a flood of interrupts/exceptions to block the delivery of the Activation-IRQ. To copy with the attack, the hypervisor configures the GIC priority register so that the Activation-IRQ is given the highest priority and all others are lower. As a result, the CPU always responds to the Activation-IRQ without being delayed. To prevent the kernel from tampering with the interrupt setting, the hypervisor sets both the GIC Distributor and the GIC priority register as inaccessible to the kernel by configuring the stage 2 translation tables.

State Transition. At runtime, the hypervisor's execution is triggered by an explicit hypcall from the kernel or an exception/interrupt destined for EL2. Initially, the hypervisor runs in the *inactive* state and enters the *active* state after receiving the Activation-IRQ. It returns to the inactive state after the acquisition session is over. When inactive, it monitors all interrupts delivered to core 0. Except for Activation-IRQ, it handles the interrupt by injecting the corresponding virtual interrupt to the GIC so that the hardware further interrupts the kernel to handle the event. When the Activation-IRQ arrives at core 0, the hypervisor switches its state and sends an IPI to a randomly chosen secondary core (e.g., core 2) as the DOE core and resumes the kernel. We choose a secondary core for the DOE for two reasons. First, normal hardware events do not disrupt the DOE as they are delivered to core 0. Hence, we only deal with malicious events delivered to the DOE. Secondly, the kernel can still attend to the interrupts delivered to core 0 which is crucial to keep the device alive.

As a result of the IPI sent from the hypervisor, the DOE core is trapped to EL2 and the hypervisor starts its execution there. The DOE consists of an isolated physical core, an isolated memory page frames and a secure I/O interface. To prevent the adversary from preempting the DOE from its core, the hypervisor filters all Software Generated Interrupts (including IPIs) bound for the DOE. The implementations details of how the hypervisor handles the interrupts are presented in Sect. 4.2.

3.4   Device Operation Environment (DOE)

In DSCOPE, the hypervisor is only for security and dependability assurance. We leave all functionality for data acquisition or other device operation to the DOE so that (1) it avoids bloating the hypervisor code; (2) it allows users to flexibly choose their preferred secure actions according to the ongoing attack.

DOE Components. The DOE is a computing environment comprising the D-core, a UART port and a segment of physical memory. The UART port is used by the DOE code to communicate with the user's trusted PC. The physical memory segment is priorly reserved by the hypervisor.

Architectural Setting. The DOE core runs at EL1. Namely, the acquisition agent runs with the kernel privilege and never downgrades itself to the user-privilege. The VA-IPA-PA mappings consists of two parts. The *local* mappings map the DOE's own code and data to the DOE physical memory segment. VAs in the local mappings are in the lower half of the 48 bits address space and are translated via TTBR0.

The *device* mappings are for the kernel VA range, i.e., the higher half of the 48 bits address space. Instead of copying the kernel's stage 1 translation tables to the DOE, the hypervisor copies TTBR1 used by the kernel to the DOE core. The hypervisor clones the stage 2 translation table used for the kernel to the DOE core, with all pages' execution permissions removed. With this setup, the DOE code reads and writes the kernel's virtual memory in the same view as the kernel without the risk of kernel code being executed in the DOE.

The environment uses a synchronous UART I/O channel with the external PC. We choose UART as the DOE's I/O port because its control and data interfaces are rather simple. To receive data from the PC, the DOE software continuously polls the UART port. As compared with normal DMA based UART operations, the polling software is much simpler. More importantly, it avoids conflicts between the interrupt handling and the hypervisor's protection of the DOE.

Code Components. Initially, the software loaded to the DOE by the hypervisor consists of the *UART library*, the *manager* and the *default agent*. They are all copied to the physical memory frames reserved during system bootup for the hypervisor and are (re)mapped to the DOE's space upon its creation. The URAR library provides functions for communication with the external PC; the manager provides basic system service such (un)loading an agent and handling exceptions; the default agent offers a primitive acquisition capability, i.e., receiving commands from the PC and returning the needed kernel objects.

Agent Importation & Execution. A DOE agent is a chunk of binary code performing the expected device operations. DSCOPE requires the agent to be DOE-contained in the sense that it does not use any code outside of the DOE memory. The agent uses the UART library to communicate with the connected PC and directly references the kernel virtual addresses. An imported agent is loaded to the predefined virtual address. Since the DOE does not enclose a memory manager for dynamic memory (de)allocation, the agent has to manage its own memory layout the DOE code runs in EL1. The manager can dynamically configure the stage 1 translation tables to provid the needed local mappings.

The agent exclusively occupies the DOE core without being interrupted. It yields the DOE core to the manager after its mission is accomplished. Runtime exceptions, e.g., divided-by-zero, are handled by the manager by default. The agent can register a call-back function for the manager to invoke. Otherwise, the manager unloads the agent and requests the hypervisor to terminate the DOE.

3.5 Protection on DOE

To ensure security and reliability of the DOE, the hypervisor isolates all its hardware resources against the kernel, including the DOE core, the memory pages and the UART port.

Core Isolation. The protection on the DOE core prevents the denial-of-service attacks from the kernel which may send IPIs such as an INIT signal to disrupt the agent's execution. In DSCOPE, core isolation means that a physical CPU core is exclusively occupied by DOE when DSCOPE is in active state. Once DSCOPE being activated, the DOE core does not receive external interrupts until it is released by the hypervisor.

Memory Isolation. Memory isolation blocks any unauthorized access to the physical memory frames used by the DOE. The physical memory frames used by the hypervisor (including the DOE) are reserved during boot up and are not used in stage 2 translation tables for the kernel. Since the kernel cannot modify the stage 2 translation tables, the adversary cannot access those memory frames. Note that before hypervisor launches the DOE, it flushes all TLBs in the DOE core so that the adversary cannot leave any poisonous mappings for the DOE.

I/O Isolation. I/O isolation ensures that the trusted PC communicates with the DOE with no risk of data leakage, modification or disconnection. It is realized by blocking the kernel's memory accesses to any UART registers, since all I/O ports in ARM processors use MMIO only. Specifically, when setting up the DOE, the hypervisor unmaps the UART registers from the stage 2 translation tables used by the kernel, and remaps it to the stage 2 tables for the DOE.

4   Implementation

We have implemented a prototype of DSCOPE on a Raspberry Pi 4 development board. The board is equipped with a Broadcom BCM2711B0 processor with 4 cores and 4 GB RAM. Figure 2(a) shows our prototype. Port 1 is the secure UART interface that can be connected to trusted PC using a cable. Port 2 mimics a button in an off-the-shelf device. The two cables are connected to the GND pin and GPIO 04 (which is chosen as the Activation-IRQ) respectively. A user triggers the Activation-IRQ by tapping the ends of the cables together to generate the signal.

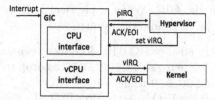

(a) A Raspberry Pi 4 board installed with DSCOPE.

(b) DSCOPE's interrupt handling process.

Fig. 2. DSCOPE prototype on a Raspberry board

In our DSCOPE prototype, the DSCOPE hypervisor consists of 922 SLOC assembly code and 1100 SLOC C code. The DOE manager includes 307 SLOC C code and the UART library has 197 SLOC C code. Since the loader and the UART library run inside the DOE instead of in EL2, the TCB of DSCOPE only has 2022 SLOC C code excluding the bootloaders.

4.1   Hypervisor Implementation

During initialization, the hypervisor recognizes the range of physical memory addresses and sets the register HCR_EL2 to enable the stage 2 address translation. The hypervisor populates the stage 2 translation tables with one-to-one mapping using the 4KB page size. It reserves 512 KB from 0x0 - 0x80000 for the hypervisor code and 64 MB from 0xF4000000 - 0xF8000000 for the stage 2 translation tables and the DOE software. The reserved memory cannot be accessed by code with EL1 or EL0 privileges. Furthermore, the hypervisor sets up the exception table and handlers for EL2 exceptions and EL2-IRQ so that it can handle the stage-2 page faults and hypcalls from the DOE.

After initializing the basic memory mappings, the hypervisor configures the GIC. First, it sets HCR_EL2.IMO/FMO bit to 1, which instructs the hardware to route all non-secure physical interrupts to EL2 for handling. Secondly, it sets the virtual CPU interface control register GICH_HCR.EN to 1 to enable vGIC and vCPU interface. It also configures the CPU interface register GICC_CTLR.EOIMode to separate End Of Interrupt (EOI) and Deactivate Interrupt (DI) signals. This step prevents interrupts from being blocked because the hypervisor can drop the interrupt priority in GIC via EOI. The base address of GIC CPU interface is remapped to the vCPU interface by the stage 2 translation tables. Lastly, the hypervisor sets register GICD_IPRIORITYR to assign the highest priority to GPIO 04 IRQ which is selected as the Activation-IRQ.

4.2   Interrupt Handling

The hypervisor is empowered to intercept, filter and dispatch all external interrupts and software generated interrupts. As shown in Fig. 2(b), the hypervisor detects the Activation-IRQ and dispatches other IRQs as vIRQs to the kernel via the GIC. When a physical IRQ occurs, the hypervisor uses the following steps to handle the event:

1. Read the GIC CPU interface register GICC_IAR to get IRQ number;
2. Write register GICC_EOIR to drop the priority. For SGI/IPI, it writes register GICC_DIR to deactivate IRQ;
3. If the IRQ is Activation-IRQ, the manager is to handle it. Otherwise, it writes register GICH_LR and sets HCR_EL2.VI to 1 so that the IRQ is forwarded as a virtual IRQ to the kernel at the same core;

As a result, the kernel is interrupted and reads GICC_IAR which is redirected to GICV_IAR to get vIRQ number. After completing handling the vIRQ, the kernel writes GICC_DIR which is redirected to GICV_DIR to deactivate IRQ.

The physical address of GICD_SGIR is protected by the hypervisor so that a kernel's access to it triggers a stage 2 page fault. When active, the hypervisor blocks the access and the kernel cannot deliver an SGI to the DOE core; when inactive, it emulates the access to trigger the SGI.

4.3   Device Operation Environment

The DOE is built on the fly by the hypervisor after receiving the Activation-IRQ. The hypervisor saves the CPU context of the DOE core including the values in register TTBR0 and TTBR1, SP_EL1 and ELR_EL2. It flushes the TLB and invalidate caches for the DOE memory. It builds the stage 1 translation tables for the local mappings within the DOE and re-configures the stage 2 translation table for memory isolation. Lastly, it switches to EL1 and passes the control to the DOE manager.

Memory Space with Data Consistency. All the code and data in the DOE are located in the 4 GB virtual address range from 0x0 to 0x00000000-

FFFFFFFF. The TTBR1_EL1 register of the DOE core is set with the same value as other cores's TTBR1_EL1 which points to the root of the stage 1 translation table for the kernel VA (i.e., from 0xFFFFFF8000000000 above) translation. As a result, the DOE agent runs in the user-space VA range and can access the kernel's virtual memory since it is granted with the EL1 privilege. This address mapping setup makes kernel memory read/write as native as accessing the agent's own memory.

The isolation between the DOE and the kernel is achieved via the stage 2 address translation. The hypervisor maintains two sets of stage 2 translation tables. One is used for the kernel and the applications on top of it. These tables covers all physical memory frames except those pages reserved for the hypervisor and the DOE. The other set is use for the DOE core and encloses mappings to the DOE memory and identical mappings to the kernel memory.

UART Library. The UART library provides several functions for code in the DOE to communicate with trusted external PC. It is loaded at a fixed virtual address. The library has a function that polls register UART_LSR (mapped to physical address 0xFE215014) to acquire the present UART status, as well as read and write functions to access register UART_LSR (mapped to physical address 0xFE215010) for data communications.

DOE Loader. The DOE loader is the first piece of code running inside the DOE after the launching. Similar to the UART library, it is loaded at a fixed virtual address. Its main functionality is to communicate with the console at the external PC via the URART channel. Since accessing the kernel memory is trivial, the loader can also introspect the kernel. Specifically, it receives three types of commands from the PC, including importing an incident response agent, introspection, and termination. For the importing command, it accepts and loads the binary image of the agent to the DOE memory. For the introspection command, it receives the starting kernel virtual address and the amount of bytes to read and then returns the fetched memory chunk to the PC.

4.4   DOE Agent

A DOE agent is a raw binary without using the ELF or kernel object format. As the DOE does not provide standard C libraries except the UART library, an agent is required to be self-contained. The entry point of a DOE agent is set to a fixed virtual address defined by DSCOPE. The loader starts the agent execution from the default entry point. After the agent is executed, the loader erase agent code and data in the memory.

4.5   Case Studies

To show DSCOPE's capability, we develop two use cases: live kernel object acquisition and CPU status acquisition.

Live Kernel Object Acquisition. We implement a kernel introspection agent that parses and dumps kernel objects to the external PC. Since DSCOPE does not force the kernel to stop execution, the agent introspects the kernel memory during kernel execution. The agent is compiled with the definitions of various kernel object structures and those static addresses of kernel symbols. The agent supports traversal of the task_struct object list. It lists all process identifiers in the running kernel. In specific, it locates the kernel symbol init_task base virtual address to get whole process identifiers and then lists the PID, command, state, stack address and next. For each process, the agent reads 1,776 byte from the starting virtual address of its task_struct. A screen snapshot of the agent's output is shown in Fig. 3(a).

The agent also dumps all entries of the system call handler table used by the running kernel by accessing the virtual address of sys_call_table, which helps the user to check whether they are hooked by a rootkit. To collect I/O related intelligence, the agent lists the device's I/O port status by accessing the memory-mapped status registers of each port and the PIDs of the current interrupt request. These information helps the user to assess whether the device has suspicious I/O operations.

CPU Status Acquisition. Although memory acquisition could be performed from the outside using special hardware, CPU status acquisition has to be done within the device. In the event of kernel panic, the kernel panic handler is expected to save all CPU cores' contexts to the kernel log. However, under DSCOPE's threat model, the kernel log could be a faked one. Hence, our second use case of DSCOPE is to collect the genuine CPU contexts.

The basic approach of CPU introspection is to preempt the kernel from its CPU core and trap them to the hypervisor. Initially, only the DOE core is fully controlled by the agent. To introspect another CPU core's context, the agent uses a hypcall to invoke the hypervisor at the DOE core to send SGIs to other cores. As a result, the recipient cores are trapped the hypervisor which responds to the event by saving all general-purpose registers and special registers on EL0/1. Figure 3(b) is a screenshot of the CPU introspection output.

(a) Live acquisition of the running processes from the device

(b) Live acquisition of CPU states

Fig. 3. Screenshots from two use cases

5 Evaluation

In this section, we shed light on how DSCOPE resists several types of attacks against its dependability and the reliability of the DOE, followed by various experiments that validate our analysis. We also measure the performance of DSCOPE and report the results.

5.1 Reliability of DScope Launch

The major attack vector is the influence of the kernel adversary on the hypervisor state. The adversary attempts to hinder the hypervisor from entering the active state or to force it to return to the inactive state.

Masking Interrupts. Because only the Activation-IRQ triggers DSCOPE to enter the active state, the kernel adversary may try to mask interrupts in order to prevent CPU cores being trapped into the hypervisor. Masking interrupt on all physical cores leads the CPU not to respond to interrupts. Benefit from vGIC virtualizing interrupts, the kernel only can mask EL1-IRQ since masking EL2-IRQ requires the EL2 privilege. In our system design, the external hardware interrupt is treated as an EL2-IRQ and the kernel only handles vIRQs which are virtualized by GIC. Hence kernel interrupt masking cannot prevent the Activation-IRQ from being delivered.

IRQ Flooding. The kernel adversary may continuously generate interrupts by reading or writing GPIO registers or IPIs to generate a flood of IRQs. The swarm of IRQs can fill up the IRQ queue in the GIC so that the Activation-IRQ cannot be forwarded to the CPU. DSCOPE counters this attack by leveraging the interrupt priority settings. The hypervisor assigns the Activation-IRQ with the highest priority by setting register GICD_IPRIORITYR. Since the interrupts generated by the kernel always have a lower priority, the GIC is ensured to deliver the Activation-IRQ to the CPU interface. Note that the priority register is inaccessible to the kernel. Thus, the IRQ flooding attack cannot block the Activation-IRQ delivery.

Device Restart and Shutdown. The kernel adversary may attempt to reboot the device so that the hypervisor is reset to the inactivate state. To deal with the attack, the hypervisor intercepts all SGIs and discards the CPU INIT signals if it is currently in the active state. Besides, the stage 2 translation table protects the registers related to power management to prevent a power off operation.

5.2 Reliability Experiments

The experiments aim at measuring whether DSCOPE can be successfully launched at the presence of a compromised or crashed kernel. We intentionally load several buggy drivers to the kernel running on the Raspberry Pi board and implement five different ways to test DSCOPE's reliability.

Kernel Panic. We introduce kernel panic by using the Linux shell command $echo c sysrq-trigger, which directly crashes the kernel. We configure the device to restart in 20 s after kernel panic and test whether the user can activate DSCOPE within the time frame. The experiment shows that the user can still launch the DOE during kernel panic.

Kernel Crash. This experiment tests DSCOPE's dependability on kernel crash. We change PXN and XN bit to 1 in all kernel page table entries, which makes all kernel code not executable. The DSCOPE activation is not dependent on the kernel because the Activation-IRQ is delivered via a hardware event. The DOE agent does not have dependence on kernel code either. In the experiment, the hypervisor still receives the Activation-IRQ and launches the DOE at a randomly chosen core.

Attack 1. Our injected driver in the kernel disables all I/O interfaces by removing the relevant drivers in the kernel, including the UART, ethernet, Wi-Fi, GPIO and Touchscreen. The goal is to prevent users from interacting with the hypervisor or the device. The experiment shows that the DOE loader can still use the UART to communicate with the PC. DSCOPE has an isolated I/O port that is only accessed by the DOE core.

Attack 2. Our injected driver in the kernel masks interrupts on all CPU cores by setting the DAIF bits. In an ARM processor, these bits mask EL1 interrupts delivered to the core. Because the hypervisor intercepts all IRQs, an EL2-bound interrupt is still delivered to the primary core which is trapped to the hypervisor. The experiment shows that DSCOPE responds as expected when the user taps the two lines shown in Fig. 2(a) to trigger the Activation-IRQ.

Attack 3. We modify the kernel so that it stops updating the watchdog on all cores when DSCOPE is active. Failure to update the watchdog on time will cause the device to restart. The hypervisor filters and drops the CPU INIT signal. The experiment shows that the device remains running when DSCOPE in the active state.

In short, the experiment results show that the hypervisor can be successfully launched and function properly in all these experiments, which demonstrates that DSCOPE is resilient against the kernel's denial of service attacks.

5.3 Security and Reliability of DOE

Next, we analyze how the DOE's security and reliability is safeguarded against the kernel adversary's attack.

SGI DoS. A direct operation to break core isolation is SGI DoS. The physical cores controlled by the kernel adversary send a flood of SGIs to the DOE core. The aim is to preempt the DOE agent and starve it of the CPU time. As explained in Sect. 3, the hypervisor filters and drops all IRQs destined to the DOE core after the DOE is set up. Therefore, the SGI DoS attack is unable to disrupt the DOE agent execution.

Break Memory Isolation. There are two potential factors that break memory isolation. One is the malicious behavior from the kernel and the other is the programming bug inside the DOE software. DSCOPE realizes two-way memory isolation. On the one hand, the stage 2 translation tables used for the kernel do not have the mappings to physical pages used by the DOE. Thus, the kernel cannot access to the DOE memory. On the other hand, kerne code pages are deprived of execution permissions in the stage 2 translation tables used by the DOR core. Hence, a buggy execution of the DOE code cannot pass the control to the kernel code. Besides, the hypervisor flushes the TLB on the DOE core and invalids caches, which ensures that the DOE software does not use stale data.

5.4   Security Assessment

We run experiments to test the security of DSCOPE against kernel attacks. In the experiments, we insert malicious code into a device driver whose execution can be triggered by using a shell command. The first attack uses the kernel function `cpumask_set_cpu(CPU_ID, &tthread_cpumask)` to stop the DOE core after the DOE is launched. This function masks the selected core by sending IPIs. The experiment shows that the DOE core does not receive the offensive IPI as expected. The hypervisor successfully stops its delivery and logs the IPI request from the isolated I/O port.

To verify one-way read/write access between the DOE and the kernel, our offensive kernel code attempts to access the DOE memory. The experiment reports the stage-2 page faults and traps the CPU into stage-2 exception handler. We instrument stage-2 page fault handler to print out the target physical address in the DOE and the virtual address that generated this page fault. The experimental result validates the memory isolation of the DOE.

5.5   Performance Evaluation

The performance evaluation measures the impact of DSCOPE on the normal use of device as well as the overheads of the hypervisor and the agents in an acquisition session.

Overhead of Interrupts Handling. The hypervisor enables interrupt virtualization and changes the workflow of interrupts handling. Compared no virtualization, the overhead of interrupt handling is slightly increased. To measure the overhead, we use the Performance Monitors Cycle Count Register (PMCCNTR) to count the CPU cycles of an interrupt handling. In order to avoid the interference caused by interrupt priority, we set a GPIO IRQ to the highest priority as the test IRQ. With DSCOPE, the time interval from the moment when the hypervisor starts to handle the test IRQ to the moment when the kernel reads the IRQ ID from vCPU interface is about 28,462 cycles in average. Without interrupt virtualization, it takes about 670 cycles for the kernel to access GIC CPU interface and get the IRQ ID. The mainly cost is caused by virtualizing IRQ and the imposed restriction on GIC vCPU interface access.

Overhead of Boot-up and Context Switch. We assess the overhead added to device boot up time by measuring the boot-up time between device power-on to displaying the login interface. The average boot up time of the original device is 30.76 s. When device is equipped with DSCOPE, the average boot up time grows to 35.29 s. The overhead is mainly incurred by configuring the memory virtualization and configuring vGIC.

To measure the context switch time, we use PMCCNTR to measure the time for DSCOPE activation and inactivation. The activation cost consists of the time interval between the Activation-IRQ arrival and sending IPI to the DOE core and the time interval between the DOE receiving this IPI and the agent starts to run. The time cost IPI delivery cannot be measured because each core has its own PMCCNTR. The inactivation cost is between the hypervisor issuing ERET instruction and the kernel getting the control of the DOE core. Our experiments report that, the first part of activation costs 5,895 CPU cycles and the second part takes 537,435 CPU cycles in average, which adds up to 543,330 cycles. The inactivation costs 730 cycles in average.

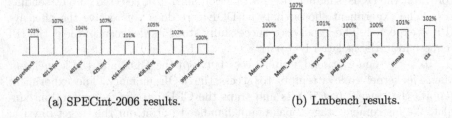

(a) SPECint-2006 results.   (b) Lmbench results.

Fig. 4. Performance overhead. The numbers are the percentage of the score with DSCOPE compared to the score without DSCOPE.

Performance Benchmarks. We run benchmarks to assess the system performance impact up the device when the hypervisor is inactive. We choose two standard test suits: SPECint-2006 [23] and Lmbench [18]. Each benchmark uses the standard test inputs. We use the Linux command time to get the average execution time of the test suite, with and without DSCOPE. The experimental results are reported in Fig. 4(a) and Fig. 4(b).

The experimental results show that DSCOPE incurs modest performance loss to the device, as the performance drops between 0% to 7%. The main reason of extra overhead on device is due to memory and interrupt virtualization. Compared the system without virtualization, the IPA-to-PA translation and virtualizing interrupts consume more CPU time. We also compare the kernel and the DOE agent's speed of reading the kernel memory. The TLB is flushed and cache is invalid before each memory experiment. When reading 1024 bytes from the kernel virtual memory, the DOE agent only takes 100 more CPU cycles than the kernel.

6   Conclusion

This paper proposes DScope as a reliable data acquire system on ARM devices. By leveraging ARM virtualization extension and interrupt virtualization, DScope can be activated by a user at any time, even if the device kernel is corrupted by malware. The user can securely acquire various types of volatile data from device with mapping consistency. We implement the DScope prototype on a Raspberry Pi4 development board with an ARM64 processor and demonstrate its strengths in both kernel memory data and CPU register status acquisition. We also measure the reliability of DScope by various experiments including kernel failure and attacks. The experimental results show that DScope is resistant to denial-of-service attacks, easy to deploy, and lightweight in terms of performance overhead.

Acknowledgement. We thank anonymous reviewers and the shepherd for their revision suggestions. This research/project is supported by the National Research Foundation, Singapore, and Cyber Security Agency of Singapore under its National Cybersecurity R&D Programme, National Satellite of Excellence in Mobile Systems Security and Cloud Security (NRF2018NCR-NSOE004-0001). Any opinions, findings and conclusions or recommendations expressed in this material are those of the author(s) and do not reflect the views of National Research Foundation, Singapore and Cyber Security Agency of Singapore.

References

1. Alder, F., Van Bulck, J., Piessens, F., Mühlberg, J.T.: Aion: enabling open systems through strong availability guarantees for enclaves. In: Proceedings of the 2021 ACM SIGSAC Conference on Computer and Communications Security, pp. 1357–1372 (2021)
2. Aliaj, E., Nunes, I.D.O., Tsudik, G.: {GAROTA}: generalized active {Root-Of-Trust} architecture (for tiny embedded devices). In: 31st USENIX Security Symposium (USENIX Security 2022), pp. 2243–2260 (2022)
3. ARM. Generic Interrupt Controller Architecture version 2.0 (2013)
4. Bahram, S., et al.: DKSM: subverting virtual machine introspection for fun and profit. In: Proceedings of the 29th IEEE Symposium on Reliable Distributed Systems (SRDS), pp. 82–91. IEEE (2010)
5. Chen, X., et al.: Overshadow: a virtualization-based approach to retrofitting protection in commodity operating systems. In: Proceedings of the 13th International Conference on Architectural Support for Programming Languages and Operating Systems (ASPLOS) (2008)
6. Cheng, Y., Ding, X., Deng, R.H.: Efficient virtualization-based application protection against untrusted operating system. In: Proceedings of the 10th ACM Symposium on Information, Computer and Communications Security (ASIACCS) (2015)
7. Dall, C., Nieh, J.: KVM/ARM: the design and implementation of the Linux ARM hypervisor. ACM SIGPLAN Not. **49**(4), 333–348 (2014)
8. Dolan-Gavitt, B., Leek, T., Zhivich, M., Giffin, J., Lee, W.: Virtuoso: narrowing the semantic gap in virtual machine introspection. In: Proceedings of the 32nd IEEE Symposium on Security and Privacy (SP), pp. 297–312. IEEE (2011)

9. Erlingsson, U., Abadi, M., Vrable, M., Budiu, M., Necula, G.C.: XFI: software guards for system address spaces. In: Proceedings of the 7th Symposium on Operating Systems Design and Implementation, pp. 75–88 (2006)

10. Fu, Y., Lin, Z.: Space traveling across VM: automatically bridging the semantic gap in virtual machine introspection via online kernel data redirection. In: Proceedings of the 33rd IEEE Symposium on Security and Privacy (SP), pp. 586–600. IEEE (2012)

11. Herder, J.N., Bos, H., Gras, B., Homburg, P., Tanenbaum, A.S.: Fault isolation for device drivers. In: 2009 IEEE/IFIP International Conference on Dependable Systems & Networks, pp. 33–42. IEEE (2009)

12. Hofmann, O.S., Kim, S., Dunn, A.M., Lee, M.Z., Witchel, E.: Inktag: secure applications on an untrusted operating system. In: Proceedings of the 18th International Conference on Architectural Support for Programming Languages and Operating Systems (ASPLOS) (2013)

13. Huber, M., Hristozov, S., Ott, S., Sarafov, V., Peinado, M.: The lazarus effect: healing compromised devices in the internet of small things. In: Proceedings of the 15th ACM Asia Conference on Computer and Communications Security, pp. 6–19 (2020)

14. Hwang, J.-Y., et al.: Xen on ARM: system virtualization using Xen hypervisor for ARM-based secure mobile phones. In: Proceedings of the 5th IEEE Consumer Communications and Networking Conference, CCNC (2008)

15. Jain, B., Baig, M.B., Zhang, D., Porter, D.E., Sion, R.: SoK: introspections on trust and the semantic gap. In: Proceedings of the 35th IEEE Symposium on Security and Privacy (SP) (2014)

16. Kwon, D., et al.: Hypernel: a hardware-assisted framework for kernel protection without nested paging. In: Proceedings of the 55th Annual Design Automation Conference, pp. 1–6 (2018)

17. Manes, V.J.M., Jang, D., Ryu, C., Kang, B.B.: Domain isolated kernel: a lightweight sandbox for untrusted kernel extensions. Comput. Secur. **74**, 130–143 (2018)

18. McVoy, L.: lmbench: portable tools for performance analysis. http://www.bitmover.com/lmbench/

19. Payne, B.D., Carbone, M., Sharif, M., Lee, W.: Lares: an architecture for secure active monitoring using virtualization. In: Proceedings of the 2008 IEEE Symposium on Security and Privacy (S&P) (2008)

20. Saberi, A., Fu, Y., Lin, Z.: Hybrid-bridge: efficiently bridging the semantic gap in virtual machine introspection via decoupled execution and training memoization. In: Proceedings of the 21st Annual Network and Distributed System Security Symposium (NDSS) (2014)

21. Seshadri, A., Luk, M., Qu, N., Perrig, A.: Secvisor: a tiny hypervisor to provide lifetime kernel code integrity for commodity OSes. In: Proceedings of the 21st ACM Symposium on Operating Systems Principles (SOSP) (2007)

22. Sharif, M.I., Lee, W., Cui, W., Lanzi, A.: Secure in-VM monitoring using hardware virtualization. In: Proceedings of the 16th ACM Conference on Computer and Communications Security, pp. 477–487. ACM (2009)

23. SPEC. Standard performance evaluation corporation. http://www.spec.org/cpu2006/index.html

24. Srinivasan, D., Wang, Z., Jiang, X., Xu, D.: Process out-grafting: an efficient out-of-VM approach for fine-grained process execution monitoring. In: Proceedings of the 18th ACM Conference on Computer and Communications Security, pp. 363–374. ACM (2011)

25. Sun, H., Sun, K., Wang, Y., Jing, J., Jajodia, S.: TrustDump: reliable memory acquisition on smartphones. In: Kutyłowski, M., Vaidya, J. (eds.) ESORICS 2014. LNCS, vol. 8712, pp. 202–218. Springer, Cham (2014). https://doi.org/10.1007/978-3-319-11203-9_12

26. Swift, M.M., Martin, S., Levy, H.M., Eggers, S.J.: Nooks: an architecture for reliable device drivers. In: Proceedings of the 10th Workshop on ACM SIGOPS European Workshop, pp. 102–107 (2002)

27. Vasudevan, A., Chaki, S., Jia, L., McCune, J., Newsome, J., Datta, A.: Design, implementation and verification of an extensible and modular hypervisor framework. In: Proceedings of the 34th IEEE Symposium on Security and Privacy (S&P) (2014)

28. Wahbe, R., Lucco, S., Anderson, T.E., Graham, S.L.: Efficient software-based fault isolation. In: Proceedings of the Fourteenth ACM Symposium on Operating Systems Principles, pp. 203–216 (1993)

29. Wang, J., Zhang, F., Sun, K., Stavrou, A.: Firmware-assisted memory acquisition and analysis tools for digital forensics. In: 2011 Sixth IEEE International Workshop on Systematic Approaches to Digital Forensic Engineering, pp. 1–5. IEEE (2011)

30. Wang, J., Li, A., Li, H., Lu, C., Zhang, N.: RT-TEE: real-time system availability for cyber-physical systems using arm trustzone. In: 2022 IEEE Symposium on Security and Privacy (SP), pp. 352–369. IEEE (2022)

31. Xu, M., et al.: Dominance as a new trusted computing primitive for the internet of things. In: 2019 IEEE Symposium on Security and Privacy (SP), pp. 1415–1430. IEEE (2019)

32. Zhao, S., Ding, X.: FIMCE: a fully isolated micro-computing environment for multicore systems. ACM Trans. Priv. Secur. (TOPS) 21(3), 1–30 (2018)

33. Zhao, S., Ding, X., Xu, W., Gu, D.: Seeing through the same lens: introspecting guest address space at native speed. In: Proceedings of the 26th USENIX Security Symposium (2017)

34. Zhou, Y., Wang, X., Chen, Y., Wang, Z.: ARMLock: hardware-based fault isolation for ARM. In: Proceedings of the 2014 ACM SIGSAC Conference on Computer and Communications Security, pp. 558–569 (2014)

SPLITS: Split Input-to-State Mapping for Effective Firmware Fuzzing

Guy Farrelly[1(✉)], Paul Quirk[2], Salil S. Kanhere[3], Seyit Camtepe[4], and Damith C. Ranasinghe[1]

[1] University of Adelaide, Adelaide, Australia
{guy.farrelly,damith.ranasinghe}@adelaide.edu.au
[2] Defence Science and Technology Group, Edinburgh, Australia
paul.quirk@defence.gov.au
[3] University of New South Wales, Sydney, Australia
salil.kanhere@unsw.edu.au
[4] CSIRO Data61, Marsfield, Australia
seyit.camtepe@data61.csiro.au

Abstract. Ability to test firmware on embedded devices is critical to discovering vulnerabilities prior to their adversarial exploitation. State-of-the-art automated testing methods rehost firmware in emulators and attempt to facilitate inputs from a diversity of methods (interrupt driven, status polling) and a plethora of devices (such as modems and GPS units). Despite recent progress to tackle peripheral input generation challenges in rehosting, a firmware's expectation of multi-byte magic values supplied from peripheral inputs for string operations still pose a significant roadblock. We solve the impediment posed by multi-byte magic strings in monolithic firmware. We propose *feedback mechanisms* for input-to-state mapping and retaining seeds for targeted replacement mutations with an efficient method to solve multi-byte comparisons. The feedback allows an *efficient* search over a *combinatorial solution-space*. We evaluate our prototype implementation, SPLITS, with a diverse set of 21 real-world monolithic firmware binaries used in prior works, and 3 *new* binaries from popular open source projects. SPLITS automatically solves 497% more multi-byte magic strings guarding further execution to uncover new code and bugs compared to state-of-the-art. In 11 of the 12 real-world firmware binaries with string comparisons, including those *extensively* analyzed by prior works, SPLITS outperformed, statistically significantly. We observed up to 161% increase in blocks covered and discovered *6 new bugs* that remained *guarded* by string comparisons. Significantly, deep and difficult to reproduce bugs guarded by comparisons, identified in prior work, were found consistently.

Keywords: Fuzzing · Monolithic Firmware · Microcontroller

1 Introduction

Embedded device proliferation is creating new targets and opportunities for adversaries. Microcontrollers running firmware are becoming integral compo-

G. Tsudik et al. (Eds.): ESORICS 2023, LNCS 14347, pp. 290–310, 2024.
https://doi.org/10.1007/978-3-031-51482-1_15

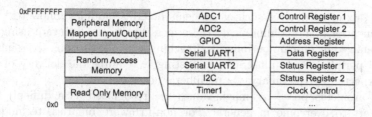

Fig. 1. Example of peripherals in a microcontroller's memory address space. Each peripheral contains multiple memory mapped registers within the peripheral's Memory Mapped Input/Output (MMIO) region a firmware can interact with.

nents of safety and security critical systems. In general, embedded devices take input from a diverse set of inputs and provide output in a unique manner, far different from those typically found on desktop computers. Integrated peripheral devices, such as timers or serial ports, manage communications with the user, often without any supervisory control from an operating system—*importantly*, the lack of supervisory control reduces the ability to detect faults and abort [25]. But, security is a crucial enabler for connected devices, making scalable and automated methods to identify software bugs and vulnerabilities prior to public release a research and societal imperative.

Fuzz testing, or fuzzing, is a de-facto industry standard for software testing and can play a crucial role in developing secure connected devices through scalable and automated testing of firmware. In fuzzing, inputs are automatically generated and run to uncover unusual program behavior [16]. But, the unique characteristics of embedded devices and their firmware present challenges for adopting fuzzing tools [25]. Fuzzing firmware based on their execution on physical devices [10,18,24,29,33] is hampered by dependence on execution on low performance embedded processors limiting fuzzing performance. To improve fuzzing throughput, the firmware can be rehosted [13] within an emulated environment on a high performance processor. While progress is made towards re-hosting and fuzzing Unix-based firmware [5,20,30,34,35], fuzzing monolithic embedded firmware presents a unique set of challenges [7,9,12,14,21,25,27,36]. A problem for rehosting for fuzzing arises from developing methods to automatically provide peripheral inputs to the multitude of memory mapped interfaces a firmware may access on these devices as illustrated in Fig. 1. In recent works [12,14,27,36,37], fuzzer generated test cases are fed to the framework rehosting the firmware, which uses this input stream to provide values to a set of peripheral registers, representing an interface used by a peripheral device (such as a modem or sensor). These approaches focus on ensuring data from peripherals can be successfully generated for the target.

A Firmware Fuzzing Roadblock. Existing methods to automatically manage peripheral inputs do not consider the problem posed by multi-byte magic values expected in peripheral inputs by firmware binaries. We observe software used to communicate with external devices often depends on magic bytes. For example, external devices such as modems or GPS modules follow text based communications, and communicate these messages to the firmware using interfaces managed by on-chip peripherals. Reaching key code sections accessing these external peripherals, as illustrated in Listing 1, requires the delivery of magic bytes expected by the binary, via peripheral accesses.

The problems posed by magic-values are recognized as a difficult hurdle for fuzzers to overcome in general. For non-firmware binaries, techniques in [1,2,8,17] are designed specifically to overcome these hurdles. The state-of-the-art technique for the problem in non-firmware binaries relies on *input-to-state mapping*, where a sequence of bytes from the fuzzer generated input is mapped to a program state variable such as the input_buffer in our example and are subsequently subjected to a surgical replacement by the magic values. Unfortunately, it cannot be simply employed for firmware.

Solving strings with input-to-state mapping techniques poses a unique challenge in firmware fuzzing due to the *unusual* and *diverse* input methods. While desktop applications read strings from a source, such as a file, as a contiguous block, embedded firmware processes **each** input byte from a peripheral, one at a time, each requiring multiple registers within the peripheral to be read. Additionally, *many peripherals are active simultaneously*, each with multiple memory mapped registers that influence firmware execution, as shown in Fig. 1. Between each byte of data read by a given peripheral, numerous other peripheral registers are often accessed, causing the data bytes within the string sourced from the fuzzer generated input to be spread across a region. Consequently, the fuzz inputs mapping to the expected magic bytes are *unpredictably interspersed* throughout a large fuzz input. This prevents existing input-to-state mapping methods from identifying and solving string comparisons.

To address this gap, we consider a solution to the problem to advance recent progress made in monolithic firmware fuzzing to discover new software bugs previously guarded by magic-value roadblocks.

Our Approach. We propose new instrumentation and feedback to provide an effective method for input-to-state mapping and an optimized input replacement strategy to solve multi-byte string comparisons for fuzzing monolithic firmware. The feedback derived allows an *efficient* search over the resulting *combinatorial solution-space* by sequentially identifying the bytes in fuzz inputs corresponding to those used in comparisons. Subsequently, we attempt to simultaneously replace all bytes to ensure the multi-byte comparison is solved. Further, we exploit the nature of string representations to craft new instrumentation providing further feedback to the fuzzer to retain seeds for targeted replacement mutations. Together, these techniques create a robust method to overcome multi-byte magic strings by providing a faster exploration of the combinatorial search space of potential solutions for feedback driven fuzzing frameworks that *simultaneously* provide input to many memory mapped peripherals.

```
1    char* input_buffer = NULL;    During fuzzing, input_buffer values must be read
2    while(true)                    via correctly accessing the serial peripheral port
3      serial.println("AT");                          ↑
4      input_buffer = serial.getline();
5      if(strcmp(input_buffer,"OK") == 0)
6        break;
```

Listing 1: Simplified code snippet illustrating a wait for a peripheral device to respond OK to an AT command (extracted from **LiteOS IoT** binary). Failing to solve the string prevents execution of any deeper code, as the loop never exits.

Our Contributions. We make the following contributions through this study:

- We propose an effective method to overcome hurdles posed by multi-byte string comparisons common in monolithic firmware.
- To demonstrate the effectiveness of our techniques, we describe and build a prototype implementation, SPLITS, an effective method to consistently solve hard fuzzing problems dealing with multi-byte string comparisons without dependence on source code or debugging symbols for its implementation.
- In a series of extensive experiments with 24 real-world binaries, we demonstrate the method we propose is effective in significantly extending reachable code (up to 161% increase in blocks covered with SPLITS automatically solving 497% more multi-byte magic values) and discovering 6 previously unknown bugs (1 with a recent CVE assignment) guarded by string comparisons, compared to prior work; especially on binaries *extensively analyzed by prior work*. We responsibly disclose vulnerabilities to the affected groups.

To facilitate future research in the field, we will release SPLITS, the firmware data sets, and bug analysis at https://github.com/SplITS-Fuzzer. We begin with a technical primer on monolithic firmware to help understand the unique aspects that present a challenge for fuzz testing monolithic firmware.

2   Technical Primer

Monolithic Embedded Systems. Unlike Unix-based firmware, a single monolithic program controls all aspects of a device's operation. The application code, system libraries and hardware abstractions are combined into a single binary sharing the same memory space. The firmware manages all functions and interacts with peripherals such as buttons or GPS units through Memory Mapped Input/Output (MMIO), hardware interrupts and Direct Memory Access (DMA).

MMIO. MMIO is a predefined segment of memory reserved for communicating directly with peripherals through reads and writes to the peripheral's registers. As shown in Fig. 1, each peripheral has a set of data, control and status registers. **Data registers** contain the data to be read or written. **Control registers** store the parameters for the peripheral's operation, such as speed or operating mode. **Status registers** describe the current state of the peripheral, indicating the presence of new data, or any errors. For **Status** and **Control** registers, it is common for many individual bits within a register to have distinct purposes and many components of the peripheral's state are condensed to a few registers.

While peripherals such as timers and Analog to Digital Converters (ADCs) are embedded on-chip, not all peripherals are integrated directly into a microcontroller. Instead the microcontroller can be connected to other hardware components such as wireless modems. These external devices communicate with the microcontroller to provide data not observable with only the built in on-chip peripherals. To facilitate this communication, integrated peripherals are implemented to control data buses. Some examples are the serial Universal Asynchronous Receiver Transmitter (UART) and Inter-Integrated Circuit (I2C). In each case, the firmware accesses external peripherals through an MMIO interface exposed by these integrated peripherals, to read and write data to the bus.

Hardware Interrupts. Peripherals also interact with firmware by generating interrupt signals, indicating an event has occurred. The CPU immediately jumps to an interrupt handler associated with the given signal, reads the peripheral status, and performs any necessary operations to handle this signal. Depending on the current status, handling the signal may involve reading new data, writing data to the peripheral, or discarding data containing errors. Afterward, the CPU returns to its prior location to continue its previous task.

3   The Input-To-Sate Mapping Problem

The use of multi-byte magic values in the form of strings occurs regularly on embedded devices. These devices can use strings to take instructions on how they should operate, such as the use of GCode commands on a 3D Printer. Alternatively, firmware can communicate with external peripherals using strings. We observe this to be the case for AT commands used to communicate with modems, similar to the initialization example in Listing 1. Here, if the device does not respond with the string OK, the while loop will never exit, and the firmware will not proceed further. State-of-the-art methods use Input-To-State (ITS) mapping to overcome such hurdles. The goal is to solve this comparison by observing the value in *input_buffer* and locating it within the fuzzer generated test case, and replacing it with the ideal value OK.

Existing input-to-state mapping techniques are effective for binaries where fuzzer generated data is loaded as a contiguous block for processing. But, *firmware typically loads fuzzer generated input data over peripherals over a period of time*, byte by byte with frequent switching between tasks for different peripherals, and uses multiple register accesses for each byte of input. This behavior **prevents the *observed* data from being contiguous in the fuzz input.** Figure 2 shows an example of firmware using fuzzer generated input, prior to reaching the string comparison described in Listing 1, and a similar example for a desktop application. While the desktop application code loads the bytes $0 \times 61, 0 \times 36$, corresponding to the ASCII string a6, the firmware example loads ac from a UART serial port through multiple MMIO register reads, intermitted

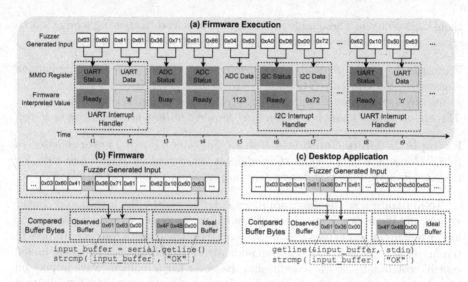

Fig. 2. Excerpt of a fuzzer generated input consumed by a sequence of register reads for multiple active peripherals. (a) The UART serial port loads the bytes a (0 × 61) at time *t2* and c (0 × 63) at time *t9*. The values read from the UART are used to form the string ac. (b) Although, adjacent in *input_buffer*, a and c are separated in the fuzzer generated input due to the unpredictable number of other peripheral register reads from *t3* to *t8*. (c) In contrast, a desktop application loads the data in a block with the bytes adjacent in the input and *input_buffer*.

by other peripheral accesses. While the string a6 does appear in the fuzzer generated input, the string ac does not. Consequently, mapping the *observed* value back to the fuzzer generated input is not trivial. This prevents existing input-to-state mapping methods from identifying and solving string comparisons.

To address this gap, we develop an input-to-state mapping technique for monolithic firmware. Through our efforts, we aim to advance recent progress made in monolithic firmware fuzzing to discover new software bugs previously guarded by magic-value roadblocks in the form of string comparisons.

4   Split Input-to-State Mapping

Consider Fig. 2. A naive approach to solve the non-contiguous string is to *attempt all possible combinations* of replacements for each character in the *observed string* with the corresponding character in the *ideal string*. While the approach may be possible for the example in Listing 1, where the string comparison only depends on solving two characters, this solution does not scale, instead creating a combinatorial problem. The number of executions required to test all possible combinations depends on two factors: *the length of the string* and *the number of candidate bytes for replacement* in the fuzzer generated input. Notably, we observe strings up to 18 characters in length, and fuzzer generated inputs with thousands of bytes. These large inputs and strings lead to creating a large search space infeasible to test effectively, as shown in the following examples.

Example 1: *Long Strings.* *Consider the string,* `rpl-refresh-routes` *observed in the **Contiki-NG** binary. When three candidates for each of the 18 characters are considered, the number of possible combinations rapidly explodes. This string would require more than three hundred million combinations be tested.*

Example 2: *Many Candidate Bytes.* *Consider the string* `poweron` *observed in the **Console** binary. When 16 candidates for each of the seven characters are considered, more than two hundred million combinations would be tested.*

To illustrate how the naive approach is influenced by the inclusion of longer strings and more candidates for each character, we refer to the naive search ① in Fig. 3. This example uses a four character string, each with four occurrences in the fuzzer generated input that are candidates for replacement, resulting in 256 possible combinations. Each additional character has a multiplicative impact on the number of combinations to test. The number of occurrences of this additional character in the fuzz input defines the scale of this multiplicative impact. While constraints can be implied, such as those discussed in Sect. 4.2, to remove some combinations, a naive approach is impractical and inefficient, as it does not prevent the extreme growth in search space resulting from this method.

4.1   Feedback Guided Search

Rather than testing possible combinations of replacements, we consider a more scalable approach guided by *whether a given byte influences the comparison.*

Comparison Feedback. To successfully replace memory comparisons based on non-contiguous accesses, without introducing an explosion in candidate replacements, we attempt to solve each byte individually. We propose monitoring the data present in the *observed* and *ideal* value buffers, and **use the content of the buffers as a feedback mechanism**. If the current byte has successfully been updated within the *observed buffer*, we only consider combinations that include this byte. If this value remains unchanged, or the comparison is not reached, we proceed to the next candidate location within the input and no longer consider any replacements that include this byte. This is done until all bytes in the *observed buffer* match the byte at the corresponding index in the *ideal buffer*, or an *observed buffer* byte could not be located in the input.

Figure 3 ② shows the feedback guided search in an example, progressively locating the 'A', 'B', 'C' and 'D' characters within an input that loads `ABCD` into a buffer. Bytes that have been confirmed to be a part of the observed buffer are highlighted in green. Tested bytes that do **not** correspond to a byte in the *observed buffer* are shown in red; such as the first 'A' tested once before exclusion. Additionally, the fourth 'A' character is quickly discarded from the search space (shown in gray), as a valid replacement for this character in the *observed buffer* has already been identified. When compared to the naive search, the number of

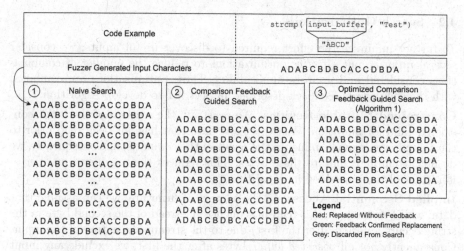

Fig. 3. Example of naive vs. feedback guided search of the observed *input_buffer* string "ABCD" within the fuzzer generated input characters of four As, Bs, Cs and Ds for replacement with "Test". In ①, the 4 occurrences of the character 'D', creates four additional fuzz inputs to test **for each combination** of the string "ABC", causing the search space to be four times larger than searching for the string "ABC" within the input. But, for the feedback guided searches ② & ③ the 4 occurrences of 'D' only adds, overall, at most four inputs to test.

firmware executions required to solve the string comparison is greatly reduced. As each candidate byte in the fuzzer generated input can only be considered for replacement once, *this method only has linear complexity with regard to the string length, and number of candidates for each character.*

Length Feedback. Comparison feedback alone is not adequate for an effective search and replacement strategy. *Strings must be the same length to be equal.* In cases where the *observed string*—values generated by the fuzzer for a peripheral—is shorter than the *ideal string*, we do not have any knowledge of which bytes need to be mutated to extend the *observed string* to the required length. But, during fuzzing, we can expect many executions to contain different strings of varying lengths. However, due to the coverage metrics used by greybox fuzzers, if the inputs only reach the same code, they are rarely saved for further processing. Thus, we rarely recall seeds with long enough strings to attempt replacement of the *observed string*. To address this issue, we include additional coverage instrumentation. We exploit the null byte in string formats to determine their length. By searching for null terminators in the *observed* and *ideal* buffers, we can determine the length of the *observed string* and *ideal string*. When a string comparison is identified, we ascertain the string lengths, and count previously unseen *observed string* lengths similar to the length of the *ideal string* as interesting. This ensures we save inputs that load sufficient data into the *observed string buffer* for successful replacement with the *ideal string*.

4.2 Search Optimizations

To further minimize the effort required to discover useful inputs, we consider several *intuitive* but *effective* optimizations to reduce the number of combinations considered and improve applicability. These optimizations are combined with the comparison feedback described in Sect. 4.1 to develop Algorithm 1.

Constrained Mutable Regions. We constrain the sections of the input considered valid for mutation. We expect any data that has not been read prior to the comparison, cannot influence the result of the comparison. Consequently, we do not attempt to mutate these bytes. This reduces the maximum number of iterations of the inner loop in Algorithm 1.

Implied Sequential Access. In the context of firmware, we can assume that data, whilst not adjacent, is read in sequence (i.e. read of the second byte in the string occurs a period after the first) due to the stream-like nature of the input. Consequently, for all *observed buffer* bytes after the first, we exclude any input bytes that have not been read since the previously solved byte in the *observed buffer* was accessed. This reduces the range of j in the inner loop of Algorithm 1.

Algorithm 1: Feedback Guided Search & Replacement Algorithm for solving a string comparison. A comparison identifiable by cmp_id, reached when executing the firmware with *input*, requires the *observed_string* to match the *ideal_string*. GetReadBytes returns the number of input bytes read at the time of comparison, and *InsertDelimiter* replaces a byte in a string with common tokenization delimiters.

---
input: *input, ideal_string, observed_string, cmp_id*
1 *original_input* ← *input*
2 *last_index* ← 0
   /* For each byte value to be replaced   */
3 **for** $i = 0$ **to** *observed_string.length* **do**
4   **for** $j = $ *last_index* **to** GetReadBytes(cmd_id) **do**
         /* If this input byte is a candidate for replacement   */
5   **if** *observed_string$_i$* = *input$_j$* **then**
6   *input$_j$* ← *ideal_string$_i$*
7   Execute(*input*)
8   *new_observed* ← GetObserved(*cmp_id*)
9   **if** *new_observed.exists* **and** *new_observed$_i$* = *ideal_string$_i$* **then**
10   *last_index* ← $j + 1$
11   **break** /* Solved. Move to next byte.   */
12   **else**
13   *input$_j$* ← *original_input$_j$* /* Not solved. Restore byte   */
14   **if** $j = $ GetReadBytes(*cmp_id*) **then**
15   **return** /* Unable to map byte   */
16   **if** $i >= $ *ideal_string.length* **then**
17   InsertDelimiter(*observed_string, i*) /* Shorten observed string */
18   **return**

String Contractions. For strings to be equivalent, both strings must be the same length. While we can not extend the *observed string*, we can attempt to shorten it. When the *observed string* is longer than the ideal string, we identify the byte corresponding to the next character in the *observed string* and attempt replacement of this byte with a set of common token delimiters such as space and newline, contracting the string to the correct size.

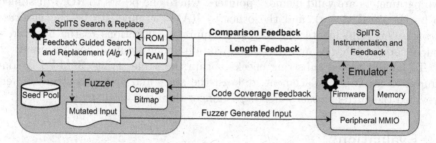

Fig. 4. SPLITS design overview. The Instrumentation and Feedback component provides string comparison and length feedback. **Length Feedback** is implemented by setting bits within the existing fuzzer coverage bitmap (Sect. 4.1). **Comparison Feedback** provides the compared strings and which bytes of the mutated input have been read to the SPLITS Search & Replace module, where the comparison is solved, guided by incremental feedback (Algorithm 1).

In Fig. 3, we illustrate the impact of using the optimizations in block ③. The optimizations reduce the number of executions required to identify the bytes in the comparison compared to the search in ② guided solely by feedback.

5   Implementation

We provide an overview of a realization of our techniques for a monolithic firmware fuzzer in Fig. 4. To test the efficacy of our approach, we implemented our method with FUZZWARE [27]. We also apply the FERMCov technique described in EMBER-IO [12] as it can increase the effectiveness of the framework. In particular, FUZZWARE's emulator was modified to detect potential calls to string comparison functions, and report the location and buffer contents to the fuzzer, AFL++ [16]. We implement our string replacement on top of AFL++'s existing *cmplog* interface. AFL++ was configured to use random bytes for colorization, and only consider string comparisons for input-to-state solving.

Given that embedded system fuzzing frameworks such as FUZZWARE use the AFL++ generated input as a stream, where each byte is only read once and in order, we use the cursor location within the stream to determine which data has been read at a given time. All bytes at a lower index than the current cursor have been read, and equal or higher indexes are unread. We pass the cursor index at the time of comparison from the SPLITS feedback inside the emulator back to AFL++ as an extension to the *cmplog* interface. This knowledge of unread bytes is used as described in Sect. 4.2. The index of the previously solved byte is determined internal to AFL++ during SPLITS' replacements.

Similar to the original REDQUEEN [2] implementation, we detect comparison functions by hooking instructions used to call functions, and analyzing the parameters. In the case of ARM, we hook the branch linked (BL) instruction, and read the R0 and R1 registers, corresponding to the first two function parameters. A function is considered a potential memory comparison function when the first two parameters are valid memory pointers, where one points to ROM (assumed to be the *ideal string*), and the other to RAM (assumed to be the *observed string*). Our implementation does not require modifications to the firmware's source code or binaries, nor does it depend on debug symbols being present.

To handle nested substring checks within the same string, SPLITS is configured to attempt replacement at both the start and end of a string buffer, provided the current *observed string* is longer than the *ideal string*.

6   Evaluation

To determine SPLITS' effectiveness at solving non-contiguous string comparisons, we evaluate it on a set of monolithic real-world firmware. We analyzed the binaries used in evaluations from existing firmware fuzzing frameworks P^{2}IM [14], μEmu [36], FUZZWARE [27] and EMBER-IO [12] that emulate memory mapped IO. From the 21 real-world firmware used in the coverage comparisons, nine contain functionality guarded by string comparison functions such as *strcmp*, *strncmp* and *strstr*. We additionally included three *new* targets containing string comparisons. Each binary is fuzzed for 24 h in five trials. To ease the analysis, we considered the binaries in the following groupings:

- *Magic-String-Binaries.*We examined a set of 24 real-world binaries and observed magic values used in string comparisons in 12 of the binaries. We employed this set for our extensive evaluations.
- *Other-Binaries.*The remaining 12 real-world binaries that did not make use of any string comparisons to guard code execution.

We conduct evaluations *with* and *without* SPLITS. Here, the fuzzer without our techniques is the state-of-the-art FUZZWARE improved with FERMCov (denoted simply as FUZZWARE) while the SPLITS denoted implementation is FUZZWARE improved with FERMCov along with our proposed techniques. FUZZWARE [27] has previously shown higher code coverage and bug finding performance when compared to prior works such as P^{2}IM [14] and μEmu [36]. ICICLE with CompCov is included for a point of comparison as CompCov instrumentation could solve some string comparisons. We also included the recent state-of-the art monolithic firmware fuzzing framework, EMBER-IO. Tests were performed using an AMD Threadripper 3990X. We used the gathered coverage information and crashing inputs to answer the following questions:

1. How successful is SPLITS at solving string comparisons? (Sect. 6.1)

2. Does the solving of string comparisons provide a significant increase in reachable code? (Sect. 6.2)
3. Does SPLITS impact fuzzing firmware with no comparisons? (Sect. 6.2)
4. How does SPLITS impact the discovery of firmware bugs? (Sect. 6.3)

Table 1. The number of reached string comparisons guarding code solved across five 24 h trials in the *Magic-String-Binaries*. *Total* represents the number of unique comparisons solved at least once across all of the trials. SPLITS outperforms state-of-the-art fuzzing techniques and is demonstrably highly effective and yields *consistent* performance across repeated trials.

Firmware	FUZZWARE				ICICLE (CompCov)				SPLITS			
	Min	Med	Max	Total	Min	Med	Max	Total	Min	Med	Max	Total
3D Printer	0	0	0	0	0	0	1	1	4	4	4	4
Console	1	1	2	2	2	3	6	9	15	15	15	15
GPS Tracker	0	0	0	0	0	0	0	0	4	4	4	4
LiteOS IoT	0	0	1	1	0	0	1	1	1	1	1	1
RF Door Lock	0	0	1	1	0	1	1	1	1	1	1	1
Steering Control	0	0	0	0	0	0	0	0	2	2	2	2
uTasker MODBUS	0	0	0	0	0	0	0	0	44	45	45	45
uTasker USB	0	0	0	0	0	0	0	0	31	33	34	34
Zephyr SocketCan	2	26	30	30	29	32	33	40	52	55	60	65
ChibiOS RTC	0	0	1	2	0	0	2	2	14	14	14	14
Contiki-NG Shell	0	0	0	0	0	0	0	0	14	14	14	14
RiotOS TWR	0	0	0	0	0	0	0	0	13	13	16	16

6.1 Effectiveness at Solving Strings

Table 1 shows the ability of FUZZWARE, SPLITS and ICICLE with CompCov to solve multi-byte string comparisons that guard further code exploration. The results show using FUZZWARE alone struggled to solve the majority of the string comparisons. For those that were solved, the ability to solve a given string was rarely consistent across the five trials. ICICLE with CompCov was able to solve some strings unreachable by FUZZWARE in the 3D Printer, Console and Zephyr SocketCan binaries. In contrast, SPLITS was able to perform significantly better and more consistently; solving all of the same strings across all trials for eight of the twelve binaries tested (i.e. the *Min* and *Total* results were equal). In the remaining cases, the majority of strings were consistently solved, but a handful were not consistent as additional constraints prevented the fuzzer from reaching the string comparison. These constraints included the number of parameters given after a command, or other aspects of the system state that must be correctly set in conjunction with the provided string.

Performance Analysis. For a deeper understanding of the effectiveness of our approach, we evaluated the efficiency with which comparisons are solved by SPLITS compared to the state-of-the-art in **Appendix A.1**

6.2   Code Coverage Analysis

We analyze code coverage over the two categories of firmware we devised (*Magic-String-Binaries* and *Other-Binaries*) to understand the effectiveness of SPLITS and determine if the introduction of the techniques impacts fuzzing performance.

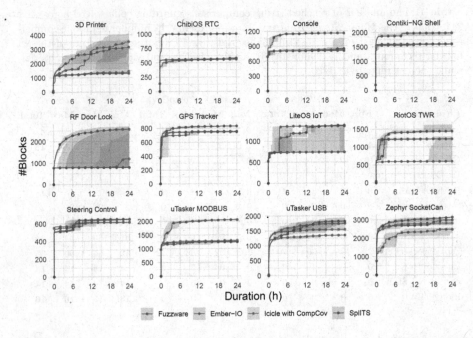

Fig. 5. *Magic-String-Binaries.* Comparison of coverage achieved by: FUZZWARE, SPLITS, EMBER-IO and ICICLE with CompCov for *Magic-String-Binaries*. Bands represent the range of coverage observed over five 24 h trials.

The introduction of SPLITS has a large impact on code coverage for several of the firmware, shown in Fig. 5 and **Appendix A.2**. Of the twelve Magic-String-Binaries, eleven had higher results deemed statistically significant when applying a Mann-Whitney U test at the 0.01 significance level. When compared to other frameworks, SPLITS saw an increase deemed statistically significant in 9 and 10 of the 12 binaries for EMBER-IO and ICICLE respectively.

Compared to the other tested firmware fuzzing frameworks, SPLITS saw more than a 50% increase in code coverage in both the uTasker MODBUS and the ChibiOS RTC binaries. We observed improvements upwards of 37% for the Console binary, 23% for the Contiki-NG Shell binary, and 17% for the RiotOS TWR binary in median blocks covered when compared to the other frameworks. The GPS Tracker and Zephyr SocketCan binaries each saw an increase in median code coverage between 5 and 10% compared to the next highest framework.

The comparisons guarding initialization in the RF Door Lock and LiteOS IoT binaries significantly impact code coverage. FUZZWARE could not consistently find a solution in 24 h, allowing an increase of more than 80% in minimum and median coverage for SPLITS. Due to FUZZWARE and EMBER-IO both solving the string comparison in the RF Door Lock in a single trial, statistical significance could not be established. In contrast, ICICLE with CompCov allowed solving the RF Door Lock binary's string comparison in most trials. EMBER-IO passed the two byte string comparison in all trials for LiteOS IoT.

Block coverage in the 3D Printer increases more than 100% when SPLITS is applied compared to FUZZWARE. Most of the commands given to the 3D Printer firmware are parsed byte by byte, rather than as a string. The string comparisons come from a handful of exceptions, such as the emergency stop command M112. The number of code blocks reachable from these special cases is too small to account for the change increase in coverage from enabling SPLITS. Further investigation reveals that solving a single command can provide a mutable case with the correct format. After the M112 emergency stop command was solved with SPLITS, mutation yielded discovery of the similar M111 and M113 commands. EMBER-IO was also able to uncover many of these commands.

Given the large difference in the number of solved strings between FUZZWARE and SPLITS on the uTasker USB firmware, we consider the difference in the number of blocks reached comparatively small. Further investigation revealed that SPLITS and FUZZWARE explored different parts of the firmware. Of the 2266 unique blocks executed across all trials, 226 were only reached using FUZZWARE, while 437 blocks could only be reached when SPLITS was applied.

Code Coverage of Other-Binaries. SPLITS is intended to solve strings, the attempts to solve strings require firmware executions to both search for, and attempt to solve potential string comparisons. To determine whether the additional processing impacts fuzzing of firmware with no string comparisons, we tested the *Other-Binaries* and compare the coverage results to FUZZWARE without SPLITS applied. We defer the results to **Appendix** A.2. In summary, none of the tests revealed a statistically significant difference in coverage achieved; this suggests that fuzzing performance is not impacted by SPLITS.

6.3   Bug Discovery

While code coverage is a useful metric for comparing the performance of fuzzing frameworks, fuzzing aims to identify bugs. We deduplicated the reported crashes and investigated any crashes in these binaries identified with SPLITS that were not previously found and reported by FUZZWARE.

Analysis of Newly Discovered Bugs. After triaging the deduplicated crashes, we identified the following new firmware bugs, and verified they are not false positives. We responsibly disclosed any vulnerabilities to the appropriate vendor.

(1) Zephyr SocketCan. *CVE-2023-0779.* Within Zephyr's network component, the pkt command provides information about internal packet buffers. The function takes an address pointer as a user entered parameter. This pointer is not validated before it is dereferenced, allowing a user to point anywhere in memory.

(2) Console. Within the Console binary, we identified an out-of-bounds read bug. Commands take input from the user regarding dates, without validation. Entering months greater than 12 causes data from outside an array to be read. We note this bug was concurrently discovered in ICICLE [7], when used with CompCov [16], which we replicated in one of our five trials.

(3) uTasker MODBUS & uTasker USB. The uTasker binaries previously tested in FUZZWARE [27] were compiled with the memory debugger enabled. This allows reading and writing arbitrary memory. While attempts to access unmapped memory ideally would be restricted, we do not consider this a vulnerability, as these commands should be disabled in release versions of firmware.

(4) Contiki-NG Shell. The Contiki-NG Shell binary does not always validate the number of parameters given to a shell command. Attempting to call a vulnerable command with fewer parameters causes the parameter pointer to be set to null. This null pointer is not checked prior to being dereferenced.

(5–6) GPS Tracker. We uncovered two new crashes, both null pointer dereferences caused by a lack of error checking. For the first bug, the code assumes a call to *strtok* will always return at least one token, and fails to consider the case where the input is an empty string. The second bug fails to consider a received string may not contain an expected value. Searching for the expected substring results in a null pointer being returned when it is not found, then dereferenced. This bug is identical in nature to a known bug in this firmware, and appears to be caused by copy-pasting the flawed code to other sections of the firmware.

Analysis of Existing Bugs Guarded by String Comparisons. Notably, the inclusion of SPLITS does not change the execution of a given fuzzer generated input. Other mutation stages such as *havoc* and *splice* employed by AFL++ can still produce inputs that trigger the crashes previously reported by FUZZWARE. We observe two bugs previously reported by FUZZWARE are guarded by string comparisons. The GPS Tracker contains a null pointer dereference when parsing AT commands. In our tests, none of the five FUZZWARE trials triggered this bug. The RF Door Lock contains a bug in the main loop, requiring the string comparison in initialization to be solved. This deeper bug was triggered in one of our five FUZZWARE trials, as the others were unable to proceed past initialization. SPLITS, was able to reproduce both bugs in **all** five trials.

7   Discussion

Comparison Functions. Predominantly, we observed standard C functions for comparing strings. But, in the two uTasker binaries, a custom function performs string comparisons, *fnCheckInput*. However, the custom function is detected as a string comparison function and appropriately solved. This suggests SPLITS can be applicable outside of the standard C functions. Notably, the use of functions to perform comparisons is extremely common but it could be performed inline, preventing the string comparison from being detected and solved using SPLITS. However, we have not observed this problem in our testing.

Comparison Detections. We observed some cases of false positive detection of string comparison functions. One example is printing to a serial port. The static string to be printed is detected as an *ideal string*, while the pointer to the serial device is detected as an *observed buffer*. This has little significance. The only impact from these false positives is taking extra computation time but time loss is already minimized, as we do not expect to be able to map the input to many of the serial port's internal variables. If a byte cannot be mapped, further processing of this comparison is abandoned.

Applicability to Other Frameworks. While we have implemented SPLITS on top of FUZZWARE [27], it is also applicable to other monolithic embedded firmware fuzzing frameworks such as P^{2}IM [14], μEmu [36] and Ember-IO [12]. In the case of Ember-IO, there is an additional requirement that *peripheral input playback* was not the source of any of the bytes in the *observed value* buffer; as only fuzzer generated input bytes can be located using input-to-state mapping. We consider DMA out of the scope, and the application of SPLITS to works that handle DMA such as DICE [23] and SEmu [37] has not been considered.

8 Related Work

Embedded Firmware Fuzzing. In general, for Unix-based firmware, several approaches have been developed [5,20,30,34,35]. While acknowledging these efforts, in this study, we focus on fuzzing approaches for monolithic firmware.

Monolithic Embedded Firmware Fuzzing. To function on monolithic firmware, some works replace hardware interactions at a Hardware Abstraction Layer [9,21], assisted by manual effort. To automate this process, works such as P^{2}IM [14] and μEmu [36] use heuristic based models to classify registers and infer the behavior of each classification. Several works have explored the use of symbolic execution as a tool to assist in firmware testing [4,11,19,22,36]. SEmu [37] instead models the behavior of peripheral registers by processing the manufacturer's manuals. Approaches such as EMBER-IO [12] and FUZZWARE [27] fuzz all registers, and simplify the process by reducing the amount of mutation required. The concurrent work Hoedur [28] addresses the problems of interspersed input accesses by separating the input into multiple streams, one for each register.

Input-to-State Correspondence Methods. Early methods to assist multi-byte comparisons such as LAF-INTEL [1] and CompCov [16] replace these comparisons with a series of easier to solve single byte comparisons. Alternate approaches used symbolic execution [3,31] or taint tracking [6,17,26,32] as a means to uncover paths with difficult to solve constraints. Eclipser [8], REDQUEEN [2] and WEIZZ [15] use input-to-state analysis for non-firmware binaries to inform replacement mutations. These desktop-focused approaches assume contiguity of inputs when compared to the program state when solving string comparisons.

9 Conclusion

To allow firmware fuzzers to appropriately solve string comparisons found in many firmware, we developed SPLITS. When integrated with FUZZWARE [27] and AFL++ [16], our instrumentation and mutation techniques were effective in finding test cases suitable for string replacement, and efficiently performing the replacement to reach deeper code. Eleven of the 12 tested firmware containing string comparisons demonstrated statistically significant improvements in block coverage compared to the baseline FUZZWARE with 6 *new* bugs (with one recent CVE assignment) in firmware found through the inclusion of SPLITS.

Acknowledgments. This research was supported by the Next Generation Technologies Fund from the Defence Science and Technology Group, Australia and through the Australian Government's Research Training Program Scholarship (RTPS).

A Appendix

A.1 Detailed Performance Analysis

For a deeper analysis of the effectiveness of our approach, we selected three sets of firmware based on their use of strings to determine the efficiency with which comparisons are solved by SPLITS compared to the state-of-the-art fuzzers.

As shown in Table 2, SPLITS was able to quickly and consistently solve the *error checks* in the LiteOS IoT and RF Door Lock binaries. In the 3D Printer and Steering Control tests, using strings *to receive data*, SPLITS solved all of these comparisons. In cases where multiple, similar length, strings are compared in quick succession, SPLITS would solve each of these strings within seconds of each other. For *configuring interfaces*, such as the console binary, with SPLITS, all **15** string comparisons were solved in every trial. FUZZWARE solved the shortest string, ps consistently, and the second shortest string rtc only in a single trial. Across these binaries, ICICLE with CompCov solved more strings than FUZZWARE due to CompCov instrumentation, but still lacked consistency and the process took considerably longer compared to SPLITS.

A.2 Code Coverage (Magic-String-Binaries and Other-Binaries)

Table 3 and Table 4 show the coverage achieved in the *Magic-String-Binaries* and *Other-Binaries* respectively. The highest minimum, median and maximum values for each firmware are shown in **bold**. P-values indicating statistical significance are calculated using Mann Whitney U tests, conducted at a 0.01 significance level.

Table 2. Time to solve a sample of string comparisons over five 24 h fuzzing campaigns. The fastest minimum, median and maximum values for each firmware are shown in **bold** and gray regions show failures.

Firmware	String	Fuzzware			Icicle (CompCov)			SpLITS		
		Min	Med	Max	Min	Med	Max	Min	Med	Max
LiteOS IoT	OK	2h13m	>24h	>24h	18h23m	>24h	>24h	**19m**	**1h2m**	**1h32m**
RF Door Lock	OK\r\n	1h1m	>24h	>24h	2h53m	20h28m	>24h	**2m**	**4m**	**10m**
3D Printer	M108	>24h	>24h	>24h	>24h	>24h	>24h	**11m**	**23m**	**44m**
3D Printer	M112	>24h	>24h	>24h	11h7m	>24h	>24h	**11m**	**23m**	**44m**
3D Printer	M410	>24h	>24h	>24h	>24h	>24h	>24h	**11m**	**23m**	**44m**
3D Printer	M110	>24h	>24h	>24h	>24h	>24h	>24h	**46m**	**1h33m**	**1h59m**
Steering Control	steer	>24h	>24h	>24h	>24h	>24h	>24h	**6m**	**8m**	**13m**
Steering Control	motor	>24h	>24h	>24h	>24h	>24h	>24h	**6m**	**8m**	**13m**
Console	ps	3m	41m	2h22m	**2m**	24m	1h25m	2m	**3m**	**7m**
Console	reboot	>24h	>24h	>24h	13h47m	>24h	>24h	**2m**	**6m**	**7m**
Console	help	>24h	>24h	>24h	3h40m	21h52m	>24h	**2m**	**6m**	**6m**
Console	saul	>24h	>24h	>24h	9h3m	>24h	>24h	**2m**	**6m**	**7m**
Console	write	>24h	>24h	>24h	>24h	>24h	>24h	**54m**	**1h25m**	**4h25m**
Console	read	>24h	>24h	>24h	>24h	>24h	>24h	**51m**	**1h4m**	**3h22m**
Console	all	>24h	>24h	>24h	>24h	>24h	>24h	**1h5m**	**1h14m**	**4h19m**
Console	rtc	14h30m	>24h	>24h	4h58m	>24h	>24h	**2m**	**3m**	**7m**
Console	poweron	>24h	>24h	>24h	9h25m	>24h	>24h	**7m**	**1h26m**	**1h40m**
Console	poweroff	>24h	>24h	>24h	9h38m	>24h	>24h	**7m**	**1h26m**	**1h40m**
Console	clearalarm	>24h	>24h	>24h	>24h	>24h	>24h	**7m**	**1h26m**	**1h40m**
Console	getalarm	>24h	>24h	>24h	18h40m	>24h	>24h	**7m**	**1h26m**	**1h40m**
Console	setalarm	>24h	>24h	>24h	20h37m	>24h	>24h	**31m**	**1h48m**	**4h28m**
Console	gettime	>24h	>24h	>24h	>24h	>24h	>24h	**7m**	**1h25m**	**1h39m**
Console	settime	>24h	>24h	>24h	>24h	>24h	>24h	**31m**	**2h15m**	**3h17m**

Table 3. *Magic-String-Binaries.* Fuzzing minimum, median and maximum block coverage achieved with each fuzzing framework over five 24 h trials.

Firmware	Blocks in Firmware	Fuzzware			Ember-IO			Icicle (CompCov)			SpLITS			p-val to Fuzzware	p-val to Ember-IO	p-val to Icicle
		Min	Med	Max	Min	Med	Max	Min	Med	Max	Min	Med	Max			
3D Printer	8045	1229	1289	1383	1575	**3517**	4059	1311	1445	2988	2695	3134	3614	<0.01	0.465	0.016
Console	2251	803	805	844	804	843	856	808	830	1063	**1157**	**1160**	**1161**	<0.01	<0.01	<0.01
GPS Tracker	4194	747	748	754	756	756	759	748	750	753	**827**	**830**	**833**	<0.01	<0.01	<0.01
LiteOS IoT	2423	736	737	1346	1347	1348	1350	736	736	1313	**1358**	**1366**	**1368**	<0.01	<0.01	<0.01
RF Door Lock	3320	781	782	2548	782	782	2662	780	1177	2380	**2539**	**2553**	**2687**	0.015	0.067	<0.01
Steering Control	1835	609	613	620	638	644	648	610	613	615	**643**	**648**	**652**	<0.01	0.169	<0.01
uTasker MODBUS	3780	1244	1246	1280	1219	1252	1311	1246	1303	1303	**2042**	**2052**	**2100**	<0.01	<0.01	<0.01
uTasker USB	3491	1734	1745	1775	1341	1351	1360	1520	1540	1862	**1792**	**1815**	**1934**	<0.01	<0.01	0.047
Zephyr SocketCan	5943	2689	2976	3029	2272	2468	2565	2733	2806	2809	**3093**	**3126**	**3135**	<0.01	<0.01	<0.01
ChibiOS RTC	3013	559	578	593	554	558	565	554	567	575	**1002**	**1005**	**1007**	<0.01	<0.01	<0.01
Contiki-NG Shell	4776	1593	1594	1596	1564	1595	1596	1584	1587	1590	**1874**	**1973**	**1993**	<0.01	<0.01	<0.01
RiotOS TWR	4261	1219	1222	1224	593	593	1224	1208	1218	1291	**1415**	**1436**	**1618**	<0.01	<0.01	<0.01

Table 4. *Other-Binaries.* Minimum, median and maximum block coverage achieved with each fuzzing framework over five 24 h trials. No binaries showed a statistically significant difference.

Firmware	Blocks in Firmware	FUZZWARE			SPLITS			
		Min	Med	Max	Min	Med	Max	p-value
6LoWPAN Receiver	6977	2732	**3149**	**3206**	**2830**	3056	3119	0.175
6LoWPAN Sender	6980	2772	2972	3161	**2786**	**3113**	**3273**	0.347
CNC	3614	**2561**	**2718**	**2733**	2209	2510	2611	0.016
Drone	2728	**1826**	**1828**	**1843**	713	1734	1837	0.076
Gateway	4921	**2908**	**2939**	**3127**	2408	2686	2939	0.036
Heat Press	1837	**550**	**554**	**564**	549	550	556	0.164
PLC	2303	**637**	**644**	**907**	629	642	650	0.344
Reflow Oven	2947	**1192**	**1192**	**1192**	**1192**	**1192**	**1192**	N/A
Robot	3034	**1305**	**1313**	1315	1298	1306	**1319**	0.249
Soldering Iron	3656	**2302**	2353	2457	2229	**2457**	**2465**	0.528
Thermostat	4673	3245	3410	3497	**3308**	**3430**	**3504**	0.251
XML Parser	9376	3239	3634	3826	**3418**	**3850**	**4004**	0.175

References

1. Circumventing fuzzing roadblocks with compiler transformations. https://lafintel.wordpress.com/2016/08/15/circumventing-fuzzing-roadblocks-with-compiler-transformations/ (2016)
2. Aschermann, C., Schumilo, S., Blazytko, T., Gawlik, R., Holz, T.: REDQUEEN: fuzzing with input-to-state correspondence. In: Symposium on Network and Distributed System Security (NDSS) (2019)
3. Cadar, C., Dunbar, D., Engler, D.: KLEE: unassisted and automatic generation of high-coverage tests for complex systems programs. In: USENIX Symposium on Operating Systems Design and Implementation (OSDI) (2008)
4. Cao, C., Guan, L., Ming, J., Liu, P.: Device-agnostic firmware execution is possible: a concolic execution approach for peripheral emulation. In: Annual Computer Security Applications Conference (ACSAC) (2020)
5. Chen, D., Egele, M., Woo, M., Brumley, D.: Towards automated dynamic analysis for Linux-based embedded firmware. In: Network and Distributed System Security Symposium (NDSS) (2016)
6. Chen, P., Chen, H.: Angora: efficient fuzzing by principled search. In: 2018 IEEE Symposium on Security and Privacy (SP), pp. 711–725 (2018)
7. Chesser, M., Nepal, S., Ranasinghe, D.C.: Icicle: a re-designed emulator for grey-box firmware fuzzing. In: ACM SIGSOFT International Symposium on Software Testing and Analysis (ISSTA) (2023)
8. Choi, J., Jang, J., Han, C., Cha, S.K.: Grey-Box concolic testing on binary code. In: International Conference on Software Engineering (ICSE), pp. 736–747 (2019)

9. Clements, A.A., et al.: HALucinator: firmware re-hosting through abstraction layer emulation. In: USENIX Security Symposium (USENIX Sec) (2020)
10. Corteggiani, N., Camurati, G., Francillon, A.: Inception: system-wide security testing of real-world embedded systems software. In: USENIX Security Symposium (USENIX Sec) (2018)
11. Davidson, D., Moench, B., Ristenpart, T., Jha, S.: FIE on Firmware: finding vulnerabilities in embedded systems using symbolic execution. In: USENIX Security Symposium (USENIX Sec) (2013)
12. Farrelly, G., Chesser, M., Ranasinghe, D.C.: Ember-IO: effective firmware fuzzing with model-free memory mapped IO. In: ACM Asia Conference on Computer and Communications Security (ASIA CCS) (2023)
13. Fasano, A., et al.: SoK: enabling security analyses of embedded systems via rehosting. In: ACM Asia Conference on Computer and Communications Security (ASIA CCS), pp. 687–701 (2021)
14. Feng, B., Mera, A., Lu, L.: P2IM: scalable and hardware-independent firmware testing via automatic peripheral interface modeling. In: USENIX Security Symposium (USENIX Sec) (2020)
15. Fioraldi, A., D'Elia, D.C., Coppa, E.: WEIZZ: automatic grey-box fuzzing for structured binary formats. In: ACM SIGSOFT International Symposium on Software Testing and Analysis (ISSTA), pp. 1–13 (2020)
16. Fioraldi, A., Maier, D., Eißfeldt, H., Heuse, M.: AFL++: combining incremental steps of fuzzing research. In: USENIX Workshop on Offensive Technologies (WOOT) (2020)
17. Gan, S., et al.: GREYONE: data flow sensitive fuzzing. In: USENIX Security Symposium (USENIX Sec) (2020)
18. Gustafson, E., et al.: Toward the analysis of embedded firmware through automated re-hosting. In: International Symposium on Recent Advances in Intrusion Detection (RAID) (2019)
19. Johnson, E., et al.: Jetset: targeted firmware rehosting for embedded systems. In: USENIX Security Symposium (USENIX Sec) (2021)
20. Kim, M., Kim, D., Kim, E., Kim, S., Jang, Y., Kim, Y.: FirmAE: towards large-scale emulation of IoT firmware for dynamic analysis. In: Annual Computer Security Applications Conference (ACSAC) (2020)
21. Li, W., Guan, L., Lin, J., Shi, J., Li, F.: From library portability to para-rehosting: natively executing microcontroller software on commodity hardware. In: Network and Distributed System Security Symposium (NDSS) (2021)
22. Liu, Y., Hung, H.W., Sani, A.A.: Mousse: a system for selective symbolic execution of programs with untamed environments. In: European Conference on Computer Systems (EuroSys) (2020)
23. Mera, A., Feng, B., Lu, L., Kirda, E.: DICE: Automatic emulation of DMA input channels for dynamic firmware analysis. In: IEEE Symposium on Security and Privacy (SP) (2021)
24. Muench, M., Nisi, D., Francillon, A., Balzarotti, D.: Avatar^2: a multi-target orchestration platform. In: Workshop on Binary Analysis Research (BAR) (2018)
25. Muench, M., Stijohann, J., Kargl, F., Francillon, A., Balzarotti, D.: What you corrupt is not what you crash: challenges in fuzzing embedded devices. In: Network and Distributed System Security Symposium (NDSS) (2018)
26. Rawat, S., Jain, V., Kumar, A., Cojocar, L., Giuffrida, C., Bos, H.: VUzzer: application-aware evolutionary fuzzing. In: Network and Distributed System Security Symposium (NDSS) (2017)

27. Scharnowski, T., et al.: Fuzzware: using precise MMIO modeling for effective firmware fuzzing. In: USENIX Security Symposium (USENIX Sec) (2022)
28. Scharnowski, T., Wörner, S., Buchmann, F., Bars, N., Schloegel, M., Holz, T.: HOEDUR: embedded firmware fuzzing using multi-stream inputs. In: USENIX Security Symposium (USENIX Sec) (2023)
29. Spensky, C., et al.: Conware: automated modeling of hardware peripherals. In: ACM Asia Conference on Computer and Communications Security (ASIA CCS) (2021)
30. Srivastava, P., Peng, H., Li, J., Okhravi, H., Shrobe, H., Payer, M.: FirmFuzz: automated IoT firmware introspection and analysis. In: International ACM Workshop on Security and Privacy for the Internet-of-Things (IoT SP) (2019)
31. Stephens, N., et al.: Driller: augmenting fuzzing through selective symbolic execution. In: Network and Distributed System Security Symposium (NDSS) (2016)
32. Wang, T., Wei, T., Gu, G., Zou, W.: TaintScope: a checksum-aware directed fuzzing tool for automatic software vulnerability detection. In: IEEE Symposium on Security and Privacy (SP), pp. 497–512 (2010)
33. Zaddach, J., Bruno, L., Balzarotti, D., Francillon, A.: AVATAR: a Framework to Support Dynamic Security Analysis of Embedded Systems' Firmwares. In: Network and Distributed System Security Symposium (NDSS) (2014)
34. Zheng, Y., Davanian, A., Yin, H., Song, C., Zhu, H., Sun, L.: FIRM-AFL: high-throughput greybox fuzzing of IoT firmware via augmented process emulation. In: USENIX Security Symposium (USENIX Sec) (2019)
35. Zheng, Y., Li, Y., Zhang, C., Zhu, H., Liu, Y., Sun, L.: Efficient greybox fuzzing of applications in Linux-based IoT devices via enhanced user-mode emulation. In: ACM SIGSOFT International Symposium on Software Testing and Analysis (ISSTA) (2022)
36. Zhou, W., Guan, L., Liu, P., Zhang, Y.: Automatic firmware emulation through invalidity-guided knowledge inference. In: USENIX Security Symposium (USENIX Sec) (2021)
37. Zhou, W., Zhang, L., Guan, L., Liu, P., Zhang, Y.: What your firmware tells you is not how you should emulate it: a specification-guided approach for firmware emulation. In: ACM SIGSAC Conference on Computer and Communications Security (CCS) (2022)

μIPS: Software-Based Intrusion Prevention for Bare-Metal Embedded Systems

Luca Degani[1,4(✉)], Majid Salehi[2,3], Fabio Martinelli[4], and Bruno Crispo[1]

[1] University of Trento, Trento, Italy
{luca.degani,bruno.crispo}@unitn.it
[2] imec-DistriNet, KU Leuven, Belgium
[3] Nokia Bell Labs, Antwerp, Belgium
majid.salehi@nokia-bell-labs.com
[4] Istituto di Informatica e Telematica - Consiglio Nazionale delle Ricerche, Pisa, Italy
fabio.martinelli@iit.cnr.it

Abstract. Many embedded systems are low-cost bare-metal systems where the firmware executes directly on hardware without an OS. Bare-metal systems typically lack many security primitives, including the well-known Address Space Layout Randomization (ASLR) and Data Execution Prevention (DEP), and their integrity can be compromised using a single vulnerability. Proposed defenses have not yet been deployed due to their requirements for firmware source code availability or hardware modifications. We present μIPS, the first Intrusion Prevention System (IPS) for bare-metal systems that requires no modification to the hardware and can be applied to stripped binaries without access to the source code. μIPS enforces fine-grained control-flow protection targeting both forward and backward edges. To achieve that, μIPS introduces a novel Trusted Execution Environment (TEE) to provide memory isolation at runtime while handling the hardware limitations of bare-metal systems. μIPS also provides Remote Integrity Check (RIC) mechanism to validate the integrity of control-flow protection policies and the TEE code, and secure Over-The-Air (OTA) update mechanism to deploy the updated policies. We evaluate μIPS against *ten* real-world representative firmware. μIPS imposes a 31% execution overhead on average on binary instrumented firmware. μIPS reduces exposure to Return-Oriented Programming (ROP) attacks by 99%.

Keywords: Embedded Systems Security · Intrusion Prevention System · Trusted Execution Environment

1 Introduction

With the wide adoption of Internet of Things (IoT) technologies, embedded systems permeate every area of our lives, from motor control chips in cars over

G. Tsudik et al. (Eds.): ESORICS 2023, LNCS 14347, pp. 311–331, 2024.
https://doi.org/10.1007/978-3-031-51482-1_16

Industrial Control Systems (ICSs) to smart consumer devices such as remote-controlled light bulbs, refrigerators, smart scales, and many more. The rise of embedded systems has opened new doors for cybercriminals. Devices have become a prime target for attackers, with reported attacks doubling every six months [27,38]. Many of the reported attacks resulted in severe consequences in cyber-physical systems (*e.g.,* TRENDnet Webcam and Jeep Hack [4]).

A big share of already deployed IoT devices are on bare-metal embedded systems, which is a particularly vulnerable and constrained subclass of embedded systems. They execute a single statically linked binary firmware that provides specific application logic and system functionality without privilege separation between them. Most firmware for bare-metal systems are developed in C or C++, which are not memory-safe programming languages. Consequently, bare-metal systems can suffer from control-flow hijacking attacks. Due to the resource constraints, bare-metal systems lack traditional protection mechanisms that are available in desktop systems [24,37], such as DEP, stack canaries, and ASLR. Furthermore, existing techniques [5,8,9,12,14,23,41] to protect these systems against control-flow hijacking attacks have not yet been deployed because they either require firmware source code availability, hardware modifications, or offer limited security guarantees.

In this paper, we propose μIPS, an intrusion prevention system that prevents control-flow hijacking attacks in bare-metal systems. μIPS tackles the previously mentioned limitations of state-of-the-art and enables fine-grained Control-Flow Integrity (CFI) and shadow stack protection mechanisms for Commercial-offthe-shelf (COTS) firmware. In addition, for every violation of the CFI policy, μIPS can emit an alert to a Security Information and Event Management (SIEM) or a log aggregation system before restoring to a working state of the device.

Due to the lack of a Memory Management Unit (MMU), embedded systems cannot provide fine-grained memory isolation, a mandatory primitive for control-flow protection. However, many modern embedded systems have a peripheral called the Memory Protection Unit (MPU) that can enforce access protections to different regions of the physical memory. At first glance, it may appear that memory isolation can be achieved in a straightforward manner by utilizing the MPU. However, this is not the case, due to the lack of privilege isolation, the MPU protection can be readily disabled [8] if privilege separation is not properly used or used at all. However, as recently demonstrated in [9850322], configuring and preventing intentional MPU misconfigurations presents many caveats that hinder the process, or even discourage a developer into using the MPU.

For solving these challenges, μIPS provides a TEE that monitors and limits memory accesses according to its control-flow protection policy. Specifically, μIPS TEE leverages a static binary instrumentation approach to reduce execution privileges of the entire firmware and a strict MPU configuration to provide access to the authorized instructions. Furthermore, μIPS provides the ability to perform a RIC procedure for validating the integrity of MPU configuration and the TEE code. Moreover, μIPS enables a remote host to perform encrypted OTA firmware updates in the case of a change to the control-flow protection policies.

By doing so, μIPS achieves control-flow protection without any access to the firmware source code or modification to the hardware. In addition to control-flow protection, this setting allows the development of an intrusion notification mechanism required for IPSs. Such a mechanism is part of the TEE and requires an exclusive access to the network interface to guarantee the integrity of the communication stack, thus preventing any interference from on-device malware.

We evaluated μIPS against ten representative firmware, comprising CPU and I/O bound, benchmarks, crypto and real-world Internet of Things (IoT) applications. μIPS achieves an average execution overhead of 31%. Additionally, we evaluated the effectiveness of μIPS by counting the maximum number of ROP gadgets available at any given time during firmware execution, using the Ropper [31]. μIPS reduces the number of ROP gadgets by 99% for all the firmware we tested.

In short, the contributions of this paper are:

- The first IPS for bare-metal systems that detects and blocks control-flow violations. μIPS proposes a fine-grained CFI and shadow stack mechanism on top of the primitives offered by the TEE. μIPS supports stripped firmware binaries.
- A full-featured TEE for bare-metal systems, providing a security layer that enables the isolation and monitoring of potentially vulnerable applications running on the device. μIPS offers security primitives such as RIC and OTA secure firmware updates for validating the integrity of control-flow protection policies and TEE code and secure deployment of updated policies respectively.
- An evaluation of a μIPS prototype on a representative set of *ten* real-world firmware. μIPS incurs 31% execution overhead on average on instrumented firmware binaries. μIPS effectively reduces exposure to ROP attacks by 99%. To foster further research, we will make our μIPS and evaluation dataset available open source upon the acceptance of the paper.

2 Background

Trusted Execution Environment. TEEs provide an isolation layer to protect the access and execution of sensitive code, data and peripherals. Without isolation, any instruction can access the entire memory, possibly leaking crypto secrets or modifying peripherals registers. For instance, security peripherals such as the MPU can be re-configured or even disabled at runtime, thus bypassing them [8]. When a TEE is provided, it would be possible to perform cryptographic operations for security services safely. Unfortunately, most of the bare-metal systems lack TEEs [29].

Memory Protection Unit. Most of the bare-metal systems use MPUs to enforce access controls (*i.e.*, read, write, and execute) on memory regions for both privileged and unprivileged modes. Unlike the MMU, an MPU does not support virtual addressing and instead enforces permissions of physical address ranges. Furthermore, MPU has limited number of supported regions varies from 8 to 16 depending on the model and configuration of the processors. For example, the MPU in ARMv7-M, only supports access control enforcing up to eight memory regions, numbered 0–7, with the following restrictions: (1) A region must be a power of two and from 32 Bytes to 4 GBytes in size; (2) A region must be size-aligned (*e.g.*, if the size is 2 KByte, then the valid starting address must be a multiple of 16 KByte); (3) Regions may overlap, with the region with the larger number taking precedence in case of permissions conflict.

3   Threat Model and Assumptions

Threat Model. In the design of μIPS, we consider an embedded device connected to a network through an unspecified medium (*e.g.*, Wi-Fi) and running firmware where at least one vulnerability is present. The firmware can also includes malicious software components. The threat is posed by an attacker who may or may not have access to the firmware binary (or source code) but has the knowledge of a write-what-where vulnerability in the target device. Through the vulnerability, she can achieve remote code execution, either injecting malicious code or resorting to ROP style attacks [32]. Since we protect against control-flow hijacking attacks, Data-Oriented Programming (DOP) attacks that target non-control data are out of scope. We also assume that the attacker cannot physically tamper with the device or, if the case, that it is not possible to flash the device with another firmware nor replace the flash memory chip. The attacker sits in the same device network over which can launch attacks.

Assumptions. We assume the hardware platform is equipped with an MPU and supports two privilege modes of execution (*i.e.*, privileged and unprivileged). Our target bare-metal system executes a single statically linked firmware binary with no protections. Indeed, in bare-metal systems, there are no dynamically linked or shared libraries. We examined more than 100 MCUs from ARM Cortex-M3, M4, and M7 series, and all except one were equipped with an MPU. Additionally, MCUs from other manufacturers, like Atmel's AVR32, also feature an MPU. Thus the MPU requirement is reasonable as present on most of the actual Micro-Controller Unit (MCU) configurations. These conditions and requirements are shared among state-of-the-art works [8], apart from the binary support that is novel and we claim is fundamental for firmware protection.

4   Design

In this section, we present the design of μIPS, detailing each component and the respective interactions. μIPS specifically requires a MPU and an underlying architecture supporting at least two privilege levels, such as ARMv7-M and RISC-V. It is composed of three core components: (1) The CFI and shadow stack protection mechanisms securing both forward edges (*i.e.*, function pointers and virtual table pointers) or backward edges (*i.e.*, return addresses) of the control-flow. (Sect. 4.1) (2) A notification system that sends an alert after a control-flow violation occurs. (Sect. 4.2) (3) The TEE that isolates security services of μIPS from the potentially vulnerable firmware and restores the device after an attack. (Sect. 4.3)

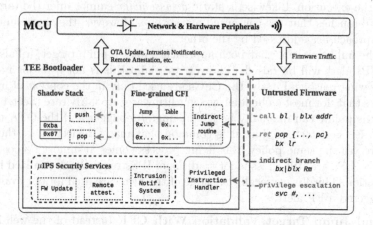

Fig. 1. An overview of the μIPS architecture. (Color figure online)

We design CFI, shadow stack protections, and the notification system on top of the TEE, without which their integrity cannot be guaranteed; an attacker would be able to disable the CFI protection by simply overwriting a memory region if unprotected. μIPS TEE delivers a trusted computing architecture combining an MPU configuration and specialized software tailored for bare-metal systems. Figure 1 depicts the overview of μIPS.

4.1 Control-Flow Protection

μIPS implements a fine-grained control-flow protection mechanism to eliminate, when possible, or mitigate the possibility that the execution flow deviates from the original Control Flow Graph (CFG). The protection should cover both forward and backward edges of a CFG. Our design combines *indexed hooks* [18,19] and a shadow stack to deliver fine-grained control-flow protection. The former guards the forward edges while the latter secures the backward ones of a CFG. μIPS implements the protection system and the policy inside the TEE; therefore, the potentially vulnerable firmware cannot tamper with it.

Policy Generation. To enforce a fine-grained control-flow protection policy, μIPS requires the CFGs of each firmware function. Due to the difficulty in recovering the symbol and relocation information discarded during compilation, extracting CFG from stripped binaries is still an open problem. To extract the CFGs from the stripped binary, we employ a *disassembler* and combine it with *symbolic execution*. In this way, μIPS can get the best of both worlds.

More specifically, CFGs constructed through *symbolic execution* include indirect branch edges thanks to the dynamic analysis of the approach. Conversely, *disassemblers* consider each function while extracting CFGs with a much lower probability of missing one. *Symbolic execution* can miss functions if not covered during the execution. Likewise, a static *disassembler* cannot infer the targets of indirect branches that are computed at runtime. However, the shortcomings of each approach are addressed by the other.

In the unlikely event that both approaches miss a jump target, a False Positive (FP) alert will be raised. However, we claim this is not a major issue for the following reasons. Firstly, the CFGs are used only in the context of indirect branches that, for most embedded systems firmware, are fairly rare (Sect. 6). Secondly, the policy can manually be fixed using a debugger and the OTA update once an FP is detected. Since it is common that many devices share the same firmware yet the same policy, this fixing process comes at almost no cost. Furthermore, FPs are still an issue for traditional IPSs requiring specialized human intervention. Thirdly, we recall that none of the firmware used for our evaluation has triggered a FP alert.

Call and Jump Target Validation With CFI. Instead of the well-known label-based approaches such as Bin-CFI [40], KCoFI [11], CPI [17], and CCFIR [39], µIPS employs *indexed hooks*. Specifically, label-based approaches use only one label for the targets of all the indirect branches; these coarse-grained approaches can lead to the *destination-equivalence* problem and be subverted [1]. µIPS overcomes this problem by leveraging *indexed hooks*.

For each indirect branch, µIPS maintains a list of valid targets generated statically at deployment time. Each indirect branch is validated at runtime thanks to instructions inserted at deployment time by our static binary instrumentation component. The instrumentation consists of a sequence of Assembly instructions that invokes the TEE's CFI module through a SuperVisor Call (SVC) instruction, passing the branch target address as a parameter (blue diagram in Fig. 1). Since exception handlers always execute in privileged mode, µIPS executes the SVC instruction which is a software exception to switch to the privileged mode. The TEE recovers the SVC instruction address as the jump location and verifies in its *indexed hooks* tables whether such a location can jump to the requested target. If it is the case, the TEE downgrades its privileges and jumps to the target address; otherwise, if a violation is detected, the intrusion notification module is invoked and the board is rebooted. By doing so, the intrusion is immediately reported and blocked, preventing a device hijack.

Return Address Validation With Shadow Stack. In each function prologue, our instrumentation component inserts Assembly instructions that save the return address to the shadow stack by calling an SVC; the SVC invokes a specific TEE function that pushes the address onto the shadow stack (green diagram in Fig. 1). When a function is about to return (*i.e.*, in the epilogue), another set of inserted instructions performs a second SVC. Then, the tainted return address will be passed to the TEE function to verify if it matches with the one on top of the shadows stack. If it succeeds, the value is popped, privileges are dropped and the execution jumps to the return address. Conversely, if the two values mismatch, an intrusion is notified, and the device is rebooted.

4.2 Intrusion Notification

Compared to other CFI solutions, μIPS notifies an endpoint about the prevented intrusion when a control-flow violation is detected. μIPS provides an intrusion notification module (Fig. 1). The notification module is built on top of a communication stack that lies in TEE for its isolation. Indeed, part of the communication stack is the network interface peripheral that is, in most cases, used by the potentially vulnerable firmware. Consequently, μIPS cannot restrain the firmware from using it, nor can it require a secondary peripheral. Thus, after detecting a violation, μIPS TEE logs it in a protected flash memory region, which is part of its designated space and used for permanent storage. In total, μIPS stores 16 bytes of data containing the expected branch/return address and the tainted one. The TEE checks whether this region contains data at the device boot time. If so, the TEE initializes the network peripheral, sends the alert until an acknowledgment is received otherwise will retry, clears the memory region, and reboots itself to a normal state. In this way, the potentially vulnerable firmware is never executed while signaling the violation; thus, it cannot interfere with it, so the integrity and availability of the network communication is guaranteed. Additionally, most drivers of standard peripherals, such as those from STM32, are available as source code; thus, we analyse the correctness of the network driver code and then include it in the TEE to avoid malicious peripheral driver in the TEE. The overall intrusion notification process is depicted in Fig. 2.

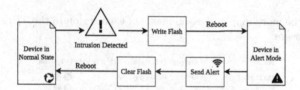

Fig. 2. The μIPS intrusion notification process.

μIPS requires the configuration of the intrusion notification module at deployment time. More specifically, if the embedded device hosts a TCP/IP NIC (*e.g.,* cellular, Wi-Fi or Ethernet), it can directly communicate to a SIEM endpoint to signal any message given the addresses. Otherwise, if the device uses another connectivity medium, such as LoRaWAN or BLE, a gateway notification module is required to forward the alert to the SIEM. While for the first scenario, only network and SIEM related information are required, the deployment in the second scenario is more complex due to the presence of an intermediator and requires a case-by-case analysis. Notably, the communication channel must be encrypted, and each message holds a timestamp for authentication to avoid replay attacks.

4.3 Trusted Execution Environment

Through *memory isolation*, μIPS assures *integrity* to the TEE and its security services. To achieve it, μIPS installs a custom bootloader that performs a sequence of actions. It starts with the configuration of the MPU to provide the Root-of-Trust (RoT) to the rest of the system and stores the cryptographic secrets (*i.e.*, a unique symmetric key for the device) in a secure memory segment (Sect. 4.3). To avoid privilege escalation scenarios, it registers *interrupt* and *exception handlers* to execute privileged tasks for the potentially vulnerable firmware (Sect. 4.3). After setting up the data structures of the CFI (Sect. 4.1) and other security services, it checks for a firmware update, authenticates itself, and signals the successful boot procedure to a remote endpoint (Sect. 4.4). Lastly, μIPS boots the potentially vulnerable firmware.

Memory Layout and MPU Configuration. μIPS splits the MCU memory into six regions described in Table 1. FLASH, RAM and RAM2 are assigned to the potentially vulnerable firmware. The first corresponds to the flash memory where the firmware is stored, therefore it should be readable and executable. The second and third are the two RAM banks available on the hardware, therefore both should be readable and writable but not executable (*i.e.*, W⊕X security policy). Also, these three regions can be accessed by the μIPS TEE to fulfill tasks parts of its security services, such as OTA updates and RIC. RAM_BOOT is a 32 bytes RAM region assigned exclusively to the TEE. The flash region where the TEE is stored is FLASH_BOOT. It can be accessed (rwx) only by itself. Lastly, FLASH_BOOT_NOPRI is a segment where the sequence to execute the firmware in unprivileged mode is stored. As such, it is not writable nor readable by the vulnerable firmware.

Table 1. μIPS memory map and assignments of each region to the TEE or potentially vulnerable firmware.

Name	Origin	Length	TEE	FW	MPU Region
FLASH_BOOT	0x08000000	0x20000 B	✓	✗	⓿ ❶
FLASH_BOOT_NOPRI	0x08020000	0x1000 B	✓	✗	⓿ ❶
FLASH	0x80221000	0xdf000 B	✗	✓	⓿
RAM_BOOT	0x20000000	0x20 B	✓	✗	❷ ❸
RAM	0x20000040	0x17FE0 B	✗	✓	❷
RAM2	0x10000000	32 KB	✗	✓	⓿

μIPS leverages the MPU to provide memory isolation. Since the number of supported regions in the MPU is limited and there are memory regions that are not naturally aligned nor sized as powers of two, we cannot readily generate a one-to-one mapping to an MPU configuration. To solve this problem, we exploit the MPU region prioritisation, where higher memory region numbers have precedence, in order to generate the fine-grained policy shown in Fig. 3. Regions ⓿ and ❷ enforce the W⊕X privilege in the entire flash memory and RAM, limiting unprivileged accesses. The access to the chunks of memory assigned to the TEE, part of the bigger ⓿ and ❷, is restricted by ❶ and ❸, denying read and write operations to the potentially vulnerable firmware. The peripherals address space has been protected using two entries **4** and **5** as this entire address space (two Gigabytes) could not be covered with a single one. The remaining space references a second RAM bank (**6**) and several configurable board features provided by the vendor (**7**). Figure 3 also depicts the permissions attributed to each region for the two privilege levels. Notably, the TEE RAM region is marked as executable to allow the execution of virtual functions, a mechanism for the emulation of untrusted privileged instructions (Sect. 4.3).

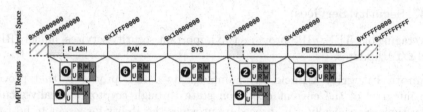

Fig. 3. The μIPS memory layout highlighting the eight configured MPU memory regions and the respective access control attributes.

Privileged Instruction Virtualization. μIPS blocks the execution of any privileged instruction by the potentially vulnerable firmware that could undermine the integrity and security of the embedded device. μIPS executes the firmware by default in unprivileged mode; it identifies instructions requiring privileged execution and executes only those instructions in privileged mode. For example, instructions that access to the program status register like the MSR and CPS need to be executed in privileged mode. Since, μIPS enforces unprivileged mode for all instructions, executing such instructions triggers a *Hard Fault* exception. μIPS captures that exception by its TEE. μIPS detects the Hard Fault root cause and, through a pattern matching sequence, extracts the address being accessed by the instruction and audits its permissions to do so. If it is an allowed operation, the TEE runs it for the potentially vulnerable firmware and returns from the exception, otherwise the board is rebooted. Exception or interrupt handlers also need to execute in privileged mode. For handling such cases, μIPS leverages an *interrupt deprioritization* technique to block the untrusted code from privileged escalation.

Interrupt deprioritization comprises three tasks: (1) An *Exception Catcher* that catches the firmware exception by replacing the original exception handler. The replacement happens by swapping the firmware Interrupt Vector Table (IVT) with a custom one that includes *Exception Catcher* entries. (2) An *Exception Simulator* that drops the privileges, re-enables the interrupts, and executes the original exception handler. Interrupts must be re-enabled since, if the original exception handler contains a privileged instruction, such instruction will trigger a fault that otherwise would be ignored and not captured by the TEE. (3) After the handler has finished the execution, an *Exception Return* is needed to return from the triggered exception correctly. To do so, the *Exception Return* triggers another exception that is captured by the TEE, restores the stack as it was originally and performs the standard exception return procedure.

Exception handlers may contain instructions that require privileges (*e.g.*, an access to the *Private Peripheral Bus*), being meant to be executed in *handler mode*. In this case, once the problematic instruction is executed without the privileges, it triggers a Hard Fault exception that is captured by the TEE. Then, μIPS handles such instructions as mentioned above.

4.4   Security Services

Leveraging our TEE, μIPS provides two important security services, namely RIC and OTA updates.

Remote Integrity Check. μIPS implements a RIC procedure that proves the integrity of the current execution state through cryptographically-secure algorithms. Specifically, RIC procedure provides the ability for a remote host to authenticate not only the potentially vulnerable firmware but also the current MPU configuration and the TEE code. After an integrity check request, μIPS computes the checksums of the aforementioned components, encrypts them and sends them back to the verifier for the verification. To avoid replay attacks, a nonce or a timestamp is included in the messages.

Over-The-Air Updates. μIPS necessitates a practical approach for deploying the CFI policy along with the firmware. If the generated policy is overly strict, leading to a FP alert, an OTA update can quickly deploy the updated policy without manual device flashing, which is impractical for production-grade systems. μIPS updates the potentially vulnerable firmware and its CFI via a request-read-flash loop. During the TEE booting time, it sends checksums of the firmware and policy to an update server, which holds a table of the latest version hashes for each device component. If a received checksum does not match its table entry, an update process begins. This involves clearing the firmware flash memory, requesting and writing firmware chunks, and then rebooting. If the checksum still mismatches after reboot, the update process restarts, avoiding device bricking. The CFI update follows the same process. Message integrity, including data chunks, is ensured through symmetric encryption, and the update routine runs in the TEE, which exclusively accesses the network peripheral since the potentially vulnerable firmware never starts.

4.5 μIPS Deployment

Compared with state-of-the-art, μIPS supports binary firmware deployments. We believe this is a milestone for the protection of embedded systems as the source code requirement is often impractical for the reasons explained above. Binary deployment accepts a firmware binary image as input and leverages the static binary instrumentation component to insert required instructions. More

precisely, μIPS binary instrumentation component statically rewrites potentially unsafe assembly instructions to guarantee protection. Such instructions
are replaced with a call to a supervisor routine. This happens through an SVC
call. μIPS replaces indirect branches with an SVC to invoke the CFI forward-edge
checker. In functions prologues and epilogues, the instrumentation inserts code
to *push* and *pop/return* from the shadow stack. The binary instrumentation also
has to move the binary segments according to the μIPS memory layout. The output of this process is a translated binary that can be loaded into the μIPS TEE.
To enable the control-flow protection, the μIPS *CFI Policy Builder* processes
the binary and generates the policy (Sect. 4.1).

5 Implementation

To validate the design, we implemented μIPS for the ARMv7-M architecture,
enabling it to protect a wide range of deployed bare-metal systems [15]. Our μIPS
implementation provides (1) the TEE, (2) the static binary instrumentation
component, and (3) the CFI policy builder.

We implemented μIPS TEE in the C and Assembly programming languages
with 2810 sloc in total, excluding peripheral drivers and the Hardware Abstraction Layer (HAL) libraries. We built the Static Binary Instrumentation on top
of μSBS [28,30]. μSBS has been extended to support the rewriting of TBB, TBH
and ADR LDR instructions. Indeed, TBB instructions and offsets are converted
into TBHs and TBHs into ADR LDRs. μIPS's Binary Instrumentation counts 1238
Python 3 sloc. The instrumented assembly instructions are listed in Table 2.
Each instruction is replaced with a call to a supervisor routine through an SVC
call. In ARMv7-M, SVC assembly instructions are followed by a number that
indicates the handler that should be invoked. To avoid consuming the limited
SVC handlers (256), that can be used by the firmware, μIPS uses a single one,
thus requiring a Procedure ID (PID) parameter to select the TEE routine to
call. For indirect branches, in addition to the PID parameter, the branch target address is also passed. We implemented CFI Policy Builder in 170 sloc
of Python 3 code, using the **angr** symbolic execution engine [34,35] and the
radare2 disassembler [26].

Table 2. List of instructions replaced by μIPS to instrument the potentially vulnerable firmware. The symbols ✗ and ✚ means that instructions are *replaced* or *added*
respectively. * *In the case of a BX lr return sequence, the instruction is replaced.*

Instruction	Context	New Inst.	Params.	Op.
BX—BLX *Rm*	Indirect Branch	SVC branch	*PID Address*	✗
push {*Rm* ...}	F. Prologue	SVC push SHDW	*PID*	✚
pop {*Rm* ... PC} or BX *lr*	F. Epilogue	SVC pop SHDW	*PID*	✚*

6   Evaluation

μIPS is the first TEE and CFI protection supporting stripped binary firmware, making it applicable to realistic scenarios where the source code is unavailable. μIPS design impacts the performance of an embedded device in terms of flash memory occupation and execution time. Measuring such overheads is not trivial due to the lack of a suitable evaluation benchmark. Ideally, the evaluation set should include CPU-intensive, IO-intensive, mixed and real-world applications, possibly exploiting as many features as possible of our representative device. For our evaluation, we selected *ten* open-source, real-world applications that are described in Sect. 6.1.

The evaluation is performed using the STM32 B-L475E-IOT01A evaluation board from STMicroelectronics. The board houses an 80 MHz Cortex-M4 core, 1 Mbyte of flash memory, and 128 Kbytes of RAM. It provides plenty of connectivity options, including Wi-Fi, NFC, BLE, and support for Sub-GHz bands. Each of the firmware binaries tested has been compiled from the source with the -O3 GCC flag that enables all compiler optimizations and debugging information have been stripped.

6.1   Evaluation Dataset

The details about the firmware selected for the evaluation of μIPS are presented in Table 7 in Appendix A. A brief description for each firmware is as follows. *Blink* is a firmware that blinks an LED and is provided by the board manufacturer. *BSP Sensors* is a firmware that reads temperature and pressure sensors and reports the result over a UART interface. *WiFi Client* and *HTTP Server* are two *IoT-like* firmware that, after connecting to a WiFi network, exchange data via a TCP connection and host a web-server respectively. *SHA-256*, *Fibonacci-Iter* and *Fibonacci-Rec* are three CPU-bound firmware developed for the evaluation of μIPS. The first computes 100000 SHA-256 hashes of three strings of different lengths. The last two implement the Fibonacci algorithm with an input of 1000000 in the case of the iterative version and 30 for the recursive one. Finally, *BLE-IoT* and *HTTP-IoT* read six sensors data and send them to a Bluetooth Low Energy (BLE) gateway and an HTTP server respectively.

6.2   Memory Footprint

μIPS usage of flash memory is twofold: the TEE and the instrumentation. While the TEE size is the same for each deployment, the firmware instrumentation highly depends on the application. In this specific case, the number of indirect branches and functions that are the instrumented locations accounts the most for the memory footprint increase. In Table 3, we measure the memory footprint of μIPS on the firmware listed in the first column. In the second and third ones, we compare the size of the instrumented Binary files and non-instrumented ones. In addition to the code, an ELF file contains metadata, symbols and deployment instructions, that is not required for the firmware to run. Therefore, since only a portion of an ELF file is actually deployed on the embedded devices, in the fourth and fifth columns, we measure the BIN sizes (*i.e.*, the blobs containing only the bytes that will be flashed). Table 3 shows that μIPS instrumented ELFs incur in 32% memory increase on average, from the 24% of the *BLE-IoT* firmware to the 40% of the *HTTP Server*. The difference is bigger for the BIN formats where the lowest increase amounts at 51%, the average at 78% and the highest at 113%.

In addition to an hashmap and a function for the runtime resolution of indirect branches, μIPS instrumentation injects *nine* assembly instructions before an indirect branch, *nine* in a function prologue and *nine* in the epilogue. However, as reported in Table 2, the direct branch and, only under specific circumstances (*i.e.*, the instruction is a BX *lr*), the epilogue instrumentation replaces a single instruction decreasing to *eight* added instructions. Counting replacements when applicable, the assembled instructions correspond to increments of 26, 30, and 28 bytes in bytes for each of the three occurrences, respectively.

Table 3. Memory footprint of the μIPS instrumentation on a representative set of firmware.

Firmware	ELF Size		Binary Size	
	Orig.	Instrumented	Orig.	Instrumented
Blink	16488 B	22158 B (+34%)	4604 B	7897 B (+72%)
BSP Sensors	184096 B	246025 B (+34%)	41068 B	87263 B (+112%)
WiFi Client	189836 B	264552 B (+39%)	45576 B	97210 B (+113%)
HTTP Serv.	201208 B	280769 B (+40%)	50436 B	105874 B (+110%)
SHA-256	18940 B	24822 B (+31%)	6568 B	10347 B (+58%)
Fib-Iter	16360 B	21561 B (+32%)	4392 B	7439 B (+69%)
Fib-Rec	16400 B	21666 B (+32%)	4968 B	8176 B (+65%)
BLE-IoT	83225 B	102817 B (+24%)	21296 B	32217 B (+51%)
HTTP-IoT	118292 B	148636 B (+26%)	30360 B	47514 B (+57%)
Average		**+32%**		**+78%**

6.3 Execution Overhead

μIPS instrumentation introduces a runtime overhead on indirect branches, function calls, and returns. Firmware with numerous indirect branches or frequent small function invocations will likely have higher overhead. In Table 4, we quantify the μIPS instrumentation impact on runtime. On average, it amounts to a 31% increase where the maximum value is 71%. For these measurements, each firmware has been run from a reset state until its main task has been accomplished and the execution time measured. For instance, for the blink firmware we measured the time between the power on of the device and the first blink. The experiments have been repeated *ten* times, and the values measured using a high-resolution logic analyzer. As the table shows, the recursive Fibonacci firmware incurs the biggest overhead due to the number of function calls caused by the recursion.

Table 4. Execution overhead of the μIPS binary instrumentation. Each experiment measures the execution time of the firmware main task from a reset state.

Firmware	Exec. time to main task (ms)	
	Original	Binary Instr.
Blink	1.59 ms	1.74 ms (**+9%**)
BSP Sensors	303.55 ms	329.9 ms (**+9%**)
WiFi Client	682.83 ms	983.3 ms (**+44%**)
HTTP Serv.	669.73 ms	970 ms (**+45%**)
SHA-256	1273.04 ms	1497.73 ms (**+18%**)
Fib-Iter	1504.51 ms	1604.11 ms (**+7%**)
Fib-Rec	7786.50 ms	13287.66 ms (**+71%**)
BLE-IoT	997.46 ms	1411.61 ms (**+42%**)
HTTP-IoT	1273.24 ms	1710.08 ms (**+34%**)
Average		**+31%**

Furthermore, to quantify the contribution of each instrumented component (branch, prologue, and epilogue) to the performance, we traced a 30 s execution of each firmware, counted the number of components hit, and measured their execution time. We report the results in Table 5. The function calls and returns are the two components that almost equally weigh the most on the overall execution time. The two firmware dealing with the network, *WiFi Client* and *HTTP Server*, present many more indirect branches than the others. We believe it is due to the number of callbacks that the firmware registers to handle network events. Lastly, the overall performance percentage increase is very similar to the values reported in Table 4, obtained with a more precise instrument, thus proving the goodness of the measures. Indeed, the average overhead increase measured amounts to 31% as for the other experiments. Indeed, the binary instrumentation overhead is inherited from μSBS. Thus, any improvement from binary instrumentation could benefit μIPS; this is an orthogonal problem to μIPS and can be improved as future work.

Table 5. Statistics on the number of *indirect branches*, *function calls* and *returns* during a 30 s execution of each firmware and the measured μIPS runtime overhead.

Firmware	Runtime Stats (30s)			Overhead over 30s exec. (ms)			
	I. Branch	Call	Return	I. Branch	Call	Return	Overall
Blink	2	14788	14787	0.36 ms	1544.02 ms	1603.76 ms	**3148.14 ms (10%)**
BSP Sensors	72	6856	6855	12.91 ms	715.84 ms	743.47 ms	**1472.22 ms (5%)**
WiFi Client	5816	57463	57462	1042.64 ms	5999.74 ms	6232.16 ms	**13274.55 ms (44%)**
HTTP Serv.	5632	56978	56977	1009.65 ms	5949.05 ms	6179.56 ms	**13138.27 ms (44%)**
SHA-256	14	30430	30429	2.51 ms	3177.16 ms	3300.24 ms	**6479.91 ms (22%)**
Fib-Iter	2	4738	4737	0.36 ms	494.70 ms	513.76 ms	**1008.82 ms (3%)**
Fib-Rec	2	104472	104471	0.36 ms	10907.9 ms	11330.6 ms	**22238.91 ms (74%)**
BLE-IoT	9	57862	57861	1.61 ms	6041.40 ms	6275.44 ms	**12318.46 ms (41%)**
HTTP-IoT	66	45624	45623	11.83 ms	4763.58 ms	4948.14 ms	**9723.55 ms (32%)**
Average							**+31%**

6.4 ROP Gadgets Reduction

μIPS instrumentation replaces indirect branches and return instructions with a sequence of MOVs and an SVC instruction. This leads to a remarkable reduction of ROP gadgets in the instrumented firmware. ROP gadgets are sequences of instructions part of the firmware that are chained together to perform a control-flow hijacking attack, reusing existing code. A peculiarity of ROP gadgets is that they end with a return or branch instruction. Since μIPS replaces all the return instructions, most of the gadgets should no more be usable. Indeed, we show the reduction of ROP gadgets in Table 6. To extract the gadgets we used the open-source *Ropper* [31] application. In the results, we do not consider those in the μIPS TEE, as they are inaccessible to an attacker due to the MPU policy requiring privileges to access the TEE memory segment. As mentioned, μIPS is able to remove all the gadgets in most of the firmware. However, in four firmware, we found a single gadget, BX pc, that cannot be used to build an exploit chain since its effect is a jump to the subsequent instruction. Such an instruction is used to switch between the *ARM* and *THUMB* instruction sets. Furthermore, we present a detailed security analysis in Appendix B.

Table 6. Count of ROP gadgets in the original and instrumented firmware.

Firmware	ROP Gadgets count				
	Original	uniq.	Instr.	uniq.	Decrease
Blink	240	190	0	0	-100%
BSP Sensors	3880	2957	2	1	-99%
WiFi Client	4044	3084	2	1	-99%
HTTP Serv.	4458	3399	2	1	-99%
SHA-256	275	222	0	0	-100%
Fib-Iter	232	185	0	0	-100%
Fib-Rec	239	190	0	0	-100%
BLE-IoT	745	537	0	0	-100%
HTTP-IoT	1436	1034	13	1	-99%

7 Discussion

Limited Flash Memory Size. For certain applications, μIPS runtime overhead and the memory footprint may be non-negligible. However, we note that compared with the previous generation of MCUs (*e.g.*, 8 bit AVR), the technology has evolved proposing cores with higher clock speeds where the performance is sometimes not entirely used by the application. Likewise, embedded flash memories are bigger, in the order of Megabytes, in contrast to the Kilobytes of the previous generation. As shown in Sect. 6, current firmware are typically less than 100 KB in size, thus cannot fill such memory chips.

Supported Architectures. In this paper, we presented μIPS making references to ARMv7-M features, but we point out that those are available on other architectures too. More specifically, properties like privileged execution, interrupt prioritization, MPU support, and vector tables are not unique to this platform or the board used for the evaluation. The implementation for a different architecture will probably differ from the presented one, and so will the performance impact; still, no specific architecture features are required for μIPS, apart from the MPU.

Protection Policy. There are several IPSs for general purpose computers that can cover more attacks and provide more services than μIPS. Nevertheless, μIPS is the first solution for bare-metal systems that not only detects attacks but also reports them. Furthermore, unlike solutions proposed for bare-metal systems, μIPS do not require source code or hardware modification. Thus, although μIPS only supports control-flow protection policies, it provides building blocks to mitigate and report more types of attacks in bare-metal systems. We leave such improvements to future work.

8 Related Works

Control-Flow Protections. Several CFI solutions [3,13,36] utilize remote attestation mechanisms where the analysis/detection agent is deployed on a remote server. However, the effectiveness of these systems depends on how embedded devices respond when asked to send captured logs to an external server. CFI CaRE [23] proposes a CFI method on forward-edges and a hardware isolated shadow stack for protecting the backward edges. CFI CaRE leverages hardware-enforced isolated execution mechanism provided by ARM-TrustZone [6]. However, ARMv7-M, as the most prevalent architecture, does not support TrustZone.

There are a number of solutions [2,5,8,14,41] that modify a compiler to mitigate control-flow hijacking attacks. Silhouette [41] uses LLVM compiler to enforce return address integrity and control-flow integrity in bare-metal systems. Kage [14] extends Silhouette compiler and modifies FreeRTOS to provide an implementation of CFI for real-time embedded systems. μRAI [5] proposes a technique that moves return addresses from writable memory to readable and executable memory at compile time. It reserves a single general purpose register to indicate the correct return location. The authors also couple μRAI with a CFI for forward edges. However, these compiler-based approaches are impractical for COTS binaries and have not yet been widely adopted.

Trusted Execution Environments. Intel Software Guard Extension (SGX) [10] is a hardware-based TEE that extends the Instruction Set Architecture (ISA) of Intel processors for isolating trusted code. Indeed, SGX executes trusted code within hardware-enforced protected areas in memory. ARM-TrustZone [6] is a hardware-based TEE for ARM processors, which enforces an access control mechanism to isolate security critical applications inside the same physical core. However, both SGX and ARM-TrustZone rely on complex and expensive hardware features that are not provided in bare-metal embedded systems. Sancus [21] extends the memory access logic and instruction set of a TI MSP430 microcontroller to create isolated software modules with a hardware-based TCB. TrustLite [16], TyTAN [7], and VRASED [22] are hardware/software co-design, so-called hybrid architectures, that try to minimize modifications to the underlying hardware and provide confidentiality and integrity guarantees. However, they require customized hardware support on every device, which is difficult to provide in bare-metal embedded systems. Unlike these systems, μIPS TEE requires no hardware modification and can be readily deployed in bare-metal embedded systems. Furthermore, our design is not limited to any architecture and can be applied in all bare-metal systems equipped with an MPU.

9   Conclusion

Protecting bare-metal embedded systems from memory corruption and control-flow hijacking attacks is challenging. Indeed, due to resource constraints, standard and state-of-the-art security mechanisms in conventional computer systems such as DEP and control-flow hijacking protections are not commonly adopted in these systems. In this paper, we presented μIPS, the first intrusion prevention system for bare-metal embedded systems. μIPS introduces a novel TEE that bridges the security gap by bringing memory isolation and privilege separation into these systems. Featuring its TEE, μIPS enables the implementation of a control-flow protection mechanism for potentially vulnerable firmware binaries. We evaluated the efficiency and efficacy of μIPS. Evaluation results demonstrated that μIPS incurs a modest runtime overhead, while effectively neutralizing various malicious attacks in different attack vectors.

Acknowledgement. This work is partially funded by the EU under Horizon Europe Programme - GA 101070537 - CrossCon and GA 101086308 - DUCA. Views and opinions expressed are however those of the author(s) only and do not necessarily reflect those of the European Union or CINEA). Neither the EU nor the granting authority can be held responsible for them.

A   Firmware Information

We present in Table 7 the detailed information about the real firmware used in our evaluation (Sect. 6).

Table 7. The representative set of firmware used for the evaluation of μIPS.

Firmware	Type	Domain	Source	URL
Blink	I/O	Sample	STM32	STM32 Cube IDE samples
BSP Sensors	I/O	Peripherals	Arm Mbed	https://tinyurl.com/m938ujky
WiFi Client	IoT/misc	Network	Arm Mbed	https://tinyurl.com/yydzumcz
HTTP Server	IoT/misc	Web Protocol	Arm Mbed	https://tinyurl.com/ydytamdk
SHA-256	CPU	Crypto	Custom	https://tinyurl.com/4nbu7yb5
Fibonacci-Iter	CPU	Benchmark	Custom	https://tinyurl.com/yc7f7bbt
Fibonacci-Rec	CPU	Benchmark	Custom	https://tinyurl.com/4tj582xm
BLE-IoT	IoT/misc	Peripherals	Open Source	https://tinyurl.com/jckvwuh2
HTTP-IoT	IoT/misc	Web Protocol	Open Source	https://tinyurl.com/jckvwuh2

B   Security Analysis

To demonstrate the ability of μIPS to prevent *any* control-flow hijacking attack, we modified the HTTP Server firmware introducing three types of memory corruption vulnerabilities: a *buffer overflow* [25], a *format string* enabling *arbitrary write* [33] and a *stack pivot* [20]. We analyze each of the three and describe how μIPS prevents the exploitation.

Buffer Overflow. A buffer overflow allows an attacker to overwrite values on the stack. The ARMv7-M architecture can store a return address either in a special register called Link Register (LR) or on the stack. Consequently, since the LR register is not memory mapped, the attacker can tamper with the execution flow by overwriting the return address only when stored on the stack. However, if the attacker succeeds, once the vulnerable function returns, the μIPS instrumentation invokes the TEE to check if the return address equals the one on top of the shadow stack. Since it has been manipulated, this check will fail, and the attack prevented. Furthermore, μIPS blocks shellcode-based buffer overflow attacks as the stack is non-executable due to the W$\oplus$X policy enforced by the MPU.

Arbitrary Write. With an arbitrary write, an attacker can precisely overwrite data on arbitrary memory locations, including the stack, flash memory, and even peripheral registers. Like buffer overflow, the attacker can overwrite the saved return address on the stack, but the attack would be detected with the μIPS shadow stack. It is also possible to overwrite the flash memory including the code regions; however, the MPU denies this operation by enforcing the W⊕X policy. Additionally, the attacker may attempt to write to the memory-mapped MPU configuration registers to disable or relax the MPU policy. Still, this operation requires privileges that are never granted to potentially vulnerable firmware. An attacker may also attempt to leverage a gadget that pops an address from the stack to the LR, but such a gadget never exists because the LR is written only by branch-with-link instructions. Finally, an attacker may corrupt the exception handler data structure where registers, including the Program Counter (PC), are saved to restore the execution once an interrupt has finished. However, such an operation requires privileges that are never granted to the firmware. As a result, μIPS prevents the attack in all the presented cases.

Stack Pivot. If an attacker controls the position of the stack, *e.g.,* through the Stack Pointer (SP) register, it can relocate it to point to a buffer it controls so that, once the function returns, it pops the return address from the stack. This attack assumes that the return address is stored on the stack, not in the LR. However, the μIPS instrumentation invokes the TEE to validate the return address with the one on top of the shadow stack. Since the two values differ, μIPS prevents the attack.

References

1. Abadi, M., Budiu, M., Erlingsson, U., Ligatti, J.: Control-flow integrity. In: Proceedings of the 12th ACM Conference on Computer and Communications Security (CCS), pp. 340–353. ACM (2005). https://doi.org/10.1145/1102120.1102165
2. Abbasi, A., Wetzels, J., Holz, T., Etalle, S.: Challenges in designing exploit mitigations for deeply embedded systems. In: Proceedings of the 2019 IEEE European Symposium on Security and Privacy (EuroS&P), pp. 31–46. IEEE (2019)
3. Abera, T., et al.: C-flat: control-flow attestation for embedded systems software. In: Proceedings of the 2016 ACM SIGSAC Conference on Computer and Communications Security (CCS), pp. 743–754 (2016)
4. IoT for all: The 5 Worst Examples of IoT Hacking and Vulnerabilities in Recorded History. https://www.iotforall.com/5-worst-iot-hacking-vulnerabilities. Accessed May 2023
5. Almakhdhub, N.S., Clements, A.A., Bagchi, S., Payer, M.: μrai: Securing embedded systems with return address integrity. In: Proceedings of the Network and Distributed Systems Security Symposium (NDSS) (2020)
6. ARM: Trustzone for cortex-m (2022). https://www.arm.com/technologies/trustzone-for-cortex-m. Accessed May 2023
7. Brasser, F., El Mahjoub, B., Sadeghi, A.R., Wachsmann, C., Koeberl, P.: Tytan: tiny trust anchor for tiny devices. In: Proceedings of the 52nd Annual Design Automation Conference (DAC), pp. 1–6 (2015)
8. Clements, A.A., et al.: Protecting bare-metal embedded systems with privilege overlays. In: Proceedings of the 2017 IEEE Symposium on Security and Privacy (SP), pp. 289–303. IEEE (2017)
9. de Clercq, R., et al.: Sofia: software and control flow integrity architecture. In: Proceedings of the 2016 Design, Automation & Test in Europe Conference & Exhibition (DATE) (2016)

10. Costan, V., Devadas, S.: Intel sgx explained. Cryptology ePrint Archive (2016)
11. Criswell, J., Dautenhahn, N., Adve, V.: Kcofi: complete control-flow integrity for commodity operating system kernels. In: Proceedings of the 2014 IEEE Symposium on Security and Privacy (SP), pp. 292–307 (2014). https://doi.org/10.1109/SP.2014.26
12. De, A., Basu, A., Ghosh, S., Jaeger, T.: Hardware assisted buffer protection mechanisms for embedded RISC-V. IEEE Trans. Comput.-Aided Des. Integr. Circuits Syst. **39**(12), 4453–4465 (2020)
13. Dessouky, G., Abera, T., Ibrahim, A., Sadeghi, A.R.: Litehax: lightweight hardware-assisted attestation of program execution. In: Proceedings of the 2018 IEEE/ACM International Conference on Computer-Aided Design (ICCAD) (2018)
14. Du, Y., Shen, Z., Dharsee, K., Zhou, J., Walls, R.J., Criswell, J.: Holistic Control-Flow protection on Real-Time embedded systems with kage. In: Proceedings of the USENIX Security Symposium (USENIX Security) (2022)
15. Insights, I.: Mcclean report 2022 (2022). https://www.icinsights.com/services/mcclean-report/. Accessed May 2023
16. Koeberl, P., Schulz, S., Sadeghi, A.R., Varadharajan, V.: Trustlite: a security architecture for tiny embedded devices. In: Proceedings of the Ninth European Conference on Computer Systems, pp. 1–14 (2014)
17. Kuznetsov, V., Szekeres, L., Payer, M., Candea, G., Sekar, R., Song, D.: Code-Pointer integrity. In: Proceedings of the 11th USENIX Symposium on Operating Systems Design and Implementation (OSDI), pp. 147–163. USENIX Association (2014). https://www.usenix.org/conference/osdi14/technical-sessions/presentation/kuznetsov
18. Li, J., Tong, X., Zhang, F., Ma, J.: Fine-CFI: fine-grained control-flow integrity for operating system kernels. IEEE Trans. Inf. Forensics Secur. **13**(6), 1535–1550 (2018). https://doi.org/10.1109/TIFS.2018.2797932
19. Li, J., Wang, Z., Bletsch, T., Srinivasan, D., Grace, M., Jiang, X.: Comprehensive and efficient protection of kernel control data. IEEE Trans. Inf. Forensics Secur. **6**(4), 1404–1417 (2011). https://doi.org/10.1109/TIFS.2011.2159712
20. McAfee: Emerging 'Stack Pivoting' Exploits Bypass Common Security. https://www.mcafee.com/blogs/other-blogs/mcafee-labs/emerging-stack-pivoting-exploits-bypass-common-security. Accessed May 2023
21. Noorman, J., et al.: Sancus: low-cost trustworthy extensible networked devices with a zero-software trusted computing base. In: Proceedings of the 22nd USENIX Security Symposium (USENIX Security 13), pp. 479–498 (2013)
22. Nunes, I.D.O., Eldefrawy, K., Rattanavipanon, N., Steiner, M., Tsudik, G.: VRASED: a verified hardware/software co-design for remote attestation. In: Proceedings of the 28th USENIX Security Symposium (USENIX Security 19) (2019)
23. Nyman, T., Ekberg, J.-E., Davi, L., Asokan, N.: CFI CaRE: hardware-supported call and return enforcement for commercial microcontrollers. In: Dacier, M., Bailey, M., Polychronakis, M., Antonakakis, M. (eds.) RAID 2017. LNCS, vol. 10453, pp. 259–284. Springer, Cham (2017). https://doi.org/10.1007/978-3-319-66332-6_12
24. Oleksenko, O., Kuvaiskii, D., Bhatotia, P., Felber, P., Fetzer, C.: Intel mpx explained: a cross-layer analysis of the intel mpx system stack. In: Proceedings of the ACM on Measurement and Analysis of Computing Systems **2**(2) (2018)
25. One, A.: Smashing the stack for fun and profit. Phrack magazine **7**(49), 14–16 (1996)
26. Pancake: radare. https://www.radare.org/r/. Accessed May 2023
27. Post, T.: IoT Attacks Skyrocket, Doubling in 6 Months. https://threatpost.com/iot-attacks-doubling/169224/. Accessed May 2023

28. Salehi, M., Degani, L., Roveri, M., Hughes, D., Crispo, B.: Discovery and identification of memory corruption vulnerabilities on bare-metal embedded devices. IEEE Trans. Dependable Secure Comput. **20**, 1124–1138 (2022)
29. Salehi, M., Hughes, D., Crispo, B.: Microguard: securing bare-metal microcontrollers against code-reuse attacks. In: Proceedings of the 2019 IEEE Conference on Dependable and Secure Computing (DSC), pp. 1–8. IEEE (2019)
30. Salehi, M., Hughes, D., Crispo, B.: μSBS: static binary sanitization of bare-metal embedded devices for fault observability. In: Proceedings of the 23rd International Symposium on Research in Attacks, Intrusions and Defenses (RAID) (2020)
31. Schirra, S.: Ropper. https://github.com/sashs/Ropper. Accessed May 2023
32. Shacham, H.: The geometry of innocent flesh on the bone: return-into-LIBC without function calls (on the x86). In: Proceedings of the 14th ACM Conference on Computer and Communications Security, New York, NY, USA (2007)
33. Shankar, U., Talwar, K., Foster, J.S., Wagner, D.: Detecting format string vulnerabilities with type qualifiers. In: Proceedings of the 10th USENIX Security Symposium (USENIX Security 01) (2001)
34. Shoshitaishvili, Y., Wang, R., Hauser, C., Kruegel, C., Vigna, G.: Firmalice-automatic detection of authentication bypass vulnerabilities in binary firmware. In: Proceedings of the Network and Distributed Systems Security Symposium (NDSS) (2015)
35. Shoshitaishvili, Y., et al.: Sok:(state of) the art of war: offensive techniques in binary analysis. In: Proceedings of the IEEE Symposium on Security and Privacy (SP). IEEE (2016)
36. Sun, Z., Feng, B., Lu, L., Jha, S.: Oat: Attesting operation integrity of embedded devices. In: Proceedings of the 2020 IEEE Symposium on Security and Privacy (SP), pp. 1433–1449. IEEE (2020)
37. Szekeres, L., Payer, M., Wei, T., Song, D.: Sok: eternal war in memory. In: Proceedings of the 2013 IEEE Symposium on Security and Privacy (SP). IEEE (2013)
38. Today, I.W.: IoT Cyberattacks Escalate in 2021, According to Kaspersky. https://www.iotworldtoday.com/2021/09/17/iot-cyberattacks-escalate-in-2021-according-to-kaspersky. Accessed May 2023
39. Zhang, C., et al.: Practical control flow integrity and randomization for binary executables. In: Proceedings of the 2013 IEEE Symposium on Security and Privacy (SP), pp. 559–573 (2013). https://doi.org/10.1109/SP.2013.44
40. Zhang, M., Sekar, R.: Control flow integrity for COTS binaries. In: Proceedings of the 22nd USENIX Security Symposium (USENIX Security 13), pp. 337–352. USENIX Association (2013). https://www.usenix.org/conference/usenixsecurity13/technical-sessions/presentation/Zhang
41. Zhou, J., Du, Y., Shen, Z., Ma, L., Criswell, J., Walls, R.J.: Silhouette: efficient protected shadow stacks for embedded systems. In: Proceedings of the 29th USENIX Security Symposium (USENIX Security 20), pp. 1219–1236 (2020)

Aion: Secure Transaction Ordering Using TEEs

Pouriya Zarbafian[1(✉)] and Vincent Gramoli[1,2]

[1] University of Sydney, Sydney, Australia
pouriya.zarbafian@sydney.edu.au
[2] Redbelly Network, Sydney, Australia
vincent.gramoli@redbelly.network

Abstract. In state machine replication (SMR), preventing reordering attacks by ensuring a high degree of fairness when ordering commands requires that clients broadcast their commands to all processes. This is impractical due to the impact on scalability, and thus it discourages the adoption of a fair ordering of commands. Alternative approaches to order-fairness allow clients do send their commands to only one process, but provide a weaker notion of order-fairness. In particular, they disadvantage isolated processes. In this paper, we introduce Aion, a set of order-fair protocols for SMR. We first leverage trusted execution environments (TEEs) to enable processes to compute the times when commands are broadcast by their issuers. We then integrate this information into existing consensus protocols to devise order-fair SMR protocols that are both leader-based and leaderless. To realize order-fairness, Aion only requires that a client sends its commands to a single process, while at the same time enabling precise ordering during synchronous periods.

Keywords: Order-fairness · Trusted execution environment · State machine replication

1 Introduction

The state-machine replication (SMR) paradigm [28] has been used in distributed systems for decades despite the fact that its specification does not require any particular ordering: the SMR specification requires an identical order at each correct replica, but it does not specify which orders are valid. The lack of ordering requirement in SMR has only become critical recently with the advent of blockchain technology [43] and decentralized finance where malicious participants have leveraged this shortcoming to reorder transactions [11] and reap hundreds of millions of dollars [46].

Multiple solutions [9,24,26,55,58] have been devised to ensure fairness in the ordering of commands. A first paradigm [9,23,24] requires clients to submit their commands to all processes so that commands can later be ordered using the relative ordering of commands at a majority of processes. However, having

G. Tsudik et al. (Eds.): ESORICS 2023, LNCS 14347, pp. 332–350, 2024.
https://doi.org/10.1007/978-3-031-51482-1_17

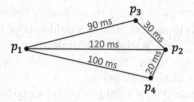

Fig. 1. Network delays between processes.

all clients broadcast their commands is costly and therefore impractical. In a second paradigm [58], a client only submits its command c to a single process p_i so that p_i can forward c to other processes and collect ordering information for c. This new approach is a practical trade-off as it circumvents circular dependencies and broadcasts by clients at the cost of weakened fairness for *isolated* processes. Process isolation is illustrated in Fig. 1. Due to the network delays between processes, process p_1 is isolated from processes p_2, p_3, p_4: p_2, p_3, p_4 are close to each other and distant from p_1. Consider a scenario where process p_1 broadcasts a command c_1 at time $t_1 = 0$ ms, and where process p_2 broadcasts a command c_2 at time $t_2 = t_1 + 50$ ms. Due to the network distribution of Fig. 1, a supermajority of $2f + 1 = 3$ processes observe c_2 before c_1 (cf. Table 1), and thus c_2 must be ordered before c_1 despite the fact that c_1 was broadcast before c_2. Note that it may sometimes be more interesting to prefer processes with shorter delays in order to improve throughput. In contrast, our approach proposes a solution to determine the sending time of commands. For some domains, such as decentralized finance, our approach provides more fairness by removing biases due to network delays.

Table 1. Times when commands c_1 and c_2 are received by processes. Process p_1 broadcasts c_1 at time $t_1 = 0$ ms, whereas p_2 broadcasts c_2 at time $t_2 = 50$ ms. Reception times are computed by adding the times when commands are broadcast (i.e., 0 or 50) to the network delays (c.f. Fig. 1).

	p_1	p_2	p_3	p_4
$c_1, t_1 = 0$ ms	$0 + 0 = 0$	$0 + 120 = 120$	$0 + 90 = 90$	$0 + 100 = 100$
$c_2, t_2 = 50$ ms	$50 + 120 = 170$	$50 + 0 = 50$	$50 + 30 = 80$	$50 + 20 = 70$

One could think of naively compensating this imbalance by using the knowledge of network delays between processes. A process p_i that receives a command c from p_j at a time t_0, and that knows the network delay d_{ji} between p_j and p_i, can compute the time t_c when c was broadcast by p_j using $t_c = t_0 - d_{ji}$. Unfortunately, such scheme cannot be implemented candidly in the Byzantine model. For instance, a Byzantine process p_B could make its distances to other processes appear larger by delaying the sending of all of its messages by an amount $d_B > 0$. If p_B stops delaying its messages before sending a new command c', a process p_i receiving c' at time t'_0 would believe that c' was sent at time $t_{c'} = t'_0 - (d_{ji} + d_B) < t'_0 - d_{ji}$, and c would unfairly preempt earlier commands. A novelty of our solution is to combine cryptographic challenges [15] with TEEs to determine safe values of network delays.

To prevent process isolation, it would be sufficient to be able to verify network delays. In this paper, we present Aion[1], a set of leader-based and leaderless protocols that leverage trusted execution environments (TEEs) to solve process isolation. First, we take advantage of the security guarantees provided by TEEs to devise a challenge-response protocol that enables processes to compute safe values of network delays, and we use an additional protocol such as [4] to increase the reliability of TEEs clocks. As far as we know, we propose the first solution that relies on an additional protocol to secure the TEE clocks. The challenges prevent Byzantine processes from advertising network delays that are shorter than the actual network delays. Note that a Byzantine process can still advertise larger network delays simply by retaining messages. Then, we rely on the fact that the network is synchronous most of the time and that network delays are stable [40], and require that measured network delays remain constant. This ensures that if a Byzantine process has inserted biases to increase the values of its network delays, then it has to abide by those new values. As a result, processes can determine the times when commands are sent in a safe way because it prevents Byzantine processes from preempting older commands.

Notice that it is not possible to directly use the timestamps provided by a TEE because a Byzantine process could generate commands with valid timestamps using its TEE, and could then broadcast these commands at a future time in order to preempt commands that it observes. In the financial domain, this is characterized as a front-running attack [16] and can have detrimental economic repercussions. Another novelty of our protocol is to complement the timestamps provided by TEEs with the verification of network delays to ensure the freshness of commands. Aion is designed to achieve an accurate ordering of commands when the network is behaving synchronously. However, networks can suffer various kinds of failure [10], and can behave asynchronously as a result of these failures. In these scenarios, the network delays are unknown, and protocols that assume an upper-bound on message delivery may see their safety properties violated [44]. Therefore, we devise partially synchronous protocols in order to preserve safety during asynchronous periods. We discuss the loss of liveness and mitigation strategies during asynchronous periods in Sect. 8.2.

Although enforcing a fair ordering of commands helps at mitigating ordering attacks in blockchains, it is not sufficient by itself to completely prevent them [23] as this requires either a commit-reveal scheme [22,37] or a combination of both a commit-reveal scheme and fair ordering [55]. In this paper, we only focus on extending the SMR specification with fair ordering. Nevertheless, a commit-reveal scheme such as in [37] or [55] could be added to our protocols to achieve

---

[1] Aion is a Hellenistic deity that symbolizes a cyclic time. The name Aion stems from the fact that our protocols rely on repeating and constant network delays.

the desired result. Requiring a fair ordering from the output of an SMR is not trivial because most of the existing SMR protocols do not support it off the shelf. A leader-based protocol such as HotStuff [54] requires a preliminary sequencing step as in [58]. Other leaderless protocols are either tolerant to crash faults only [6,47], or require an additional commit protocol as in [55]. Hence, we show how our protocol for a fair ordering of commands can be integrated into existing SMR protocols. Specifically, we make the following contributions:

- We leverage TEEs to devise a protocol that enables processes to safely measure network delays. The novelty of our approach resides in using TEEs so that the measurements of network delays can be used without compromising safety.
- We build upon safe values of network delays and compute the times when commands are broadcast with proven accuracy during synchronous periods, while preserving safety during asynchronous periods.
- We integrate the sending times of commands with both leader-based and leaderless consensus protocols to implement Aion, a set of SMR protocols with fair ordering. Thus, we show that our approach is modular and practical due its low overhead of only two message delays.

The rest of this paper is organized as follows. We present related work in Sect. 2, and our computational model in Sect. 3. We introduce the timestamping protocol in Sect. 4, and use it to build the ordering protocol in Sect. 5. We build upon the ordering protocol to build Leader-Based Aion in Sect. 6, and Leaderless Aion in Sect. 7. We discuss our results in Sect. 8, and we conclude in Sect. 9.

2   Related Work

Order-fair protocols were first investigated by Kelkar et al. [24] with Aequitas. In Aequitas, a client must broadcast its commands to all processes, and commands are ordered based on the local orderings of commands observed by processes. For instance, a command c_1 must be ordered before a command c_2 if a sufficient fraction of the processes have observed c_1 before c_2. However, in large SMR systems, the number of clients is orders of magnitude larger than the number of processes [19,20,55,58]. Requiring that clients broadcast their commands to all processes incurs an extra linear multiplicative cost on communication and message complexity, and renders the approach intrinsically impractical on a large scale.

Cachin et al. [9] extend this paradigm by showing related lower bounds. Specifically, they determine the differential number of processes required to ensure any ordering on the commands that are output. Pompē [58] introduces a new ordering paradigm whereby a client only sends its commands to a single process who forwards them to all processes. Commands are then ordered based on the times when other processes have received the forwarded commands. Although Pompē does not require clients to broadcast their commands to all processes in order to achieve a fair ordering of commands, it suffers from process isolation (cf. Sect. 1). To reduce the latency of Pompē, Lyra [55] uses the network delays measured between processes so that processes can predict the times when their commands are received by other processes. Interestingly, the knowledge of network delays can also be used to compute the times when commands are sent. Our contribution is to use network delays to compute the times when commands are sent, and to leverage TEEs to make these computations safe.

Cryptographic challenges were introduced by Dwork and Naor [15] as a way to limit junk emails. They are commonly used as way to prevent denial-of-service attacks in networks [17,27,51,53]. In blockchains, lottery-like methods are widely used as a means to preserve safety against Byzantine processes. Proof of works were introduced by Hashcash [7] and are used in Bitcoin [43] and Ethereum [52] to mine new blocks and extend the ledger. Ouroboros [25] and Algorand [20] are based on proof-of-stake mechanisms that use verifiable random functions [39].

Stathakopoulou et al. [50] use TEEs to add fairness to the ordering of commands. Their approach focuses on preventing front-running attacks, and therefore relies on obfuscating commands until they are committed, while delegating the actual ordering to the total broadcast layer. Therefore, their approach is closer to a commit-reveal scheme [22]. Gupta et al. [21] also leverage trusted components in SMR, but focus instead on improving liveness and reducing communication complexity, and although their protocol supports concurrent executions of consensus, it does not implement order-fairness. In blockchains, multiple protocols rely on TEEs for implementing SMR. TEEs are used to improve scalability [33], limit the behavior of Byzantine processes [56], or secure off-chain commands [31,32], but they do not consider fairness in the ordering of commands.

3   Model

3.1   Processes

We examine a system of n processes denoted by Π. We assume the existence of a dynamic adversary that can corrupt up to $f < \frac{n}{3}$ processes. As a result, and because SMR requires consensus [3], our protocols for SMR are resilience optimal in non-synchronous environments. Processes that are controlled by the adversary are denoted *Byzantine* and can act arbitrarily [29], whereas non-corrupted processes are denoted *correct*. Processes communicate via authenticated and reliable channels that preserve the integrity of messages.

3.2   Network

We assume that the network is partially synchronous [14]. In a partially synchronous network, messages can be delayed up to a *global stabilization time* (GST) whose value is unknown. After GST, the network behaves synchronously and network delays between correct processes are bounded by a known value Δ.

During synchronous periods, we assume that the network delays are stable and that the fluctuations in network delays between any two processes are bound by $\lambda > 0$. This assumption relies on recent studies on the probability distributions of network delays [40]. For stable networks, λ is usually less than one millisecond [41]. Let d_{ij} denote the network delay between p_i and p_j. During a synchronous period T, we have

$$\forall t_1, t_2 \in T, \forall p_i, p_j \in \Pi, |(d_{ij} \text{ at } t_1) - (d_{ij} \text{ at } t_2)| \leq \lambda.$$

3.3 Trusted Execution Environments

We assume the existence of Trusted Execution Environment (TEE) technology. A TEE provides a secure environment that ensures that each process executes the protocol correctly. Formally, a TEE guarantees the following properties [48]:

– authenticity of the code executed by each process,
– integrity and confidentiality of runtime states (memory, registers, I/O,...),
– a trusted time service,
– remote attestation in order to prove correctness to a third-party.

We also assume that TEEs are resilient to both software and hardware attacks. As a result, when a process becomes corrupted, the adversary can only take control of resources outside of the TEE (e.g. operating system, network,...). Such technology is implemented, for instance, by hardware with Intel Software Guard Extensions (SGX) [38] or ARM TrustZone [1].

3.4 Clocks

We assume that each process p_i has a trusted local clock denoted $\mathsf{clock}_i()$ that is managed by the TEE environment and that returns timestamps in $\mathbb{N}$. This is implemented, for instance, in Intel SGX. Although Intel SGX provides access to a secure timer, a privileged user can still manipulate this timer [5]. Consequently, we propose that the local clock be secured with an additional protocol such as TimeSeal [4] to secure the value of $\mathsf{clock}_i()$. TimeSeal adopts a holistic approach to obtain a reliable time stack by securing the timer, ensuring that the timer can be read in a timely manner, and protecting timekeeping software. During asynchronous periods, the offsets between clocks can grow unboundedly. But after GST, the network is synchronous and the offsets between any two clocks are bounded by $\delta > 0$. Clock synchronization [35] can achieve a value of δ less than a millisecond, and typically in the order of tens of microseconds [30].

3.5 Intervals

We divide the set $\mathbb{N}$ of all possible timestamps into consecutive intervals of size ℓ. Let I_k denote the kth interval,

$$\forall k \in \mathbb{N}, I_k = [k\ell, (k+1)\ell).$$

We also define the interval mapping function $\mathcal{I}$ that maps any timestamp t to its corresponding interval $\mathcal{I}(t)$ such that $t \in I_{\mathcal{I}(t)}$,

$$\forall t \in \mathbb{N}, \mathcal{I}: \mathbb{N} \longrightarrow \mathbb{N},$$
$$t \longmapsto k \mid k\ell \leq t < (k+1)\ell.$$

In the rest of the paper, when the context is unambiguous, we simply refer to $I_{\mathcal{I}(t)}$ by $\mathcal{I}(t)$. Intervals are used as a basis for implementing a *total order broadcast* [12]: to build a totally ordered set of commands, correct processes reach agreement on the set of commands in each interval.

3.6 Cryptography

We assume the existence of collision-resistant hash functions and a public key infrastructure. Each process has a public-private key pair [13] denoted (PK_i, SK_i). The private key of each process resides inside the memory of the TEE and is protected against unauthorized access. Let $\langle v \rangle_i$ denote that the value v has been signed using the private key SK_i of process p_i.

$$\langle v \rangle_i = \mathsf{private\text{-}sign}(SK_i, v)$$

We also assume the existence of a $(2f + 1, n)$ threshold signature scheme [49]. Finally, we assume a computationally-bounded adversary that cannot break the security of cryptographic schemes.

3.7 Consensus

To decide the content of each interval, we rely on a generic consensus abstractions [45]. Such abstractions enable all correct processes to agree on the set of commands in each interval. We consider protocols that have the classical *termination* and *agreement* properties, but also an *external validity* property [8]. External validity relies on a predicate γ and requires that any decided value contains correctly signed inputs from at least $2f + 1$ distinct processes. More formally, we define the predicate

$$\gamma: v \mapsto |v| \geq 2f + 1 \ \wedge \ \forall \langle x \rangle_i \in v, \mathsf{public\text{-}verify}(PK_i, \langle x \rangle_i).$$

We assume the following properties for the consensus problem:

- **Termination.** Each correct process eventually decides a value.
- **Agreement.** All correct processes decide the same value.
- **External Validity.** If a correct process decides a value v, then $\gamma(v)$ holds.

For Leader-Based Aion (Sect. 6), we assume the existence of a leader-based consensus protocol, denoted leader-propose, where a leader proposes a value, i.e., the sequence of commands for an interval, and processes agree on whether to output or not the value of the leader. For instance, HotStuff [54] implements such abstraction. For Leaderless Aion (Sect. 7), we assume the existence of a leaderless consensus protocol denoted leaderless-propose, where instead of being proposed by a leader, the decided value comes from all processes. Such abstraction is implemented, for instance, by BFT-Archipelago [2].

Table 2. Symbols

Symbol	Description
$\mathcal{C}$	The set of all possible commands
GST	Global Stabilization Time
$\mathsf{clock}_i()$	Clock of process p_i
δ	Offset between clocks
Δ	Upper bound on network delays
λ	Fluctuation in network delays
ℓ	Length of an interval
I_k	Interval $[k\ell, (k+1)\ell)$
$\mathcal{I}$	Interval mapping function
$\langle v \rangle_i$	Value v signed by the private key of p_i
γ	External validity predicate

4 Timestamping Protocol

In this section, we present the protocols used by processes to determine the time when a command is broadcast. First, the Network Challenge protocol (Sect. 4.1) enables processes to obtain reliable values of network delays. Then, these network delays are used in the Timestamp Validation protocol (Sect. 4.2) to determine if the timestamps requested for commands are valid.

4.1 Network Challenge

The *Network Challenge* protocol is used by processes to measure network delays. To this end, processes regularly challenge other processes by sending them cryptographic nonces. The Network Challenge protocol is presented in Algorithm 1. To prevent Byzantine processes from generating a dictionary of responses to the challenges, and thus to ensure the freshness of the timestamps received, challenges that are sent by a process p_i are signed by p_i (line 6). When a process p_j receives a challenge $\langle u \rangle_i$ from p_i, p_j answers with the signed value $\langle i, u, t \rangle_j$ containing the secure timestamp t generated for u, and the values u and i to certify that the TEE of p_j created the timestamp t for the challenge u sent by p_i (line 12). Upon receiving a response $\langle i, u, t \rangle_j$ to its challenge from p_j, p_i computes the network delay d_{ji} from p_j to p_i using $d_{ji} = \mathsf{clock}_i() - t$ (line 16). Each process maintains an array D that stores the values of network delays obtained with these challenges.

4.2 Timestamp Validation

The *Timestamp Validation* protocol enables processes to validate the timestamp of a command by inferring the time when the command was sent. It combines the network delays obtained via the Network Challenge protocol with a requirement

Algorithm 1. Network Challenge Protocol

1: **State**
2:    $U \leftarrow []$ ▷ challenges sent by p_i
3:    $D \leftarrow []$ ▷ network delays computed by p_i

4: **function** CHALLENGE(p_j)
5:    $u \leftarrow$ nonce()   ▷ generate challenge
6:    $\langle u \rangle_i \leftarrow$ private-sign(SK_i, u)   ▷ sign challenge
7:    send(CHALLENGE, $\langle u \rangle_i$) to p_j ▷ send challenge to p_j
8:    $U[j] \leftarrow u$ ▷ store challenge

9: **upon** receiving a message (CHALLENGE, $\langle u \rangle_j$) from p_j **do**
10:    **if** public-verify($PK_j, \langle u \rangle_j$) **then**   ▷ verify signature
11:        $t \leftarrow$ clock$_i$()
12:        $\langle j, u, t \rangle_i \leftarrow$ private-sign($SK_i, (j, u, t)$)   ▷ sign response
13:        send(RESPONSE, $\langle j, u, t \rangle_i$) to p_j ▷ respond to p_j's challenge

14: **upon** receiving a message (RESPONSE, $\langle j, u, t \rangle_j$) from p_j **do**
15:    **if** public-verify($PK_j, \langle j, u, t \rangle_j$) $\wedge C[j] = u$ **then**
16:        $d_{ji} = $ clock$_i$() $- t$ ▷ compute network delay
17:        $D[j] \leftarrow d_{ji}$ ▷ update network delays
18:        $U[j] \leftarrow \perp$ ▷ discard challenge

on these message delays to remain constant. The requirement on stable network delays is based on recent studies and experiments on the probability distributions of network delays [40].

Algorithm 2. Timestamp Validation

1: **function** VALIDATE(c, t, j)   ▷ validation of c and t received from p_j
2:    $t_{send} \leftarrow$ clock$_i$() $- D[j]$ ▷ compute send time of c
3:    **if** $|t_{send} - t| \leq \lambda + \delta$ **then**   ▷ check the timestamp of c
4:        **return** true   ▷ accept t
5:    **else**
6:        **return** false   ▷ reject t

Algorithm 2 shows the protocol for deciding whether to accept or reject commands based on their requested timestamps. A process simply computes the time when it believes the command was sent (line 2), and compares it to the timestamp of the command (line 3). During synchronous periods, the error when estimating the send time of a command is bounded by $2(\delta + \lambda)$.

Lemma 1. *After GST, a correct process p_i validates a command c that has a requested timestamp t (Algorithm 2) only if the difference between t and the actual send time t_{actual} of c is less than $2(\lambda + \delta)$.*

$$\forall p_i \in \{p \in \Pi \mid p \text{ is correct}\}, p_i \text{ accepts } (c,t) \Rightarrow |t - t_{actual}| \leq 2(\lambda + \delta)$$

Proof. If a correct process p_i validates (c,t), then p_i determined that c was sent at a time t_{est}, and that $|t_{est} - t| \leq \lambda + \delta$. Process p_i computed t_{est} using a challenge, and particularly by using the timestamp included in the response to the challenge and the network delay that p_i computed based on the challenge. After GST, the offsets between the clocks of processes are bounded by δ, and Byzantine processes cannot drift from the expected network latencies by more than a quantity λ, so the margin of error for challenges is $\lambda + \delta$. As a result, the margin of error of t_{est} is $\lambda + \delta$, and thus $|t - t_{actual}| \leq 2(\lambda + \delta)$.

5 Ordering Phase

The *ordering* phase, borrowed from Pompē [58], enables a process p_i to request a timestamp t for a command c and to schedule (c,t) so that c is included in $\mathcal{I}(t)$. The aim of the ordering phase is to ensure that if the network is behaving synchronously and that a correct process terminates the ordering phase for (c,t), then c is guaranteed to be included in the interval $\mathcal{I}(t)$. This protocol is used as a preliminary step both in Leader-Based Aion (Sect. 6) and in Leaderless Aion (Sect. 7).

5.1 Stability of Committed Intervals

In an SMR, all correct processes output commands in the same order. Specifically, a command is only output when all of its preceding commands have been delivered. Therefore, after a command c is output, no new command can be output before c. We refer to this property as the *stability* of committed intervals: once the consensus instances for the k first intervals have terminated, and that the sets of commands in these intervals are known, no other command can be added to an interval I_m such that $m \leq k$. Hence, the ordering phase must preserve the stability of committed intervals.

In order to guarantee that the commands that have been successfully ordered are committed in their corresponding intervals, while at the same time preserving the stability of committed intervals, we rely on standard quorum intersections [36]. On the one hand, a command (c,t) is successfully ordered for the interval $\mathcal{I}(t)$ if at least $2f+1$ processes accept to schedule c in $\mathcal{I}(t)$. On the other hand, using the external validity predicate (Sect. 3.7), Aion protocols (Sects. 6, 7) determine the content of each interval by collecting the commands that have been ordered by at least $2f + 1$ processes. As a result, if a command (c,t) is ordered by at least $2f + 1$ processes in the interval $\mathcal{I}(t)$, then c is guaranteed to be output in the interval $\mathcal{I}(t)$.

Algorithm 3. Ordering Protocol

1: **State**
2:     $S \leftarrow [\mathcal{C} \rightarrow []]$ ▷ shares collected by p_i
3:     $C \leftarrow [\mathbb{N} \rightarrow []]$ ▷ commands ordered for each interval
4:     $nextSub \leftarrow 0$ ▷ next interval submitted by p_i

5: **function** ORDER(c)
6:     $t \leftarrow \text{clock}_i()$
7:     broadcast(REQUEST, (c, t))   ▷ request timestamp t for c

8: **upon** receiving a message (REQUEST, (c, t)) from p_j **do**
9:     **if** VALIDATE(c, t, j) **then**
10:         $\pi_{c,t} \leftarrow$ share-sign(ACCEPT$\|c\|t$)   ▷ encryption share of acceptance
11:         send(ACCEPT, $c, \pi_{c,t}$) to p_j
12:     **else**
13:         send(REJECT, c) to p_j

14: **upon** receiving a message (ACCEPT, $c, \pi_{c,t}$) from p_j **do**
15:     $S[c][j] \leftarrow \pi_{c,t}$ ▷ store share from p_j
16:     **if** $|S[c]| \geq 2f + 1$ **then**
17:         $\Pi_{c,t} \leftarrow$ share-sombine($S[c]$)   ▷ create proof of acceptance
18:         broadcast(ORDER, $c, \Pi_{c,t}$)

19: **upon** receiving a message (ORDER, $c, \Pi_{c,t}$) from p_j **do**
20:     **if** threshold-verify($\Pi_{c,t}$) **then**
21:         $C[nextSub] \leftarrow C[nextSub] \cup (c, \Pi_{c,t})$
22:         **if** $\mathcal{I}(t) \geq I_{nextSub}$ **then**
23:             send(INTERVAL, $c, \mathcal{I}(t)$) to p_j ▷ p_i submits c in $\mathcal{I}(t)$
24:         **else**
25:             send(INTERVAL, $c, I_{nextSub}$) to p_j ▷ p_i submits c in $I_{nextSub}$

5.2 Ordering Protocol

The ordering protocol is presented in Algorithm 3. First, a process p_i broadcasts a command c and a requested timestamp t (line 7). Processes validate the timestamp t of p_i using the Timestamp Validation protocol (Algorithm 2). When a process p_j accepts t, p_j also sends a threshold encryption share $\pi_{c,t}$ (line 10) to p_i. Then, p_i waits until it has collected at least $2f + 1$ encryption shares (line 16), and combines these shares into a full proof $\Pi_{c,t}$ (line 17) that it broadcasts. When processes receive the full proof $\Pi_{c,t}$, they verify the aggregated signature (line 20) and reply with the interval where they order (c, t) (lines 23 and 25). The Aion protocols in the following sections (Sects. 6, 7) determine the content of each interval I_k by collecting the commands that have been ordered in I_k by at least $2f + 1$ processes. If a process p_j has not yet submitted the commands that it has ordered for $\mathcal{I}(t)$, then it accepts to order (c, t) in $\mathcal{I}(t)$ (line 23). Otherwise, p_j includes (c, t) in its submission for the next interval (line 25).

Lemma 2. *If a command (c, t) is ordered in an interval I_k by at least $2f + 1$ processes, and if the content of I_k is determined by collecting the commands ordered in I_k by at least $2f + 1$ processes, then (c, t) is output in I_k.*

Proof. If (c, t) is ordered in I_k by $2f + 1$ processes, then at least $f + 1$ correct processes will include (c, t) in their submissions for I_k. The content of I_k includes submissions from at least $f + 1$ correct processes, and therefore there is at least one correct process that ordered (c, t) in I_k and whose submission is used for determining the content of I_k.

Note that if a command (c, t) is ordered in $\mathcal{I}(t)$ by less than $2f + 1$ processes, it may or may not be output in $\mathcal{I}(t)$ depending on the set of $2f + 1$ processes whose submissions are used for the interval $\mathcal{I}(t)$. Assume that a command does not get ordered in the requested interval by at least $2f + 1$ processes, and that the process that requested the ordering receives a set $I = \{I_k\}$ of ordered intervals, where $|I| \geq 2f + 1$. Let I_{min} be the lowest interval among the $f + 1$ highest intervals in I. Then, the command is guaranteed to be output no later than in the interval I_{min}.

6   Leader-Based Aion

In this section, we present Leader-Based Aion, an order-fair SMR protocol, by integrating the previous ordering step (Sect. 5) with a leader-based consensus protocol. Our leader-based protocol is analogous to Pompē [58] and consists of (1) an ordering step (Sect. 5) that is executed continuously by processes, and (2) a consensus step for each interval. During synchronous periods, a correct process p_i successfully orders a command (c, t) and all correct processes have received a full proof $\Pi_{c,t}$ and ordered (c, t) in the interval $\mathcal{I}(t)$ after 3 rounds (cf. Algorithm 3). Consequently, processes can start the agreement protocol to decide the content of an interval $I_k = [k\ell, (k + 1)\ell)$ when their clocks reach the value $(k + 1)\ell + 3\Delta$.

The Leader-Based Aion protocol is presented in Algorithm 4. When a process p_i learns that the agreement protocol for the interval I_k can be started (line 6), and that p_i is the leader for the interval I_k, p_i broadcasts a COLLECT message to start collecting submissions for I_k (line 9). In response, processes sign their submissions (line 13) before sending them to p_i. The signatures are used to verify that the proposal of p_i for I_k contains submissions from at least $2f + 1$ distinct processes, and that therefore it satisfies external validity (cf. Sect. 3.7). When p_i has collected at least $2f + 1$ submissions (line 19), p_i starts a consensus instance over its proposal for I_k (line 21). If the leader is Byzantine, processes can deterministically decide on a new leader in case the proposal is invalid or the absence thereof.

Theorem 1. *A protocol using Algorithm 4 to output sets of commands in consecutive decided intervals starting with I_0 implements an order-fair SMR.*

Algorithm 4. Leader-Based Aion

1: **State**
2:     $C \leftarrow [\mathbb{N} \rightarrow []]$ ▷ commands ordered for each interval
3:     $L \leftarrow [\mathbb{N} \rightarrow []]$ ▷ submissions collected for each interval
4:     $nextSub \leftarrow 0$ ▷ next interval submitted by p_i
5:     $collecting \leftarrow$ false

6: **upon** clock$_i() \geq (k+1)\ell + 3\Delta$ **do**   ▷ I_k can be decided
7:     **if** $i \equiv k \pmod{n}$ **then**   ▷ p_i is the leader of I_k
8:         $collecting \leftarrow$ true
9:         broadcast(COLLECT, k)

10: **upon** receiving a message (COLLECT, k) from p_j **do**
11:     **if** $j \equiv k \pmod{n}$ **then**   ▷ verify leader
12:         **wait until** clock$_i() \geq (k+1)\ell + 3\Delta$ ▷ wait for interval
13:         $\langle C_k \rangle \leftarrow$ private-sign($SK_i, C[k]$)   ▷ sign submission
14:         send(SUBMIT, $\langle C_k \rangle$) to p_j ▷ send submission to leader
15:         $nextSub \leftarrow nextSub + 1$

16: **upon** receiving a message (SUBMIT, C_k) from p_j **do**
17:     **if** $collecting \wedge$ public-verify(PK_j, C_k) **then**   ▷ verify signature
18:         $L[k] \leftarrow L[k] \cup C_k$ ▷ add submission to proposal
19:         **if** $\|L[k]\| \geq 2f + 1$ **then**
20:             $collecting \leftarrow$ false
21:             leader-propose($k, L[k]$)   ▷ leader proposes $L[k]$ for I_k

Proof. The agreement property of the consensus protocol ensures that each correct process outputs the same set of commands for each interval. The fact that output commands come for consecutive intervals, and starting with the first interval, guarantees the stability of the commands that are output. The order-fairness property comes from Lemma 1 and the fact that the leader must collect submissions from at least $2f + 1$ processes (Lemma 2).

7   Leaderless Aion

In this section, we present Leaderless Aion, an order-fair implementation of an SMR, by combining the ordering step (Sect. 5) with a leaderless consensus protocol.

7.1   Leaderless Consensus

Without a leader, agreeing on a set of commands for an interval is not straightforward. For instance, two correct processes may submit two sets of commands of equal size that only differ by one command. To achieve consensus without a leader, [2] relies on an *adopt-commit* object. Intuitively, an adopt-commit object enables processes to adopt the highest value that they witness, and later to commit to this value once enough processes have adopted it. Thus, the consensus algorithm uses consecutive rounds where processes converge towards the highest value. For two sets of commands, we define the highest value as the largest set. In case of a tie, two sets can be sorted deterministically using a lexicographical order.

7.2 Leaderless SMR Protocol

Leaderless Aion comprises the ordering phase that is executed continuously by processes, and a decision phase for each interval. The decision phase consists of an exchange step followed by a consensus step. To preserve the guarantees of the ordering phase (Lemma 2), processes first exchange their sets of ordered commands before executing the consensus protocol.

Algorithm 5 presents our leaderless algorithm for order-fair SMR. First, when a process observes that the interval I_k can be decided (line 5), it broadcasts the set of commands that it has ordered for I_k (line 7). Then, once a process has received the sets of at least $2f + 1$ processes (line 12), it joins the consensus instance for the interval I_k (line 13). The exchange step ensures that the value that it broadcasts satisfies the external validity property (cf. Sect. 3.7).

Theorem 2. *A protocol using Algorithm 5 to output sets of commands in consecutive determined intervals starting with I_0 implements an order-fair SMR.*

Proof. The proof is analogous to the leader-based case. It results directly from the agreement property of the consensus protocol combined with the stability of the commands that are output, Lemma 1, and Lemma 2.

Algorithm 5. Leaderless Aion

1: **State**
2:   $C \leftarrow [\mathbb{N} \to []]$ ▷ commands ordered for each interval
3:   $E \leftarrow [\mathbb{N} \to []]$ ▷ sets received for each interval
4:   $nextSub \leftarrow 0$ ▷ next interval submitted by p_i

5: **upon** $\mathsf{clock}_i() \geq (k+1)\ell + 3\Delta$ **do**   ▷ I_k can be decided
6:   $\langle C_k \rangle \leftarrow \mathsf{private\text{-}sign}(SK_i, C[k])$ ▷ sign set ordered by p_i for I_k
7:   $\mathsf{broadcast}(\textsc{exchange}, \langle C_k \rangle)$ ▷ broadcast ordered set
8:   $nextSub \leftarrow nextSub + 1$

9: **upon** receiving a message $(\textsc{exchange}, C_k)$ from p_j **do**
10:   **if** $\mathsf{public\text{-}verify}(PK_j, C_k)$ **then**   ▷ verify signature
11:     $E[k] \leftarrow E[k] \cup C_k$ ▷ store set of p_j.
12:     **if** $|E[k]| \geq 2f + 1$ **then**
13:       $\mathsf{leaderless\text{-}propose}(k, E[k])$ ▷ propose $E[k]$ for I_k

---

8   Discussion

8.1   Comparison to Pompē and Aequitas

In Aequitas [24], a command c_1 must be ordered before a command c_2 if a predetermined proportion of processes have observed c_1 before c_2. The ordering paradigm of Pompē [58] is strictly weaker than that of Aequitas. In Pompē, to require that c_1 be ordered before c_2, it is not sufficient that all processes observe c_1 before c_2; it must also be that all correct processes observe c_1 before any of them observe c_2. Nevertheless, Pompē is an attractive trade-off because, on the one hand, it does not require building graphs of potentially cyclic dependencies between commands, and on the other hand, clients can send their commands to a single process.

In Aequitas, although the paradigm is fairer than Pompē, a client still has to send its commands to all processes, and thus, clients can also be disadvantaged based on their distances to the set of all processes. By assigning timestamps to commands, we lean towards Pompē's paradigm which is more scalable [23,55, 58]. However, instead of computing a timestamp using the median value of the timestamps observed by processes, we compute the send timestamp of a single process. This enables clients to chose the processes they send their commands to. The results in [9] rely on differential validity for consensus [18] and show that when $f = \lceil \frac{n}{3} \rceil - 1$, for two commands c_1 and c_2, if a single correct process observes c_2 before c_1, then it cannot be required from any protocol to output c_1 before c_2. By leveraging secure timestamping and allowing clients to chose a single process, a client can select the process it is the closest to. This diminishes the influence of network delays, both between clients and processes and between processes, and thus reduces the fairness gap between the two paradigms.

8.2   Byzantine Behaviors and Asynchrony

The use of TEEs prevents Byzantine processes from lying about the values of their clocks or from using the values of another clock. Byzantine processes may still introduce biases in the measurements of network delays. First, they can try to beat the network and reduce network delays by using the lack of triangle inequality in networks delays [34]. Byzantine processes may also induce longer network delays by simply retaining messages. In both cases, biases are handled by verifying network delays: if a Byzantine process introduces a bias, it has to commit to that bias, and therefore cannot take advantage of it. Actual variations in network delays are taken into account by the Network Challenge protocol. If a process detects a change in its network delays, it can impose a cooldown period on impacted processes before starting to validate their commands again. The cooldown period allows pending commands from other processes to be committed before using new values of network delays.

During asynchronous periods, or in the presence of an adversary controlling the network, the network delays are unknown, and the clocks can become desynchronized. In this case, our protocols lose liveness but maintain safety. An increase in the offsets between the clocks of processes only diminishes the level of fairness in the ordering of the commands that are output. Finally, various attacks have been identified against the security of TEEs [42,57], but are out of the scope of this paper.

9   Conclusion

In this paper, we presented Aion, a set of protocols that enable a secure ordering of commands. Aion leverages TEEs to help determine the times when commands are broadcast, and uses this information to realize leader-based and leaderless SMR protocols with an accurate ordering of commands. Essentially, Aion protocols do not require clients to broadcast their commands to all processes, and do not disadvantage processes based on their network delays to other processes.

Acknowledgements. This work is supported in part by the Australian Research Council Future Fellowship funding scheme (#180100496).

References

1. Alves, T.: TrustZone: integrated hardware and software security. Inf. Q. **3**, 18–24 (2004)
2. Antoniadis, K., Desjardins, A., Gramoli, V., Guerraoui, R., Zablotchi, I.: Leaderless consensus. In: 2021 IEEE 41st International Conference on Distributed Computing Systems (ICDCS), pp. 392–402. IEEE (2021)
3. Antoniadis, K., Guerraoui, R., Malkhi, D., Seredinschi, D.-A.: State machine replication is more expensive than consensus. In: Schmid, U., Widder, J. (eds), 32nd International Symposium on Distributed Computing (DISC 2018), volume 121 of Leibniz International Proceedings in Informatics (LIPIcs), pp. 7:1–7:18. Schloss Dagstuhl–Leibniz-Zentrum fuer Informatik, Dagstuhl, Germany (2018)
4. Anwar, F.M., Garcia, L., Han, X., Srivastava, M.: Securing time in untrusted operating systems with timeseal. In: 2019 IEEE Real-Time Systems Symposium (RTSS), pp. 80–92 (2019)
5. Anwar, F.M., Srivastava, M.: Applications and challenges in securing time. In: 12th USENIX Workshop on Cyber Security Experimentation and Test (CSET 19) (2019)
6. Arun, B., Peluso, S., Palmieri, R., Losa, G., Ravindran, B.: Speeding up consensus by chasing fast decisions. In: 2017 47th Annual IEEE/IFIP International Conference on Dependable Systems and Networks (DSN), pp. 49–60 (2017)
7. Back, A., et al.: Hashcash-a denial of service counter-measure (2013)
8. Cachin, C., Kursawe, K., Petzold, F., Shoup, V.: Secure and efficient asynchronous broadcast protocols. In: Kilian, J. (ed.) CRYPTO 2001. LNCS, vol. 2139, pp. 524–541. Springer, Heidelberg (2001). https://doi.org/10.1007/3-540-44647-8_31
9. Cachin, C., . Mićić, J., Steinhauer, N., Zanolini, L.: Quick order fairness. In: Eyal, I., Garay, J. (eds.) Financial Cryptography and Data Security. FC 2022. Lecture Notes in Computer Science, vol. 13411, pp. 316–333. Springer, Cham (2022). https://doi.org/10.1007/978-3-031-18283-9_15

10. Chiesa, M., Kamisiński, A., Rak, J., Retvari, G., Schmid, S.: A survey of fast-recovery mechanisms in packet-switched networks. IEEE Commun. Surv. Tutorials **23**(2), 1253–1301 (2021)

11. Daian, P., et al.: Flash boys 2.0: frontrunning in decentralized exchanges, miner extractable value, and consensus instability. In: 2020 IEEE Symposium on Security and Privacy, pp. 910–927. IEEE (2020)

12. Défago, X., Schiper, A., Urbán, P.: Total order broadcast and multicast algorithms: taxonomy and survey. ACM Comput. Surv. **36**(4), 372–421 (2004)

13. Diffie, W., Hellman, M.: New directions in cryptography. IEEE Trans. Inf. Theory **22**(6), 644–654 (1976)

14. Dwork, C., Lynch, N., Stockmeyer, L.: Consensus in the presence of partial synchrony. J. ACM (JACM) **35**(2), 288–323 (1988)

15. Dwork, C., Naor, M.: Pricing via processing or combatting junk mail. In: Brickell, E.F. (ed.) CRYPTO 1992. LNCS, vol. 740, pp. 139–147. Springer, Heidelberg (1993). https://doi.org/10.1007/3-540-48071-4_10

16. Eskandari, S., Moosavi, S., Clark, J.: Transparent dishonesty: front-running attacks on blockchain. In: 3rd Workshop on Trusted Smart Contracts (WTSC) (2019)

17. Fallah, M.: A puzzle-based defense strategy against flooding attacks using game theory. IEEE Trans. Dependable Secure Comput. **7**(1), 5–19 (2008)

18. Fitzi, M., Garay, J.A.: Efficient player-optimal protocols for strong and differential consensus. In: Proceedings of the Twenty-Second Annual Symposium on Principles of Distributed Computing, pp. 211–220 (2003)

19. Gelashvili, R., et al.: Block-STM: scaling blockchain execution by turning ordering curse to a performance blessing. In: Proceedings of the 28th ACM SIGPLAN Annual Symposium on Principles and Practice of Parallel Programming, pp. 232–244 (2023)

20. Gilad, Y., Hemo, R., Micali, S., Vlachos, G., Zeldovich, N.: Algorand: scaling byzantine agreements for cryptocurrencies. In: Proceedings of the 26th Symposium on Operating Systems Principles, pp. 51–68 (2017)

21. Gupta, S., Rahnama, S., Pandey, S., Crooks, N., Sadoghi, M.: Dissecting BFT consensus: in trusted components we trust! In: Proceedings of the Seventeenth European Conference on Computer Systems (EuroSys), (2023)

22. Heimbach, L., Wattenhofer, R.: SoK: preventing transaction reordering manipulations in decentralized Finance. In: 4th ACM Conference on Advances in Financial Technologies (2022)

23. Kelkar, M., Deb, S., Long, S., Juels, A., Kannan, S.: Themis: fast, strong order-fairness in byzantine consensus. In: ConsensusDays 21 (2021)

24. Kelkar, M., Zhang, F., Goldfeder, S., Juels, A.: Order-fairness for byzantine consensus. In: Micciancio, D., Ristenpart, T. (eds.) Advances in Cryptology – CRYPTO 2020: 40th Annual International Cryptology Conference, CRYPTO 2020, Santa Barbara, CA, USA, August 17–21, 2020, Proceedings, Part III, pp. 451–480. Springer International Publishing, Cham (2020). https://doi.org/10.1007/978-3-030-56877-1_16

25. Kiayias, A., Russell, A., David, B., Oliynykov, R.: Ouroboros: a provably secure proof-of-stake blockchain protocol. In: Katz, J., Shacham, H. (eds.) CRYPTO 2017. LNCS, vol. 10401, pp. 357–388. Springer, Cham (2017). https://doi.org/10.1007/978-3-319-63688-7_12

26. Kursawe, K.: Wendy, the good little fairness widget: achieving order fairness for blockchains. In: Proceedings of the 2nd ACM Conference on Advances in Financial Technologies, pp. 25–36 (2020)

27. Laishun, Z., Minglei, Z., Yuanbo, G.: A client puzzle based defense mechanism to resist dos attacks in WLAN. In: 2010 International Forum on Information Technology and Applications, vol. 3, pp. 424–427. IEEE (2010)

28. Lamport, L.: In: Time, Clocks, and the Ordering of Events in a Distributed System, pp. 179–196. Association for Computing Machinery (2019)

29. Lamport, L., Shostak, R., Pease, M.: In: The Byzantine Generals Problem, pp. 203–226. Association for Computing Machinery (2019)

30. Lenzen, C., Sommer, P., Wattenhofer, R.: Optimal clock synchronization in networks. In: Proceedings of the 7th ACM Conference on Embedded Networked Sensor Systems, pp. 225–238 (2009)

31. Liao, J., Zhang, F., Sun, W., Shi, W.: Speedster: an efficient multi-party state channel via enclaves. In: Proceedings of the 2022 ACM on Asia Conference on Computer and Communications Security, pp. 637–651 (2022)

32. Lind, J., Naor, O., Eyal, I., Kelbert, F., Sirer, E.G., Pietzuch, P.: Teechain: a secure payment network with asynchronous blockchain access. In: Proceedings of the 27th ACM Symposium on Operating Systems Principles, pp. 63–79 (2019)

33. Liu, J., Li, W., Karame, G.O., Asokan, N.: Scalable byzantine consensus via hardware-assisted secret sharing. IEEE Trans. Comput. **68**(1), 139–151 (2018)

34. Lumezanu, C., Baden, R., Spring, N., Bhattacharjee, B.: Triangle inequality and routing policy violations in the internet. In: Moon, S.B., Teixeira, R., Uhlig, S. (eds.) PAM 2009. LNCS, vol. 5448, pp. 45–54. Springer, Heidelberg (2009). https://doi.org/10.1007/978-3-642-00975-4_5

35. Lundelius, J., Lynch, N.: A new fault-tolerant algorithm for clock synchronization. In: Proceedings of the Third Annual ACM Symposium on Principles of Distributed Computing, pp. 75–88 (1984)

36. Malkhi, D., Reiter, M.: Byzantine quorum systems. Distrib. Comput. **11**(4), 203–213 (1998)

37. Malkhi, D., Szalachowski, P.: Maximal extractable value (MEV) protection on a DAG. In: 4th International Conference on Blockchain Economics Security and Protocols (2022)

38. McKeen, F., et al.: Innovative instructions and software model for isolated execution. In: HASP 2013: Proceedings of the 2nd International Workshop on Hardware and Architectural Support for Security and Privacy, vol. 10, p. 1 (2013)

39. Micali, S., Rabin, M., Vadhan, S.: Verifiable random functions. In: 40th Annual Symposium on Foundations of Computer Science (cat. No. 99CB37039), pp. 120–130. IEEE (1999)

40. Mouchet, M., Vaton, S., Chonavel, T.: Statistical characterization of round-trip times with nonparametric hidden Markov models. In: 2019 IFIP/IEEE Symposium on Integrated Network and Service Management (IM), pp. 43–48. IEEE (2019) ¡error l="308" c="Invalid ¡error l="306" c="Invalid ¡error l="307" c="Invalid ¡error l="308" c="Invalid command: paragraph not started." /¿ command: paragraph not started." /¿ command: paragraph not started." /¿ command: paragraph not started." /¿

41. Mouchet, M., Vaton, S., Chonavel, T., Aben, E., Den Hertog, J.: Large-scale characterization and segmentation of internet path delays with infinite HMMs. IEEE Access **8**, 16771–16784 (2020)

42. Murdock, K., Oswald, D., Garcia, F.D., Van Bulck, J., Gruss, D., Piessens, F.: Plundervolt: software-based fault injection attacks against intel SGX. In: 2020 IEEE Symposium on Security and Privacy (SP), pp. 1466–1482. IEEE (2020)

43. Nakamoto, S.: Bitcoin: A Peer-to-peer Electronic Cash System. Decentralized Business Review, p. 21260 (2008)

44. Natoli, C., Gramoli, V.: The blockchain anomaly. In: 2016 IEEE 15th International Symposium on Network Computing and Applications (NCA), pp. 310–317. IEEE (2016)

45. Pease, M., Shostak, R., Lamport, L.: Reaching agreement in the presence of faults. J. ACM **27**(2), 228–234 (1980)

46. Qin, K., Zhou, L., Gervais, A.: Quantifying blockchain extractable value: how dark is the forest? In: 2022 IEEE Symposium on Security and Privacy (SP), pp. 198–214 (2022)

47. Rezende, T.F., Sutra, P.: Leaderless state-machine replication: specification, properties, limits. In: 34th International Symposium on Distributed Computing (DISC 2020), volume 179 of Leibniz International Proceedings in Informatics (LIPIcs), pp. 24:1–24:17 (2020)

48. Sabt, M., Achemlal, M., Bouabdallah, A.: Trusted execution environment: what it is, and what it is not. In: 2015 IEEE Trustcom/BigDataSE/Ispa, vol. 1, pp. 57–64. IEEE (2015)

49. Shamir, A.: How to share a secret. Commun. ACM **22**(11), 612–613 (1979)

50. Stathakopoulou, C., Rüsch, S., Brandenburger, M., Vukolić, M.: Adding fairness to order: preventing front-running attacks in BFT protocols using tees. In: 2021 40th International Symposium on Reliable Distributed Systems (SRDS), pp. 34–45. IEEE (2021)

51. Wang, X., Reiter, M.K.: Defending against denial-of-service attacks with puzzle auctions. In: 2003 Symposium on Security and Privacy, 2003, pp. 78–92. IEEE (2003)

52. Wood, G., et al.: Ethereum: a secure decentralised generalised transaction ledger. Ethereum Proj. Yellow Pap. **151**(2014), 1–32 (2014)

53. Wu, Y., Zhao, Z., Bao, F., Deng, R.H.: Software puzzle: a countermeasure to resource-inflated denial-of-service attacks. IEEE Trans. Inf. Forensics Secur. **10**(1), 168–177 (2014)

54. Yin, M., Malkhi, D., Reiter, M.K., Gueta, G.G., Abraham, I.: Hotstuff: BFT consensus with linearity and responsiveness. In: Proceedings of the 2019 ACM Symposium on Principles of Distributed Computing, pp. 347–356 (2019)

55. Zarbafian, P., Gramoli, V.: Lyra: fast and scalable resilience to reordering attacks in blockchains. In: 2023 IEEE International Parallel & Distributed Processing Symposium. IEEE (2023)

56. Zhang, J., et al.: TBFT: efficient byzantine fault tolerance using trusted execution environment. In: ICC 2022 - IEEE International Conference on Communications, pp. 1004–1009 (2022)

57. Zhang, Y., Zhao, M., Li, T., Han, H.: Survey of attacks and defenses against SGX. In: 2020 IEEE 5th Information Technology and Mechatronics Engineering Conference (ITOEC), pp. 1492–1496. IEEE (2020)

58. Zhang, Y., Setty, S., Chen, Q., Zhou, L., Alvisi, L.: Byzantine ordered consensus without byzantine oligarchy. In: Proceedings of the 14th USENIX Conference on Operating Systems Design and Implementation, pp. 633–649 (2020)

Towards a Privacy-Preserving Attestation for Virtualized Networks

Ghada Arfaoui[1], Thibaut Jacques[1,2(✉)], Marc Lacoste[1], Cristina Onete[2], and Léo Robert[3]

[1] Orange, Cesson-Sévigné, France
thibaut.jacques@orange.com
[2] XLIM, University of Limoges, Limoges, France
[3] MIS, Université de Picardie Jules Verne, Amiens, France

Abstract. TPM remote attestation allows to verify the integrity of the boot sequence of a remote device. *Deep Attestation* extends that concept to virtualized platforms by allowing to attest virtual components, the hypervisor, and the link between them. In multi-tenant environments, deep attestation solution offer security and/or efficiency, but no privacy.

In this paper, we propose a privacy preserving TPM-based deep attestation solution in multi-tenant environments, which provably guarantees: **(i) Inter-tenant privacy**: a tenant is cannot know whether other VMs outside its own are hosted on the same machine; **(ii) Configuration hiding**: the hypervisor's configuration, used during attestation, remains hidden from the tenants; and **(iii) Layer linking**: tenants can link hypervisors with the VMs, thus obtaining a guarantee that the VMs are running on specific hardware. We also implement our scheme and show that it is efficient despite the use of complex cryptographic tools.

Keywords: Deep Attestation · Multi-tenant · 5G · Privacy

1 Introduction

The use of virtualization has revolutionized mobile networks (5G and beyond). Virtual Network Functions (VNFs) can be easily added, removed, or migrated to form slices (also called tenants), propose new services on demand, and meet the heterogeneous, stringent requirements of verticals (*e.g.*, e-health, banking, etc.). The flexibility of virtualization, however, induces an inevitable loss of control and a need to regularly confirm that the resulting network can be trusted.

A solution recommended by the European Telecommunications Standards Institute (ETSI) is *remote attestation* [10]. It enables a prover to convince an authorized verifier that it conforms to some specifications (and thus that it has specific properties). In this paper, we focus on the type of attestation that verifies the integrity state of a component. Recently, at ACNS 2022, [1] proposed a solution to attest VNFs and their underlying infrastructure, offering both security and scalability *for single tenant use, i.e.*, one entity operates all VNFs *and* the underlying infrastructure. However, new mobile network generations are

G. Tsudik et al. (Eds.): ESORICS 2023, LNCS 14347, pp. 351–370, 2024.
https://doi.org/10.1007/978-3-031-51482-1_18

typically multi-tenant environments (*i.e.*, the operator provides slices/tenants to different verticals). In that setting, the solution of [1] becomes inefficient. Moreover, privacy concerns arise (*e.g.*, the operator does not want to reveal its network nodes configuration), which are not addressed.

1.1   Our Contribution

We consider the typical multi-tenant architecture shown in Fig. 1, which is equipped with a hardware Trusted Platform Module (TPM) and spawns a virtual TPM (vTPM) for each VM it manages. VMs can be operated by tenants, and one tenant can have multiple VMs. Every tenant has a dedicated verifier to perform attestation. Our work makes a triple contribution.

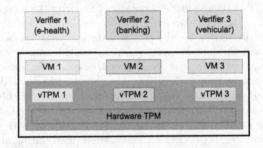

Fig. 1. Multi-tenant architecture where each VNFs belongs to a different tenant.

A New Protocol. We propose a primitive called privacy-preserving multi-tenant attestation (PP-MTA), which provides attestation, but also layer-binding and privacy: *Inter-tenant privacy* (no tenant can learn if other tenants share the same platforms as its own VMs) and *Configuration hiding* (the hypervisor attestation convinces a tenant that the hypervisor is well-configured without revealing the configuration). These strong properties are achieved with no modification to the TPM, and rely on ZK-SNARKs, vector-commitment schemes, and secure-channel establishment.

Formal Analysis. We formally model and prove the security and privacy of our protocol. We *extend* the layer-binding properties defined in [1] to a multi-tenant environment, and *add* definitions for *inter-tenant privacy* and *configuration-hiding*. We formally quantify the privacy of our protocol, with more details in the full version of this paper [2]. The security of our scheme relies on standard ACCE-secure channels, secure vector commitments, and zero-knowledge succinct non-interactive arguments of knowledge (ZK-SNARKs), but also two new properties: partner-hiding authenticated key-exchange (AKE) and collision-resistant vector commitments (see Appendix A and B).

Implementation. We provide an implementation of our protocol, with several benchmarks. Despite relying on ZK-SNARKs, known for poor performance, our scheme remains fast enough for real-world use.

1.2 Background and Related Work

Our work builds on TPM-based remote-attestation, for which we recall some basics below. We also recall the syntax of vector commitment and ZK-SNARK. Finally we review related work on attestation with a focus on [1].

Vector Commitment. Introduced in [6], vector commitment schemes allow a user to commit to a list of values (rather than to a single message). Vector commitments can be opened partially, by index (opening information exists separately per committed value). After a setup phase $\mathsf{VC.Setup}(1^\lambda, q) \to \mathsf{ppar}$, one can commit to a sequence of values $\mathsf{VC.Com}(v) \to (c, aux)$. Given an opening $\mathsf{VC.Open}(m, i, aux) \to \pi_i$, one can verify that a value is contained in the commitment $\mathsf{VC.Ver}(m, c, i, \pi_i) \to b \in \{0, 1\}$.

ZK-SNARK. Zero-Knowledge Succinct Non-Interactive Arguments of Knowledge (ZK-SNARKs) [4] are generic NIZK proof systems. Given an NP statement, one can prove knowledge of a valid witness without revealing it. A common reference string (CRS) is generated during setup: $\mathsf{ZKP.Setup}(R) \to \mathsf{CRS}$. Given the CRS, a statement x_{ZK}, and a witness w_{ZK} such that $(x_{ZK}, w_{ZK}) \in R$, one can compute $\mathsf{ZKP.Prove}(\mathsf{CRS}, R, x_{ZK}, w_{ZK}) \to \pi_{ZK}$ and verify the proof $\mathsf{ZKP.SkVer}(\mathsf{CRS}, R, x_{ZK}, \pi_{ZK}) \to b \in \{0, 1\}$.

TPM Remote Attestation. This type of attestation, which allows the verification of the integrity state of a target, has two main phases: (1) the TPM measures all the code involved in the boot process and securely stores the measurements in the *Platform Configuration Registers (PCR)*; (2) upon request, the TPM signs with an attestation key (AK) the target configuration (PCR values) and sends the result. The receiver of the attestation checks the validity of the signature and of the PCR-values. Thus, classical attestation requires verifiers to know a full set of valid PCR-values (*i.e.*, valid configurations) – which, in some environments, is a privacy threat.

Property-Based Attestation. Property-based attestation (PBA) [19] aims to improve privacy in TPM remote attestation. Indeed, [19] showed that binary attestation can enable easier configuration leakage. PBA provides a privacy-friendly attestation mechanism by verifying that the target satisfies some high-level properties (rather than sending PCR measurements). A property can be achieved by multiple configurations. While some PBAs [7,17] use a Trusted Third Party (TTP), its existence is not always guaranteed. Alternatively, some PBAs [8,11] leverage zero-knowledge proofs of membership of a configuration among a set of valid configurations – at the expense of modifying TPM specifications. PBA achieves a different kind of privacy than Direct Anonymous Attestation (DAA) [5]. While DAA prevents linking attestations to a specific TPM (or multiple attestation to the same TPM), PBA aims to protect the *content* of the attestation itself. In our work, we focus on classical attestation in a multi-tenant environment, for which DAA is unnecessary.

Deep Attestation. Attesting a virtual component (*e.g.*, a VM) implies attesting the underlying virtualization infrastructure, a process called *deep attestation*

(DA). In *single-channel* DA [10, 16, 21, 23], the integrity of a VM is verified simultaneously with attesting its hypervisor, and the linking of the two components *layer binding*. This approach can ensure trust, scales badly for a large number of VMs. Conversely, *multiple-channel* DA [9, 10, 23] drops layer-binding to provide independent (and efficient) VM and hypervisor attestations.

Comparison to [1]. The DA scheme by [1] provides both layer-binding DA that scales as well as multiple-channel attestation, and requires no modification of the TPM. Hypervisor attestations also incidentally attest the public keys of the VMs they manage. As a result, the verifier can link those attestations with those of the VMs. Unfortunately, this solution does not scale in multi-tenant environments (e.g., 5G and beyond) for which *inter-tenant privacy* is required. Moreover, as the scheme builds on standard DA, the verifier learns, from the attestation quote, the current PCR-configurations of the physical machine. This is a privacy risk for the platform owner (e.g., the operator).

Attestation in the Cloud. Although other works have explored attestation for trust in cloud-like environments [3, 15, 18, 20, 22, 24, 25], none focused on DA. Such solutions require full trust in the infrastructure provider. DA enables stronger security and privacy, making less trust assumptions on the provider.

2 Technical Overview

In this section we give an overview of our solution for DA in multi-tenant environments.

Use Case and Problem Statement. We consider a use-case similar to that of Keylime [14, 21]. This solution found in cloud infrastructures provides system integrity monitoring based on TPM attestations. Keylime allows deploying an agent on each target VM: the agent sends, every few seconds, an attestation to a cloud verifier. Keylime is efficient even in very large cloud-infrastructures [12]. Unfortunately, it is limited to VM attestations (rather than to linked hypervisor/VM attestations). Moreover, it provides neither tenant privacy nor hypervisor configuration privacy.

Ideally, we would like to provide linkable attestation in multi-tenant settings, such that the resulting solution is practical (scalable and efficient), secure, provides strong privacy for both the tenants and for the provider of the physical infrastructure and requires no modification of the TPM.

Solution Outline. A naïve application of [1] to multi-tenant scenarios provides layer-linking but not privacy. The result also scales poorly.

Hypervisor-configuration hiding requires that attestation quotes, signed by a physical root of trust (TPM), only prove the validity of the PCR-measurement, without revealing it. The naïve approach of the TPM computing a zero-knowledge proof would require TPM modifications. This is precisely what we want to avoid. In our solution, this is achieved by the use of ZK-SNARKs.

Moreover, the protocol in [1] is designed for environments where a single entity owns the infrastructure and all the VMs. Naïvely reusing that solution in multi-tenant environments creates a significant bottleneck when multiple tenants request attestations simultaneously; this could be resolved by *batching* [20] hypervisor attestations for multiple tenants. Batching is challenging to achieve simultaneously with inter-tenant privacy and layer-linking. As layer-linking requires VM attestations to be linked to their managing hypervisor's attestation, the latter has to include some binding information to the VMs it is managing. Yet, in multi-tenant environments such VMs might belong to distinct users; each user must only verify the binding of its own VMs to the hypervisor. To bridge that gap, we use vector-commitment schemes to store (in a hidden form) linking information to VMs hosted on the hypervisor. This allows each tenant to open some specific positions in that commitment, learning nothing about other positions.

Our Solution. We introduce several new elements to the layer-linking DA solution of [1]. A trivial, but necessary modification is at setup: unlike [1], we need to account for the *ownership*, by a tenant, of a VM. In our infrastructure, tenants will have to use long-term credentials in order to register new VMs.

As VM attestations are independently requested by VM-owners, we can simply use typical multiple-channel attestation for this step. Our key contribution, however, is a novel hypervisor-attestation method which is scalable (as it allows for simultaneous attestation requests to be batched), linkable to VM attestations, and guaranteeing inter-tenant privacy and hypervisor-configuration hiding.

The hypervisor may receive one or more attestation requests from one or more tenants. Requests are buffered if the TPM is busy. As soon as the TPM is free, the hypervisor makes an attestation request for the aggregated queries, using a special nonce computed as follows.

For each tenant, the hypervisor retrieves linking information and concatenates it with that tenant's nonces (per each VM). Then it assigns a random position in a vector commitment to each tenant, places the concatenated linking-values for the tenant at that position, and commits to the resulting vector[1]. This is the nonce used in the attestation request.

The unmodified TPM computes and signs a regular attestation quote (revealing the PCR values). The hypervisor receives the signed quote and computes a ZK-SNARK confirming its validity without revealing the configuration. Then, the hypervisor computes, for each tenant, an opening to the vector for its attributed positions. Each tenant can verify the ZK-SNARK and use the opening information to retrieve its linking information, thus ensuring layer-linking.

3   Model

Our security model applies to the virtualization architecture shown in Fig. 1. Tenants associated with unique identities T can register a number of virtual machines VM on a hypervisor H.

Each hypervisor H has a physical root of trust represented by a TPM TPM. We assume each physical machine (with a unique hypervisor H) upper-bounds

---

[1] If not all tenants simultaneously request attestations, or if the platform contains less tenants than its capacity, remaining vector positions are filled with dummy values.

the number of tenants N_T it can host, and the number of VMs N_{VM} each tenant can have on $\mathcal{H}$. Such bounds do exist in practice, usually driven by physical constraints. For the sake of legibility, we assume *universal* bounds (for all hypervisors), rather than *local*, hypervisor-specific ones.

We call the list of tuples of PCR measurements and accepted values during hypervisor attestation the *configuration* of the hypervisor. We assume the existence of a set (of more than one element) CONF of possible configurations for each hypervisor. In the quote, the current configuration is represented as the hash of the list of PCRs.

Security/Privacy Notions. We formally define the privacy properties required for our protocol and the adversary model in Sects. 3.2 and 3.3. For attestation security we require an extension of the linking property formalized by [1], adapted to the multi-tenant setting. In a nutshell, this notion requires that no malicious party (even a malicious hypervisor) be able to fool a tenant into falsely believing that a VM is hosted by the hypervisor when in fact it is not. The full formalization of this property is in the extended version [2].

3.1 Primitive Syntax

We formally define a new primitive called privacy-preserving multi-tenant attestation (PP-MTA). It consists of 9 PPT algorithms: PP-MTA = (Setup, HSetup, TKGen, VMReg, HAttest, VMAttest, VfHAttest, VfVMAttest, Link) with:

Setup(1^λ) → {ppar, spar}: On input of a security parameter λ, this algorithm outputs public parameters ppar (including the bounds N_T, N_{VM}, and valid configuration-set CONF), and private parameters spar (which may be instantiated to $\bot$ if not useful). The public parameters are input implicitly for every subsequent algorithm.

HSetup(ppar) → {$\mathcal{H}$.pk, $\mathcal{H}$.sk, AK.pk, AK.sk, $\mathcal{H}$.Conf, $\mathcal{H}$.state}: This algorithm s-ets up the (honest) hypervisor $\mathcal{H}$, by associating it with a public key $\mathcal{H}$.pk, a private key $\mathcal{H}$.sk, public- and private- attestation credentials (AK.pk, AK.sk), and a configuration $\mathcal{H}$.Conf $\in$ CONF. The hypervisor "inherits" the universal bounds N_T and N_{VM} from ppar. The hypervisor maintains state $\mathcal{H}$.state related to hosted tenants and their VMs.

TKGen(ppar) → {T.pk, T.sk}: This algorithm generates public and private keys for a single tenant T. All parties have access to all the public keys. Only the tenant has access to its private key.

VMReg($\mathcal{H}$, T.sk, VMdesc) → {(VM, VAK.pk), VAK.sk, $\mathcal{H}$.state} $\cup \bot$: This algorithm performs the registration, by tenant T, of a VM of description VMdesc on the machine with hypervisor $\mathcal{H}$. If the tenant's request exceeds either the hypervisor's capacity to host new tenants N_T, or its capacity for VMs for this tenant N_{VM}, then the algorithm returns $\bot$. Otherwise, the hypervisor creates the required VM, for which it returns a handle VM, as well as a tuple of public/private parameters, corresponding to the *attestation* keypair for that VM, as stored by the vTPM: (VAK.pk, VAK.sk). The algorithm also requires mutual authentication of the tenant and the hypervisor, enabling $\mathcal{H}$

to update its state $\mathcal{H}$.state. If the authentication fails, the algorithm returns $\perp$. Otherwise it returns to the tenant the handle VM and the public keys and VAK.pk.

$\texttt{HAttest}\langle \mathcal{T}(\mathcal{T}.\text{sk}, \text{nonce}_\mathcal{T}), \mathcal{H}(\mathcal{H}.\text{sk}, \text{AK}.\text{sk}, \mathcal{H}.\text{state}, \mathcal{H}.\text{Conf})\rangle \rightarrow \{\text{ATT}_{\mathcal{H},\mathcal{T}}\}$:
The hypervisor attestation protocol is an interactive algorithm between a tenant $\mathcal{T}$ which takes as input its private key and a fresh nonce $\text{nonce}_\mathcal{T}$ and the hypervisor with input its long-term credentials $\mathcal{H}$.sk, AK.sk, its current state $\mathcal{H}$.state, its configuration $\mathcal{H}$.Conf. It outputs an attestation $\text{ATT}_{\mathcal{H},\mathcal{T}}$.

$\texttt{VfHAttest}(\text{ATT}_{\mathcal{H},\mathcal{T}}, \text{nonce}_\mathcal{T}, \text{link}_\mathcal{T}) \rightarrow \{0,1\}$: Given as input a hypervisor attestation $\text{ATT}_{\mathcal{H},\mathcal{T}}$, a nonce $\text{nonce}_\mathcal{T}$ and linking information $\text{link}_\mathcal{T}$, this verification algorithm outputs 1 if the attestation is valid and 0 otherwise.

$\texttt{VMAttest}\langle VM(\text{VAK}.\text{sk}), \mathcal{T}(\mathcal{T}.\text{sk}, \text{nonce})\rangle \rightarrow \{\text{ATT}_{VM}\} \cup \perp$: The interactive VM attestation protocol takes place between a tenant (using its key $\mathcal{T}$.sk and a fresh nonce nonce) and a VM that the tenant owns (associated with its private key VAK.sk). The output could be $\perp$ (typically if the tenant does not own VM) or a VM attestation ATT_{VM}.

$\texttt{VfVMAttest}(\text{ATT}_{VM}, \text{nonce}, \text{link}) \rightarrow \{0,1\}$: Given as input a VM attestation ATT_{VM}, a nonce nonce and linking information link, the VM attestation-verification algorithm outputs 1 if the attestation is valid and 0 otherwise.

$\texttt{Link}(\text{ATT}_{\mathcal{H},\mathcal{T}}, \text{nonce}_\mathcal{T}, \text{link}_\mathcal{T}, \text{ATT}_{VM}, \text{nonce}, \text{link}) \rightarrow \{0,1\}$: Given as input a tuple consisting of a hypervisor attestation quote $\text{ATT}_{\mathcal{H},\mathcal{T}}$ and hypervisor attestation linking information $\text{link}_\mathcal{T}$, and a tuple consisting of a VM attestation quote ATT_{VM} and VM attestation linking information link, the linking algorithm outputs 1 if the two attestation are linked and 0 if they are not.

3.2 Inter-tenant Privacy

Intuitively, inter-tenant privacy ensures that a malicious, but legitimate tenant cannot tell whether or not VMs from other tenants are running on the same hypervisor as its own VMs. In the real-world, tenants might be well-aware that they are sharing resources with other tenants. However, by considering a much stronger privacy notion, we ensure that this (and potentially other) information is not leaked by the attestation. This makes our protocol usable in all situations, not just those in which some leakage is acceptable. The definition we provide (and prove for our protocol) only guarantees that leakage is avoided at the protocol-level: the adversary may have alternative means of knowing about VMs co-hosted on the same hardware.

Formally, inter-tenant privacy is defined as a game (depicted in Fig. 2a) between a challenger $\mathcal{G}$ and an adversary $\mathcal{A}$. The challenger runs the setup algorithm $\texttt{Setup}(1^\lambda)$. It then sets up a hypervisor $\mathcal{H}$ by running $\texttt{HSetup}(\text{ppar})$. $\mathcal{G}$ initiates $\mathcal{L}_H := \emptyset$ and $\mathcal{L}_C := \emptyset$. The challenger draws a random bit $b \xleftarrow{r} \{0,1\}$. The adversary, given ppar and the length of the security parameter (in unary) 1^λ, as well as the handle $\mathcal{H}$, can then use the following oracles:

$\texttt{oHonTReg}_b(\{\text{VMDesc}_i\}_{i=1}^\ell)$: this oracle depends on bit b. Given as input a set of VM descriptions VMDesc_i, this oracle internally runs the key-generation algorithm TKGen(ppar), receiving either $\perp$ (too many tenants) or a handle $\mathcal{T}$ and keys $\mathcal{T}$.pk, $\mathcal{T}$.sk. The oracle adds $\mathcal{T}$ to $\mathcal{L}_H$ and increments a variable $n_{\mathcal{T}}$ (that stores the number of tenants on that hypervisor) by 1. Assuming that oHonTReg did not output $\perp$: if $b = 1$, the oracle runs VMReg($\mathcal{H}, \mathcal{T}$.sk, VMDesc$_i$) for each VM in the input set, obtaining handles VM, keys VAK.pk, VAK.sk, and an updated hypervisor state $\mathcal{H}$.state, containing tuples of the form $(\mathcal{T}, VM_i, \text{VAK.sk}_i, \text{VAK.pk}_i, \text{REAL})$ for each VM. If $b = 0$, then the VMs are not truly created: instead, the oracle generates random values VAK.pk$_i$ for each $i = 1, \ldots, \ell$, and handles VM_i, updating the hypervisor state with tuples of the form $(\mathcal{T}, VM_i, \text{VAK.pk}_i, \text{FAKE})$. Finally, the oracle outputs the following values to the adversary: $\mathcal{T}, \{VM_i\}_{i=1}^{\ell}$ as well as keys: $\mathcal{T}$.pk, $\{\text{VAK.pk}_i\}_{i=1}^{\ell}$. If $\ell > N_{VM}$, the output of VMReg will be $\perp$, forwarded to the adversary instead of the VM information. The adversary can, in parallel, use TKGen algorithm to register malicious tenants: these will be added by the challenger to $\mathcal{L}_C$.

$\underline{\text{oVMReg}(\mathcal{T}, \text{VMDesc})}$: given as input a (registered) tenant $\mathcal{T} \in \mathcal{L}_H$ and a VM with description VMDesc, this oracle internally runs VMReg($\mathcal{H}, \mathcal{T}$.sk, VMDesc). If the bound N_{VM} has still not been reached for tenant $\mathcal{T}$ then the algorithm outputs $(VM, \text{VAK.pk})$ as in the previous oracle. The hypervisor state $\mathcal{H}$.state is updated. A malicious tenant can always register a new VM by running the VMReg algorithm directly.

$\underline{\text{oHAttest}(\mathcal{T})}$: given as input a registered tenant $\mathcal{T} \in \mathcal{L}_H$, this oracle simulates running HAttest between $\mathcal{T}$ and the hypervisor $\mathcal{H}$. The adversary gains a transcript τ_{HAtt} of the protocol run (or $\perp$ if e.g., $\mathcal{H}$ does not exist or if $\mathcal{T}$ has no VMs registered on $\mathcal{H}$). If the VMs created for this tenant were fake (the bit b picked by the challenger is 0), the hypervisor attestation is done over the current configuration and the VMs currently existing on the machine.

Since the adversary is a collusion of valid tenants, it does not need oracle access to VM attestations: it can simply run the correct algorithms.

Definition 1 (Inter-tenant privacy). *A PP-MTA scheme* PP-MTA= *(Setup, HSetup, TKGen, VMReg, HAttest, VMAttest, VfHAttest, VfVMAttest, Link) is $(N_{\mathcal{T}}, N_{VM}, \epsilon)$-inter-tenant private if, and only if, for every probabilistic polynomial adversary $\mathcal{A}$, the following holds:*

$$\text{Adv}_{\text{PP-MTA}}^{\text{TPriv}}(\mathcal{A}) := \left| \Pr[\mathcal{A} \text{ wins } G_{\text{TPriv}}(\lambda)] - \frac{1}{2} \right| \leq \epsilon.$$

The value $\text{Adv}_{\text{PP-MTA}}^{\text{TPriv}}(\mathcal{A})$ is called the advantage *of $\mathcal{A}$ against the inter-tenant privacy of PP-MTA. Asymptotically, we call a PP-MTA scheme* inter-tenant private *if ϵ is a negligible function of the security parameter λ.*

3.3 Hypervisor-Configuration Hiding

Intuitively, hypervisor-configuration ensures that an adversary (which can be a group of colluding, legitimate tenants) cannot learn the precise configuration

$$
\begin{array}{l}
\text{Game } G_{\mathsf{TPriv}}(\lambda) \\
\hline
\{\mathsf{ppar}, \mathsf{spar}\} \leftarrow \mathsf{Setup}(1^\lambda) \\
\{\mathcal{H}.\mathsf{pk}, \mathcal{H}.\mathsf{sk}, \mathsf{HAK}.\mathsf{pk}, \mathsf{HAK}.\mathsf{sk}, \mathcal{H}.\mathsf{Conf}\}, \\
\mathcal{H}.\mathsf{state} \leftarrow \mathsf{HSetup}(\mathsf{ppar}) \\
b \xleftarrow{r} \{0,1\} \\
d \leftarrow \mathcal{A}^{\mathsf{oHonTReg}_b(\cdot), \mathsf{oVMReg}(\cdot, \cdot), \mathsf{oHAttest}(\cdot)}(1^\lambda) \\
\hline
\mathcal{A} \textbf{ wins iff.: } d = b
\end{array}
$$

(a) Inter-tenant

$$
\begin{array}{l}
\text{Game } G_{\mathsf{CHid}}(\lambda) \\
\hline
\{\mathsf{ppar}, \mathsf{spar}\} \leftarrow \mathsf{Setup}(1^\lambda) \\
b \xleftarrow{r} \{0,1\} \\
d \leftarrow \mathcal{A}^{\mathsf{oChooseConfig}_b(\cdot)}(1^\lambda) \\
\hline
\mathcal{A} \textbf{ wins iff.: } d = b
\end{array}
$$

(b) Hypervisor Configuration

Fig. 2. The privacy games

of the hypervisor: just that this configuration is one of potentially many valid configurations. Technically, the property is formalized using a oChooseConfig oracle, which allows the adversary to choose two configurations, one of which will be used in fact for attestation. The adversary's task is to distinguish between those configurations.

In the hypervisor configuration-hiding game (Fig. 2b), the adversary gets access to the following oracle:

- oChooseConfig$_b(\mathcal{H}.\mathsf{Conf}_0, \mathcal{H}.\mathsf{Conf}_1) \to \{\mathsf{OK}\} \cup \bot$: This oracle can only be called once. Given as input two hypervisor configurations $\mathcal{H}.\mathsf{Conf}_0$ and $\mathcal{H}.\mathsf{Conf}_1$, this oracle checks that $\mathcal{H}.\mathsf{Conf}_0 \in \mathsf{CONF}$ and $\mathcal{H}.\mathsf{Conf}_1 \in \mathsf{CONF}$. It ensure that $\mathcal{H}$ has not yet been set up (e.g., through HSetup). If either verification fails, the oracle outputs $\bot$. If verification succeeds, the oracle calls HSetup, forcing the picked hypervisor configuration $\mathcal{H}.\mathcal{H}.\mathsf{Conf}$ to be $\mathcal{H}.\mathsf{Conf}_b$.

Definition 2 (Configuration hiding). *A PP-MTA scheme* PP-MTA= *(Setup, HSetup, TKGen, VMReg, HAttest, VMAttest, VfHAttest, VfVMAttest, Link) is ϵ-configuration-hiding if, and only if, for every probabilistic polynomial adversary $\mathcal{A}$, the following holds:*

$$
\mathsf{Adv}_{\mathsf{PP\text{-}MTA}}^{\mathsf{CHid}}(\mathcal{A}) := \left| \Pr[\mathcal{A} \text{ wins } G_{\mathsf{CHid}}(\lambda)] - \frac{1}{2} \right| \leq \epsilon.
$$

The value $\mathsf{Adv}_{\mathsf{PP\text{-}MTA}}^{\mathsf{CHid}}(\mathcal{A})$ *is called the* advantage of $\mathcal{A}$ against the configuration-hiding of PP-MTA. *Asymptotically, a PP-MTA scheme is* configuration-hiding *if ϵ is negligible in the security parameter λ.*

4 Construction

In this section we instantiate the PP-MTA primitive using a signature scheme (SigKGen, SigSig, SigVer), a collision-resistant hash function H, a vector commitment scheme (VC.Setup, VC.Com, VC.Open, VC.Ver), a ZK-SNARK scheme (ZKP.Setup, ZKP.Prove, ZKP.SkVer, ZKP.SkSim), and a secure-channel establishment protocol: AKE = (AKE.KGen, AKE.AKE, AKE.Enc, AKE.Dec).

4.1 Setup

We first instantiate the global-setup and hypervisor-setup algorithms (Setup, HSetup), then set up the tenants with long-term parameters.

Global Setup. The goal is to instantiate the scheme's global public and private parameters: $\{\mathsf{ppar}, \mathsf{spar}\} \leftarrow \mathsf{Setup}(1^\lambda)$. Two universal bounds are chosen: a maximal number of tenants per physical machine N_T and a maximal number of VMs per hosted tenant N_{VM}. These bounds are later crucial in avoiding trivial inter-tenant privacy attacks. A set of *plausible* configurations CONF is chosen for the hypervisor. We set up the vector commitment and ZK-SNARK:

$$(\mathsf{ppar}_{\mathsf{VC}}) \leftarrow \mathsf{VC.Setup}(1^\lambda, N_T) \text{ and } (CRS, \tau) \leftarrow \mathsf{ZKP.Setup}(R)$$

The vector-commitment length is a constant N_T. Given the following zero-knowledge proof:

$$\{(\mathsf{quote}, \sigma) : \mathsf{SigVer}(\mathsf{AK.pk}, \mathsf{quote}, \sigma, c) == 1 \wedge \mathsf{quote}.\mathcal{H}.\mathsf{Conf} \in \mathsf{CONF}\}$$

we fix the statement:

$$(x_{ZK}) \leftarrow \{\mathsf{SigVer}(\mathsf{AK.pk}, \mathsf{quote}, \sigma, c) == 1 \wedge \mathsf{quote}.\mathcal{H}.\mathsf{Conf} \in \mathsf{CONF}\}$$

At the end of the global setup, we set $\mathsf{ppar} := (N_T, N_{VM}, \mathsf{CONF}, \mathsf{ppar}_{\mathsf{VC}}, CRS, x_{ZK})$ and $\mathsf{spar} := \tau$.

Hypervisor Setup. We instantiate the algorithm $\{\mathcal{H}.\mathsf{pk}, \mathcal{H}.\mathsf{sk}, \mathcal{H}.\mathsf{Conf}\} \leftarrow \mathsf{HSetup}(\mathsf{ppar})$ as follows. To begin the hypervisor will require two pairs of keys, one for the AKE protocol, the other, for attestation, as follows:

$$(\mathcal{H}.\mathsf{pk}, \mathcal{H}.\mathsf{sk}) \leftarrow \mathsf{AKE.KGen}(\mathsf{ppar}) \text{ and } (\mathsf{AK.pk}, \mathsf{AK.sk}) \leftarrow \mathsf{SigKGen}(\mathsf{ppar})$$

The hypervisor picks a configuration $\mathcal{H}.\mathsf{Conf} \xleftarrow{r} \mathsf{CONF}$ uniformly at random and sets $\mathcal{H}.\mathsf{state} = \emptyset$.

Tenant Setup. The tenants generate TKGen long-term keys $\{T.\mathsf{pk}, T.\mathsf{sk}\}$ which are, in fact, AKE keys $(T.\mathsf{pk}, T.\mathsf{sk}) \leftarrow \mathsf{AKE.KGen}(\mathsf{ppar})$.

4.2 Registration

A tenant and a hypervisor run the following algorithm to register a VM of a given description on the given hypervisor: $\{(VM, \mathsf{VAK.pk}, \mathsf{VAK.sk}), \mathcal{H}.\mathsf{state}\} \cup \perp \leftarrow \mathsf{VMReg}(\mathcal{H}, T.\mathsf{sk}, \mathsf{VMdesc})$.

As depicted in Fig. 3, when a registration request is made, $\mathcal{H}$ and T run AKE.AKE (using their long-term credentials) to establish a secure channel, over which they can communicate in a confidential and authentic manner. Over this secure channel, T requests the registration of a VM with description VMdesc. The hypervisor verifies it can still allow tenants to register a new VM (w.r.t. N_{VM}). If this is not so, the algorithm aborts. Otherwise, the hypervisor generates attestation (signature) keys for the newly-registered VM: $(\mathsf{VAK.sk}, \mathsf{VAK.pk}) \leftarrow \mathsf{SigKGen}(\mathsf{ppar})$. The keys VAK.sk and $T.\mathsf{pk}$ will be stored in the vTPM corresponding to the new VM.

Once the VM is created, $\mathcal{H}$ updates its internal state $\mathcal{H}.\mathsf{state}$ with entries $(VM, \mathsf{VAK.pk}, T)$. Still over the secure channel, the hypervisor sends the VM handle VM and public keys VAK.pk to T.

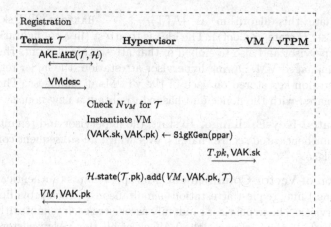

Fig. 3. Registration

4.3 Hypervisor Attestation

```
Hypervisor Attestation

Tenant T                        Hypervisor                    TPM
              AKE.AKE(T, H)
         ←─────────────────→

              nonce_T
         ───────────────────→
              Wait until TPM is available
              i_T ← {1, 2, ..., (N_T)}
              link_T ← H.state(T.pk)
              v ← (..., (nonce_T|link_T)^{i_T}, ...)^{N_T}
              c, aux ← VC.Com(v)
                                         c
                                 ───────────────────→
                                         σ ← SigSig(AK.sk, quote, c)
                                     quote, σ
                                 ←───────────────────
              π_{i_T} ← VC.Open(c, i_T, aux)
              w_{ZK} ← SnarkCirc(AK.pk, quote, σ, c, CONF)
              π_{ZK} ← ZKP.Prove(CRS, R, x_{ZK}, w_{ZK})
              π_{ZK}, π_{i_T}, c, i_T
         ←─────────────────────
ATT_{H,T} ← (π_{ZK}, π_{i_T}, c, i_T)
```

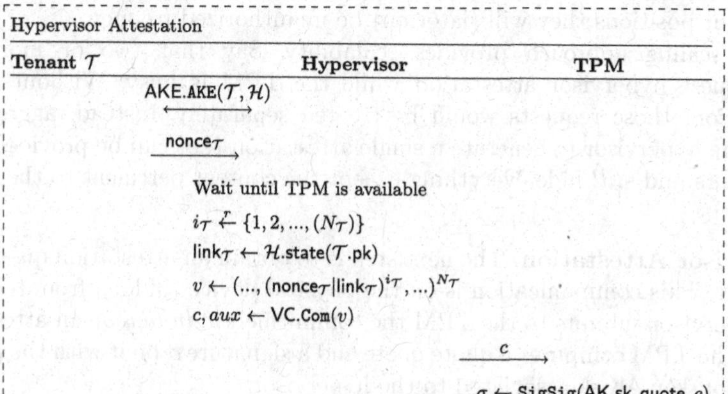

Fig. 4. Hypervisor Attestation upon the i-th tenant's request. However, multiple requests can be batched by aggregating all the nonces through the commitment.

We instantiate this algorithm as $\{\text{ATT}_{\mathcal{H},\mathcal{T}}\} \leftarrow \text{HAttest}\langle \mathcal{T}(\mathcal{T}.\text{sk}, \text{nonce}_\mathcal{T}),$ $\mathcal{H}(\mathcal{H}.\text{sk}, \text{AK}.\text{sk}, \mathcal{H}.\text{state}, \mathcal{H}.\text{Conf})\rangle$. The idea is to attest (in a configuration-hiding way) the hypervisor and also to embed in that attestation elements that characterise each managed VM. During hypervisor attestation, the latter retrieves the public attestation-key stored on each of the vTPMs it manages[2]. Those values are concatenated with the nonce and hashed to obtain a new nonce.

Authenticated Key-Exchange. To start, the hypervisor and tenant establish a mutually-authenticated secure channel, over which all subsequent communication takes place.

Preparation of Vector Commitment. Multiple tenants (authenticated over a secure channel) may request attestations simultaneously, each providing a nonce to the hypervisor. The hypervisor randomly associates each tenant with an index $i \in \{1, \ldots N_\mathcal{T}\}$. It then retrieves the VAK.pk of all the VMs registered by the tenant(s) requesting an attestation and concatenates, for each tenant, the nonce that tenant provided and the VAK.pk of all the VMs the latter owns. The list of VAK.pk per tenant constitutes its linking information (link in Fig. 4). If less than $N_\mathcal{T}$ request an attestation, empty position in the vector are filled with random values, and the commitment is always of constant size.

The vector commitment must be hiding, as tenants should learn no information about positions they will (later on) be unauthorized to open.

Our scaling approach provides scalability. Say that two or more tenants request hypervisor attestation while the TPM is busy. Without nonce-aggregation, those requests would be treated separately. Instead, aggregation allows the hypervisor to generate a single attestation that can be provided to all the tenants and *still* hide everything except the content pertinent to the tenant itself.

Hypervisor Attestation. The next step is to obtain an attestation quote from the TPM. This communication is on the physical device (hidden from tenants). The hypervisor submits to the TPM the commitment c *in lieu of* an attestation nonce. The TPM computes a quote quote and a signature σ on it with the private attestation key AK.sk associated to the hypervisor.

Proof of Attestation. The hypervisor, having received the quote and signature computes a proof of ownership of a valid attestation. Note that the attestation quote (and corresponding signature) reveal the configuration of the hypervisor, which we want to hide from the tenants. Thus, the hypervisor proves that it has a valid attestation from the TPM for a configuration within the set CONF, with respect to nonce c, *i.e.*, it needs to compute:

$\text{ZK-SNARK}\{(\text{quote}, \sigma) : \text{SigVer}(\text{AK}.\text{pk}, \text{quote}, \sigma, c) == 1 \wedge \text{quote}.\mathcal{H}.\text{Conf} \in \text{CONF}\}$

We can compile this computation into an arithmetic circuit. Then, a ZK-SNARK will allow the hypervisor to prove it has run this algorithm for some

---

[2] This idea appears in [1] but there the instantiation consists of simply including a set of public keys into the nonce. This achieves layer-linking but no inter-tenant privacy. In our approach, the instantiation requires vector commitments and ZK-SNARKs.

public set CONF, the nonce c, with respect to AK.pk, and that the algorithm output 1, all this without revealing the quote quote nor the signature σ.

Opening. Finally, the hypervisor needs to provide to each tenant its partial vector-commitment opening (*i.e.*, each tenant can only open the position corresponding to the index the hypervisor associated with that tenant at the beginning of its attestation). The hypervisor sets, for each tenant $\text{ATT}_{\mathcal{H},\mathcal{T}}$ to contain: the proof of attestation π_{ZK}, the vector commitment c; the position i on which the tenant is placed; and the opening information π_t for that position.

4.4 VM Attestation

This algorithm $\{\text{ATT}_{VM}\} \leftarrow \text{VMAttest}(VM(\text{VAK.sk}, \text{VAK.pk}), \mathcal{T}(\mathcal{T}.\text{sk}, \text{nonce}))$ (Fig. 5) generates a quote that only the tenant owning the VM can actually see and verify. The tenant and VM run an AKE protocol to establish a secure channel, over which $\mathcal{T}$ requests an attestation and forwards a nonce. The VM retrieves the linking information (VAK.pk) and concatenates it with the nonce to obtain a value later hashed to lkaux. Then, the VM requests a signed quote for lkaux and forwards the response to the tenant over the secure channel.

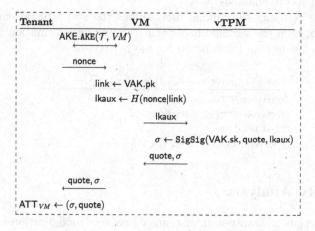

Fig. 5. VM Attestation

4.5 Verification

Hypervisor Attestation Verification. We instantiate the algorithm $\{0,1\} \leftarrow$ VfHAttest($\text{ATT}_{\mathcal{H},\mathcal{T}}, \text{nonce}_{\mathcal{T}}, \text{link}_{\mathcal{T}}$) as depicted in Fig. 6a. The tenant opens the commitment c at the relevant index, then checks that it opens to the concatenation of the nonce $\text{nonce}_{\mathcal{T}}$ and linking information $\text{link}_{\mathcal{T}}$ (if this fails, the algorithm outputs 0). Then the tenant verifies the ZK-SNARK proof and outputs 1 if both verifications succeed.

Verification of VM Attestation. In this case, the verification is straightforward, as the tenant only retrieves the lkaux value and checks that the signature and received quote verify.

VfHAttest(ATT$_{\mathcal{H},\mathcal{T}}$, nonce$_{\mathcal{T}}$, link$_{\mathcal{T}}$) → {0, 1} :	VfVMAttest(ATT$_{VM}$, nonce, link) → {0, 1} :
Parse ATT$_{\mathcal{H},\mathcal{T}}$ as $(\pi_{ZK}, \pi_{i_{\mathcal{T}}}, c, i_{\mathcal{T}})$	Parse ATT$_{VM}$ as (quote, σ)
VC.Ver$((\text{nonce}_{\mathcal{T}} \| \text{link}_{\mathcal{T}}), c, i_{\mathcal{T}}, \pi_{i_{\mathcal{T}}})$	lkaux ← H(nonce $\|$ link)
ZKP.SkVer$(CRS, R, x_{ZK}, \pi_{ZK})$	SigVer(VAK.pk, quote, σ, lkaux)
If all verification pass output 1, otherwise 0	If all verifications work output 1, otherwise 0
(a) Hypervisor	(b) VM

Fig. 6. Verification

Linking Attestations. The link algorithm {0, 1} ← Link(ATT$_{\mathcal{H},\mathcal{T}}$, nonce$_{\mathcal{T}}$, link$_{\mathcal{T}}$, ATT$_{VM}$, nonce, link) will attempt to link the hypervisor and the VM attestation given in input. Any party in possession of the input values can run the linking – however, note that attestation quotes are only received over mutually-authenticated secure channels.

The party verifying the linking first verifies the two attestations – if both come through, then the verifier checks that the linking information for the VM is included in the linking information for the hypervisor.

Link(ATT$_{\mathcal{H},\mathcal{T}}$, nonce$_{\mathcal{T}}$, link$_{\mathcal{T}}$, ATT$_{VM}$, nonce, link) → {0, 1}:
VfHAttest(ATT$_{\mathcal{H},\mathcal{T}}$, nonce$_{\mathcal{T}}$, link$_{\mathcal{T}}$)
VfVMAttest(ATT$_{VM}$, nonce, link)
Check link ∈ link$_{\mathcal{T}}$
If all verifications work output 1, otherwise 0

5   Security Analysis

Our construction guarantees inter-tenant privacy, configuration-hiding, and layer-linking. The latter property is defined by [1], and we do not reiterate its syntax. Below, we give concrete statements characterizing the security of our scheme, leaving the proofs to the full version [2]. The non-standard assumptions of partner-hiding AKE and collision-resistant vector commitments are required for inter-tenant privacy and layer-linking respectively, and are presented in Appendices A and B. Note that the TLS 1.3 protocol is initiator-hiding (Theorem 1) and Merkle-tree-based vector commitment schemes are collision-resistant (Theorem 3), as we prove in the full version [2].

Theorem 1 (Inter-tenant privacy). *The* PP-MTA *scheme provides inter-tenant privacy given the use of: an initiator-hiding and (minimally) ACCE-security of the AKE protocol and a hiding vector commitment. More formally, if* *there exists an adversary $\mathcal{A}$ that breaks the inter-tenant privacy of* PP-MTA *with advantage* $\mathsf{Adv}_{\text{PP-MTA}}^{\text{TPriv}}(\mathcal{A})$, *then there exist adversaries* $\mathcal{B}_1, \ldots, \mathcal{B}_4$ *such that:*

$$\mathsf{Adv}_{\text{PP-MTA}}^{\text{TPriv}}(\mathcal{A}) \leq \mathsf{Adv}_{\text{AKE}}^{\text{IHide}}(\mathcal{B}_1) + N_{\mathcal{T}} \cdot \mathsf{Adv}_{\text{AKE}}^{\text{Auth}}(\mathcal{B}_2)$$

$$+ q_{\text{oHAttest}} \cdot \mathsf{Adv}_{\text{AKE}}^{\text{SC}}(\mathcal{B}_3) + q_{\text{HAttest}^*} \cdot \mathsf{Adv}_{\text{VC}}^{\text{VCHide}}(\mathcal{B}_4),$$

where q_{oHAttest} *represents the number of queries the adversary makes to the* oHAttest *oracle, and* q_{HAttest^*} *is the number of honest hypervisor-attestation sessions started by the adversary (on its own behalf) in its* PP-MTA *game.*

Theorem 2 (Configuration hiding). *The PP-MTA scheme is configuration hiding if:* ZK-SNARK *is zero-knowledge and* CONF *is large (exponential size in the length of the security parameter). More formally, if there exists an adversary $\mathcal{A}$ that breaks the inter-tenant privacy of* PP-MTA *with* $\mathsf{Adv}_{\text{PP-MTA}}^{\text{CHid}}(\mathcal{A})$, *then there exists adversary $\mathcal{B}$ such that:* $\mathsf{Adv}_{\text{PP-MTA}}^{\text{CHid}}(\mathcal{A}) \leq q_{\text{oHAttest}} \cdot \mathsf{Adv}_{\text{ZK-SNARK}}^{\text{ZK}}(\mathcal{A})$ *where* q_{oHAttest} *is the number of queries $\mathcal{A}$ makes to the hypervisor-attestation algorithm.*

Theorem 3 (Linkability security). *The PP-MTA scheme has linkability security if: the hash function H and* VC *are collision resistant, the* ZK-SNARK *is sound, and the signature scheme* SIG=(SigKGen, SigSig, SigVer) *is EUF-CMA. More formally, if there exists an adversary $\mathcal{A}$ that breaks the linkability security of* PP-MTA *with* $\mathsf{Adv}_{\text{PP-MTA}}^{\text{Link}}(\mathcal{A})$, *then there exist adversaries* $\mathcal{B}_1, \ldots, \mathcal{B}_5$ *such that:*

$$\mathsf{Adv}_{\text{PP-MTA}}^{\text{Link}}(\mathcal{A}) \leq \frac{1}{N_{\mathcal{P}}} + \mathsf{Adv}_{\text{H}}^{\text{Coll}}(\mathcal{B}_1) + \mathsf{Adv}_{\text{VC}}^{\text{Coll}}(\mathcal{B}_2)$$

$$+ 2 \cdot (N_{VM} \cdot \mathsf{Adv}_{\text{VC}}^{\text{VCBind}}(\mathcal{B}_3) + \mathsf{Adv}_{\text{ZK-SNARK}}^{\text{ZK}}(\mathcal{B}_4) + \mathsf{Adv}_{\text{Sig}}^{\text{EUF-CMA}}(\mathcal{B}_5))$$

where q_{att} *is the number of queries $\mathcal{A}$ makes to the* oHAttest *and* oVMAttest *oracles, and n is the size of committed vectors.*

6   Implementation

We implemented the scheme described in Sect. 4. We instantiated the ZK-SNARK as in [13] and used a Merkle-tree-based vector commitment scheme (combined with a basic hash-based commitment for hiding).

Figure 7 compares a traditional attestation and our hypervisor attestation. We can see that the ZK-SNARK adds a significant overhead but the total time is still low enough (2.4 s) for practical use. This is especially true with a high number of tenants requests (like in 5G and beyond). With a classic sequential processing of the requests it would take minutes to answer all the tenants whereas in our case despite having a relatively high base computing time, the attestation scales very well as depicted on Fig. 7a. Attestation time increases by only 8% for a tenant requests increase of 900%. Additional results and experimental setup are available in the extended version [2].

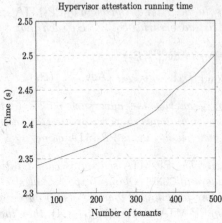

Hypervisor attestation running time

Attestation	Mean	Median
Traditional (s)	0.94	0.94
Hypervisor (s)	2.40	2.40
SNARK (s)	1.46	1.46
Commitment (ms)	9.06	8.98

Verification	Mean	Median
Traditional (ms)	2.42	2.36
Hypervisor (ms)	25.06	25.05
SNARK (ms)	25.02	24.99
Commitment (ms)	0.043	0.063

(a) Scaling (configuration set of size 128).   (b) Time to perform attestation

Fig. 7. Benchmarks

7   Conclusion and Discussion

In this work, we proposed a scalable and efficient TPM attestation scheme for multi-tenant environments. Our scheme does not require modification to the TPM nor unrealistic trust assumptions (e.g., Attestation proxy). It provides strong privacy for both tenants and the hypervisor, and guarantees layer-binding.

Our scheme achieves privacy by relying on vector commitment and ZK-SNARK. The latter primitive incurs a relatively high overhead but it remains stable even with a drastically high number of attestation requests (which is the case in multi-tenant environments like 5G) without requiring any TPM modification. In addition, if in some cases the configuration hiding property is not needed – but still have a high number of attestation requests –, due to the modularity of our construction, our scheme can still work efficiently by simply omitting the ZK-SNARK module.

Acknowledgements. We thank the anonymous reviewers for their constructive comments. This study was partially supported by the French ANR, grant 18-CE39-0019 (MobiS5).

A   Collision-Resistance of Vector Commitment

The goal of a malicious hypervisor could be to find a collision by keeping the values of a given tenant with its correct index but modifying the other positions to find a collision with a previous committed vector. An other attack could also happened if the nonce of a given tenant would match with a previous nonce. In that case, the hypervisor could simply send the old attestation with the same proof of membership in the vector. Finally, the malicious hypervisor could also compute a collision which occurs with probability $\frac{q}{2^{n+1}}$ for q attestation queries and vector commitment of size n.

We thus define the collision resistance of vector commitment to avoid the above attacks. We propose a security game, $G_{\mathsf{VC-Coll}}(\lambda, n)$ (see Fig. 8a), to define the collision resistance of vector commitment. This game is the same as for hash functions but for vector commitment.

Definition 3 (VC collision-resistance). *We say that* VC *is* (λ, n)−*collision resistant if for all adversary* $\mathcal{A}$, *the probability of winning game* $G_{\mathsf{VC-Coll}}(\lambda, n)$ *is negligible.*

Game $G_{\mathsf{VC-Coll}}(\lambda, n)$
$\{\mathsf{ppar}\} \leftarrow \mathsf{VC.Setup}(1^\lambda, n)$
$(v, v') \leftarrow \mathcal{A}(\mathsf{ppar})$
$\mathcal{A}$ wins iff.: $\exists i$ such that $v[i] \neq v'[i]$ and $\mathsf{VC.Com}(v) = \mathsf{VC.Com}(v')$

(a) VC Collision Resistance

Game $G_{\mathsf{InitHide}}(\lambda, N_\mathcal{P})$
Game setup for all $\mathcal{P} \in \mathbb{P}$ with $|\mathbb{P}| = N_\mathcal{P}$
$b \xleftarrow{} \{0, 1\}$
$\mathsf{state} \leftarrow \mathcal{A}^{\mathsf{oNewSession}(\cdot,\cdot,\cdot),\mathsf{oSend}(\cdot,\cdot),\mathsf{oReveal}(\cdot)}(1^\lambda)$
$\mathsf{state} \leftarrow \mathcal{A}^{\mathsf{oNewSession}_{b,\mathsf{Initiator}}(\cdot,\cdot),\mathsf{oSend}_b(\cdot,\cdot)}(1^\lambda, \mathsf{state})$
$d \leftarrow \mathcal{A}^{\mathsf{oNewSession}(\cdot,\cdot,\cdot),\mathsf{oSend}(\cdot,\cdot),\mathsf{oReveal}(\cdot)}(1^\lambda)$
$\mathcal{A}$ wins iff.: $d = b$

(b) Initiator hiding

Fig. 8. The security games

B Security of Partner-Hiding

Our solution requires secure channels, constructed from AKE schemes. Indeed, consider the VM attestation algorithm from Sect. 4. The tenant and VM use a mutually-authenticated AKE to establish a secure channel over which attestation data is sent. This is sufficient to ensure that attestation quotes remain confidential for an adversary that controls neither the tenant nor the TPM. However, channel-security is insufficient for inter-tenant privacy, where an adversary (possibly a collusion of tenants) must be unable to know if another tenant's VMs exist, or not, on the same machine as the adversary's. With regular AKE, this cannot be guaranteed even with mutual authentication. We require a stronger assumption, which we dub *Partner-Hiding*, in which an adversary not in possession of the long-term credentials of either endpoint cannot learn whether it faces a real or simulated entity as one endpoint.

Security Game. We consider two-party AKE protocols, for which the endpoints are parties $\mathcal{P} \in \mathbb{P}$. The protocol runs in *sessions* between an *instance* of one endpoint and an instance of the other. We denote i-th instance of party $\mathcal{P}$ as $\pi_\mathcal{P}^i$. Each $\mathcal{P}$ is associated with a tuple of long-term parameters $(\mathsf{sk}, \mathsf{pk})$ and each instance keeps track of the following *attributes*:

- $\pi_\mathcal{P}^i.\mathsf{sid}$: the session identifier of instance $\pi_\mathcal{P}^i$ is a concatenation of session-specific values, which might be public (included in public information, such as the transcript) or secret. The session identifier is protocol-specific.

- $\pi_{\mathcal{P}}^i$.pid: the partner identifier of instance $\pi_{\mathcal{P}}^i$, which must be a party $\mathcal{Q} \in \mathbb{P} \backslash \mathcal{P}$.
- $\pi_{\mathcal{P}}^i.\alpha$: the acceptance flag α takes three values: $\bot$ (which stands for unset), 0 (reject), and 1 (accept). It models the result of the authentication performed by $\pi_{\mathcal{P}}^i$.pid.
- $\pi_{\mathcal{P}}^i$.k: the session key of instance $\pi_{\mathcal{P}}^i$, which starts out as equal to a special symbol $\bot$, but may take a true value once that key has been computed.

The AKE protocol is run between an *initiator* (*i.e.*, the party instance that starts the protocol) and the *responder* (*i.e.*, the party instance that goes second).

We define Partner-Hiding in terms of an adversary $\mathcal{A}$ that is a Person-in-the-Middle. The security game will, in a nutshell, guarantee that an adversary is unable to tell the difference between an interaction with a real, uncorrupted party, and an interaction with a simulator (which only has access to the security parameter, but not to any of the private keys generated in the game). Whereas this weak form of partner-hiding suffices for our needs, we also provide in the appendix a stronger notion, in which arbitrary corruptions are possible.

In our weak partner-hiding game, the adversary can control honest parties and instances by means of oracles:

- $\pi_{\mathcal{P}}^i \leftarrow$ oNewSession($\mathcal{P}, \mathcal{Q}$, role): the (honest) session creation oracle will initiate a new instance $\pi_{\mathcal{P}}^i$ with partner identifier $\pi_{\mathcal{P}}^i$.pid $= \mathcal{Q}$, such that $\pi_{\mathcal{P}}^i$ plays the role designated by role (either initiator or responder) in its session.
- $m^* \leftarrow$ oSend($\pi_{\mathcal{P}}^i, m$): the (honest) sending oracle models sending message m to an already-existent instance $\pi_{\mathcal{P}}^i$. It is expected that $\pi_{\mathcal{P}}^i$ returns a message m^*, which is the protocol-specific reply (potentially an error symbol $\bot$) as a response. A special $m =$ Start sent to a instance of an initiator is used to jump-start the session (thus yielding m^* as the first message of the actual session).
- $k \leftarrow$ oReveal($\pi_{\mathcal{P}}^i$): the revelation oracle allows the adversary to learn already-established session keys k.
- $\pi_{\mathcal{P}}^i \leftarrow$ oNewSession$_{b,\text{role}}(\mathcal{P}, \mathcal{Q})$: this is the left-or-right version of the oNewSession oracle above, for which the roles will be restricted according to which notion we want to guarantee between initiator- and responder-hiding. If $b = 0$, this oracle creates an instance of the party $\mathcal{P}$, with partner identifier $\mathcal{Q}$, such that $\mathcal{P}$ will have a role as either the initiator or the responder of the session. On the i-th call to the oracle oNewSession$_b(\mathcal{P}, *)$, the created instance will be indexed as $\pi_{\mathcal{P}}^i$. The oracle forwards the handle $\pi_{\mathcal{P}}^i$ to the adversary. If $b = 1$, the oracle call is forwarded to a simulator Sim, which is only given the security parameter, but no party information.
- $m^* \leftarrow$ oSend$_b(\pi_{\mathcal{P}}^i, m)$: this left-or-right version of the sending oracle allows the message m to be either forwarded to $\pi_{\mathcal{P}}^i$ (if $b = 0$) or to the simulator Sim otherwise. In both cases the adversary expects a message m^*. As before, a special message $m =$ Start will jump-start the session.

The security game begins with the setup of all the honest parties $\mathcal{P} \in \mathbb{P}$. The adversary receives all the public keys, whereas the challenger keeps track of all the private keys. The simulator will be given no information at all, apart from the security parameter.

There are two phases to the game. In the learning phase, the adversary will use the honest session-creation and sending oracles, as well as the session-key revelation oracle, in order to observe honest sessions and interact with the honest parties.

In the second phase of the game, the adversary gains access only to the left-or-right instance-creation and sending oracles. We distinguish between the two following notions:

– **Initiator-hiding.** In this case, the oNewSession$_{b,\text{role}}$ oracle has role set to Initiator. Hence, in the challenge phase, the adversary will only be able to create new instances that are protocol initiators.
– **Responder-hiding.** Conversely, in this case oNewSession$_{b,\text{role}}$ oracle has role set to Responder. Hence, in the challenge phase, the adversary will only be able to create new instances that are protocol responders.

Finally, the adversary will be allowed a final learning phase, identical to the first one. When the adversary is ready to end the game, it will output a bit d, which will be its guess for the bit b used by the challenger during the challenge phase.

It should be noted that at the transition to each new phase, all ongoing sessions are aborted.

Definition 4 (Initiator-Hiding security). *Consider an authenticated key-exchange protocol* AKE. *This protocol is* $(N_{\mathcal{P}}, q_{\text{oNewSession}}, q_{\text{oNewSession}_{b,\text{Role}}}, \epsilon)$-*initiator hiding if for any PPT adversary* $\mathcal{A}$ *making at most* $q_{\text{oNewSession}}$ *queries to the (learning)* oNewSession *oracle and at most* $q_{\text{oNewSession}_{b,\text{Role}}}$ *queries to the (challenge)* oNewSession$_{b,\text{role}}$ *oracle, if we denote* $\text{Adv}_{\text{AKE}}^{\text{IHide}}(\mathcal{A}) := \left|\Pr[\mathcal{A} \text{ wins } G_{\text{InitHide}}(\lambda, N_{\mathcal{P}})] - \frac{1}{2}\right|$, *then it holds that:*
$$\text{Adv}_{\text{AKE}}^{\text{IHide}}(\mathcal{A}) \leq \epsilon.$$
The value $\text{Adv}_{\text{AKE}}^{\text{IHide}}(\mathcal{A})$ *is the* advantage *of adversary* $\mathcal{A}$. *If* ϵ *is asymptotically negligible in the security parameter, then we call the authenticated key-exchange protocol* initiator-hiding.

References

1. Arfaoui, G., et al.: A cryptographic view of deep-attestation, or how to do provably-secure layer-linking. In: ACNS 2022 (2022)
2. Arfaoui, G., Jacques, T., Lacoste, M., Onete, C., Robert, L.: Privacy-preserving Attestation for Virtualized Network Infrastructures. Cryptology ePrint Archive, Paper 2023/735 (2023)
3. Berger, S., Goldman, K., Pendarakis, D., Safford, D., Valdez, E., Zohar, M.: Scalable attestation: a step toward secure and trusted clouds. In: IC2E (2015)
4. Bitansky, N., Canetti, R., Chiesa, A., Tromer, E.: From extractable collision resistance to succinct non-interactive arguments of knowledge, and back again. In: ITCS (2012)

5. Brickell, E., Camenisch, J., Chen, L.: Direct anonymous attestation. In: CCS 2004 (2004)
6. Catalano, D., Fiore, D.: Vector commitments and their applications. In: PKC (2013)
7. Chen, L., Landfermann, R., Löhr, H., Rohe, M., Sadeghi, A.R., Stüble, C.: A protocol for property-based attestation. In: ACM STC (2006)
8. Chen, L., Löhr, H., Manulis, M., Sadeghi, A.R.: Property-based attestation without a trusted third party. In: ISC (2008)
9. Eckel, M., Fuchs, A., Repp, J., Springer, M.: Secure attestation of virtualized environments. In: Hölbl, M., Rannenberg, K., Welzer, T. (eds.) ICT (2020)
10. ETSI: GS NFV-SEC 007 v1.1.1. Technical report (2017)
11. Fajiang, Y., Jing, C., Yang, X., Jiacheng, Z., Yangdi, Z.: An efficient anonymous remote attestation scheme for trusted computing based on improved CPK. Electron. Commerce Res. **19**, 689–718 (2019)
12. Foy, K.: Keylime software is deployed to IBM cloud (2021)
13. Groth, J.: On the size of pairing-based non-interactive arguments. In: Fischlin, M., Coron, J.-S. (eds.) EUROCRYPT 2016. LNCS, vol. 9666, pp. 305–326. Springer, Heidelberg (2016). https://doi.org/10.1007/978-3-662-49896-5_11
14. Keylime dev: Keylime (2022)
15. Larsen, B., Debes, H.B., Giannetsos, T.: Cloudvaults: integrating trust extensions into system integrity verification for cloud-based environments. In: Boureanu, I., et al. (eds.) ESORICS 2020. LNCS, vol. 12580, pp. 197–220. Springer, Cham (2020). https://doi.org/10.1007/978-3-030-66504-3_12
16. Lauer, H., Kuntze, N.: Hypervisor-based attestation of virtual environments. In: UIC-ATC (2016)
17. Poritz, J.A., Schunter, M., Herreweghen, E.V., Waidner, M.: Property attestation – scalable and privacy-friendly security assessment of peer computers. Technical report, IBM (2004)
18. Ruan, A., Martin, A.: Repcloud: achieving fine-grained cloud TCB attestation with reputation systems. In: STC (2011)
19. Sadeghi, A.R., Stüble, C.: Property-based attestation for computing platforms: caring about properties, not mechanisms. In: NSPW (2004)
20. Santos, N., Rodrigues, R., Gummadi, K.P., Saroiu, S.: Policy-Sealed data: a new abstraction for building trusted cloud services. In: USENIX Security (2012)
21. Schear, N., Cable, P.T., Moyer, T.M., Richard, B., Rudd, R.: Bootstrapping and maintaining trust in the cloud. In: ACSAC (2016)
22. Schiffman, J., Moyer, T., Vijayakumar, H., Jaeger, T., McDaniel, P.: Seeding clouds with trust anchors. In: CCSW (2010)
23. TCG: Virtualized trusted platform architecture specification. Technical report (2011)
24. Xin, S., Zhao, Y., Li, Y.: Property-based remote attestation oriented to cloud computing. In: CIS (2011)
25. Zhang, T., Lee, R.B.: Cloudmonatt: an architecture for security health monitoring and attestation of virtual machines in cloud computing. In: ISCA (2015)

An Empirical Study of the Imbalance Issue in Software Vulnerability Detection

Yuejun Guo[1] , Qiang Hu[2]([✉]) , Qiang Tang[1] , and Yves Le Traon[2]

[1] ITIS, Luxembourg Institute of Science and Technology, Esch-sur-Alzette, Luxembourg
{yuejun.guo,qiang.tang}@list.lu

[2] SnT, University of Luxembourg, Luxembourg City, Luxembourg
{qiang.hu,yves.letraon}@uni.lu

Abstract. Vulnerability detection is crucial to protect software security. Nowadays, deep learning (DL) is the most promising technique to automate this detection task, leveraging its superior ability to extract patterns and representations within extensive code volumes. Despite its promise, DL-based vulnerability detection remains in its early stages, with model performance exhibiting variability across datasets. Drawing insights from other well-explored application areas like computer vision, we conjecture that the imbalance issue (the number of vulnerable code is extremely small) is at the core of the phenomenon. To validate this, we conduct a comprehensive empirical study involving nine open-source datasets and two state-of-the-art DL models. The results confirm our conjecture. We also obtain insightful findings on how existing imbalance solutions perform in vulnerability detection. It turns out that these solutions perform differently as well across datasets and evaluation metrics. Specifically: 1) *Focal loss* is more suitable to improve the precision, 2) *mean false error* and *class-balanced loss* encourages the recall, and 3) *random over-sampling* facilitates the F1-measure. However, none of them excels across all metrics. To delve deeper, we explore external influences on these solutions and offer insights for developing new solutions.

Keywords: Software security · Vulnerability detection · Deep learning · Imbalance

1 Introduction

The existence of software vulnerability is an inevitable risk in the software development life cycle, which raises significant concern since the vulnerability can be exploited by cybercriminals to run malicious code, install malware, and steal sensitive data. Discovering vulnerabilities in advance of the final deployment is ever required to enhance software security.

This work is funded by the European Union's Horizon Research and Innovation Programme under Grant Agreement n°101070303.

Manually identifying a function as vulnerable or not is tough concerning the required domain expertise and time. Fortunately, the rapid progress of deep learning (DL) largely automates this process [42]. In this paper, we are interested in applying DL to software vulnerability detection at the function level, which enables early detection of vulnerabilities during the programming stage. Figure 1 shows an example of a vulnerable function tagged with ID CVE-2017-7597[1]. The detailed information is that tif_dirread.c in LibTIFF 4.0.7 has an "outside the range of representable values of type float" undefined behavior issue, which might allow remote attackers to cause a denial of service (application crash) or possibly have unspecified other impacts via a crafted image.

```
1    static enum TIFFReadDirEntryErr
2 ▾  TIFFReadDirEntryCheckedRational (TIFF * tif, TIFFDirEntry * direntry,
3 ▾                      double *value){
4      UInt64Aligned_t m;
5      assert (sizeof (double) == 8);
6      assert (sizeof (uint64) == 8);
7      assert (sizeof (uint32) == 4);
8 ▾    if (!(tif->tif_flags & TIFF_BIGTIFF)){
9          enum TIFFReadDirEntryErr err;
10         uint32 offset = direntry->tdir_offset.toff_long;
11         if (tif->tif_flags & TIFF_SWAB)
12       TIFFSwabLong (&offset);
13         err = TIFFReadDirEntryData (tif, offset, 8, m.i);
14         if (err != TIFFReadDirEntryErrOk)
15       return (err);
16       }
17     else
18       m.l = direntry->tdir_offset.toff_long8;
19     if (tif->tif_flags & TIFF_SWAB)
20       TIFFSwabArrayOfLong (m.i, 2);
21     if (m.i[0] == 0)
22       *value = 0.0;
23     else
24       *value = (double) m.i[0] / (double) m.i[1];
25     return (TIFFReadDirEntryErrOk);
26   }
```

Fig. 1. An example of vulnerable code: a C-language function from the LibTIFF project [41]. This function is tagged with the "Denial of Service" vulnerability in the Lin2018 dataset (please refer to Sect. 4.1 for more details). The code framed in a red rectangle highlights a concern about handling cases of division by zero when $m.i[1] == 0$.

Although various DL models [9,17,19,37] have been designed for vulnerability detection, the imbalance issue that causes a high false positive rate or false negative rate [10] is usually ignored. In this paper, "imbalance" refers to the numeral difference where the number of vulnerable code is much less than secure code in a dataset. In practice, software vulnerabilities do exist but rarely (e.g., 1 vulnerability in every 500 C-language functions) in source code programmed by experienced software developers. This imbalance problem is widely studied in other areas, such as computer vision (CV) and natural language processing

---

[1] https://www.cvedetails.com/cve/CVE-2017-7597/?q=CVE-2017-7597.

(NLP), and to tackle it, both data and model-level methods have been proposed. The main idea is to put more importance on the minority set. Data-level methods straightforwardly down-sample [15] the majority set or over-sample [55] the minority set to ensure the numeral balance of data. Model-level approaches focus on the loss function [13,32] that guides the training procedure via adjusting the weights of majority and minority sets.

Although DL-based vulnerability detection is gaining attention, how the imbalance issue affects the "performance" of DL models in this specific area is still an open question. What makes things more complex is that, the model performance is evaluated by various metrics in the literature [26], such as accuracy [35], precision, and false positive rate. This makes it very difficult to compare their performance. For instance, the state-of-the-art (SOTA) model Code-BERT [35] is reported to achieve over 60% detection accuracy, while the false negative rate is 70%. The model is acceptable if accuracy is the evaluation criterion but useless in the case of a false negative rate.

In this paper, we conduct a comprehensive study on the imbalance issue in DL-based vulnerability detection. Through a series of experiments, our findings are summarized as follows. First of all, our first experimental results show that the imbalance problem tends to cause a model to gain a relatively low loss on secure code compared to the vulnerable one during the training procedure. Thus, The false negative rate is high.

Second, we experiment on how the imbalance solutions adapted from the CV and NLP domains perform in vulnerability detection. Our results show that:

- Compared to accuracy and false positive rate, precision, recall, and F1-measure are more informative when evaluating a DL model for vulnerability detection.
- None of the existing solutions from other domains performs perfectly across all selected datasets and models. Model-level solutions are beneficial to precision and recall. Data level solutions are more helpful to F1-measure.

Third, apart from the designed methodology, we explore how external factors affect the effectiveness of existing solutions, where these factors come from source code, such as the appearance of vulnerability types in the training procedure and test time and the detection difficulty of vulnerable code. Our experiment results show that external factors, such as the absence of vulnerabilities, identification difficulty of certain vulnerability types, and data distribution need to be considered when designing a new solution specifically for vulnerability detection.

For the readers to validate our findings, the experiment datasets and artifacts (including all solutions) for reproduction are made available on Git[2].

2   Background and Related Work

2.1   Software Vulnerability Detection

A software vulnerability is a security flaw and glitch found in source code. Detecting vulnerabilities has attracted considerable interest in the security community.

---

[2] https://github.com/testing-cs/vulnerability-detection.git

Manually checking source code is straightforward, but even for experts, this task is tedious and subjective because of great code complexity and diverse programming languages. At a higher level, there is the popular fuzzing [1] technique that automates the task. The basic idea of fuzzing is to generate a large number of test cases that are fed into the target program for execution. When a crash is triggered, it will be first determined as a bug or not and further identified as a vulnerability or not by exploitability analysis [16]. Since fuzzing highly relies on the generated test cases and the target program is required to be executed to monitor the behavior, it cannot be applied during a very early stage, such as the programming time.

Traditional detection tools like static analyzers [2] often require manual feature engineering by security researchers and target specific vulnerabilities, which is less efficient [43]. Deep learning (DL) facilitates the static analysis without running the target program and is feasible to function at different code module granularity [12], such as file level [18], function level [29,30,35,53], and program slice level [27,28]. Various DL models have been developed in the literature to support automated vulnerability detection. Simple examples [26] include multilayer perception (MLP), convolutional neural network (CNN), long short-term memory (LSTM), gated recurrent unit (GRU), bidirectional LSTM, and bidirectional GRU. Advanced ones dedicated to the structural representation of source code with graph neural networks, such as Devign [53] proposed by Zhou et al.. More recently, the application of foundation models is changing the domination of these task-specific models, which is discussed in the next subsection.

2.2   Recap of (foundation) DL Models

In classical DL, a model is initially randomly parameterized. Given a large set of labeled data, the model is trained with a certain number of epochs to achieve a satisfying performance for a given task. Therefore, this type of model is also called the task-specific model. Depending on the data type, model architecture, and learning task, the training procedure can take minutes or days. For instance, given the ImageNet-1k dataset to obtain an image classification model with ResNet-50, the 90-epoch training takes 14 days on a NVIDIA M40 GPU [51].

Different from task-specific models, foundation models, aka pre-trained models [20][3], break the limitation of relying on labeled data and have been a new paradigm of artificial intelligence (AI) [6]. Generally, a foundation model is trained using a huge volume of unlabeled data at scale and can be used for a wide range of downstream tasks. Via a few epochs' fine-tuning, the model can achieve SOTA performance. Foundation models have been increasingly developed and brought dramatic improvements in various communities, such as computer vision, natural language processing, and software engineering. Example models are the bidirectional encoder representations from transformers (BERT) [14],

---

[3] The term "foundation model" is used in this paper because, in the literature, a "pre-trained model" also has the meaning of a model trained by someone else and targeting a similar task [11,24].

generative pre-trained transformer 3 (GPT-3) [7], Roberta [33], ViLBERT [34], VideoBERT [45], CodeBERT [17], and GraphCodeBERT [19].

2.3 Solutions for Addressing Imbalance

There are mainly two types of methods for the imbalance issue, data level and model level [8]. Data level solutions focus on balancing the data size between minority and majority, such as down-sampling on majority and over-sampling on minority. The basic re-sampling strategy is in a random manner where samples are randomly selected to be removed [15] or duplicated [22]. An advanced over-sampling is to introduce new data based on neighboring samples [10] or synthesized [55]. However, advanced solutions [38] are data-dependent and some are inapplicable to source code. For instance, SMOTE [10] generates a new sample by joining k minority class nearest neighbors in the feature space, but generated code are likely to be invalid concerning both the syntax and semantics. Shu *et al.* [44] proposed Dazzle that leverages the Wasserstein Generative Adversarial networks as an over-sampling solution for software vulnerability detection. However, how to ensure the correctness of generate code is not addressed.

Model-level solutions, also known as cost-sensitive learning [13], assume the costs (represented by the loss) caused by different errors are unequal. The most common way is to put higher weight on the loss of the minority and less on the majority. Typical solutions include calculating the loss on minority and majority separately [49], effective number-based re-weighting [13], and misclassification-focused [32]. All these solutions adjust the decision boundary during the training procedure. Another method, threshold-moving [21] adjusts the boundary in the test time, which is simple but sensitive to the change in data.

Most existing solutions are initially proposed and studied in computer vision [8,13,32] and natural language processing [13,49]. In this paper, we investigate their effectiveness for software vulnerability detection.

3 Empirical Study Design

Fig. 2 gives an overview of our study design. In total, four research questions are framed:

RQ1: How does imbalance impact model performance in vulnerability detection?
RQ2: Which metrics are appropriate for evaluating detection models?
RQ3: How effective are existing solutions in mitigating imbalance in vulnerability detection?
RQ4: What external factors may hinder the solutions to work?

3.1 Sketch of DL-Based Vulnerability Detection Task

Generally, deep learning approaches formalize the vulnerability detection task as a binary classification problem, i.e., identifying a given code sample as secure (the label is 0) or vulnerable (the label is 1) [53]. Formally, let $\mathcal{D} = \{x, y\}$ be a

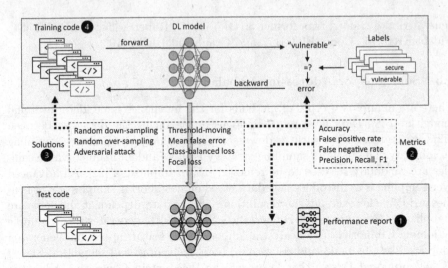

Fig. 2. Overview of the empirical study. During the training procedure (top), a foundation DL model is fine-tuned to minimize the error between predicted and ground truth labels. In the test time (bottom), the trained model is used to make predictions on test data. ❶❷❸❹ refer to four research questions.

source code set with samples, where $x \in X$ and $y \in Y$ represent a source code sample and its corresponding label ($Y = \{0, 1\}$), respectively. f_θ is such a binary classifier parameterized by θ that maps the data space X to the label space Y. The training procedure of the model is to find the optimal θ^* that minimizes the error between prediction and ground truth as shown in Fig. 2. Formally, the optimization objective is defined by:

$$\theta^* = \underset{\theta \in \Theta}{\arg\min}\, \ell\left(f_\theta, X, Y\right) \tag{1}$$

where ℓ is a loss function that captures the error between the predicted labels by f_θ and ground truth labels. The loss function can be in different forms, such as cross-entropy loss, mean squared error, and hinge embedding loss. For vulnerability detection, the cross-entropy loss is mostly applied and in this form, the objective becomes to minimize the cross entropy over all samples:

$$\ell = \frac{1}{N} \sum_{i=1}^{N} CE\left(p_i, y_i\right) \tag{2}$$

where

$$CE\left(p_i, y_i\right) = \begin{cases} -\log\left(p_i\right) & y_i = 1 \\ -\log\left(1 - p_i\right) & y_i = 0 \end{cases} \tag{3}$$

Note that in Eq. (2), the loss is an average over all samples. That is, all samples are equally treated regardless of being secure or vulnerable, which is reasonable when data are evenly distributed in two types. However, in reality, the number of vulnerable code is usually much less than secure ones, which causes the imbalance issue for training.

Remarkably, let p $(0 \leq p \leq 1)$ be the predicted probability of x being vulnerable. In binary classifiers, usually, a decision threshold is set at 0.5. Namely, if $p > 0.5$, x is determined as vulnerable, otherwise secure.

3.2   Imbalance Solutions

In total, we examine seven methods that are widely adopted in the literature to handle the imbalance problem. These methods cover both the data and model-level solutions. Note that data level (marked with *) solutions only carry out on the training set during the training time. Let N_s and N_v denote the number of secure and vulnerable code, respectively. $N_d = N_s - N_v$.

*Random down-sampling [15]. N_d secure code are randomly selected and removed from the training set.

*Random over-sampling [22]. As opposed to down-sampling, N_d vulnerable code are randomly selected from and replicated to the training set.

*Adversarial attack-based augmentation [50,52]. An advanced over-sampling method that generates new vulnerable code via adversarial attack. In this paper, we perform the variable renaming-based adversarial attack that changes the name of local variables. The advantage is that the generated code can pass the compiler and remain executable. To ensure that the substitute name is natural to software developers, we use the masked language prediction function of CodeBERT [17] to produce the candidates.

Threshold-moving [21], also known as threshold-tuning, post-scaling, and thresholding. It adjusts the decision threshold and is applied during the test time. Concretely, the model is trained using the training set and then used to predict the probabilities of samples in the validation set. Given a candidate threshold set, the performance on the validation set is evaluated on each candidate and the threshold producing the best performance is selected as the optimal one for the prediction on the test set. In this paper, we set the candidate threshold to range from 0 to 1 with a 0.01 interval.

Mean False Error (MFE) Loss [49]. The concept comes from the "false positive rate" and "false negative rate". The goal is to make the loss more sensitive to the errors caused by the minority set by computing the loss on different sets separately. The original base loss is the mean squared error for image classification and document classification tasks. We adapt it to the cross entropy error to fit vulnerability detection models. Formally,

$$\ell_{mfe} = \frac{1}{N_s} \sum_{i=1}^{N_s} CE\left(p_i, y_i\right) + \frac{1}{N_v} \sum_{j=1}^{N_v} CE\left(p_j, y_j\right) \tag{4}$$

Class-Balanced (CB) Loss [13]. This method addresses the imbalance issue by introducing the effect number that refers to the expected volume of samples of a given set. Formally,

$$\ell_{cb} = \frac{1}{N} \sum_{i=1}^{N} \frac{1-\beta}{1-\beta^{N_{y_i}}} CE\left(p_i, y_i\right) \tag{5}$$

where $N_{y_i} = N_v$ if $y_i = 1$ otherwise N_s. As recommended [13], we set $\beta = 0.9999$.

Focal Loss (FL) [32]. The idea is to put more focus on hard, misclassified samples meanwhile reduce the loss for well-classified samples. For instance, given three vulnerable code x_1, x_2, and x_3, the model predicts them as vulnerable with 0.9, 0.5, and 0.2 probability, respectively. x_1 is well-classified. x_2 is hard to classify. x_3 is misclassified as secure. Formally,

$$\ell_{fl} = -\frac{1}{N} \sum_{i=1}^{N} \left(1 - p_t\right)^{\gamma} \log\left(p_t\right) \tag{6}$$

where

$$p_t = \begin{cases} p_i & y_i = 1 \\ 1 - p_i & y_i = 0 \end{cases} \tag{7}$$

when $\gamma = 0$, Eq. (6) is equivalent to Eq. (2). As recommended [32], we set $\gamma = 2$.

3.3 Evaluation Metrics

We investigate all the following six metrics which have been used in different papers to evaluate software vulnerability detection models [9,17,19,28,53].

Accuracy [17,19,53] is the percentage of samples that are correctly classified by a model. This metric may give a fake good performance. For instance, if a test set has 100 code where only one is vulnerable. A model classifies all samples as secure, so its accuracy is 99%, which is nearly perfect. However, this model is useless as a detection model.

False positive rate (FPR) [28] measures the ratio of misclassified secure code to the total number of secure samples. A low value means the model learns very well from secure code.

False negative rate (FNR) [28] computes the ratio of misclassified vulnerable code to the total number of vulnerable samples. This metric focuses on the ability to figure out vulnerable code. A low value indicates a strong ability.

Precision [53], also known as positive predictive rate, is the fraction of correctly classified vulnerable code among samples classified as vulnerable.

Recall [53], the opposite of FNR, is the fraction of correctly classified vulnerable code among all vulnerable samples. In practice, precision and recall are often in tension. Improving precision will cause recall to decay, and vice versa.

F1-measure (F1) [53] is defined as the harmonic mean of precision and recall. It balances the importance between precision and recall.

4   Experimental Setup

All experiments were conducted on a high-performance computer (HPC) cluster and each cluster node runs a 2.20GHZ Intel Xeon Silver 4210 GPU with an NVIDIA Tesla V100 32G GPU. Models are trained and tested using the PyTorch 1.7.1 framework with CUDA 10.1.

4.1   Datasets

As listed in Table 1, nine function-level datasets from three open-source repositories on GitHub are considered in the experiments. All the datasets are C-language and the related projects are popular among software developers. Devign [40] is provided by Zhou *et al.* [54] and consists of two datasets collected from the FFmpeg [5] and QEMU [4] projects, respectively. Labels of source code are manually annotated by professional security researchers. Lin2018 [31][4] includes six datasets from Asterisk [3], FFmpeg [5], LibPNG [46], LibTIFF [41], Pidgin [39], and VLC media player [48], respectively. For each project, source code are manually labeled by Lin *et al.* according to the CVE and NVD records. CodeXGLUE [36] provides a mixture version of two datasets from FFmpeg and QEMU in Devign.

Table 1. Datasets overview. IR: imbalance ratio ($\frac{\#Secure}{\#Vulnerable}$).

Source	Project	Project description	#Vulnerable	#Secure	#Total	IR
Devign	FFmpeg	A cross-platform to record, convert and stream audio and video.	4,981	4,788	9,769	0.96
	QEMU	A generic and open source machine emulator and virtualizer.	7,479	10,070	17,549	1.35
	Asterisk	A framework for building communications applications.	56	17,070	17,126	304.82
	FFmpeg	A cross-platform to record, convert and stream audio and video.	213	5,550	5,763	26.06
	LibPNG	Official PNG reference.	44	577	621	13.11
	LibTIFF	TIFF library and utilities.	96	731	827	7.61
	Pidgin	A multi-platform instant messaging client.	29	8,612	8,641	296.97
Lin2018	VLC	A cross-platform multimedia player.	43	6,113	6,156	142.16
CodeXGLUE	Devign	Mixture of FFmpeg and QEMU.	12,460	14,858	27,318	1.19

To have a closer view of the vulnerabilities existing in these datasets, we provide Table 2. In total, 25 vulnerabilities are included and a certain vulnerability may have more than one CVE record with different CVSS scores, e.g., Bypass a restriction or similar.

4.2   Models

Two SOTA foundation models, CodeBERT [17] and GraphCodeBERT [19], for natural language and programming language, are leveraged in this paper. Both

---

[4] Notice: the number of data is a bit different from the original paper in [30] because we remove empty source code files from the provided datasets. Empty files cause compiling bugs and degrade the model performance.

Table 2. List of vulnerabilities. The common vulnerability scoring system (CVSS) score measures the severity of a certain vulnerability type.

ID	Vulnerability Type	CVSS	ID	Vulnerability Type	CVSS
1	Bypass a restriction or similar	4.3–7.5	14	Execute Code	5.8–9.3
2	Cross Site Scripting	4.3	15	Execute Code Gain privileges	6.5
3	Denial Of Service	2.6–7.8	16	Execute Code Memory corruption	6.8
4	Denial Of Service Execute Code	6.8–9.3	17	Execute Code Memory corruption Obtain Information	6.8
5	Denial Of Service Execute Code Memory corruption	6.8–10.0	18	Execute Code Overflow	6.0–10.0
6	Denial Of Service Execute Code Overflow	6.5–10.0	19	Execute Code Overflow Bypass a restriction or similar	6.8
7	Denial Of Service Execute Code Overflow Memory corruption	6.8	20	Execute Code Overflow Memory corruption	6.8
8	Denial Of Service Memory corruption	6.8	21	Gain privileges	9.0
9	Denial Of Service Obtain Information	4.3–10	22	Obtain Information	4.3–5.0
10	Denial Of Service Overflow	2.6–9.3	23	Overflow	4.3–10
11	Denial Of Service Overflow Memory corruption	4.3–6.8	24	Overflow Memory corruption	5.0
12	Denial Of Service Overflow Obtain Information	5.8	25	Unspecified	4.3–10.0
13	Directory traversal	5.8–9.3			

models follow BERT [14] and use multi-layer bidirectional Transformer [47] as the backbone. CodeBERT is pre-trained on 2.1M bimodal data and 6.4M unimodal codes. GraphCodeBERT is pre-trained on the CodeSearchNet [23] dataset consisting of 2.3M functions paired with natural language descriptions. The main difference between CodeBERT and GraphCodeBERT is that the source code in CodeBERT is represented as a sequence of tokens, while GraphCodeBERT takes the data flow of source code as its input.

Our implementation is adapted from the GitHub repositories provided by CodeXGLUE[5] for CodeBERT and by Microsoft[6] for GraphCodeBERT, respectively. The base models for fine-tuning are loaded from Hugging Face[7][8] from Hugging Face.

4.3   Training

Each model is fine-tuned 50 epochs and the "best" one is saved for evaluation. For reproduction, we follow the default setting in original implementations to set the random seed at 123456. In each dataset, we proportionally (8:1:1) split the dataset into a training set, a validation set, and a test set (the training and validation sets are involved in the training procedure, and the test set is only for testing.). Vulnerable and secure code are randomly divided into these three sets with the same imbalance ratio as in Table 1.

5   Results

5.1   RQ1: Influence of Imbalance in Vulnerability Detection

Experiments. We train CodeBERT and GraphCodeBERT with default settings, ignoring the imbalance. For each trained model, we check if the imbalance causes a bias towards secure code by comparing loss and accuracy across individual sets.

---

[5] https://github.com/microsoft/CodeXGLUE.
[6] https://github.com/microsoft/CodeBERT.
[7] https://huggingface.co/microsoft/codebert-base.
[8] https://huggingface.co/microsoft/graphcodebert-base.

Table 3. Model accuracy and loss on secure and vulnerable code. **Baseline**: model accuracy on all code. The best performance is highlighted.

Source	Project	Accuracy (%)			Total Loss		Average loss	
		Baseline	Vulnerable	Secure	Vulnerable	Secure	Vulnerable	Secure
CodeBERT								
Devign	FFmpeg	56.71	62.17	51.04	537.37	449.77	0.72	0.63
	QEMU	64.31	40.96	81.67	1361.10	583.43	1.21	0.39
Lin2018	Asterisk	99.77	44.44	99.96	33.75	3.18	3.75	0.00
	FFmpeg	97.46	36.36	99.88	124.56	2.92	3.77	0.00
	LibPNG	95.83	50.00	100.00	14.25	0.65	1.78	0.01
	LibTIFF	88.89	53.33	93.69	49.34	30.54	3.29	0.28
	Pidgin	99.85	60.00	100.00	17.14	0.08	3.43	0.00
	VLC	99.89	85.71	100.00	3.07	0.08	0.44	0.00
CodeXGLUE	Devign	61.49	31.95	86.59	1716.89	531.24	1.37	0.36
GraphCodeBERT								
Devign	FFmpeg	56.99	74.87	38.39	437.05	559.02	0.58	0.78
	QEMU	65.38	52.98	74.59	1001.18	776.03	0.89	0.51
Lin2018	Asterisk	99.81	44.44	100.00	31.18	0.90	3.46	0.00
	FFmpeg	97.35	51.52	99.16	134.98	37.00	4.09	0.04
	LibPNG	96.88	62.50	100.00	16.16	0.68	2.02	0.01
	LibTIFF	92.06	33.33	100.00	47.81	1.31	3.19	0.01
	Pidgin	99.85	60.00	100.00	13.18	0.39	2.64	0.00
	VLC	99.68	57.14	100.00	11.77	1.26	1.68	0.00
CodeXGLUE	Devign	62.81	58.25	66.69	1047.34	806.85	0.83	0.55

Results. Table 3 shows the results. Regardless of the model and evaluation metric, the model performs better on the secure set than on the vulnerable one. Considering the accuracy, except for the FFmpeg dataset in Devign, both models achieve higher accuracy on secure code. Particularly, 100% secure code can be perfectly identified in several datasets, such as LibPNG, LibTIFF, Pidgin, and VLC. However, the performance in identifying vulnerable code is less satisfying. For instance, in Asterisk from Lin2018, GraphCodeBERT can correctly identify all secure code but only 44.44% vulnerable code. On the other hand, with respect to the loss between prediction and ground truth, the loss on secure code is, in general, much lower than on vulnerable code. For instance, on average, CodeBERT has no loss on each secure code for Pidgin from Lin2018, but 0.44 on the vulnerable one. This indicates that during the training procedure, the model tends to learn more from the secure code. When summing over all code, the imbalance makes it worse, e.g., GraphCodeBERT has, in total, 0.39 loss on secure code but 13.18 on vulnerable one. The reason is that, during the training procedure, the loss is calculated as an average (Eq. (2)) or sum over all samples (both the majority secure and minority vulnerable). This methodology weakens the influence of vulnerable code and gives "fake" feedback to the training that the model is performing well, which is the essence of the imbalance issue.

Answer : The imbalance encourages a DL model to gain more knowledge from secure code, which leads to poor performance on detecting vulnerable code, e.g., 44.44% accuracy (55.56% false negative rate).

5.2 RQ2: Analysis of Evaluation Metrics

Experiments. In the default setting of CodeBERT and GraphCodeBERT, for each trained model, different metrics are used to evaluate the model performance.

Results. Table 4 lists the model performance. From the perspective of identifying vulnerable code, accuracy and FPR are not informative enough and can be misleading. For instance, Table 3 shows that CodeBERT only successfully detects 44.44% vulnerable code in Asterisk from Lin2018. However, the output accuracy

Table 4. Model performance (%) using different evaluation metrics. Accuracy is the default metric of CodeBERT and GraphCodeBERT.

Source	Project	Accuracy	FPR	FNR	Precision	Recall	F1
CodeBERT							
Devign	FFmpeg	56.71	48.96	37.83	56.92	62.17	59.42
	QEMU	64.31	18.33	59.04	62.42	40.96	49.46
Lin2018	Asterisk	99.77	0.04	55.56	80.00	44.44	57.14
	FFmpeg	97.46	0.12	63.64	92.31	36.36	52.17
	LibPNG	95.83	0.00	50.00	100.00	50.00	66.67
	LibTIFF	88.89	6.31	46.67	53.33	53.33	53.33
	Pidgin	99.85	0.00	40.00	100.00	60.00	75.00
	VLC	99.89	0.00	14.29	100.00	85.71	92.31
CodeXGLUE	Devign	61.49	13.41	68.05	66.94	31.95	43.26
GraphCodeBERT							
Devign	FFmpeg	56.99	61.61	25.13	55.83	74.87	63.96
	QEMU	65.38	25.41	47.02	60.78	52.98	56.61
Lin2018	Asterisk	99.81	0.00	55.56	100.00	44.44	61.54
	FFmpeg	97.35	0.84	48.48	70.83	51.52	59.65
	LibPNG	96.88	0.00	37.50	100.00	62.50	76.92
	LibTIFF	92.06	0.00	66.67	100.00	33.33	50.00
	Pidgin	99.85	0.00	40.00	100.00	60.00	75.00
	VLC	99.68	0.00	42.86	100.00	57.14	72.73
CodeXGLUE	Devign	62.81	33.31	41.75	59.77	58.25	59.00

is almost perfect at 99.77%. The overall accuracy hides the actual performance of detecting vulnerable code. FPR only considers the detection of secure code, which misses the main purpose of vulnerable detection, namely to identify vulnerabilities at an early stage. Recall (the opposite of FNR) is equivalent to the individual accuracy on the vulnerable code in Table 3 and can tell how the model identifies vulnerable code. However, recall ignores the secure code. Precision covers this shortage by including misclassified secure code. If one only cares about detecting vulnerable code and ignores the cost of manually filtering secure code afterward, recall is the best option. If one wishes to have fewer errors in the identified vulnerable code, precision can be taken. As a balanced version between precision and recall, F1 can be used when an overall score is preferred.

Answer : Precision, recall and F1 provide more informative and comprehensive insights on model performance than accuracy. FPR might be useful in some situations to limit the impact of false positives (e.g., static analysis), but precision can serve a similar purpose as a higher precision generally implies a lower FPR.

5.3   RQ3: Effectiveness of Solutions for Addressing Imbalance

Experiments. We train CodeBERT and GraphCodeBERT following the methodology of different solutions for handling the imbalance issue. Based on the selected evaluation metrics, precision, recall, and F1, by RQ2, the effectiveness of solutions is investigated.

Results. Table 5 and Table 6 show the results on CodeBERT and GraphCode-BERT, respectively. Note that in FFmpeg, Devign, the number of vulnerable programs (4981) is greater than the secure one (4788), thus, no re-sampling-based solutions are applied. Regardless of the dataset, model, and evaluation metric, random down-sampling performs the worst since massive information about the secure code is eliminated. In particular, when the imbalance ratio is high and the data size is small (e.g., Asterisk from Lin2018), the remaining data is insufficient to support the model training. The focal loss stands out as the optimal choice for improving precision. The reason is that focal loss puts more effort into hard and misclassified samples during the training procedure whether those samples are vulnerable or secure. Thus, the model can more precisely predict a code sample to be vulnerable or secure. Two model-level solutions, MFE and CB, are the worst regarding precision. The reason is that, the methodology of these two solutions is to put relatively more attention to the vulnerable code during the training procedure, thus, more vulnerable code should be correctly identified than the baseline. This is confirmed by the results of recall where both solutions outperform the others. While in this case, the focal loss gains low recall. With respect to the overall performance F1, random over-sampling seems to be the best in most cases for both models.

Answer: No single existing solution is the best to address the imbalance issue across all evaluation metrics. Specifically, to focal loss is the best option for improving precision. MFE and CB shall be used for optimizing recall. Random over-sampling is the best option when focusing on the overall F1 performance. Nevertheless, the pursuit of a new, task-specific solution to address the imbalance issue remains imperative.

5.4   RQ4: Investigation of External Factors

Experiments. Based on Table 5 and Table 6, we dig into the prediction results to explore possible external factors.

Table 5. CodeBERT trained using different solutions for imbalance issues. **Baseline**: the default setting. **Down-R**: random down-sampling. **Over-R**: random over-sampling. **Over-A**: adversarial attack-based augmentation. For each dataset, the best solution under a given metric is highlighted.

Source	Project	Baseline	Down-R	Over-R	Over-A	Thresholding	MFE	CB	FL
Precision									
Devign	FFmpeg	56.92	–	–	–	0.00	67.72	63.14	88.24
	QEMU	62.42	60.51	62.33	71.12	0.00	55.36	55.17	93.04
Lin2018	Asterisk	80.00	0.00	75.00	100.00	0.00	66.67	54.55	100.00
	FFmpeg	92.31	3.23	76.19	65.38	100.00	34.29	38.71	90.00
	LibPNG	100.00	66.67	100.00	85.71	0.00	62.50	70.00	100.00
	LibTIFF	53.33	66.67	60.00	80.00	72.73	57.14	53.33	80.00
	Pidgin	100.00	0.00	100.00	75.00	100.00	60.00	0.00	0.00
	VLC	100.00	0.00	100.00	100.00	100.00	0.00	0.00	0.00
CodeXGLUE	Devign	66.94	59.52	62.03	62.72	100.00	58.38	59.82	85.49
Recall									
Devign	FFmpeg	62.17	–	–	–	0.00	31.42	47.86	4.01
	QEMU	40.96	50.49	49.07	29.39	0.00	71.33	75.96	9.53
Lin2018	Asterisk	44.44	0.00	66.67	44.44	0.00	44.44	66.67	33.33
	FFmpeg	36.36	3.03	48.48	51.52	36.36	72.73	72.73	54.55
	LibPNG	50.00	25.00	62.50	75.00	0.00	62.50	87.50	62.50
	LibTIFF	53.33	40.00	40.00	26.67	53.33	53.33	53.33	26.67
	Pidgin	60.00	0.00	60.00	60.00	60.00	60.00	0.00	0.00
	VLC	85.71	0.00	85.71	57.14	85.71	0.00	0.00	0.00
CodeXGLUE	Devign	31.95	47.33	52.59	45.98	5.02	53.55	47.81	13.15
F1									
Devign	FFmpeg	59.42	–	–	–	0.00	42.92	54.45	7.67
	QEMU	49.46	55.05	54.91	41.59	0.00	62.33	63.92	17.29
Lin2018	Asterisk	57.14	0.00	70.59	61.54	0.00	53.33	60.00	50.00
	FFmpeg	52.17	3.13	59.26	57.63	53.33	46.60	50.53	67.92
	LibPNG	66.67	36.36	76.92	80.00	0.00	62.50	77.78	76.92
	LibTIFF	53.33	50.00	48.00	40.00	61.54	55.17	53.33	40.00
	Pidgin	75.00	0.00	75.00	66.67	75.00	60.00	0.00	0.00
	VLC	92.31	0.00	92.31	72.73	92.31	0.00	0.00	0.00
CodeXGLUE	Devign	43.26	52.73	56.92	53.06	9.56	55.86	53.14	22.79

Results. Note that in some cases, the model performance degrades after applying a solution. For instance, in Pidgin from Lin2018, CodeBERT with the default setting gains 100% precision and 60% recall, but 75% precision and the same recall by adversarial attack-based augmentation. We found that by over-R, over-A, thresholding, and MFE, CodeBERT identifies the same vulnerable samples as the baseline, and the code with the Overflow vulnerability (ID 23 in Table 2) is always misclassified. This is because this vulnerability type does not appear in the training or validation sets (as shown in Fig. 3(b)) and the model cannot gain knowledge of this specific vulnerability type. Introducing more vulnerable

Table 6. GraphCodeBERT trained using different solutions for imbalance issue. **Baseline**: the default setting. **Down-R**: random down-sampling. **Over-R**: random over-sampling. **Over-A**: adversarial attack-based augmentation. For each dataset, the best solution under a given metric is highlighted.

Source	Project	Baseline	Down-R	Over-R	Over-A	Thresholding	MFE	CB	FL
Precision									
Devign	FFmpeg	55.83	–	–	–	0.00	59.48	56.76	86.36
	QEMU	60.78	58.43	61.19	65.28	93.33	56.70	54.93	85.15
Lin2018	Asterisk	100.00	0.00	44.44	100.00	100.00	38.46	23.53	100.00
	FFmpeg	70.83	24.53	70.97	70.37	75.00	28.00	17.39	62.50
	LibPNG	100.00	66.67	83.33	85.71	0.00	66.67	66.67	100.00
	LibTIFF	100.00	0.00	100.00	77.78	0.00	55.56	47.06	100.00
	Pidgin	100.00	0.00	100.00	75.00	0.00	50.00	20.00	66.67
	VLC	100.00	0.00	83.33	100.00	0.00	75.00	75.00	100.00
CodeXGLUE	Devign	59.77	58.25	59.75	60.05	100.00	60.36	60.86	90.21
Recall									
Devign	FFmpeg	74.87	–	–	–	0.00	52.41	65.11	5.08
	QEMU	52.98	54.94	53.07	37.67	6.23	64.02	62.51	15.32
Lin2018	Asterisk	44.44	0.00	44.44	44.44	33.33	55.56	44.44	22.22
	FFmpeg	51.52	78.79	66.67	57.58	45.45	84.85	84.85	60.61
	LibPNG	62.50	75.00	62.50	75.00	0.00	75.00	75.00	62.50
	LibTIFF	33.33	0.00	40.00	46.67	0.00	66.67	53.33	26.67
	Pidgin	60.00	0.00	80.00	60.00	0.00	80.00	60.00	80.00
	VLC	57.14	0.00	71.43	85.71	0.00	85.71	85.71	71.43
CodeXGLUE	Devign	58.25	55.70	56.89	54.50	4.54	61.04	57.85	13.94
F1									
Devign	FFmpeg	63.96	–	–	–	0.00	55.72	60.65	9.60
	QEMU	56.61	56.63	56.84	47.77	11.69	60.14	58.48	25.96
Lin2018	Asterisk	61.54	0.00	44.44	61.54	50.00	45.45	30.77	36.36
	FFmpeg	59.65	37.41	68.75	63.33	56.60	42.11	28.87	61.54
	LibPNG	76.92	70.59	71.43	80.00	0.00	70.59	70.59	76.92
	LibTIFF	50.00	0.00	57.14	58.33	0.00	60.61	50.00	42.11
	Pidgin	75.00	0.00	88.89	66.67	0.00	61.54	30.00	72.73
	VLC	72.73	0.00	76.92	92.31	0.00	80.00	80.00	83.33
CodeXGLUE	Devign	59.00	56.95	58.29	57.14	8.69	60.70	59.31	24.15

samples can just cause the overfitting problem. Another case is in LibTIFF from Lin2018, the thresholding, MFE, and CB identify the same vulnerable samples as the baseline and miss five vulnerability types, Denial Of Service (ID 3,) Denial Of Service Execute Code Overflow (ID 6), Denial Of Service Overflow (ID 10), Execute Code Overflow (ID 18), and Overflow (ID 23). All these types are included in the training procedure (training and validation sets) (see Fig. 3(a)). All the trained models with or without solutions reach 53.33% recall, these solutions can only increase the correctness of secure code because, by the corresponding training methodology, the model already reaches the limit of identifying certain types of vulnerability. In addition, thresholding tends to ruin the model entirely, such as FFmpeg from Devign and LibPNG from Lin2018, which is caused by the distribution shift between the validation set in the training time and the test set in the test time. Distribution shift [25] is a research topic per se and is not further explained in this paper.

Answer : External factors including the absence of vulnerability types in the training time, inherent identification difficulty of certain vulnerability types, and the distribution shift in data should be considered when developing a new solution.

5.5   Insights

Selecting evaluation metrics: In vulnerability detection, when selecting a metric to evaluate a model's performance, accuracy is the least suitable metric. Recall should be used if only the detection on vulnerable code matters. Precision should be selected if one wishes to have less secure code in identified vulnerable code. F1 can be considered from an overall perspective.

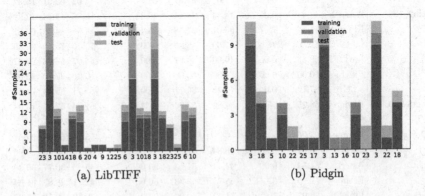

(a) LibTIFF   (b) Pidgin

Fig. 3. Vulnerability type distribution in each split set (training, validation, and test). x-axis: vulnerability type ID (Please refer to Table 2 for more details.). y-axis: number of samples in the corresponding set. Source: Lin2018.

Designing solutions: When designing a solution to address imbalance, one should consider the evaluation metric first. If the goal is to improve precision or recall, modifying the loss function is more efficient than manipulating training data. Minority over-sampling brings benefits to the overall evaluation. Vulnerability type and difficulty in data should be considered when a solution fails.

6   Conclusion

This work studies the imbalance issue in software vulnerability detection. Seven solutions proposed in other domains are investigated on nine open-source datasets and two state-of-the-art deep learning models (CodeBERT and Graph-CodeBERT). We found the defaulting setting of CodeBERT and GraphCode-BERT makes the training procedure focus more on the secure code, which causes a high false negative rate (e.g., 68.05%). Existing solutions perform differently over various datasets and models, which calls for a new solution specifically for vulnerability detection. With the insights stated in the paper, this will be an interesting future work. Furthermore, we explore external factors like the vulnerability type distribution that should be aware of when designing such a new solution. There are many future research topics. The observations from this paper should be tested on other datasets and for other programming languages. Related to this, the observations should also be tested on other ML models other than CodeBERT and GraphCodeBERT. External factors, which can affect the performances, should be explored in more depth. This is particularly important if a solution is about to be deployed in practice.

References

1. Amankwah, R., Kudjo, P., Yeboah, S.: Evaluation of software vulnerability detection methods and tools: a review. Int. J. Comput. Appl. **169**, 22–27 (2017). https://doi.org/10.5120/ijca2017914750
2. Arusoaie, A., Ciobâca, S., Craciun, V., Gavrilut, D., Lucanu, D.: A comparison of open-source static analysis tools for vulnerability detection in c/c++ code. In: 19th International Symposium on Symbolic and Numeric Algorithms for Scientific Computing, pp. 161–168. IEEE (2017). https://doi.org/10.1109/SYNASC.2017.00035
3. Asterisk team: Asterisk website (2022). https://www.asterisk.org/. Accessed 25 Aug 2023
4. Bellard, F.: Qemu wesite (2022). https://www.qemu.org/. Accessed 25 Aug 2023
5. Bellard, F.: FFmpeg team: Repository of ffmpeg on github (2023). https://github.com/FFmpeg/FFmpeg. Accessed 25 Aug 2023
6. Bommasani, R., Hudson, D.A., Adeli, E., et al.: On the opportunities and risks of foundation models. CoRR abs/2108.07258 (2021). https://arxiv.org/abs/2108.07258
7. Brown, T., Mann, B., Ryder, N., et al.: Language models are few-shot learners. In: Advances in Neural Information Processing Systems, pp. 1877–1901. Curran Associates, Inc. (2020). https://proceedings.neurips.cc/paper_files/paper/2020/file/1457c0d6bfcb4967418bfb8ac142f64a-Paper.pdf

8. Buda, M., Maki, A., Mazurowski, M.A.: A systematic study of the class imbalance problem in convolutional neural networks. Neural Netw. **106**, 249–259 (2018). https://doi.org/10.1016/j.neunet.2018.07.011

9. Chakraborty, S., Krishna, R., Ding, Y., Ray, B.: Deep learning based vulnerability detection: are we there yet? IEEE Trans. Softw. Eng. **48**(09), 3280–3296 (2022). https://doi.org/10.1109/TSE.2021.3087402

10. Chawla, N.V., Bowyer, K.W., Hall, L.O., Kegelmeyer, W.P.: Smote: synthetic minority over-sampling technique. J. Artif. Intell. Res. **16**(1), 321–357 (2002). https://doi.org/10.1613/jair.953

11. Choi, S., Yang, S., Choi, S., Yun, S.: Improving test-time adaptation via shift-agnostic weight regularization and nearest source prototypes. In: Computer Vision - ECCV 2022, pp. 440–458. Springer, Cham (2022). https://doi.org/10.1007/978-3-031-19827-4_26

12. Croft, R., Xie, Y., Babar, M.A.: Data preparation for software vulnerability prediction: a systematic literature review. IEEE Trans. Softw. Eng. **49**, 1044–1063 (2022). https://doi.org/10.1109/TSE.2022.3171202

13. Cui, Y., Jia, M., Lin, T.Y., Song, Y., Belongie, S.: Class-balanced loss based on effective number of samples. In: IEEE/CVF Conference on Computer Vision and Pattern Recognition, pp. 9260–9269. IEEE (2019). https://doi.org/10.1109/CVPR.2019.00949

14. Devlin, J., Chang, M., Lee, K., Toutanova, K.: Bert: pre-training of deep bidirectional transformers for language understanding. In: Proceedings of the Conference of the North American Chapter of the Association for Computational Linguistics: Human Language Technologies, pp. 4171–4186. Association for Computational Linguistics (2019). https://aclanthology.org/N19-1423.pdf

15. Drummond, C., Holte, R.: C4.5, class imbalance, and cost sensitivity: why undersampling beats oversampling. In: International Conference on Machine Learning Workshop on Learning from Imbalanced Data Sets II, Washington, DC, USA (2003). https://www.site.uottawa.ca/~nat/Workshop2003/drummondc.pdf

16. Fell, J.: A review of fuzzing tools and methods. PenTest Magazine (2017)

17. Feng, Z., Guo, D., Tang, D., et al.: Codebert: a pre-trained model for programming and natural languages. In: Findings of the Association for Computational Linguistics: EMNLP 2020, pp. 1536–1547. Association for Computational Linguistics (2020). https://doi.org/10.18653/v1/2020.findings-emnlp.139

18. Garg, A., Degiovanni, R., Jimenez, M., Cordy, M., Papadakis, M., Le Traon, Y.: Learning from what we know: how to perform vulnerability prediction using noisy historical data. Empir. Softw. Eng. **27**(7) (2022). https://doi.org/10.1007/s10664-022-10197-4

19. Guo, D., Ren, S., Lu, S., et al.: Graphcodebert: pre-training code representations with data flow. In: International Conference on Learning Representations (2021). https://openreview.net/pdf?id=jLoC4ez43PZ

20. Han, X., Zhang, Z., Ding, N., et al.: Pre-trained models: past, present and future. AI Open **2**, 225–250 (2021). https://doi.org/10.1016/j.aiopen.2021.08.002

21. He, H., Ma, Y.: Imbalanced Learning: Foundations, Algorithms, and Applications, 1st edn. Wiley-IEEE Press, Hoboken (2013)

22. Huang, C.Y., Dai, H.L.: Learning from class-imbalanced data: review of data driven methods and algorithm driven methods. Data Sci. Finan. Econ. **1**(1), 21–36 (2021). https://doi.org/10.3934/DSFE.2021002

23. Husain, H., Wu, H.H., Gazit, T., Allamanis, M., Brockschmidt, M.: Codesearchnet challenge: evaluating the state of semantic code search. CoRR abs/1909.09436 (2019). https://arxiv.org/abs/1909.09436

24. Kim, J., Feldt, R., Yoo, S.: Guiding deep learning system testing using surprise adequacy. In: 41st International Conference on Software Engineering, pp. 1039–1049. IEEE Press (2019). https://doi.org/10.1109/ICSE.2019.00108
25. Koh, P.W., Sagawa, S., Marklund, H., et al.: Wilds: a benchmark of in-the-wild distribution shifts. In: 38th International Conference on Machine Learning, pp. 5637–5664. PMLR (2021)
26. Li, Z., Zou, D., Tang, J., Zhang, Z., Sun, M., Jin, H.: A comparative study of deep learning-based vulnerability detection system. IEEE Access **7**, 103184–103197 (2019). https://doi.org/10.1109/ACCESS.2019.2930578
27. Li, Z., Zou, D., Xu, S., Jin, H., Zhu, Y., Chen, Z.: Sysevr: a framework for using deep learning to detect software vulnerabilities. IEEE Trans. Depend. Secure Comput. **19**(04), 2244–2258 (2022). https://doi.org/10.1109/TDSC.2021.3051525
28. Li, Z., et al.: Vuldeepecker: a deep learning-based system for vulnerability detection. In: 25th Annual Network and Distributed System Security Symposium. The Internet Society (2018). https://doi.org/10.14722/ndss.2018.23158
29. Lin, G., Xiao, W., Zhang, J., Xiang, Y.: Deep learning-based vulnerable function detection: a benchmark. In: Zhou, J., Luo, X., Shen, Q., Xu, Z. (eds.) ICICS 2019. LNCS, vol. 11999, pp. 219–232. Springer, Cham (2020). https://doi.org/10.1007/978-3-030-41579-2_13
30. Lin, G., et al.: Cross-project transfer representation learning for vulnerable function discovery. IEEE Trans. Ind. Inf. **14**(7), 3289–3297 (2018). https://doi.org/10.1109/TII.2018.2821768
31. Lin, G., et al.: Repository of lin2018 on github (2019). https://github.com/DanielLin1986/TransferRepresentationLearning. Accessed 25 Aug 2023
32. Lin, T.Y., Goyal, P., Girshick, R., He, K., Dollár, P.: Focal loss for dense object detection. IEEE Trans. Pattern Anal. Mach. Intell. **42**(2), 318–327 (2020). https://doi.org/10.1109/TPAMI.2018.2858826
33. Liu, Y., Ott, M., Goyal, N., et al.: Roberta: a robustly optimized bert pretraining approach. CoRR abs/1907.11692 (2019). https://arxiv.org/abs/1907.11692
34. Lu, J., Batra, D., Parikh, D., Lee, S.: Vilbert: pretraining task-agnostic visiolinguistic representations for vision-and-language tasks. In: 33rd Conference on Neural Information Processing Systems (2019)
35. Lu, S., Guo, D., Ren, S., Huang, J., et al.: Codexglue: a machine learning benchmark dataset for code understanding and generation. In: Thirty-fifth Conference on Neural Information Processing Systems Datasets and Benchmarks Track. OpenReview.net (2021). https://openreview.net/forum?id=6lE4dQXaUcb
36. Lu, S., Guo, D., Ren, S., et al.: Implementation of codexglue. https://github.com/microsoft/CodeXGLUE (2022). Accessed 25 Aug 2023
37. Mazuera-Rozo, A., Mojica-Hanke, A., Linares-Vásquez, M., Bavota, G.: Shallow or deep? an empirical study on detecting vulnerabilities using deep learning. In: IEEE/ACM 29th International Conference on Program Comprehension, pp. 276–287 (2021). https://doi.org/10.1109/ICPC52881.2021.00034
38. Mendoza, J., Mycroft, J., Milbury, L., Kahani, N., Jaskolka, J.: On the effectiveness of data balancing techniques in the context of ml-based test case prioritization. In: 18th International Conference on Predictive Models and Data Analytics in Software Engineering, pp. 72–81. Association for Computing Machinery, New York (2022). https://doi.org/10.1145/3558489.3559073
39. Pidgin team: Pidgin website (2020). https://pidgin.im/. Accessed 25 Aug 2023
40. Pinconschi, E.: Repository of devign on github (2020). https://github.com/epicosy/devign. Accessed 25 Aug 2023

41. Sam Leffler, S.G.: Repository of libtiff on gitlab (2020). https://gitlab.com/libtiff/libtiff. Accessed 25 Aug 2023

42. Sharma, T., et al.: A survey on machine learning techniques for source code analysis. CoRR abs/2110.09610 (2021). https://arxiv.org/abs/2110.09610

43. Shen, Z., Chen, S., Coppolino, L.: A survey of automatic software vulnerability detection, program repair, and defect prediction techniques. Secur. Commun. Netw. **2020** (2020). https://doi.org/10.1155/2020/8858010

44. Shu, R., Xia, T., Williams, L., Menzies, T.: Dazzle: using ooptimized generative adversarial networks to address security data class imbalance issue. In: 19th International Conference on Mining Software Repositories, pp. 144–155. Association for Computing Machinery, New York (2022). https://doi.org/10.1145/3524842.3528437

45. Sun, C., Myers, A., Vondrick, C., Murphy, K., Schmid, C.: Videobert: a joint model for video and language representation learning. In: IEEE/CVF International Conference on Computer Vision (ICCV), pp. 7463–7472. IEEE Computer Society, Los Alamitos (2019). https://doi.org/10.1109/ICCV.2019.00756

46. Truta, C., Randers-Pehrson, G., Dilger, A.E., Schalnat, G.E.: Repository of libpng on github (2023). https://github.com/glennrp/libpng. Accessed 25 Aug 2023

47. Vaswani, A., Shazeer, N., Parmar, N., et al.: Attention is all you need. In: 31st Conference on Neural Information Processing Systems. Curran Associates, Inc. (2017). https://proceedings.neurips.cc/paper_files/paper/2017/file/3f5ee243547dee91fbd053c1c4a845aa-Paper.pdf

48. VLC team: Vlc media player website (2023). https://github.com/videolan/vlc. Accessed 25 Aug 2023

49. Wang, S., Liu, W., Wu, J., Cao, L., Meng, Q., Kennedy, P.: Training deep neural networks on imbalanced data sets. In: International Joint Conference on Neural Networks, pp. 4368–4374. IEEE (2016). https://doi.org/10.1109/IJCNN.2016.7727770

50. Yang, Z., Shi, J., He, J., Lo, D.: Natural attack for pre-trained models of code. In: International Conference on Software Engineering, pp. 1482–1493. Association for Computing Machinery (2022). https://doi.org/10.1145/3510003.3510146

51. You, Y., Zhang, Z., Hsieh, C., Demmel, J.: 100-epoch imagenet training with alexnet in 24 minutes. CoRR abs/1709.05011 (2017). https://arxiv.org/abs/1709.05011

52. Zhang, H., Li, Z., Li, G., Ma, L., Liu, Y., Jin, Z.: Generating adversarial examples for holding robustness of source code processing models. In: Proceedings of the AAAI Conference on Artificial Intelligence, pp. 1169–1176 (2020). : https://doi.org/10.1609/aaai.v34i01.5469

53. Zhou, Y., Liu, S., Siow, J., Du, X., Liu, Y.: Devign: effective vulnerability identification by learning comprehensive program semantics via graph neural networks, pp. 10197–10207. Curran Associates Inc., Red Hook (2019)

54. Zhou, Y., Liu, S., Siow, J., Du, X., Liu, Y.: Devign: effective vulnerability identification by learning comprehensive program semantics via graph neural networks. In: 33rd International Conference on Neural Information Processing Systems, pp. 10197–10207. Curran Associates Inc., Red Hook (2019). https://dl.acm.org/doi/pdf/10.5555/3454287.3455202

55. Zou, Y., Yu, Z., Vijaya Kumar, B.V.K., Wang, J.: Unsupervised domain adaptation for semantic segmentation via class-balanced self-training. In: Ferrari, V., Hebert, M., Sminchisescu, C., Weiss, Y. (eds.) ECCV 2018. LNCS, vol. 11207, pp. 297–313. Springer, Cham (2018). https://doi.org/10.1007/978-3-030-01219-9_18

AttnCall: Refining Indirect Call Targets in Binaries with Attention

Rui Sun[✉] , Yinggang Guo , Zicheng Wang , and Qingkai Zeng

State Key Laboratory for Novel Software Technology, Nanjing University,
Nanjing, China
{rabbit,gyg,wzc}@smail.nju.edu.cn, zqk@nju.edu.cn

Abstract. Accurate Control Flow Graphs are crucial for effective binary program analysis, while solving indirect function call targets is its major challenge. Existing static analysis methods heavily rely on domain-specific patterns, resulting in an abundance of false positive edges due to limited expert knowledge. Concurrently, learning-based approaches often depend on heuristic analysis during the code representation stage, which prevents the model from fully comprehending program semantics.

To address these limitations, this paper presents AttnCall, a novel neural network learning framework that leverages the attention mechanism to automatically learn the matching relationship between function callsites and callees' context semantics. AttnCall refines the identification of indirect call targets through the learned matching patterns, eliminating the drawbacks of existing techniques. Additionally, we propose an end-to-end code representation scheme that effectively embeds the semantics of callsites and callees without relying on heuristic rules.

The evaluation of AttnCall focuses on the task of predicting indirect function call targets. The results demonstrate that AttnCall surpasses state-of-the-art approaches, achieving 31.4% higher precision and 5% higher recall. Moreover, AttnCall enhances model interpretability, allowing for a better understanding of the underlying analysis process.

Keywords: Binary Analysis · Control Flow Graph · Indirect Call · Deep Neural Network · Attention Mechanism

1 Introduction

Studying the code reuse attacks [30] for almost two decades, Control Flow Integrity (CFI) [1,2] has become an engaging research subject for security professionals. The CFI mechanism restricts the program's control flow within the Control Flow Graph (CFG) defined by the designer, which ensures that attackers cannot hijack the control flow to arbitrary addresses. Despite the fact that many CFI security solutions have been proposed [16,18,23,32,40], they lack sufficient security guarantees because of the imprecise CFG. In addition, CFG also plays an important role in program analysis, while coarse-grained CFG lead to imprecise analysis results [31].

© The Author(s), under exclusive license to Springer Nature Switzerland AG 2024
G. Tsudik et al. (Eds.): ESORICS 2023, LNCS 14347, pp. 391–409, 2024.
https://doi.org/10.1007/978-3-031-51482-1_20

The primary challenge in the construction of CFG lies in accurately determining the legitimate targets for indirect branches [31]. While the backward control flow can be effectively protected by shadow stack mechanisms [5], the identification of indirect function call targets remains an open problem. Indirect function calls involve using the address stored in function pointers as the target for control flow transfer, making pointer analysis a potential solution [10]. Unfortunately, Rice's theorem dictates that solving pointer analysis for general programs is an undecidable problem [7,29]. Consequently, there is no theoretically precise solution for resolving indirect function calls. Existing methods predominantly rely on coarse-grained static analysis techniques to approximate the targets for indirect function calls.

For instance, TypeArmor [34] adopts a strategy of selecting matching functions with the same number of function arguments as the indirect callsite. BPA [19] utilizes the Value Set Analysis (VSA) framework to analyze the potential value set of function pointers used by indirect branches. Both of them rely on identifying patterns within the binary instructions to refine the targets of indirect calls. However, their reliance on heuristic rules and the absence of source-level information contribute to low precision outcomes.

CALLEE [41] represents the first attempt at utilizing a learning-based approach for solving this problem. In order to determine whether the indirect callsite and callee match, it employs contrastive learning [39] to build a Siamese neural network that calculates the difference score between callsites and callees. However, CALLEE' training data does not include the complete execution flow of function jumps. Instead, they design heuristic rules to slice the code context of function calls and select instructions that they consider important for training. Due to the lack of complete contextual semantics, CALLEE also lost some precision in results.

In recent years, the Transformer architecture [35] has achieved tremendous success in the field of natural language processing. By incorporating the attention mechanism, deep learning models can focus more on the salient parts of input sequences, mimicking human attention and enhancing model performance. Beyond that, the Transformer has also shown potential in the field of program analysis. By applying it, researchers have achieved impressive results in tasks such as code similarity comparison [17,36], binary type recovery [27] and code generation [38]. In light of this, we can leverage the Transformer architecture to automatically discover the semantic matching patterns in the process of function calls. The attention mechanisms inherent in Transformers can assist in eliminating the need for manual code slicing or searching for instruction usage patterns in binary code.

In this paper, we present AttnCall, a novel neural network model designed to address the challenge of determining legitimate targets of indirect calls in binaries. AttnCall leverages the powerful Transformer architecture and incorporates two separate encoder input layers to capture the context of both function callsites and callees. By integrating the attention mechanism, we can guide the model to automatically focus on key instructions that contribute to the semantic understanding of function jumps. Therefore, we don't need heuristic rules to slice the code, as AttnCall can automatically embed the complete code semantics in an end-to-end code representation manner. By creating a training task centered around the control flow of function calls, the attention mechanism in AttnCall emphasize the identification of context-matching patterns between callsites and callees. This enables the model to better understand the complex relationships and dependencies involved in function calls.

In summary, we make the following contributions:

- We present and open-source AttnCall[1], the first Transformer-based architecture designed to comprehend the semantic matching patterns of the indirect function calls in binaries.
- We design an end-to-end code representation learning scheme, that performs effective representation learning of function call semantics without introducing any heuristic rules.
- We utilize AttnCall for the task of predicting legal targets of indirect calls in binaries, achieving 31.4% precision improvement over the state-of-the-art work.
- We conducted extensive evaluations that demonstrates the soundness of the results in contribution 3, the effectiveness of techniques in contributions 1 and 2, as well as the interpretability of the model.

The rest of this paper is organized as follows. Section 2 introduces the background and related work. Section 3 gives an overview of AttnCall. Section 4 details the methodology of important parts. The evaluation is provided in Sect. 5. Section 6 discusses the limitations. Finally, Sect. 7 concludes the paper.

2   Related Work

We discuss related work in indirect call targets refining, DNN-based Binary Analysis, and Attention Mechanism.

2.1   Indirect Call Targets Refining

The key aspect of reconstructing program CFGs is to solve the legal targets of indirect calls [19]. Researchers have proposed many different approaches to this problem. It is worth noting that the binary level will introduce additional challenges compared with the source code level, since binaries lack source level information such as symbol information.

Control Flow Classification. Indirect control flow exhibits specific characteristics during runtime that can be leveraged to narrow down potential targets. CCFIR [40] defines Address-Taken (AT) functions, asserting that only functions

---

[1] https://github.com/anonmai/AttnCall.

whose addresses are taken during the compilation phase can be assigned to function pointers. Lockdown [26] adopts a module perspective, restricting indirect branches to jump only to functions within the same module or imported from other modules. BinCC [37] proposes the concept of code continent, which categorizes basic blocks into internal nodes and boundary nodes. Internal nodes have deterministic targets, while boundary nodes have range-based targets. BBB-CFI [14] presents a lightweight binary Control Flow Integrity (CFI) scheme, in which indirect control flow can only jump to basic block boundaries. In summary, these approaches adopt a coarse-grained partitioning of the control flow, aiming to obtain more restricted but less precise results for indirect branch targets.

Type-Based Analysis. Indirect function calls represent a distinct category within function calls, where the target function's prototype must match the callsites. Different approaches have been developed to address this challenge, starting from the source code to the binary level. LLVM-CFI [32] introduces a function prototype matching mechanism during the compilation stage. It restricts indirect function calls to target functions with the same function prototype. TypeArmor [34] extends this idea to the binary level and only performs coarse-grained matching using the number of function arguments. τCFI [25] includes register width as an additional matching criterion, which narrows down targets at the binary level. However, approaches based on function prototype analysis face the problem of function prototype recovery accuracy at the binary level. Even if function types are recovered accurately, there can be still a significant number of function sets with identical types, leading to numerous false positive edges. In addition to this, type analysis struggles to handle cases involving type casting [11].

Value-Based Analysis. Indirect function calls involve function pointers, which are a special type of pointer that holds function addresses. Therefore, traditional value-based methods can also be applied to solving function pointer values. Angr [31] and IDA Pro [15] use symbolic execution and constraint solving techniques to determine the specific values of function pointers. Although this method provides mathematical correctness guarantees, the solved values are often not precise. BPA [19], based on the Value Set Analysis (VSA) [4], takes advantage of the block characteristics of data usage in binary code and constructs a coarse-grained VSA architecture to solve function pointer values. However, the accuracy of its results is comparable to that of methods based on type matching.

Learning-Based Analysis. CALLEE [41] is the first deep learning-based approach to solve indirect call targets. It learns a matching model for callsites and callees from a large number of program jump pair samples. Inspired by question-answering systems [39], CALLEE employs contrastive learning and constructs a Siamese neural network to calculate the contextual difference score between callsites and callees. However, CALLEE relies heavily on expert knowledge. It designs heuristic rules for selectively slicing programs, which limits the model's ability to learn knowledge from code semantics. Furthermore, Siamese neural networks are primarily designed for evaluating the similarity between data instances with shared characteristics. This may not be ideal for matching the context of callsites and callees, as they possess distinct characteristics. These limitations indicate the need for further advancements in learning-based approaches to address the challenges of solving indirect targets. By overcoming the reliance on heuristic rules and considering the unique characteristics of callsites and callees, more architecture should be developed to improve the precision and reliability of indirect target resolution in binary programs.

2.2 DNN-Based Binary Analysis

Existing work utilizing Deep Neural Networks (DNNs) has made significant progress in binary analysis areas such as binary information recovery and code similarity comparison. EKLAVYA [6] uses RNNs to learn function types from disassembled code. Asm2vec [9] treats code as text and generates vector representations of assembly code based on the doc2vec model for similarity comparison. jTrans [36] believes that code contains structural information and is not simply plain text. Therefore, it adopts the Transformer architecture and adds jump vectors to the embedding layer, which guides the model to learn the contextual sequence relationships caused by direct jump instructions. The widespread use of DNNs in the field of program analysis motivates us to explore the capabilities of DNNs for refining indirect call targets.

2.3 Attention Mechanism

The inspiration for attention mechanisms comes from the human visual attention system. In 2014, RNNsearch [3] first applied the attention mechanism to the neural machine translation (NMT) task. It can automatically learn which parts of the source sentence to focus on during the translation process, thus improving translation quality. Vaswani et al. proposed the Transformer model [35] in 2017, which is entirely based on attention mechanisms. It abandons the structures of both convolutional neural networks (CNNs) and recurrent neural networks (RNNs), thereby significantly enhancing computational efficiency and performance.

In the realm of natural language processing tasks, pre-trained models such as BERT [8], GPT [28], and RoBERTa [22] have embraced the Transformer architecture. These models leverage self-attention mechanisms for efficient feature extraction and context modeling, leading to remarkable performance enhancements. Based on the Transformer architecture, there are also some code pre-trained models, such as CodeBERT [12] and PalmTree [21], which aim to optimize code representations to be suitable for downstream program analysis tasks.

The typical Transformer architecture utilizes one encoder to accept the input sequence, and one decoder to output the result sequence. It constructs the relationships within the two sequences through self-attention mechanisms. Additionally, each layer of the decoder contains a cross-attention module to establish the contextual relationship between the source and target sequences. This enables the decoder to focus on relevant parts of the source sequence when generating the target sequence, thereby improving the model's performance.

In the scenario presented in this paper, we also have two sequence inputs – the context of callsites and the context of callees. Therefore, we can use the attention mechanism to establish the contextual relationship between the two sequences, which helps the neural network to recognize the pattern matching relationship of function calls from the semantic context.

3 Overview

In this section, we present the overall architecture of AttnCall. As shown in Fig. 1, the AttnCall mainly consists of two parts: the model training module and the target binary prediction module.

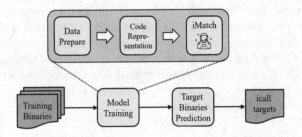

Fig. 1. Overview of the AttnCall architecture.

In the model training module, there are three steps: data preparation, code representation, and intelligent matching learning. Given the large-scale binaries required for training, we first preprocess the data by disassembling and sampling. Then, we convert the sampled code into vectors that can be recognized by deep learning models. Finally, the samples are fed into the intelligent matching model *iMatch* for training. In the target binary prediction module, we use the trained model to predict the targets of indirect function calls in the target binary. We will briefly explain each part below.

3.1 Workflow of the Model Training

1. **Data Prepare.** First, we disassemble the input binary files, to obtain the disassembled code and Direct Control Flow Graph (DCFG). DCFG can be analyzed and sliced for all function callsites. Specifically, for a function callsite, slice backward to the caller function header, providing the top context for the call, and slice forward to the callee function tail, forming the call's bottom context. We employ random slicing, which means that only one path

is randomly selected at each branch instruction. This is because each path contains all the context that the function call possesses. Combine the top context and bottom context as a positive sample for the function call. We then replace the bottom context with any incorrect context to serve as a negative sample.

2. **Code Representation**. Prior to model training, the code must be represented as vectors or tensors. In this work, we designed an end-to-end embedding approach, where we make embedding the learning process into the front end of the training process, rather than performing it in stages. This allows the representation learning process to be more closely aligned with the training task and to be more automated, avoiding excessive human involvement. Specifically, this step is divided into three processes: symbolization, vectorization, and pooling. We will detail it in Sect. 4.1

3. **Train an iMatch Model**. For the top and bottom contexts represented as vectors, we constructed a neural network model based on the Transformer architecture, using an encoder for the top context and another encoder for the bottom context. The model outputs a matching score between the top and bottom contexts.

3.2 Target Binaries Prediction

This module takes the target binaries for prediction. It identifies all indirect call sites, and performs backward slicing to obtain the top context. It then identifies all legitimate functions and performs forward slicing to obtain the bottom context. The module combines all top and bottom contexts and inputs them into the previously obtained model, scoring each paired sequence to determine if the top and bottom contexts match. A match between top and bottom context signifies a legitimate indirect call target.

4   Methodology

4.1 Context Representation

Before the code representation learning, instructions must be symbolized to avoid the Out-of-Vocabulary (OOV) phenomenon. Then, the instructions also need to go through a vectorization process, which convert natural language symbols into machine-readable vectors. Finally, we introduce a pooling layer to pool the split instruction fragments into complete instructions.

Symbolization. The overall goal of symbolization is to replace open-set token collections with closed-set ones. An open set is a collection where unrecognized types are present, while a closed set is the opposite. For our model, the number of vocabulary items such as immediate values and addresses is too large as the training process grows. Therefore, they are considered as open-set collections.

A common strategy for handling open-set collections is to replace samples in the same category with a single symbol. For example, we can replace all addresses with [addr] and all immediate values with [num]. However, in open-set collections, some vocabulary items appear frequently and play an important role in the context's semantic information, which is useful for model learning, such as small numbers. Therefore, we adopt a compromise strategy in that we reserve these small numbers.

Vectorization. If we directly include all instruction tokens into the model training, the model will fail to recognize the instruction boundaries and understand the instruction semantics. Therefore, Instruction2Vec [20] adopts a fixed-length vector strategy to represent instructions, designing a fixed symbol count of 9-element vector based on the maximum number of elements in each instruction. However, Instruction2Vec does not represent the semantics of indirect references. Building on this, we add an extra element for each operand to indicate whether it is an indirect reference or not. If the token *ind* exists, it indicates that the operand is an indirect operand and the inverse indicates a direct operand.

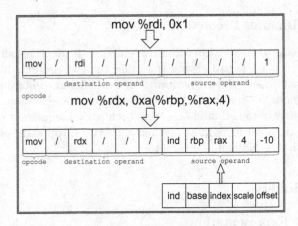

Fig. 2. The instruction vector

Formally, we represent each instruction using an 11-element vector:

- The first element represents the operator of the instruction.
- The second to sixth elements represent the destination operand.
- The seventh to eleventh elements represent the source operand.

To illustrate this representation, we provide two examples in Fig. 2. Each operand in the vector spans five elements: the first indicates indirect addressing, the second represents the base register or single operand location, the third denotes the index register, the fourth signifies the scale size, and the fifth stands for the offset size. For pointer operands, we deduce the ptr address as $base + index *$

scale + *offset*. The pointer operand vector is shown at the bottom of Fig. 2. This vector-based representation allows us to capture the essential features and characteristics of each instruction in a compact and structured manner.

Pooling. In order to learn the code representation, related work [9,12,21] generally adopts NLP-based sequence relationship learning models, which treat instructions as sentences and operators, registers, immediate values, punctuation, etc., as vocabulary. However, the model can hardly understand the semantics of individual instructions, as the CPU executes one instruction at a time. Alternatively, some approaches [6,42] treat functions/basic blocks as sentences and a single instruction as vocabulary. This approach helps the machine understand the semantics at the instruction level, but it may lead to an infinite expansion of vocabulary. To address these challenges, we propose a pooling layer in our design. As depicted in Fig. 3, the 11-element vector representing an instruction is pooled into a condensed 3-element vector.

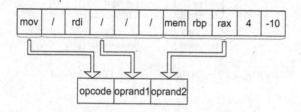

Fig. 3. The pooling process

4.2 Structure of the DNN Model

To match the context of the callsite and the callee, we have built a neural network model based on the Transformer architecture to predict their matching score. As shown in Fig. 4, the model has an encoder on the left side, which takes the top context as input, and another encoder on the right side, which takes the bottom context as input. The left encoder is a stack composed of N identical layers, each containing a multi-head self-attention layer and a feed-forward neural network. The right encoder is also a stack composed of N identical layers. Similar to the left one, each layer contains a multi-head self-attention layer and a feed-forward neural network, with an additional cross-attention layer, where K and V are taken from the output of the left encoder stack. A linear layer is added to the end of the right encoder stack to convert the output into a 0/1 classification result.

4.3 Target Binaries Prediction

We employ this model to predict indirect function calls, evaluating semantic matching degrees between the indirect call and candidate functions. This app-

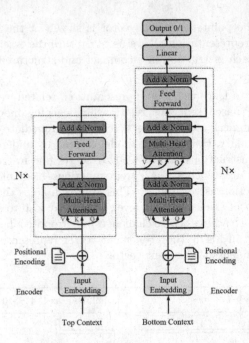

Fig. 4. The structure of the DNN Model

roach inherently presumes that semantic matching patterns for direct and indirect function calls are equivalent. It is reasonable since their ways of handling parameters are identical. The sole distinction lies in the storage of jump targets for function calls — hard-code or in the register/memory. Consequently, their dependencies on the callee context are also consistent.

Address-Taken Functions. In our methodology, we select Address-Taken (AT) functions as candidate functions from the target binaries. AT functions are those whose addresses are "taken" into variables during compilation. Specifically, indirect calls invariably consume a function pointer, assigned either an function address during initialization or execution. As such, only AT functions can potentially serve as targets for indirect function calls.

We assign the contexts of indirect callsites as tops and the contexts of candidate functions as bottoms. Given m tops and n bottoms, we arrange and combine them into $m \times n$ matching pairs, feeding each pair into the model to generate a matching degree score. Specifically, we set a threshold based on the model's output score d to determine if a top and bottom constitute a match. As the binary classifier layer outputs values between 0 and 1, we establish a balanced threshold value of 0.5.

$$\text{matching} = \begin{cases} \text{yes} & \text{if } d \geq \text{threshold,} \\ \text{no} & \text{if } d < \text{threshold.} \end{cases}$$

5 Evaluation

Our evaluation aims to answer the following questions:

- Does AttnCall can determine whether a function call is legitimate? (S5.1)
- Which semantic is important in the function call? (S5.2)
- How accurate is AttnCall compared to the baselines on the indirect call target prediction task? (S5.3)
- Whether the results are sound for static analysis? (S5.4)
- Does the model have interpretability? (S5.5)

5.1 Experiment Setup

Our dataset is gathered from BinaryCorp of jTrans [36], extracted from Arch-Linux's official repositories and Arch User Repository(AUR). It contains the majority of popular open-source software and builds them with different compiler optimizations to yield different binaries. We disassemble these binaries with Angr [31] to collect training examples. Direct function calls serve as positive samples, while fabricated function call pairs constitute negative samples. We construct negative samples by replacing the bottom instruction in positive samples with random continuous instructions from binaries. In total, we collected 54 million positive samples and 324 million negative samples. These samples were divided into training and testing sets in a ratio of 80% to 20%, respectively. The training and test results are shown in Setting 1 of Table 1. The high accuracy shows that AttnCall succeeds to determine whether a function call is legitimate or not.

Then, we use AttnCall to predict the targets of indirect function calls. The average indirect call target (AICT) [23] metric is presented to compare the precision with related work. To show the soundness of prediction results, we collect ground truth for benchmarks with Intel Pin [24]. We use the same benchmark as BPA: the SPEC CPU 2006 benchmark and 5 sever applications (thttpd-2.29, memcached-1.5.4, lighttpd-1.4.48, exim-4.89, and nginx-1.10). We build the learning model with TensorFlow 2.12 [13]. The code is public in https://github.com/anonmai/AttnCall for future research.

Table 1. Overall Performance of AttnCall

Setting	Ablation	Train				Test			
		Accuracy	Precision	Recall	F1	Accuracy	Precision	Recall	F1
1	none	98.18%	96.97%	99.47%	98.20%	96.66%	97.07%	96.22%	96.64%
2	opcode	95.30%	86.47%	96.46%	91.19%	95.10%	87.04%	94.45%	90.59%
3	reg	94.30%	84.30%	94.86%	89.27%	91.74%	83.74%	83.11%	83.42%
4	num	97.90%	96.47%	99.44%	97.93%	96.32%	95.52%	97.78%	96.63%

5.2   Ablation Study

To evaluate which key parts in the semantic context of function jumps affect the performance of AttnCall, we conduct ablation experiments on opcode, registers, and immediate in the context, respectively. The ablation study results are shown in Setting 2–4 of Table 1.

- **Effect of the operator**. We symbolize all opcodes as a single symbol *[op]*. The results are shown in Setting 2 of Table 1. Because of the significant decline in precision, we find that the opcode plays an important role in the semantic matching of function calls.
- **Effect of the register**. We ablate the type information of registers and symbolize all register types as a single symbol *[reg]*. The results, depicted in Setting 3 of Table 1, shows the maximum reduction in precision amongst our comparisons. This indicates that the type information of registers holds paramount importance in our model.
- **Effect of the number**. We note that small constants frequently occur and typically serve to represent offsets in data structures. We symbolize small constants in the same way as large constants, using [num]. The results, depicted in Setting 4 of Table 1, show only a negligible impact, suggesting that numbers in the context are not as critical as other features.

5.3   Comparison on the Indirect Call Prediction

We use the trained model AttnCall to predict the targets of the indirect function calls as shown in Sect. 4.3.

Table 2. AICT evaluation results

Binary	Functions	Instrs	icallsites	AICT				
				AT	Arity	BPA	CALLEE	AttnCall
401.bzip2	79	21k	22	2.0	1.0	2.0	1.4	1.0
458.sjeng	145	32k	3	7.0	7.0	7.0	7.0	6.0
433.milc	245	31k	6	2.0	2.0	2.0	2.0	3.0
482.sphinx3	336	45k	10	6.0	2.3	1.3	5.6	5.7
456.hmmer	506	88k	11	22.0	22.0	2.9	7.2	6.6
464.h264ref	533	161k	371	39.0	30.6	4.3	20.9	21.5
445.gobmk	2537	213k	46	1790.0	1395.7	884.6	672.4	422.3
400.perlbench	1793	306k	141	721.0	580.4	400.3	354.0	313.2
403.gcc	4678	969k	459	1211.0	650.0	534.8	338.0	274.0
thttpd	117	18k	1	17.0	17.0	8.0	/	7.0
memcached	244	37k	75	24.0	20.8	1.0	11.3	2.1
lighttpd	360	66k	126	52.0	27.8	35.5	31.7	17.4
exim	622	168k	89	85.0	40.4	31.1	22.4	15.1
nginx	1118	232k	409	753.0	441.6	444.0	383.0	296.5
Average	950.9	170k	126.4	380.2	238.4	209.3	142.8	99.4

The prediction results will be compared with several closely relevant solutions including CCFIR [40], TypeArmor [34], BPA [19] and CALLEE [41]. We choose Average Indirect Call Targets (AICT) [23] as the evaluation metric, which can well reflect the accuracy of indirect function call prediction [19]. We use the same benchmark as BPA: the SPEC CPU 2006 benchmark and 5 sever applications (thttpd-2.29, memcached-1.5.4, lighttpd-1.4.48, exim-4.89, and nginx-1.10).

The results are displayed in Table 2. Column *Functions* and *Instrs* represent the count of all functions and instructions in a binary, respectively. Column *icall-sites* indicates the number of indirect callsites. In the group of AICT columns, AT is a strategy the same as CCFIR [40], which allows an indirect call to target all Address-Taken functions; Arity is the conservative arity-matching based CFG construction, which is an implementation of TypeArmor [34]. Since BPA [19] and CALLEE [41] have not been open-sourced, we adopt the results from their paper. The last column AttnCall is our work, which shows 31.4% reduction in AICT, compared with CALLEE [41]. Thus, we can conclude that AttnCall outperforms the state-of-the-art work in the precision of indirect call prediction.

5.4   Soundness Evaluation of Indirect Call Prediction

We evaluate the soundness of AttnCall's predictions for indirect function call targets. Due to static analysis limitations, we cannot obtain the precise set of valid targets for indirect function calls. As a result, we resort to dynamic testing to approximate the ideal set of valid targets. Through dynamic testing, we capture a comprehensive range of valid targets and compute the recall rate, which represents the percentage of dynamic targets that are correctly identified in the predicted set. However, it should be noted that the actual recall will be lower than the evaluated recall rate. We mitigate this disparity by conducting as many dynamic tests as possible.

To collect dynamic paths of SPEC2006 binaries, we leverage Intel's Pin tool [24]. We use their extensive reference as the input dataset, which encompasses a wide range of inputs. If all dynamic paths of the indirect calls appear in the prediction results, we will treat the prediction results as sound. Hence, we use the recall metric to represent the soundness of the refinement targets. The following formula is to calculate the average recall rate for all indirect function callsites in the target binaries:

$$R_c = \frac{1}{n} \sum_{i=1}^{n} Rc_i \quad where \ Rc_i = \frac{TP_i}{TP_i + FN_i} \tag{1}$$

Here, TP_i and FN_i represent the numbers of true positives and false negatives, respectively, for indirect function callsite i. A true positive indicates that the target appears in both the predicted set and the dynamically recorded set. A false negative indicates that the target appears in the dynamically recorded set but not in the predicted set. Table 3 presents the recall performance of AttnCall on various benchmarks at different levels of optimization.

Table 3. The recall rate of AttnCall

Opt- level	401. bzip2	458. sjeng	433. milc	482. sphinx3	456. hmmer	464. h264ref	445. gobmk	400. perlbench	403. gcc
O0	100%	100%	100%	100%	100%	92.31%	96.93%	78.41%	93.16%
O1	100%	100%	100%	100%	100%	99.10%	99.64%	94.37%	91.78%
O2	100%	100%	100%	100%	90%	100%	95.08%	97.44%	92.31%
O3	100%	100%	100%	100%	100%	91.07%	44.74%	90.83%	87.30%

As reflected in the table, our method yields an average recall of 95.42% on the benchmark dataset. This recall metric is 5.0% higher than that of the state-of-the-art work CALLEE [41]. This substantial recall rate achieved by AttnCall underscores its efficacy in delivering a sound Control Flow Graph (CFG) for binary program analysis, applicable to tasks like code similarity detection, fuzzing, and vulnerability discovery. In conclusion, AttnCall demonstrates significant proficiency in attaining high soundness while predicting indirect call targets for binary analysis.

5.5   Interpretability

Embedding Model. We employ T-SNE [33] to transform high-dimensional vectors into a two-dimensional space to verify whether the embedding model properly classifies words with varying semantics, as depicted in Fig. 5. The figure clearly exhibits tokens with similar semantics clustering together, such as registers, arithmetic operators, and jump operators. Consequently, we deduce that our code representation learning has successfully captured the semantics of assembly instructions.

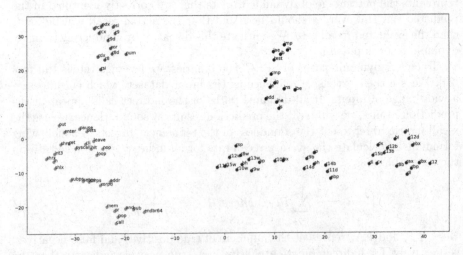

Fig. 5. The T-SNE visualization of tokens in AttnCall

Case Study. We employ a cross-attention mechanism in AttnCall to facilitate the interpretation of the deep learning network. This cross-attention learning layer builds an association between the function callsites and their corresponding callees. Using the attention values, we can evaluate the degree of correlation between two instructions. Higher attention values imply a stronger relevance between instructions, while lower values signify a relatively weaker association.

Fig. 6. The case of the cross attention visualization

Figure 6 presents a case study of an indirect function call. The left portion of the figure displays an example of C code. In this example, Function 1 defines a function pointer with a parameter list of one integer type. It is then assigned the value of Function 2, and the function pointer is called. The center part shows the execution flow of the disassembled code when such an indirect call take place. AttnCall will identify highly correlated instructions from such code snippets. The right segment depicts the cross-attention value matrix that AttnCall learned for this particular case. As seen in the matrix diagram, instructions related to the function parameter types (e.g. *mov edi eax*) have obtained the highest attention weights. This case illustrates AttnCall's successful extraction of the most crucial instructions in the matching pattern during a function call.

Study on Function Call Patterns. The Ablation Study results led us to ascertain the significant role of registers in AttnCall. To deepen our comprehension of learned matching patterns, we conducted a statistical analysis on highly attended tokens. The findings are collated in Table 4. The table's first row represents operand types, signified by their base registers. Indirect addressing is indicated by it in parentheses. The second and third rows respectively illustrate the frequencies with which these operand types appear at callsites and callees.

Table 4. High attention operand statistics

op type	esi	rsi	edi	rdi	(rdi)	edx	ecx	rax	(rip)	rbx
callsite	28.18%	19.93%	2.17%	14.92%	0.07%	2.74%	2.28%	8.45%	7.02%	0.83%
callee	3.04%	2.09%	1.24%	0.97%	16.09%	3.83%	1.52%	12.12%	13.35%	13.20%

The analysis reveals that certain registers play more significant roles in function calls. Specifically, the registers *esi/rsi* and *rdi* emerge as the most important in callsites, representing the first and second arguments of function calls. For callees, the most significant registers are *(rdi)* and *(rip)*, which correspond to the second argument and global variable. The prominence of indirect addressing is particularly evident in the callee context, as callee functions often utilize passed pointers to reference data. The statis shows AttnCall's ability to capture semantics of function calls, echoing the manner in which humans understand it.

In summary, our analysis demonstrates that AttnCall effectively learns the function call semantics and capture the relevance and importance of different tokens in the contexts. We can draw the following conclusion: AttnCall has good interpretability and can learn patterns consistent with expert knowledge.

6   Discussion

The core aim of this paper is to improve the precision of recognizing legitimate targets for indirect calls. Although we have achieved improved precision compared to related work, our recall rate has not reached 100%. This falls short for security mechanisms like Control Flow Integrity (CFI) [2], as any false negative could disrupt the correct execution of the program. Nevertheless, for indirect branches with less than 100% recall, a hybrid strategy involving type matching can be employed to complement our approach.

While our evaluation focused primarily on the soundness of the refined targets, future research can explore the impact of these refinements on various downstream tasks to measure their effectiveness in improving code analysis and related applications, such as code similarity detection, fuzzing, and vulnerability discovery. Nonetheless, the substantial soundness demonstrated by the refined results sufficiently qualifies them for use in program analysis solutions.

7   Conclusion

In this work we present AttnCall, the first Transformer-based learning model to predict indirect function call targets in binaries. Employing the Transformer framework, AttnCall automatically discerns the correlation between callsites and callees, without any heuristic rules. By leveraging attention mechanisms, manual selection of significant instructions is rendered unnecessary. The model autonomously identifies instructions warranting high attention in both contexts. Experimental results demonstrate that our model outperforms SOTA work in indirect call prediction and attains soundness contrasted with dynamically collected ground truth. Crucially, we highlight the interpretability of our model. By visualizing the embeddings and attention mechanisms, we deduce that the model exhibits a level of understanding of the code that is comparable to human comprehension. Overall, AttnCall offers a promising solution for accurately refining legitimate targets of indirect calls in binary programs, with the strengths of the Transformer architecture and attention mechanism.

References

1. Abadi, M., Budiu, M., Erlingsson, Ú., Ligatti, J.: Control-flow integrity. In: Proceedings of the 12th ACM Conference on Computer and Communications Security, CCS '05, pp. 340–353. Association for Computing Machinery, New York (2005). https://doi.org/10.1145/1102120.1102165
2. Abadi, M., Budiu, M., Erlingsson, Ú., Ligatti, J.: Control-flow integrity principles, implementations, and applications. ACM Trans. Inf. Syst. Secur. **13**(1), 1–40 (2009). https://doi.org/10.1145/1609956.1609960
3. Bahdanau, D., Cho, K., Bengio, Y.: Neural machine translation by jointly learning to align and translate (2015). https://doi.org/10.48550/arXiv.1409.0473
4. Balakrishnan, G., Reps, T.: Analyzing memory accesses in x86 executables. In: Duesterwald, E. (ed.) CC 2004. LNCS, vol. 2985, pp. 5–23. Springer, Heidelberg (2004). https://doi.org/10.1007/978-3-540-24723-4_2
5. Burow, N., Zhang, X., Payer, M.: SoK: shining light on shadow stacks. In: 2019 IEEE Symposium on Security and Privacy (SP), Oakland, pp. 985–999 (2019). https://doi.org/10.1109/SP.2019.00076
6. Chua, Z.L., Shen, S., Saxena, P., Liang, Z.: Neural nets can learn function type signatures from binaries. In: Proceedings of the 26th USENIX Security Symposium, Security, pp. 99–116 (2017). https://doi.org/10.5555/3241189.3241199
7. Debray, S., Muth, R., Weippert, M.: Alias analysis of executable code. In: Conference Record of the Annual ACM Symposium on Principles of Programming Languages, POPL, pp. 12–24. ACM (1998). https://doi.org/10.1145/268946.268948
8. Devlin, J., Chang, M.W., Lee, K., Toutanova, K.: BERT: pre-training of deep bidirectional transformers for language understanding (2019). https://doi.org/10.48550/arXiv.1810.04805
9. Ding, S.H.H., Fung, B.C.M., Charland, P.: Asm2Vec: boosting static representation robustness for binary clone search against code obfuscation and compiler optimization. In: 2019 IEEE Symposium on Security and Privacy (SP), SP, pp. 472–489 (2019). https://doi.org/10.1109/SP.2019.00003
10. Emami, M., Ghiya, R., Hendren, L.J.: Context-sensitive interprocedural points-to analysis in the presence of function pointers. ACM SIGPLAN Not. **29**(6), 242–256 (1994). https://doi.org/10.1145/773473.178264
11. Farkhani, R.M., Robertson, W., Jafari, S., Kirda, E., Arshad, S., Okhravi, H.: On the effectiveness of type-based control flow integrity. ACM Int. Conf. Proc. Ser. **12**, 28–39 (2018). https://doi.org/10.1145/3274694.3274739
12. Feng, Z., et al.: CodeBERT: a pre-trained model for programming and natural languages (2020). https://doi.org/10.48550/arXiv.2002.08155
13. Google: create production-grade machine learning models with TensorFlow. https://www.tensorflow.org//
14. He, W., Das, S., Zhang, W., Liu, Y.: BBB-CFI: lightweight CFI approach against code-reuse attacks using basic block information. ACM Trans. Embed. Comput. Syst. **19**(1), 1–22 (2020). https://doi.org/10.1145/3371151
15. Hex-Rays: The IDA pro disassembler and debugger (2008). https://www.hex-rays.com/products/ida/
16. Hu, H., et al.: Enforcing unique code target property for control-flow integrity. In: Proceedings of the 2018 ACM SIGSAC Conference on Computer and Communications Security, CCS, pp. 1470–1486. ACM, New York (2018). https://doi.org/10.1145/3243734.3243797

17. Jiang, S., Fu, C., Qian, Y., He, S., Lv, J., Han, L.: IFAttn: binary code similarity analysis based on interpretable features with attention. Comput. Secur. **120**, 102804 (2022). https://doi.org/10.1016/j.cose.2022.102804

18. Khandaker, M.R., Liu, W., Naser, A., Wang, Z., Yang, J.: Origin-sensitive control flow integrity. In: Proceedings of the 28th USENIX Security Symposium, Security, pp. 195–211 (2019). https://doi.org/10.5555/3361338.3361353

19. Kim, S.H., Sun, C., Zeng, D., Tan, G.: Refining indirect call targets at the binary level. In: Proceedings 2021 Network and Distributed System Security Symposium. No. February in NDSS, Internet Society, Reston, VA (2021). https://doi.org/10.14722/ndss.2021.24386

20. Lee, Y.J., Choi, S.H., Kim, C., Lim, S.H., Park, K.W.: Learning binary code with deep learning to detect software weakness. In: In KSII The 9th International Conference on Internet (ICONI) 2017 Symposium, ICONI, p. 5 (2017)

21. Li, X., Qu, Y., Yin, H.: PalmTree: learning an assembly language model for instruction embedding. In: Proceedings of the 2021 ACM SIGSAC Conference on Computer and Communications Security, CCS, pp. 3236–3251. ACM, Virtual Event Republic of Korea (2021). https://doi.org/10.1145/3460120.3484587

22. Liu, Y., et al.: RoBERTa: a robustly optimized BERT pretraining approach (2019). https://doi.org/10.48550/arXiv.1907.11692

23. Lu, K., Hu, H.: Where does it go? Refining indirect-call targets with multi-layer type analysis. In: Proceedings of the ACM Conference on Computer and Communications Security, CCS, pp. 1867–1881. Association for Computing Machinery, New York (2019). https://doi.org/10.1145/3319535.3354244

24. Luk, C.K., et al.: Pin: building customized program analysis tools with dynamic instrumentation. ACM SIGPLAN Not. **40**(6), 190–200 (2005). https://doi.org/10.1145/1064978.1065034

25. Muntean, P., Fischer, M., Tan, G., Lin, Z., Grossklags, J., Eckert, C.: τ CFI: type-assisted control flow integrity for x86-64 binaries. In: Bailey, M., Holz, T., Stamatogiannakis, M., Ioannidis, S. (eds.) RAID 2018. LNCS, vol. 11050, pp. 423–444. Springer, Cham (2018). https://doi.org/10.1007/978-3-030-00470-5_20

26. Payer, M., Barresi, A., Gross, T.R.: Fine-grained control-flow integrity through binary hardening. In: Almgren, M., Gulisano, V., Maggi, F. (eds.) DIMVA 2015. LNCS, vol. 9148, pp. 144–164. Springer, Cham (2015). https://doi.org/10.1007/978-3-319-20550-2_8

27. Pei, K., et al.: StateFormer: fine-grained type recovery from binaries using generative state modeling. In: Proceedings of the 29th ACM Joint Meeting on European Software Engineering Conference and Symposium on the Foundations of Software Engineering, ESEC/FSE 2021, pp. 690–702 (2021). https://doi.org/10.1145/3468264.3468607

28. Radford, A., Narasimhan, K., Salimans, T., Sutskever, I.: Improving language understanding by generative pre-training, p. 12. arXiv (2018)

29. Ramalingam, G.: The undecidability of aliasing. ACM Trans. Program. Lang. Syst. (TOPLAS) **16**(5), 1467–1471 (1994). https://doi.org/10.1145/186025.186041

30. Shacham, H.: The geometry of innocent flesh on the bone. In: Proceedings of the 14th ACM Conference on Computer and Communications Security - CCS '07, CCS, p. 552. ACM Press, New York (2007). https://doi.org/10.1145/1315245.1315313

31. Shoshitaishvili, Y., et al.: SOK: (state of) the art of war: Offensive techniques in binary analysis. In: Proceedings - 2016 IEEE Symposium on Security and Privacy, SP 2016, SP, pp. 138–157 (2016). https://doi.org/10.1109/SP.2016.17

32. Tice, C., et al.: Enforcing forward-edge control-flow integrity in {GCC} {&} {LLVM}. {USENIX} Security, pp. 941–955 (2014). https://doi.org/10.5555/2671225.2671285

33. Van der Maaten, L., Hinton, G.: Visualizing data using t-SNE. J. Mach. Learn. Res. **9**(11) (2008)

34. Van der Veen, V., et al.: A tough call: mitigating advanced code-reuse attacks at the binary level. In: 2016 IEEE Symposium on Security and Privacy (SP), pp. 934–953. IEEE, Oakland (2016). https://doi.org/10.1109/SP.2016.60

35. Vaswani, A., et al.: Attention is all you need. In: Advances in Neural Information Processing Systems, NIPS, vol. 30. Curran Associates, Inc. (2017)

36. Wang, H., et al.: jTrans: jump-aware transformer for binary code similarity detection. In: Proceedings of the 31st ACM SIGSOFT International Symposium on Software Testing and Analysis, ISSTA, pp. 1–13. ACM, Virtual South Korea (2022). https://doi.org/10.1145/3533767.3534367

37. Wang, M., Yin, H., Vasisht Bhaskar, A., Su, P., Feng, D.: Binary code continent: finer-grained control flow integrity for stripped binaries. In: Proceedings of the 31st Annual Computer Security Applications Conference on - ACSAC 2015, ACSAC. ACM Press, New York (2015). https://doi.org/10.1145/2818000.2818017

38. Yang, G., Chen, X., Zhou, Y., Yu, C.: DualSC: automatic generation and summarization of shellcode via transformer and dual learning. In: 2022 IEEE International Conference on Software Analysis, Evolution and Reengineering (SANER), pp. 361–372 (2022). https://doi.org/10.1109/SANER53432.2022.00052

39. Yu, L., Hermann, K.M., Blunsom, P., Pulman, S.: Deep learning for answer sentence selection. arXiv preprint: arXiv:1412.1632 (2014). https://doi.org/10.48550/arXiv.1412.1632

40. Zhang, C., et al.: Practical control flow integrity and randomization for binary executables. In: Proceedings - IEEE Symposium on Security and Privacy, Oakland, pp. 559–573 (2013). https://doi.org/10.1109/SP.2013.44

41. Zhu, W., et al.: CALLEE: recovering call graphs for binaries with transfer and contrastive learning. In: 2023 IEEE Symposium on Security and Privacy (SP), pp. 2357–2374. IEEE (2023). https://doi.org/10.1109/SP46215.2023.10179482

42. Zuo, F., Li, X., Young, P., Luo, L., Zeng, Q., Zhang, Z.: neural machine translation inspired binary code similarity comparison beyond function Pairs. In: Proceedings 2019 Network and Distributed System Security Symposium, NDSS (2019). https://doi.org/10.14722/ndss.2019.23492

Acumen: Analysing the Impact of Organisational Change on Users' Access Entitlements

Selasi Kwashie[1,2,3]($\boxtimes$) (iD), Wei Kang[1,2] (iD), Sandeep Santhosh Kumar[1] (iD), Geoff Jarrad[1,2] (iD), Seyit Camtepe[1,2] (iD), and Surya Nepal[1,2] (iD)

[1] CSIRO Data61, Adelaide, Australia
skwashie@csu.edu.au,
{wei.kang,Sandeep.SanthoshKumar,geoff.jarrad,seyit.camtepe,
surya.nepal}@data61.csiro.au
[2] Cyber Security CRC, Joondalup, Australia
[3] AI & Cyber Futures Institute, Charles Sturt University, Bathurst, Australia

Abstract. Planned organisational changes are frequent occurrences in large enterprises due to the dynamicity of employees' roles, evolution of teams, units and divisions as a result of mergers, demergers, and general restructuring. To safeguard system security and employees' productivity, it is paramount for system administrators to keep track and remediate all users' changing access needs. This paper studies the impact of (planned) organisational changes on the access privileges of employees in line with access control policies. Our solution, Acumen, uses binary decision diagrams (BDDs) to encode XACML policies via a Boolean function conversion, and performs semantic interpretation of organisational changes for analysis over the BDDs. The BDD structure is versatile, enabling succinct representation as well as effective and efficient symbolic operations and visualisation. We demonstrate the efficacy of Acumen with two data sets via a series of case studies on: a) a commonly used benchmark access control policy data in the literature; and b) a proprietary data set containing planned organisational changes in a large real-world financial institution with a dynamic business environment. The empirically results show Acumen to be effective and efficient.

Keywords: Access control · Change impact analysis · BDDs

1 Introduction

In modern enterprises with dynamic business environments, employees' duties and roles often change due to project/business demands and/or organisational restructuring (e.g., mergers, demergers, creation of new teams, etc.). In these settings, the twofold demands of staff productivity and system security call for an efficient and effective analysis and management of users' access entitlements. However, in practice, system administrators find it difficult to keep up with

---

S. Kwashie, W. Kang, and S. Santhosh Kumar—Equal contributions.

© The Author(s), under exclusive license to Springer Nature Switzerland AG 2024
G. Tsudik et al. (Eds.): ESORICS 2023, LNCS 14347, pp. 410–430, 2024.
https://doi.org/10.1007/978-3-031-51482-1_21

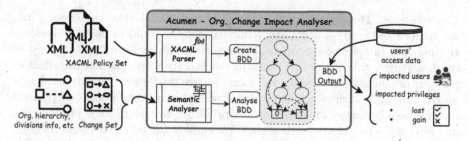

Fig. 1. Overview of the proposed solution.

users' changing need for access due to the arduous and non-automatic nature of their processes. Thus, managing access privileges properly tends to be rather time-consuming and complicated in large enterprises, where an ordinary change in an organisational structure could impact tens or even hundreds of employees.

This paper investigates the design of an automatic system for assessing the impact of planned organisational changes on access privileges of subjects (i.e., users, teams, etc.) in large dynamic organisations.

Motivation & Problem Description. Consider a large organisation, say a multi-national financial institution (e.g., one with thousands of staff, hundreds of teams across tens of divisions/units). In general, there are formal policies for administering and provisioning of access privileges to any user of an organisation's IT and business systems. However, the dynamicity of users' daily duties and fluidity of teams in modern organisations may require the movement of users and/or resources (resp., teams) to different roles (resp., units) in the defined organisational structure, often within short notice. It, thus, behooves system administrators to quickly and correctly provision access to users/teams in light of the intended changes and in accordance with the access control policies, to ensure there is no: (a) productivity loss due to unassigned access privileges; and (b) security breach/violations due to unrevoked access privileges.

This work provides a tool, Acumen, that enables system admins to analyse organisational changes w.r.t. access control policies and organisational structure, for remediation of access requirements in line with terms (a) and (b) above.

Overview of Proposed Solution. A general overview of our proposed solution, Acumen, is depicted in Fig. 1. We adopt *binary decision diagrams* (BDDs) as the cornerstone data structure of our solution, as it allows a symbolic representation and manipulation of Boolean functions (cf. [6, Ch. 7] and [5]). The solution has three components viz.: 1) an XACML Parser – parses access control policies (in XACML format) as Boolean functions to be encoded into a BDD; 2) a Semantic Analyser – synthesises change scenarios within the organisational structure for analysis *w.r.t.* access control policy rules over the BDD; and a 3) BDD Output – coalesces output from the BDD with users' identity data to present lists of impacted users and their associated lost/gained accesses.

Contributions. The contributions of this paper are summarised as follows. First, we propose and study a new change impact analysis problem using access control policies. In spite of its practical relevance in the real-world, to the best of our knowledge, this is the first work in the literature to examine the effect of planned organisational changes on users' access privileges. Second, we design an effective and efficient solution to analyse and reveal the impact of planned organisational changes on users' access privileges to ensure high productivity and reduce the risk of system breaches. We employ the binary decision diagram (BDD) data structure to losslessly encode access control policies, and to enable a swift analysis/manipulation of change operations over the encoded policies. Last, we empirically evaluate the performance of our solution through case studies with both open- and close-source access control policies data. In particular, we show that the proposed solution is scalable in large real-world organisational change analysis settings; and demonstrate the effectiveness of the solution with a well-known benchmark access control policy data set. The experimental results show the solution to be effective and efficient.

Related Work. Access control policy (ACP) analysis is a well-studied subject in the literature. A recent survey [12] categorises existing ACP analysis works into two major groups: a) ACP quality assessment; and b) ACP design and optimisation. Although the ACP analysis considered in this work is new and differs from those in existing works, it loosely relates to some of the problems in the latter group. Specifically, the *change impact analysis* and the *similarity analysis* problems are closer. Given a set of ACPs, existing change impact analysis works [11,13,17,24] focus on assessing: the impact of a proposed change to the configuration/specification of ACPs; or the differences among versions of the same policy set due to evolution of specifications. On the other hand, ACP similarity analysis works [7,14–16] seek to discover the relationships amongst the set of ACPs to enable policy integration, and collaboration across organisations. In contrast, we consider the effect of proposed organisational changes (in the form of subject property-value changes) on users' (resp. teams', units', etc.) access entitlements according to specifications of ACPs. In the context of our work, once we encode all relevant change and organisational hierarchy information, existing ACPs solutions like Margrave [11] and EXAM [15] can be co-opted to address a specific sub-task, viz.: assess the similarity of pre- and post- change BDDs. However, they cannot identify the impacted rules.

Several techniques have been explored to address the ACP analysis problems. In particular, model-checking-based methods are common as they enable complete and lossless encoding of the ACP rules. For example, Fisler et al. [11] uses multi-terminal BDDs (MTBDDs), Turkmen et al. [24] employs SMT-solvers [2], while Lin et al. [15] employs both MTBDDs and SAT-solvers. Another common approach is the use of formal methods, as seen in [7,13,14].

2   Preliminaries

In this section, we present the concepts used in the paper.

2.1   XACML Policies

The OASIS standard for representing access control policies is XACML [19]. There are three main, hierarchical elements in XACML: *policy set*; *policy*; and *rule*. A *policy set* is composed of either nested *policy sets* or *policies*, and a *policy* is composed of *rules*. Hence, in general, the root-level *policy set* can be decomposed into a large set of individual *rules*.

Policy sets, policies and rules all specify *subjects*, *resources* (or objects), and *actions*. A *subject* represents the entity requesting access. A *resource* represents the data, service or system component for which access is requested. An *action* specifies the type of access requested on the resource. They all can have one or more attributes. Collectively, the subject, resource and action comprise the *target*, which specifies a set of Boolean expressions that determine if the element is relevant to the request.

Rules additionally specify *conditions* and *effects*. The *conditions* specify Boolean expressions for the attributes of interest, which determine if the rule is satisfied or not. The *effect* specifies whether a successful rule will *permit* or *deny* access to the given resource.

Attribute Expressions. Agrawal et al. [1] categorised the different types of Boolean expressions that appear in policies. We list the atomic structures of this categorisation to understand the scope of our attribute expressions:

1. *Variable equality constraints* of the type $a \rhd v$, where $\rhd \in \{=, \neq\}$.
2. *Variable inequality constraints*, $a \rhd v$, where $\rhd \in \{<, \leq, >, \geq\}$.
3. *Regular expression constraints* of the type $a \rhd L(r)$, where a is a string-valued attribute, $\rhd \in \{\in, \notin\}$, and $L(r)$ is the language generated by regular expression r.
4. *Real valued linear constraints* of the type $\sum_{j=1}^{m} a_j x_j \rhd c$, where $x_j \in \mathbb{R}$ are numeric attributes, with real-valued coefficients $a_j \in \mathbb{R}$ and comparison value $c \in \mathbb{R}$, for operator $\rhd \in \{=, <, \leq, >, \geq\}$.

For our purposes, we require only the one-variable equality and inequality constraints, with operator $\rhd \in \{=, \neq, <, \leq, >, \geq\}$. Thus, we define a Boolean *attribute expression* as a triplet of the form $(a, \rhd, v)$, or simply $a \rhd v$, which compares a single attribute a with the given value v using the operator $\rhd$.

Policy Expressions. In practice, each XACML access policy can be translated into an amalgamation of Boolean expressions, obtained by combining the *target* and *condition* expressions of the policy and its rules. A detailed representation of this process is specified by Lin et al. [15, Def. 2]. Since the effect of a rule is to permit or deny access to the resource, the end result of the amalgamation is that each policy can be represented by the dual Boolean expressions f_{permit} and f_{deny}. Hence, access to the resource is explicitly permitted by a policy if f_{permit} evaluates to *true* for a given request, and access is explicitly denied under the policy if f_{deny} evaluates to *true*. The policy is in conflict if $f_{\text{permit}} \wedge f_{\text{deny}}$ can be true; and it is indeterminate if $f_{\text{permit}} \vee f_{\text{deny}}$ can be false.

Collectively, access to the resource is permitted if it is permitted by at least one policy in the policy set, and is denied if it is denied by at least one policy. Conflict arises if access is permitted by one policy but denied by another. The access is indeterminate if no policy permits or denies access.

In scenarios with no explicit denial mechanism, there is no f_{deny} expression, and hence access to the resource is permitted under the policy if f_{permit} is true. However, if f_{permit} is false, then the policy does not apply. Access to the resource is then permitted if at least one policy permits access, otherwise access is denied.

2.2   Binary Decision Diagrams

A binary decision diagram (BDD) is a data structure used to represent a logical expression. BDDs provide a way of representing large, complex Boolean functions effectively. It enables us to represent and manipulate Boolean functions symbolically [6, Ch. 7]. A detailed introduction can be found in [9, Sec. 7.1.4].

Graph Representation. A BDD typically takes the form of a directed acyclic graph with a single root node and two terminal nodes. The terminal nodes are labelled *true* and *false*, corresponding to each possible result obtained by evaluation of the Boolean function. Each parent node in the graph has an associated Boolean variable, and two child nodes: the *high* child is reached along the *high* edge if the variable is *true*; and the *low* child is reached along the *low* edge if the variable is *false*. To evaluate the BDD, we start from the root node and traverse the graph based on the variable assignments, finally arriving at one of the terminal nodes providing the final evaluation. Due to reduction

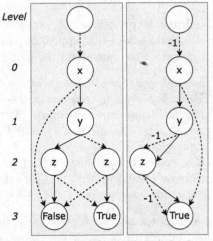

Fig. 2. An exemplar BDD for the logical expression $x \wedge (y \veebar z)$: (*left*) without; and (*right*) with complementary edges.

rules, BDDs emphasise reusability of sub-graphs, and lack redundant nodes – making representation concise.

Complementary Edges. BDDs can also be represented in a more compact form, using complementary edges. Complementary edges are similar to normal edges in BDDs but they negate the sub-graph to which the edge is directed. The use of complementarity reduces the number of nodes required to express Boolean functions as BDDs. It also eliminates the requirement of two terminal nodes since the negation of the *true* node is *false*. Complementarity must be a property of either the low or the high edges, but not both, to maintain the canonical property of BDDs [8].

As an example, consider the function $f(x, y, z) = x \wedge (y \veebar z)$, where $\veebar$ is the logical XOR operator. The BDD of this function with complementarity (labelled -1) on the low edges is illustrated in Fig. 2. The edge pointing from the empty node to the root node is an external reference which can also be a complementary edge. A solid line represents the *high* edge for which the parent node variable is true; a dashed line indicates the converse (*low* edge). A -1 indicates that the resulting Boolean value is to be negated.

BDD Complexity. A BDD may be constructed from a Boolean function using Shannon's decomposition, as described by Bryant [4]. The number of nodes in a BDD is in the worst case exponential and in the best case polynomial or even linear in the number of function variables. For this reason, we strive to minimise the creation of new variables, and maximise the reuse of existing variables.

Note that when constructing a BDD, its size can strongly depend on the variable ordering chosen [20]. We impose a reordering of the Boolean variables, such that a low order index corresponds to a high frequency of occurrence. This simple ordering heuristic has proven effective in promoting the reusability of nodes in the BDD. We remark that other variable ordering schemes, such as Rudell's shifting algorithm [21], are also effective in reducing the size of a BDD.

3   Problem Formulation

We present the formal problem definition and sketch of the solution below.

Problem Definition. Let $\mathcal{P}, \mathcal{H}, \mathcal{C}$ denote the sets of XACML access control policies, organisational hierarchies, and proposed organisational changes respectively. The set $\mathcal{P} = \{P_1, \cdots, P_{|\mathcal{P}|}\}$ of policies is defined non-empty; and $\mathcal{H} = \{h_1, \cdots, h_{|\mathcal{H}|}\}$ and $\mathcal{C} = \{c_1, \cdots, c_{|\mathcal{C}|}\}$ are possibly empty sets. A hierarchy $h \in \mathcal{H}$ is a tree encoding the organisational structure amongst sets of units/teams in the organisation – each node storing relevant attribute value pairs, and a list of references to other nodes. A proposed change $c \in \mathcal{C}$ is of the form $c := (a, u, v)$, where a is an attribute (e.g., of user/resource/organisational hierarchy) with current value u, and proposed change value v.

The purpose of an *organisational change analysis* is to determine which policies (or rule(s) within a policy) will be triggered by the changes. In particular, we wish to know which resource entitlements might be lost and/or gained by subjects affected by the changes. A subject S of a policy rule possesses a set $\mathcal{A} = \{A_1, A_2, \ldots\}$ of descriptive attributes, given by attribute expressions (cf., Sect. 2.1) of the form $A = (a, \rhd, v)$. For each *change instance*, $c \in \mathcal{C}$, a subject will potentially be affected if it possesses attribute a with value u, i.e. if $(a, =, u) \in \mathcal{A}$. Change analysis then determines the effect on the subject's entitlements caused by changing the attribute to the alternative value, i.e. to $(a, =, v)$. More formally, the *organisational change analysis problem* is defined as follows in Definition 1.

Definition 1 (Organisational Change Analysis Problem). *Given the sets* $\mathcal{P}, \mathcal{H}, \mathcal{C}$, *the organisational change analysis problem is to produce the set* $\mathcal{I} = \{I_1, \cdots, I_{|\mathcal{I}|}\}$ *of all impacted access entitlements/privileges that might be loss (resp., gain) by any subject (e.g., users, teams, etc.) in* $\mathcal{P}$ *due to* $\mathcal{C}$ *(w.r.t.* $\mathcal{H}$*).*

An impacted resource $I \in \mathcal{I}$, *is given as* $I := (R_{\mathcal{C}} \subseteq P, E_{\text{gain}}, E_{\text{lost}})$, *where* $P \in \mathcal{P}$, E_{gain} *and* E_{lost} *specify the sets of entitlements gained and lost, respectively, by the affected subjects.*   □

A Sketch of the Proposed Solution. To achieve the above-mentioned goal, first, we employ binary decision diagrams (BDDs) to perform a concise and lossless representation of XACML access policies. This encoding enables an efficient and effective symbolic and logical manipulation as well as visualisation of the access control policies (in Sect. 4). Next, given a set of change scenarios within an organisation, we perform semantic analysis with respect to organisational hierarchies (if exist); and transform said changes into logical functions for infusion into the encoded policy BDDs for change operations (in Sect. 5). Finally, the output of the change analysis shows the impact of the (proposed) change – detailing triggered rules (resp., policies), gained and lost entitlements.

4   Representing XACML Policies with BDDs

In order to implement XACML policies and rules, it is necessary to have an algorithmic framework for unambiguously representing and evaluating the various Boolean expressions. Here, we examine the reframing of XACML access control policies into an equivalent BDD representation via Boolean functions.

4.1   Rules and Policies

We assume a three-level hierarchy, such that a policy set $\mathcal{P}$ is represented as a set of (non-nested) policies, $\mathcal{P} = \{P_1, P_2, \ldots\}$, and each policy P is a set of rules, $P = \{R_1, R_2, \ldots\}$. Each rule R is represented as a triplet $R = (S, E, d)$, where: (i) the subject S is a Boolean expression constructed using attribute expressions; (ii) the entitlement E is the privilege granted by the rule and specifies the allowed action on the resource; and (iii) the decision $d \in \{permit, deny\}$ specifies the effect of the rule when S is satisfied for an applicable request. This definition mostly follows from [3,23], except that the action and object elements are here expressed as the combined element E rather than as separate elements. In the terminology of Sect. 2.1, the elements S and E are jointly specified by the *target* and *conditions* of an XACML rule, where d is the *effect*. Thus, the current representation is equivalent to XACML.

4.2   Boolean Rule Functions

Here, we consider the representation of rule conditions via Boolean functions. To illustrate the process, consider a three-rules policy for different entitlements permissible on the same resource in Table 1 – we specify the rules

Table 1. An example Policy consisting of three rules

Rule	Subject (S)	Entitlement (E)	Effect (d)
R_1	(Group == A) & (Level == 1) & (OrgID == 001)	(action : "Read") & (resource : "client record")	*permit*
R_2	((Group == A) | (Group == B)) & (Level != 1) & (OrgID == 001)	(action : "Delete") & (resource : "client record")	*deny*
R_3	(Group == B) & (Level >= 2) & ((OrgID == 001) | (OrgID == 002) | (OrgID == 005))	(action : "Write") & (resource : "client record")	*permit*

as they might be written in some programming language, to help distinguish the raw rules from our later logical manipulations of Boolean functions.

In order to represent these rules as Boolean functions, we regard each attribute expression $A = a \triangleright v$ (see Sect. 2.1) as a logical proposition encoded by some Boolean variable x, such that x is *true* when A is satisfied. Therefore, each attribute expression is initially replaced with a distinct Boolean variable. Then, we improve the succinctness of the representation by further allowing a single Boolean variable s to encapsulate multiple attribute expressions. This operation is important for efficiently processing disjunction of attribute expressions defined on the same attribute name. For our exemplar rules shown in Table 1, the conditions (Group == A) \| Group == B) and (OrgID == 001) \|

Table 2. Boolean variables & expressions mappings

Variables	Expressions
x_1	(Group == A)
x_2	(Level == 1)
x_3	(OrgID == 001)
x_4	(Group == B)
x_5	(Level >= 2)
x_6	(OrgID == 002)
x_7	(OrgID == 005)
s_1	$(x_1 \lor x_4)$
s_2	$(x_3 \lor x_6 \lor x_7)$

... == 005) within the subjects of R_2 and R_3 respectively are equivalent to such multiple queries. Consequently, by replacing multiple attribute expressions with a single variable, we decrease the total number of variables and improve conciseness of representation. After these replacements, in general, each Boolean variable represents an arbitrary Boolean function of attribute expressions.

That is, for rules in Table 1, we first replace each distinct attribute expression with the variables $x_1, \ldots, x_7$. Next, we replace the nested structures of multiple attribute expressions with the new variables s_1, s_2 (see Table 2 for details of mappings). Table 3

Table 3. Rule subjects as Boolean functions

Rule	Boolean function (S)	
	direct	compact
R_1	$x_1 \land x_2 \land x_3$	$x_1 \land x_2 \land x_3$
R_2	$(x_1 \lor x_4) \land \lnot x_2 \land x_3$	$s_1 \land \lnot x_2 \land x_3$
R_3	$x_4 \land x_5 \land (x_3 \lor x_6 \lor x_7)$	$x_4 \land x_5 \land s_2$

shows a *direct* versus *compact* Boolean function representations of the rule-subject expressions in Table 1.

4.3   Boolean Policy Functions

For conciseness, we aim to represent all the rules in a given policy by a single Boolean function, $f(\mathbf{x})$, obtained as the disjunction of the individual rule functions. Since this may involve combining rules for both the *permit* and

---

Algorithm 1 Combining rule functions into a policy function

Require: Policy P // set of rule functions
1: $P' \leftarrow false$ // initialise policy function
2: $A \leftarrow \text{dict}()$ // initialise expression/variable map
3: $N \leftarrow \lceil \log_2 |P| \rceil$ // number of indicator variables
4: **for all** $R_k \in P$ **do**   // iterate over policy rules
5:    **for all** $A \in R_k$ **do**   // iterate over attribute expressions
6:        $X \leftarrow \text{lookup}(A, A)$ // map expression to policy variable
7:        $R_k \leftarrow \text{replace}(R_k, A, X)$ // replace expression by variable
8:    **end for**
9:    $R'_k \leftarrow \text{indicator}(k, N) \wedge R_k$ // add unique rule identifier
10:   $P' \leftarrow P' \vee R'_k$ // disjunction of rule functions
11: **end for**
12: **return** P', A

---

deny decisions, in the notation of Sect. 2.1, it is equivalent to $f = f_{\text{permit}} \vee f_{\text{deny}}$. However, we must also be able to identify which particular rule(s) would be triggered by any specified request (cf. Algorithm 1). To do this, we first augment each rule function by a unique Boolean identifier function.

If there are $m = |P|$ rules in a given policy, then it suffices to introduce $n = \lceil \log_2 m \rceil$ Boolean indicator variables, $i_1, \ldots, i_n$, such that the unique identifier for each rule is a function $\iota(i_1, \ldots, i_n)$ of the indicators. The indicator function may be obtained by first encoding the rule index as a sequence of n bits, and then translating this bit sequence into a conjunction of (possibly negated) indicator variables.

Thus, for our three example rules from Table 3, we require two indicator variables, i_1 and i_2. If we re-index the rules via the bit sequences 00, 01, 10, then the overall policy function becomes:

$$f(\mathbf{x}) = \quad (\neg i_1 \wedge \neg i_2) \wedge (x_1 \wedge x_2 \wedge x_3)$$
$$\vee \; (\neg i_1 \wedge i_2) \wedge (s_1 \wedge \neg x_2 \wedge x_3)$$
$$\vee \; (i_1 \wedge \neg i_2) \wedge (x_4 \wedge x_5 \wedge s_2). \tag{1}$$

Note that the number of distinctly labelled variables in the policy function is minimised by reusing the same Boolean variable for the same attribute expression across all rules in the policy.

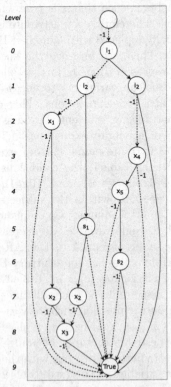

Fig. 3. BDD of the example policy

4.4   Policy Decision Diagrams

In order to represent a policy function as a BDD, we first ensure that the reordered variables (cf. Sect. 2.2) commence with the rule indicator variables. Then, in its unsimplified form, the policy BDD is a shared graph comprised of the individual rule BDDs, each branching from the root node via its individual indicator function. Further, we simplify the policy BDD by coalescing nodes and sub-graphs that recur across different rules. The resulting simplified BDD is, thus, an effective way of representing many Boolean functions [18].

For our example policy function in Eq. (1), the simplified policy BDD is shown in Fig. 3. Note that even after simplification, different nodes might still correspond to the same Boolean variable.

5   Organisational Change Impact Analysis

This section covers the interpretation and representation of organisational changes (*w.r.t.* existing organisational structures) as well as the actual analysis of impact with BDDs. A snippet of the procedure is captured in Algorithm 2.

5.1   Interpreting Attribute Changes

Given a set C of changes, each *change instance* $c \in C$ is specified as a list of *atomic changes*, $c = [\Delta_1, \cdots, \Delta_m]$. An atomic change, Δ, has the form $\Delta : a(u, v)$ – stating a change of value u to v for attribute a.

Thus, a change instance with more than one atomic change requires a careful evaluation and interpretation of its semantics due to possible interactions among the constituent atomic changes. To see this, suppose we have a change instance $c_1 = [\Delta_1 : \text{Group}(A, B)]$. Clearly, a subject with attribute Group's value being "A" might be affected by this change. Now, consider $c_2 = [\Delta_1, \Delta_2 : \text{OrgID}(001, 005), \Delta_3 : \text{OrgID}(002, 005)]$, in which case a potentially impacted subject must belong to Group A and have OrgID being either *001* or *002*.

Consequently, for any $c \in C$, we construct a Boolean expression to find its subject matches correctly via conjunction (designated by attribute name) of disjunctions (grouped by attribute name) of its atomic change terms. However, for practical purposes the Boolean expression is converted into disjunctive normal form (DNF), and transformed into a set of mutually exclusive change mappings. That is, C is reinterpreted as C' such that $\forall\, c = [\Delta_1, \cdots, \Delta_m] \in C$, there exists its set of mutually exclusive change mappings, $m(c) = \{\alpha_1 \to \beta_1, \cdots, \alpha_k \to \beta_k\} \in C'$, where α_i is a set of the existing subject attribute-value assignments, and β_i is the corresponding set of new attribute-value assignments.

In our example, the Boolean expression for c_2, will be: $(\text{Group} == A) \wedge ((\text{OrgID} == 001) \vee (\text{OrgID} == 002))$; with DNF equivalent of: $(\text{Group} == A) \wedge (\text{OrgID} == 001) \vee (\text{Group} == A) \wedge (\text{OrgID} == 002)$. Further, its set of mutually exclusive change mappings, $m(c_2) = \{\{\text{Group} = A, \text{OrgID} = 001\} \to \{\text{Group} = B, \text{OrgID} = 005\}, \{\text{Group} = A, \text{OrgID} = 002\} \to \{\text{Group} = B, \text{OrgID} = 005\}\}$.

Algorithm 2. Change analysis

Require: BDD, $\mathcal{C}, \mathcal{H}$

1: $C' \leftarrow semantic(\mathcal{C}, \mathcal{H})$ `// interpret C w.r.t. H`
2: $g_i \leftarrow$ BDD; $g_f \leftarrow$ BDD   `// initialisation`
3: **for all** $m(c) = \{\alpha_0 \rightarrow \beta_0, \cdots\} \in C'$ **do**
4:     $g_i \leftarrow subst\_BDD(g_i, \alpha_0^k); g_f \leftarrow subst\_BDD(g_f, \beta_0^k)$ `// assert c in BDDs`
5: **end for**
6: $a2na \leftarrow g_i \wedge \overline{g_f}$ `// detect changes from A to NA`
7: $na2a \leftarrow \overline{g_i} \wedge g_f$ `// detect changes from NA to A`
8: $r\_a2na \leftarrow determine\_rules(a2na)$ `// identify rules per Section 5.4`
9: $r\_na2a \leftarrow determine\_rules(na2a)$
10: $E_{\text{lost}} \leftarrow det\_entitlements\_lost(r\_a2na, a2na)$ `// ent'lments to be lost`
11: $E_{\text{gained}} \leftarrow det\_entitlements\_gained(r\_na2a, na2a)$ `// ent'lments to be gained`
12: $R_{\mathcal{C}} \leftarrow \{r\_na2a, r\_a2na\}$
13: **return** $(R_{\mathcal{C}}, E_{\text{gained}}, E_{\text{lost}})$

We remark that proposed changes can be over the organisational hierarchy $\mathcal{H}$. In our particular case, $\mathcal{H}$ is represented with a general tree. Each node denotes a unit within the organisations with a subject attribute and associated access entitlements specified in the access control policies $\mathcal{P}$. Parent-child relations are represented by edges in the tree with associated access inheritance defined in $\mathcal{P}$, analogous to hierarchical RBAC (RBAC1) [22]. The root node represents the whole organisation, and is linked with universal access privileges. Therefore, a change instance $c \in \mathcal{C}$ might involve moving/merging of (sub)-path(s) in the tree. We note our reinterpretation of $\mathcal{C}$ as $\mathcal{C}'$ includes all semantics of $\mathcal{H}$ (cf. line 1 in Algorithm 2).

5.2 Representing Attribute Changes

Here, we encode the proposed change information into the policy BDDs. Recall that each policy $P \in \mathcal{P}$ has a corresponding Boolean function $f(P)$, and an associated BDD, $BDD(P)$. Hence, for each policy, we wish to encode the proposed changes into a *change BDD*, in order to facilitate change analysis of each policy.

We compute two new Boolean functions from $f(P)$ to represent the changes $m(c) = \{\alpha_0 \rightarrow \beta_0, \cdots, \alpha_k \rightarrow \beta_k\} \in C'$, namely:

$$f_{\text{pre}} \doteq \bigvee_{m(c) \in C'} \mathsf{ast}(f(P), \{\alpha_0, \cdots, \alpha_k\}); \quad f_{\text{post}} \doteq \bigvee_{m(c) \in C'} \mathsf{ast}(f(P), \{\beta_0, \cdots, \beta_k\}),$$

where the function $\mathsf{ast}(f(P), \{d_1, \ldots, d_k\})$ asserts every subject attribute-value assignments d_i in $f(P)$. That is, for any Boolean variable x in $f(P)$ with the attribute expression $A : a \triangleright v$ and an attribute assignment $(a = u) \in d$, x is set to the Boolean value evaluation of the expression

Table 4. Asserting change mappings over rule Boolean functions

Rule	Group=A	Group=B	XOR
R_1	$\mathsf{x}_2 \wedge \mathsf{x}_3$	$false$	$\mathsf{x}_2 \wedge \mathsf{x}_3$
R_2	$\neg\mathsf{x}_2 \wedge \mathsf{x}_3$	$\neg\mathsf{x}_2 \wedge \mathsf{x}_3$	$false$
R_3	$false$	$\mathsf{x}_5 \wedge \mathsf{s}_2$	$\mathsf{x}_5 \wedge \mathsf{s}_2$

$u \triangleright v$ (i.e., *true* or *false*). Note that a variable x might contain one or more general attribute expressions of the form $a \triangleright v$, e.g. $a = u$, $a > v$, $a \neq v$, etc., and thus each A might affect multiple variables.

For our running example, recall the policy in Table 1 is encoded as a Boolean function in Eq. 1 (cf. Table 3 for expressions for each rule). Given the change instance $c_1 = [\Delta_1 :$ Group(A, B)], $m(c_1) = \{\{$Group $=$ A$\} \rightarrow \{$Group $=$ B$\}\}$. To compute f_{pre}, the value of attribute Group is set to "A" and evaluated in all Group-expressions within Boolean variables in Eq. 1. Table 4 shows the effect of asserting c_1 over rule-subject functions in Table 3. Note that only the Boolean variables x_1, x_4, s_1 contain Group-expressions. Thus, for this assertion, all but x_4 evaluate to *true*, with the resultant rule-subject expressions in the Group=A-column of Table 4. Indeed, the value of x_4 (i.e., *false*) renders the entire R_3 expression *false*. Similarly, for f_{post} computation using $\{$Group $=$ B$\}$, the resulting rule-subjects are as shown in column Group=B of Table 4 – there, R_1 expression is *false* due to the evaluation of x_1. The last column is the XOR of both cases.

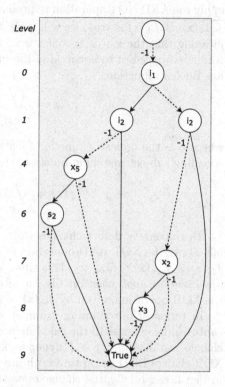

Fig. 4. The XOR change BDD for the example policy and change instance c_1.

More formally, the change functions f_{pre} and f_{post} for our running example is given as:

$$f_{\mathrm{pre}}(\mathbf{x}) = (\neg i_1 \wedge \neg i_2) \wedge (x_2 \wedge x_3) \vee (\neg i_1 \wedge i_2) \wedge (\neg x_2 \wedge x_3), \text{ and}$$
$$f_{\mathrm{post}}(\mathbf{x}) = (\neg i_1 \wedge i_2) \wedge (\neg x_2 \wedge x_3) \vee (i_1 \wedge \neg i_2) \wedge (x_5 \wedge s_2), \text{ respectively.}$$

In the following, we discuss how the BDDs corresponding to f_{pre} and f_{post} are combined into a single change BDD for analysis.

5.3   Change Decision Diagrams

The change BDD represents the logical combination of the pre-change and post-change functions, $f_{\mathrm{pre}}(\mathbf{x})$ and $f_{\mathrm{post}}(\mathbf{x})$, respectively (see Sect. 5.2). The specific combination operation required depends upon the type of change to be detected. For example, suppose that attribute set A matches some rule R_i with decision $d \in \{permit, deny\}$, and fails to match some other rule R_j. Further suppose that under the changed attribute set A', rule R_i no longer matches but now rule R_j

does. Thus, we say that the status of rule R_i has changed from *applicable* to *not applicable*, and conversely rule R_j has changed from *not applicable* to *applicable*.

Notionally, to detect potential changes from *applicable* to *not applicable*, we apply the AND NOT operation to produce the change function $f_{ch}(x) = f_{pre}(x) \wedge \overline{f_{post}(x)}$. If $f_{ch}(x)$ is true, we will know that $f_{pre}(x)$ is true and $f_{post}(x)$ is false, meaning that the status becomes from *applicable* to *not applicable*. In practice, care must be taken to not modify the unique rule identifiers. Hence, if policy P has Boolean function:

$$f(x) = \bigvee_{R_i \in P} \iota_i(x) \wedge g_i(x),$$

where ι_i is the indicator function identifying rule R_i, and g_i is the rule's corresponding subject matching function, then the required negation is defined as

$$\overline{f(x)} \doteq \bigvee_{R_i \in P} \iota_i(x) \wedge \neg g_i(x).$$

To conversely detect changes from *not applicable* to *applicable*, we notionally apply the NOT AND operation to produce the alternative change function $f_{ch}(x) = \overline{f_{pre}(x)} \wedge f_{post}(x)$. This time, when $f_{ch}(x)$ is true, it changes from *not applicable* to *applicable*. Finally, to detect changes in both directions we apply the XOR operation, given by $f_{ch}(x) = f_{pre}(x) \wedge \overline{f_{post}(x)} \vee \overline{f_{pre}(x)} \wedge f_{post}(x)$.

In terms of our running example, recall that the XOR column of Table 4 captures the changes to the rule-functions, *w.r.t.* the policy function (Eq. 1) and change instance $m(c_1) = \{\{\text{Group} = \text{A}\} \to \{\text{Group} = \text{B}\}\}$. The corresponding XOR change BDD to capture both directions of change in entitlement is shown in Fig. 4. Essentially, the change operations prune the policy BDD (in Fig. 3) to one in Fig. 4 with only relevant variables to ease further analysis.

5.4   Identifying Rules Affected by Change

The change BDD with Boolean function $f_{ch}(x)$, defined in Sect. 5.3, specifies the subset of policy rules potentially affected by the proposed attribute changes. However, apart from the indicator variables $i = (i_1, i_2, \dots)$ that help identify the rules, there will typically remain other variables, namely $z = x \backslash i$, that represent attribute conditions with undetermined truth values. In the absence of any particular subject with specified attributes, it impossible to judge whether these attribute conditions will be satisfied or not. Hence, we notionally consider the subset of all subjects for which the change BDD will be satisfied.

Theoretically, this means eliminating the remaining variables $z = (z_1, z_2, \cdots, z_n)$ by evaluating $f(x)$ over all possible combinations of truth values, giving:

$$f'_{ch}(i) \doteq \bigvee_{x \backslash i \in \mathbb{B}^n} f_{ch}(x),$$

Table 5. Summary of Datasets

Datasets	DS1	DS2
XACML Policies	101 policies, specifying rules for over 120K unique entitlements	46 rules for 11 entitlements
Users' Access Data	About 50K users with 32 attributes and over 2M unique user-permission assignments	19 users with 9 attributes over 40 resource items
Org. hierarchies	7K unique teams across 14 divisions in multiple cities	2 Departments

where $\mathbb{B} = \{true, false\}$. In practice, the change BDD can be reduced simply by replacing each sub-graph, with root node corresponding to undecidable variable z_i, by a direct edge to the *true* node. Consequently, the reduced change BDD corresponding to $f'_{ch}(\mathbf{i})$ now directly specifies the rules potentially affected by the changes.

Finally, for our running example, the BDD in Fig. 4 is reduced to that in Fig. 5, and we can determined affected rules as follows. Given that i_1 is absent in the diagram, this means the first bit of the index sequences can be 0 or 1 (i.e., 0_, 1_). Next, we determine i_2 bit-value(s) by traversing the BDD from the *root* to the *terminal* node. For case $i_2 = 0$, we reach the *terminal* node via an even number of complementary edges. Hence, $i_2 = 0$ is *true*, since the even complementary edges cancel out. However, case $i_2 = 1$ is *false* as we get to the *terminal* node via an odd number of complementary edges. Hence, the index of the affected rules are: 00 and 10 corresponding to rules R_1 and R_3 in Table 1 (cf. re-indexing of rules in Subsect. 4.3).

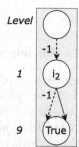

Fig. 5. BDD of affected rules

6   Empirical Evaluation

In this section, we summarise the experimental evaluation of Acumen.

6.1   Datasets and Experimental Settings

Two collections of datasets are used in our experimental study, viz.: a) DS1 – a set of 101 real-world XACML access control policies (ACPs) from a large organisation with 50K users and complex organisational structures and hierarchies; and b) DS2 – a set of 46 rules generated from a well-known ACPs dataset in the literature (e.g., used in [25] for mining attribute-based ACPs; see Appendix B for more details). A brief description of the datasets are presented in Table 5.

Due to privacy and security reasons, we are unable to present the real data including the attribute names and values, and the BDD generated using DS1 for change impact analysis. However, we refer interested readers to Appendix A for the distribution of entitlements to illustrate the challenges brought about by organisational changes and the necessity for an effective and automated solution to change impact analysis in large organisations.

The developed solution is implemented in Python 3.8.12 and we used the `autoref` module in the PyPi `dd` package [10] to construct and manipulate the BDDs. The experiments are conducted on a laptop running Windows 10 with 8 GB RAM and an i7-1065G7 CPU processor.

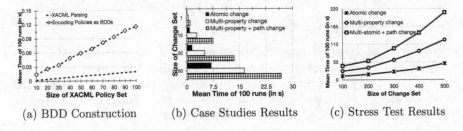

(a) BDD Construction   (b) Case Studies Results   (c) Stress Test Results

Fig. 6. Analysis of Time Performance of Acumen

6.2   Efficiency Study

We present an efficiency study over DS1, the real-world data from a large organisation. The rules in the parsed XACML policy set consists 542 distinct attribute expressions of the forms specified in Sect. 2.1. The Boolean policy functions constructed from all rules required 274 shared Boolean variables, comprising: 7 indicator variables to uniquely identify each rule; 217 variables corresponding to individual attribute expressions of the form $a \triangleright v$; and a further 50 compound variables corresponding to various disjunctions of attribute expressions (typically specifying lists of allowed or disallowed attribute values). In exception of *Exp-1a*, which varies the policy set size, we use the entire set in all experiments.

Exp-1a: Efficiency of Constructing BDDs. The BDD constructed from the policy functions comprised 525 nodes, where a node corresponds to a specified variable. The small size of the BDD is due to the effect of variable ordering. For our experiments, the most frequently appearing variables were placed earlier in the ordering to promote re-usability of nodes. Indeed, Fig. 6(a) show linear time performances for parsing and encoding different sizes of policy set into a BDD.

Exp-1b: Efficiency of Change Analysis. The performance of Acumen is characterised by the sizes of the policy and change sets, and the complexity of change instances. Thus, we evaluate Acumen *w.r.t.* these parameters, using their historic real-world settings seen in our partner organisation. The plot in Fig. 6(b) presents the mean of 100 experiments in the following scenarios: 1) Atomic changes – involving only single attribute-values (black bars); 2) Multiple attribute-value changes – involving change instances with up to five attributes (cf. clear bars);

and 3) Multiple attribute-values & organisational hierarchy path changes. This includes case 2) change instances and changes involving the move of teams/individuals across different paths/levels in the organisational structure (i.e., patterned bars). Overall, we observe a near-linear time performance with respect to both increasing change instance complexity and change set size. Notable, a set of 50 complex changes can be performed under 30 s.

Exp-1c: Stress Test of Change Analysis. Furthermore, we perform extensive stress testing of Acumen by increasing the size of changes (up to 500) and their complexity, captured by Fig. 6(c). The cross-, circle-, and square-marked lines show the performance on atomic, multi-attribute (up to 20 attributes), and multi-attribute (20–30 attributes) and path changes, respectively. The plots show a consistent near-linear performance, demonstrating the scalability of Acumen. Indeed, a set of 500 most-complex changes is performed in about $3\frac{1}{2}$ min.

6.3   Case Studies: Change Analysis in DS2

Next, we demonstrate the effectiveness of Acumen to analyse user/resource changes in the DS2 dataset. Due to space constraints, we shall defer some details of this study to Appendix B. For the goal in this section, however, the following suffices to illustrate the change analysis performance.

There exist two categories of tasks for any project in the DS2 dataset (i.e., proprietary and non-proprietary tasks) with explicit rules on which users can request to work on either category (see Tables 6 and 7) as presented in Appendix B.

Now, suppose we want to investigate changes to users' access entitlements due to an impending restructuring of the organisation. In particular, we want to know access entitlement changes for users that might transition from employees to contractors, with a change of expertise from design to coding. In DS2, we compile 8 rules to capture different values allowed for user attributes such as isEmployee and userExpertise. Figure 8 shows the original BDD generated using only the 8 rules for illustration purpose and the change BDD after imposing organisational changes mentioned above; with a brief discussion in Appendix B.2.

7   Conclusion

This paper proposes Acumen, a tool for evaluating the effect of planned organisational changes on users' access entitlements based on defined access control policies. Acumen consists of three core components, viz.: a module for parsing and transforming XACML policies into Boolean functions for encoding as binary decision diagrams (BDDs); a semantic analytic module for synthesising the change information in the context of organisational structures and hierarchies; and an output module for coalescing BDD outputs with users' access data. Given a change scenario, Acumen returns the set of impacted users and their associated lost/gained access privileges—*which may be very difficult to detect manually*—to prevent potential business disruption and security breaches. We conduct an empirical evaluation of the proposed solution in a case study of planned organisational changes within a dynamic real-world enterprise. The results show Acumen is scalable, efficient and effective; and useful for remediating the effect of planned changes in the organisation.

Acknowledgement. The work has been supported by the Cyber Security Research Centre Limited whose activities are partially funded by the Australian Government's Cooperative Research Centres Programme.

A   Distribution of Entitlements and Its Implications

Here, we present a t-SNE plot to illustrate the distribution of entitlements in high dimensional user-profile feature space; and discuss its implications and the necessity for automated change analysis.

Figure 7 is generated using 20% of randomly selected samples from DS1. It has over 837K dots (with overlapping) which seem to be randomly and evenly distributed in a sphere, where each dot is an entitlement instance and the colours represent the entitlement IDs. Among the 837K entitlement instances, there are over 60K unique entitlements – as one entitlement can be assigned to multiple subjects (e.g., users). Clearly, dots with dark colours dominate, meaning that the entitlements with smaller IDs are

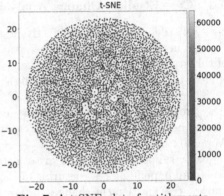

Fig. 7. A t-SNE plot of entitlements.

assigned much more frequently. According to our distribution analysis, the first 270 entitlements accounts for 50% of the total instances, and the first 5000 entitlements 75%. As the most common 270 entitlements appear in half of the instances, on average each of these entitlements will be assigned to roughly 1550 users. Thus, a single organisational change can affect the profiles of users, and consequently the access of an average of 1550 users can be impacted, rendering manual maintenance of access entitlements and analysis of change impact infeasible.

B   The Project Management Policy: A Case Study

DS2 is an ABAC policy data for a project management system used in [25]. However, the access control rules are not strictly represented using attribute expressions in the form of $a \triangleright v$ as we do in this work. Thus, we transformed the rules into their attribute expression equivalent so that they can be analysed by our algorithms. We refer interested readers to [25] for the complete dataset.

Table 6. Users Attribute Data: Technical Workers – Proj11

	UserID	Expertise	Project	isEmployee	Tasks
1	des11	design	proj11	True	proj11task1a, proj11task1propa
2	code11	coding	proj11	True	proj11task2a, proj11task2propa

Table 7. Resources Attribute Data: Proj11 Tasks

	Project	isProprietary	ReqExpertise	Tasks
1	proj11	False	coding	proj11task2a, proj11task2
2	proj11	True	coding	proj11task2propa, proj11task2prop
3	proj11	False	design	proj11task1a, proj11task1
4	proj11	True	design	proj11task1propa, proj11task1prop

B.1   Policy Rules, Users and Resource Data

The original DS2 consists of 11 policies. For ease of comprehension, we use a single policy from the set for this discussion. The chosen policy's tenet in natural language format as they appear in [25] states: *"an employee working on a project can read and request to work on any task whose required areas of expertise are among his/her areas of expertise"*.

We represent this policy by a set of eight rules, using the attribute expression in Sect. 2.1. Snippets of relevant users attribute data and resource attribute data in Tables 6 and 7 respectively, that support our discussion.

B.2   Change BDD

The BDD to support the case study in Sect. 6.3 is presented in Fig. 8. In Fig. 8(b), we can see two roots. The subgraph rooted at node @-1 captures the change BDD for rules changing from *not applicable* to *applicable*. On the other hand, the other subgraph rooted at @13 shows the change BDD capturing rules impacted from *applicable* to *not applicable*. To find those rules, we search for all the paths connecting any number of the indicator nodes down to variable nodes that are connected with the terminal node with solid arrow(s). Then we can easily obtain the binary representations of the four impacted rule ids 4, 5, 6 and 7 by decoding the arrows in each path above and replacing the solid lined arrow ($\rightarrow$) with 1 and the dashed lined arrow ($\dashrightarrow$) with 0 respectively. Therefore, the entitlements related to rules 4, 5, 6 and 7 will be lost due to the change.

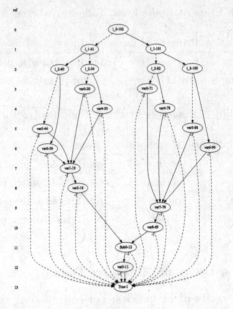

(a) Original BDD

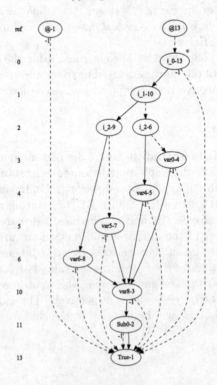

(b) Change BDD

Fig. 8. Change analysis using BDD

References

1. Agrawal, D., Giles, J., Lee, K., Lobo, J.: Policy ratification. In: Proceedings of Sixth IEEE International Workshop on Policies for Distributed Systems and Networks, Los Alamitos, CA, USA, pp. 223–232. IEEE Computer Society (2005)
2. Barrett, C., Tinelli, C.: Satisfiability modulo theories. In: Clarke, E., Henzinger, T., Veith, H., Bloem, R. (eds.) Handbook of Model Checking, pp. 305–343. Springer, Cham (2018). https://doi.org/10.1007/978-3-319-10575-8_11
3. ter Beek, M., Gnesi, S., Montangero, C., Semini, L.: Detecting policy conflicts by model checking UML state machines, pp. 59–74 (2009)
4. Brace, K.S., Rudell, R.L., Bryant, R.E.: Efficient implementation of a BDD package. In: Proceedings of the 27th ACM/IEEE Conference on Design Automation, pp. 40–45. IEEE/ACM, ACM Press (1991)
5. Bryant, R.E.: Binary decision diagrams. In: Clarke, E., Henzinger, T., Veith, H., Bloem, R. (eds.) Handbook of Model Checking, pp. 191–217. Springer, Cham (2018). https://doi.org/10.1007/978-3-319-10575-8_7
6. Clarke, E.M., Henzinger, T.A., Veith, H., Bloem, R.: Handbook of Model Checking, 1st edn. Springer, Cham (2018). https://doi.org/10.1007/978-3-319-10575-8
7. Craven, R., Lobo, J., Ma, J., Russo, A., Lupu, E., Bandara, A.: Expressive policy analysis with enhanced system dynamicity. In: Proceedings of the 4th International Symposium on Information, Computer, and Communications Security, pp. 239–250 (2009)
8. van Dijk, T., Pol, J.: Sylvan: multi-core framework for decision diagrams. Int. J. Softw. Tools Technol. Transf. **19**, 675–696 (2017)
9. Knuth, D.E.: The Art of Computer Programming, vol. 4A, 6th edn. Addison-Wesley, Boston (2015)
10. Filippidis, I., Haesaert, S., Livingston, S.C., Wenzel, M.: California Institute of Technology (2022)
11. Fisler, K., Krishnamurthi, S., Meyerovich, L., Tschantz, M.: Verification and change-impact analysis of access-control policies, pp. 196–205 (2005)
12. Jabal, A.A., et al.: Methods and tools for policy analysis. ACM Comput. Surv. (CSUR) **51**(6), 1–35 (2019)
13. Koch, M., Mancini, L.V., Parisi-Presicce, F.: On the specification and evolution of access control policies. In: Proceedings of the Sixth ACM Symposium on Access Control Models and Technologies, SACMAT 2001, pp. 121–130. Association for Computing Machinery, New York (2001)
14. Kolovski, V., Hendler, J., Parsia, B.: Analyzing web access control policies. In: Proceedings of the 16th International Conference on World Wide Web, pp. 677–686 (2007)
15. Lin, D., Rao, P., Bertino, E., Li, N., Lobo, J.: Exam: a comprehensive environment for the analysis of access control policies. Int. J. Inf. Secur. **9**(4), 253–273 (2010)
16. Lin, D., Rao, P., Bertino, E., Lobo, J.: An approach to evaluate policy similarity. In: Proceedings of the 12th ACM Symposium on Access Control Models and Technologies, pp. 1–10 (2007)
17. Martin, E., Xie, T.: A fault model and mutation testing of access control policies. In: Proceedings of the 16th International Conference on World Wide Web, pp. 667–676 (2007)
18. Minato, S.I., Ishiura, N., Yajima, S.: Shared binary decision diagram with attributed edges for efficient boolean function manipulation, vol. VLD89, pp. 52–57 (1990)

19. OASIS: extensible access control markup language (XACML) (2013)
20. Rice, M., Kulhari, S.: A survey of static variable ordering heuristics for efficient BDD/MDD construction. University of California, Technical report (2008)
21. Rudell, R.: Dynamic variable ordering for ordered binary decision diagrams. In: Proceedings of the 1993 IEEE/ACM International Conference on Computer-Aided Design, ICCAD 1993, pp. 42–47. IEEE Computer Society Press, Washington, DC (1993)
22. Sandhu, R., Ferraiolo, D., Kuhn, R., et al.: The NIST model for role-based access control: towards a unified standard. In: ACM Workshop on Role-Based Access Control, vol. 10 (2000)
23. Shu, C.C., Yang, E., Arenas, A.: Detecting conflicts in ABAC policies with rule-reduction and binary-search techniques, pp. 182–185 (2009)
24. Turkmen, F., den Hartog, J., Ranise, S., Zannone, N.: Analysis of XACML policies with SMT. In: Focardi, R., Myers, A. (eds.) POST 2015. LNCS, vol. 9036, pp. 115–134. Springer, Heidelberg (2015). https://doi.org/10.1007/978-3-662-46666-7_7
25. Xu, Z., Stoller, S.D.: Mining attribute-based access control policies. IEEE Trans. Dependable Secure Comput. **12**(5), 533–545 (2015)

Author Index

G. Tsudik et al. (Eds.): ESORICS 2023, LNCS 14347, pp. 431–432, 2024.
https://doi.org/10.1007/978-3-031-51482-1

Printed in the United States
by Baker & Taylor Publisher Services